CIW Security
Professional
Certification Bible

CIW Security Professional Certification Bible

Mandy Andress, Philip Cox, Ed Tittel, Series Editor

Hungry Minds™

Best-Selling Books • Digital Downloads • e-Books • Answer Networks • e-Newsletters • Branded Web Sites • e-Learning

New York, NY ✦ Indianapolis, IN ✦ Cleveland, OH

CIW Security Professional Certification Bible

Published by
Hungry Minds, Inc.
909 Third Avenue
New York, NY 10022
www.hungryminds.com

Library of Congress Catalog Card No.: 2001092746

ISBN: 0-7645-4822-0

Printed in the United States of America

10 9 8 7 6 5 4 3 2 1

1P/QX/QZ/QR/IN

Distributed in the United States by Hungry Minds, Inc.

Distributed by CDG Books Canada Inc. for Canada; by Transworld Publishers Limited in the United Kingdom; by IDG Norge Books for Norway; by IDG Sweden Books for Sweden; by IDG Books Australia Publishing Corporation Pty. Ltd. for Australia and New Zealand; by TransQuest Publishers Pte Ltd. for Singapore, Malaysia, Thailand, Indonesia, and Hong Kong; by Gotop Information Inc. for Taiwan; by ICG Muse, Inc. for Japan; by Intersoft for South Africa; by Eyrolles for France; by International Thomson Publishing for Germany, Austria, and Switzerland; by Distribuidora Cuspide for Argentina; by LR International for Brazil; by Galileo Libros for Chile; by Ediciones ZETA S.C.R. Ltda. for Peru; by WS Computer Publishing Corporation, Inc., for the Philippines; by Contemporanea de Ediciones for Venezuela; by Express Computer Distributors for the Caribbean and West Indies; by Micronesia Media Distributor, Inc. for Micronesia; by Chips Computadoras S.A. de C.V. for Mexico; by Editorial Norma de Panama S.A. for Panama; by American Bookshops for Finland.

For general information on Hungry Minds' products and services please contact our Customer Care department within the U.S. at 800-762-2974, outside the U.S. at 317-572-3993 or fax 317-572-4002.

For sales inquiries and reseller information, including discounts, premium and bulk quantity sales, and foreign-language translations, please contact our Customer Care department at 800-434-3422, fax 317-572-4002 or write to Hungry Minds, Inc., Attn: Customer Care Department, 10475 Crosspoint Boulevard, Indianapolis, IN 46256.

For information on licensing foreign or domestic rights, please contact our Sub-Rights Customer Care department at 212-884-5000.

For information on using Hungry Minds' products and services in the classroom or for ordering examination copies, please contact our Educational Sales department at 800-434-2086 or fax 317-572-4005.

For press review copies, author interviews, or other publicity information, please contact our Public Relations department at 317-572-3168 or fax 317-572-4168.

For authorization to photocopy items for corporate, personal, or educational use, please contact Copyright Clearance Center, 222 Rosewood Drive, Danvers, MA 01923, or fax 978-750-4470.

About the Authors

Mandy Andress (CISSP, SSCP, CPA, CISA) has over five years experience with security technologies. Before starting ArcSec Technologies, Mandy worked for Exxon, USA and several Big 5 accounting firms, including Deloitte & Touche and Ernst & Young. After leaving the Big 5, Mandy became Director of Security for Privada, Inc., a privacy startup in San Jose.

Mandy has also written numerous security articles for magazines such as *InfoWorld*, *Information Security Magazine*, and *eSecurity Advisor*. Mandy has spoken at several industry conferences, including Networld+Interop and TISC. She is also the author of *Surviving Security: How to Integrate People, Process, and Technology*. Mandy is currently President and Founder of ArcSec Technologies, a security consultancy.

Philip Cox is a consultant of SystemExperts Corporation, a consulting firm that specializes in system security and management. He is a well-known authority in the areas of system integration and security. He is the lead author of *Windows 2000 Security Handbook* and Technical Editor of *Hacking Linux Exposed,* both from Osborne McGraw-Hill. His experience includes Windows NT/2000, UNIX, and IP based networks integration, Secure network design and implementation, and Information Security Policy development. Phil frequently writes and lectures on issues dealing with UNIX & NT integration, and Information Security. He holds a BS in Computer Science.

Shawn Porter (contributing writer) is a *Windows 2000 Magazine* author and a network administrator in Calgary, AB Canada. His areas of expertise are in computer security and computer/network troubleshooting. A nine-year veteran of the computer industry, Shawn has many years of hands-on experience in many facets of computers, including time spent as a computer journalist for the newspaper *The Vernon SUN*. Previously, Shawn was an owner of a successful computer service-oriented company in Vernon, BC. Shawn has obtained numerous technical certifications, including Microsoft's MCSE certification and CIW Security Professional.

Ed Tittel, Series editor, is a 19-year computer industry veteran. He is currently the president of LANWrights, Inc. and Vice President of IT Certifications at LeapIt.com. Ed stays busy writing books (he has 110 titles to his credit), magazine articles, teaching, and consulting.

Credits

Acquisitions Editor
Greg Croy

Project Editor
Marcia Brochin

Technical Editor
Mark T. Edmead

Copy Editors
Gabrielle Chosney
Kevin Kent

Editorial Managers
Ami Sullivan
Kyle Looper

Project Coordinator
Regina Snyder

Graphics and Production Specialists
Joyce Haughey
Gabriele McCann
Barry Offringa
Jill Piscitelli
Betty Schulte
Laurie Stevens
Brian Torwelle

Quality Control Technicians
Carl Pierce
Marianne Santy
Robert Springer

Permissions Editor
Carmen Krikorian

Media Development Specialist
Gregory Stephens

Media Development Coordinator
Marisa Pearman

Proofreading and Indexing
TECHBOOKS Production Services

Preface

This book is designed to help you prepare for the CIW Security Professional Exam (1D0-470). CIW certification is recognized as a leading industry standard for the Internet industry, accredited by the Association of Internet Professionals (AIP), and endorsed by the International Webmasters Association (IWA).

The exams are developed to certify an individual's expertise with Internet-related technologies and topics. CIW exams are currently offered at over 1,000 testing locations worldwide.

The CIW Security Professional Exam tests the candidate on a broad base of general knowledge related to developing and managing a security infrastructure.

This book provides information about everything covered on the exam. In addition, we cover many topics in more detail than the exam, and have used our experience in the security industry to provide you with a practical guide to security in the real world. For this reason, this book is much more than a study guide for the CIW Security Professional Exam. You'll also find that this book is useful as an introduction and guide to planning, building, and managing a security infrastructure that you will be able to refer to long after you've passed the CIW Security Professional Exam.

How This Book Is Organized

This book is divided into five parts. To get the maximum benefit, we recommend that you carefully study all of the material in each part and complete all of the exercises and sample exam questions.

The parts are roughly evenly divided between five main aspects of security: Security concepts, network security, operating system security, intrusion detection and response, and security auditing and analysis. The exam does a good job of balancing theoretical and technical security principles, but because of the complexity of some security topics, we tend (correctly, we feel) to put greater emphasis on practical concepts and testing your knowledge of the big picture.

If you're short on time and you want to do the bare minimum amount of work to get the maximum amount of knowledge before taking the CIW Security Professional Exam, you should be sure to closely study specific parts and chapters within these parts. We've noted these parts in this section. Of course, we hope that you'll come back to our book after you've successfully passed the exam to complete the exercises and get valuable hands-on experience with security tools.

Part I: Introducing Computer Security Concepts

This part begins by answering several fundamental questions, including:

- ✦ What is security?
- ✦ Why do you need security?
- ✦ What are the basic concepts of security?

After defining the fundamental terms, laying out the case for security, and explaining the basic concepts, we discuss some general concepts and principles, such as encryption and TCP/IP, that are critical to understanding more complex security concepts and issues.

Part II: Network Security

Part II focuses on network security concepts, beginning with a discussion on the types of security incidents and attacks that you may encounter.

Chapters 6 and 7 continue the network security discussion by focusing on boundary security devices and configurations that can help you secure your network from the attacks discussed in Chapter 5. Chapter 6 focuses on the types of boundary devices that are available, while Chapter 7 delves into details on the most common boundary device—the firewall.

Part III: Operating System Security

In Part III, we move from the network perimeter to the operating systems that are running on each server and workstation. We begin by discussing basic risks and threats to the operating system in Chapter 8. Chapter 9 is a theoretical discussion of operating system security principles.

Beginning in Chapter 10, we get more hands-on and technical, discussing specific ways to harden various operating systems. Chapters 11 and 12 delve into detail on two specific areas—system files and user accounts, respectively.

Part IV: Intrusion Detection and Response

Part IV gets into detail about potential attacks that can be launched against your network and systems and how to deal with those attacks. Chapter 13 begins with a general discussion of attack scenarios, common targets, etc. Chapter 14 continues the theoretical discussion by showing ways to detect and prevent network and system attacks.

Beginning the practical discussion, Chapter 15 goes into detail on Intrusion Detection Systems and how they function to help detect network and host-based attacks in your organization. Chapter 16 discusses what you need to do in the event that a successful attack is launched against your network.

Part V: Security Auditing, Analysis, and Intrusion Detection

Part V discusses the most important security concept — ongoing maintenance and monitoring. Chapter 17 begins with a theoretical discussion of the concepts of security auditing. Chapter 18 discusses practical, hands-on tools and techniques that you can use to audit your network.

Chapter 19 discusses the theoretical principles behind security management and control procedures and some of the methods that attackers can use to exploit those controls as well as ways you can mitigate the risk of the attacker's actions. Chapter 20 focuses on log files and how beneficial thorough log analysis can be. Chapter 21 helps you to understand the results of your audit and the steps that you need to take after the audit is complete.

Back Matter

The Back Matter contains several useful appendices that are designed to provide references to more in-depth information on topics covered in the book and to help you make the best use of this book.

Of particular interest is Appendix C, the sample exam. We recommend that you don't look at this sample exam until you've read the entire book. If you can correctly answer at least 45 of the 60 questions in this sample exam, you're probably ready to take the real thing.

After you're sure that you'll pass with flying colors, Appendix D will give you all the information that you need to find a testing location, get signed up, and get certified. Appendixes E and F will provide useful information on well-known ports and Web resources.

How Each Chapter Is Structured

This book is designed to provide you with the best possible learning and exam preparation experience. The structure of each chapter, and the specific elements used, are designed to present the exam material in a clear and easy-to-learn way.

The elements that you'll find in each chapter are:

✦ A list of exam objectives covered in this chapter

✦ A chapter pre-test

✦ Clear, concise text on each topic

✦ Step-by-step instructions on how to perform specific tasks

✦ Screen shots and graphics to aid in your understanding

✦ A Key Point Summary

✦ A comprehensive Study Guide that contains:

- Exam-style assessment questions
- Scenario problems for you to solve
- Lab exercises to perform on your computer
- Answers to chapter pre-test questions, assessment questions, and scenarios

✦ A list of resources for more information on the topics discussed

How to Use This Book

This book can be used either by individuals working independently or by groups in a formal classroom setting.

We recommend that you read this book sequentially. The chapters are designed to be studied in order, meaning that it's best to complete Chapter 1 before moving on to Chapter 2 (and so on). Some of the chapters can stand alone, but in many cases, the topics presented in a chapter are based on knowledge obtained in preceding chapters. Additionally, some Lab Exercises require completion of Lab Exercises in previous chapters to work properly. (In most cases, this is noted at the beginning of the Lab Exercise.)

When studying each chapter, we recommend the following approach: First, read the Chapter Pre-Test. Answer as many of the questions as you can. For those questions that you are unsure of, be on the lookout for the answers as you read the chapter. After you've read the chapter, use the Key Point Summary as a guide to what you have just learned. If any of the key points are unfamiliar to you, review that section of the chapter.

Next, complete the assessment questions. If you're unsure of an answer, make your best guess. When you're done, check your answers. For any incorrect answers, review the topic by re-reading the appropriate section of the chapter. Next, complete the Scenario(s) to test how you would apply the knowledge learned in the chapter to a real-world situation. Finally, get hands-on experience with the Lab Exercises.

Prerequisites

This book assumes the same level of knowledge that the CIW Security Professional Exam assumes — that is, a broad general knowledge of basic security principles and concepts. Just as the CIW Foundations Exam (1D0-410) is a prerequisite to the CIW Security Professional Exam, knowledge of the foundations of Web development are a prerequisite for readers of this book.

Hardware and Software That You'll Need

Although we've tried to keep requirements to a bare minimum, you will need access to various hardware and software to be able to do the Lab Exercises in this book.

Here are what we consider to be the minimum hardware requirements, although you may be able to get by with less if you're creative and patient:

+ Intel-based computer with Pentium/133MHz processor, 64MB of RAM, and 2GB of hard drive space.
+ CD-ROM drive
+ Access to the Internet

Optional equipment that you may benefit from using includes:

+ Network adapter card
+ Printer

Here is the software that you'll need:

+ Windows 98, Windows 2000, or Windows NT is recommended, but many of the exercises in the book can be completed with other operating systems as well. A Linux system can be highly beneficial.

Conventions Used in This Book

This book uses a number of standards and conventions to help you process the material efficiently. It's helpful to familiarize yourself with the following items before reading the book.

New Terms

Many terms are unique to e-commerce. These terms can be confusing to e-commerce novices. New or potentially unfamiliar terms, such as *intellectual property*, are italicized in their first appearance in the book. In most cases, we define a new term right after its first mention. Unfamiliar words that are italicized but not followed by definitions can be looked up in the Glossary at the end of the book.

Code

All code listings in this book are presented in typewriter font, like this:

```
<time>6:00 A.M.</time>
```

This type of font is also used to identify names of files, folders, URLs, and code that you are to enter into a program in the Lab Exercises.

Icons

Several types of icons are used throughout this book to draw your attention to matters that deserve a closer look:

This icon is used to highlight a common mistake that could be made in working with the technology or topic being discussed. It represents our effort to steer you clear of potential problems.

This icon points you to another place in this book for more coverage of a particular topic. It may point you back to a previous chapter where important material has already been covered, or it may point you ahead to let you know that a topic will be covered in more detail later.

This icon points out important information or advice for those preparing to take the CIW E-commerce exam.

Sometimes things work differently in the real world than how they are described in books and on the CIW E-commerce exam. This icon draws your attention to our real-world experiences, which will hopefully help you on the job, if not on the exam.

This icon highlights a particular exam objective that's covered in the section where the icon appears. Use this visual clue to focus your study.

This icon is used to draw your attention to a little piece of friendly advice, a helpful fact, a shortcut, or a bit of personal experience that may be of use to you.

How to Contact Us

We've done our best to ensure that this book is technically accurate and free from errors. Our editors and technical reviewer have also worked their tails off to achieve this goal.

However, there will inevitably be some items that we have overlooked. So, if you find an error, or have a comment or insight that you'd like to share, please send us an e-mail message at CIWecomm@minnickweb.com.

We promise to read all of our readers' e-mails and include corrections and ideas in subsequent editions, if possible. Due to the high volume of e-mail that we receive, however, it may not be possible to respond to each e-mail. Please don't take it personally if you don't receive a response.

And one last request: For technical issues with the software used in this book, please contact the software vendor.

Good luck on the exam!

Acknowledgments

I would like to thank Ed Tittel for giving me the opportunity to work on this project. To Dawn Rader and the rest of the LANWrights team: Thanks for keeping everything working smoothly and answering all my questions! Finally, I would like to thank my partner Heather for putting up with all those hours I spent locked in my office on the weekends so I could meet my deadlines. — *Mandy Andress*

Thanks to Ed Tittel for allowing me to participate in the book. — *Phil Cox*

I would like to thank LANWrights for this great opportunity, Dawn you rock! Naturally, I also thank my beautiful wife Nicole for supporting me during my various projects and for making those all-important junk food runs for me! — *Shawn Porter*

Contents at a Glance

Contents

· ·

Part III: Operating System Security   173

Part V: Security Auditing, Analysis, and Intrusion Detection
379

Introducing Computer Security Concepts

◆   ◆   ◆   ◆

This part of the book serves as an introduction to most of the security concepts discussed throughout the remainder of the book.

Chapter 1, *A Security Primer*, examines the fundamental points of network and system security. This discussion includes information on overall computer security, including what data should be protected and what the data needs to be protected from. The chapter discusses the sources of system and network intrusion, where the biggest security risks lie, and how to assess security threats. The chapter concludes with an examination of the various security standards, and how to formally assess operating system security.

Basic Principles of System and Network Security discusses common security principles, explores methods for building a security policy that will meet the needs of your organization, and how to apply security practices, principles, and policies. Additionally, this chapter explores the three major areas of security risk — physical, software, and human. It shows how to integrate security with other business strategies. The chapter concludes with some common security checklists to help you formally assess your security needs.

Using Encryption Technologies begins with a general discussion of encryption and trusts. It then takes a more detailed look at encryption technologies, techniques, and strengths, and examines the processes of encryption in regard to

(continued)

Continued

network services and protocols. The chapter explores secure protocols, such as SSL, VPN, ISAKAMP, and IPSec. The chapter provides pointers to security associations and the Internet Key Exchange, and concludes with a discussion of PKI, digital certificates, and encryption alternatives.

Securing TCP/IP explores Internet Protocol security issues. To really break down IP, this chapter provides a layer-by-layer examination of IP's relationship with the OSI Reference Model.

A Security Primer

EXAM OBJECTIVES

- ✦ Explain the need for security
- ✦ List hacker motivations
- ✦ Describe how increased security mechanisms can result in increased latency
- ✦ Define authentication
- ✦ Explain access control
- ✦ Discuss data integrity
- ✦ Define data confidentiality
- ✦ Explain non-repudiation
- ✦ Identify security-related organizations, warning services, and certifications

CHAPTER PRE-TEST

1. What does security mean?

2. What are you protecting?

3. What are you protecting against?

4. What are the major security services?

5. What are the major security mechanisms?

✦ Answers to these questions can be found at the end of the chapter. ✦

Security is growing increasingly important in today's business environment. It has always been important; companies need to protect their data and sensitive corporate information (such as trade secrets and salary information) from malicious users, spies, and other sundry evildoers. But in today's fast-paced, online-based business world, security is critical to maintain success, profitability, and reputation.

The Internet is inherently insecure. It was designed as an open network, allowing anyone with a computer and an access provider to connect. Companies are now using the Internet as a means of communication, commerce, and collaboration; furthermore, they are demanding security technologies be developed to help secure these communications and processes. The security products industry is expected to grow to $7.4 billion in 2003, and the security services market is expected to reach $14 billion in 2003.

Defining Security

What exactly is security? It is hard to pin down an exact definition because it encompasses so many areas. In general, computer security is preventing attackers from achieving unauthorized access to or unauthorized use of computers and networks. Security encompasses network security, system security, and physical security, as well as manual processes and controls for dealing with people.

Security is more than the products and services most people associate with the industry. Renowned security expert Bruce Schneier continues to repeat his mantra that security is a process and a state of mind, not just a product or collection of products installed at a company. Security is a moving target because new flaws or vulnerabilities are constantly found in applications and products and because the computing environment in a company's network is always changing.

What Are You Protecting?

One of the main steps in security is defining what you are going to protect; for now, consider the main areas: data and information resources.

Data

Data is an integral part of any company. Very little of the information retained by a company is deemed unnecessary. Why else would you spend time and resources saving and protecting it? Depending on the industry, data such as customer information, design plans, secret formulas, and source code may be critical to a company's future success. What would happen if this data were destroyed, modified, or obtained by competitors?

Tip   In protecting data, you are protecting three things: availability, integrity, and confidentiality.

Availability

Protecting the availability of data is ensuring it is accessible to those who use the data when they need to use it. This area was not focused on very much until the denial-of-service (DoS) attacks hit the Internet in February 2000. Prior to these attacks, technology issues or maintenance problems were the main cause of availability problems. With the DoS attacks of 2000, it was shown that a few determined individuals could bring the Internet to its knees. If a company is running an e-commerce site through which the majority of revenues are obtained from online orders or displayed ad impressions, any downtime when the site is not accessible to customers can cost the company millions of dollars.

Integrity

 Objective   Discuss data integrity

Protecting the integrity of data is ensuring that the data will not been modified in any way, whether while in transit or in storage. If a company sends payroll data to a processing center over the Internet, how would the payroll department like a zero added to the HR Director's amount paid as the data is in transit, changing the amount to be paid from $5,000 to $50,000? It wouldn't be processing too many more payroll cycles in that manner, would it? Or, what if a zero were added to each salary field in the HR database, increasing everyone's salary by a magnitude of 10? Protecting data integrity prevents these kinds of errors.

Confidentiality

 Objective   Define data confidentiality

Protecting the confidentiality of data means ensuring that only authorized individuals can see the data. Access controls and authorization models help define who can see what, whereas cryptography and encryption technologies help prevent data from being seen by *sniffers* as it travels over public networks.

When most people think about security, they focus on confidentiality. Yes, secrecy is important, but the availability and integrity of data is just as crucial. A software company might lose millions of dollars if the source code to its applications is found and leaked to the public. The company might also lose millions of dollars if it becomes the victim of a DoS attack and customers cannot access the Web site to order products. Additionally, if the source code is modified slightly when being transferred from one machine to another, causing the application to crash the system instead of functioning properly, customers will not continue to buy the software, and word will spread quickly about the poor quality of the product.

Intangibles

This brings up another area of discussion, the intangible aspects of security. What happens if an attacker compromises your network and systems, stealing customer credit card numbers, corporate bank account numbers, or employee social security numbers? Customers might not be willing to take the risk to order something from your Web site or even do business with the company. When consumer confidence is shaken, it takes considerable work, and often a considerable amount of money, to regain that confidence.

Resources

Resources include all the components that compose company systems and networks. This includes end user resources, such as desktop computers and laptops, and server resources, such as Web servers, application servers, e-mail servers, FTP servers, and so on. One of the most overlooked resource areas is that of network resources. The hubs, switches, routers, and protocols that make communication possible are often highly susceptible to attack.

Information storage resources, such as Storage Area Networks (SANs) and databases, are critical in today's Information Age. These resources often contain the company jewels and should be protected accordingly, but they are often the most overlooked areas in a company's security plan.

What Are You Protecting Against?

Now that you have a general idea of what you are protecting, you need to know what it is that you are protecting against. The discussion here focuses on the general areas of attack. Specific types of attacks are discussed later in the book.

Active versus passive

Before you read about the main categories of attacks, it is worth mentioning that there are two types of attack approaches, active and passive. With active attacks, the attacker is doing something, whether it is making a phone call, submitting exploit code, poking around in a system they compromised, or launching a packet flood; they are physically involved in the process. This is in contrast to passive attacks in which the attacker sits back to see what happens. The best example of a passive attack is a sniffer. An attacker places a sniffer somewhere on a network and then waits to see what type of information he or she gets. Some sniffers even alert an attacker when it recognizes a user-id/password combination.

Attack categories

Security vulnerabilities can be broken down into three main categories: intrusion, denial of service, and theft.

Intrusion

Intrusion is the most common and well-known type of attack. Here, an attacker physically breaks into a system. This is done for a variety of reasons. Some attackers want to use the systems as launch points for other attacks, some are malicious and want to wreak havoc wherever they can, and others do it just for fun. You can read more about specific groups to watch out for in the "Sources of Attack" section later in the chapter.

An attacker can gain access to a system many ways. One of the easiest is through social engineering, the act of using weaknesses in human nature to gain user-ids and passwords to a system. One of the most popular social engineering attacks is to call up an employee pretending to be a system administrator. Violators tell the employee that they are having a few problems with the employee's account and that he or she needs to change his or her password immediately. To save the employee time, violators then suggest having the employee tell them his or her new password so that they can enter it into the system for him or her. *Voila*, the violators have a username and a password that may allow substantial system access or access to a system that contains valuable information.

Another avenue into a system is a *brute-force attack*, in which a violator tries all combinations of user-ids and passwords until he or she finds one that works. With a little thought and research, a brute-force attack is not as difficult and time-consuming as it sounds. Most people choose very guessable passwords.

The main entry point, though, is through vulnerabilities in applications and operating systems. Bugs in code, default configurations left unchanged, and misconfiguration of resources can leave a company wide open to attacks, without anyone's even realizing it. Keeping up-to-date with all the new vulnerabilities and exploits released is a full-time job in itself but is not considered a priority for many people, at least not until their systems are compromised by a bug in their Web server even though a patch fixing that bug was released two months ago.

Denial-of-service

Unlike intrusions, a *denial-of-service attack* does not cause any damage to data or resources. A denial-of-service attack is designed to prevent the use of important resources. In some cases, this attack can be more devastating than intrusion attacks if the sole purpose is to harm the targeted company. The denial-of-service attacks in February 2000 against Yahoo!, eBay, CNN, and other high-profile sites cost those companies millions of dollars in lost revenue, as well as a dip in consumer confidence.

Denial-of-service attacks are not limited to Web servers. Mail servers can be flooded with so many incoming mail messages that the system becomes overwhelmed and crashes. This attack is also known as a mail bomb. A denial-of-service attack can also be aimed at a network, filling it with so much extraneous traffic that authorized traffic cannot get through.

Disabling a user account is another type of denial-of-service attack. For security reasons (to protect against brute-force intrusion attacks), many user accounts are disabled after a specified number of failed login attempts and must be reset by an administrator. If the authorized user of the account wants to log in to the system and is unable to do so, then it constitutes a denial of service.

Information theft

Information theft is exactly what it seems; an attacker steals information. This could be user-ids and passwords, credit card numbers, network design documents, source code, or anything else the attacker may feel is valuable to the company or to the attacker him or herself. Information theft does not necessarily mean an intrusion has occurred. Passive information theft is very possible and is often the easiest way to gather user-id/password combinations.

Information theft is not always a technical feat, either. Dumpster diving is an effective way to gather information. Rifling through a company's garbage turns up a surprising amount of useful information. You might be surprised how many people throw away documents that contain passwords and other account information. Most attackers are looking for user-ids and passwords when stealing information, but others may be looking for those company secrets that give them a competitive advantage in the marketplace, an act considered industrial espionage.

Sources of Attacks

 List hacker motivations

Now that we have discussed what you are protecting and what you are protecting against, we need to define the term *attacker* in a little more detail.

An attacker is anyone looking to do something that is not authorized on a system or network. Many varieties of attackers exist, and many stereotypes go along with them. However, attackers do share a few common characteristics. They do not want to get caught, so they hide their identity and location as much as possible. If they gain access to your system(s), then they want to keep that access and cover their tracks as best as they can.

A discussion of all the groups and subgroups of attackers is beyond the scope of this book, but a few main categories include hackers, script-kiddies, crackers, spies, and insiders.

Hackers

Hackers are typically highly intelligent individuals who attempt to break in to a system to prove they can. They do not have malicious intent; they are not out to destroy data or steal information for competitors. Mainly, they want to prove their technical prowess and break in to highly secure networks and systems. They may find new vulnerabilities or develop new exploits in order to compromise a system. Hackers are most likely to use intrusion attacks against your systems.

Script kiddies

Script kiddies are generally adolescent individuals who are bored and looking for something to do. They are not usually exceptionally advanced in their technological knowledge; they download exploit scripts from the Internet to see what happens when they are run. If they do manage to compromise a system, they are often easily caught because they do not know enough to cover their tracks. Script kiddies are motivated by ego. To them, this is a game of one-upmanship, seeing who can break in to the coolest or most well-known system. Script kiddies will launch intrusion attacks, denial-of-service attacks, and information theft attacks against your systems.

Crackers

Crackers are the people the media often refers to as hackers. Crackers are like hackers, except for their motivation. Crackers are malicious. They either have something personal against the company they are attacking, or they have a personal message and are trying to find a way to get that message out. Many crackers vandalize Web sites to get their message to the public. Most crackers will launch intrusion attacks against your systems, but they are not beneath denial-of-service attacks if they have a personal vendetta against the company and want to cause problems. They will utilize information theft attacks to help them gain access to your systems.

Spies

Industrial espionage is growing quickly, with competing companies trying to find out what the other is doing by breaking into systems. *Spies* will most often launch information theft attacks because they are looking only for information. They are not trying to destroy the company they are attacking or cause any major damage.

Insiders

Insiders are probably the largest and most dangerous group of attackers, but are often overlooked. Insiders can include employees, contractors, consultants, accountants, lawyers, and any other individual trusted by the company. Generally, insiders are not a threat unless they become disgruntled. If unhappy, they may sabotage a system; delete, modify, or destroy data; or perform any number of actions to harm the company.

There have been numerous instances of programmers coding *logic bombs* in company systems and applications. Logic bombs are unauthorized pieces of code set to execute at a specific time or when specific conditions are met. One disgruntled system administrator knew he was getting fired and set the backup process to delete all contents of the backup tapes. Before he left, he coded a small batch file set to delete the entire contents of critical production systems. When this batch file ran, the company could not restore the system from the backup tapes because they were empty!

Dealing with insiders is a tricky issue because a certain amount of trust must be placed in employees. Proper controls and segregation of duties are the best way to mitigate the risk of insider attacks.

Understanding Security Issues and Risks

No system is completely secure, unless it is disconnected from the network, turned off, and thrown in a locked safe. This is not a practical solution. You can create a secure system that will keep out all but the most determined attackers, though. Adding more security than that is usually not cost-effective; you do not want to spend more money on security than the worth of the resources or data you are securing. For example, you do not want to implement a multi-million dollar Public Key Infrastructure (PKI) to protect data that is only worth $100,000 to the company.

Security is fallible. It relies on human intervention, and humans are imperfect, illogical beings. The most detailed security policies and procedures will not be effective if not implemented correctly. The best example is user passwords. A secure password is something not easily remembered by a human. Thus, we either write down our passwords, or we make them something easily remembered (and subsequently easily guessed by an attacker).

Another example of the interaction between humans and security technology deals with usability. System users want everything to be quick and easy. If the company has implemented a secure authentication system in which a card must be inserted into the system to log on, then the user will most likely keep that card in the system at all times, even when they go home at night, rendering the additional security provided by the technology completely useless. Achieving a balance between usability and security is key.

Security processes and technology also add additional overhead, increasing transaction latency (delay). For example, e-commerce sites' using SSL to encrypt customers' communications in order to protect private information such as credit card numbers increases communication time. SSL-enabled sites take a little longer to encrypt the data and send it to the customer than do non-SSL-enabled sites. Customers are willing to accept this increased latency because they value the security of their information.

Security is not a panacea; it cannot protect everything 100 percent. Security is a tool used to mitigate risk, to create a balance. This is very difficult to achieve and is actually an ongoing process, with the balance swaying from one side to the other and security professionals trying to maintain equilibrium. Attackers are always on the lookout for new holes and vulnerabilities in systems, so security professionals must always be on alert.

Developing a Security Plan

Each chapter of this book deals with a component of the security plan, but there are a few characteristics that should be considered before diving in to various security technologies. A security plan should be flexible, scalable, easy to use, and informative.

Flexible

A flexible security plan provides for changes in the corporate computing environment. If the company changes from a product-oriented business to a services-oriented business, then different data and resources are considered critical. A security plan must be able to be modified quickly and efficiently to reflect the changes in the company's direction.

Scalable

A scalable security plan allows the security infrastructure to grow as the company grows. This is key with today's fast-growing companies. I have often seen small companies with great security plans, but as the company grew, they could not successfully scale the security to the new company size, which left them vulnerable to attack.

Easy to use

A difficult security plan is often equivalent to no security plan. If security is too difficult and cumbersome for users, they will find ways around it, providing no security protection for the company.

Informative

A good security plan provides a means for alarming and reporting. You need to know when a security breach has occurred so you can research what damage, if any, was done and how to fix the problem so it won't happen again. The reporting needs to be detailed and timely. You don't need a report telling you a month after the fact that one of your systems was breached.

Security Standards

Since security is such a large, overwhelming area, formal standards have been developed to help define what is secure.

International Standards Organization

The International Standards Organization (ISO) developed document 7498-2, "Information Processing Systems — Open Systems Interconnection — Basic Reference Model — Part 2: Security Architecture." This document describes security architecture concepts such as security services and security mechanisms. It also outlines how security services can be placed in OSI Reference Model.

 Cross-Reference For more information on the OSI Reference Model, consult Chapter 4.

Security services

The ISO standard defines several key security services, as outlined in Table 1-1. You will learn more about these in later chapters.

Table 1-1 Definitions of Security Services	
Security Service	**Function**
Authentication	Authentication is the process of proving that you are who you say you are, establishing proof of identity. This can be achieved through the use of passwords, smart cards, biometrics, or a combination thereof.
Access control	Access controls provide a means of determining who can access what system resources. After a user is authenticated to a system, defined access controls tell the system where the user can go. For example, ordinary system users should not have access to areas where account passwords are stored. Access control services prevent this from occurring.
Data confidentiality	Data confidentiality protects data from being viewed by unauthorized individuals.
Data integrity	Data integrity protects data from being modified, retaining the consistency and original meaning of the information.
Non-repudiation	Repudiation is the ability for an individual to deny participation in a transaction. If a customer places an order and a non-repudiation security service is not built in to the system, the customer could deny ever making that purchase. Non-repudiation services provide a means of proving that a transaction occurred, whether it was an order being placed at an online store or an e-mail message being sent and received.

Security mechanisms

ISO 7498-2 also defines security mechanisms. A security mechanism is a technology, whether it is software or a procedure, that implements one or more security services. The main security mechanisms are defined in Table 1-2.

Table 1-2 Definitions of Security Mechanisms	
Security Mechanism	*Function*
Encryption	Encryption is the process of converting data to an unrecognizable form. It supports security services such as authentication, confidentiality, integrity, and non-repudiation. You will learn more about encryption technologies in Chapter 3.
Digital signatures	Digital signatures help guarantee the authenticity of data, much like a written signature verifies the authenticity of a paper document. They support security services such as authentication and non-repudiation.
Access control	Access control is a process that ensures a person or system has the permission to use a requested resource. These controls can be built directly into the operating system, incorporated into applications, or implemented as add-on packages. One example of an access control mechanism is a firewall.
Data integrity checks	Data integrity checks include mechanisms such as parity checks and checksum comparisons. These support the data integrity service and require the sender and receiver to compare check sequences to ensure the data has not been modified.
Authentication exchange	Authentication exchange is a communication mechanism between a requester and a verifier to assure the verifier of the requester's identity. This communication can occur between the sender and the receiver in the case of mutual authentication or between the sender, receiver, and a third party in the case of third-party authentication.
Traffic padding	Traffic padding is a mechanism that disguises data characteristics to provide protection against traffic analysis. This mechanism can include the padding of data (adding irrelevant and unnecessary data to a message) or sending dummy messages to disguise traffic.

Specific versus pervasive mechanisms

As defined by ISO, a security mechanism can be specific or pervasive. A specific security mechanism implements only one security service at a time. One example of a specific security mechanism is encryption. Although encryption can be used to implement data confidentiality, integrity, and non-repudiation security services, the means of implementation requires a different security mechanism for each service.

A pervasive security mechanism implements multiple security services. Usually, pervasive mechanisms are a list of procedures. Examples of pervasive mechanisms include incident detection and response procedures and audit logs.

Other standards

In addition to the standards set by ISO, there are other standards that have been developed, as discussed in the following sections.

British Standard 7799

British Standard 7799: Part 2: 1998 Specification for Information Security Management Systems provides a series of mandatory controls that a company must successfully implement before obtaining certification.

The controls cover the following areas in a significant level of detail:

✦ Information security policy

✦ Security organization

✦ Assets classification and control

✦ Personnel security

✦ Physical and environmental security

✦ Computer and network management

✦ System access control

✦ System development and maintenance

✦ Business continuity planning

✦ Compliance

Orange Book

The Orange Book is the nickname of the Trusted Computer System Evaluation Criteria (TCSEC) developed by the United States in the early 1980s. It gained its name from the color of the book cover. It is one book in a series of standards often called the Rainbow Series because each book has a different colored cover.

The Orange Book defines a series of levels of secure systems, starting with level D (least secure) and rising to level A1 (the most secure). Although the Orange Book is useful, its relevance in the security world has diminished a bit in recent years. Mainly, the standards are dated and designed specifically for government organizations. The rapid advancement in technology and the high levels of security required by the government make these standards difficult for a company to implement.

For more detailed information on the Orange Book levels of secure systems, see Chapter 9.

Common Criteria

Common Criteria (`www.commoncriteria.org`) is a joint effort between the United States, Canada, France, Germany, and the United Kingdom to develop an international standard of criteria for evaluation of IT security. The criteria stems from the Trusted Computer System Evaluation Criteria (TCSEC) and the Federal Criteria for Information Technology Security (FC) developed by the United States, the Information Technology Security Evaluation Criteria (ITSEC) developed by the European Commission, and the Canadian Trusted Computer Product Evaluation Criteria (CTCPEC).

Security Organizations

 Identify security-related organizations, warning services, and certifications

Numerous security-related organizations exist around the world to help keep people informed and up-to-date on innovations and findings in the security industry.

SANS Institute

Founded in 1989, the System Administration, Networking, and Security (SANS) Institute is one of the leading security organizations. It is a research and education organization focused on sharing the lessons and skills learned by its government, corporate, and educational entity members. The Institute's online content is free to the public, and offers many training classes and seminars throughout the world (`www.sans.org`).

Computer Security Institute

Founded in 1974, the Computer Security Institute (CSI) provides information and seminars to computer and network security professionals. CSI sponsors the annual Computer Security Conference and Exhibition, the NetSec Conference, and numerous technical security seminars (`www.gocsi.com`).

Warning Services

Many companies have recently launched warning services, sending an e-mail or page to a specified individual when a new vulnerability or exploit is found in products they use. Even with the introduction of these new services, the best warning system is still monitoring the BugTraq mailing lists. BugTraq, now located at `www.securityfocus.com`, is the premiere mailing list for security vulnerabilities. Starting in 1993, almost every known vulnerability and exploit has been posted on the BugTraq mailing list for other security experts to read, test, and comment on. A Windows NT specific mailing list, NT Bugtraq, was created by Russ Cooper and can be found at `www.ntbugtraq.com`.

Certifications

As in any field, people like to have a validation of skills to help show that a purported security professional has a base level of knowledge. Although certifications in the security field are rather new, a few recognized credentials exist.

CISSP

The Certified Information Systems Security Professional (CISSP) certification is quickly becoming the standard for security professionals, much like the CPA certification for public accountants. The CISSP is administered by the International Information Systems Security Certifications Consortium (ISC)2, which can be found at `www.isc2.org`. Pass an exam and work in the security industry for a minimum of three years and you will achieve the CISSP certification. The exam covers ten domains in the Common Body of Knowledge (CBK) of security:

- ✦ Access control systems and methodology
- ✦ (Computer) operations security
- ✦ Cryptography
- ✦ Application systems and development
- ✦ Business continuity and disaster recovery planning
- ✦ Telecommunications and network security
- ✦ Security architecture and models
- ✦ Physical security
- ✦ Security management practices
- ✦ Law, investigation, and ethics

This certification is focused on the development of security information security policies, standards, and procedures. Corporate positions such as Chief Information Officer (CIO), Chief Security Officer (CSO), and Director of Security are the focus for this certification.

The CISSP Web site can be found at `http://www.isc2.org/cissp_examination.html`.

SSCP

`http://www.isc2.org/sscp_examination.html`

(ISC)2 has recently introduced a new certification, the Systems Security Certified Practitioner (SSCP). This certification is aimed at network, system, and security administrators, those individuals who implement security technologies and work with them on a daily basis. The exam covers seven security domains:

✦ Access control

✦ Administration

✦ Audit and monitoring

✦ Risk, response, and recovery

✦ Cryptography

✦ Data communications

✦ Malicious code

The goal of this certification is to make system administrators more security conscious. Similar to the CISSP certification, SSCP requires passing an exam and one year of direct work experience.

The SSCP Web site can be found at `http://www.isc2.org/sscp_examination.html`.

SANS Institute

`http://www.sans.org/giactc.htm`

SANS Institute recently began offering certifications through their Global Incident Analysis Center (GIAC). The SANS/GIAC certifications are focused on hands-on, how-to knowledge, not just theory. To achieve certification, a candidate must pass an exam and submit a practical paper on a relevant topic. SANS certifications include LevelOne Security Essentials and LevelTwo Subject Area Modules. Currently, LevelTwo subjects include the following:

- ✦ Firewalls, perimeter protection, and virtual private networks
- ✦ Intrusion detection in depth
- ✦ Advanced incident handling and hacker exploits
- ✦ Securing Windows
- ✦ Securing UNIX

The SANS Institute's Web site can be found at `http://www.sans.org/giactc.htm`.

Certified Internet Webmaster (CIW)

The Certified Internet Webmaster (CIW) certification was developed by ProsoftTraining to validate an individual's Internet skills. One component of this certification is the Security Professional Exam, which is the reason you are reading this book. This exam is aimed at individuals looking to secure systems and networks connected to the Internet.

Vendor certifications

Many vendors offer certifications for their products. Certifications offered by companies such as Cisco and Check Point have become highly recognized in the industry and are often required for product-specific positions.

Key Point Summary

This chapter presents an introduction to security principles that will be built on throughout future chapters.

- ✦ Security is preventing attackers from unauthorized access to or unauthorized use of computers and networks. It is all encompassing and includes more than specific technologies and products; it is a process and a mentality, something that should be considered in every situation.
- ✦ Security protects data and resources from intrusion, denial of service, and theft.
- ✦ There are many types of attackers and reasons for launching attacks. The main groups include hackers, script kiddies, crackers, spies, and insiders.
- ✦ No system is ever completely secure. Companies use security to mitigate risk and weigh the cost of implementing a security technology against the benefits received by it.

✦ Security must be user-friendly and understood by everyday system users. If a security implementation is too complex, users will find a way around it, exposing the company's systems and networks to attack.

✦ A security plan should be flexible, scalable, easy to use, and informative.

✦ The International Standards Organization (ISO) developed standard 7498-2 regarding information security. In this standard, ISO defines security services: authentication, access control, data confidentiality, data integrity, and non-repudiation. ISO also defines security mechanisms: encryption, digital signatures, access control, data integrity checks, authentication exchange, and traffic padding.

✦ Other important standards include British Standard 7799, the Orange Book, and the Common Criteria.

✦ The SANS Institute and CSI are two of the more well-known security organizations that provide training and information for security professionals.

✦ Warning services provide security professionals timely information on new exploits and vulnerabilities, allowing them to act quickly and decisively to protect their data and resources.

✦ Numerous security certifications exist, including the CISSP, SSCP, SANS/GIAC, CIW, and vendor certifications.

✦   ✦   ✦

STUDY GUIDE

This Study Guide presents five assessment questions to test your knowledge of the chapter objectives.

Assessment Questions

1. A good security plan should be:

    A. Long and complicated

    B. Flexible, scalable, easy to use, and informative

    C. Scalable and easy to use

    D. Informative and flexible

2. Which security service provides a means of proving that a transaction occurred?

    A. Access control

    B. Authentication

    C. Non-repudiation

    D. Data confidentiality

3. Which security mechanism disguises data characteristics to protect against traffic analysis?

    A. Authentication exchange

    B. Data integrity checks

    C. Digital signatures

    D. Traffic padding

4. The digital signature mechanism supports which security services?

    A. Authentication and on-repudiation

    B. Authentication, confidentiality, integrity, and non-repudiation

    C. Access control

    D. Data integrity

5. The most dangerous and overlooked source of attack against a company is often:

   A. Hackers

   B. Spies

   C. Insiders

   D. Script kiddies

Answers to Chapter Questions

Chapter Pre-Test

1. Security is preventing attackers from achieving unauthorized access to or unauthorized use of computers and networks.

2. You are protecting your data, resources, and intangible areas such as company reputation and customer confidence.

3. You are protecting against intrusion, denial of service, and theft.

4. The major security services are authentication, access control, data confidentiality, data integrity, and non-repudiation.

5. The major security mechanisms are encryption, digital signatures, access control, data integrity checks, authentication exchange, and traffic padding.

Assessment Questions

1. **B.** A good security plan should be flexible, scalable, easy to use, and informative.

2. **C.** Non-repudiation is the security service that proves a transaction occurred.

3. **D.** Traffic padding is the security mechanism that disguises data characteristics to provide protection against traffic analysis.

4. **A.** The digital signature mechanism supports the authentication and non-repudiation security services. Choice B lists the services supported by encryption. Choice C is the service supported by the access control mechanism, and Choice D is the service supported by the data integrity checks mechanism.

5. **C.** Insiders are the most dangerous and overlooked group of attackers.

Basic Principles of System and Network Security

✦ ✦ ✦ ✦

- ✦ Understand the importance of a formalized security policy
- ✦ Understand the major authentication methods
- ✦ Understand the need for access control
- ✦ Understand the function of an access control list
- ✦ Understand the purpose of auditing
- ✦ Identify the three main encryption methods
- ✦ Understand the business impact of security solutions

CHAPTER PRE-TEST

1. What is an access control list?

2. What are the six main elements of security?

3. List two types of authentication methods.

4. Why are business issues important to consider?

5. Why is auditing important?

The basic principles of security help define what should and should not be considered when implementing a security strategy. All decisions should be based on the needs and priorities of the company, so a systematic approach should be used to make sure all aspects of the company and its resources are analyzed.

Chapter 1 discussed the basics of security at a high level, focusing on international standards and definitions. This chapter discusses in more detail each of the elements necessary for an effective security infrastructure.

Understanding Common Security Elements

There are six main security elements, shown in Figure 2-1, required for any security infrastructure. Like the food group pyramid you might remember from growing up, the bottom element of the security pyramid is the base and must be in place to create a strong foundation. In the security world, this base is the corporate security policy, discussed in more detail later in the chapter in the section "Applying Security Practices, Principles, and Policies."

User authentication is the process of determining who someone is. This helps to ensure that only authorized users access a system or network. There are several ways to achieve this, though they are not all 100 percent accurate. Encryption is the process of hiding the true message in a form indecipherable to anyone but the intended recipient. This process helps prevent data from being read by network traffic sniffing or the reading of confidential files not meant to be seen by the general public. Access control ensures that only the appropriate people can access a specified resource. Coupled with authentication, access control is one of the most powerful security elements. Audit and administration are necessary, ongoing elements that help you maintain a strong security infrastructure. Periodic audits help you ensure the company is following the corporate security policy, and timely administration helps keep everything up-to-date.

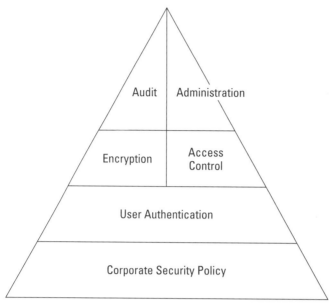

Figure 2-1: The six elements of an effective security infrastructure require a corporate security policy as a basic foundation.

The Positive Power of Paranoia

Security is all about being paranoid. The more paranoid you are, the stronger your security infrastructure will be. Of course, you can take your levels of paranoia a bit too far and cross the point where additional security mechanisms are just a waste of money, and an inconvenience to your users. What paranoia does accomplish, though, is keeping you on your toes, always suspecting that someone is trying to break into a system or the network. This keeps you alert and on the lookout for strange and unusual activity.

Administrators help implement and enforce the corporate security policy and audit user activity. In some companies, a separate audit organization is created to perform all auditing functions. An effective audit group is one that maintains a healthy level of paranoia.

Building a Security Policy

The basic foundation of any security infrastructure is the security policy. An effective security infrastructure helps secure resources, but more importantly, provides a formal written policy for everyone to follow.

A security policy sets the guidelines for the entire organization. Be aware, though, that the security policy must reflect the culture and goals of the company. Implementing a security policy that states no employees may have Internet access when the company regularly uses the Internet for business purposes does not provide any protection. In fact, it makes the rest of the security policy difficult to implement because that one section will be ignored. If that section can be ignored, so can others. Your security policy becomes useless.

A security policy defines how to protect your resources, but you need to know what resources need protection and how much protection they need. Follow these six steps:

1. Classify your systems.

2. Determine security priorities for each system.

3. Assign risk factors.

4. Define acceptable and unacceptable activities.

5. Decide how you will educate employees about security.

6. Determine who will administer your policy.

After classifying all your resources, implement the security policy on a resource-by-resource basis. For example, the security policy for an end user's workstation might ensure that no highly confidential files are stored there and that the system is running the latest antivirus software, while the security policy for a mail server might discuss items such as encrypting outgoing mail to certain parties; specifying what services, such as Telnet, can and cannot be running on the system; and so on. The main point is that each resource has specific security needs and should be analyzed accordingly.

Resource classification

The first step in developing a security policy is to classify all your resources. These resources must be classified based on their importance to the company. A three-level classification system is often the most helpful:

Level I

Level I systems are central to the business's operations. For example, an Internet portal company might classify its Web servers as Level I systems. Employee databases, user account databases, and e-mail servers all count as Level I resources based on their importance to the company and the critical data they contain.

Level II

Level II systems are necessary to the company, but are not critical to daily operation. These systems could be out a day or two and not cause any major losses to the company. For example, if the company contact database was down for a few days, this might annoy some people, but it would not cause a great monetary loss to the company.

Level III

Level III systems are those that are not needed by the company on a daily basis. A desktop system is an example of a Level III system. If a desktop goes down, the employee can use another system without interrupting his or her work too much. Also, a system is Level III as long as it does not affect any system in Levels I and II.

Table 2-1 summarizes the classification levels.

Table 2-1 Resource Classification Summary			
Level	**Data**	**Systems**	**Security**
Level I — Critical	Production data, data requiring high levels of data integrity.	Systems that would disrupt normal business operations when lost, mission-critical systems, such as Web servers, certificate servers, database servers, mail servers.	Focused security policy, system level audit, continuous monitoring, dedicated security.
Level II — Significant	Data that could damage the company if lost or if it becomes part of the public domain.	Daily business systems that could sustain up to 48 hours of downtime.	Normal security, plus focused system audits.
Level III — Routine	Operational data.	Systems whose complete loss would not significantly damage the company.	Normal security policy.

Categorize resources wisely

Make sure you categorize your systems wisely. Administrators often categorize a majority of their systems as Level I. Securing Level I systems takes considerable time, money, and resources. Classify only those mission-critical systems as Level I.

Analyze each resource carefully, making sure the decided impact of the loss of the system on the company is accurate. Use the following criteria to categorize resources:

- ✦ **Level of traffic** — The more traffic the machine receives, the higher the criticality.

- ✦ **Sensitivity of information** — The more sensitive the information, the higher the criticality.

- ✦ **Operating system** — Some operating systems are more secure than others. An unhardened Windows NT system would have a higher criticality than a Solaris system would.

Prioritize resources

After classifying each resource as Level I, II, or III, prioritize each system within a category based on perceived threats and the actions to be taken to protect against those threats. The resources with the highest criticality and perceived threat are the highest priority. Priorities should be based on the significance of the system to the company. For example, a data gathering company might classify its database servers as a higher priority than its mail server. This list of prioritized resources is essential because you do not want rash decisions made during a crisis. Everything should already be analyzed and defined before a crisis occurs.

Time and money are of the utmost importance when prioritizing systems. Most companies have a limited amount of both, so both should be distributed wisely. Make sure the highest priority systems receive enough time and money to adequately secure them. If time and money are running out, then make sure the less critical systems, such as Level III systems, have at least enough security to protect them against their major threats. For example, antivirus software is usually a must for Level III systems.

Assign risk factors

After categorizing and prioritizing systems, assign risk factors to each resource based on the probability of attack by an outside hacker or a malicious user. The basic rule for assigning risk factors is the more sensitive or critical the resource, the higher the risk factor.

As with everything else that has been discussed, risk factors are unique to each company. Some use a scale of 1–10, whereas others use High, Medium, and Low as their risk factor scale. Assign risk levels that are appropriate for your company based on the function of the resource in the corporate environment and the goals of the company.

Define acceptable and unacceptable activities

The next step in establishing a security policy is to define the acceptable and unacceptable activities for each resource. Each company has different opinions on what is acceptable and unacceptable; therefore, this is specific to the needs of your company. One business may feel it is okay to allow end users to open Windows shares on their desktop machines, while another may not.

Acceptable activities

Acceptable activities vary from resource to resource and from user to user. A policy for a corporate mail server may specify that users can only connect to the server using a company-specified e-mail client to check their mail. Administrators, of course, have additional acceptable activities that are required to maintain the system.

Unacceptable activities

Unacceptable activities also vary from resource to resource. You can approach unacceptable activities in a variety of ways. You can explicitly define acceptable activities and state that everything else is unacceptable, or you can explicitly state what is unacceptable. Each method has pros and cons. Listing acceptable activities might hinder users in their job functions if the acceptable activities list is too narrow. On the other hand, you might open loopholes through the security policy by listing unacceptable activities and accidentally omitting something important.

Most companies take the approach of listing unacceptable activities. This means the policy must be reviewed and updated frequently, but a publicly accessible list helps create a more effective policy.

If and when an action is challenged, security policies are your legal standing. Make sure your security policy accurately and thoroughly reflects what activities can and cannot be performed and defines the appropriate disciplinary action that must be taken when the policy is not followed.

Define measures to apply to resources

Once resources have been identified and their uses determined, then it is time to identify the appropriate technology that should be used to implement the policy. Security technologies can include the purchase of firewalls, antivirus software, encryption technologies, and authentication devices such as smartcards.

This step is very important and should closely follow the prioritized resource list. Some security technologies require more time and money to implement and administer, so these solutions should be implemented only on the most critical resources. Always perform a cost-benefit analysis, making sure the security measures you implement do not cost more than the replacement of the resource you are protecting.

A good way to start is to list the measures you wish to implement on each resource. For example, on the mail server you may want to implement attachment and content filtering as well as encryption.

Define education standards

The best way to ensure that the security policy is followed and implemented correctly is to educate the end user. By knowing why the security measure is in place and how important it is to the success of the company, users are more likely to follow the security policy than to think it is intrusive and a waste of time and to find ways to circumvent it.

Users need to be educated on the significance and importance of selecting strong passwords. Programmers need to be educated on how to program securely, protecting against buffer overflow attacks and backdoors. Administrators need to be educated on how to securely configure a system.

Each type of user requires a different level of training. Administrators are more technical by nature, and their job requires they have a full understanding of resource security and how to implement and administer it. Executives need to understand the importance of security to their company to help them make more informed decisions on security policy. Users need to understand their role in the security process. They need to be aware of security threats and vulnerabilities and how they are a critical component of the security infrastructure.

Administering the policies

One of the most essential components of the security policy is the assignment of specific roles and responsibilities for administering the policy. If this is not included, everybody will point the finger the other way, and nothing will get accomplished. Responsibilities must be clearly defined and delineated.

In smaller companies, everything may fall on the shoulders of one or two individuals. In larger corporations, often separate groups handle network security, auditing, and administration.

User Authentication

Moving up to the next level in the pyramid, I want to discuss the importance of user authentication in a security infrastructure.

Authentication is the process of verifying the identity of the user or system trying to access a resource. You encounter authentication almost every day of your life. Signing your name on a credit card receipt is one form of authentication. The merchant compares that signature to the one on the back of your credit card. Entering your PIN at the ATM machine is another form of authentication.

Authentication methods

 Understand the major authentication methods

There are four main methods you use to prove you are who you say you are:

◆ Proving what you know

◆ Showing what you have

◆ Demonstrating who you are

◆ Identifying where you are

Proving what you know

Proving what you know is the most common form of authentication used on the Internet and systems today. The best example is an access password. When you log on to a computer to access its resources, your bank account to access your balance, or your brokerage account to check on your stocks, you have to enter a password to access the information and resources. If you give your password to someone else, that person can access everything you can access. The same goes for a cracker or malicious user that figures out your password.

Showing what you have

This method of authentication is a little more complex than proving what you know because you need something physical. The best example is a building access card, such as those annoying little pieces of plastic you have to keep with you at all times so you can enter your office. Authentication here is based on possession. The system assumes that if you have possession of the card, you are entitled to enter the building. But if this is the only measure in place, it is useless if a user's card is stolen.

The best way to mitigate this risk is by combining methods. The most common way of doing this today is combining what you know with what you have, often referred to as two-factor authentication. A good example is accessing an ATM machine. You must have the card (something you have) and the PIN (something you know) to access your account. If your card is stolen, the thief will not be able to make cash withdrawals out of an ATM machine because he or she does not have the PIN (unless you wrote it on the back of the card). If your PIN is compromised, the thief cannot do anything with it unless he or she also has the card. In computer systems, two-factor authentication includes smartcards, digital certificates, and SecurID.

Smartcards

Smartcards are credit card–sized devices that contain a microchip. This microchip can contain quite a bit of information about a user, including name, Social Security number, drivers license number, address, and digital certificate.

American Express launched its Blue Card, shown in Figure 2-2, which is a smart-card. The chip on the Blue Card is read-only and can be accessed only through the American Express card reader. The Blue Card helps provide two-factor authentication for purchases over the Internet because the purchaser must have the physical card inserted in the reader for the transaction to process correctly.

Figure 2-2: The American Express Blue Card uses smartcard technology to help secure transactions.

There are many types of smartcards available. Stored value cards may be used to create a cashless system. Stored memory cards are read-only, and the contents cannot be altered once created. Some cards require readers, although others do not. The best smartcard for your company depends on how you intend to use the technology.

Smartcards are not cheap. A card and reader can cost up to $100 per person. Thus, this is not the best technology to use unless you really need a strong authentication system, as may be required on some Level I systems.

Smartcard use is expected to grow rapidly in the United States in the next few years. Smartcards have been used in Europe for quite some time. For more information on smartcards, take a look at the following:

✦ http://www.visa.com/pd/smart/main.html

✦ http://www.smart-card.com/

✦ http://www.smartcardforum.org/

SecurID

SecurID, currently sold by RSA, is another option for two-factor authentication. With SecurID, users are given a token (shown in Figure 2-3) that changes the random number displayed every 60 seconds. To log in to a system using SecurID, the user must enter a PIN as well as the number displayed on the token.

For more information on SecurID, take a look at www.rsasecurity.com/product/securid.

Figure 2-3: SecurID tokens can be used for two-factor authentication.

Demonstrating who you are

Authentication by demonstrating who you are is based on some human characteristic that cannot be easily duplicated, also known as biometrics. Biometric authentication is expensive, but it is becoming cheaper as new technologies are developed. Biometrics includes everything from fingerprints to retinal scans to voice recognition.

There are still issues with the accuracy of biometric authentication, though. The possibility of a false positive or false negative still exists. With a false positive, an individual not authorized to access a resource may be granted access. With a false negative, an authorized individual may be denied access. Hopefully, advances in the technology will alleviate these issues.

Identifying where you are

Identifying where you are determines a user's identity based on his or her location, often by IP address. The largest threat here is spoofing, or someone fooling the system into thinking he or she is an authenticated user. If someone sits at your machine or spoofs your IP address, he or she can gain access to all the resources you can access.

Cross-Reference   Spoofing is thoroughly defined in Chapter 5.

Another form of location authentication is reverse DNS. Before the relaxation of the use of 128-bit encryption, many companies performed reverse DNS lookups to make sure the request was coming from a U.S.-based system. This method is easily circumvented with IP spoofing.

Encryption

 Identify the three main encryption methods

Moving up to the next level of the security element pyramid, I want to discuss the role of encryption.

 Encryption technologies are discussed in greater detail in Chapter 3.

Encryption is used to make a document on network traffic indecipherable to anyone but the intended recipient. Because the Internet is a public network, encryption technology is often used to protect sensitive and confidential data that travels through it, protecting it from the prying eyes of network sniffers. The following sections explore encryption in further detail.

Encryption types are divided into three main categories. Each category has its own unique purpose in the security world and its own set of algorithms.

 Encryption is discussed in detail in Chapter 3.

Symmetric

Symmetric encryption encrypts and decrypts data with the same key. This speeds up the process, but also introduces problems with key management.

Asymmetric

Asymmetric encryption uses a different key for encryption and decryption. This process is slower than symmetric encryption, but eliminates some of the key management issues of symmetric encryption.

Hash encryption

Hash encryption performs a one-way mathematical function on data and creates a fixed-length "hash code." This hash code can be used to check data integrity because the same set of data always generates the same hash code. Theoretically, no two sets of data generate the same hash code. By comparing hash codes from before and after the data traveled through the Internet, you can easily tell if anything has been modified in transit.

Access Control

 Understand the need for access control

The next security element I discuss is access control. Access control works in conjunction with authentication to make sure authorized individuals access authorized resources. Two main types of access control technologies are access control lists and execution control lists.

The authentication process helps prove your identity and that you are authorized to access a given resource. Access control is the next step in the process, which controls exactly what resources you can use and gain access to on a system.

Access control lists

 Understand the function of an access control list

Access control lists are one of the most common ways to limit user access to resources. By definition, an access control list is a table listing individual users and groups and what access rights each has to a particular object, such as a file or directory. The most common privileges are read, write, and execute.

For example, a public file directory on a network might give everyone read and execute privileges, but deny write access so a file cannot be modified without the owner's permission. Another example is giving only system administrators execute privileges for the firewall administration program. If someone tries to access a resource and he or she is denied, an exception message should be displayed and the event should be logged, especially for critical resources such as password files.

Execution control lists

Execution control lists (ECLs) are relatively new to the security arena. These lists focus on individual applications and what system resources those applications can access. Web browsers such as Netscape Navigator and Microsoft's Internet Explorer are prime examples of applications that would use execution control lists.

Numerous security vulnerabilities exist in Web browser applications, especially those using ActiveX and Java applets, that allow malicious users to access various system resources that should not be accessed. ECLs can help prevent this. ECLs control what resources an application can access and can deny any request to a resource that is not permitted.

Auditing

 Understand the purpose of auditing

The next level in the security element pyramid brings me to an introductory discussion of auditing.

 For a detailed discussion on auditing, refer to Chapter 17.

Auditing is an ongoing process essential to any security infrastructure. It can take many forms, from log analysis to periodic system audits. Many systems today provide auditing, or logging, features that help administrators keep track of specific events that are important to them, such as incorrect login attempts, accesses to the administrator account, and so on.

The main purpose of auditing is to make sure the security policy is properly implemented. Reviewing system configurations ensures that only authorized services are running on systems. Reviewing access control lists ensures that only authorized individuals are granted access to specific files, directories, and programs.

Passive and active auditing are the two main categories of auditing techniques.

Passive auditing

Passive auditing, such as logging, is anything that is recorded without the intervention of an administrator or auditor. With logging, trigger events are recorded automatically. The appropriate individual then reviews the logs and investigates and resolves any anomalies. Passive auditing is not real time or preventative.

Active auditing

Active auditing is the process of taking immediate action to an event, such as terminating a login when unacceptable activity occurs or blocking access to certain Web sites and servers.

There must be a balance between auditing and other administrative tasks that need to be performed. Auditing can be very resource intensive on both systems and people. If you find your administrators are spending most of their time auditing, then you may want to consider hiring a full-time auditor or reexamine the auditing needs of your company. Too much auditing is counterproductive, but too little auditing threatens the security of your resources and the strength of your security infrastructure.

Applying Security Practices, Principles, and Policies

When combining all elements of security into the corporate security policy and then creating the procedures to implement the appropriate security technology, consider three main areas:

✦ Physical security

✦ Software security

✦ Human security

Physical security

Physical security involves protecting physical assets. Building access systems, door locks, fire extinguishers, halon systems, raised floors, fire-resistant safes, security alarms, smoke detectors, environment control systems, off-site storage of critical documents, and backup tapes are all part of physical security.

Physical security is important and is often the most visible component of a security infrastructure. It's hard to miss the raised floors in the computer room and the building access control system. Protecting the physical assets is just as important as protecting the electronic assets. If a fire breaks out in the computer room and your company has a water sprinkler system, your computer systems will be ruined, as well as all the data stored on them unless you have an adequate physical security system in place.

 Tip   Crackers and malicious users are often where companies focus their attention; you need to make sure you don't overlook the obvious.

Software security

Software security is an all-encompassing area that includes everything electronic: network security, system security, database security, and so on. This is the area where companies focus most of their resources, time, and money. Security technologies that fit in this category include just about everything you are familiar with, including firewalls, encryption, access control lists, and authentication mechanisms.

Human security

Human security is the most important element of security but is also the most overlooked. Human security involves making users aware of what the security issues are and how they can help create a secure corporate culture. The key to human security is education. Without proper education, users will continue to open e-mail attachments that overload the network with bogus e-mails or erase the contents of their hard drive. They will continue to select weak passwords, leaving even the most security-conscious administrators vulnerable to a security breach.

Integrating Security with Other Strategies

A security infrastructure should not exist in a vacuum. It should combine with and fit within the goals and direction of the company. Security should not be an afterthought on any project; it should be considered an essential component from day one. For example, a company looking to create an Internet presence by allowing customers to access account information online should start considering the security implications of the project immediately. Tech support personnel need to be trained on how to handle users that have forgotten their password so the company is not susceptible to social engineering attacks. The design of the system should be analyzed to make sure it does not create significant security holes in the company's network.

By including security in all aspects of the business, you not only create a company with a security-conscious culture, but you also create an effective security infrastructure that helps you maintain an advantage over your competitors. Creating an effective security infrastructure helps protect the intangibles such as reputation and customer satisfaction because you are not susceptible to successful attacks. If an attacker does manage to penetrate your various levels of security, you have the correct procedures in place to deal with that security breach effectively and efficiently.

Business Issues for Security

 Understand the business impact of security solutions

Security is all about trade-offs. You mitigate business risk by implementing security measures. You determine what security measures to implement based on a risk and cost-benefit analysis.

Make sure that any security mechanism implemented does not place an undue burden on the users. This decreases productivity and the effectiveness of the security mechanism because users find ways to circumvent it. Security solutions should be easy for the end user to install and use.

Key Point Summary

This chapter continues the introduction to security principles that will be discussed in more detail in future chapters.

✦ There are six main security elements: corporate security policy, user authentication, encryption, access control, auditing, and administration.

✦ User authentication is the process of determining who someone is.

✦ Encryption is the process of hiding the true message in a form indecipherable to anyone but the intended recipient.

✦ Access control ensures that only the appropriate people access a specified resource.

✦ Auditing and administration are necessary, ongoing elements that help you maintain a strong security infrastructure. Periodic audits help you ensure that the company is following the corporate security policy, and timely administration helps keep everything up-to-date.

✦ Maintaining a healthy level of paranoia helps improve the effectiveness of a security infrastructure because it keeps you alert and conscious to strange and unusual activity.

✦ The basic foundation of any security infrastructure is the security policy.

✦ The following six steps should be followed to create a strong security policy:

• 1 — Classify your systems.

• 2 — Determine security priorities for each system.

• 3 — Assign risk factors.

• 4 — Define acceptable and unacceptable activities.

• 5 — Decide how you will educate employees about security.

• 6 — Determine who will administer your policy.

✦ Classifying your resources into Level I, II, or III helps determine the criticality of the system to the corporation and the level of time and money that should be spent protecting it.

✦ Acceptable and unacceptable activities should be explicitly defined for each resource.

✦ All employees should be educated about the importance of security and the role they play in the security infrastructure.

✦ Administrators of the security policy must be explicitly defined within the policy to ensure all aspects of the policy are implemented and reviewed periodically.

✦ There are four main types of authentication methods:

- Proving what you know
- Showing what you have
- Demonstrating who you are
- Identifying where you are

✦ The combination of proving what you know and showing what you have is also known as two-factor authentication and is the most commonly used method today when looking for a stronger authentication method than just a password.

✦ Smartcards and SecurID are two examples of two-factor authentication technology available today.

✦ Demonstrating who you are is also known as biometric authentication.

✦ Identifying where you are is the weakest form of authentication.

✦ The three main encryption categories are symmetric, asymmetric, and hash encryption.

✦ An access control list is a table listing individual users and groups and what access rights each has to a particular object, such as a file or directory.

✦ Execution control lists control what resources an application, such as a Web browser, can access and deny any request to a resource that is not permitted.

✦ Auditing is essential to any security infrastructure and is an ongoing process.

✦ Two types of auditing are passive and active.

✦ To create a complete security system, you must combine all the security elements with security policies and procedures; this includes providing physical security, software security, and human security.

✦ Security solutions should be easy for the end user to install and use.

✦   ✦   ✦

STUDY GUIDE

This Study Guide presents five assessment questions to test your knowledge of the exam objectives.

Assessment Questions

1. An example of passive auditing is

   A. Disabling a login when an intruder starts port scanning the network

   B. Blocking access to a porn site when it is discovered that employees are accessing it during the work day

   C. Shutting down the Telnet server discovered in a routine network port scan

   D. Examining a log of invalid login attempts

2. I want to provide a strong, but accurate level of authentication. Which is the best method to use?

   A. Fingerprints

   B. SecurID

   C. Reverse DNS

   D. Password

3. What is the first step in creating a security policy?

   A. Classify your systems

   B. Determine security priorities

   C. Assign risk factors

   D. Define acceptable and unacceptable activities

4. Access control lists work in conjunction with what other security element?

   A. Encryption

   B. Authentication

   C. Audit

   D. Administration

5. Web browsers often use what technique to protect resources from malicious Java or ActiveX programs?

　　A. Two-factor authentication

　　B. Encryption

　　C. Execution control lists

　　D. Auditing

Lab Exercise

Lab 2-1 Viewing access control settings in Windows NT

1. Open Windows Explorer.

2. Select any directory and right-click.

3. Select Properties.

4. Select the Security tab.

5. Select Permissions.

6. Default permissions in NT give everyone Full Control (see Figure 2-4). Remove "Everyone" and give a specific user read access to the directory.

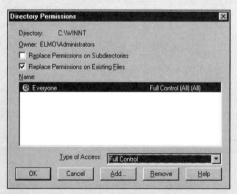

Figure 2-4: Default access in Windows NT gives everyone Full Control.

Answers to Chapter Questions

Chapter Pre-Test

1. An access control list is a table listing individual users and groups and what access rights each has to a particular object, such as a file or directory. The most common privileges are read, write, and execute.

2. The six main elements of security are corporate security policy, user authentication, encryption, access control, audit, and administration.

3. There are four main types of authentication methods: what you know, what you have, who you are, and where you are.

4. Security works only when it is developed to fit within the needs and goals of the company. Ignoring business issues will create a security infrastructure that is impossible to implement and administer, making it useless and ineffective.

5. Auditing helps maintain the effectiveness and accuracy of the security infrastructure. Periodic audits ensure the security policy is implemented correctly and that all individuals and resources are in compliance with the written standard.

Assessment Questions

1. **D.** Passive auditing involves examining log files or other documents after the fact, looking for anomalies.

2. **B.** SecurID, or two-factor authentication, is the best answer. Biometrics provides strong authentication, but the technology is not very accurate. Passwords are more accurate than biometrics if the passwords are chosen well, but two-factor authentication provides a stronger level of authentication than a password does by itself. Reverse DNS is very weak and should never be considered as a means of authentication on a system containing information of any value.

3. **A.** Classifying your systems is the first step in developing a corporate security policy.

4. **B.** Access control lists work with the authentication element to help ensure authorized individuals access only authorized resources on specific systems.

5. **C.** Web browsers may use execution control lists to protect the system from malicious ActiveX or Java applets.

Using Encryption Technologies

◆ ◆ ◆ ◆

EXAM OBJECTIVES

- ✦ Understand different encryption algorithms

- ✦ Deploy PGP in Windows NT and Linux

- ✦ Understand symmetric, asymmetric, and hash encryption

- ✦ Understand how digital signatures work

- ✦ Understand how SSL and S-HTTP work

- ✦ Understand the use of digital certificates and signatures

- ✦ Understand the importance of trusts

CHAPTER PRE-TEST

1. What is symmetric encryption? Name one symmetric algorithm.

2. What is asymmetric encryption? Name one asymmetric algorithm.

3. Why is trust important?

4. What is a hash?

5. What is a digital signature?

✦ Answers to these questions can be found at the end of the chapter. ✦

Encryption is a widely used security technology that is growing in importance every day. Online shopping is an accepted means of purchasing a product because credit card numbers are secured during transit using encryption. Popular wireless technologies use encryption to keep sniffers from reading signals as they fly through the air. Numerous other uses of encryption surround you each day, some of which you may not even recognize.

Chapter 2 briefly discussed encryption and its importance as a security technology. This chapter discusses encryption in-depth, detailing its components and uses.

Understanding Encryption and Trusts

 Understand the importance of trusts

Encryption's main purpose is to protect the data so that only "trusted" people can access it but un-trusted people cannot. With a phone conversation, for example, you can hear the voice of the person on the other end, so you are pretty sure you are talking to the person you intended to speak with.

With online communications, however, it is difficult to identify the person on the other end of the communications line. You cannot see or hear them, so it's more difficult to know whether you are communicating with the right person or server.

Trust relationships are important in the encryption process. A simple example of creating a trust relationship is encrypting files using asymmetric encryption so only the intended recipient can view the contents.

Trust relationships can be created manually or automatically. Manual trust relationships require you to perform some action to establish trust. To use symmetric encryption, you must distribute keys to all parties with whom you communicate. These keys are used to encrypt/decrypt messages and files.

Secure Sockets Layer (SSL) and IPSec are examples of automatic trust relationships. The intricacies of SSL are discussed later in this chapter; for now, all you need to know is that the key exchange takes place automatically. Subsequently, you have established a level of trust without any interaction.

Encryption Techniques and Technologies

 Understand symmetric, asymmetric, and hash encryption

Cryptography involves securing the transmission and storage of data. Its purpose is to protect data from the eyes of unintended viewers. Cryptography can also be used to control access to computers and networks. Cryptography involves the processes of encryption/decryption. Encryption protects data from attackers (a person or system that intends to compromise a system) by scrambling the information (or plaintext) into an unreadable form (or ciphertext). This scrambling process is based on algorithms that use various forms of substitution or transposition to encrypt the message.

Rounds, parallelization, and strong encryption

Before diving into a discussion about encryption, you need to understand some basic terms. *Algorithms*, the foundation for the encryption process, are mathematical constructs that are applied through various applications in order to secure transmissions or storage. *Decryption* is the process of using the same algorithm to restore the information into readable form. A *round* is a discrete part of the encryption process. An algorithm generally goes through several rounds when generating an encryption/decryption key. The higher the number of rounds, the better. Some algorithms, especially symmetric key algorithms, process half the data in one round, the other half in a second round, and then combine everything in a final third round, making the encryption that much stronger. The separation also speeds up processing time.

Parallelization refers to the method of using multiple processes, processors, or machines working together to try and crack an algorithm. *Strong encryption* refers to an encryption process that uses at least a 128-bit key. New technologies are always being developed to create longer keys, so this definition may change in the future. In the past, the U.S. government did not allow products containing strong encryption to be exported. As of January 2000, this policy changed to allow the export of products with strong encryption.

Symmetric-key encryption

 Understand different encryption algorithms

The private key method (or symmetric method) encryption process uses one key for both encryption and decryption, as shown in Figure 3-1.

Private key encryption is fast and efficient, making it ideal for large data transmissions. Furthermore, private key encryption is effective when used in conjunction with public key encryption (discussed later in the chapter). However, because the private key method uses the same key for both encryption and decryption, the sender and receiver must exchange keys before the data transmission, which raises a vital problem. The private key must be transmitted over a secure channel to the receiver. But how is a channel secured? If a secure channel existed, encryption wouldn't be needed. So, the receiver and sender must devise a method for safely exchanging the key prior to transmission.

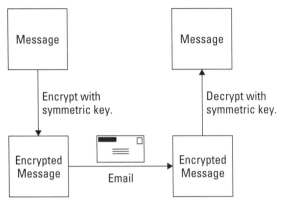

Figure 3-1: Symmetric key encryption uses the same key for encryption and decryption.

Also, the private key method requires a large amount of keys. Usually, people transmit data to and receive data from more than one party. Each pair of senders and receivers must possess a special key, which means each party maintains multiple keys — something that can be difficult to manage. Many businesses interact with millions of one-time customers daily, making this solution infeasible. Therefore, the private key method is best used in environments where the private key can be exchanged easily and where frequent communication between parties exists. For instance, the private key method is optimally used in internal communication between colleagues.

Symmetric algorithms

Many symmetric algorithms exist, including the Data Encryption Standard (DES), Triple DES, RSA algorithms RC2, RC4, RC5, RC6, MARS, Twofish, and Rijndael.

Data Encryption Standard

DES is one of the most widely accepted, publicly available cryptographic systems today. DES was developed by IBM in the 1970s. Although it was later adopted by the U.S. government as a national standard, it has always been controversial. Many fear that DES has a weakness only known by the National Security Agency (NSA). The fear stems from the possibility that the DES algorithm could be cracked by a brute force attack, an attack requiring lots of money and processing power. Critics of DES believe that the NSA has the ability to launch a successful brute force attack. Additionally, the NSA reduced the proposed key size (64 bits) by 8 bits before the approval of the 56-bit key. Consequently, some believe the U.S. government has the knowledge and capability to crack the DES algorithm. Although DES' abilities have been questioned, the majority of these claims remain unconfirmed. DES uses a 56-bit key (as compared to 40 – 128 bits). The larger the key, the more secure the transmission. DES processes 64-bit inputs into 64-bit ciphertext. Essentially, this algorithm goes through 16 iterations that interlace blocks of plaintext and combine in values obtained from the key.

How does the DES algorithm work? The process starts when the original message is divided into 64-bit blocks.. Each block is then permutated to change the order of its bits. Next, this plaintext block is split into two 32-bit blocks (the right and left blocks).

Simultaneous to the division and permutation of the original message, the 56-bit key is divided into two 28-bit halves (the right and left half). Each half is circular-shifted to the left, reconnected, transposed, and enlarged to 48 bits. (The two key halves are saved and used for the following iteration.)

Then, the right half of the plaintext blocks (32-bit) is expanded to 48-bits and is permutated.

Next, the new 48-bit plaintext block is crossed over with the 48-bit key blocks. This result is converted to 32 bits using a substitution function. This 32-bit block is crossed over with the left half of the plaintext block (the left half of the original 64-bit block), forming two new 32-bit halves.

The process then starts again with the circular shifting of the new 32-bit halves. There are 15 more iterations of this sequence.

Obviously, this explanation is a simplified version of the many complex details involved with the DES algorithm. DES is a standard algorithm used in single key encryption; however, there are many alternatives, including International Data Encryption Algorithm (IDEA) and Ron Rivest's RC ciphers.

Triple DES

DES uses a 56-bit key and is not deemed sufficient to encrypt sensitive data. Triple DES goes through three iterations of DES, effectively encrypting the data with a 168-bit key, strong enough to secure sensitive information. The data is first encrypted using a 56-bit DES key, decrypted with another 56-bit DES key, and finally encrypted again with the original 56-bit DES key.

Because Triple DES contains several levels of encryption, you are better protected against man-in-the-middle attacks.

DES is a very fast algorithm, and although Triple DES is a little slower, it is still faster than some other symmetric encryption algorithms. Triple DES' main advantage, though, is that it is compatible with all software and hardware that support DES.

RSA algorithms

Ron Rivest, Adi Shamir, and Leonard Adleman are best known for inventing the public-key RSA algorithm in 1977. They also developed the RC series of symmetric algorithms — RC2, RC4, RC5, and RC6. This series uses variable-length keys up to 128 bits. RC2 and RC4 are the most commonly used symmetric key algorithms for commercial applications.

RC2 (Rivest Cipher No. 2) and RC5 were developed by Ron Rivest. RC2 is a block-mode cipher, meaning it encrypts data in 64-bit blocks. As a variable-length key, RC2 can use key lengths from 0 to infinity. Of course, the larger the key length, the slower the encryption process.

RC5 is similar to RC2 because it is a block cipher, but RC5 uses a variable block size, key length, and number of processing rounds. The general recommendation for RC5 is to use a 128-bit key and 12 to 16 processing rounds for a secure algorithm.

RC4, developed by Ron Rivest in 1987, is a stream cipher, meaning it encrypts all the data in real time. This differs from block ciphers, which break the data into smaller chunks for processing. RC4 allows a variable key length, but a 128-bit key is standard.

RC6 represents a new family of encryption algorithms developed in 1998. A theoretical weakness was discovered in RC5 regarding how it processed encryption in certain rounds. RC6 was designed to fix this flaw.

IDEA

The International Data Encryption Algorithm (IDEA) was originally developed in 1990 as the Proposed Encryption Standard (PES). In 1992, it was renamed IDEA. IDEA is a block cipher that uses 64-bit data blocks and a 128-bit key. Even though some consider IDEA a stronger algorithm than RC4 and Triple DES, it has not gained wide acceptance and usage in the market.

Blowfish and Twofish

The Blowfish and Twofish algorithms were developed by Bruce Schneier, famed cryptographer, author of *Applied Cryptography*, and founder of Counterpane. Blowfish, a very flexible symmetric key algorithm often used in Secure Shell (SSH), is a variable-round black cipher that can use a variable key length up to 448 bits.

Twofish, Schneier's latest algorithm, uses a 128-bit block and is much faster than Blowfish. Twofish supports 28-, 192-, and 256-bit keys and is designed to work on smart cards.

Skipjack

Skipjack is a symmetric key algorithm designed by the U.S. National Security Agency (NSA) and found in the Fortezza and Clipper chips. It uses an 80-bit key and 32 rounds on 64-bit data blocks. The math behind this algorithm is top-secret.

MARS

MARS is a block cipher algorithm developed by IBM. It uses 128-bit blocks and supports keys longer than 400 bits. MARS provides stronger security and better performance speed than DES. Like Twofish, it is designed to work on smart cards.

Rijndael and Serpent

The Rijndael algorithm is a block cipher that supports 128-, 192-, or 256-bit keys. This algorithm is designed to work quickly over ATM networks, ISDN lines, and high-definition television (HDTV). Rijndael was recently accepted as the new Advanced Encryption Standard (AES).

Serpent, a 128-bit block cipher that supports key sizes up to 256 bits, is comparable to DES in how it processes information, but it is optimized for Intel-based chips.

Advanced Encryption Standard (AES)

AES is the encryption algorithm that will replace DES as the national standard. Some feel DES and Triple DES are no longer adequate algorithms for their security needs. NIST recently announced that the Rijndael algorithm will replace DES.

Asymmetric Encryption

A second method of encryption is public key, or asymmetric, encryption. This form of cryptography involves two keys: a private key and a public key. Every user has a public key, which is distributed freely, and a private key, which is kept secret. For transmission, the data is first encrypted with the recipient's public key by the sender. Next, the data is sent to the recipient, who decrypts it with their personal private key. Therefore, to send an encrypted message, according to the public key method, the sender must first obtain the intended recipient's public key (see Figure 3-2).

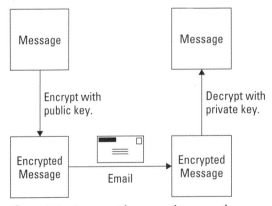

Figure 3-2: Asymmetric encryption uses the public key for encryption and the private key for decryption.

The asymmetric technique is simple; yet producing two keys that work together to provide a high level of security can be complex. This added complexity, however, increases the use of public key cryptography. Messages and data can be exchanged without first communicating a private key. Also, because of the public key method, documents can contain digital signatures authenticating the data source. Due to the high level of security provided by this method, it is most often applied to electronic commerce. Several public key schemas exist; however, the most popular and well-known technique involves RSA (the Rivest, Shamir, and Adleman algorithm).

The RSA algorithm

The RSA algorithm randomly generates a very large prime number public key. The algorithm uses this prime number to generate another number — the private key. The private key is derived through complex mathematical functions. The RSA algorithm is founded on four basic properties:

✦ **Property 1** — The deciphering (decryption) of an enciphered (encrypted) message yields the original message. This property is represented by the following equation:

```
D (E (M)) = M
```

D represents the action of deciphering, E represents the action of enciphering, and M represents the original message.

✦ **Property 2** — Relatively, E and D are easily computed.

✦ **Property 3** — Knowing E does not reveal an easy way to compute D. In other words, only the holder of D can decipher (decrypt) a message.

✦ **Property 4** — The converse of the first property is true. Therefore, a deciphered message can be encrypted to result in the original message M.

These properties seem simple enough (and they are for small numbers of 10 to 20 digits); however, the RSA algorithm generally uses numbers up to 154 digits (512-bits) for each of the public and private keys. The RSA algorithm is based on a one-way, or trap door, function. A function is known as a trap door function if it meets the first three properties above. A trap door function is easy to compute in one direction but not the other. It is labeled a "trap door" function because the inverse of the function is easily computed if you know the private (trap door) information (or, for encryption purposes, the private key).

RSA implementation

Various programs implement the RSA algorithm through three steps:

1. The program converts the message into a representative integer between 0 and (n-1). If the message is large, the program will break it down into blocks. Each block is represented by its own integer less than n-1.

2. By raising each of the integer values to the Eth power, the program encrypts the message. The resulting value is divided by n. The remainder is saved as the encrypted message. This type of arithmetic is known as modulo arithmetic, which retains only the remainder from a division operation. The original message is now an encrypted message, C.

3. To decrypt C, the recipient raises the message to the Dth power. Then, the recipient uses n to perform modulo division on the result. The result is the blocks within the decrypted message, which the program converts back to text.

In practice, the user distributes the encryption key (E, n) and keeps the decryption key (D, n) private.

The math of RSA
The RSA algorithm goes through four steps.

1. The algorithm finds two large primary numbers (p & q).

2. Next, n is calculated, such that n = p*q.

3. E (the public exponent) is selected. E must be less than n and relatively prime to (p-1)*(q-1).

4. D (the private exponent) is computed such that ED = 1 mod ((p-1)*(q-1)).

As mentioned earlier, (E, n) is the public key, and (D, n) is the private key.

RSA is the most popular public key algorithm. In the past, it was very expensive to license and use. However, in September 2000, the RSA patent expired, making it freely available to the public.

Diffie-Hellman — The primary alternative to RSA
Several alternatives exist to the RSA algorithm. The Diffie-Hellman Algorithm represents the most popular of these. While similar to the RSA algorithm, the strength of each algorithm is based on separate factors. The RSA factor of strength lies in the difficulty of finding the prime factors of a large integer. The Diffie-Hellman factor of strength is the difficulty of computing discrete logarithms in a finite field generated by a large primary number. Although both algorithms are similar in mathematical theory, their implementation is somewhat different. The implementation is affected by the expiration of the Diffie-Hellman patent in September 1997. This algorithm has been released to the public. Until 2000 when the RSA patent expired, many chose to use Diffie-Hellman to avoid paying licensing fees.

Digital Signature Algorithm
NIST introduced the Digital Signature Algorithm (DSA) and made it available to the public. Because DSA was not proprietary, it was used in many products, such as Linux.

Hash encryption
Hash encryption converts data from a variable length to a fixed length 128-bit piece of data called a hash value. Theoretically, no two data will produce the same hash value. The hash process is irreversible — you cannot recover the original data by reversing the hash process.

Users most often utilize hashes when there is information they never want decrypted or read. For example, UNIX passwords are only stored on the system as hashes. When you log on to a UNIX system and enter your password, the system calculates the hash and compares it to the one on file for your userid. If they match, you are granted system access.

Hash algorithms

Several hash algorithms exist, including MD2, MD4, MD5, and the Secure Hash Algorithm (SHA).

MD2, MD4, and MD5

The MD series comprises a group of one-way hash algorithms developed by Ron Rivest. MD4 and MD5 are faster than the original MD2 and are also used more often. MD4 was susceptible to attack, so Rivest developed MD5. MD5 is stronger than MD4 and still produces a 128-bit hash. MD5 is discussed in RFC 1321.

Secure Hash Algorithm

Secure Hash Algorithm (SHA) was developed by NIST and the NSA and produces a 160-bit hash value. SHA was intended to be the standard hash algorithm for government communications.

SHA is similar to MD5 in structure, though it is slower and more secure. Its increased security stems from the fact that its hash value is 25 percent larger than the value created by MD5.

Digital signatures

 Understand how Digital Signatures work

Digital Signature (DS) is the technique of appending a string of characters to an electronic message to authenticate the sender. Some DS techniques also provide an integrity check to ensure the data was not altered during transit. A DS is applied to the message, in essence sealing it from modification. These Signatures are based on public key encryption. Because DS is based on an asymmetric scheme, it helps ensure the integrity and confidentiality of the message. The two components of a DS are the original message and the sender's private key that is used to encrypt the message.

DS, as appended to messages, typically employs hexadecimal representations for the body of the signature. This is an integer that uses a single byte for each character. The DS simply takes a text message and treats it as if it were a number consisting of a sequential string of hexadecimal digits. The process of creating a DS is as follows:

1. The original text message is sent through a hashing algorithm, discussed earlier, which creates a string of hexadecimal characters known as the *message digest.*

2. The algorithm used to form the message digest seals the message so that if any character in the plaintext message is changed, the digest will also change. The message digest, generated for use with digital signatures, is a fixed length, short enough to be encrypted with the sender's private key.

3. The message digest is encrypted with the sender's private key, resulting in the *digital signature.*

4. The sender encrypts the digital signature with a *new random key.*

5. The sender encrypts the new random key with the recipient's public key, resulting in a *digital envelope.* A digital envelope is a type of security that uses two layers of encryption to protect a message.

6. The encrypted message, encrypted digital signature, and encrypted digital envelope are sent over the Internet to the recipient.

7. The recipient decrypts the digital envelope with his/her private key in order to obtain the random key.

8. The random key allows the recipient to decrypt the digital signature and the original message.

9. The recipient then decrypts the digital signature with the sender's public key, exposing the original message digest.

10. The original message digest is assembled using a *cyclic redundancy check,* which samples bits horizontally according to some repetitive scheme across characters in the plaintext message field. The recipient must have the hashing algorithm used by the sender.

11. The decrypted, original message is sent through the algorithm. This produces a new message digest.

12. This new message digest is compared to the original message digest in order to verify the digital signature. Even the change of a single bit in the digest will result in a failure to verify the signature.

A digital signature provides the same significance as a handwritten signature. DS accomplishes this task by satisfying two needs: identifying the signer and verifying the content.

Identifying the signer

Digital signatures provide greater reliability for identification of the possessor of the private key as the signer of a particular message than does a conventional signature on a paper document. The difficulty arises when trying to associate the holder of a specific private key with an individual person. A solution to this problem is to bring in a third party to electronically verify the identity of the key-holder and to certify that information to the recipient. These third parties are known as Certificate Authorities (CAs).

Verifying the content

Digital signatures provide a seal on an electronic message. By using a hashing algorithm, digital signatures can verify that the contents of a message remain unchanged from the version that was signed with the private key. The recipient can be assured that the message was not intercepted en route, and the sender can be assured that the recipient did not alter the message.

Electronic fund transfer systems, Electronic Data Interchange (EDI), and database integrity maintenance all employ digital signatures:

✦ In electronic fund transfer systems, a person who requests a transfer of a specific amount from one account to another over an unprotected network risks having that message altered by an unauthorized third party. If the message is signed with a digital signature, the recipient can verify that the message is authentic.

✦ Electronic Data Interchange (EDI) is the computer-to-computer interchange of messages representing business documents. EDI business documents replace handwritten signatures with digital signatures.

✦ In a database environment, a manager may want to verify digital signatures for any person who attempts to append, update, or modify any information. If the signature is verified, the manager knows the database has not been altered, deleted, or entered by an unauthorized third party.

Digital certificates

 Understand the use of digital certificates and signatures

Digital certificates electronically identify an individual. A digitally signed statement from a trusted third party verifies the identity and public key of an individual or computer. Digital certificates are the electronic equivalent of a driver's license or birth certificate. A digital certificate can be obtained from a public certificate authority or from a private authority running its own certificate server. Digital certificates are composed of

✦ Sender's public key

✦ Sender's name

✦ Expiration date of sender's public key

✦ Name of the certificate issuer

✦ Serial number of the certificate

✦ Digital signature of the issuer

Certificate Authorities guarantee that when a user downloads a file sent from Sender, sender is the person that actually signed the file. This verification acts as a notary seal on a document. The Certificate Authority verifies the person's identity and then sends the person their digital certificate, which contains information about the person's identity and a copy of their public key. The certificate is encrypted by the Certificate Authority's private key.

When a person signs a document, a software program will append their digital signature and their digital certificate to the document. When the recipient receives the file containing the sender's digital signature and digital certificate, they can verify that no one has forged the document. The software program verifies the digital signature by comparing the sender's public key contained in their digital signature with the copy contained in the sender's digital certificate. The success of authenticating software programs depends on two assumptions. First, users cannot easily determine the private key from the public key. Second, someone does not steal the person's certificate and private key.

These encryption and secure exchange systems are used, both individually and together, to secure transactions in electronic commerce. This segment of online activity is expected to grow tremendously in the next few years. Business-to-consumer electronic commerce sales are estimated to grow to $7 billion in the next few years, whereas business-to-business transactions will be worth a total of more than $150 billion. With this expected amount of growth, it is important to understand how these encryption technologies work together to ensure secure transaction processing.

Using Encryption Processes

The encryption algorithms and crypto-systems discussed above can be combined to secure communications, such as e-mail, e-commerce transactions, and network security.

E-mail

Several encryption technologies exist to provide secure messaging. The most commonly used are Pretty Good Privacy (PGP) and Secure Multi-Purpose Internet Mail Extension (S/MIME).

PGP

 Deploy PGP in Windows NT and Linux

PGP, developed by Philip Zimmerman, provides a confidentiality and authentication service that can be used for e-mail and file-storage applications. PGP uses cryptographic algorithms, integrated into a general-purpose application that is independent of operating systems and processors. PGP and its documentation, including source code, are freely available on the Internet. For a more thorough exploration of PGP, refer to the lab exercises at the end of this chapter.

S/MIME

S/MIME is a secure method of sending e-mail that uses the RSA public-key encryption system. S/MIME is included in the latest versions of the Web browsers from Microsoft and Netscape and has also been endorsed by other vendors that make messaging products. RSA has proposed S/MIME as a standard to the Internet Engineering Task Force (IETF).

MIME is described in RFC 1521 and spells out how an electronic message will be organized. S/MIME describes how encryption information and a digital certificate can be included as part of the message body. S/MIME follows the syntax provided in the Public-Key Cryptography Standard (Public-Key Cryptography System) format #7.

Web server encryption

 Understand how SSL and S-HTTP work

Secure Sockets Layer (SSL) is the de facto secure protocol for e-commerce transactions. Although SSL does not provide mechanisms for handling payment, it does offer confidentiality in Web sessions, authenticity of Web servers and, optionally, verification of end users. The second, less commonly used, secure protocol is Secure HTTP (S-HTTP). S-HTTP is a connectionless protocol that wraps messages in a secure digital envelope.

Secure Sockets Layer

Secure Sockets Layer (SSL) provides a secure channel between Web clients and Web servers that choose to use the protocol for Web sessions. Unlike the standard Internet protocols such as TCP/IP, SSL must be selectively employed by the Web client and server in order to use the protocol. A Web client can usually invoke the protocol to connect to an SSL-enabled server by clicking on a designated SSL Web page link.

SSL is a layered approach to providing a secure channel. That is, SSL is simply another layer in the network protocol stack that rides on top of the TCP/IP stack. SSL provides secure communications, authentication of the server, and data integrity of the message packet. Because SSL resides on top of the TCP/IP layers, it can potentially secure the communications of any number of application-level protocols that communicate over the Net. Currently, SSL secures only Web sessions.

SSL secures the channel by providing end-to-end encryption of the data that is sent between a Web client and a Web server. Although an intermediary may be able to see the data in transmission, the encryption will effectively scramble the data so that it cannot be intelligently interpreted. However, the technology should not be oversold. Data that resides on the Web client's machine and on the Web server's machine, before it is encrypted and after it is decrypted, is only as secure as the host machine's.

In addition to securing the channel via encryption, SSL provides authentication of the merchant's server. This means that if the channel has been successfully secured, the Web client is assured that the server has been endorsed by a Certification Authority (CA) that the Web client trusts. The CA will endorse only the identity of the Web server. End users can be sure of the identity of the Web site to which they are connected, but there is no assurance of the quality of the Web content.

SSL uses two different encryption technologies, public key (asymmetric) encryption and private key (symmetric) encryption, to authenticate the Web server and/or client and encrypt the communication channel. Public key encryption is used to authenticate the server and/or client and to exchange a private session key between the Web server and client. The exchange of the private session key makes symmetric encryption possible in securing communications. The strict use of public key encryption to conduct secure sessions is inefficient. Its performance would be too slow and impractical for Web sessions. Symmetric encryption and decryption, by contrast, is performed significantly faster than public key encryption. A performance penalty exists when using SSL or any encryption algorithm in general; however, the delay imposed by symmetric encryption is acceptable in most Internet applications.

When initiating a secure connection, the consumer's browser sends a "Client Hello" to the server that consists of the browser-supported suite of secure protocols and a random challenge string generated by the browser. The random challenge string is unique to this session and will be used at the close of the initialization to verify that a secure session has been established. The suite of secure protocols consists of the following:

✦ Key exchange algorithms for agreement on a private session key

✦ Private key encryption protocols for transaction confidentiality

✦ Hashing algorithms for data integrity

Before setting up the secure connection, SSL will attempt to authenticate the server. In response to the "Client Hello," the server will respond with a "Server Hello," consisting of an X.509 standard server certificate, an acknowledgment that the server can support the protocols requested by the client, and a random connection identifier. As with the random challenge string, the connection identifier will be used at the close of the protocol to determine if a secure session has been established.

The merchant's certificate must be endorsed by a trusted Certification Authority for server authentication.

1. The client's browser will check the digital signature on the server certificate against the public key of the CA stored in the browser's table of CAs.

2. If the merchant server certificate is endorsed by a Certification Authority, it will be signed through use of the CA's private key.

3. The endorsement of the Certification Authority is verified when the browser checks the signature using the public key stored in its table of CA's public keys.

Once the merchant server has been authenticated by the browser client, the browser will generate a master secret to be shared between the server and client. This secret serves as a seed to generate a number of keys used for both symmetric encryption and data integrity. The master secret is encrypted with the server's public key and sent to the merchant.

From this point on, public key encryption is no longer necessary for this session. Efficient private key encryption algorithms, such as RC2 (40-bit encryption) and RC4 or RC6 (128-bit), can be used to secure all subsequent messages during this session. From the master secret, both the server and client will generate two sets of symmetric key pairs to secure incoming and outgoing messages. Because the server and client have agreed to a common protocol and are both using the same master secret, they will generate identical symmetric key pairs. One key pair is used to encrypt outgoing traffic from the client and to decrypt incoming traffic to the server. In other words, the client's outgoing write key equals the server's incoming read key.

The other symmetric key pair is used to encrypt the server's outgoing messages and decrypt the client's incoming messages. For security purposes, the client browser generates the master shared secret to provide assurance from the client's perspective that the server is not reusing the same symmetric encryption key pairs for other sessions. In addition, the master secret is randomly generated for each new session. Even if this key were compromised by chance, it could not be used to decrypt other sessions with other merchants or future sessions with the same merchant.

Two final handshakes verify the secure setup of the session.

✦ The "Client Finish" encrypts the server's random connection identifier using the client-write key. If the server started with the same shared secret, the server's read key will decrypt the random connection identifier. The server will know that a secure connection has been established if the decrypted connection identifier is the same as the one the server sent during the "Server Hello."

✦ The "Server Finish" completes the setup of the secure channel.

The server uses the server-write key to encrypt the challenge string sent by the client during the Client Hello. The encrypted challenge key is sent back to the client. The client decrypts the challenge using the client's read key and compares it with the challenge originally sent to the server. If the comparison checks properly, the client will have assurance that a secure connection has been established. Recall that the random challenge was sent to the server during the Client Hello in plaintext form that could possibly have been intercepted by a third party. Although this may have seemed foolish at the time, the final step of encrypting and decrypting the random challenge provides the assurance of security. Because the master secret is known only to the server and client and was subsequently used as a seed in encrypting and decrypting the random challenge, the client can be assured that a secure connection has been established with the server challenged during the Client Hello.

Through this series of handshakes involving public and private key cryptography, the Web shopper can be assured of a secure connection to an authenticated merchant server.

Secure Hypertext Transfer Protocol

The Secure Hypertext Transfer Protocol (S-HTTP) is a secure extension of HTTP. S-HTTP provides a means for communicating securely with a Web server. The protocol was designed to provide broad support for a number of different secure technologies, including symmetric encryption for data confidentiality, public key encryption for client/server authentication, and message digests for data integrity.

In contrast to SSL, the negotiation of secure properties occurs through an exchange of packet headers in S-HTTP. While SSL uses special handshakes to establish the parameters of the secure connection, S-HTTP defines a specific security negotiation header for packets sent during the Web session. The security negotiation headers may define the following:

✦ The choice of secure technologies (symmetric encryption, client/server authentication, data integrity)

✦ The specific algorithms that the party will support

✦ The direction in which the party desires the property to be enforced (sending or receiving)

✦ The mode in which the property is requested (required, optional, refuse)

Once the secure properties for a session have been negotiated, S-HTTP secures the session by encapsulating the data within a secure envelope. The secure envelope supports confidentiality of the Web session contents, message integrity, and authentication of clients and servers.

Secure network protocols

Virtual Private Networks are becoming a popular method for securing remote access connections.

A Virtual Private Network (VPN) is a private data network that makes use of the public telecommunication infrastructure, maintaining privacy through the use of a tunneling protocol and security procedures. A virtual private network can be contrasted with a system of owned or leased lines that can only be used by one company. The purpose of a VPN is to provide the same capabilities at much lower cost by using the shared public infrastructure of the Internet rather than a private one.

Using a virtual private network involves encrypting data before sending it through the public network and decrypting it at the receiving end. An additional level of security involves encrypting not only the data but also the originating and receiving network addresses. Microsoft, 3Com, and several other companies have developed the Point-to-Point Tunneling Protocol (PPTP) to do just that.

In addition to offering direct cost savings over other communications methods (such as leased lines and long-distance calls), VPNs offer other advantages, including indirect cost savings as a result of reduced training requirements and equipment, increased flexibility, and scalability.

In VPNs, *virtual* implies that the network is dynamic, with connections set up according to organizational needs. It also means that the network is formed logically, regardless of the physical structure of the underlying network (the Internet, in this case). Unlike the leased lines used in traditional corporate networks, VPNs do not maintain permanent links between the end points that make up the corporate network. Instead, a connection is created between two sites when it is needed, and torn down when no longer necessary, making the bandwidth and network resources available for other uses. So, the connections making up a VPN do not have the same physical characteristics as the hard-wired connections used on the LAN.

Tunnels can consist of two types of end points, either an individual computer or a LAN with a security gateway, which might be a router or firewall. Only two combinations of these end points are usually considered in designing VPNs:

✦ **LAN-to-LAN tunnels.** A security gateway at each end point serves as the interface between the tunnel and the private LAN. Users on either LAN can use the tunnel transparently to communicate with each other.

✦ **Client-to-LAN tunnels.** This tunnel type is usually set up for a mobile user who wants to connect to the corporate LAN. The client (the mobile user) initiates the creation of the tunnel on his end in order to exchange traffic with the corporate network. To do so, he runs special client software on his computer to communicate with the gateway protecting the destination LAN.

Four different protocols have been suggested for creating VPNs over the Internet:

✦ Point-to-point tunneling protocol (PPTP)

✦ Layer-2 forwarding (L2F)

✦ Layer-2 tunneling protocol (L2TP)

✦ IP security protocol (IPSec)

One reason for the number of protocols is that, for some companies, a VPN is a substitute for remote-access servers, enabling mobile users and branch offices to dial into the protected corporate network via their local ISP. For others, a VPN may consist of traffic traveling in secure tunnels over the Internet between protected LANs. The protocols that have been developed for VPNs reflect this dichotomy. PPTP, L2F, and L2TP are largely aimed at dial-up VPNs, whereas IPSec's main focus has been LAN-to-LAN solutions.

The most commonly used protocol for remote access to the Internet is point-to-point protocol (PPP). PPTP builds on the functionality of PPP to provide remote access that can be tunneled through the Internet to a destination site. As currently implemented, PPTP encapsulates PPP packets using a modified version of the generic routing encapsulation (GRE) protocol, which gives PPTP the flexibility of handling protocols other than IP, such as Internet packet exchange (IPX) and network basic input/output system extended user interface (NetBEUI).

Because of its dependence on PPP, PPTP relies on the authentication mechanisms within PPP, namely password authentication protocol (PAP) and Challenge Handshake Authentication Protocol (CHAP). Because there is a strong tie between PPTP and Windows NT, an enhanced version of CHAP, MS-CHAP, is also used, which utilizes information within NT domains for security. Similarly, PPTP can use PPP to encrypt data, but Microsoft has also incorporated a stronger encryption method, called Microsoft point-to-point encryption (MPPE), for use with PPTP.

Aside from the relative simplicity of client support for PPTP, one of the protocol's main advantages is that PPTP is designed to run at OSI Layer 2, or the link layer, as opposed to IPSec, which runs at Layer 3. By supporting data communications at Layer 2, PPTP can transmit protocols other than IP over its tunnels. PPTP does have limitations, though. For example, it does not provide strong encryption for protecting data, nor does it support any token-based methods for authenticating users.

Layer 2 Forwarding (L2F) also arose in the early stages of VPN development. Paralleling PPTP's design, L2F utilized PPP for authentication of the dial-up user, but it also included support for TACACS+ and RADIUS for authentication from the beginning. L2F differs from PPTP because it defines connections within a tunnel, allowing a tunnel to support more than one connection. There are also two levels of authentication of the user, first by the ISP prior to setting up the tunnel and then when the connection is set up at the corporate gateway. Because L2TP is a Layer-2 protocol, it offers users the same flexibility as PPTP for handling protocols other than IP, such as IPX and NetBEUI.

L2TP was created by an IETF working group as a replacement for PPTP and L2F. L2TP was designed to address the shortcomings of these past protocols and become an IETF-approved standard. L2TP uses PPP to provide dial-up access that can be tunneled through the Internet to a site. However, L2TP defines its own tunneling protocol, based on the work done on L2F. L2TP transport is being defined for a variety of packet media, including X.25, frame-relay, and ATM. To strengthen the encryption of the data it handles, L2TP uses IPSec's encryption methods.

Because it uses PPP for dial-up links, L2TP includes the authentication mechanisms within PPP (PAP and CHAP). Similar to PPTP, L2TP supports PPP's use of the extensible authentication protocol for other authentication systems, such as RADIUS. PPTP, L2F, and L2TP do not include encryption or processes for managing the cryptographic keys required for encryption in their specifications. The current L2TP draft standard recommends that IPSec be used for encryption and key management in IP environments; future drafts of the PPTP standard may do the same.

The last, and perhaps most important protocol, IPSec, grew out of efforts to secure IP packets as the next generation of IP (IPv6) was being developed. IPSec can now be used with IPv4 protocols as well. Although the requests for comment (RFCs) defining the IPSec protocols have already been part of the IETF's standards track since mid-1995, engineers continue to refine the protocols.

IPSec allows the sender (or a security gateway acting on the sender's behalf) to authenticate or encrypt each IP packet or apply both operations to the packet. Separating the application of packet authentication and encryption has led to two different methods of using IPSec, called modes. In *transport mode*, only the transport-layer segment of an IP packet is authenticated or encrypted. The other approach, authenticating or encrypting the entire IP packet, is called *tunnel mode*. Although transport-mode IPSec can prove useful in many situations, tunnel-mode IPSec provides more protection against certain attacks and traffic monitoring that might occur on the Internet.

IPSec is built around a number of standardized cryptographic technologies to provide confidentiality, data integrity, and authentication. For example, IPSec uses:

✦ Diffie-Hellman key exchanges to deliver secret keys between peers on a public net

✦ Public-key cryptography for signing Diffie-Hellman exchanges, to guarantee the identities of the two parties and avoid man-in-the-middle attacks

✦ Data Encryption Standard (DES) and other bulk encryption algorithms for encrypting data

✦ Keyed hash algorithms (HMAC, MD5, SHA) for authenticating packets

✦ Digital certificates for validating public keys

Two ways currently exist to handle key exchange and management within IPSec's architecture: manual keying and IKE for automated key management. Both of these methods are mandatory requirements of IPSec. Although manual key exchange might be suitable for a VPN with a small number of sites, VPNs covering a large number of sites or supporting many remote users benefit from automated key management.

IPSec is often considered the best VPN solution for IP environments, as it includes strong security measures in its standards set, including:

✦ Encryption

✦ Authentication

✦ Key management

Because IPSec is designed to handle only IP packets, PPTP and L2TP are more suitable for use in multiprotocol non–IP environments, such as those using NetBEUI, IPX, and AppleTalk.

IPSec details

IPSec combines the aforementioned security technologies into a complete system that provides confidentiality, integrity, and authenticity of IP datagrams. IPSec actually refers to several related protocols as defined in the new RFC 2401-2411 and 2451 (the original IPSec RFCs 1825-1829 are now obsolete). These standards include

✦ **IP Security Protocol,** which defines the information to add to an IP packet to enable confidentiality, integrity, and authenticity controls, as well as define how to encrypt the packet data.

✦ **Internet Key Exchange (IKE),** which negotiates the security association between two entities and exchanges key material. Using IKE is not necessary, but manually configuring security associations is a difficult and manually intensive process. IKE should be used in most real-world applications to enable large-scale secure communications.

IPSec packets

IPSec defines a new set of headers to be added to IP datagrams. These new headers are placed after the IP header and before the Layer 4 protocol (typically Transmission Control Protocol [TCP] or User Datagram Protocol [UDP]). These new headers provide information for securing the payload of the IP packet as follows:

✦ **Authentication header (AH).** This header, when added to an IP datagram, ensures the integrity and authenticity of the data, including the invariant fields in the outer IP header. It does not provide confidentiality protection. AH uses a keyed-hash function rather than digital signatures, because digital signature technology is too slow and would greatly reduce network throughput.

✦ **Encapsulating security payload (ESP).** This header, when added to an IP datagram, protects the confidentiality, integrity, and authenticity of the data. If ESP is used to validate data integrity, it does not include the invariant fields in the IP header.

AH and ESP can be used independently or together, although for most applications, one of them is sufficient. For both of these protocols, IPSec provides an open framework for implementing industry-standard algorithms, rather than defining a specific security algorithm to use. Initially, most implementations of IPSec will support MD5 from RSA Data Security or the Secure Hash Algorithm (SHA) as defined by the U.S. government for integrity and authentication. The Data Encryption Standard (DES) is currently the most commonly offered bulk encryption algorithm, although RFCs are available that define how to use many other encryption systems, including IDEA, Blowfish, and RC4.

In transport mode, only the IP payload is encrypted, and the original IP headers are left intact. This mode has the advantage of adding only a few bytes to each packet. It also allows devices on the public network to see the final source and destination of the packet. This capability allows you to enable special processing (for example, quality of service) in the intermediate network based on the information in the IP header. However, the Layer 4 header will be encrypted, limiting the examination of the packet. Unfortunately, bypassing the IP header in the clear, transport mode allows an attacker to perform some traffic analysis. For example, an attacker could see when Cisco's CEO sent packets to another CEO. However, the attacker would not be able to determine if the packets were e-mail or another application.

In tunnel mode, the entire original IP datagram is encrypted, and becomes the payload in a new IP packet. This mode allows a network device, such as a router, to act as an IPSec proxy.

In tunnel mode, the following steps occur:

1. The router performs encryption on behalf of the hosts.
2. The source's router encrypts packets and forwards them along the IPSec tunnel.
3. The destination's router decrypts the original IP datagram and forwards it on to the destination system.

The major advantage of tunnel mode is that the end systems do not need to be modified to enjoy the benefits of IP Security. Tunnel mode also protects against traffic analysis. With tunnel mode, an attacker can only determine the tunnel endpoints and not the true source and destination of the tunneled packets, even if they are the same as the tunnel endpoints.

As defined by the IETF, IPSec transport mode can only be used when both the source and the destination systems understand IPSec. In most cases, you deploy IPSec with tunnel mode. Doing so allows you to implement IPSec in the network architecture without modifying the operating system or any applications on your PCs, servers, and hosts.

Security Association

IPSec provides many options for performing network encryption and authentication. Each IPSec connection can provide either encryption, integrity, or both. When the security service is determined, the two communicating nodes must determine exactly which algorithms to use (for example, DES or IDEA for encryption; MD5 or SHA for integrity). After deciding on the algorithms, the two devices must share session keys. The Security Association is the method that IPSec uses to track all the particulars concerning a given IPSec communication session. A Security Association (SA) is a relationship between two or more entities that describes how the entities will use security services to communicate securely. The nomenclature gets a little confusing at times, because SAs are used for more than just IPSec. For example, IKE SAs describe the security parameters between two IKE devices.

The Security Association is unidirectional, meaning that for each pair of communicating systems, there are at least two security connections (one from A to B and one from B to A). The Security Association is uniquely identified by a randomly chosen unique number called the security parameter index (SPI) and the IP address of the destination. When a system sends a packet that requires IPSec protection, it looks up the Security Association in its database, applies the specified processing, and inserts the SPI from the Security Association into the IPSec header. When the IPSec peer receives the packet, it looks up the Security Association in its database by destination address and SPI and processes the packet as required.

Internet Key Management Protocol

IPSec assumes that a Security Association is in place, but does not have a mechanism for creating that association. The IETF chose to break the process into two parts: IPSec provides the packet-level processing, and the Internet Key Management Protocol (IKMP) negotiates security associations. After considering several alternatives, including the Simple Key Internet Protocol (SKIP), the IETF chose IKE as the standard method of configuring security associations for IPSec.

IKE creates an authenticated, secure tunnel between two entities and negotiates the security association for IPSec. This process requires that the two entities authenticate themselves to each other and establish shared keys.

IKE provides a very flexible framework for authentication that supports multiple authentication methods. The two entities must agree on a common authentication protocol through a negotiation process. At this time, the following mechanisms are generally implemented:

✦ **Pre-shared keys.** The same key is pre-installed on each host. IKE peers authenticate each other by computing and sending a keyed hash of data that includes the pre-shared key. If the receiving peer is able to independently create the same hash using its pre-shared key, it knows that both parties must share the same secret, thus authenticating the other party.

✦ **Public key cryptography.** Each party generates a pseudo-random number and encrypts it in the other party's public key. The ability for each party to compute a keyed hash containing the other peer's number, decrypted with the local private key as well as other publicly and privately available information, authenticates the parties to each other. Currently, only the RSA public key algorithm is supported.

✦ **Digital signature.** Each device digitally signs a set of data and sends it to the other party. This method is similar to public key cryptography, except that it provides nonrepudiation. Currently, both the RSA public key algorithm and the digital signature standard (DSS) are supported.

Both digital signature and public key cryptography require the use of digital certificates to validate the public/private key mapping. IKE allows the certificate to be accessed independently (for example, through DNSSEC) or by having the two devices explicitly exchange certificates as part of IKE.

Both parties must have a shared session key in order to encrypt the IKE tunnel. The Diffie-Hellman protocol is used to agree on a common session key. The exchange is authenticated as described above to guard against "man-in-the-middle" attacks.

Using IKE with IPSec

Two steps, authentication and key exchange, create the IKE SA, a secure tunnel between the two devices. One side of the tunnel offers a set of algorithms, and the other side must then accept one of the offers or reject the entire connection. When the two sides have agreed on which algorithms to use, they must derive key material to use for IPSec with AH, ESP, or both together. IPSec uses a different shared key than IKE. The IPSec shared key can be derived by using Diffie-Hellman again to ensure perfect forward secrecy, or by refreshing the shared secret derived from the original Diffie-Hellman exchange that generated the IKE SA by hashing it with pseudo-random numbers. The first method provides greater security but is slower. After this process is complete, the IPSec SA is established.

IPSec gives you the power to enable confidentiality, integrity, and authenticity in your network infrastructure. The Internet holds unlimited promise for changing the way you do business, but not without first addressing the security risks. IPSec provides a key piece of the solution, because it allows you to embed security at the network layer. It will work in concert with your other security mechanisms and help your organization become a global networked business.

Public Key Infrastructure

The accepted technology standard for identifying people is public key infrastructure (PKI), but PKI solutions are often expensive, complex systems that are difficult to deploy, administer, and use. PKI has been touted as the next big thing for years but has yet to gain wide acceptance (primarily due to trust issues, because you cannot currently attach a certificate to a specific person, and the lack of easy-to-use applications).

Managed PKI versus CA service

A managed PKI includes the entire life cycle of certificates and keys, including

✦ Rollover

✦ Recovery

✦ Enforcement

✦ Handling

✦ Integration

A CA service merely provides basic certificate issuance and revocation capabilities. A CA is only involved in a PKI a small percentage of the time — to issue, revoke, and roll over certificates. A managed PKI is involved over the entire life of the entity.

A CA service is much simpler and easier to roll out than a managed PKI. Verisign is a great example of a CA service. If all you are looking for are certificate issuance and revocation options, such as getting an SSL certificate for your Web server, then a CA service is the right choice for you. With a CA service, you do not have an easy means of managing keys and certificates. What happens when someone's key is compromised?

Additionally, with a CA service, you must work with a third party to provide key management and policy enforcement. What good is a certificate if it cannot be used anywhere?

CA services are ideal for large environments where you do not have control over the end user, such as an Extranet. If you allow your business partners or suppliers to access information on your internal network, you may want to provide stronger authentication than just a user id and password by using certificates. Because your Extranet has the possibility of maintaining thousands of users, you do not want to manage all their certificates and keys. A CA service can handle certificate issuance and revocation for you.

 Cross-Reference   Authentication is discussed in detail in Chapter 5.

Another difference between a CA service and a managed PKI is control. A CA service is usually run by a third party from whom you purchase services. A managed PKI is run in-house and controlled by you. You have complete control of your organization's keys. Entrust is a great example of a managed PKI. Their PKI solution allows you to control every aspect of the PKI, from certificate issuance down to the end-user client software. Many managed PKI providers leave the client software to a third party and focus solely on the key and certificate management cycle, which means you have to deal with yet another company to integrate your PKI to the end user. I would recommend choosing a managed PKI that includes client applications if you have complete control over the end user. This will make your life easier during integration.

Before beginning the analysis process to decide what product to purchase, you need to decide if you require Certificate services or key management services (managed PKI). Once you make this decision, your list of potential solutions will be much shorter.

Overall, a managed PKI is usually the best choice if you are planning to roll out a company-wide PKI to provide strong authentication and e-mail security. A managed PKI is complex and requires integration and compatibility with whatever applications you want to use it with. Although compatibility issues are decreasing, many still exist and cause quite a few headaches when trying to implement a managed PKI.

Key Point Summary

This chapter discusses encryption processes and techniques you can use to secure your organization's data and communications.

✦ The main purpose of encryption is to establish trust between the communicating parties.

✦ Trust relationships can be created manually or automatically. With manual trust relationships, you need to perform some action to establish trust. Automatic trust relationships are created without any user interaction.

✦ Cryptography involves securing the transmission and storage of data. Its purpose is to protect data from the eyes of unintended viewers. Cryptography can also be used to control access to computers and networks. It involves the processes of encryption/decryption.

✦ Encryption protects data from attackers (a person or system that intends to compromise a system) by scrambling the information (or plaintext) into an unreadable form (or ciphertext).

✦ Algorithms are the foundation for the encryption process. They are mathematical constructs that are applied through various applications in order to secure transmissions or storage.

✦ A round is a discrete part of the encryption process. An algorithm generally goes through several rounds when generating an encryption/decryption key. The higher the number of rounds, the better.

✦ Parallelization refers to the method of using multiple processes, processors, or machines working together to try and crack an algorithm.

✦ Strong encryption refers to an encryption process that uses at least a 128-bit key.

✦ The private key method (or symmetric method) is an encryption process where one key is used for both encryption and decryption.

✦ Private key encryption is fast and efficient, making it ideal for large data transmissions.

✦ Because the same key is used for both encryption and decryption, the sender and receiver must exchange keys before the data transmission.

✦ Many symmetric algorithms exist, including the Data Encryption Standard (DES), Triple DES, RSA algorithms RC2, RC4, RC5, RC6, MARS, Twofish, and Rijndael.

✦ Asymmetric encryption uses two keys, public and private, for encryption and decryption.

✦ Hash encryption converts data from a variable length to a fixed length 128-bit piece of data called a hash value.

✦ Several hash algorithms exist, including MD2, MD4, MD5, and the Secure Hash Algorithm (SHA).

✦ Digital signature (DS) is the technique of appending a string of characters to an electronic message to authenticate the sender. Some DS techniques also provide an integrity check to ensure the data was not altered during transit.

✦ The primary function of a digital signature is to provide the same significance as handwritten signatures. DS accomplishes this task by satisfying two needs: identifying the signer and verifying the content.

✦ Digital certificates electronically identify an individual.

✦ A certificate is a digitally signed statement from a trusted third party that verifies the identity and public-key of an individual or computer.

✦ Digital certificates are composed of Sender's public key, Sender's name, Expiration date of sender's public key, Name of the certificate issuer, Serial number of the certificate, and Digital signature of the issuer.

✦ Certificate Authorities (CAs) guarantee that when a user downloads a file sent from Sender, Sender is the person that signed the file.

✦ PGP provides a confidentiality and authentication service that can be used for e-mail and file-storage applications.

✦ S/MIME (Secure Multi-Purpose Internet Mail Extensions) is a secure method of sending e-mail that uses the RSA public-key encryption system.

✦ Secure Sockets Layer (SSL) is the de facto secure protocol for e-commerce transactions.

✦ Secure Sockets Layer (SSL) provides a secure channel between Web clients and Web servers that choose to use the protocol for Web sessions. Unlike the standard Internet protocols such as TCP/IP, SSL must be selectively employed by the Web client and server in order to use the protocol. Usually, by simply clicking on a designated SSL Web page link, a Web client will invoke the protocol to connect to an SSL-enabled server.

✦ The Secure Hypertext Transfer Protocol is a secure extension of HTTP.

✦ In contrast to SSL, the negotiation of secure properties occurs through an exchange of packet headers in S-HTTP. Whereas SSL used special handshakes to establish the parameters of the secure connection, S-HTTP defines a specific security negotiation header for packets sent during the Web session.

✦ A virtual private network (VPN) is a private data network that makes use of the public telecommunication infrastructure, maintaining privacy through the use of a tunneling protocol and security procedures.

✦ In VPNs, *virtual* implies that the network is dynamic, with connections set up according to organizational needs. It also means that the network is formed logically, regardless of the physical structure of the underlying network.

✦ The IP Security Protocol defines the information to add to an IP packet to enable confidentiality, integrity, and authenticity controls, as well as defining how to encrypt the packet data.

✦ Internet Key Exchange negotiates the security association between two entities and exchanges key material. It is not necessary to use IKE, but manually configuring security associations is a difficult and manually intensive process. IKE should be used in most real-world applications to enable large-scale secure communications.

✦ Authentication Header (AH) ensures the integrity and authenticity of the data, including the invariant fields in the outer IP header. It does not provide confidentiality protection. AH uses a keyed-hash function rather than digital signatures, because digital signature technology is too slow and would greatly reduce network throughput.

✦ Encapsulating security payload (ESP) protects the confidentiality, integrity, and authenticity of the data. If ESP is used to validate data integrity, it does not include the invariant fields in the IP header.

✦ A Security Association (SA) is a relationship between two or more entities that describes how the entities will use security services to communicate securely.

✦ The Internet Key Management Protocol (IKMP) negotiates security associations. IKE is the standard method used.

✦ You can authenticate to IPSec using a pre-shared key, digital certificates, or digital signatures.

✦ The accepted technology standard for identifying people is PKI (public key infrastructure).

✦ A managed PKI includes the entire life cycle of certificates and keys, including rollover, recovery, enforcement, handling, and integration.

✦ A CA service merely provides basic certificate issuance and revocation capabilities. A CA is only involved in a PKI a small percentage of the time, namely to issue, revoke, and roll over certificates.

✦   ✦   ✦

STUDY GUIDE

This Study Guide presents five assessment questions and ten lab exercises to test your knowledge of the exam topic area.

Assessment Questions

1. You want to share large encrypted files with a small number of people. What encryption method should you choose?

   A. Symmetric

   B. Asymmetric

   C. Hash

   D. Digital

2. Which of the following algorithms is used for creating hash values?

   A. RSA

   B. DSA

   C. SHA

   D. DES

3. Asymmetric encryption uses which of the following?

   A. The same key for encryption and decryption

   B. A different key for encryption and a different key for decryption

   C. A total of three keys

   D. A total of four keys

4. What is a Triple DES?

   A. A Hash algorithm

   B. A symmetric algorithm

   C. An asymmetric algorithm

   D. A tri-symmetric algorithm

5. What technology is primarily used to secure e-commerce?

    A. Digital certificates

    B. Digital signatures

    C. S-HTTP

    D. SSL

Lab Exercises

Lab 3-1 Installing PGP in Windows NT

 Deploy PGP in Windows NT and Linux

1. If you do not have Outlook Express installed on your system, download it from `www.microsoft.com`.

2. Download PGP v6.5.8 from `web.mit.edu/network/pgp.html`.

3. Run setup.exe.

4. Click Next on the Welcome screen.

5. Click Yes on The Software License Agreement.

6. Click Next on the Important Product Information screen.

7. Enter your name and company on the User Information screen.

8. Accept the default installation path by clicking Next or select your own path by selecting Browse.

9. On the Select Components screen, make sure you have the Outlook Express Plugin checked and click Next.

10. Click Next to start copying files.

11. When prompted, select the network adapter you want protected by PGPnet (a lock will appear in the box). This allows you to communicate securely using IPSec.

12. When asked if you have any existing keyrings you would like to use, select No.

13. When you see the Setup Complete screen, make sure the "Yes, I want to restart my computer" box is checked and click Finish.

Lab 3-2 Generating a key pair in PGP on Windows NT

1. From the Start menu, select Programs ⇨ PGP ⇨ PGPkeys.

2. The Key Generation Wizard will start. Click Next on the Welcome screen.

3. Enter the Full Name and E-mail Address that will be associated with this key. Click Next when finished.

4. On the next screen, select Diffie-Hellman/DSS as your Key Pair Type. Click Next.

5. The Key Pair Size establishes encryption strength. The higher the key size, the stronger the encryption. The default 2048 bits is sufficient for our use. Make sure it is selected and click Next.

6. Choose the default selection: Key pair never expires. Click Next.

7. Select your passphrase. This phrase is what is used to protect your private key. Only you should know your passphrase. Select something difficult to guess, but not so difficult that you won't remember it. Enter your passphrase in the Passphrase box.

8. Enter the passphrase again in the Confirmation box. Click Next.

9. PGP will now generate your key pair. When you see the word Complete, the process is finished. Click Next to continue.

10. Leave the "Send my key to the root server now" box unchecked and click Next.

11. Click Finish to end the Key Generation Wizard.

12. Your PGPkeys window will open. PGP comes with many keys pre-installed. Find the key you just created. Right-click and select Key Properties. Notice that your key is fully trusted.

13. Click the Subkeys tab. Your subkey is used for encryption and can be revoked at any time if you think it has been compromised.

Lab 3-3 Exporting PGPkeys

For this lab, you will need to find a partner to exchange keys with.

1. Launch PGPkeys if it is not already open.

2. Find your public key and right-click. Select Export.

3. The Export Key to File box opens. Keep the default settings and save the file.

4. A file with the name associated with the key and an .asc extension should appear in the saving location.

5. Launch Microsoft Outlook Express. (Make sure it is configured to send and receive e-mail.)

6. Send a message to your partner and attach your key file to the message as an attachment. Have your partner do the same, sending you his key file.

7. When you receive your partner's message with his key attached, save the attachment to your system.

8. Now add your partner's key to your key ring. In PGPkeys, select Keys ⇨ Import.

9. In the dialog box that opens, select the file location of your partner's key and click Open.

10. The Select Key(s) dialog box will open. Highlight your partner's key and select Import.

11. You now have your partner's key in your keyring. But his key is not signed, so it is not trusted. Change this by right-clicking your partner's key and selecting the Sign option.

12. Highlight your key and select the "Allow signature to be exported" checkbox.

13. When you are prompted for a passphrase, enter the passphrase you selected during the installation process to protect your private key.

14. When a green icon appears next to your partner's key, it is now signed.

15. Right-click your partner's key and select Key Properties.

16. At the bottom, slide the bar from Untrusted to Trusted.

Lab 3-4 Exchanging encrypted messages using PGP on Windows NT

For this lab, you will need to find a partner to exchange messages with.

1. Open Outlook Express and type a message to your partner.

2. Before sending the message, select the PGP Encrypt and PGP Sign icons.

3. Enter your passphrase for your private key when prompted.

4. Have your partner do the same to send you a message.

5. When you receive the encrypted message your partner sent you, double-click it to open it in its own window.

6. Click the Decrypt PGP Message icon.

7. When prompted for the passphrase for your private key, enter it. This will decrypt the message that your partner encrypted with your public key.

8. You can now read the message, as well as see who signed it.

Lab 3-5 Encrypting files with PGP on Windows NT

For this lab, you will need a partner to exchange files with.

1. On your system, select a file you want to encrypt. If you want, you can create a test file in Notepad to use for this lab.

2. From the Start menu, select Programs ⇨ PGP ⇨ PGPtools.

3. Select the Encrypt/Sign icon.

4. The Select File dialog box opens. Select the file you want to encrypt.

5. The PGP Key Selection dialog box will now open.

6. Select your partner's key and double-click on it.

7. Your partner's key should not be listed in the Recipients screen. Click OK.

8. When prompted, enter the passphrase for your private key.

9. PGP will now encrypt the file. It automatically adds the .pgp extension.

10. Have your partner perform the same steps and exchange encrypted files.

11. Double-click the encrypted file you received from your partner.

12. When prompted, enter the passphrase for your private key. When you enter the correct passphrase, PGP will prompt you for an output file name. Save the file as its original name.

13. When PGP has finished processing the file, the PGPlog dialog box will open and show that the file was properly signed. Close this window.

Lab 3-6 Installing and generating a key pair using gpg on Red Hat Linux

 Deploy PGP in Windows NT and Linux

1. Download the rpm for gpg, version 1.0.1.

2. Install the rpm.

3. Run the key generation program by typing the following:

   `/usr/bin/gpg -gen-key`

4. When prompted for the kind of key you want, select choice 1, the default DSA and ElGamal key.

5. When prompted, enter 2048 as your key size.

6. Type yes when asked if you really need such a large key size.

7. When prompted, enter 0 to say the key never expires.

8. When prompted, enter Y to confirm that your key should never expire.

9. Enter the Real Name, Comment, and E-mail Address to be associated with this key when prompted.

10. Confirm the information you entered is correct by pressing the letter "o" and hitting Enter.

11. Select a passphrase to protect your private key.

12. Confirm the passphrase by entering it again.

13. Gpg will now generate your key. It's a good idea to move the mouse and type on the keyboard to help generate random information for the system to use. This process may take a while.

14. To confirm that gpg has created a private key, enter the following information:

    ```
    /usr/bin/gpg -list-secret-keys
    ```

15. To confirm you have a public key, enter the following information:

    ```
    /urs/bin/gpg -list-keys
    ```

16. To verify that you have signed your key, enter the following information:

    ```
    /usr/bin/gpg -list-sigs
    ```

17. You now have a key pair to trade with your partners.

Lab 3-7 Exporting and exchanging keys in gpg on Red Hat Linux

For this lab, you will need a partner to exchange keys with.

1. To export your key, enter the following information:

    ```
    gpg -export > yourname.asc
    ```

2. Copy this file where your partner can easily access it, such as the /home/ftp directory.

3. Have your partner pick up your public key and place their key in the same directory.

4. Now that you have your partner's public key, you need to import it into your key ring. Enter the following to import your partner's key:

    ```
    gpg -import partnername.asc
    ```

5. To confirm that your partner's key was imported, issue the following command:

    ```
    gpg -list-keys
    ```

6. Now that you have added your partner's key to your key ring, you need to sign the key and make it trusted. Start this process by issuing the following command:

    ```
    gpg -sign-key <username>
    ```

7. When asked "Are you sure you want to sign this key?", enter Yes.

8. When prompted, enter your passphrase protecting your private key.

9. To make sure you have signed the key, enter the following command:

```
gpg -list-sigs
```

10. You can now encrypt messages and files to your partner.

Lab 3-8 Encrypting files with gpg on Red Hat Linux

In this lab, you will need a partner to exchange files with.

1. Select a file to encrypt, or use a text editor to create a new file.

2. Encrypt the selected file by entering the following command:

```
gpg -encrypt -r <partners_public_key_name> <filename>
```

3. Gpg will encrypt the file and attach the .gpg extension.

4. Now, send this encrypted file to your partner through e-mail or have him pick it up off the FTP server. Have your partner encrypt a file for you.

5. To decrypt the encrypted file your partner gave you, issue the following command:

```
gpg -decrypt <filename>.gpg
```

6. Enter your passphrase that protects your private key.

7. You should see a message that says "If you want to create a new file that contains this message, enter the following command:"

```
gpg -decrypt <filename>.gpg > <filename>
```

8. You can now read the file your partner sent you.

Lab 3-9 Installing and generating a key pair using gpg on Red Hat Linux

In this lab, you will need a partner to exchange signature files with.

1. To verify signatures, you first need to create a signature file. Create a text file by issuing the following command:

```
touch <username>
```

2. Create a cleartext signature file by issuing the following command:

```
gpg -clearsign <username>
```

3. When prompted, enter your passphrase.

4. Gpg will generate a new text file name, <username>.asc. Use cat to read this file if you want to see its contents.

5. Copy the file to your FTP directory or e-mail it to your partner. Have your partner do the same for you.

6. Once you have your partner's signature file, you can use them to verify signed files and messages.

Lab 3-10 Signing files with gpg on Red Hat Linux

In this lab, you will need a partner to exchange files with.

1. Select a file to be signed and sent to your partner. You can also create a new file in a text editor.

2. Sign the file by issuing the following command:

```
gpg -se -r <partner's_public_key> <filename>
```

3. When prompted, enter your passphrase.

4. Gpg adds a .gpg extension to this file when it signs it. Copy this file to your FTP directory or e-mail it to your partner. Have him do the same for you.

5. Once you have your partner's signed file, verify the signature by issuing the following command:

```
gpg -verify <partner's_sig>.asc <partner's_file>.gpg
```

Answers to Chapter Questions

Chapter Pre-Test

1. Symmetric encryption is the process of converting plaintext to ciphertext and back again using the same key. DES is a symmetric key encryption algorithm.

2. Asymmetric encryption is the process of converting plaintext to ciphertext and back again using different keys. RSA is an example of an asymmetric key algorithm.

3. Trust is important because it is what encryption provides. Without encryption technologies, you would not be able to trust who you were communicating with.

4. A hash is a fixed length (usually 128-bit) message derived through a hash algorithm from variable length data.

5. A digital signature is an electronic signature that can be used by someone to authenticate the identity of the sender of a message or the signer of a document.

Assessment Questions

1. **A.** Symmetric encryption is much faster than asymmetric encryption. Because you have a small group of people, it is easy to manage the required keys.

2. **C.** SHA is a hashing algorithm.

3. **B.** Asymmetric encryption uses a different key for encryption and decryption.

4. **B.** Triple DES is a symmetric algorithm.

5. **D.** SSL is the technology most often used to secure e-commerce.

Securing TCP/IP

◆ ◆ ◆ ◆

CHAPTER PRE-TEST

1. The only layer in the DARPA model that does not correspond to a layer in the OSI Model is the application layer. True or False?

2. File Transfer Protocol (FTP) uses port 28 to communicate. True or False?

3. Telnet is secure because it encrypts all traffic. True or False?

4. UDP is a reliable, connection-oriented protocol. True or False?

5. Although HTTP is a commonly used TCP/IP protocol, it does not use any encryption or security for communication. True or False?

✦ Answers to these questions can be found at the end of the chapter. ✦

There would be no Internet without TCP/IP (Transmission Control Protocol/Internet Protocol). Unfortunately, when TCP/IP was first invented, it was designed to run on a private network (namely, the Department of Defense network). This private network was secure from the outside world; consequently, TCP/IP was designed with little or no security protocols. It is for this reason that TCP/IP is inherently an insecure protocol. There are, however, ways to secure TCP/IP, as described in this chapter.

To understand how TCP/IP-based attacks work, you must first understand the TCP/IP protocol stack and how it works. The U.S. Department of Defense Advanced Research Projects Agency (DARPA) created TCP/IP in 1969, as the result of a resource-sharing experiment called Advanced Research Projects Agency Network (ARPANET). The original purpose of TCP/IP was to provide high-speed communication network links.

TCP/IP Security Issues

 Understanding the TCP/IP protocol stack.

The TCP/IP protocol maps to a conceptual model known as the DARPA model. As shown in Figure 4-1, the DARPA model is broken into four layers: application, transport, Internet, and network interface. Each layer of the model corresponds to one or more layers of the seven-layer Open Systems Interconnection (OSI) Model. Discussion of the OSI Model and how it ties in with the DARPA model occurs later in this chapter.

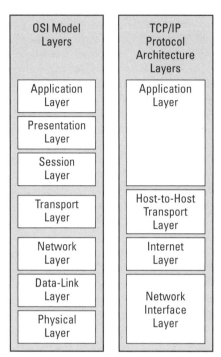

Figure 4-1: TCP/IP in the layered DARPA model

Application layer

The application layer provides the ability to access the service of the other layers and defines the protocols that applications use to exchange data. Application layer protocols are constantly evolving, and new applications are being developed. Some of the more widely used protocols are listed here.

✦ **HTTP (Hypertext Transfer Protocol)** — Transfers files that users commonly see when viewing Web pages on the World Wide Web.

✦ **FTP (File Transfer Protocol)** — Transfers files from one host to another.

✦ **Telnet** — Is a terminal emulation protocol typically used for the remote management of network devices and remote logins.

✦ **SMTP (Simple Mail Transfer Protocol)** — Transfers electronic mail.

✦ **DNS (Domain Name System)** — Resolves host names to an IP address. For example, when an Internet user types www.lanw.com in his or her browser, DNS will automatically resolve the name to the proper IP address, allowing the Web site to be displayed.

+ **RIP (Routing Information Protocol)** — Is used between routers and other network devices to exchange routing information.

+ **SNMP (Simple Network Management Protocol)** — Is used for network management and information collection.

Caution   All of these protocols have some security issues you need to be aware of. Further information will be provided in this chapter; however, it is recommended that you understand each of these protocols and their functions.

Transport layer

The transport layer provides the application layer with session and datagram communication services. The transport layer is made up of two core protocols: Transmission Control Protocol (TCP) and User Datagram Protocol (UDP).

TCP

TCP is a reliable one-to-one, connection-oriented communications service. TCP is responsible for the establishment of connections, sequencing, acknowledgment of packets sent, and recovery of lost packets during transmission.

UDP

UDP is an unreliable, one-to-one, one-to-many, connectionless-oriented communications service. UDP is typically used to transmit small, single packets of data, for which the overhead of a TCP connection is undesirable or reliability of delivery is handled by another method, usually in the application layer.

Internet layer

The Internet layer addresses packet and routing functions. The Internet layer is made up of four core protocols.

+ **Internet Protocol (IP)** — Is a routable protocol responsible for IP addressing, fragmentation of packets, and reassembly of packets.

+ **Address Resolution Protocol (ARP)** — Is responsible for the resolution of the Internet layer address to the network interface layer address, such as a hardware address.

+ **Internet Control Message Protocol (ICMP)** — Is responsible for providing diagnostic functions and reporting errors regarding the delivery of IP packets.

+ **Internet Group Management Protocol (IGMP)** — Is responsible for managing IP multicast groups.

Network interface layer

The network interface layer, sometimes referred to as the network access layer, is responsible for the sending and receiving of TCP/IP packets from the network medium. TCP/IP was designed to be network access method independent, allowing for multiple network types to communicate.

TCP/IP DARPA Model and the OSI Model

 Exploring the OSI Model

As previously mentioned, the TCP/IP DARPA model and the OSI Model correspond. Some layers of the DARPA model correspond to more than one layer of the OSI Model.

Mapping the layers

The network interface layer of the DARPA model encompasses the physical and data link layers of the OSI Model. The Internet layer of the DARPA model corresponds with the network layer of the OSI Model. The host-to-host transport layer of the DARPA model encompasses both the transport layer and the session layer of the OSI Model. Finally, the application layer of the DARPA model corresponds with the presentation layer of the OSI Model. The application layer of the OSI Model is the only layer that does not correlate with the DARPA model. Table 4-1 lists the different layers in the DARPA and the OSI models.

| Table 4-1 | |
| **DARPA and OSI Model Layers** | |
DARPA Model	*OSI Model*
Application	Application
Application	Presentation
Application	Session
Transport	Transport
Internet	Network
Network	Data Link
Network	Physical

Security issues with TCP/IP — DARPA in depth

 Examining specific protocols and their exploits

I will again look at each layer of the TCP/IP DARPA model beginning with the network interface layer and address the security issues surrounding each.

As you have already read, the network interface layer is responsible for sending and receiving packets. Typically, hacker attacks and exploits do not engage this layer, but it is important to know how this layer works and which protocols are used.

IP

The Internet layer is an easy target for hackers and malicious users. As mentioned earlier in this chapter, the Internet Protocol (IP) is an integral part of the Internet layer; IP is routable and is responsible for the addressing of network communications. An IP address is a 32-bit address that uniquely identifies a host on a TCP/IP network. The IP address contains a 20-byte header and a number of informational and control fields, such as source IP address, destination IP address, IP version numbering, length, type of service, and other configurations. The openness of IP addressing is what makes it an easy target for hackers and malicious users.

Some popular attacks using the IP protocol are IP spoofing, in which an attacker changes or forges his IP address to make it appear that packets are actually coming from someone other than him. At the Internet layer, it is impossible to determine if the source address information in the IP datagram is valid or not.

Routing protocols

Source routing is also a popular attack found at the Internet layer. An attacker can modify or create IP datagrams that will travel to the destination via a preset route. This attack type is often used to bypass firewalls and proxy servers.

ICMP

The smurf attack is a denial-of-service attack that uses IP spoofing. In a smurf attack, an attacker sends an ICMP (ping) packet to multiple computers or network broadcast addresses, but the attacker replaces the source address in the IP datagram with the address of the computers he wishes to attack. When the "pinged" computers reply, the ICMP messages go to the forged address causing enough network traffic to stop legitimate services from accessing the network.

As mentioned earlier in the chapter, ICMP is used for diagnostic purposes. The most commonly used ICMP command is the PING command. This command, regardless of what operating system is running, sends an ICMP ping request to a host. Receiving an ICMP reply tells you that the host is up and responding. For obvious reasons, this ability can be quite useful when diagnosing network-related problems. Unfortunately, ICMP is also very useful to attackers, mostly for denial-of-service (DoS) attacks and reconnaissance work.

The high-profile distributed denial-of-service (DDoS) attacks, which occurred in February of 2000, used ICMP to consume the targeted network resources, causing legitimate traffic to fail. Other attacks like WinNuke, which is Microsoft Windows specific, also involve ICMP packets that have been modified.

Reconnaissance can be performed using ICMP by conducting "ping sweeps" where an attacker pings multiple network addresses to map out which hosts are responding and which ones are not. Some research in the last few years has also made it possible to identify the operating system of the remote systems using ICMP.

Because of the relative ease of use in attacks, many corporate routers and firewalls do not respond to ICMP traffic. For example, typing **Ping** www.microsoft.com at a command prompt will result in receiving no ICMP replies.

Transport layer

Next is the host-to-host transport layer, also referred to as the transport layer. This section covers the TCP and UDP protocols.

TCP

The Transmission Control Protocol (TCP) in the transport layer is used to create a connection between two hosts to facilitate communications. TCP is the protocol used for most Internet services. Understanding how this connection is carried out and how it can be exploited for malicious uses is very important.

TCP handshake

Stepping through TCP/IP handshaking

TCP connections are carried out with what is called a handshake (a number of steps that allow two systems to connect to each other for communication). In the TCP header, there is a flag field. These flags establish the steps in the TCP handshake. The flags are as follows:

- ✦ **SYN**—Used to synchronize TCP sequence numbers
- ✦ **FIN**—Used to signal the end of a data transmission
- ✦ **ACK**—Used to acknowledge TCP packets

Additionally, a TCP packet has four different states: active open, active close, passive open, and passive close.

SYN and ACK

A TCP connection handshake is accomplished in the following manner. Computer A wants to initialize communications with Computer B. Computer A sends an active open TCP packet with the SYN flag set. The SYN flag synchronizes the two clients. The initial SYN packet also contains the desired port number for the connection (more on port numbers in the "UDP and TCP ports" section) and a randomly generated Initial Sequence Number (ISN), which is used in synchronization. Computer B replies to Computer A with a passive open TCP packet that has the SYN and ACK flags set. This is referred to as a SYN-ACK. Computer B also includes, for the purpose of synchronization, its randomly generated ISN. Finally, Computer A sends one last TCP packet with the ACK flag set. The communication handshake is now complete and the computers are free to transmit data.

FIN and ACK

Once the two computers have finished transmitting data, the TCP connection must be terminated. This process is completed in three steps. Computer B sends an active close TCP packet with the FIN flag set. This stops data flow from Computer A. Computer A then replies with a passive close TCP packet that has both the FIN and ACK flags set. This is sometimes referred to as a FIN-ACK. Computer B then completes the operation by sending one final packet with the ACK flag set.

The TCP handshaking process has been the facilitator of a variety of denial-of-service (DoS) attacks. One such attack is known as a SYN flood. A SYN flood sends multiple SYN requests to a host without completing the second and third steps of the handshaking process. If enough SYN requests are sent to a host, the host will be busy waiting for replies from the attacker and will be unable to reply to legitimate connection attempts.

An attacker who is able to predict the connection sequence numbers of a TCP handshake could hijack a TCP session. This TCP-based attack was made famous on Christmas Day of 1994 by Kevin Mitnick's alleged strike against Tsutomu Shimomura. I won't go into great detail on how this can be accomplished, as you will not be tested on it, but it is important to realize that any Windows NT Server or Workstation that does not have at least Service Pack 6 installed is vulnerable to sequence prediction. Microsoft improved on the randomness of the sequence numbers issued in Service Pack 6.

At the time of this writing, there is a tremendous amount of research being carried out by private organizations on other denial-of-service attacks that could be carried out by exploiting this handshaking process. Once such organization is BindView's RAZOR security team (http://razor.bindview.com).

UDP

UDP, the other protocol in the transport layer, is an unreliable, connectionless protocol that is used for broadcast-type communications. The nature of this protocol makes exploiting it for malicious purposes difficult and uncommon.

UDP and TCP ports

TCP and UPD communications use ports. These ports allow for multiple TCP/IP applications to coexist on a singular host. An application can use any number of the 65,536 possible ports. Of these 65,536 ports, 1023 are well-known registered ports.

You do not need to memorize the first 1023 well-known ports; however, you should know the ports most often used by applications.

Caution   Just because the first 1,023 ports are known registered ports, do not assume that traffic received on these ports is safe. Reports of Trojans horses and other malicious activity over these ports have surfaced. Currently, no method in place prevents a malicious user from using one of the well-known ports for an unknown application. Most Internet applications can be customized to run on any port the user desires.

Application layer

The application layer is the layer that users are most familiar with. Applications, such as Web browsers and mail clients, function at this level. Because of the diverse nature of TCP/IP applications, the application layer is the most difficult to secure.

Client/Server applications

Client-side applications are especially difficult to secure, as it is difficult if not impossible to control the environment of the applications communicating with your servers. Malicious users can easily modify their own applications to communicate with your servers in detrimental ways. Client applications either initiate communications via TCP or UDP, depending on the application. They also use ports to communicate. Unlike TCP/IP server applications, the client-side applications are not concerned with specific port numbers when communicating. As was mentioned earlier, the first 1023 ports are reserved; this means a client normally establishes a TCP connection using ports between 1024 and 5000. For example, when a client uses a Web browser, the browser initiates the TCP session with the Web server. Although the client knows to talk to the Web server over port 80, the server communicates with the client over a dynamically selected port assigned by the client during the first SYN step of the handshaking process.

TCP/IP servers and daemons

Objective   Reviewing common TCP and UDP ports and their use

On the server side of TCP/IP applications, TCP and UDP ports are used to distinguish between requests from different server applications. Unlike client applications, server applications are always running or listening for connections. During the startup of a typical host, the server applications also begin monitoring their assigned ports for connection requests. These applications are known as services in Microsoft products and as daemons in UNIX and Linux products.

Application vulnerabilities

As previously mentioned, server applications almost always use the same ports. The first 1023 ports are reserved for common Internet applications. Server applications are a popular target for malicious users. In some cases, attackers have been known to load their own server-side applications to ensure continued connectivity with a targeted host.

Exam Tip   The following sections review these specific implementations of Internet applications: Simple Mail Transfer Protocol (SMTP), File Transfer Protocol (FTP), Network News Transfer Protocol (NNTP), Hypertext Transfer Protocol (HTTP), Simple Network Management Protocol (SNMP), Domain Name System (DNS), and Telnet.

SMTP

SMTP transfers e-mail from one server to another. SMTP uses TCP port 25 to communicate. When an e-mail message is sent from a client application to the SMTP server, the server uses what is called an MX record (located in the DNS tables) to determine the destination IP address of the message. Standard TCP communications are used to route the message to its destination.

Sendmail, a UNIX-based SMTP server application, has had many past security issues that made running it risky. Microsoft Exchange Server, the Microsoft implementation of an SMTP server, has also had security issues in the past. Each vendor has addressed the issues and in most environments SMTP offers little risk in itself. However, SMTP still serves as a vehicle for attackers.

Attacks such as mail bombs, in which an attacker sends multiple (usually thousands) messages to an SMTP server, cause either the server or the e-mail client trying to download the messages to stop responding from the sheer volume of incoming messages. SMTP servers can also be used in what is called mail relaying. Typically, spammers (the initiators of these mass mailings) will use SMTP servers open to relaying to hide their real location when sending thousands of unsolicited spam messages. E-mail messages can also be forged by attackers and used in a variety of ways, from minor pranks to social engineering attacks.

The most dangerous risk involved with SMTP is the sending and receiving of viruses and Trojan horse applications. Recent infections like the Melissa and I Love You virus have proven just how easily SMTP can be exploited to perform an attacker's bidding. Though the Melissa and I Love You virus incidents were not targeted attacks, the even more recent Microsoft QAZ attack proved that SMTP could be used for direct assaults.

The easiest way to defend against most SMTP-based attacks is to not allow mail relaying and to educate e-mail client users on the dangers of opening unsolicited or unknown e-mail messages that contain attachments. It is also recommended that you install SMTP Gateway virus- or content-scanning applications that will check e-mail messages for malicious content before passing them on to the users.

Caution   SMTP gateway scanners can detect only known malicious e-mail attachments and are effective only if constantly updated by the product vendors.

FTP

The File Transfer Protocol (FTP) is used to transfer files from one host, the FTP server, to another, the FTP client. Almost every implementation of TCP/IP includes some sort of FTP program. FTP uses TCP port 21 to maintain a control connection between hosts. A data connection is established using an ephemeral port. While the connection on port 21 is busy sending and receiving control messages and commands, data is sent via a connection that is reestablished for each set of data to be transferred.

Hackers can use FTP for a variety of reasons. Recent buffer overflow exploits in WU-FTP, an FTP server package that runs on UNIX/Linux operating systems, have enabled hackers to gain root access on affected servers. FTP traffic, including authentication, is sent in clear text. This means that if a malicious user were monitoring network traffic with a sniffer, he or she would capture the usernames and passwords used to login to the FTP server. In the case of Microsoft Internet Information Server, these accounts could also be used to gain access to other resources, as they are set up and managed as regular user accounts on the server.

Hackers often use FTP servers with poorly configured write permissions as a drop point for tools or even as a relay for attacks. Software pirates, not to be confused with hackers, have even been known to use open, writeable FTP servers as a drop point for illegally copied software.

One historically popular FTP attack was the FTP Bounce attack. Essentially, an attacker would use multiple vulnerable FTP sites to launch a denial-of-service attack on another site.

Standard recommendations can help administrators operate an FTP server as securely as possible. First, as with all Internet services, if it is not required, then do not run it. If FTP is required, then it should be run outside of the corporate firewall in what is sometimes called the demilitarized zone (DMZ). To prevent the sniffing of usernames and passwords, allow anonymous access only. The FTP server should be segregated on a separate partition or volume from the operating system, and quotas should be enforced on any writeable directories. Following the previous suggestions prevents malicious users from jumping outside the boundaries of the FTP server and accessing the operating system. Disk quotas prevent possible logging issues caused by the server's hard drive becoming full. Enabling and reviewing all possible audit logs on a daily basis, watching for suspicious activity, is also helpful.

NNTP

The Network News Protocol (NNTP) is very similar to SMTP in architecture. The major difference is that all messages are stored on a central news server, in what are known as newsgroups, and the client connects to the server to retrieve and post messages. Just like SMTP servers, NNTP servers can be used to maliciously send viruses and Trojan horses. NNTP runs on TCP port 119 and can be used in conjunction with Secure Sockets Layer (SSL), which authenticates the session.

HTTP

The Hypertext Transfer Protocol (HTTP) is the most widely used protocol. When an Internet user accesses a Web page, it is transferred to the user using this protocol. The World Wide Web, as we know it, is based on HTTP.

Just like FTP servers, Web servers should be isolated outside of the corporate firewalls in a DMZ. In general, HTTP in itself is not a high risk, but the addition of CGI scripts and other Web enhancements have opened HTTP up to a variety of exploits. These exploits can lead to a number of things, including unauthorized access to sensitive information and the altering of Web content (defacing).

To date, there are easily over 350 separate CGI and other scripting vulnerabilities. Hackers and security professionals alike can use CGI scanners like VLAD (`http://razor.bindview.com`) or whisker (`www.wiretrip.net/rfp`) to quickly scan for known CGI vulnerabilities.

Unless SSL is in use, HTTP traffic, including any basic authentication events, is sent in clear text and can easily be intercepted.

SNMP

Although the Simple Network Management Protocol (SNMP) was a good idea at the time of creation (remember, TCP/IP was created back in 1969), it has proven to be very insecure. SNMP is used to manage network devices and to trap certain events as configured by the network administrator. Using UDP ports 161 and 162, SNMP-compliant network devices allow network administrators to manage and, in some cases, make configuration changes remotely.

SNMP uses "community names" as its only means of authentication. If you know the correct community name string, then you can easily connect to any SNMP service and collect the data the string has to offer or change configuration data. Unfortunately, default community names are constantly used and not changed by administrators. It has been suggested that a proper SNMP service is a viable solution on private networks. I tend to disagree, as internal security threats are just as prevalent, if not more prevalent, than external threats are. SNMP transmits data in clear text and does not currently support any type of encryption. Your network administrators will hate you, but I recommend that SNMP not be enabled on any critical devices.

DNS

Domain Name System (DNS), as already mentioned, is what resolves host names to IP addresses. DNS uses both UDP port 53, for name resolution, and TCP port 53, for Zone Transfers. DNS is a common attack point for hackers. Multiple vulnerabilities in BIND and other DNS-related services have led to a large amount of successful attacks on UNIX hosts. DNS cache poisoning is also a popular attack; this is when an attacker inserts wrong information into a Zone Transfer, causing certain host names to resolve to the wrong IP address. I recommend you place your DNS servers outside the firewall, in the DMZ, and restrict Zone Transfers. If you are running DNS on the UNIX platform, be sure to use the latest version and patch version of all DNS-related services, especially BIND.

Telnet

Telnet is the final protocol you'll need to understand for the exam. However, I recommend that after the exam you investigate all the protocols related to TCP/IP and their vulnerabilities.

Telnet, TCP port 23, allows for remote terminal access and can be used to administer UNIX machines. By default, Microsoft Windows NT 4.0 does not provide Telnet services, but they are provided by add-ons in the Windows NT Resource Kit. Microsoft Windows 2000 does have Telnet services installed. On UNIX platforms, the use of Remote Shell (rsh) and Remote Login (rlogin) accomplish the same functionality as Telnet.

Running Telnet is discouraged. As with most of the other protocols, SMTP, HTTP, and so on, information is sent in clear text. A hacker can either capture the authentication information by using a sniffer or hijack a Telnet session that is in progress. Both of these threats are very real and used often. Instead of running Telnet, try using Secure Shell (SSH). SSH runs over port 22 and encrypts all data communications.

TCP/IP Addressing

 Understanding IP address classes

Every TCP/IP host is identified by a logical IP address. The IP address is a network layer address and has no dependence on the data link layer address (MAC address). Each host that wants to communicate TCP/IP on a network has to have a unique IP address. Each IP address includes a network ID and a host ID.

The network ID, sometimes referred to as the network address, identifies the systems that are located on the same physical network bound by IP routers. All hosts on the same physical network have the same network ID. The network ID is unique for every network.

The host ID, sometimes referred to as the host address, identifies each IP host on the network.

For example, if my network ID was 192.168.1.0, my host ID could be anything between 192.168.1.2 and 192.168.1.255. Try not to dwell on this example just yet. It will become clearer in the paragraphs to follow.

An IP address is 32 bits long and is segmented into four 8-bit fields called octets. Each octet is converted into a decimal number in a range from 0 to 255, separated by a period. This format is called dotted decimal notation. For example, the IP address 11000000 10101000 00000011 00011000 in binary format converts to 192.168.3.24 in dotted decimal format.

Five different IP address classes were created to accommodate networks of various sizes, and they are as follows (an operating system such as Microsoft Windows supports only Class A, B, and C addresses assigned to hosts):

✦ **Class A** — These addresses are assigned to networks with a very large number of hosts. A Class A address allows for 126 networks and 16,777,214 hosts per network. The first octet of a Class A address represents the network ID and the last three represent the host ID. A class A network address would be 192.0.0.0 and hosts can be anything from 192.1.1.1 to 192.255.255.255.

✦ **Class B** — These addresses allow for 16,384 networks and 65,534 hosts. The first two octets represent the network ID, and the last two represent the host ID. For example, if my network ID is 192.168.0.0, then I can have hosts on any IP address between 192.168.1.1 and 192.168.255.255.

✦ **Class C** — Probably the most commonly used addresses, these allow for 2,097,152 networks and 254 hosts per network. The first three octets are the network ID, and the last octet is the host ID. For example, if my network ID is 192.168.50.0, then I can have hosts on any IP address between 192.168.50.1 and 192.168.50.255.

✦ **Class D** — These addresses are reserved for IP multicast addresses.

✦ **Class E** — These addresses are experimental addresses reserved for future use.

The network ID identifies the TCP/IP hosts that are located on the same physical network. All hosts on the same physical network must be assigned the same network ID in order to communicate with each other.

The host ID identifies a TCP/IP host within a network. The combination of the network ID and host ID make up an IP address.

Class A, Class B, and sometimes Class C networks are far too large to be practical. In an effort to create smaller network IDs for common distribution and use, subnetting is used. Subnetting is the process by which a network address class is divided up into smaller network addresses. In order to identify each new subnetted network ID, subnet masks must also be used. A subnet mask is a numerical value used to determine which part of the IP address is the network ID and which part is the host ID.

The TCP/IP packet structure

 Deconstructing TCP/IP packets

Data that is sent across a TCP/IP network is bundled into packets. The OSI Model is used to determine how a network constructs packets and which portion of the DARPA TCP/IP model matches which level of the operating system. Each network device and service could operate at a different level of the model.

An example of how this process works can be explained as follows. A user, smanzuik@razor.bindview.com, composes and sends an e-mail to steve@securesolutions.org. The e-mail client program first transmits the message to the mail server at razor.bindview.com. The SMTP server at razor.bindview.com then issues commands to the stack telling it to create a mail session to the SMTP mail server at securesolutions.org. The stack puts a header on this message stating that it is destined for remote TCP port 25 (SMTP). The entire TCP packet is then packaged as data in an IP datagram. As previously stated, the datagram includes the client IP address and the destination IP address. The datagram is then put into a physical media packet, in most cases Ethernet, which includes the physical address of the packet's first hop on its way to securesolutions.org. As the packet traverses the network, it is examined and repackaged at each stop before it finds its way to securesolutions.org.

Once the packet reaches securesolutions.org, the SMTP mail server strips off pieces of the packet until it is left with the e-mail to be delivered.

Firewalls and VPN solutions that are able to control the encapsulation process can improve security on a network.

Denial-of-service attacks

 Categorizing denial-of-service attacks

As previously stated, a denial-of-service (DoS) attack is any attack that prevents legitimate users from accessing network resources (for example, SYN floods that affect services at the Internet layer or buffer overflows that attack the application layer).

This chapter is focused on TCP/IP security; therefore, I will focus on DoS attacks that occur at the Internet layer and not on buffer overflows, which affect specific applications. As discussed earlier, almost all TCP/IP implementations are vulnerable to one DoS attack or another.

Completely removing the threat of DoS attacks is quite difficult. A countless number of DoS attacks are grouped into one of three categories: local DoS attacks, remote DoS attacks, and distributed DoS attacks (DDoS). Local DoS attacks serve little purpose, as they have to be run locally on a host.

Local DoS attacks

Used for pranks more than for malicious activity, local DoS attacks like CPU Hog can cause Windows NT hosts to crash by taking advantage of the way Windows NT schedules concurrently running applications. CPU Hog has been addressed by Microsoft and can be fixed by applying the latest service pack.

Remote DoS attacks

The more commonly seen DoS attacks are classified as remote DoS attacks. An older (and no longer effective) example of a remote DoS attack is WinNuke. WinNuke, as suggested by its name, affects Windows operating systems. An attacker could send what is known as out of band data to TCP port 139 or a Windows host, causing the host to either crash with a blue screen or stop responding. As with CPU Hog, Microsoft has addressed this issue, and installing the latest service pack can prevent it. Ping of Death, another DoS attack, has affected most operating systems. The Ping of Death uses extra large ICMP packets. A pinged host is ordinarily sent an ICMP packet that is 64 bits in size. Ping of Death, however, sends an ICMP packet size of 65,537 bits, causing a variety of results depending on the operating system. Most vendors have issued patches to address this issue. Depending on your operating system, you may want to consult with your operating system vendor. Certain brands of routers may also block ICMP packets. Another DoS attack that affects various operating systems is LAND. A LAND attack floods a host with TCP SYN packets specifying the target host's address as both the source and destination address and using the same TCP port on the target host as both source and destination port number. The result of this attack varies depending on the operating system, but most TCP/IP stacks are unable to handle such packets and crash. Most vendors have addressed this attack and patches are available. You can also apply filters on most firewall products to protect against this attack.

A variant on the smurf attack discussed at the beginning of this chapter is known as Fraggle. Much like the smurf attack, the Fraggle attack uses UDP echo packets instead of ICMP echo packets.

Distributed DoS attacks

The third category of DoS attacks, DDoS attacks, is the latest and probably most dangerous form of DoS attacks. Originally discovered in the summer of 1999, DDoS attacks have been given a lot of media attention because some large corporate Web sites have been victims of these attacks. As hinted to by the name, distributed denial-of-service attacks are conducted against one host by many. An attacker first gains access to multiple hosts on the Internet; the typical target is university hosts that have large and speedy connections to the Internet. Once the hosts are compromised, the attacker loads a client portion of the attack software. Also called zombies, these DDoS clients simply listen and wait for commands from the server. Once the attacker has a number of zombies under his control, he can use them to launch a variety of DoS attacks on a target. Unlike the traditional DoS attack, the attacker does not use his own system to launch the attack; instead, he commands multiple compromised hosts to coordinate a mass attack.

Tools used to accomplish such attacks are TFN, TFN2K, mstream, Shaft, Stacheldraht, Trin00, WinTrin00, and Freak88. Although there are not many ways to effectively defend against such attacks, the most important method is to prevent your systems from becoming a part of these attacks. Keep your systems patched and monitor vigilantly to help prevent your systems from being involved in these attacks. If everyone becomes good Internet citizens and keeps their own systems from being used, then these attacks become ineffective.

Some good information on distributed attacks and defenses can be found at `http://razor.bindview.com` and `http://packetstorm.securify.com`. There is also a tool, aptly named Zombie Zapper, that helps detect and remove the client portions of DDoS tools. Zombie Zapper can be found at `http://razor.bindview.com`.

Key Point Summary

This chapter discussed the TCP/IP protocol and some of its security risks. I have only scratched the surface of TCP/IP security and given you what you need to know for the exam. I strongly recommended that you check out some of the books and Web sites listed in the final section of this chapter, "For More Information."

+ I presented each layer of the TCP/IP DARPA model and how each layer corresponds to layers in the OSI Model. Know each layer of both models and how they correspond. Be sure to know each layer of the DARPA model and what it does.

+ I explained the TCP handshaking process and how it can be exploited. Remember, the handshake is a three-way process starting with the initial SYN, a SYN-ACK, and finally an ACK. TCP sessions are synchronized with random and unique session numbers, and these so-called random numbers can be predicted and exploited in session hijacking.

+ 65,536 possible TCP and UDP ports can be used in communications. The first 1023 ports are well-known registered ports, and the others are open to be used by any application. You do not need to know all 1023 ports, but I recommend that you memorize the most common services and the ports they use.

+ I presented the different protocols that operate on the application layer and addressed the most common ones: SMTP, HTTP, Telnet, SNMP, and FTP. Each protocol has its weaknesses and recommendations to secure them. Know these protocols, their weaknesses, and ways to address those weaknesses.

+ The surface of IP addressing and subnetting was scratched; this chapter has provided you with only the information required for the exam. There are many publications available on the TCP/IP protocols that go into further detail. I recommend further study on this issue because a deep understanding of TCP/IP is very beneficial to a security professional. However, for the purpose of the exam, be sure to know what the different address classes are and what they look like.

+ TCP/IP packet encapsulation has also been briefly covered with review of how a TCP/IP packet is created and routed across networks to its final destination.

+ Finally, denial-of-service attacks were examined in more detail covering local DoS attacks like CPU Hog, remote attacks like Ping of Death, and DDoS attacks and how all these attacks work.

✦   ✦   ✦

STUDY GUIDE

This section allows you to apply what you've learned to exercises and to answer the following questions about this chapter. The answers to these questions are revealed in the "Answers to Chapter Questions" section of this chapter.

Assessment Questions

1. Which of the following describes the TCP handshaking process?

   A. ACK—SYN—ACK/ACK

   B. SYN—SYN/ACK—ACK

   C. SYN—SYN—ACK

   D. ACK—ACK—SYN

2. Which of the following protocols does NOT use plain text for communication?

   A. SMTP

   B. SSL

   C. Telnet

   D. HTTP

3. Which port does the SMTP use?

   A. 21

   B. 23

   C. 25

   D. 80

4. Which port does Telnet use?

   A. 21

   B. 23

   C. 25

   D. 80

5. Which port does HTTP use?

    A. 21

    B. 23

    C. 25

    D. 80

Lab Exercise

Lab 1-1 Using Trace Route (TraceRT)

This lab illustrates the use of the Trace Route utility to trace the route a packet takes from the source to the destination computer.

1. From a Microsoft Windows system, type the following at a DOS prompt:

```
Tracert
```

Press Enter. You should be presented with the following:

```
Microsoft (R) Windows 98
 (C) Copyright Microsoft Corp 1981-1999.

C:\>tracert

Usage: tracert [-d] [-h maximum_hops] [-j host-list] [-w
timeout] target_name

Options:

    -d                 Do not resolve addresses to hostnames.
    -h maximum_hops    Maximum number of hops to search for
target.
    -j host-list       Loose source route along host-list.
    -w timeout         Wait timeout milliseconds for each
reply.

C:>\
```

2. Next, type the following:

```
tracert www.lanw.com
```

Press Enter. You should see something similar to the following listing:

```
Tracing route to www.lanw.com [206.224.65.194]

over a maximum of 30 hops:

  1   <10 ms    27 ms    55 ms  24.66.196.1
  2    55 ms    14 ms   <10 ms  24.64.0.8
```

```
   3    82 ms    28 ms    27 ms   rc2wh-atm1-0-
1.vc.shawcable.net [204.209.214.69]
   4    41 ms    28 ms    28 ms   rclwt-atm1-0-
1.wa.shawcable.net [204.209.214.114]
   5    28 ms    27 ms    28 ms   ibr01-p1-2.tkwl01.exodus.net
[209.1.169.221]
   6    41 ms    28 ms    96 ms   bbr02-g4-0.tkwl01.exodus.net
[216.34.64.164]
   7    41 ms    41 ms    41 ms   bbr02-p2-0.sttl01.exodus.net
[216.32.132.121]
   8    82 ms    69 ms    69 ms   bbr01-p0-0.okbr01.exodus.net
[216.32.132.90]
   9   110 ms    96 ms   151 ms   bbr01-p1-0.dlls01.exodus.net
[209.185.9.33]
  10   110 ms   151 ms   110 ms   bbr02-p3-0.aust01.exodus.net
[209.1.169.93]
  11    96 ms   124 ms    96 ms   dcr01-g2-0.aust01.exodus.net
[216.34.160.17]
  12   110 ms   110 ms    96 ms   acr01-p0-1-
0.aust01.exodus.net [216.34.160.218]
  13   110 ms   110 ms   110 ms   aus-bb-S2-0-
DS3.illuminati.net [216.34.164.6]
  14   110 ms   110 ms    96 ms   www.lanw.com [206.224.65.194]

Trace complete.
```

Answers to Chapter Questions

Chapter Pre-Test

1. **True.** The only DARPA layer that does not correspond to an OSI layer is the application layer.

2. **False.** FTP uses port 21 to communicate.

3. **False.** Telnet uses plain text to transfer information on the network.

4. **False.** UDP is an unreliable, connectionless-based protocol. TCP is a reliable, connection-oriented protocol.

5. **True.** HTTP tends to be an unsecure protocol. It is the Web server that is responsible for controlling security.

Assessment Questions

1. **B.** The handshake process is as follows: Computer A sends an active open TCP packet with the SYN flag set. Computer B replies to Computer A with a passive open TCP packet that has the SYN and ACK flags set. This is referred to as a SYN-ACK. Finally, Computer A sends one last TCP packet with the ACK flag set.

2. B. SSL is the only protocol listed that uses encryption when sending data (such as usernames and passwords) over the network. The others use plain text.

3. C. The SMTP protocol uses port 25 for its communication.

4. B. The Telnet protocol uses port 23 for its communication.

5. D. The HTTP protocol uses port 80 for its communication.

For More Information

Throughout this chapter, I have referenced other sources of information. Although these sources of information will not necessarily prepare you for the exam, they will help give you a deeper understanding of the issues. I strongly recommend that these sources be explored.

✦ *Internetworking with TCP/IP Volume I,* Comer, Douglas, Prentice Hall, March 2000, ISBN # 0130183806

✦ *Internetworking with TCP/IP Volume II,* Comer, Douglas E. and Stevens, David L., Prentice Hall, June 1998, ISBN # 0139738436

✦ *Internetworking with TCP/IP Volume III,* Comer, Douglas E. and Stevens, David L., Prentice Hall, May 1997, ISBN # 0138487146

✦ Papers on distributed denial-of-service attacks, `http://packetstorm.securify.com/papers/contest/`

✦ Distributed Denial of Service Defense Tactics, Simple Nomad, `http://www.razor.bindview.com/publish/papers/DDSA_Defense.html`

✦ Zombie Zapper tool, `http://www.razor.bindview.com/tools/ZombieZapper_form.shtml`

✦ Microsoft White Paper on TCP/IP, `http://www.microsoft.com/windows2000/techinfo/reskit/samplechapters/cnbb/cnbb_tcp_kscb.asp`

✦ *Security Problems in the TCP/IP Protocol Suite*, S.M. Bellovin, `http://www.ja.net/CERT/Bellovin/TCP-IP_Security_Problems.html`

✦ Computer Emergency Response Team (CERT) DoS tips, `http://www.cert.org/tech_tips/denial_of_service.html`

Network Security

This part of the book begins the examination into network concepts and technologies.

Security Incidents and Attacks examines protecting against system attacks. This discussion includes information on viruses, Trojan horses, DoS attacks, brute-force attacks, system bugs, backdoors, and man-in-the middle attacks. This chapter also discusses the more subtle forms of intrusion: Social engineering and unauthorized access.

Understanding Boundary Devices discusses the purpose of using a firewall on networks that are connected to the Internet. It explores the various types of firewalls, including packet filters, proxy servers, and stateful inspection. This chapter goes into the actual deployment of firewall technologies, including bastion hosts, DMZs, and NAT, and discusses advanced firewall functions and features, such as authentication, remote access, alerts, alarms, logs, proxy clients, remote access servers and virtual private networks.

Implementing Firewalls begins with a general discussion of firewall deployment issues, and then takes a more detailed look at how to create a secure firewall, work with bastion hosts, and understand firewall equipment. The chapter includes a discussion of the basic types of firewalls: Screening routers, single- and dual-homes bastion hosts, and screened subnet firewalls. The chapter ends with details on how to implement a simple firewall strategy.

Security Incidents and Attacks

EXAM OBJECTIVES

- ✦ Understand the different types of security attacks
- ✦ Identify attack incidents
- ✦ List the main types of viruses
- ✦ Understand why buffer overflow attacks are so dangerous
- ✦ Understand how humans are the weakest link
- ✦ List the contents of a root kit
- ✦ Understand the importance of controlling information leakage

CHAPTER PRE-TEST

1. What is a brute-force attack?

2. What is social engineering and why is it so successful?

3. What is a man-in-the-middle attack?

4. List two viruses that spread quickly and caused a lot of damage to corporate and government networks.

5. Name two popular DoS attacks that have seen widespread use in the past couple of years.

✦ Answers to these questions can be found at the end of the chapter. ✦

Tего his chapter discusses the types of attacks you may face in the real world, as well as some of the tools used to launch these attacks. By understanding the attacks launched against you and recognizing them, you can respond quickly to any incident that occurs.

Along with the types of attacks, you must also be familiar with the various tools and programs available to an attacker. Knowing your enemy (and the types of tools he or she uses) is the first step to a strong defense. Put yourself in their shoes and take a look at your network and systems to see how vulnerable you really are.

 We discuss various types of attacks individually in this chapter, but in reality, such attacks are most often used in conjunction with one another to compromise a system or network.

Understanding Attacks and Security Incidents

There are numerous types of system attacks that occur every day, all over the world. Before the specifics of the various attacks are outlined, we need to discuss a few of the general principles regarding attacks.

 Understand the different types of security attacks

Identify attack incidents

Attacks can be active or passive. *Active attacks* are those that require action by the attacker, such as launching scripts or programs that exploit vulnerabilities in an application. *Passive attacks* do not require interaction by the attacker. The best example is a network sniffer. Once the sniffer is in place, the attacker just sits back and waits until it captures some valuable information, such as a username and password combination.

Attacks can be internal or external, meaning they can originate from inside or outside your network. Although external attackers get the most press and notoriety, the internal attackers are the most dangerous. Disgruntled employees, contractors, and other individuals with access to the company network can cause immense damage and monetary loss. Internal attackers are so dangerous for several reasons. Companies want to completely trust their employees, and the way most organizations neglect to implement proper internal security controls shows this implicit trust. Organizations spend lots of money on firewalls and intrusion detection systems to protect their network from the external attackers, but they overlook their internal security, leaving the network wide open for an internal attack. Internal attacks can be as minor as someone's gaining access to the server room and shutting off the computers or as major as someone's deleting production source code, modifying database records, or changing payroll information.

In the Real World The main goal of hackers when trying to break into networks is to gain internal access and rights. Once a hacker has penetrated a system, he or she should be considered inside users, typically with rights that far exceed what they had before. Without any internal security in place, they could potentially go anywhere on the network, or at a minimum, have a chance at gaining better access to other network resources.

Attacks can be described as front door or backdoor. Front-door attacks try to bypass or defeat authentication processes. Examples of front-door attacks include guessing username and password combinations and cracking passwords. In a front-door attack, the intruder appears to be a legitimate system user. Backdoor attacks take advantage of undocumented (and sometimes documented) points of access in application or operating system code placed there by the programmers. Although many system administrators are not aware of these backdoors, attackers are. Exploiting backdoors provides access, often with high privileges, and bypasses authentication systems in the process.

Attacks can be direct or indirect. Direct attacks try to directly access the system by either guessing a user's password or exploiting a vulnerability in the operating system or in an application running on the system. Indirect attacks use other means of gathering information, such as social engineering or dumpster diving.

Cross-Reference When you realize you have been the target of an attack, you need to respond quickly and efficiently. Chapter 16 discusses this in more detail.

Viruses

A *virus* is a piece of programming code that creates an unexpected and generally undesirable event, such as deleting the contents of a hard drive or eating up all system resources on a machine. A virus can also be pretty harmless and just flash a message on the screen.

A virus is often designed to spread to other systems automatically. A worm is a special type of virus that can automatically replicate itself and spread quickly to many systems.

Viruses can be transmitted by sending them as attachments to an e-mail, by downloading an infected program from the Internet, or through the sharing of floppy disks or CDs. A security company recently sent out a CD containing various shareware security applications to its customers. Many of the files on the disk were infected with viruses. Whether this was intentional or not is unknown.

Some viruses wreak havoc as soon as their code is executed, whereas others lie dormant until circumstances cause their code to be executed by the computer (for example, when the system hits a specific date or launches applications in a certain order or when the user hits a specific key sequence). These time-delayed viruses are often called *logic bombs*.

Three main general classes of viruses exist. These virus types are discussed in the following sections.

 List the main types of viruses

File infectors

File infector viruses usually attach themselves to program files, such as .COM or .EXE files. Some can infect any program for which execution is requested, including .SYS, .HLP, .PRG, and .MNU files. When the program is loaded, the virus is also loaded and possibly executed. Other file infector viruses arrive as wholly contained programs or scripts sent as an attachment to an e-mail.

System or boot-record infectors

System or *boot-record infector* viruses infect executable code found in certain system areas on a disk. They attach to the boot sector on diskettes or the master boot record (MBR) on hard disks. A typical boot-record virus is transmitted via a disk. When your operating system is running, files on the disk can be read without triggering the virus. However, if you leave the disk in the drive and then restart your system, the computer will find the disk with its virus, load it, and the virus will make using your hard disk impossible, either by denying access to or deleting the entire contents of the drive. Such attacks are just one reason why you should make sure you always have a bootable floppy disk on hand.

Macro viruses

Macro viruses infect your Microsoft Word or Excel application and typically insert unwanted words or phrases. These are among the most common viruses, and they tend to do the least damage.

The most recent virus outbreaks have exploited Microsoft Exchange and the Outlook mail client. The Melissa, I Love You, and Navidad viruses of 1999 and 2000 caused millions of dollars in damage around the world, often causing large corporations to take their e-mail systems offline for several days.

The best protection against a virus is to run antivirus software on all your systems. Companies such as Symantec, F-Secure, and McAfee are experts in the antivirus field. Most antivirus software available today will scan your master boot record and all files on your hard drive as well as any floppy disks inserted in your drives and any e-mail attachments you receive. Antivirus software that can scan e-mail attachments is a must have for anyone using e-mail.

Many people find antivirus software annoying and will disable it or not keep it updated with the latest virus signatures. They will learn their lesson soon enough. From time to time, you may get an e-mail message warning of a new virus. Unless the warning is from a source you recognize, chances are good that the warning is a hoax.

Trojan Horses

A *Trojan horse* is a seemingly harmless program or piece of data that contains malicious or harmful code. This malicious code will often try to gain control of your system and cause damage, such as ruining the file allocation table on your hard disk. A Trojan horse can be considered a virus if it is widely distributed.

Popular Windows Trojan horses today are BackOrifice, NetBus, and SubSeven. BackOrifice, available from `http://www.cultdeadcow.com/tools/`, is a Windows 9*x* remote administration tool. It allows the user to remotely send and receive files, view cached passwords, reboot the system, launch processes, create file shares, and modify Registry keys. NetBus is similar to BackOrifice, but provides a better interface, graphical remote control, and more configuration options. SubSeven, based on the number of scans you receive for this on your cable modems, is the most popular Trojan horse today. SubSeven is more stable than BackOrifice or NetBus and provides capabilities such as launching port scans from the victim's system, printing, port redirection, and mouse hijacking.

You can do many things to protect yourself from Trojan horses. System administrators should verify that all software installed on a system comes from a trusted source and has not been modified in transit. This task can be accomplished through the verification of digital signatures or checksums when files are downloaded. If you cannot download the software, you may wish to receive the program on a disk with the manufacturer's logo. This method does not remove the complete possibility that the application might be infected with a Trojan horse, but does reduce the chance.

Do not execute any unsolicited e-mail attachments. Even if the message comes from a trusted party, recent attacks, such as the I Love You Virus, have shown how opening any unsolicited attachments — no matter who they are from — is dangerous.

Most important, educate your end users to greatly reduce your risk of being successfully attacked with Trojan horses.

History of the Trojan Horse

The term Trojan horse comes from Homer's *Iliad*. In the Trojan War, the Greeks presented the citizens of Troy with a large wooden horse in which they had secretly hidden their warriors. During the night, the warriors emerged from the wooden horse and overtook the city.

Denial-of-Service Attacks

A *denial-of-service attack* is aimed at depriving an organization of a resource they expect to be able to use. In today's world, denial-of-service attacks refer to attacks that prevent you from using your computing resources, whether it be your mail server, Web server, or database server.

Denial-of-service attacks are usually intentional attacks against a specific system or network. The attacker may have a personal grudge against the company or may just want to target a high-profile organization. The distributed denial-of-service attacks against Amazon and CNN in February of 2000 are the best examples of this type of attack. Distributed denial-of-service attacks use a group of computers in different locations, often unknown to the system owner, to launch an attack against a specific target.

Most often, denial-of-service attacks are caused by flooding, sending more data or TCP/IP packets to a resource than it can handle. One of the earliest denial-of-service attacks was the 1988 Morris worm that brought down the Internet. An error in a piece of code developed by Robert Morris caused the code to replicate itself so fast that it consumed almost all system resources and spread to other computers on the Internet.

Flooding attacks are easy to carry out, especially since programs such as Trinoo and tribal flood network are freely available on the Internet. These programs allow you to create a denial-of-service attack against a specific target. They are also key in carrying out distributed denial-of-service attacks.

Other denial-of-service attacks include locking an account after a set number of failed login attempts or causing a system to reboot. An attacker can attempt to log in to a user account with an incorrect password(s), but once the attacker has reached the failed login attempts limit (usually three), the system is unavailable for the real user until the administrator resets the account or the set amount of time passes and the account resets itself. Because the legitimate account owner cannot log in to the system, the attacker has created a denial of service. Other methods allow an attacker to shut down or reboot a server, making it unavailable for use.

Denial-of-service attacks can also be caused accidentally. Misconfiguration or inappropriate network use can cause resources to be unavailable. The use of streaming media and peer-to-peer technology such as Napster can cause a denial of service, overloading network traffic to the point that legitimate business transactions cannot be processed.

Many methods exist to launch denial-of-service attacks and more are discovered every day as applications are analyzed for security weaknesses. The main types of exploits include buffer overflows, SYN attacks, and teardrop attacks.

Buffer overflows

 Understand why buffer overflow attacks are so dangerous

Buffer overflows are the most common type of denial-of-service attacks (they can also fall under the heading of system bugs if the overflow is unintentional). Here, an attacker sends more data than an application's buffer can hold. When the amount of data exceeds the buffer size, the extra data overflows onto the stack, often causing the application or entire system to crash. In some cases, the data can be carefully crafted to include machine code that will execute when it overflows onto the stack.

The skills necessary to identify and exploit buffer overflows are very advanced. Scripts and executables that perform these functions automatically are freely available on the Internet, making these attacks easier to execute and very dangerous, because many of them lead to complete system compromise.

One of the best examples of a buffer overflow denial of service is the *Ping of Death* attack. Here, an attacker sends an oversized ICMP (Internet Control Message Protocol) packet to a system. When the system receives the packet, it cannot handle the oversized packet and crashes.

SYN attack

A *SYN attack*, also known as a SYN flood, takes advantage of the TCP implementation. When a connection request is sent to a system, the packet contains a SYN field that represents an initial communication request. The receiving system responds with a SYN/ACK, holding the SYN packet in memory until it receives final confirmation, ACK, from the initiating system and communication between the two systems can begin. An attacker can manipulate the TCP connection process and create a Denial of Service by sending a large number of SYN packets with no corresponding ACK to cause the receiving system to hold these packets in memory, making it difficult for legitimate requests to go through. The following shows the TCP SYN/ACK communication pattern.

```
1 A <-----SYN-----> B
2 A <---SYN/ACK---> B
3 A <-----ACK-----> B
```

Teardrop attack

A *teardrop attack* exploits the IP implementation. When a packet is too large for a router to handle, it is broken into smaller packets called fragments. To reassemble the fragments into the original packet when it arrives at its destination, the fragment packets contain an offset value to the first packet. An attacker can put a confusing offset value in the second or later fragment packet that may cause the receiving system to crash when it tries to reassemble the complete packet.

As always, the best denial-of-service attack is to simply cut the wire, also known as a *physical denial-of-service* or *infrastructure denial-of-service* attack.

Brute-Force Attacks

Brute-force attacks (also known as brute-force cracking) try every known character combination to guess a user's password and defeat an authentication system or encryption key. Brute-force attacks are exhaustive and can use many system resources. If attackers are patient, though, they will most likely be successful.

Crackers are sometimes used in an organization to test network security, although their more common use is for malicious attacks. Some variations, such as L0phtCrack from L0pht Heavy Industries (now part of @Stake), start by making assumptions, based on knowledge of common or organization-centered practices, and then apply brute force to crack the rest of the data. *PC Magazine* reported that a system administrator who used the program from a Windows 95 terminal with no administrative privileges was able to uncover 85 percent of that office's passwords within 20 minutes.

Brute-force attacks are easy to recognize because they involve a high number of failed login attempts. Locking an account after three to five failed login attempts helps combat this form of attack.

Dictionary attacks are a form of brute-force attack. They use large lists of common words to try and crack an authentication scheme. With a brute-force attack, an attacker tries every single character combination including uppercase and lower-case letters, numbers, and special characters. Because most people choose poor passwords such as their name, their spouse's name, general words or places, dictionary attacks are often successful and less time consuming than other brute-force attacks.

John the Ripper is an example of a program used to launch a dictionary attack against a target. This type of attack works very well against systems running UNIX or Linux. As with brute-force attacks, some system administrators run this program to audit their user accounts, but it is mostly used for attacks.

System Bugs and Backdoors

A *bug* is a coding error in a computer program. The process of finding bugs before program users do is called *debugging*. Debugging starts after the code is first written and continues in successive stages as code is combined with other units of programming to form a software product, such as an operating system or an application. After a product is released or during public beta testing, bugs are still likely to be discovered, especially with today's desire for quick time to market. Products often go through very brief or no quality assurance testing before being released to the public. When this occurs, users have "buggy" code and have to pay close attention to updates or patches released by the vendor. If the application is not updated in a timely manner, the system is highly susceptible to attack. Most attacks today occur through systems that have not been appropriately patched. A well-designed program developed using a well-controlled process will result in fewer bugs per thousands of lines of code.

The Bugtraq database, located at www.securityfocus.com/vdb, is the place to go to find complete information on system bugs and backdoors for all operating systems and products. Bugtraq maintains stats on the vulnerabilities it receives at www.securityfocus.com/vdb/stats.html. Microsoft products have the most reported vulnerabilities. Whether this is due to the inherent insecure design of their products, or the fact that they are more carefully focused on because they are so widely used, is up for debate. See Figure 5-1 for a breakdown of the number of vulnerabilities reported each month since 1998.

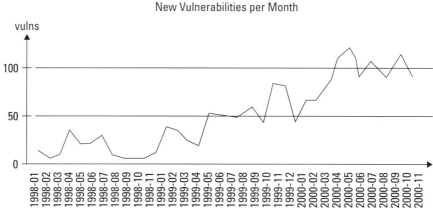

Figure 5-1: This graph shows the number of vulnerabilities reported each month. As you can see, as security has become a bigger focus, the number of reported vulnerabilities has increased dramatically.

Bug Tales

The term, *bug*, has been wrongly attributed to the pioneer programmer Grace Hopper. In 1944, Hopper, a young Naval Reserve officer, went to work on the Mark I computer at Harvard, becoming one of the first people to write programs for it. As Admiral Hopper, she later described an incident in which a technician is said to have pulled an actual bug (a moth, in fact) from between two electrical relays in the Mark II computer. In his book, *The New Hacker's Dictionary*, Eric Raymond reports that the moth was displayed for many years by the Navy and is now the property of the Smithsonian. Raymond also notes that Admiral Hopper was already aware of the term when she told the moth story. The term, *bug*, was used prior to modern computers to mean an industrial or electrical defect.

Table 5-1 presents the number of Operating System vulnerabilities on a yearly basis, as does Figure 5-2.

Table 5-1 Number of OS Vulnerabilities by Year				
OS	1997	1998	1999	2000
AIX	21	38	10	7
BSD (aggr.)	8	8	25	46
BSD/OS	6	5	4	0
BeOS	0	0	0	5
Caldera	3	2	13	19
Connectiva	0	0	0	22
Debian	3	2	32	40
FreeBSD	4	2	17	32
HP-UX	8	5	13	25
IRIX	28	14	9	13
Linux (aggr.)	12	24	99	130
MacOS	0	1	5	0
MacOS X Server	0	0	1	0
Mandrake	0	0	2	39
NetBSD	1	4	10	19
NetWare	0	0	4	3
OpenBSD	1	2	4	16
Red Hat	6	10	46	76
SCO UNIX	1	3	9	2
Slackware	4	8	11	10
Solaris	24	32	36	16
SuSE	0	0	22	27
Turbolinux	0	0	2	17
UnixWare	0	3	14	4
Windows 3.1x/95/98	1	1	46	43
Windows NT/2000	6	7	99	117

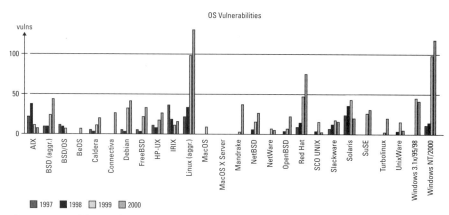

Figure 5-2: This graph shows the number of vulnerabilities by OS each year.

Table 5-2 shows the software packages with the most vulnerabilities from the year 2000.

Table 5-2 Top Vulnerable Packages 2000	
Package	*Number of Vulnerabilities*
Microsoft Windows NT 4.0	95
Microsoft Windows NT 2000	79
Red Hat Linux 6.2 i386	59
Red Hat Linux 6.2 sparc	46
Red Hat Linux 6.2 alpha	46
Red Hat Linux 6.1 i386	43
Microsoft Windows 98	43
Microsoft Windows 95	39
MandrakeSoft Linux Mandrake 7.0	34
Red Hat Linux 6.1 sparc	33
Red Hat Linux 6.1 alpha	33
Red Hat Linux 6.0 i386	31
Debian Linux 2.2	31
Microsoft IIS 4.0	24
Microsoft BackOffice 4.5	24

Package	Number of Vulnerabilities
Microsoft BackOffice 4.0	24
Red Hat Linux 6.0 alpha	23
Red Hat Linux 6.0 sparc	22
FreeBSD FreeBSD 4.0	22
Red Hat Linux 7.0	21

Root kits

 List the contents of a root kit

A *root kit* is a group of programs used by an attacker to assume complete control of a UNIX/Linux system. Root kits often include a sniffer; a Trojan horse login replacement with a backdoor; replacement programs for the `ls`, `du`, `ps`, `netstat`, and `ifconfig` utilities; and tools to adjust the timestamps and checksums of replacement programs and system log cleaners. Recently, Greg Hoglund, a regular contributor on the Bugtraq mailing list, developed a Windows NT/2000 root kit.

Man-in-the-Middle Attack

A *man-in-the-middle attack* occurs when an attacker intercepts packets intended for a different destination. The attacker will either modify the packets and send them on to their true destination or the attacker will have a server acting as the sender's intended server. During a typical man-in-the-middle attack, an attacker can intercept the packets bound for the target site and obtain the user's login information when, for instance an online banking customer attempts to log into his or her online account. During another type of man-in-the-middle attack, a session hijack, the attacker can run a Web server that appears to be the bank's Web server and capture the user's login information with the user being none the wiser because the page would look almost identical to the legitimate server.

The main difference between the above attacks is that in a session hijack, the attacker has taken control of the connection between the communicating systems. In a typical man-in-the-middle attack, the attacker just has access to the packets, not control over the entire communication medium. These attacks are difficult to execute, but can be very effective.

Spoofing

Spoofing is the process of changing the source identity of a communication. You can spoof such things as TCP/IP packets and e-mail messages. Spoofed communications are difficult to detect and are used to bypass authentication mechanisms. For example, if a system is configured to accept connections from a specific list of IP addresses, an attacker can create packets that appear to originate from one of those authorized addresses, allowing him/her to communicate with the target system. The most common TCP/IP implementation, IPv4, can fall victim to spoofing attacks quite easily. IPv4 is particularly vulnerable to spoofing because it does not have the built-in ability to actually determine the legitimate origin of the suspect packet. As such, it always believes the information contained in the packet as to its origin. Thankfully, there is a new implementation, IPv6, that is now slowly making inroads and has proven to improve protection from these types of attacks.

 Cross-Reference   See Chapter 21 for more information on IPv6 and the benefits and hazards associated with implementing it.

Attackers also spoof IP addresses during an attack to make it difficult for authorities to find their location. An attacker in Russia may make all his packets appear as if they originated from a user in San Francisco, California.

Many different types of attack programs facilitate spoofing of IP addresses during the attack. Quite often, tracking down the original packet can be very hard, and if done properly, a hacker could almost be completely untraceable.

Keep in mind that if an auditor works quickly enough, and puts in enough effort tracing back through system logs and network routers (both at the victim's site and on down the line), there is a chance that they will find the source of the attack; however, more often than not, there is little chance of finding the actual legitimate source, due to the sheer amount of routers and networks typically found between a source address and destination address on the Internet. This also assumes that the hacker hasn't at one point utilized a hijacked computer, which can make things even more difficult.

Web Bugs

A *Web bug* is a graphic on a Web page or in an e-mail message that is designed to monitor your activity. Through this graphic, companies can monitor who is reading the Web page or e-mail message. Web bugs are often invisible because they are typically only 1-by-1 pixels in size. They are represented as HTML IMG tags. For example, here are two Web bugs recently found on Quicken's home page (www.quicken.com):

```
<img src="http://ad.doubleclick.
net/ad/pixel.quicken/NEW" width=1 height=1 border=0><IMG
WIDTH=1
HEIGHT=1border=0SRC="http://media.preferences.com/ping?
ML_SD=IntuitTE_Intuit_1x1_RunOfSite_Any&db_afcr=4B31-C2FB-
10E2C&event=reghome&group=register&time= 1999.10.27.20.5 6.37">
```

The two Web bugs were placed on the home page by Quicken to provide "hit" information about visitors to DoubleClick and MatchLogic (`www.preferences.com`), two Internet advertising companies.

Ad networks use Web bugs to gain information on what sites a person is visiting or to create a personal profile. The personal profile is identified by the browser cookie of an ad network. At some later time, this personal profile, which is stored in a database server belonging to the ad network, determines what banner ads are shown to you. The following information may be sent back to the ad company:

✦ The IP address of the computer that fetched the Web bug

✦ The URL of the page that the Web bug is located on

✦ The URL of the Web bug image

✦ The time the Web bug was viewed

✦ The type of browser that fetched the Web bug image

✦ A previously set cookie value

Another use of Web bugs is to provide an independent accounting of how many people have visited a particular Web site. Web bugs are also used to gather statistics about Web browser usage at different places on the Internet.

Web bugs have several uses in e-mail messages. A Web bug can be used to find out if and when a particular e-mail message has been read. A Web bug can provide the IP address of the recipient if the recipient is attempting to remain anonymous. Within an organization, a Web bug can give an idea of how often a message is being forwarded and read.

Web bugs are especially useful to junk e-mailers or "spammers." They are used to measure how many people have viewed the same e-mail message in a marketing campaign, to detect if someone has viewed a junk e-mail message or not, and to synchronize a Web browser cookie to a particular e-mail address. This trick allows a Web site to know the identity of people who come to the site at a later date.

Tip   There is no way to detect a Web bug except to analyze the HTML code of the Web page.

Social Engineering

 Understand how humans are the weakest link

Social engineering, one of the most effective attacks, exploits the weakest component of any company's security infrastructure, the human. Social engineering uses deception or persuasion to convince someone to take an action or divulge information to the attacker.

The best social engineers are patient and research their target carefully. The more attackers know, the more they will be able to discover during conversations with their targets.

Social engineering usually occurs over the telephone, but it can also occur over e-mail, snail mail, or any other communications medium. A good example is an attacker's pretending to be a high-level executive of the target company calling the help desk claiming to have forgotten his/her password and needing it reset. Most help desk employees are intimidated by senior executives and will quickly respond to the attacker's request without too many questions. Of course, a security-conscious help desk worker will have some means of confirming identity.

Sending fake e-mail messages is a very simple process that can be achieved by using Telnet to connect to an SMTP server.

 Tip   Check the lab exercises at the end of this chapter for more information on e-mail trickery.

E-mails can be used to gather information about a target or even to receive usernames and passwords. You would be surprised how many system users will send their password to a suspected IT director over e-mail.

Unauthorized Access to Sensitive Information

 Understand the importance of controlling information leakage

As soon as you connect your systems to the Internet, you are exposed to potential attack or intrusion. The mere process of registering a domain name will provide attackers with valuable publicly available information.

You need to make a conscious effort to reduce the amount of data available to potential attackers. Some information, such as InterNIC registration information and services running on systems connected to the Internet, will always be known. Implementing mitigating controls helps reduce the risk of attacks from the outside world that might be caused by this information.

Proper configuration of DNS servers will prevent attackers from gaining information on the design and architecture of your internal network. Additionally, user account names and passwords should be guarded as one of the crown jewels of the organization because they provide attackers with easy access to your network.

Even though attackers can easily discern what services you are running on your servers, you should not allow them to find out what specific servers are running. For example, having port 80 open on a system shows the attacker that you have a Web server running, but disabling banner information keeps them from finding out you are running IIS 4.0. Attackers can still find out what server you are running, but at least you won't make it a simple process.

Key Point Summary

This chapter discusses the types of attacks you may encounter against your systems and describes how to recognize those attacks.

✦ Attacks can be active or passive. Active attacks require action by the attacker, such as launching scripts, or programs that exploit vulnerabilities in an application. Passive attacks do not require interaction by the attacker.

✦ Attacks can be external or internal, meaning they can originate outside your network or inside your network. Encryption is the process of hiding the true message in a form indecipherable to anyone but the intended recipient.

✦ Attacks can also be described as front door or backdoor. Front-door attacks try to bypass or defeat authentication processes. In a front-door attack, the attacker appears to be a legitimate system user. Backdoor attacks take advantage of "undocumented" points of access in application or operating system code placed there by the programmers.

✦ Attacks can be direct or indirect. Attackers use direct attacks to access the system by either guessing a user's password or exploiting a vulnerability in the operating system or an application running on the system. Indirect attacks use other means of gathering information, such as social engineering or dumpster diving.

✦ A virus is a piece of programming code that creates an unexpected and generally undesirable event, such as deleting the contents of a hard drive or eating up all system resources on a machine.

✦ Viruses can be transmitted by sending them as attachments to an e-mail, by downloading an infected program from the Internet, or through the sharing of floppy disks or CDs.

✦ File infector viruses usually attach themselves to program files, such as .COM or .EXE files.

✦ Boot sector viruses attach to the boot sector on diskettes or the master boot record on hard disks.

✦ Macro viruses infect your Microsoft Word or Excel application and typically insert unwanted words or phrases.

✦ The best protection against a virus is to run antivirus software on all your systems and make users aware of the virus threat.

✦ A Trojan horse is a seemingly harmless program or piece of data that contains harmful code. Popular Windows Trojan horses today are BackOrifice, NetBus, and SubSeven.

✦ A denial-of-service attack is aimed at depriving an organization of a resource they expect to be able to use. Denial-of-service attacks prevent you from using your computing resources, whether it be your mail server, Web server, or database server.

✦ Most often, denial-of-service attacks are caused by flooding, sending more data or TCP/IP packets to a resource than it can handle. Other types of denial of service include locking an account after a set number of failed login attempts or causing a system to reboot. Denial-of-service attacks can also be caused accidentally.

✦ Buffer overflows, the most common type of denial-of-service attacks, send more data than the application's buffer can hold. When the amount of data exceeds the buffer size, the extra data overflows onto the stack, often causing the application or entire system to crash. In some cases, the data can be carefully crafted to include machine code that will execute when it overflows onto the stack.

✦ A SYN attack, also known as a SYN flood, takes advantage of the TCP implementation. Sending a large number of SYN packets with no corresponding ACK will cause the receiving system to hold these packets in memory, making it difficult for legitimate requests to go through.

✦ The teardrop attack exploits the IP implementation. An attacker can put a confusing offset value in the second or later fragment packet that may cause the receiving system to crash when it tries to reassemble the complete packet.

✦ Brute-force attacks (also known as brute-force cracking) are a trial-and-error method using every known character combination to guess a user's password and defeat an authentication system or encryption key.

✦ Dictionary attacks are a form of brute-force attack. They use large lists of common words to try and crack an authentication scheme.

✦ A bug is a coding error in a computer program. Most attacks today occur through systems that have not been appropriately patched. Buffer overflows are one of the most dangerous forms of system bugs.

✦ A root kit is a group of programs used by an attacker to assume complete control of a UNIX/Linux system. Root kits often include a sniffer; a Trojan horse login replacement with a backdoor replacement programs for the `ls`, `du`, `ps`, `netstat`, and `ifconfig` utilities; and tools to adjust the timestamps and checksums of replacement programs and system log cleaners.

✦ A man-in-the-middle attack intercepts packets intended for a different destination.

✦ In a session hijack, an attacker takes control of the connection between communicating systems.

✦ Spoofing is the process of changing the source identity of a communication. You can spoof such things as TCP/IP packets and e-mail messages.

✦ A Web bug is a graphic on a Web page or in an e-mail message that is designed to monitor user activity.

✦ Social engineering is one of the most effective attacks used. It exploits the weakest component of any company's security infrastructure, the human. Social engineering uses deception or persuasion to convince someone to take an action or divulge information to the attacker.

✦ You need to make a conscious effort to reduce the amount of data available to potential attackers. Some information, such as InterNIC registration information and services running on systems connected to the Internet, will always be known. Implementing mitigating controls helps reduce the risk of threats this information can cause.

✦   ✦   ✦

STUDY GUIDE

This Study Guide presents ten assessment questions and two lab exercises to assess your understanding of the exam objectives.

Assessment Questions

1. Your system resources suddenly skyrocket to 100 percent. You have most likely been the target of what type of attack?

   A. Trojan horse

   B. Denial of service

   C. Spoof

   D. Man-in-the-middle

2. You receive a cartoon as an e-mail attachment that also installs a backdoor on your system when executed. What type of attack is this?

   A. Trojan horse

   B. Denial of service

   C. Spoof

   D. Man-in-the-middle

3. A SYN flood is what type of attack?

   A. Trojan horse

   B. Denial of service

   C. Spoof

   D. Man-in-the-middle

4. If you are using the L0phtCrack program, what type of attack are you executing?

   A. Worm

   B. Information leakage

   C. Denial of service

   D. Brute-force attack

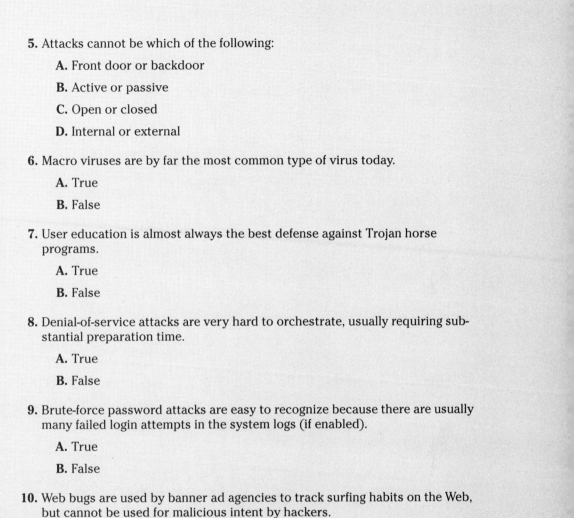

5. Attacks cannot be which of the following:

    A. Front door or backdoor

    B. Active or passive

    C. Open or closed

    D. Internal or external

6. Macro viruses are by far the most common type of virus today.

    A. True

    B. False

7. User education is almost always the best defense against Trojan horse programs.

    A. True

    B. False

8. Denial-of-service attacks are very hard to orchestrate, usually requiring substantial preparation time.

    A. True

    B. False

9. Brute-force password attacks are easy to recognize because there are usually many failed login attempts in the system logs (if enabled).

    A. True

    B. False

10. Web bugs are used by banner ad agencies to track surfing habits on the Web, but cannot be used for malicious intent by hackers.

    A. True

    B. False

Lab Exercises

Lab 5-1 Utilizing Telnet to generate a spoofed e-mail message

In this lab, you will see how easy it is to generate spoofed e-mails utilizing Telnet. By doing this, a hacker can easily appear to be a company insider.

1. Using Telnet, connect to an SMTP server on port 25.

2. Enter the following text:

```
hello <cr>
mail from: unknowing.sender@iamspoofed.com <cr>
rcpt to: gullible.recipient@company.com <cr>
data: <cr>
Type your spoofed message here. <cr>
. <cr>
quit <cr>
```

3. Send the message to an account you can access, check your mail for the message you just sent, and make sure you check the From field.

Lab 5-2 Using L0phtCrack to run a brute-force password attack

As you will see throughout this book, L0phtCrack is a powerful tool. This lab uses L0phtCrack to brute-force attack passwords dumped from the Registry.

1. Download L0phtCrack from `http://www.10pht.com/10phtcrack`.

2. Run Setup to install the program on your Windows NT system.

3. From the Tools menu, select "Dump Passwords from Registry." By choosing this option, L0phtCrack will import the passwords on your system into the application where they are ready for cracking.

4. From the Tools menu, select "Options" to define the type of attack you would like to launch on your passwords. Enable the brute-force attack if the box is not already checked and select the "A-Z, 0-9" character set.

Now you are ready to start cracking. From the Tools menu, select "Run Crack." You may be astounded at how quickly L0phtCrack cracks your passwords.

Answers to Chapter Questions

Chapter Pre-Test

1. Brute-force attacks (also known as brute-force cracking) are a trial-and-error method using every known character combination to guess a user's password and defeat an authentication system or encryption key.

2. Social engineering is one of the most effective attacks used. It exploits the weakest component of any company's security infrastructure, the human. Social engineering uses deception or persuasion to convince someone to take an action or divulge information to the attacker.

3. A man-in-the-middle attack intercepts packets intended for a different destination.

4. Two fast-spreading worms that can spread very quickly and cause damage to network resources are the Melissa virus and the I Love You virus.

5. Two of the more popular DoS attacks are Trinoo and tribal flood network.

Assessment Questions

1. **B.** A denial-of-service attack can cause your system resources to increase to 100 percent.

2. **A.** A Trojan horse is an attack that appears to be benign, but actually performs a malicious act on your system.

3. **B.** A SYN flood attack is a denial-of-service attack.

4. **D.** L0phtCrack helps you execute a brute-force attack.

5. **C.** Open or closed is not an option for an attack.

6. **A.** True. Macro Viruses are by far the most common type of virus today.

7. **A.** True. User education is almost always the best defense against Trojan horse programs.

8. **B.** False. Denial-of-service attacks are very hard to orchestrate, usually requiring substantial preparation time.

9. **A.** True. Brute-force password attacks are easy to recognize because there are usually many failed login attempts in the system logs (if enabled).

10. **B.** False. Web bugs are used by banner ad agencies to track surfing habits on the web, but cannot be used for malicious intent by hackers.

For More Information

✦ Learn about the basics of buffer overflows — `www-106.ibm.com/developerworks/library/overflows/index.html`

✦ See this page for actual sample code for a teardrop attack program — `www.windowsitsecurity.com/Articles/Index.cfm?ArticleID=9290`

✦ This is the WinNuke relief page, a general discussion of WinNuke and things to watch for — `http://www.users.nac.net/splat/winnuke/`

Understanding Boundary Devices

EXAM OBJECTIVES

- ✦ Define and describe a firewall
- ✦ Understand the purpose of a firewall and the role it plays in a company's security policy
- ✦ Define common firewall terms, such as NAT and DMZ
- ✦ Understand packet filters
- ✦ Understand application-level gateways
- ✦ Understand circuit-level gateways
- ✦ Understand stateful inspection
- ✦ Describe some advanced firewall functions and features

CHAPTER PRE-TEST

1. What are the advantages of an application-level gateway?

2. What is NAT?

3. What is a firewall?

4. What is a VPN?

5. What are the advantages of stateful inspection?

✦ Answers to these questions can be found at the end of the chapter. ✦

Door locks keep unwanted and/or malicious visitors out of your house. Only certain individuals have a key to unlock the door. All others must ring the doorbell. You can look through the peephole to see who is at your door and decide whether or not to let them in. Firewalls do the same for your network security as doorlocks and peepholes do for your home by restricting access to allowed protocols and services.

What Is a Firewall?

 Define and describe a firewall

According to *Merriam-Webster's Collegiate Dictionary*, a firewall (1759) is "a wall constructed to prevent the spread of fire." Today, a *firewall* also refers to a computer or computer software that prevents unauthorized access to private data by outside computer users.

The original firewall was used for buildings that were close together or contained multiple compartments, such as an apartment building. For safety purposes, a fireproof wall was placed on shared walls to help contain damage in the event of a fire. Most firewalls have a door that allows people to go in and out. Even though the wall provides a high level of protection from fire, it still allows access to necessary building locations.

In computer terms, a firewall provides a similar level of protection, or buffer, between your network and the outside world. It also contains doors, in the form of ports, that allow necessary services to enter your secured network from the unsecured Internet.

Early firewalls were primarily software-based, difficult to configure, and costly to manage. They used command-line interfaces, and each system had to be managed separately. They usually consisted of a single box, known as a *bastion host*, that sat between the Internet and your internal network. A firewall now refers to an area between your internal network and the Internet that consists of multiple components, including several complex machines and software applications.

Firewalls have evolved and, although functionality has generally stayed the same, usability and product packaging have greatly improved. For example:

✦ Software-based firewalls have given way to Plug and Play hardware appliances.

✦ Hybrid firewalls that include stateful inspection and application proxies are the norm.

✦ Firewalls can be managed remotely via Web browsers or centralized management applications.

✦ Integrated products now offer both firewall and virtual private networking (VPN) functionality.

✦ Vendors are also offering personal and server/host resident firewalls.

✦ Firewall solutions are now available as managed services.

To implement your firewall, you should know what services and activities your users need to access both internally and externally. These requirements often determine the type of firewall that will fit best in your environment.

What Does a Firewall Do?

 Understand the purpose of a firewall and the role it plays in a company's security policy

A firewall is the core component of your security infrastructure and probably the most critical. Without it, hackers can easily ravage your systems and resources, making them useless and a potential liability to you. A firewall in your infrastructure should meet four main goals:

✦ **A firewall should be your primary means of enforcement for your corporate security policy.** Your security policy may state that only HTTP and SMTP traffic can be initiated by individuals outside your network. This policy is enforced by creating access rules on your firewall, denying all inbound access except HTTP and SMTP to specific servers. Your security policy might also state that employees cannot listen or watch streaming media. You can easily enforce this policy by defining access rules on your firewall denying this traffic.

✦ **A firewall creates a single point of entry to your network.** This is also known as a *choke point*. All traffic into and out of your network must pass through the firewall so it can monitor, filter, and verify what travels in and out of your organization. By having all traffic pass through a single point, you can focus your security efforts on a central location instead of trying to secure numerous servers and workstations.

✦ **A firewall can log all activities and traffic that pass through it.** This allows you to see who is accessing what services, who is spending their entire day on the Web playing games, and who is visiting Web sites that violate your corporate security policy. Firewall logs also play a vital role in tracking down an attacker if your network is broken into.

✦ **A firewall protects your network by adding a layer of security between your systems and the Internet.** This is often referred to as your *network perimeter*. From the Internet, your network looks like a single system, the firewall. Potential attackers may not be able to easily tell the size or composition of your network behind the firewall.

A few advanced firewall features discussed throughout this chapter provide some additional protection. Encryption and authentication allow you to protect data as it travels on the network, as well as help verify the source of the traffic.

Firewall Terminology

 Define common firewall terms, such as NAT and DMZ

Before exploring the various types of firewall technologies available for use in your organization, you should understand a few important terms that will be used in the rest of the chapter.

Gateway

A *gateway* is a device that relays services between two systems. A gateway can be as simple as a software application, such as the Common Gateway Interface (CGI) commonly used in Web applications to transfer data from the user to the Web server, or as complex as a firewall that analyzes traffic between two networks.

Packet filter

A *packet filter* analyzes traffic on a packet-by-packet basis. Packet filters can be configured to allow or deny traffic based on protocol, such as to allow all FTP traffic or disallow all Telnet traffic. Packet filters are usually implemented on routers. When this occurs, the router is often called a *screening router*.

Circuit-level gateway

In a *circuit-level gateway*, the firewall function is divided between two hosts that relay TCP connections. You can implement a circuit-level gateway using a screening router and application firewall or with two application firewalls. The benefit of this design is that if one firewall fails or is compromised by an attacker, there is still one remaining device that functions.. Overall, circuit-level gateways are similar to packet filters, except they give you the opportunity to use network address translation.

Application gateway

Application gateways function at all levels of the OSI model. They are implemented through software and require special services to function. Application gateways are sometimes known as proxy servers, but not for this exam.

A *proxy server* communicates with external servers on behalf of the requesting internal system. Proxy servers typically refer to application gateways, but a circuit-level gateway is also a form of proxy server. For this exam, the term proxy server will be used for a server that communicates on behalf of others. When the terms application-level gateway and circuit-level gateway are used, they refer to specific services provided by a form of firewall.

Network Address Translation

Network Address Translation (NAT) is the translation of an IP address used within one network to a different IP address known within another network. Typically, a company maps its local network addresses to one or more global outside IP addresses and unmaps the global IP addresses on incoming packets back into local IP addresses. This helps ensure security, because each outgoing or incoming request must go through a translation process — called a *stateful inspection* — that also offers the opportunity to qualify or authenticate the request or match it to a previous request.

NAT is described in general terms in RFC 1631. Also discussed is NAT's relationship to Classless Interdomain Routing (CIDR) as a way to reduce the IP address depletion problem. NAT reduces the need for a large amount of publicly known IP addresses by creating a separation between publicly known and privately known IP addresses. CIDR aggregates publicly known IP addresses into blocks so that fewer IP addresses are wasted. The IP address ranges discussed in RFC 1631 are

✦ 10.0.0.0 – 10.255.255.255

✦ 172.16.0.0 – 172.31.255.255

✦ 192.168.0.0 – 192.168.255.255

Network administrators create a NAT table on the firewall that performs the global-to-local and local-to-global IP address mapping. NAT can be statically defined or it can be set up to dynamically translate to and from a pool of IP addresses. Most firewalls let you develop tables that map the following:

✦ A local IP address to one global IP address statically

✦ A local IP address to any of a rotating pool of global IP addresses that a company may have

✦ A local IP address plus a particular TCP port to a global IP address or one in a pool of them

✦ A global IP address to any of a pool of local IP addresses on a round-robin basis

Bastion host

A *bastion host* is the only computer a company allows to be addressed directly from the Internet and is designed to screen the rest of its network from security exposures. A bastion host is usually a *dual-homed host*, meaning it has two network cards and sits on two distinct networks.

A bastion host is used to deploy gateway services. A *gateway service* is a dedicated daemon that routes a specific protocol from the Internet to your internal network and vice versa. In an application-level gateway, daemons are needed for each Application-layer protocol you use. So, if you want to use e-mail and Web services through an application-level gateway bastion host, you need a POP3 daemon, SMTP daemon, and HTTP daemon. A packet-filtering router does not use daemons because it simply filters packets instead of processing them through services.

One problem with bastion hosts is the operating system required to run them. Because the bastion host is the gateway between your internal network and the Internet, the system must be very secure. To achieve a high level of security, you must harden the operating system, which means removing any unnecessary services. Most firewalls operate on top of an operating system and perform some OS hardening for you upon installation. Some even provide the ability to prohibit the installation and execution of any program the firewall does not recognize. Besides removing or disabling services, you should also unbind all protocols except TCP/IP from your network adapters.

Demilitarized zone

A demilitarized zone (DMZ) is a computer host or small network inserted as a neutral zone between a company's private network and the outside public network. It prevents outside users from gaining direct access to internal corporate servers. (The term DMZ comes from the geographic buffer zone that was set up between North Korea and South Korea following the Korean War in the early 1950s.)

In a typical DMZ configuration, a separate computer receives requests from users on your internal network for access to Web sites or other companies accessible on the Internet. The DMZ host then initiates sessions for these requests. However, the DMZ host is not able to initiate a session back into the private network. It can only forward packets that have already been requested.

Internet users outside the company can access only the DMZ host. The DMZ may typically also house your Web server, so the pages could be served to the outside world. Because the DMZ is isolated from the internal network, an attacker targeting the Web server should not be able to access any other systems. However, the DMZ doesn't provide access to any other data. In the event that an attacker penetrated the DMZ host's security, the Web pages might be corrupted, but no other company information would be exposed.

Types of Firewalls

The four main types of firewalls are

- ✦ Packet filters
- ✦ Stateful inspection
- ✦ Circuit-level gateways
- ✦ Application-level gateways

Packet filters

 Understand packet filters

Packet filters selectively route packets between trusted and untrusted networks. They allow or deny packets to reflect a site's security policy. If installed properly, a packet filter will be almost transparent to users.

Packet filters are application-independent and examine each packet at the Network layer, allowing them to deliver high performance and scalability. They are the least secure firewall, however. Because they are not application-aware, they cannot understand the context of a given communication, making them easier for hackers to fool.

Screening routers

Historically, packet filters have been implemented on routers, filtering user-defined content of a packet, such as IP addresses. A few components of a TCP/IP packet that can be filtered include

- ✦ Source address
- ✦ Destination address
- ✦ Source port
- ✦ Destination port

A router with packet filtering capability is called a *screening router*. Because a screening router functions at the network level, you can control your network traffic without making changes to your applications. Many organizations configure their external routers as screening routers to provide an extra layer of protection and filtering.

Packet filter functionality

To understand how packet filtering works, look at the difference between an ordinary router and a screening router. An ordinary router examines the destination address of each packet and selects the best way it knows to send the packet to its destination. Two ways are possible for handling the packet, based solely on its destination: the router either knows how to send the packet and does so, or doesn't know how to send the packet and returns it to its source.

A screening router, on the other hand, examines packets more closely. In addition to determining whether or not it can route a packet towards its destination, a screening router also determines whether or not it should, a decision determined by your security policy and enforced by the screening router through access control lists (ACLs).

If only a screening router sits between your internal network and the Internet, an enormous responsibility is placed on the screening router. Other than performing all routing and routing decision-making, it is a single point of failure and the only protection for your network. What happens if the router gets overloaded or attacked? If overloaded, the router will either stop functioning, creating a Denial of Service, or start allowing all traffic to pass to your internal network, providing absolutely no protection from attack. Screening routers are most often used in conjunction with another firewall.

This perimeter configuration mitigates your risk by only endangering the firewall if the screening router is compromised. The attacker then needs to penetrate the firewall to gain access to your network. Some companies place a second screening router behind the firewall.

Cross-Reference Firewall architectures are discussed in more detail in Chapter 7.

Screening routers are most often used to filter unwanted traffic before it hits the firewall, especially packets with spoofed IP addresses. Using a screening router often improves the performance of a firewall because the firewall has less traffic to deal with.

The order of rules is very important in a packet filter. Rules are read from top to bottom. Once a packet matches a rule, none of the following rules are applied. So, if your default deny everything rule is the first on your list, your packet filter will deny all traffic.

A few examples of ways you might configure a packet filter to selectively route packets to or from your site include:

✦ Block all incoming connections from systems outside the corporate network, except for incoming SMTP connections, so you can receive e-mail.

✦ Block all connections to or from specific systems or IP addresses you distrust.

To better understand how packet filters function, I will spend the last part of this section examining the use of FTP over a packet filter. Before I begin, you should know that

✦ The initial FTP connection from the client to the FTP server occurs over port 21.

✦ The actual transfer of files occurs on a random port above 1023.

You have two choices for your packet filter configuration with FTP connections. You can leave the entire upper range (greater than 1023) of ports open and allow the file transfer session to take place over the dynamically allocated port (which means exposing your internal network), or you can shut down the entire upper range of ports to secure the internal network and block all services. Your network is either wide open or completely closed. This trade-off between application support and security is not acceptable. The other firewall technologies provide solutions to this problem.

Packet filter advantages and disadvantages

Packet filters are available in most routers, so you probably already have all the components in place in your network and will not need to spend a significant amount of money to get a firewall up and running.

There are certain issues with packet filters — such as difficulty checking and filtering User Datagram Protocol (UDP) packets — that make them less than ideal as the sole perimeter security device. Additionally, they lack alerting and auditing applications, so that when the router filters out a packet, it will not alarm or alert the administrator.

Furthermore, a packet filter cannot analyze specific services. It can permit or deny a service, but it cannot protect individual operations within a service. Nor can it tell good packets from bad packets. The packet filter may be allowed to pass HTTP traffic, but it does not know if that traffic contains malicious data or code.

Packet filtering rules are difficult to configure and require a significant knowledge of TCP/IP. Some rule sets require hundreds of rules to properly implement a security policy. The configuration process may take a significant amount of time and resources.

Stateful inspection

 Understand stateful inspection

Stateful inspection is an extension of packet filtering and is often referred to as *dynamic packet filtering*. With stateful inspection, packet filtering rules are modified "on the fly" by the firewall in response to certain events. For example, an outgoing UDP packet might cause the creation of a temporary rule to allow a corresponding, answering UDP packet back in. Stateful inspection also extends packet filtering by providing extensions for authentication and filtering at the application level, functionality much more precise than the filtering possible with traditional packet filter firewalls.

Stateful inspection provides full Application-layer awareness without breaking the client/server model. With stateful inspection, the packet is intercepted at the Network layer and the firewall extracts state-related information required for security decisions from all Application layers and maintains this information in dynamic state tables for evaluating subsequent connection attempts. This provides a solution that is highly secure and offers maximum performance, scalability, and extensibility.

Stateful inspection functionality

Stateful inspection firewalls look like proxy systems from the external side because all requests appear to come from a single host (your corporate gateway). However, they look like packet filtering systems from the inside because internal hosts and users think they are talking directly to the external systems. Stateful inspection firewalls accomplish this through state tables maintaining currently active connections and through packet rewriting.

Examining an FTP connection, a stateful firewall tracks the FTP session by examining FTP Application-layer data. When the client requests that the server generate the back-connection to transfer files (port greater than 1023), the firewall extracts the port number from the request. Both client and server IP addresses and both port numbers are recorded in an FTP-data pending request list. When the FTP data connection is attempted, the firewall examines the list and verifies that the attempt is in response to a valid request. The list of connections is maintained dynamically so that only the required FTP ports are opened. As soon as the session is closed, the ports are locked, ensuring maximum security.

Stateful inspection advantages and disadvantages

Because stateful inspection does not examine the entire packet, malformed packets can make it through the inspection, attacking servers behind the firewall. A packet's payload can contain information or commands that cause applications, such as Web server's CGI script, to die or execute arbitrary code.

Additionally, although stateful inspection has reduced the need for application proxies, some multimedia applications, such as RealAudio, require firewall manufacturers to revise their stateful inspection engines.

Circuit-level gateways

 Understand circuit-level gateways

A *circuit-level gateway* translates IP addresses between the Internet and your internal systems and operates on the network level of the OSI Model. The gateway receives outbound packets and transfers them from the internal network to the external network. Inbound traffic is transferred from the outside network to the internal network.

Circuit-level gateways provide a complete break between your internal network and the Internet. Unlike a packet filter, which simply analyzes and routes traffic, a circuit-level gateway translates packets and transfers them between network interfaces. This helps shield your network from external traffic. Remember that you must not enable IP forwarding or routing on your circuit-level gateway. If you do, you will have a glorified packet filter.

The most popular circuit-level gateway is the SOCKS gateway, invented by IBM. Many products provide SOCKS supports, making it easier to implement a circuit-level gateway in your environment.

Circuit-level gateway functionality

When a request to connect to an external system is made, the circuit-level gateway receives the request and compares it to a set of rules. If the request does not violate any of the rules, the circuit-level gateway sends the request to the external system on behalf of the internal system. The packets appear to have originated from the circuit-level gateway's Internet IP address. This approach helps shield your network topology from potential attackers.

Circuit-level gateway advantages and disadvantages

The primary advantage of circuit-level gateways is NAT, which provides administrators greater flexibility when designing your network architecture. Circuit-level gateways are based on the same principles as packet-filter firewalls, so all the advantages (and disadvantages) apply.

The primary disadvantage of a circuit-level gateway is that it requires special applications to function correctly. Each application and service that must communicate with a system on the Internet must be configured to function with the circuit-level gateway. If your applications are not able to do so and cannot be modified, you may be out of luck. Additionally, new technologies cannot be used until a circuit-level gateway compliant application is developed.

Application-level gateways

 Understand application-level gateways

Application-level gateways take requests for Internet services and forward them to the actual services. Application-level gateways differ from circuit-level gateways in that they operate at the Application layer of the OSI Model.

Application-level gateways sit between a user on the internal network and a service on the Internet. Instead of talking to each other directly, each system talks to the gateway. Your internal network never directly connects to the Internet.

Application-level gateways help improve perimeter security by examining all Application layers, bringing context information into the decision process. However, they do this by breaking the client/server model. Every client/server communication requires two connections: one from the client to the firewall and one from the firewall to the server. In addition, each proxy requires a different application process, or daemon, making scalability and support for new applications a problem.

Application-level gateway functionality

To see how a proxy server functions, I will return to the FTP discussion. Using FTP over an application-level gateway requires two components: a gateway server and a proxy client. The gateway server runs on the firewall system. An FTP proxy client is a special version of a normal client program that talks to the proxy server rather than to the "real" server out on the Internet. The gateway server evaluates requests from the proxy client, and decides which to approve and which to deny based on its configuration (which is reflective of your security policy). If a request is approved, the gateway server contacts the real server on behalf of the client, and relays requests from the proxy client to the real server and responses from the real server to the proxy client.

Application-level gateway advantages and disadvantages

Transparency is the major benefit of application-level gateways. To the user, an application-level gateway presents the illusion that the user is dealing directly with the real server. To the real server, the gateway presents the illusion that the real server is dealing directly with a user on the proxy host (as opposed to the user's real host).

Application-level gateways effectively mask the origin address of the initiating connection and protect your network from intruders that are trying to gain as much information about your network as they can. Application-level gateways are used to hide your IP address, making you anonymous on the Internet. On the flip side, hackers often use application-level gateways to hide their IP addresses when attacking a server.

The application-level gateway does not always just forward users' requests. The gateway can control what users do because it recognizes network protocols and resides at the Application layer. Depending on your site's security policy, requests might be allowed or refused. For example, the FTP proxy might refuse to let users export files, or it might allow users to import files only from certain sites. More sophisticated proxy servers might allow different capabilities to different hosts, rather than enforce the same restrictions on all hosts.

Another advantage to application-level gateways is the ability to implement reverse proxies. Reverse proxies function the same way as normal proxies except that they proxy inbound, not outbound, requests. The reverse proxy server is placed outside your firewall and looks like a Web server or other device to a normal user. When a request is made to the Web server, for example, the reverse proxy server receives the request and connects to the real Web server inside your network. If someone tries to hack into your Web server, they will only hack into the reverse proxy server. Your real Web server is hidden safely on your internal network behind your firewall.

Although the application-level gateway overcomes some of the limitations of packet filtering by bringing Application-layer awareness to the decision process, it does so with an unacceptable performance penalty. Because application-level gateways are software applications that create a new connection for every communication, processing is slow and does not scale well for large environments. Additionally, each service needs its own proxy. New protocols, services, and technologies cannot be used with an application-level gateway until the appropriate components are developed.

Advanced Firewall Features

 Describe some advanced firewall functions and features

Most firewalls today are a hybrid of stateful inspection, circuit-level gateways, and application-level gateways. Only packets dealing with acceptable activities are allowed in and out of your internal network. To implement an effective firewall, you need all three firewall types in place. Some firewalls provide advanced firewall features that make them more effective in your perimeter.

Authentication

The firewall is a logical place to install authentication mechanisms to help overcome the limitations of TCP/IP. You can use a reverse lookup on an IP address to try and verify that the user is actually at his reported location. This activity helps identify and prevent spoofing attacks.

Firewalls can also provide user authentication. Some application-level gateways contain an internal user account database or integrate with UNIX and Windows domain accounts. These accounts can be used to limit activities and services by user or provide detailed logs of user activity. Because individual users can be easily identified, more granular rule sets can be implemented. For example, users in the Marketing group can use RealAudio, while other employees cannot.

You can also use authentication for remote access. Allowing employees to connect to the internal network from home or while traveling increases productivity, but how can you ensure that the person making the request is who he is supposed to be? Most firewalls support third-party authentication methods to provide strong authentication. Digital certificates, biometrics, and SecurID are examples of commonly supported authentication methods.

Logs and alarms

Almost every firewall performs some type of logging. Most packet filters do not enable logging by default because it degrades performance of traffic analysis. So, if you want logging, make sure it is enabled and active. Screening routers can only log basic packet information. Circuit-level gateways log the same information as screening routers, but they also include data on NAT. Application-level gateways can log much more information because they reside at the Application layer and have a more thorough understanding of the activities and protocols being used.

Extensive logging can help you track and potentially capture a hacker. Since your firewall is the single point of entry to your network, an attacker will have to pass through it. Your log files should provide information to show you what the hacker was up to on your systems.

Proxy client software

In order for application-level gateways to function properly, proxy clients and servers must be installed for each service used on your network. Some applications, such as Yahoo Messenger, Web browsers, and many FTP clients, are pre-configured to work with SOCKS-compliant proxy servers. Other applications must be modified to work with a proxy, and some applications are not supported by proxy servers.

Remote access servers

Remote access is the ability to get access to a computer or network from a remote location. In corporations, people who are traveling, telecommuting, or working from a branch office may need access to the company's network. Direct dial-up connections through desktop, notebook, or handheld computer modem over regular telephone lines is a common method of remote access for some companies. Remote access is also possible using a dedicated line between a computer or a remote local area network and the "central" or main corporate local area network. Wireless, cable modem, and Digital Subscriber Line (DSL) technologies offer other possibilities for remote access.

A *remote access server* is a computer and associated software that is set up to handle users seeking access to networks remotely. Sometimes called a *communication server*, a remote access server usually includes or is associated with a firewall to ensure security, and a router that can forward the remote access request to the requested section of the internal network. A remote access server may include or work with a modem pool manager so that a small group of modems can be shared among a large number of intermittently present remote access users.

Virtual private networks

Some firewalls now provide integrated virtual private network (VPN) functionality. A VPN is a private data network that makes use of the public telecommunication infrastructure, maintaining privacy through the use of a tunneling protocol and security procedures such as encryption. A virtual private network can be contrasted with a system of owned or leased lines that can only be used by one company. The idea of the VPN is to provide the same capabilities at much lower cost by using the shared public infrastructure rather than a private one. Phone companies have provided secure shared resources for voice messages. A virtual private network allows the same secure sharing of public resources for data. Companies today are looking at the possibility of using a private virtual network for both extranet, intranet, and remote access.

Using a virtual private network involves encrypting data before sending it through the public network and decrypting it at the receiving end. An additional level of security involves encrypting not only the data but also the originating and receiving network addresses.

Key Point Summary

This chapter discussed the types of firewalls you may use in your environment.

✦ A firewall provides a buffer between your network and the outside world.

✦ A firewall is the core component of your security infrastructure and probably the most critical.

✦ A firewall is your primary means of enforcement for your corporate security policy.

✦ A firewall creates a single point of entry to your network (a choke point).

✦ A firewall can log all activities and traffic that pass through it.

✦ A firewall protects your network by adding a layer of security between your systems and the Internet (your network perimeter).

✦ A gateway is a device that relays services between two systems. Gateways can be as simple as a software application, such as the Common Gateway Interface (CGI) commonly used in Web applications to transfer data from the user to the Web server, or as complex as a firewall that analyzes traffic between two networks.

✦ A packet filter analyzes traffic on a packet-by-packet basis.

✦ In a circuit-level gateway, the firewall function is divided between two hosts that relay TCP connections.

✦ Application gateways function at all levels of the OSI model. They are implemented through software and require special services to function. Application gateways are sometimes known as proxy servers, but not for this exam.

✦ A proxy server communicates with external servers on behalf of the requesting internal system. Proxy servers typically refer to application-level gateways, but a circuit-level gateway is also a form of proxy server. For this exam, the term proxy server will be used for a server that communicates on behalf of others. When the terms application-level gateway and circuit-level gateway are used, they refer to specific services provided by a form of firewall.

✦ NAT (Network Address Translation) is the translation of an IP address used within one network to a different IP address known within another network.

✦ The IP address ranges discussed in RFC 1631 are

   • 10.0.0.0 – 10.255.255.255

   • 172.16.0.0 – 172.31.255.255

   • 192.168.0.0 – 192.168.255.255

✦ A bastion host is the only computer a company allows to be addressed directly from the Internet and is designed to screen the rest of its network from security exposures. A bastion host is usually a dual-homed host, meaning it has two network cards and sits on two distinct networks.

✦ A bastion host is used to deploy gateway services.

✦ One problem with bastion hosts is the operating system required to run the system. Since the bastion host is the gateway between your internal network and the Internet, the system must be very secure.

✦ A DMZ (demilitarized zone) is a computer host or small network inserted as a neutral zone between a company's private network and the outside public network. It prevents outside users from gaining direct access to internal corporate servers.

✦ Packet filters selectively route packets between trusted and untrusted networks. They allow or deny packets in reflection of a site's security policy.

✦ Packet filters are application-independent and examine each packet at the Network layer, allowing packet filters to deliver high performance and scalability.

✦ When applied to a router, packet filters will filter user-defined content of a packet, such as IP addresses.

✦ An ordinary router looks at the destination address of each packet and selects the best way it knows to send the packet to its destination.

✦ A screening router examines packets more closely than an ordinary router. In addition to determining whether or not it can route a packet towards its destination, a screening router determines whether or not it should, a decision determined by your security policy and enforced by the screening router through access control lists (ACLs).

✦ Screening routers are most often used to filter unwanted traffic before it hits the firewall, especially packets with spoofed IP addresses.

✦ Using a screening router often improves the performance of a firewall because it has less traffic to deal with.

✦ The order of rules is very important in a packet filter. Rules are read from top to bottom. Once a packet matches a rule, none of the following rules are applied. So, if your default deny everything rule is the first in your list, your packet filter will deny all traffic.

✦ With a packet filter and services that use dynamic ports, your network is either wide open or completely closed. This trade-off between application support and security is not acceptable. The other firewall technologies provide solutions to this problem.

✦ Packet filters are available in most routers, so you probably already have all the components in place in your network and will not need to spend a significant amount of money to get a firewall up and running.

✦ A packet filter cannot analyze specific services. It can permit or deny a service, but it cannot protect individual operations within a service.

✦ A packet filter cannot tell good packets from bad packets. The packet filter may be allowed to pass HTTP traffic, but it does not know if that traffic contains malicious data or code.

✦ Packet filtering rules are also difficult to configure and require a significant knowledge of TCP/IP.

✦ Some rule sets require hundreds of rules to properly implement a security policy. This process may take a significant amount of time and resources.

✦ Stateful inspection is an extension of packet filtering and is often referred to as dynamic packet filtering.

✦ With stateful inspection, packet filtering rules are modified "on the fly" by the firewall in response to certain events.

✦ Stateful inspection provides full Application-layer awareness without breaking the client/server model.

✦ Stateful inspection firewalls look like proxy systems from the external side because all requests appear to come from a single host (your corporate gateway). They look, however, like packet filtering systems from the inside because internal hosts and users think they are talking directly to the external systems. They accomplish this through state tables maintaining currently active connections and through packet rewriting.

✦ Stateful inspection does not examine the entire packet; malformed packets can make it through the inspection, attacking servers behind the firewall.

✦ A circuit-level gateway translates IP addresses between the Internet and your internal systems and operates on the network level of the OSI Model. The gateway receives outbound packets and transfers it from the internal network to the external network. Inbound traffic is transferred from the outside network to the internal network.

✦ Circuit-level gateways provide a complete break between your internal network and the Internet.

✦ The circuit-level gateway receives the request and compares it to a set of rules. If the request does not violate any of the rules, the circuit-level gateway sends the request to the external system on behalf of the internal system. The packets appear to have originated from the circuit-level gateway's Internet IP address.

✦ The primary advantage of circuit-level gateways is NAT, which provides administrators greater flexibility when designing your network architecture.

✦ The primary disadvantage of a circuit-level gateway is that it requires special applications to function correctly. Each application and service that must communicate with a system on the Internet must be configured to function with the circuit-level gateway.

✦ Application-level gateways take requests for Internet services and forward them to the actual services.

✦ Application-level gateways differ from circuit-level gateways because they operate at the Application layer of the OSI Model.

✦ Application-level gateways help improve perimeter security by examining all Application layers, bringing context information into the decision process. However, they do this by breaking the client/server model. Every client/server communication requires two connections: one from the client to the firewall and one from the firewall to the server. In addition, each proxy requires a different application process, or daemon, making scalability and support for new applications a problem.

✦ Transparency is the major benefit of application-level gateways. To the user, an application-level gateway presents the illusion that the user is dealing directly with the real server. To the real server, the gateway presents the illusion that the real server is dealing directly with a user on the proxy host (as opposed to the user's real host).

✦ Application-level gateways effectively mask the origin address of the initiating connection and protect your network from intruders that are trying to gain as much information about your network as they can.

✦ The application-level gateway does not always just forward users' requests. The gateway can control what users do because it recognizes network protocols and resides at the Application layer.

✦ Another advantage to application-level gateways is the ability to implement reverse proxies. Reverse proxies function the same way as normal proxies except they proxy inbound requests instead of outbound requests.

✦ Although the application-level gateway overcomes some of the limitations of packet filtering by bringing Application-layer awareness to the decision process, it does so with an unacceptable performance penalty. Since application-level gateways are software applications that create a new connection for every communication, processing is slow and does not scale well for large environments.

✦ Additionally, each service needs its own proxy. New protocols, services, and technologies cannot be used with an application-level gateway until the appropriate components are developed.

✦ Most firewalls today are a hybrid — a combination of stateful inspection, circuit-level gateways, and application-level gateways.

✦ The firewall is a logical place to install authentication mechanisms to help overcome the limitations of TCP/IP. You can use a reverse lookup on an IP address to try and verify that the user is actually at his reported location. This activity helps identify and prevent spoofing attacks.

✦ Firewalls can also provide user authentication. Some application-level gateways contain an internal user account database or integrate with UNIX and Windows domain accounts.

✦ Most firewalls also support third-party authentication methods to provide strong authentication. Digital certificates, biometrics, and SecurID are examples of commonly supported authentication methods.

✦ Almost every firewall performs some type of logging.

✦ Application-level gateways can log much more information because they reside at the Application layer and have a more thorough understanding of the activities and protocols being used.

✦ In order for application-level gateways to function properly, proxy clients and servers must be installed for each service used on your network.

✦ Remote access is the ability to get access to a computer or network from a remote location.

✦ Direct dial-up connections through desktop, notebook, or handheld computer modem over regular telephone lines is a common method of remote access for some companies. Remote access is also possible using a dedicated line between a computer or a remote local area network and the "central" or main corporate local area network. Wireless, cable modem, and Digital Subscriber Line (DSL) technologies offer other possibilities for remote access.

✦ A virtual private network (VPN) is a private data network that makes use of the public telecommunication infrastructure, maintaining privacy through the use of a tunneling protocol and security procedures such as encryption.

✦ Using a virtual private network involves encrypting data before sending it through the public network and decrypting it at the receiving end. An additional level of security involves encrypting not only the data but also the originating and receiving network addresses.

✦   ✦   ✦

STUDY GUIDE

This Study Guide presents five assessment questions and four lab exercises to test your knowledge of the exam objectives.

Assessment Questions

1. What firewall type provides no direct communication between the Internet and your internal network?

A. Stateful inspection

B. Packet filter

C. Application-level gateway

D. NAT

2. Circuit-level gateways provide what key functionality?

A. IP address translation

B. Authentication

C. Remote access

D. VPN

3. Screening routers implement which firewall technology?

A. Application-level gateway

B. Packet filtering

C. Stateful inspection

D. Circuit-level gateway

4. If you require specialized client software to communicate with servers on the Internet, what type of firewall do you have?

A. Application-level gateway

B. Packet filter

C. Stateful inspection

D. Screening router

5. Firewalls help protect your network by creating a:

    A. Choke point

    B. Filter

    C. Perimeter

    D. All of the above

Lab Exercises

Lab 6-1 Configuring Microsoft Proxy Server

1. Prepare your server to use an additional IP address. Right-click Network Neighborhood and select Properties.

2. Choose the Protocols tab and double-click the TCP/IP Protocol. You must add an IP address to your network interface card.

3. Click the Advanced button to add another IP address. In the IP address section, click the Add button. Enter an IP address. For the purposes of this lab, use 192.168.1.1. The subnet mask should be 255.255.255.0. When you are finished, click Add.

4. Click OK to confirm the advanced TCP/IP settings.

5. Click OK to confirm the TCP/IP protocol configuration.

6. Click OK to confirm the Network Control Panel configuration.

7. Restart your computer and log back on as Administrator.

8. Obtain the setup files for Microsoft Proxy Server. You can download an evaluation from `www.microsoft.com`. Run setup.exe.

9. Confirm the product ID by clicking OK.

10. Click the Installation Options button to select which components of Proxy you want to have installed.

11. Select the default options and click the Continue button.

12. The next configuration will ask you which drives will contain Proxy Server's cache. These drives must be formatted with the NTFS file system and must reside on the local computer. Choose an NTFS drive and click OK.

13. Define the Local Address Table (LAT). This defines what IP addresses are internal to your network. Enter the address range from 192.168.1.1 to 192.168.1.254. Click the Add button.

14. The installation will ask you to configure the Client Installation/Configuration for Proxy Server. This setting allows clients to easily connect to and use the proxy server. Click OK to accept the default settings.

15. The next portion of the installation contains the Access Control options. Deselect both checkboxes to allow any client access to Proxy Server. Click OK to continue.

16. The program will install the necessary files on your system.

17. Click OK to accept the Packet Filtering Tool message.

18. Click OK to confirm the installation of Proxy Server.

19. Reboot your computer.

Lab 6-2 Configuring Internet Explorer for use with a proxy server

1. Make sure your computer is using a reserved IP address. Right-click Network Neighborhood and select Properties.

2. Choose the Protocols tab and double-click TCP/IP.

3. Change your IP address to a reserved IP address. For this lab, use 192.168.1.2. The subnet mask should be 255.255.255.0.

4. Right-click the Internet Explorer icon and select Properties.

5. Click the Connection tab to configure the browser to use Proxy Server. In the Proxy Server field, enter the IP address of your proxy server. For this lab, the address is 192.168.1.1. Enter **80** for the port.

6. Click OK to confirm the change. Load Internet Explorer and browse to any Internet site.

Lab 6-3 Installing Microsoft Proxy Client

1. Access the Microsoft Proxy Client by entering 192.168.1.1/msproxy in your Web browser. This will access Proxy Server on your network.

2. When given a choice, select "Run this program from its current location" radio button. Follow the installation wizard to finish installation and restart your computer.

Lab 6-4 Checking Microsoft Proxy Server logs

1. Open the c:\winnt\system32\msplogs directory on your proxy server system.

2. The save format for Microsoft Proxy logs is Wsyr|mo|dy. If today were February 3, 2000, for example, the proxy server log file would be WS000203.log.

3. Open the file and view its contents.

Answers to Chapter Questions

Chapter Pre-Test

1. Transparency is one benefit of application-level gateways. Application-level gateways also effectively mask the origin address of the initiating connection and protect your network from intruders that are trying to gain as much information about your network as they can. Finally, application-level gateways do not allow direct communications between your internal network and the Internet.

2. NAT (Network Address Translation) is the translation of an IP address used within one network to a different IP address known within another network.

3. A firewall provides a buffer between your network and the outside world. It also contains doors, in the form of ports, to allow necessary services to enter your secured network from the unsecured Internet.

4. A VPN is a private data network that makes use of the public telecommunication infrastructure, maintaining privacy through the use of a tunneling protocol and security procedures such as encryption.

5. Stateful inspection has the same advantages of packet filters. Additionally, it allows you to use services that require dynamically allocated ports by tracking the status of communications in a state table.

Assessment Questions

1. **C.** An application-level gateway provides no direct access between the Internet and your internal network.

2. **A.** Circuit-level gateways provide IP translations, also known as NAT.

3. **B.** Screening routers implement the packet filter firewall technology.

4. **A.** Application-level gateways require special client software to connect to services on the Internet.

5. **D.** A firewall creates a choke point, or single point of entry for your network. It also creates a perimeter around your internal network, providing a "buffer" layer between you and the Internet. Finally, a firewall filters traffic.

Implementing Firewalls

EXAM OBJECTIVES

- ✦ Understand bastion hosts
- ✦ Understand screening routers
- ✦ Understand screened host
- ✦ Understand screened subnet

CHAPTER PRE-TEST

1. What is a bastion host?

2. What is a screening router?

3. What are the types of bastion hosts?

4. What is the best use of a screening router?

5. Which architecture provides the highest level of security?

Chapter 6 discussed firewalls and the various types — packet filters, gateways, and stateful inspection — available for use. This chapter focuses on how a firewall fits into a network architecture to secure servers and networks.

Understanding Firewall Deployment Issues

Once you have created your security policies and decided on the type of technology you need, you are ready to decide how to implement and deploy your chosen firewall solution.

Firewall placement is critical to the security level and resource protection required in your environment. Your firewall should also create choke points. The fewer access points into your network that you have to control, the easier it is to manage your security. By forcing all traffic to a few points, you can focus your time and resources on security in those areas. This way, you get the most security with the least amount of effort.

Choke points enable easier administration. You know where all the information enters and leaves your network, so you can place comprehensive and extensive monitoring tools at these choke points.

In many ways, placement is a resource issue. If you do not place your firewall and other security resources correctly, you will need more hardware to achieve your required level of protection. Because equipment is expensive to purchase and maintain, you should give careful consideration to your resource placement plan.

Building a Firewall

Take great care when building your firewall. In Chapter 6, a bastion host was defined as any system with a direct connection to the Internet. In this chapter, bastion host also refers to a firewall device.

By definition, a bastion host, or firewall, is a publicly accessible device, so you should be very careful when constructing it. When Internet users access resources on your network, the first machine they encounter is the bastion host. Because the bastion host is directly connected to the Internet, all information on it is exposed. This high level of exposure necessitates strong security configurations.

Bastion hosts check all incoming and outgoing traffic, enforcing rules specified by your organization's internal and external sources. They should also be armed with logging and alarm functionality to record and warn of attacks.

When building a firewall, you should follow two main rules: keep it simple and make contingency plans in case the firewall is penetrated.

Simple design

An attacker most often gains access to a resource through overlooked components installed on a system. Make sure you build your bastion host with the fewest possible components. The bastion host should provide only firewall services. It should not function as a Web server, FTP server, or e-mail server. All unnecessary daemons should be removed. The fewer services you have running on your firewall, the less chance there is that an attacker will be able to exploit it.

Make contingency plans

If your architecture is properly configured, the only public access to your network will be through your firewall. However, firewalls are not foolproof. Prepare for the possibility of firewall penetration. If you have only one firewall separating your internal resources from outsiders, a compromised firewall will provide complete access to your network.

To prevent penetration, consider implementing several layers of firewall devices so you are not relying on a single device. If one firewall device is compromised, you still have several other devices to protect you. (I will discuss some layered firewall designs later in this chapter.) Your security policy should state what to do in the event of a security compromise. Consider these steps:

✦ Create an identical copy of the software.

✦ Configure an identical system and store it in a safe place.

✦ Ensure that all software necessary to install the firewall is handy.

Types of Bastion Hosts

 Understand bastion hosts

When creating a bastion host, you must remember its function in your firewall strategy. Determining the bastion host's role will help you decide what type of system, memory, components, and so on is needed and how the device should be configured. Three common bastion hosts are discussed in the following sections.

Single-homed bastion host

A single-homed bastion host is a firewall with only one network interface. Single-homed bastion hosts are generally used for application-level gateway firewalls. The external router sends all traffic to the bastion host, and all internal clients send outgoing traffic to the bastion host. The bastion host then compares the traffic to its security guidelines and acts accordingly. The main disadvantage to this firewall is that the router can be reconfigured to pass information directly to the internal network, bypassing the bastion host. Users can also reconfigure their machines to bypass the bastion host and send their outgoing information directly to the router.

Dual-homed bastion host

Dual-homed bastion hosts function identically to single-homed hosts except they have at least two network interfaces. Dual-homed hosts serve as application gateways, circuit-level gateways, and packet filters. A dual-homed host creates a complete break between the external network and internal network. This break forces all traffic to pass through the bastion host and is very similar to implementing a proxy server.

Single-purpose bastion host

A single-purpose bastion host can be either a single- or multi-homed bastion host. As your organization's needs change, new applications and technologies will be required. New technologies are often untested and can open major security holes. You should create a bastion host specifically for these needs. Do not compromise your production firewalls by installing untested applications or services on them.

For example, if you want to use a new streaming media technology, implement a single-purpose bastion host to secure this service. Because it is new, you do not know what security holes it will open on your production firewall. Implementing a single-purpose host will protect you from this possible weakness.

Internal bastion hosts

Internal bastion hosts are standard single- or multi-homed bastion hosts that reside on an internal network. Usually, they receive all incoming traffic from external bastion hosts. They can provide extra layers of security in case the external firewall is compromised.

Hardware Issues

When deciding on hardware to purchase for the firewall, companies often choose the biggest and fastest machine on the market, following the assumption that the faster machine will process incoming and outgoing traffic more quickly. This assumption is incorrect, however. A bastion host performs functions that do not require powerful systems. The operating system on which the bastion host runs will generally dictate the minimum requirements. When choosing hardware components, select known, tested technologies and not cutting-edge solutions that have not been fully tested.

Using less powerful hardware provides a few other advantages. If your firewall is compromised and the attacker installs tools or services to further penetrate your network, a less powerful system will slow the process.

The RAM and processor you purchase for your bastion host will be influenced by the role the system plays in your security infrastructure. For example, if the bastion host will act as an application gateway, you might want to purchase a larger hard drive for the caching features. You can never have too much RAM, and although a fast processor is not necessary to analyze traffic, maintaining state can be memory- and processor-intensive.

Because you must also back up your bastion host, it should have its own tape backup device. Networked backup solutions are not ideal for bastion hosts because they can open security holes into your internal network. Use a local backup solution for your bastion host.

Operating System

Depending on the type of firewall you choose to use in your environment, you may or may not have to select an operating system. Packet filters usually run on routers that use their own proprietary OS, and appliance firewalls usually use a hardened Linux or Free BSD kernel. Installing an application gateway on a computer requires that you select an operating system. The biggest factor in your decision should be your familiarity with the operating system. Hardening an operating system for use on a firewall is a complex process. If you are a Windows NT administrator, do not select Solaris as your firewall OS; select the OS with which you are most comfortable.

The services required on your network represent another factor in your OS decision. If your environment requires an application server that can filter HTTP, SMTP, and NNTP traffic, your operating system must facilitate this process. For example, you may be very familiar with Windows 98, but it does not support all common Internet protocols. The operating system you choose should, at a minimum, provide multitasking and support multiple simultaneous connections. You should also make sure that if installing a software firewall, you properly harden and secure the operating system on the computer running the firewall.

If you are building a bastion host and do not have an OS of choice, try UNIX. It is a well-understood, tested OS that has been used on the Internet for many years.

Services and Daemons

Secure each bastion host individually at all levels. Secure the firewall application, operating system, and other services. Each of these areas possesses specific vulnerabilities that must be addressed separately.

When you install an operating system, many services and daemons are installed by default. For example, all versions of UNIX install Telnet by default. Remove all unnecessary services and daemons. Ideally, a bastion host functioning as a firewall should not be running any services.

Caution   Disabling unnecessary services is not the best approach to hardening a server, because they can be re-enabled at a later time. For example, many administrators disable the Scheduler service because it runs with administrative privileges. If the bastion host is compromised, the attacker can easily re-enable the Scheduler service and run programs with administrative privileges.

Remove as many programs on the operating system as you can. On UNIX, you should remove the system administration programs, such as chmod, rm, and so on. These programs can help an attacker gain root access to your system.

Another important configuration for firewalls is to remove IP routing. If routing is enabled, the bastion host may automatically route packets without passing them through the security definitions defined in the firewall application. Removing IP routing forces the bastion host to use the firewall software to route or proxy traffic.

Removing unnecessary services and daemons is the critical step in configuring your bastion host. Without this step, your system will most likely contain security holes that can be exploited by an attacker, providing them with easy entry to your network.

Common Firewall Designs

Now that you understand how to create a secure firewall, this next section discusses placement in your architecture. The first step is to physically secure your firewall. The strongest security measures mean nothing if someone can just cut the power to your system or access it directly. Most systems provide easy access to administrator/root privileges if you have physical access to the system and a simple floppy disk.

The four common firewall designs provide various levels of security. The more sensitive the data and resources you are protecting, the more extensive your firewall solution should be. The four common firewall designs are:

✦ Screening router

✦ Single-homed bastion host

✦ Dual-homed bastion host

✦ Screened subnet

Each design implements a mixture of layers, filters, and access points to help secure information and resources. The screening router represents the simplest and most common design. The options for creating a screened host, single-homed, or dual-homed bastion host, require all traffic to pass through a single host acting as an application or circuit-level gateway. The screened subnet represents the most secure design, adding an additional layer of security with a packet filter.

Screening routers

 Understand screening routers

The screening router is a great first line of defense. Most screening routers are implemented on network routers, so you most likely have the hardware already in place. Configure the screening router to route traffic that is acceptable to your security policy. Screening routers proficiently deny ranges of IP addresses and filter unwanted TCP/IP applications. Figure 7-1 shows a screening router in a network architecture.

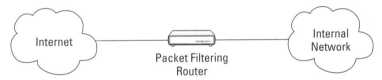

Figure 7-1: Screening routers are an inexpensive, yet powerful, security solution.

Screening routers possess several disadvantages. For one, configuration of a screening router requires a high level of TCP/IP knowledge. The screening router depends entirely on filter rules, so any errors or misconfiguration may compromise your security infrastructure.

Another disadvantage is that a single device is being used to protect the network. If an attacker compromises the screening router, there is nothing protecting your internal resources. Additionally, your screening router does not hide your internal network architecture. Anyone can see your network layout with ease.

Typically, screening routers do not include powerful logging or monitoring features. If a screening router receives traffic that violates its filters, you will not obtain much information about it, nor will you be alerted to its occurrence.

Screened host firewall (single-homed bastion)

 Understand screened host

A screened host that uses a single-homed bastion host in addition to a screening router represents a second popular firewall design. The bastion host can be either a

circuit-level or application gateway. With this design, the bastion host can hide the configuration of your internal network. Network Address Translation (NAT) gives you the ability to use any internal IP address.

The screened host firewall design passes all incoming and outgoing information through the bastion host. Figure 7-2 shows this configuration. The screening router is your first line of defense and is configured to pass all traffic to the bastion host. This routing structure allows the bastion host to analyze all traffic before it travels to the internal network. The screening router configuration routes outgoing traffic only if it originates from the bastion host. By adding this configuration to the screening router, internal systems cannot be reconfigured to bypass the bastion host.

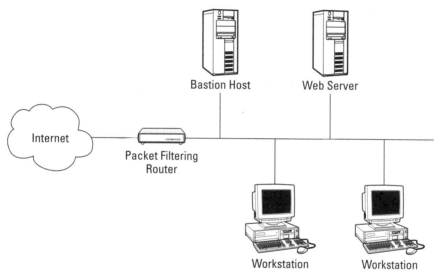

Figure 7-2: A single-homed bastion in a screened host design provides more protection than a single packet filter.

This design is superior to a packet filter screening router in several areas. It adds a bastion host, as well as circuit-level and/or application gateways. The bastion host itself provides a second layer of security that should be difficult for an attacker to penetrate if configured correctly.

The disadvantages of this design include increased cost and decreased performance. Because the bastion host processes all traffic, it takes more time to respond. Additionally, if the bastion host is an application gateway, individual applications must be configured and not all applications will function. For example, streaming video and audio may not function properly.

Screened host firewall (dual-homed bastion)

The design of the screened host firewall adds even more security to your architecture by using a dual-homed bastion host. Figure 7-3 shows this design.

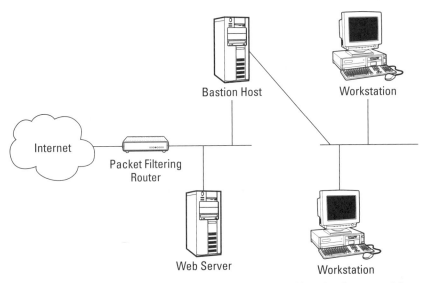

Figure 7-3: A screened host design with a dual-homed bastion host provides more protection than a single-homed bastion host.

This design is more secure because it creates a physical break between your internal network and the Internet. As with a single-homed bastion host design, all external traffic is forwarded to the bastion host for processing.

With a single-homed bastion host design, an attacker may still be able to modify the router to bypass the bastion host. A dual-homed bastion host makes this impossible. An attacker who penetrates the packet filter or dual-homed bastion host will still need to penetrate the remaining firewall and packet filter to gain access to your internal network. Dual-homed bastion hosts, like single-homed bastion hosts, allow you to use NAT to hide your internal network architecture.

Screened subnet firewall (demilitarized zone)

 Understand screened subnet

The screened subnet design represents the most secure option and is often called the demilitarized zone, or DMZ, because it creates a secure space between the Internet and your internal network. This design places all publicly accessible devices in the DMZ. The DMZ is a small, isolated network that separates your highly targeted servers from your more sensitive internal resources.

Internal and external screening routers ensure that all traffic enters and leaves through the bastion host. With this arrangement, you cannot directly access the DMZ; you must go through the bastion host. The external screening router rejects any outgoing traffic that does not originate from the bastion host. The internal router helps prevent IP spoofing and acts as a third line of defense. Like the external router, the internal router rejects any incoming traffic that did not originate from the bastion host and sends outgoing packets only to the bastion host.

The primary advantage of the screened subnet design is that an attacker must compromise three separate devices before gaining access to your internal network. Additionally, your internal network architecture remains completely hidden from public view. Only the DMZ is accessible from the Internet.

Because the internal network is completely hidden and unknown to Internet routing tables, any traffic that goes directly from the internal network to the Internet will not be replied to because the routers do not know where to send the packets. This prevents internal users from bypassing security measures; all traffic must pass through the bastion host for successful communication. In this design, you do not need a dual-homed bastion host because the routers ensure that all traffic will pass through the bastion host.

Key Point Summary

This chapter discussed the firewall designs you may use in your environment.

✦ Firewall placement is critical to the security level and resource protection you require in your environment.

✦ Your firewall should create choke points to simplify your security architecture. With fewer access points into your network that you have to control, it is easier to manage security.

✦ One benefit of choke points is easier administration. For example, you know where all the information enters and leaves your network, so you can place comprehensive and extensive monitoring tools at these points.

✦ Placement can be considered a resource issue. If you do not place your firewall and other security resources correctly, you will need more hardware to achieve your required level of protection. Because equipment is expensive to purchase and maintain, you should take time to carefully plan your resource placement.

✦ Bastion hosts check all incoming and outgoing traffic, enforcing rules specified by your organization's internal and external sources. They should also be armed with logging and alarm functionality to record and warn of attacks.

✦ When building a firewall, follow two main principles: keep it simple, and make contingency plans in case the firewall is penetrated.

✦ The most common way an attacker gains access to a resource is through over-looked components installed on a system. Make sure you build your bastion host with the fewest possible components.

✦ The fewer services you have running on your firewall, the fewer chances an attacker has to exploit it.

✦ You need to consider and prepare for the occurrence of firewall penetration. If you have only one firewall separating your internal resources from outsiders, a compromised firewall will provide complete access to your network.

✦ To prevent penetration, you might consider implementing several layers of firewall devices. This way, you are not relying on a single device.

✦ If your security is compromised, your security policy should state what to do. Consider these steps:

  • Create an identical copy of the software.

  • Configure an identical system and store it in a safe place.

  • Ensure that all software necessary to install the firewall is handy.

✦ A single-homed bastion host is a firewall with only one network interface. Single-homed bastion hosts are generally used for application-level gateway firewalls.

✦ Dual-homed bastion hosts function identically to single-homed hosts except they have at least two network interfaces. Dual-homed hosts serve as application gateways, circuit-level gateways, and packet filters. The advantage of a dual-homed host is that it creates a complete break between the external network and internal network. This break forces all traffic to pass through the bastion host.

✦ A single-purpose bastion host can be either a single- or multi-homed bastion host.

✦ The most common mistake made when deciding on which system to use for the firewall is to purchase the biggest and fastest machine on the market. The incorrect assumption is that the faster machine will process incoming and outgoing traffic quickly.

✦ Using less powerful hardware provides a few other advantages. If your firewall is compromised and the attacker installs tools or services to further penetrate your network, a less powerful system will slow the process.

✦ You must back up your bastion host, so it should have its own tape backup device. Networked backup solutions are not ideal for bastion hosts because they could open security holes into your internal network. A local backup solution should be used on your bastion host.

✦ Depending on the type of firewall you choose to use in your environment, you may or may not have to select an operating system. Packet filters usually run on routers that use their own proprietary OS, and appliance firewalls usually use a hardened Linux or Free BSD kernel. If you plan to install an application gateway on a computer, you need to select an operating system.

✦ Each bastion host should be secured individually and at all levels. You should secure the firewall application, operating system, and other services. Each of these areas has specific vulnerabilities that must be addressed separately.

✦ Removing unnecessary services and daemons is the critical step in configuring your bastion host. Without this step, your system will most likely contain security holes that can be exploited by an attacker, providing them easy entry to your network.

✦ You must physically secure your firewall. The strongest security measures mean nothing when someone can just cut the power to your system or access it directly. Most systems provide easy access to administrator/root privileges if you have physical access to the system and a simple floppy disk.

✦ The screening router is a great first line of defense.

✦ Configuration of a screening router requires a high level of TCP/IP knowledge. The screening router depends entirely on filter rules, so any errors or misconfiguration may compromise your security infrastructure.

✦ Screening routers do not include powerful logging or monitoring features. If a screening router receives traffic that violates its filters, you will not obtain much information about it, nor will you be alerted to its occurrence.

✦ The second popular firewall design is a screened host that uses a single-homed bastion host in addition to a screening router.

✦ The bastion host can be either a circuit-level or application gateway. With this design, the bastion host can hide the configuration of your internal network. NAT gives you the ability to use any internal IP addresses.

✦ The screened host firewall is designed so that all incoming and outgoing information is passed through the bastion host.

✦ The dual-homed screened host is more secure because it creates a physical break between your internal network and the Internet.

✦ The screened subnet design is the most secure and is often called the demilitarized zone, or DMZ, because it creates a secure space between the Internet and your internal network. In this design, all publicly accessible devices are placed in the DMZ. The DMZ is a small, isolated network that separates your highly targeted servers from your more sensitive internal resources.

✦   ✦   ✦

STUDY GUIDE

This study guide presents five assessment questions to test your knowledge of this exam topic area. It also presents four lab exercises to further enhance your review of the material.

Assessment Questions

1. Which firewall design is the most secure?

 A. Screened host, single-homed

 B. Screened host, dual-homed

 C. Screening router

 D. Screened subnet

2. What should not be removed from your bastion host?

 A. Unnecessary daemons and services

 B. NIC

 C. Administration programs

 D. Guest account

3. Screening routers implement which firewall technology?

 A. Application-level gateway

 B. Packet filtering

 C. Stateful inspection

 D. Circuit-level gateway

4. What is a dual-homed host?

 A. A system with at least two network interfaces

 B. An application server

 C. A system with two monitors

 D. A system with no network interfaces

5. What is an internal bastion host?

   A. A system with one connection on the internal network

   B. A system entirely on the internal network and dividing two subnets

   C. A system connected to the Internet

   D. None of the above

Lab Exercises

Lab 7-1 Installing WinRoute

1. Download the WinRoute software from `www.winroute.com`.
2. Run the installation program.
3. Accept all defaults.
4. Restart your computer.

Lab 7-2 Create an internal network with WinRoute

1. Start WinRoute Administration. Go to Start ➪ Programs ➪ WinRoute Pro ➪ WinRoute Administration.
2. In the Open Configuration dialog box, enter localhost as the WinRoute host. By default, WinRoute has no Admin password.
3. To change the password, go to Settings ➪ Accounts ➪ Edit.
4. Change the password and click OK.
5. Go to Settings ➪ Interface Table. Select the interface connecting to the internal network and click Properties.
6. Select the Perform NAT checkbox. Click OK and Apply to return to WinRoute Administration.

Lab 7-3 Establish a packet filter

1. Open the WinRoute Administration program.
2. Go to Settings ➪ Advanced ➪ Packet Filter. The Packet Filter dialog box opens.
3. Select the Any Interface icon and expand it.
4. Double-click the No Rule icon. The Add Item dialog box appears.
5. Go to the Protocol drop-down box and select ICMP.

6. Edit this rule. Keep the Source and Destination boxes at the default (Any Address).

7. In the ICMP Types dialog box, select the All checkbox.

8. In the Action area, select the Drop dialog box.

9. In the Log Packet area, select the Log into Windows checkbox and keep the Valid at value as its default (Always). Click OK.

10. Click Apply and OK to return to the main window.

11. Now, ping will not function. To view the logs to confirm this, go to View ⇨ Logs ⇨ Security Log.

Lab 7-4 Denying HTTP access

1. Go to Settings ⇨ Advanced ⇨ Packet Filter and select the Outgoing tab.

2. Select the Any Interface tab and select TCP.

3. In the Source area, allow Any Address for both Source and Destination.

4. In the Port area, select "Greater than" for source, and enter **1024**.

5. In the Destination Port area, select "Equal to" and enter **80**.

6. In the Action section, select Deny.

7. Select the "Log into window" checkbox.

8. Click OK to return to the Packet Filter Window.

9. Click Apply and OK to activate the rule.

Answers to Chapter Questions

Chapter Pre-Test

1. A bastion host is any system with a direct connection to the Internet. It can also refer to a firewall device.

2. A screening router is a router with packet filtering functionality. It serves as a great first line of defense.

3. Single-homed, dual-homed, and internal are the types of bastion hosts.

4. A screening router is best used as a first line of defense.

5. The screened subnet design provides the highest level of security.

Assessment Questions

1. D. The screened subnet design is the most secure.

2. B. You should not remove the NIC from a bastion host. This is what connects the system to the network.

3. B. Screening routers implement the packet filtering firewall technology.

4. A. A dual-homed host is a system with at least two network interfaces.

5. B. An internal bastion host is a system entirely on your internal network dividing subnets.

Operating System Security

T his part of the book introduces you to operating system security concepts.

Operating System Security Risks examines threats to operating system security, explaining types of threats and attacks. The chapter goes on to explore security risks in the Windows and Unix operating systems.

Principles of Operating System Security explores operating system security in more detail. This examination includes discussions on the levels of system security and system security mechanisms. The chapter looks at system security management of the Windows NT, Unix, and Linux operating systems.

Operating System Hardening begins with a general discussion of security maintenance and the importance of deploying operating system patches, fixes, and updates that are released by vendors. This chapter takes a look at Microsoft Service Packs and Hotfixes, as well as Linux errata, and takes a detailed look at how to secure the Windows Registry. Additional Windows coverage includes how to manage unnecessary Windows services, securing networking and system logging, and miscellaneous Windows security tricks. The chapter also covers unnecessary Unix services, working with TCPWrapper, and fingerprinting systems with checksums.

Securing File Systems and Resources examines security in terms of file systems. This discussion begins with an examination of the Windows New Technology File System (NTFS), its permissions and partitions, as well as how to manage security for move and copy operations for files and directories. In addition, the chapter discusses Windows share security, share permissions, and how to combine NTFS and share permissions. The chapter concludes with a discussion on securing

(continued)

Continued

UNIX file systems, including details on the Unix file system hierarchy and permissions, the Unix commands umask and chmod, as well as working with UIDs and GIDs.

Securing User Accounts takes a look at user accounts and passwords, and explores Windows and Unix account security mechanisms.

Operating System Security Risks

CHAPTER PRE-TEST

1. Are internal users a threat to system security?

2. By default, is Windows NT completely secure?

3. In Windows NT, what group is recommended for use instead of the Everyone group?

4. Do NIS+ and Secure RPC solve all of the security issues with NIS and RPC, respectively?

To properly protect your network resources, you must understand that each operating system comes with security threats. No operating system on the market today is completely secure. Vulnerabilities will continue to be discovered in each operating system, making it crucial for administrators to be aware of these discoveries. This chapter introduces some of the tools and resources available for administrators to stay ahead of hackers.

Operating System Security Risks

Security threats can be classified into two separate categories — accidental and intentional. Accidental threats are those caused unintentionally by users. A good example of an accidental threat was in the media recently. An employee for a major U.S. airline stumbled upon ticket pricing information for a competitor on an airport kiosk machine used by agents. The media reported that the employee did not log out of his session properly, leaving the door open for other agents to access the airline's data.

Intentional threats are planned actions by either internal users or external attackers. These threats most often grab the media's attention and cause administrators the greatest concern. Intentional threats can be divided into two types — passive and active.

A passive threat doesn't modify or alter data. Passive threats usually go unnoticed by users. An example of a passive threat is the installation of a sniffer to capture network data.

Active threats cause the most damage and are easier to identify. An active threat causes some sort of effect that the users notice.

Multiple types of attacks (of both the passive and active variety) can be accomplished either accidentally or intentionally. These types of attacks include the following:

✦ Spoofing or masquerading attacks

✦ Replay attacks

✦ Denial-of-Service (DoS) attacks

✦ Insider attacks

✦ Trapdoor attacks

✦ Trojan horses

Spoofing attacks

In a spoofing or masquerading attack, a malicious host or program attempts to masquerade as a trusted host or program. When people refer to this type of attack, they are usually talking about *IP address spoofing*, which occurs when a malicious user alters his or her IP address to either hide his or her true identity or appear to be a trusted host. In another type of masquerading attack, an attacker replaces an application or service with one that appears to be identical to the trusted application, except that it performs a malicious task (such as reissuing checks in the hacker's name).

Replay attacks

A replay attack occurs when a malicious user captures important network data, modifies it, and replays it back to the host in an attempt to gain unauthorized access.

Denial-of-Service attacks

As described in detail in Chapter 4, Denial-of-Service (DoS) attacks usually have one purpose — to cause network services to be unresponsive. A DoS attack includes any attack that prevents legitimate users from accessing a service.

Insider attacks

As its name implies, insider attacks are carried out by insiders or regular users of a network's resources. Insider attacks are thought to be one of the largest threats to corporate networks, yet many security policies fail to address them. The types of insider attacks that occur range from the stealing of proprietary documents to the circumventing of firewall and perimeter security policies.

Trapdoor attacks

Trapdoor attacks are perpetrated by attackers who don't have complete access to a system. The attacker plants malicious code to be run when another user, most likely a user with Administrative access, logs into a host. For example, an attacker may gain limited access to a host and find that he or she is able to write to certain directories — in particular, the \WINNT\PROFILES\Administrator\Start Menu\Start Up directory. The attacker then inserts malicious code, or even legitimate code, to escalate his privileges when the administrator logs in. After this is accomplished, the attacker waits for the administrator to log in to the host.

Trojan horses

Trojan horses are a variation of the trapdoor attack. A Trojan horse is normally a program that appears to be useful, but installs some sort of backdoor access or performs malicious actions on a host. Many Trojan horse programs enter networks via e-mail attachments.

Caution   Some anti-virus vendors have incorrectly labeled programs, such as L0phtcrack (used to test password strength on Windows NT hosts), as Trojan horses. Be aware that many of the security tools and scripts that you download may trigger your anti-virus software.

Keylogger programs have been labeled as Trojan horses. Most are detected by anti-virus software, but some are not. When placed on a host, a keylogger intercepts and logs all keystrokes made by a user. Certain Windows-based keyloggers have been known to replace the login prompt, thus capturing the user's login ID and password. Most keyloggers can be configured to capture all kinds of data. If a user types anything, a keylogger can be used to capture that data.

Windows NT Security Risks – Insecure Defaults

 Objective   Identify security issues and solutions specific to Windows NT

For the purpose of the exam and security in general, this section covers some of the more dangerous, high-profile risks.

Many consider security through obscurity to be the best way to protect a system. In other words, if you were to choose settings (such as installation folders) that fall outside of the norm, a hacker would find those settings much tougher to figure out. For example, Windows NT installs itself to the default directory of *%systemroot%*\Winnt. Changing this directory during installation can prevent an attacker from easily accessing files (or at least make it more difficult to locate such information). Although this approach definitely fools an inexperienced attacker, an attacker has multiple ways, depending on the server's configuration, to find the correct location of the files.

Exam Tip   For every recommendation of obscurity, there is a way around it.

If your server is configured securely and properly monitored, changing the default installation directory of Windows NT or any application is unnecessary.

Another security through obscurity recommendation is to change the default user-names to something other than the default. Microsoft and numerous security experts have recommended that the Administrator, Guest, and IUSR_*Machinename* accounts created by Internet Information Server be renamed. First, renaming the IUSR_*Machinename* account has been known to cause problems with servers that are being used to host Web pages. Second, although renaming the Administrator account slows down an inexperienced attacker, he or she can find methods to remotely determine the name of the Administrator account and when it was last used.

In the Real World
Remember that these security measures are merely recommendations. When you are turned loose on your own network, remember that these are rather trivial ways to protect your network.

Windows NT also includes hidden administrative shares that are created by default:

✦ C$

✦ D$

✦ Admin$

✦ IPC$

The dollar sign ($) signifies that the share is a hidden share that normal users can't see. Multiple ways exist to delete these shares; for example, an administrator can simply delete each share manually. Unfortunately, every time the operating system is rebooted, the shares re-create themselves. You can also use automated ways of removing these shares.

One way to remove the shares involves editing the Registry and removing the C$, D$ (and any other drives that may be present), and the Admin$ shares. If you edit the **Registry** key, *HkeyLocalMachine\System\CurrentCointrolSet\Services\ LanManServer\ParametersI*, and add the **Registry** key, *AutoShareServer*, with the DWORD value of *0*, then these administrative shares won't be automatically created.

Another way, and one that I recommend over the Registry edit, is to use the AUTOEXNT command from the *Windows NT Server 4 Resource Kit* from Microsoft Press. This tool allows administrators to specify commands to be launched as Windows NT boots. By using the NET SHARE command built into Windows NT, administrators can have the shares automatically deleted each time the system boots.

Caution
If you are running other services or applications (such as Microsoft Exchange), there will be, depending on configuration, other hidden shares. Be sure to test the results of removing these shares in a non-production environment before removing them from production servers.

Be sure to secure the directory permissions on the directory containing the AUTOEXNT tool. If an attacker is able to access this tool, he or she can add other commands to the startup of the operating system.

Default permissions comprise a large concern on Windows NT systems, in particular the use of the built-in Everyone group. A good rule to remember is that under Windows NT, Everyone means *everyone*, even anonymous Internet users. Installations of Windows NT 4 that contain Service Pack 3 or later include a group named Authenticated Users. In general, replacing the Everyone group with Authenticated Users is a good idea. Administrators should also audit the permissions on all directories and on the Registry to make sure that local and remote users don't have improper access to directories and Registry keys. A good tool to assist in this process is DUMPACL from SysInternals (`www.sysinternals.com`). This tool gives administrators an output of all the file-level permissions.

 Note   File-level permissions only function on drives formatted using NTFS. A good rule to follow is to format all drives on a Windows NT system with NTFS.

Default services running on Windows machines are also a danger to uninformed administrators. Disabling any services that aren't required is a common security recommendation. By default, Windows NT Server enables the following services:

✦ Alerter

✦ Computer Browser

✦ DHCP Client

✦ Event Log

✦ License Logging Service

✦ Messenger

✦ Net Logon

✦ Plug and Play

✦ Remote Procedure Call Service

✦ Server

✦ Spooler

✦ TCP/IP NetBIOS Helper Service

✦ Workstation

Additionally, if Internet Information Server is installed, then FTP Publishing Service, Gopher Publishing Service, and World Wide Web Publishing Service will also be enabled. Depending on the applications installed on the server and the server's required function, you may or may not need many of these services.

For example, cases have been reported in which the Messenger Service, a service that isn't essential to the operation of Windows NT, has been used in social engineering attacks. Denial of Service attacks have been discovered via the Spooler service, which is used for printing, and both the Web Publishing service and the FTP service have multiple vulnerabilities.

Windows 2000 Security Risks

 Identify security issues and solutions specific to Windows 2000

Like Windows NT, Windows 2000 has multiple risks that need to be addressed. Not only do the previously mentioned Windows NT issues exist, but Windows 2000 has introduced new configuration options and new services that bring their own level of risk.

One of the major features added by Windows 2000 is Active Directory. Active Directory serves as the operating system's primary basis for storing and disseminating critical information within one or more domains.

Like the Windows NT Registry, Active Directories control access with Access Control Lists (ACLs). Thus, administrators need to review and adjust any rights that would give internal and external users unauthorized access.

Although Active Directory controls most aspects of Windows 2000, Windows 2000 still uses a Registry. The Windows 2000 Registry and its permissions should also be reviewed and adjusted as required. As with Windows NT, all hard drives in a Windows 2000 system should be formatted with NTFS.

Windows 2000 also installs a number of services by default, such as:

- ✦ Com
- ✦ Event Service
- ✦ Computer Browser
- ✦ DHCP client
- ✦ Distributed Link Tracking Client
- ✦ DNS Client
- ✦ Event Log
- ✦ IPSEC Policy Agent
- ✦ Logical Disk Manager
- ✦ Messenger
- ✦ Net Logon
- ✦ Network Connections
- ✦ Plug and Play
- ✦ Print Spooler
- ✦ Protected Storage
- ✦ Remote Procedure Call

✦ Remote Registry Service

✦ Removeable Storage

✦ RunAs Service

✦ Security Accounts Manager

✦ Server

✦ System Event Notification

✦ Task Scheduler

✦ TCP/IP NetBIOS Helper

✦ Workstation

As with Windows NT, if Internet Information Server is installed, additional services will be installed and activated.

System Scanning and Footprinting

 Understand system scanning and footprinting

As a first step, the attacker will usually try to identify the operating system of the target, as well as identify any open TCP ports listening for connections. Both of these steps help attackers determine the existing vulnerabilities to attempt an attack on the target. These methods are also useful to administrators attempting to secure their hosts.

System scanning with NMAP

System scanning is a process in which an attacker uses an automated tool, such as NMAP, to map out a system and pinpoint potential vulnerabilities. Other commercially available scanning tools, such as BindView's BV-Control for Internet Security, take this process one step further and actually scan for specific vulnerabilities, as well as open ports.

Many types of system or port scans can be performed. NMAP, for example, can perform a variety of scan types; some are *noisy*, and can tip off the target machine's administrators, and some are more *stealthy*.

TCP connect scan

The first scan type that NMAP performs is a TCP connect scan. It is the also the most basic form of scanning. The problem with the TCP connect scan is that it completes the three-way handshaking process and actually connects to an open port, but then drops the connection. A ton of log entries are generated, which tips the administrator off to the fact that his or her system has been scanned.

TCP SYN scan

The second scan option that NMAP provides is a TCP SYN scan, also known as a *half scan* or *half-open scan*. This scan doesn't complete the three-way handshake, and therefore only opens the listening port halfway. As discussed in Chapter 4, the handshaking process starts with a SYN and then a SYN-ACK is received; after NMAP receives the SYN-ACK, it knows that the port is listening and immediately resets the connection, avoiding detection by most logging devices.

UDP port scan

NMAP also performs a UDP port scan, which, as the name suggests, scans a host for open UDP ports. This is an excellent option when looking for backdoor Trojan horses, such as BackOrifice, that listen on UDP ports. Many other scanning options exist in NMAP (the examples used in this chapter are the most commonly used scans). Additional information on NMAP is available at `www.insecure.org/nmap/nmap_manpage.html`.

Commercial scanning tools

Commercial tools, such as BV-Control for Internet Security, provide all the useful features of NMAP, but also take system scanning a step further. By integrating numerous vulnerability checks, commercial software vendors have taken much of the work out of scanning systems for vulnerabilities. When using NMAP, system administrators should manually check each service identified for vulnerabilities. This means that he or she must manually execute scripts to test for the vulnerabilities, and the scripts themselves must often be created. The commercial tools automatically run exploit scripts (included with the product) and vulnerability checks to determine if a host is vulnerable.

Another advantage of commercial scanning tools is that most vendors employ a team of security researchers who help discover new vulnerabilities and add checks for them to the scanning product. Additional information on BV-Control for Internet Security is available at `www.bindview.com`.

Remote operating system identification

Most experienced attackers also perform remote operating system identification as part of *system footprinting* (the process of sizing up the opponent, or the system being attacked). Administrators can usually tell when an inexperienced attacker is probing their systems because exploits are being tried against it for services that don't exist. An experienced attacker will avoid easy detection and ensure the highest percentage of success by attempting to exploit only those vulnerabilities that he or she is sure exist.

Numerous methods can be used to identify a remote operating system. NMAP, for example, uses TCP/IP fingerprinting, which utilizes numerous proprietary techniques to detect subtleties in the underlying operating system network stack of the computers being scanned. NMAP uses this information to create a fingerprint that is compared against a database of known fingerprints.

Another method that is used to remotely identify operating systems and that doesn't require the use of additional tools is *banner scraping*. By using the Telnet application included with most operating systems, a remote user can easily identify the remote operating systems. For example, if you want to know what operating system www.microsoft.com is running, you can launch the following commands from a command prompt:

```
root.localhost%: Telnet www.microsoft.com 80
```

This command uses Telnet to establish a connection with Microsoft.com via port 80. You will then see the following:

```
Trying www.microsoft.com...
Connect, www.microsoft.com...
Escape Character is '^]'
```

Now by issuing a simple command, you can identify the remote operating system:

```
Get HTTP/1.0/ <cr> <cr>
```

<cr> denotes carriage return. You will then see the following:

```
HTTP/1.1 400 Bad Request
Server: Microsoft-IIS/5.0
Content-Type: text/html
Content-Length: 87
<html><head><title>Error</title></head><body>The parameter is
incorrect. </body>
Disconnected.
```

The Web server application gladly informs you that the remote operating system is Microsoft Internet Information Server 5.0, which runs on Windows 2000. You can defend against this type of remote reconnaissance by most applications by simply changing the provided banner information. As with some of the Windows NT recommendations, the idea of changing the banners falls under the category of security through obscurity. An experienced attacker can easily use other methods to identify the remote operating system.

UNIX Security Risks

 Identify security issues and solutions specific to UNIX

Although it would be impossible to discuss all of the UNIX security risks, this chapter addresses the most important risks and looks in detail at the rlogin command, Telnet, Network Information System (NIS), and Network File System (NFS).

The rlogin command

The rlogin command originates from the Berkeley variety of UNIX, which contained adaptations to accommodate networks and distributed system access. The rlogin command is routinely used to bypass the normal password prompt. Because the original rlogin command was so easily exploited — and because of the vast number of incidents surrounding this command — some systems either don't support it or only support highly modified versions of it.

When rlogin is used, the command checks the user's identity on the remote system through the following two files: /etc/hosts.equiv, which isn't supported by many systems; and .rhosts, which is located in the remote user's home directory.

/etc/hosts.equiv is a system-wide file that is normally maintained by the administrator. If this file was compromised, a malicious user could remotely log on to the destination host.

For obvious reasons, both of these files, if supported by the operating system, must be protected to prevent unauthorized access.

The rlogin process uses TCP port 513 and is identified in the /etc/services file. During the rlogin process, the /etc/hosts.equiv file is checked for the requesting system's host name. If it is present, remote login continues. If it isn't present, the .rhosts file is queried for the originating host's hostname. The process assumes that the same user ID exists on both systems unless a different user ID is provided when using the rlogin command. If, for some reason, the user ID doesn't exist or the incoming system host name is not present, then rlogin automatically prompts for a password.

The syntax of the rlogin command is as follows:

```
rlogin [ -E | -ex ] [ -l username ] [ -S ] [ -L ] host
```

Telnet

Telnet is also used to gain remote access to hosts. Though similar to rlogin, Telnet's authentication process doesn't follow a trusted model like rlogin's. Telnet uses the client/server model and doesn't check for trusts. If a user can supply the correct username and password, then the session is established. No encryption takes place when transmitting data via a Telnet session. Because of this cleartext transmission, it is definitely a bad idea to use Telnet over an untrusted network, such as the Internet. It should only be used to log into devices that are not essential. A good alternative to Telnet is Secure Shell (SSH). SSH offers all the features and abilities of Telnet; furthermore, it encrypts the entire session, including the authentication process.

The Network Information System

Under UNIX operating systems, the Network Information System (NIS) represents one way to create a distributed computing environment on a local network. NIS was originally created by Sun Microsystems and was quickly adopted by other operating systems. It provides a network database of important configuration information, and helps bind a network of machines into a single usable entity.

Without NIS, companies would require a network consisting of multiple UNIX machines to have an account for each user on each host. Obviously, this would be an administrative and usability nightmare. NIS solves this problem by creating a single, centrally administered database that allows users to have a single username and password for each host in the network.

NIS also assists in managing the many necessary configuration files, which allows administrators to manage and implement configuration options on multiple hosts from a single location.

NIS is still widely used by Linux, AIX, and HP-UX networks, but Sun Microsystems has upgraded to NIS+. NIS+ includes some added functionality and is covered later in this section.

Unfortunately, the NIS service is inherently insecure, and multiple security issues exist with NIS. This section covers the following NIS security issues:

✦ The lack of authentication requirements

✦ NIS server broadcasts

✦ Plain-text distribution

The Remote Procedure Call (RPC) protocol doesn't require hosts to contact the portmapper or other RPC services to authenticate themselves. A wrapper program, which enables administrators to limit the IP addresses or domain names that are allowed access, can solve this authentication problem. Of course, a malicious user can bypass this security flaw by using IP spoofing.

You can hide your RPC servers behind firewalls and only trust certain internal hosts. However, this doesn't protect you completely, especially from internal risks. Or, you can utilize the "secure RPC" add-on. Secure RPC is an enhancement to RPC that includes a public key based host and user authentication scheme. Unfortunately, the RPC server's designers chose to use a 90-digit RSA encryption scheme that has been broken and published for quite some time.

With NIS, the ypbind process contacts its server by broadcast, creating another security risk. This means that anyone with access to the local network can set up a ypserv process and distribute forged NIS maps. Later implementations of ypbind, which include an option that allows administrators to specify the NIS servers' IP address, still don't effectively secure the service.

NIS distributes its maps in plain text. The NIS password map can be read by anyone with network access using the ypcat program, which reveals the encrypted passwords. Some NIS implementations allow for the use of a shadow password map. Unfortunately, this doesn't solve the problem of clear-text transmissions, because anyone with a packet sniffer can capture the shadow file and run it against a password-cracking utility.

Another dangerous security issue is the failure of the yppasswdd daemon to encrypt its transactions or to use any authentication. When a user changes his password via yppasswdd, it is transmitted across the network in clear-text.

New releases of Linux have included an enhanced portmap process that uses hosts.allow and hosts.deny to control access. These two files let administrators specify which hosts, by IP address, will receive access to the daemon.

To address the multiple security issues with NIS, Sun Microsystems released NIS+. NIS+ runs only on Sun Solaris systems and offers the following advantages over NIS:

✦ **More maps:** NIS+ supports more NIS maps. This allows more aspects of system configuration to be centralized in the NIS+ database.

✦ **Hierarchical database structure:** The database itself went from being a flat database in NIS to a more powerful hierarchical database structure. This gives NIS+ the ability to handle a larger installation base of Unix hosts.

✦ **Incremental updates for slave servers:** The added incremental updates feature assists in improving the overall usability of NIS. When a change is made, NIS distributes the entire NIS map to slave servers. With NIS+, only the items changed are broadcast.

✦ **Lack of stored information:** NIS+ addresses the broadcasting problems of NIS. As previously mentioned, the ypbind process contacts servers by broadcast. Under NIS+ the information on specific servers is stored, ensuring that users are contacting the correct servers.

✦ **Reasonable authentication at the host and user levels:** NIS+ supports reasonable authentication at the host and user levels. By using a system of credentials based on public key cryptography, NIS+ forces users to authenticate before altering maps.

✦ **Ability to create groups of NIS+ principals with shared information:** NIS+ facilitates sharing administrative information among those who need access.

✦ **Granting or denying access:** NIS+ also provides a level of access control that enables administrators to allow or deny access to specific groups, machines, or even individual users. The ability for administrators to control access rights on each individual NIS map field has also been implemented.

✦ **The ability to set permissions at the field level:** Specific security settings at the field level allow greater network security and administrative control.

Obviously, the additions that NIS+ provides make NIS+ much more difficult to administer, and prone to more administration mistakes than NIS. Compatibility issues also exist with NIS+; for example, in order for NIS+ to communicate with NIS, all of the additional security features must be disabled, making the use of NIS+ almost pointless.

Network File System

 Examine security using the Network File System

Network File System (NFS) distributes file systems across a network. Under NFS, some machines, called NFS clients, can mount file systems that are physically located on other machines, referred to as *NFS servers*. An NFS server that makes file systems available for remote mounting is said to export or share those file systems.

NFS is essentially a file-sharing protocol. Like NIS, NFS was created by Sun Microsystems and has many purposes in a UNIX environment:

✦ Distributed home directories allow a user to access his home directory from any workstation on the network. NFS exports the file system, making this possible.

✦ NFS makes centralized application administration possible. A large software package can be installed on one machine, and via NFS, other clients on the network can access it. Administrative changes only need to be made on the original copy of the software and the clients will automatically see the updated changes.

✦ NFS also helps administrators conserve disk space. Instead of replicating data on multiple servers in an organization, administrators can export an NFS share to multiple hosts from one UNIX server.

Two separate security issues arise with NFS. The first has to do with management issues and the administrative synchronization of user and group IDs among the various machines sharing NFS partitions, and the granting or denying of access by certain hosts or individuals to certain file systems. The second issue is more fundamental, and concerns the inherent weaknesses of NFS that make it unsafe to use on a network that is not completely trusted, such as the Internet, or with hosts that are not completely trusted.

When a client remotely mounts an NFS partition from a server, it must interpret and abide by the user and group ID information concerning file ownership on that partition. For example, if I had a machine (my_server), and NFS was used to export /export/users/data, which was then mounted on the client (my_client) as /users, then any client machine that has a user with the UID of 1001 (assuming that the directory on my_server is owned by UID 1001) can access the share point. A similar problem exists with group IDs.

To address the NFS weakness and many of the other security issues related to RPC, Secure RPC was created. Secure RPC uses a combined public-key/private-key encryption system. Unfortunately, the selected encryption scheme uses a small and easily crackable key size.

NFS transfers are unencrypted, even when Secure RPC is used. The bulk data is not encrypted, so a malicious user armed with a sniffer could read the contents of files being transferred.

By itself, RPC has no built-in authentication. Hosts that use NFS don't need to prove their identity.

Many security experts suggest that NFS only be used on a trusted network behind the protection of a firewall. Of course, this cautionary statement only addresses external risk; it doesn't protect you against internal malicious users.

Key Point Summary

This chapter discusses threats to Windows NT and UNIX system security and identifies the two types of threats:

✦ Internal accidental users

✦ External malicious attackers

This chapter reviews the different types of attacks:

✦ Spoofing or masquerading

✦ Replay attacks

✦ Denial-of-Service (DoS) attacks

✦ Insider attacks

✦ Trapdoor attacks

✦ Trojan horses

Operating system-specific security issues are examined, starting with Windows NT and its insecure default configurations. The topics that are covered include:

✦ User permissions, default access rights, and security through obscurity options that some administrators choose to implement

✦ Windows 2000 and its default insecurities

System scanning and footprinting are discussed, as well as:

✦ The freeware scanner, Nmap, and its options

✦ A superior, but commercial, scanning product — BV-Control for Internet Security. The key points to remember from this section are how system scanning and footprinting assist malicious attackers in deciding what to exploit.

This chapter covers the "senior citizen" of operating systems, UNIX, and touches on the following topics:

✦ The Berkeley r-utilities and their insecurities

✦ Telnet and the more secure option secure shell (SSH)

✦ NIS and NFS

✦ The insecurities with NIS and NFS and the failed attempt to improve and secure the services.

✦   ✦   ✦

STUDY GUIDE

This Study Guide presents five assessment questions and one lab exercise to assess your understanding of the exam objectives.

Assessment Questions

1. Which utility can be used to determine the operating system of a remote server?

   A. ping

   B. tracert

   C. telnet

   D. ifconfig

2. What is a masquerading attack?

   A. An attack that records network information, modifies it, and sends it back to the network.

   B. An attack that prevents legitimate users from accessing a server or service.

   C. An attack in which the malicious program or host attempts to disguise their true identity.

   D. An attack that is executed by another user, thereby creating a backdoor to the system.

3. What is a Denial-of-Service (DoS) Attack?

   A. An attack that records network information, modifies it, and sends it back to the network.

   B. An attack that prevents legitimate users from accessing a server or service.

   C. An attack in which the malicious program or host attempts to disguise their true identity.

   D. An attack that is executed by another user, thereby creating a backdoor to the system.

4. What are the two security threat categories?

   A. Accidental and Controlled

   B. Controlled and Intentional

   C. Accidental and Intentional

   D. None of the above

5. What are the two types of intentional attacks? Choose two of the following:

   A. Controlled

   B. Active

   C. Passive

   D. Subdued

Lab Exercise

Lab 8-1 Using NMAP from a command prompt to scan a network for well-known service ports:

Scan a Class C network of a known network for popular services:

```
nmap -fsp 21,22,23,25,80,110 microsoft.com/24
```

Scan a host for reserved ports using a standard TCP scan:

```
nmap host
```

Answers to Chapter Questions

Chapter Pre-Test

1. Yes. Internal users are a major threat to system security. A large majority (up to 70 percent) of attacks are initiated within the organization.

2. No. No operating system is completely secure, Windows NT included.

3. The Authenticated Users group should be used instead of the Everyone group.

4. No. Although NIS+ and Secure RPC solve many of the security issues with NIS and RPC respectively, they don't solve all the security issues.

Assessment Questions

1. **C.** The Telnet utility can be used to access any open port on a remote system. For more information, see the section titled, "System Scanning and Footprinting."

2. **C.** In a masquerading attack, the malicious host or program attempts to access a secure system by pretending to be a trusted system. For more information, see the section titled, "Operating System Security Risks."

3. **B.** A Denial of Service attack simply bombards the attacked system with so many requests that legitimate systems on the network can't communicate with it. For more information, see the section titled, "Operating System Security Risks."

4. **C.** For more information, see the section titled "Operating System Security Risks."

5. **A and C.** For more information, see the section titled "Operating System Security Risks."

For More Information

For additional information on Keylogger programs, visit the following Web sites:

✦ http://packetstorm.securify.com
✦ http://www.technotronic.com
✦ http://www.keyloggers.com
✦ http://home.swipenet.se/~w94075/keylogger/
✦ http://www.nmrc.org

For additional information on Windows NT security issues, visit the following Web sites:

✦ http://www.microsoft.com/security
✦ http://www.windowsitsecurity.net
✦ http://www.win2ksecadvice.net
✦ http://razor.bindview.com
✦ http://www.nmrc.org

For additional information on Windows 2000 Security Issues, visit the following Web sites:

✦ http://microsoft.com/security

✦ http://www.windowsitsecurity.net

✦ http://www.win2ksecadvice.net

✦ http://razor.bindview.com

For additional information on system scanning and footprinting, visit the following Web sites:

✦ http://www.bindview.com/products

✦ http://razor.bindview.com

✦ http://www.insecure.org

✦ http://www.wiretrip.net/rfp

✦ http://www.windowsitsecurity.net

For additional information on UNIX security issues, visit the following Web sites:

✦ http://www.securityfocus.com

✦ http://www.sun.com/security

✦ http://razor.bindview.com

Principles of Operating System Security

CHAPTER PRE-TEST

1. By default, Windows NT is a secure operating system. True or false?

2. Microsoft releases security patches in both Service Packs and Hot Fixes. True or false?

3. Windows NT is C2-compliant when first installed. True or false?

4. Windows NT uses a DIS to identify each user or group. True or false?

5. All Windows NT user and group information (including credentials) is stored in the SAM. True or false?

✦ Answers to these questions can be found at the end of the chapter. ✦

One of the main components of security, and unfortunately one of its greatest weaknesses, is the operating system. This chapter introduces you to some of the terms and definitions related to the Windows NT side of operating system security. UNIX and Linux operating system security is covered in subsequent chapters.

Why Is Security So Important?

 Understanding the need for security in UNIX and Windows NT environments

Examining industry evaluation criteria used for security

Many people mistakenly assume that if their computers are not connected to a public network such as the Internet, security is not a large concern. However, whenever one computer allows other computers to connect or transmit data, security risks and concerns arise that need to be addressed. This is true regardless of the origin of the connections or data, be it the Internet or a server on a private LAN.

The majority of corporate servers run on either Windows NT or UNIX operating systems. Because of their connectivity to the world, these systems receive an extra amount of attention — both wanted and unwanted. Obviously, the unwanted attention (of the hacker kind) needs to be addressed carefully and the data protected.

There are many definitions of security. The International Standards Organization (ISO) in ISO document ISO-7498-2 defines security as a means to reduce, to the greatest extent possible, the vulnerability of data and resources. These vulnerabilities can include any weakness that enables an unauthorized person to view, modify, or destroy data assets of an organization, or anything that prevents legitimate access.

ISO-7498-2 also defines certain security services for all levels of remote and local system and application accesses. These services were described in the OSI model that was covered in Chapter 1. Table 9-1 describes these services.

Table 9-1				
ISO-7498-2 Security Services as They Pertain to the OSI Model				
Security Service	**OSI Layer**	**OSI Layer**	**OSI Layer**	**OSI Layer**	**OSI Layer**
	Physical	**Data Link**	**Network**	**Transport**	**Application**
Authentication: Peer Entity and Data Origin	No	No	Yes	Yes	Yes

Continued

Security Service	OSI Layer Physical	OSI Layer Data Link	OSI Layer Network	OSI Layer Transport	OSI Layer Application
Access Control	No	No	Yes	Yes	Yes
Confidentiality: Connection-oriented	Yes	Yes	Yes	Yes	Yes
Confidentiality: Connectionless	No	Yes	Yes	Yes	Yes
Confidentiality: Selective Field	No	No	No	No	Yes
Traffic Flow Confidentiality	Yes	No	Yes	No	Yes
Integrity: Connection-oriented With Recovery	No	No	No	Yes	Yes
Integrity: Connection-oriented Without Recovery	No	No	Yes	Yes	Yes
Integrity: Selective Field and Connection-oriented	No	No	No	No	Yes
Integrity: Connectionless	No	No	Yes	Yes	Yes
Integrity: Selective Field Connectionless	No	No	No	No	Yes
Non-repudiation: Origin or Delivery	No	No	No	No	Yes

Table 9-1 *(continued)*

Many organizations, especially financial and governmental organizations, will not do business with other individuals and businesses who do not have proven security procedures and compliance with a third-party standard. Because security is a regional concern, many industries, organizations, and national governments enforce their own standards and policies that provide adequate security measures. However, there have been some recent efforts to create a global ISO security document.

The European Information Technology Security Evaluation Criteria (ITSEC) document BS 7799 was rewritten in 1999. It documents network threats and various controls that can be put in place to reduce the likelihood of a crippling attack. ITSEC BS 7799 defines vulnerability as something for which the systems administrator is responsible and characterizes a threat as something over which you have little control. The document outlines procedures that can be used to help secure systems. Auditing processes, auditing file systems, assessing risks, maintaining virus control, information management, e-commerce, legal issues, and reporting methods are all covered by BS 7799. Information on ITSEC is available at `www.itsec.gov.uk`.

In the United States, the National Computer Security Center (NCSC) is responsible for establishing the security criteria for trusted computer products. The NCSC created the Trusted Computer Systems Evaluation Criteria (TCSEC), Department of Defense Standard 5200.28, for establishing trust levels. The document criteria (also referred to as the "Orange Book") is intended to indicate the potential security capabilities of a system.

TCSEC has several security ratings, ranging from Level A to Level D. Level A indicates the highest possible level of security and is used on military systems, whereas Level D indicates no security. Each of the levels has a numeric sublevel (e.g., A1, B3, B2, B1, C2, C1, and D). The lower the number, the higher the level of security, as described in the following list:

✦ **Level A1 is a verified design.** This level requires rigorous mathematical proof that the system cannot be compromised, and provides all the features listed in the lower levels. An example of an A1-certified system is the Honeywell SCOMP.

✦ **Level B3 uses security domains.** This level offers data hiding and layering, preventing all interaction between layers. An example of a B3-certified system is the Honeywell Federal Systems XTS-200.

✦ **Level B2 implements structured protection at the hardware level.** Memory areas are virtually segmented and rigidly protected. An Example of a B2-certified system is the Honeywell MULTICS.

✦ **Level B1 requires labeled security protection.** At this level, the system provides more protection than the C2 and C1 levels, such as varied security levels. Also, mandatory access controls beyond those levels place resources in compartments, isolating users in cells and thus offering further protection. An example of a B1-certified system is the IBM MVS/ESA.

✦ **Level C2 implements discretionary access security.** At this level, the system differentiates between users but treats them uniquely. System-level protection exists for resources, data, files, and process. An example of a C2-certified system is Microsoft Windows NT 4.0.

✦ **Level C1 implements discretionary security protection.** At this level, the system does not differentiate between users. The System can provide rudimentary access control. A good example of a C1-certified system is a small departmental workstation with files stored in a location for common use in an area with individual use.

✦ **Level D offers no security protection whatsoever.** An example of this level is MS-DOS.

Typically, Level C is found in commercial environments, which means that the owners of the data need to be able to determine who is allowed to access the data. C1 allows users to log on with the use of group Ids, whereas C2 requires individual IDs and the use of auditing.

TCSEC is very similar to ITSEC except that ITSEC rates functionality (F) and effectives (E) separately. TCSEC Level C2 is equivalent to ITSEC Level F-C2, E2. Certain aspects of discretionary access control, object reuse, identification and authentication, and auditing are required for both C2 and F-C2, E2 certifications.

✦ **Discretionary access control** — The owner of the data or of a resource is able to control who has access to it.

✦ **Object reuse** — Object Reuse is controlled by the operating system and requires that resources such as memory can be reused without the danger of the new user obtaining the previous data.

✦ **Identification and authentication** — The ability of the system to identify and authenticate a user, and the ability to track that user's action by through identification.

✦ **Auditing** — The final requirement for C2 and F-C2, E2, and the ability of the system to allow system administrators to log and audit all security-related information.

A copy of the TCSEC document is available at `www.radium.ncsc.mil`.

Based on the ITSEC and TCSEC documents, the Common Criteria (CC) standard attempted to unify all the various regional and national security standards into one complete document. Common Criteria specifies and evaluates the security features of computer products and systems. It is the first internationally accepted standard for IT security.

Common Criteria provides two basic functions: a standardized way to describe security requirements, such as security needs, the products and systems to fulfill those needs, and the analysis and testing of those products and systems; and a reliable technical basis for evaluating the security features of products and systems. A copy of the Common Criteria is available at `http://csrc.nist.gov/cc`.

Levels of System Security

 Setting guidelines for determining three general security levels

The various operating systems used in corporate networks provide a wide range of security options. Administrators are able to adjust the security of each system depending on the services that the system is providing. Numerous ways exist to secure both Unix and Windows NT systems.

Guidelines have been created to help administrators designate security levels — low, medium, and high — for each system. Because there are multiple configurations and security adjustments that can be made depending on the operating system, these guidelines should be treated as generic and customized for each organization.

- ✦ **Low security** — The computer must be located in a secure location; it must not contain or access sensitive information. This level does not require that operating system security be applied, but the computer must be running antivirus software and must also be protected against theft.

- ✦ **Medium security** — The computer may be used to hold or access corporate data; the computer may be used by more than one user, and protection against accidental information is implemented. This level requires that auditing is enabled, file permissions and account policies implemented, and countermeasures and protections enabled in the operating system.

- ✦ **High security** — The computer may hold or access highly sensitive or valuable information and is in a high-risk situation. The operating system must be stripped of all features and services except for the bare minimum required to perform its chosen function, and additional strict countermeasures and protections must be enabled in the operating system.

Security Mechanisms

 Implementing security system mechanisms

Specific security measures can be implemented at different layers to provide security. Specific security technologies include the following:

- ✦ **Encipherment mechanisms** — Encrypt data moving among systems on a network or between two processes on a local host.

- ✦ **Digital signature mechanisms** — Function nearly the same way as encryption, but with the added feature of verifying the sender and contents.

- ✦ **Access control mechanisms** — Employ various mechanisms to ensure that the sender or receiver is authorized to conduct a specific task or procedure.

✦ **Data integrity mechanisms** — A technique to ensure that each data piece is sequenced, numbered, and time stamped.

✦ **Authentication mechanisms** — The ability to verify a user by means of a password.

✦ **Traffic padding mechanisms** — Add parts to network traffic to prevent unauthorized monitoring or sniffing. Padding makes each packet appear to be the same size, preventing a malicious user from singling out certain packets for examination.

Wide security mechanisms are not specific to any layers and include the following:

✦ **Trusted functionality** — Ensure that certain services or hosts are secure.

✦ **Security labels** — Applied to indicate the data's level of sensitivity.

✦ **Audit trails** — Usually implemented at various levels and monitored for anomalies that might be evidence of a security issue or intrusion. An audit trail is simply a record of objects that have been accessed.

✦ **Security recovery** — A set of rules to apply when dealing with a security event.

Managing System Security

 Exploring the three different areas of security management

To develop a proper security approach, policy managers need to understand the different areas of security management: system security management, security service management, and security mechanism management.

System security management is the management of the entire computer environment and its security, which involves the definition of policy, the consulting of possible service providers, and choosing a specific security mechanism or system. This area should also be responsible for the audit and recovery process and for all other security pervasive work.

Security mechanism management covers the area of data traffic or padding, generating or assigning digital signatures, encryption keys, data integrity, and access control work.

Windows NT "Out of the Box" Security

 Understanding Windows NT "out of the box" security

Microsoft knew that Windows NT would only be taken seriously in the operating system market if it were secure. Unfortunately, Windows NT entered a market that already contained some secure, established operating systems, such as Novell NetWare and the varieties of UNIX. To compete, Microsoft designed Windows NT with security in mind, allowing for permissions to be set on individual objects for different users.

The marketing group at Microsoft was quick to point out that if Windows NT was "too secure," then many organizations would not implement it until their IT staff was versed in the operating system. However, the IT staff would not be versed in the operating system unless they had the opportunity to implement Windows NT. To solve this problem, Windows NT was released as a secure operating system, but not "out of the box."

In layman's terms, "out of the box" means that although Windows NT can be secured, it has minimal security when first installed. However, the advantage is that organizations can quickly implement the operating system. A couple of examples are as follows.

As previously mentioned, Windows NT allows individual users to access different objects on the system, such as files and folders. These permissions, however, do not come into play unless the hard drives are formatted in the NTFS format. NTFS is a file system that is supported natively only by Windows NT (and Windows 2000). Converting to NTFS is easy. Converting back, however, is not.

The second example of this is the way Windows NT assigns default permissions to objects on the system. Assuming that a file exists on an NTFS volume, that file is granted the permission, Everyone Full Control. If every file and folder on the system has the Everyone Full Control permission, then everyone has access to everything. Not very secure. The opposite situation occurs with some of Windows NT's competitors (such as Novell NetWare), where the default permission is Everyone No Access, or another similar permission. The notion with Windows NT is to have the security open and then have the administrator restrict it.

Although Windows NT was designed with security in mind to meet industry and government security needs, there have been numerous security issues found with the operating system. Because Microsoft has become the market leader in both home and corporate PC operating system sales, it is also a target of scrutiny, and a target of hackers and security researchers.

Since its release, new vulnerabilities and exploits are found in Windows NT almost every week. This, combined with an influx of inexperienced and poorly trained system administrators and Microsoft Certified System Engineers (MCSE), has caused Windows NT to go from an operating system designed for security to an operating system surrounded by a multitude of security issues. The attention that Windows NT garners, however, does have a positive side; over the years, Microsoft has implemented security patches and major updates addressing Windows NT security issues and thus making Windows NT one of the more secure operating systems available today.

Microsoft refers to security patches as "hot fixes" and to major updates as "service packs." A Windows NT installation without the addition of hot fixes and service packs is very insecure. Some are quick to fault Windows NT (especially from non-Windows NT shops) and Microsoft for this insecurity, but I challenge you to find another operating system that is completely secure "out of the box" and that offers the same functionality.

In order to correct these security shortcomings and properly secure a Windows NT system (or any Windows system for that matter), administrators and system owners must always stay on top of new developments in security vulnerabilities and new fixes released by Microsoft. For instance, they can stay in the loop by monitoring `www.windowsitsecurity.com`, a Web site dedicated to Windows security issues, as well as popular security mailing lists such as Win2KsecAdvice, BestOfSecurity, and BugTraq.

Tools to evaluate Windows NT security

 Using tools to evaluate Windows NT security

Many of the vulnerabilities identified in Windows NT have been followed by the creation of software or scripts to exploit them. Usually, these programs and scripts originate from the security research world, routinely created as proof of concept and testing tools. A small amount of these programs and scripts have come from the hacking community.

Some might think that the creation of these scripts and tools by the research community is unethical. However, in order to properly demonstrate the vulnerability to Microsoft and to properly test the hot fix generated by Microsoft, they are a necessity.

Many of these tools can be used separately to test for one specific issue or another. Some organizations have gone to the trouble of developing software packages, usually available commercially, to automate the testing of multiple issues.

Other useful tools to test Windows NT security include the following:

✦ **L0phtcrack** — Available at `www.l0pht.com`, this tool is used to test the strength of Windows NT passwords. A fifteen-day trial of L0phtcrack is available for free, but it is definitely worthwhile to purchase a licensed copy.

✦ **Whisker** — Available at `www.wiretrip.net/rfp`, this tool is used to scan Web servers for CGI vulnerabilities. Whisker is a freeware Perl script that does not scan for specific NT vulnerabilities but is a good tool for testing Web servers. It also covers some important Windows NT-specific issues.

✦ **Nmap** — Available at `www.insecure.org` (and covered in Chapter 8), this tool is useful for identifying open TCP and UDP ports on a Windows NT system.

✦ **Legion** — Available at `www.technotronic.com` and `http://packetstorm.securify.com`, this tool is used to scan for and identify NetBIOS shares.

✦ **BV Control for Internet Security (formerly named HackerShield)** — Available at `www.bindview.com`, this commercial product will scan Windows NT systems' known vulnerabilities and give administrators the ability to identify what service packs and hot fixes are installed on the system.

Windows NT security architecture

A basic understanding of the underlying architecture of Windows NT is required to properly grasp security issues and their impact. Because Microsoft designed Windows NT with security in mind, security is the primary goal of its architecture.

There are six broad elements with which to achieve the appropriate security implementation for a given system: corporate security policy, user authentication, encryption, access control, audit, and administration. Windows NT contains built-in support for user authentication, access control, administration, and auditing. By design, Windows NT attempts to prevent the circumvention of security settings through these parameters.

Tip A good rule to consider is to only grant legitimate users access to resources that they require to do their jobs properly.

Components of Windows NT security

For the purpose of the CIW security exam, the components of Windows NT Security as they apply to the C2 Security Certification, discussed earlier in this chapter, are as follows:

✦ *Discretionary access control* enables an object's owner to control who can access the object and how that access occurs.

✦ *Object reuse* prevents all system applications from accessing information contained in any resource, such as memory or disk, that another application has used. This is why Windows NT does not include the functionality to undelete files.

✦ *Mandatory log on* is the Windows NT feature that forces users to log in to either the local machine or a domain controller. Other Microsoft operating systems provide the functionality of user authentication but do not prevent network resource access like Windows NT does.

✦ *Auditing* is the mechanism that Windows NT uses to monitor access to resources. Under Windows NT, auditing can be customized to monitor specific resources.

✦ *Access control* to objects is the process Windows NT uses to disallow direct access to any resource in the system. This mechanism allows specific access control to resources.

Windows NT objects

Microsoft designed Windows NT to handle all resources of any type in the system as specific objects. These objects contain the resource itself, as well as the mechanism and programs necessary to access it. The process works by encapsulating everything as objects and creating a single mechanism to use them. By doing this, Microsoft has created a single avenue for controlling access to objects. Thus, Windows NT is sometimes referred to as an object-based operating system.

The following object principles are the basis of Windows NT security:

✦ Objects represent all resources.

✦ Only Windows NT can directly access these objects.

✦ Objects may contain both data and functions.

✦ The Windows NT security subsystem verifies all access to objects.

✦ Several object types exist and determine what individual objects can do.

The primary Windows NT object types are as follows:

✦ Files

✦ Folders

✦ Printers

✦ I/O devices

✦ Windows

✦ Threads

✦ Processes

✦ Memory

The Windows NT architecture is designed to be consistent and, in theory, because all objects can only be accessed one way, the chance that the security mechanism can be bypassed is diminished.

Security components

The Windows NT security subsystem is made up of five key components: security identifiers, access tokens, security descriptors, access control lists, and access control entries. All five of these components can be used to control users' actions on both local machines and network resources.

Security identifiers

Security identifiers (SIDs) are statistically unique numbers that are assigned to each user. Every time a new user ID or group ID is created, a new SID is also created for that ID. The SID identifies the user, group, or machine on both the local computer and during communications with other resources on the network.

SID uniqueness is ensured with a formula combination of computer name, current time, and the amount of time the current user mode thread has spent using CPU time.

A SID looks like the following:

```
S-1-2-34-5678901234-5678901234-567
```

 Exam Tip   For the purpose of this exam, it is important to understand the different aspects of SIDs as they are explained throughout this book.

Access tokens

Access tokens are issued to users after they authenticate on any given resource. The token is made up of the user name, group membership names, user's SID, and the SIDs of any groups that the user belongs to.

The access token is used to access system resources. When a user attempts to access resources, the access token is given, and the resource checks the token against an access control list. If the user has the correct permissions, access is granted.

 Tip   The access token is issued during authentication. Any changes to a user's access levels require the user to log out and then back in to enable the new rights.

Security descriptors

Security descriptors hold an object's security setting. Every object in Windows NT has a security descriptor. The descriptor is made up of the object owner's SID, a group SID for use by the POSIX subsystem, a discretionary access control list, and a system access control list.

Access control lists

Access control lists (ACLs) are broken down into two different types: discretionary and system. The discretionary access control list holds a list of users, groups, and their appropriate permissions. Each user or group with specific permissions is listed in the discretionary access control list. The system access control list contains the audit information for each user and resource.

Access control entries

Access control entries are made up of the user's or group's SID and permission to an object. An access control entry exists for every object. Access control entries are made up of two types: AccessAllowed or AccessDenied. AccessDenied outweighs AccessAllowed, which means that even if a user is in a group that is allowed access, if that user is specifically named to be denied access, he will not be able to access the object.

Windows NT security subsystem

In Windows NT, the security infrastructure is known as the *security subsystem*. The security subsystem is made up of the following parts:

✦ Winlogon

✦ Graphical Identification and Authentication DLL (GINA)

✦ Local Security Authority (LSA)

✦ Security Support Provider Interface

✦ Authentication packages

✦ Security support providers

✦ Netlogon Server

✦ Security Account Manager (SAM)

Winlogon and Local Security Authority

Two of the subsystem parts, Winlogon and LSA, are shown in the Windows NT task manager, whereas the other parts consist of DLL files that are called upon and loaded by the Winlogon and LSA processes.

Winlogon is responsible for loading the GINA DLL and for monitoring the Secure Authentication Sequence. The GINA DLL provides the logon interface for the user. GINA was designed to be independent and can be replaced by a stronger authentication system if required.

During the logon process, Winlogon will look at the following Registry key to see if a value for GINA DLL exists:

```
HKLM\Software\Microsoft\WindowsNT\CurrentVersion\Winlogon
```

If no value exists, the default GINA DLL, MSGINA.DLL, is used.

The Local Security Authority (LSA) is a protected subsystem responsible for multiple tasks, such as the following:

✦ Loading of all authentication packages

✦ Retrieving any local group SIDs and user rights for the user

✦ Creating the user's access token

✦ Managing the service accounts used by locally installed services

✦ Storing and mapping user rights

✦ Managing the audit policy and settings

✦ Managing trust relationships

Security support tools

The security support provider interface was designed as specified in RFC 2743 and RFC 2744 and is responsible for providing a way for applications and services to request secure authenticated connections.

The authentication package provides the actual user authentication by verifying the information supplied through the GINA DLL and returning the SID to the LSA so it can be included in the access token.

Windows NT includes three security support drivers with the operating system, but other third-party drivers can be used. The security support drivers can be installed to support additional authentication methods.

The three included drivers are as follows:

✦ **MSNSSPC.DLL** — The Microsoft Network (MSN) challenge/response authentication scheme.

✦ **MSAPSSPC.DLL** — The distributed password authentication challenge/response scheme, which is also used by MSN.

✦ **SCHANNEL.DLL** — The authentication scheme used by certificates issued by certificate authorities such as VeriSign. This authentication is used during SSL and private communication protocol communications.

Netlogon Server

Netlogon is used to establish a secure channel for pass-through authentication. To do so, it locates a domain controller with which to establish the secure channel, passes the user's credentials, and receives the SID and user rights from the domain controller.

Security Account Manager

The Security Account Manager (SAM) is a database of users and their credentials. SAM is stored in the Registry itself. Every machine has its own SAM database.

UNIX and Linux Security

 Identifying general threats to Unix systems

The UNIX equivalent of the Windows NT Registry is a series of text files and memory resident applications. For the purpose of the exam, I will not analyze the UNIX architecture in this chapter but only discuss some general UNIX security issues.

Other than poorly configured systems, one of the most common threats to UNIX and Linux systems are buffer overflows. A buffer overflow occurs when a user or process attempts to place more data into a buffer or fixed array than was originally allocated.

Some buffer overflows cause the system to crash; others allow the execution of arbitrary commands, giving an attacker root access.

 For more detailed information on the various buffer overflows that have been found in UNIX and Linux and how to secure against them, refer to Chapter 10.

Key Point Summary

This chapter reviews the need for security in UNIX and Windows NT environments, including the following:

✦ Industry evaluation criteria used for security, such as ITSEC, TCSEC, and Common Criteria

✦ Guidelines for determining general security levels and mechanisms used to implement security systems

✦ The three different areas of security management, as well as Windows NT security, tools used to evaluate NT security, and the Windows NT security architecture

✦ UNIX and Linux security and the threat of buffer overflows

✦   ✦   ✦

STUDY GUIDE

This Study Guide consists of five assessment questions, one scenario, and one lab exercise to test your knowledge of the material contained in this chapter. The answers are presented in the "Answers to Chapter Questions" section at the end of the chapter.

Assessment Questions

1. Windows NT is compliant with the _____ system security level.

   A. A1

   B. B1

   C. C1

   D. C2

   E. D

2. What type of access control list stores audit information?

   A. Discretionary

   B. User

   C. System

   D. Secure

3. What type of access control list stores user and group permissions?

   A. Discretionary

   B. User

   C. System

   D. Secure

4. Which of the following is an example of a Windows NT SID?

   A. JSmith-1-2-34-5678901234-5678901234-567

   B. SID-1-2-34-5678901234-5678901234-567

   C. S-1-2-34-5678901234-5678901234-567

   D. JSmith

5. Which of the following is NOT a Windows NT object?

    A. File

    B. Process

    C. Floppy drive

    D. Printer

    E. Memory

Scenario

You are an administrator at a local real estate office. You get permission to install Windows NT as a corporate server. The server is connected to the Internet and will house all the corporate documents. You install Windows NT on the system and upgrade it with Service Pack 2. Is the system now secure from attack? If you answer No, what additional steps should you have taken to secure the system?

Lab Exercise

Lab 9-1 Using L0phtCrack 2.5 on a Windows NT system to test its password security

1. Download and install L0phtCrack 2.5 from `www.l0pht.com`.

2. Choose the `Dump Password from Registry` option from the Tools menu.

3. Enter the name of a Windows NT server on your network using the `\\servername` format and click OK.

4. The server will be contacted and the usernames downloaded from its Registry.

5. To crack the passwords, choose the `Run Crack` option from the Tool menu. The amount of time it takes to crack the passwords will depend on the number of accounts and the complexity of the passwords.

Answers to Chapter Questions

Chapter Pre-Test

1. **False.** Although Windows NT can be a secure operating system, it needs to be configured as such.

2. **True.**

3. **False.** Windows NT must be configured for C2-compliance. There is a utility in the Windows NT Server Resource Kit to accomplish this.

4. **False.** Windows NT uses a SID to identify each user or group.

5. **True.**

Assessment Questions

1. **D.** Windows NT can be configured to be C2-compliant. For more information, see the section titled "Why is Security So Important?"

2. **C.** Audit information is stored in the System ACL. For more information, see the section titled "Access Control Lists."

3. **A.** User and group permissions are stored in the Discretionary ACL. For more information, see the section titled "Access Control Lists."

4. **C.** S-1-2-34-5678901234-5678901234-567 is an example of a SID. For more information, see the section titled "Security Components."

5. **C.** A floppy drive is not a Windows NT object. For more information, see the section titled "Windows NT 'Out of the Box' Security."

Scenario Question

The answer would be a resounding NO. Service Pack 2 for Windows NT was notoriously flawed. It caused more security holes than it fixed. To protect the system as much as possible, Service Pack 6a should be applied followed by the newest service packs for all the applications running on the server and any relevant Hot Fixes that were released after Service Pack 6a.

For More Information

For more information on the topics covered in this chapter, visit the following sites:

✦ **L0phtCrack** — www.l0phtcrack.com. A tool for testing username/password combination on your Windows NT system.

✦ **Whisker** — www.wiretrip.net/rfp. A tool for scanning Web servers for CGI vulnerabilities.

✦ **ITSEC** — www.itsec.gov.uk.

✦ **TCSEC** — www.radium.ncsc.mil.

✦ **Common Criteria** — csrc.nist.gov/cc.

Operating System Hardening

EXAM OBJECTIVES

- ✦ Implement operating system bug fixes and patches
- ✦ Understand the Windows NT Registry and its security
- ✦ Describe the process of controlling Windows NT and UNIX Services and Daemons
- ✦ Understand how to use audit logs in Windows NT to monitor your systems

CHAPTER PRE-TEST

1. All Windows NT Services are secure. True or false?

2. The C2Config tool is a great starting point for securing your Windows NT and UNIX systems. True or false?

3. Although UNIX services tend to be more secure than those for Windows NT, they still have security holes. True or false?

4. There is a way to physically remove installed services from Windows NT. True or false?

5. It is not recommended to audit every successful and failed event under Windows NT. True or false?

✦ Answers to these questions can be found at the end of the chapter. ✦

In a perfect world, operating systems would be easy to secure, and once secured, they would never be compromised. But this is the real world, and systems simply don't function that way. Therefore, the system administrator takes on the additional role of a security officer. The administrator must ensure that operating systems remain secure in the event of any and all security flaws and holes that may come to light.

This chapter introduces some of the tasks that need to be performed — and the tools to perform them with — to ensure that your Windows NT and UNIX systems remain protected from potential internal and external attacks from hackers.

OS Patches, Fixes, Uprevs, and Updates

As operating system security holes and flaws are discovered, the operating system vendors will release bug fixes and patches. The size and complexity of the fixes and patches depend on the "size" of the security hole. The more complex the repair of the hole, the larger the fix. It is important to understand the differences between a fix and a patch.

A bug fix repairs the security hole or flaw. The reason for the security hole is detected and then corrected. Once the bug fix has been applied, the security hole can no longer be used to gain unauthorized access to the network or system.

A patch, however, is more of a band-aid solution than a true fix. The patch will temporarily secure the hole until a more permanent solution can be found. That permanent solution is the bug fix.

Because operating systems tend to be fairly large complex systems, new security holes are found almost every day. Therefore, a large number of bug fixes and patches may be available. For this reason, vendors usually recommend that not all bug fixes and patches be applied. Instead, only the fixes and patches that directly correspond to security holes in applications and components that exist on your systems should be applied. For example, if a server does not run Microsoft's Internet Information Server (IIS), then any fixes and patches for IIS need not be applied.

Each vendor maintains a database of the available patches and bug fixes. The administrator must monitor these databases (they are usually available on the Internet or through a mailing list). The following sections introduce the terms used for Windows NT and Linux operating systems.

Microsoft service packs and hot fixes

Windows NT 4.0 Server is a huge operating system made up of millions of lines of code, developed by hundreds of different programmers. Not surprisingly, Windows NT has its fair share of bugs and security holes, but most of these bugs do not affect the security of your Windows NT systems. Unfortunately, just one security hole can bring down your system or endanger your network.

Microsoft releases bug fixes in one of two methods: service packs (SPs) and hot fixes. Service packs are fairly major operating system updates. Each subsequent SP contains all the bugs fixed in the previous SPs and hot fixes. Service packs do not need to be installed in the order in which they were released. For example, the current SP (as of this writing) for Windows NT 4.0 is Service Pack 6a (although Service Pack 7 is currently being developed). When a new system is installed with Windows NT, all the administrator has to do to apply all the bug fixes and patches released until the newest SP is apply SP 6a.

Until recently, SPs included not only fixes and patches, but also program enhancements and features (such as more advanced utilities and tools). For example, Service Pack 5 gave Windows NT systems the ability to recognize the new NTFS file system for the next version of the Windows NT family of products, Windows 2000. This addition of features and enhancements, however, greatly increased the size of the service packs. In fact, it was not uncommon for a service pack to be 30 or more megabytes in size. After many administrators complained, Microsoft promised to make two versions of the service packs available: a service pack containing all the fixes and patches, and a service pack containing all the fixes, patches, enhancements, and features. Administrators can now choose which versions they wish to install on their system.

Service packs only come out every 12 to 18 months. Unfortunately, security holes are found at a much faster rate. To solve this problem, Microsoft releases hot fixes on a regular basis. Hot fixes repair a single operating system bug or security hole. Not all hot fixes need to be applied; only the ones that pertain to the tasks performed by your systems. Additionally, hot fixes must be installed in a very specific order, or the system can become unstable.

The Windows NT service packs are available from the Microsoft Web site located at www.microsoft.com/ntserver; the hot fixes are available at the Microsoft FTP site at ftp.microsoft.com/bussys/winnt/winnt-public/fixes.

Both the service packs and hot fixes tend to replace system files. The newer service packs (those released after SP 5) include an option to back up the old (replaced) file. Always choose the backup option to ensure that if the system becomes unstable after the SP installation, it can be recovered from the backed up files. Hot fixes, however, do not provide this functionality, so back up the system before applying any hot fixes.

Caution Almost every hot fix requires the system be rebooted. Do not install multiple hot fixes without rebooting between their application. If you don't reboot, the system may become unstable or may not start upon rebooting.

UNIX patches and fixes

The varied UNIX vendors offer many different versions of the same patches and fixes, and each has a different method for applying them. Each vendor also assigns different names for these patches and fixes. Solaris, for example, calls them Security Patches, whereas Red Hat Linux calls them Errata.

 Tip Solaris' Security Patches and Red Hat Linux's Errata are essentially the same. They are both a collection of bug fixes and patches that help protect the operating system from any new security holes. The Red Hat Linux Errata can be found at www.redhat.com/corp/support/errata.

As with the Windows NT service packs and hot fixes, you should back up the system before applying UNIX patches and bug fixes, as they replace important operating system files.

Securing the Windows Registry

In previous versions of Windows (before Windows NT 4.0 and Windows 95) all configuration information about the operating system and its environment was stored in .INI files. Every component in Windows and every application either had their own .INI file or had a section on a shared .INI file, such as the Win.ini or System.ini files. This not only made Windows difficult to configure, but difficult to secure.

With the 32-bit versions of Windows (Windows NT 4.0 and Windows 95) Microsoft opted to store all of this system and application configuration information in a new database known as the Registry. This central repository of configuration information not only simplified control over the system and its settings, but allowed security to be applied to each component within the Registry.

Figure 10-1 illustrates how the Microsoft Registry Editor distinguishes between secured and unsecured sections of the Registry. Note that the Security and SAM containers have a gray color associated with them, whereas the rest are black. This gray color denotes that security settings are applied. By default, only the Security and SAM containers are secured.

Administrators make legitimate changes to the Registry on a daily basis — not by editing it directly, but by using built-in control panels. Most administrators secure their file systems using NTFS permissions but neglect to do the same with the Registry (although the process of securing the Registry is very similar).

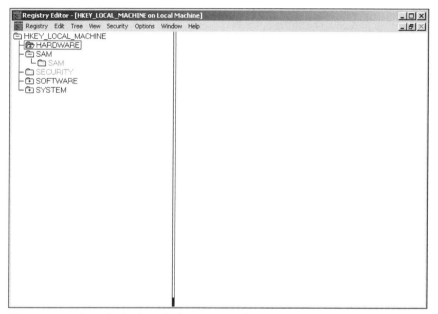

Figure 10-1: Security in the Windows NT Registry

Many of the security exploits that exist today take advantage of the lack of security (by default) in the Windows Registry. Hackers access and modify entries in the Registry that have not been secured properly.

Although securing the Registry is a relatively easy task, knowing which parts of the Registry to secure and what levels of security to assign to those parts is not. As of this writing, Microsoft hasn't published any complete documents on which portions of the Registry need to be secured.

Registry overview and structure

As previously mentioned, the Registry is a database that stores all the configuration and security information for the Windows NT system. In fact, the Registry is a set of databases rather than a single database. Copies of some of these databases are stored in the %winroot%\System32\Config folder on the Windows NT system. The remaining databases are stored in the system's memory.

Should a system's security be overcome and the system attacked, these settings can be used to help recover the system during such a system failure. The Rdisk.exe command is executed to create a backup of the Registry, which is saved to the %winroot%\system32\Repair folder and can then be copied to a floppy disk that is known as the Emergency Repair Disk (ERD). The ERD can then be used to attempt recovery of a failed Windows NT system using the R option in the Windows NT Setup program.

Because copies of some of the Registry databases exist in both the Config and Repair folders, you should make sure that they are secured using Windows NT's NTFS permissions.

Caution Editing the Registry is not for the inexperienced. One wrong move and the system can be rendered inoperable. Exercise extreme caution when manually editing the Registry, and use the control panels for all possible settings. In other words, if you don't know what the Registry setting you are modifying does and how it is configured, don't touch it.

Windows NT ships with two versions of the Registry Editor, Regedit.exe and Regedt32.exe. These two applications do not appear in any of the Start menus by default (so that regular users are not automatically given access to them) and must be executed from either the Command Prompt or from the Run dialog box. Figure 10-2 shows Regedit.exe, the Windows 95 version of the Registry Editor. Notice that you cannot modify security permissions on the Registry, because the Windows 95 version of the Registry cannot be secured using permissions.

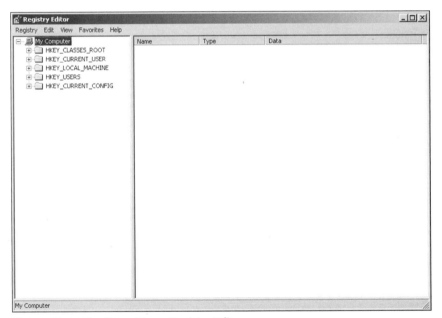

Figure 10-2: The Regedit.exe Registry Editor

Microsoft includes the Regedit.exe version of the Registry Editor in Windows NT (even though it does not perform all the desired tasks) for the following reasons:

✦ The Regedit application has much better search capabilities and options when compared to the Regedt32 application. Regedit enables you to search for Keys, Values, and Data (explained later in this section), whereas Regedt32 can only search for Keys.

✦ With the Regedit application, you can import and export Registry keys enabling you to easily transfer Registry entries from one system to another.

The Regedt32 Registry Editor, shown in Figure 10-3, gives you several options that are not available on its Windows 95 counterpart.

✦ Regedt32 can be configured in Read-Only mode to prevent users from modifying the Registry.

✦ Loading and unloading large portions of the Registry is possible with this tool.

✦ Regedt32 can be used to secure each of the components in the Registry.

The Registry is subdivided into five main sections, also known as subtrees. Table 10-1 lists each of the subtrees, their acronym, and a description of the information they store.

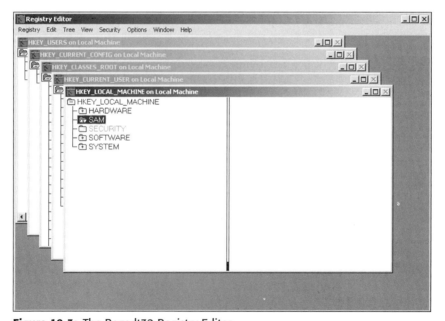

Figure 10-3: The Regedt32 Registry Editor

Table 10-1
The Registry Subtrees

Subtree	Acronym	Description
HKEY_LOCAL_MACHINE	HKLM	This subtree contains all configuration information for this system. Data within this subtree includes all the services that are currently installed on the system and how they are configured, all device drivers and their configurations, and all software configuration information.
HKEY_USERS	HKU	This subtree contains two different subkeys: Default and one described by a Security Identifier (SID). The Default subkey contains all the information that is to be used when a user presses the Ctrl+Alt+Delete keys to log onto the system. The SID subkey contains all the configuration information for the user that is currently logged onto the system.
HKEY_CURRENT_USER	HKCU	This subtree is actually the same subkey as HKU\SID. Any information modified here will also be modified in the HKU subkey. This configuration information is stored locally on the system in the user's profile directory (%winroot%\profiles\username) in the NTUser.Dat file.
HKEY_CLASSES_ROOT	HKCR	This subtree contains all information used for backwards-compatibility with previous applications and all file extension mappings. This is simply a pointer to HKLM\Software\Classes.
HKEY_CURRENT_CONFIG	HKCC	The HKCC subtree contains all information about the current hardware profile. This information is collected from the SOFTWARE and SYSTEM subkeys of the HKLM subtree.

The most important subtree in the Registry is the HKLM subtree, since it stores most of the configuration information for the Windows NT operating system. Table 10-2 lists the five subkeys that exist within the HKLM subtree and their descriptions.

Table 10-2
The HKEY_LOCAL_MACHINE Subtrees

Subtree	Description
Hardware	This subkey contains all the hardware information for any devices currently installed on the system. This subkey is dynamically built every time the system boots up.
SAM	The Security Accounts Manager (SAM) subkey contains the user account and password information for the users logging onto the system.
Security	All security information about this system is stored in this subkey.
Software	All application configuration information is stored in this subkey. Anytime a new application is installed, assuming that it is Windows NT- or 95-aware, it will create a new subkey in the Software subkey and store its configuration information.
System	This subkey stores all device and service information for the system.

Registry security defaults

As previously mentioned, the Registry can be secured using the Regedt32 Registry Editor application. Table 10-3 lists the 10 different permissions that can be specified on any part of the Registry.

Table 10-3
The Registry Permissions

Permission	Description
Query Value	Allows for the value of an entry to be read.
Set Value	Allows for the value of an entry to be set.
Create Subkey	Allows for the creation of a subkey.
Enumerate Subkey	Allows for the objects contained within a subkey to be listed.
Notify	Allows for the setting of audit notification events to be set to an object.
Create Link	Allows for a symbolic link to a Registry key to be created.
Delete	Allows for the deletion of a key.
Write DAC	Allows for the Discretionary ACL of the key to be modified. Similar to the Change Permissions right in NTFS permissions.

Permission	Description
Write Owner	Allows a user or group to take ownership of a key. Similar to the Take Ownership right in NTFS permissions.
Read Control	Allows for the security information of a key to be displayed.

Dealing with Unnecessary Windows Services

The creation of Windows NT marked Microsoft's first real entry into the Network Operating System market. In order to compete and take market share away from the current leaders, Microsoft made Windows NT easy to use, inexpensive when compared to their competitors, and extremely robust. Windows NT, therefore, comes preconfigured with components that are not used in most installation. These components are known as Services.

Windows Services overview

Services are mini-applications or tasks that the server performs. Instead of appearing as actual applications, these Services run in the background. This is how Windows NT differs from Windows 98, for example. Most applications that are designed to run on Windows NT systems have their own services. Therefore, when an administrator or user installs more applications or components (both from Microsoft and third-party vendors), more Services get installed on the system.

You can modify Windows NT in several different ways so that unnecessary or unwanted Services are removed or disabled. The remainder of this section deals with the removal of a Service from the Windows NT operating system; the next two sections will look at disabling services using the Windows NT Network and Service control applets and the C2Config utility respectively.

Caution Make sure you have a good backup before forcibly removing Services from Windows NT. Removing built-in Windows NT Services is a permanent, one-way process. The only way to recover deleted Services is either from a backup or by re-installing the operating system.

The easiest way to forcibly remove a Windows NT Service is to use the SC command. The SC command allows an administrator to find which file or files on the system make up the Service and then remove the Service from the Registry.

The following example deals with one of the most common Services used for attack on Windows NT systems (mostly because it runs with full System permissions), the Scheduler Service. Enter the following command:

```
sc qc schedule
```

The SC program will return a response similar to the following output:

```
[SC] GetServiceConfig SUCCESS

SERVICE_NAME: schedule
 TYPE : 10 WIN32_OWN_PROCESS
 START_TYPE : 2 AUTO_START
 ERROR_CONTROL : 1 NORMAL
 BINARY_PATH_NAME : C:\WINNT\system32\AtSvc.exe
 LOAD_ORDER_GROUP :
 TAG : 0
 DISPLAY_NAME : Schedule
 DEPENDENCIES :
 SERVICE_START_NAME : LocalSystem
```

This output notifies the administrator of a few important items. The executable file for the Service is the AtSvc.exe file stored in the c:\winnt\system32 folder. Also, the service is set to start automatically, has no dependent services, and runs under the LocalSystem security context.

You can now delete the Service by issuing the following command:

```
sc delete schedule
```

You should get an output similar to

```
[SC] Delete Service SUCCESS
```

Because the executable controlling this Service is no longer needed, you can remove it by issuing the following command:

```
Del c:\winnt\system32\AtSvc.exe
```

The Schedule Service is now removed from the Registry and from the system completely. This process can be used to remove any Service from the system.

Using the Network and Services applets

To many administrators, physically removing a Service permanently from the operating system is a scary thought. Luckily, you do not have to go to such drastic measures if you prefer not to. Instead, you can simple disable the Service so that is does not start by itself or by another Service by using the Network and Services control panel applets.

The Network control panel

Many Services, such as the FTP and World Wide Web Services, are installed as optional components in Windows NT. If these are not necessary, you can remove them by using the Network control panel.

The Network control panel has a Services tab associated with it that lists all option-ally installed network components. Select the Services tab, highlight the unwanted Service, and click the Remove button to remove the Service. Under normal opera-tions, you will need to reboot Windows NT before you can remove any Services.

The Services control panel

If the Service to be disabled is not listed in the Services tab of the Network control panel or a reboot is not desired, it can be disabled using the Services control panel applet.

The Services control panel applet lists all the services currently installed on the system, their current state (running, paused, or stopped), their startup mode (auto-matic, manual, or disabled), and their security context (either running as the LocalSystem account or as a specific user). Of most interest in this case is the startup mode.

Setting a Service to manual will leave the Service stopped when the operating sys-tem starts in all instances unless an application or another Service requires it to start. To fully disable a Service, highlight the Service, click the Startup button, select the Disable radio button, and click OK. As long as there are no other Services dependent on this Service, you will be returned to the Services control panel. If dependencies exist, you will be presented with a dialog box listing all the depen-dencies and asking you whether they should be stopped as well.

Disabling a Service rather than deleting it makes the state of the Service easily reversible. If you find yourself in need of the disabled Service, simply enable it.

The following is a recommended list of Services that should be removed or dis-abled from your system:

- ✦ Alerter
- ✦ Clipbook Server
- ✦ Computer Browser
- ✦ DHCP Client
- ✦ Directory Replicator (assuming that this server is not a domain controller)
- ✦ Messenger
- ✦ Remote Procedure Call Locator
- ✦ SNMP Trap Service
- ✦ Spooler (assuming that clients print directly to the printer, rather than through a Windows NT server)
- ✦ TCP/IP NetBIOS Helper
- ✦ Telephony Service

Using the C2Config utility

As mentioned in earlier chapters, Windows NT is C2-compliant. This means that with some changes, Windows NT can become compliant with the C2 level of security. To assist in this compliance, Microsoft released a tool in the Windows NT Server Resource kit known as C2Config. C2Config uses a wizard-like interface to easily meet each of the requirements of C2.

C2Config includes the following options:

- ✦ File System Security
- ✦ OS Configuration
- ✦ OS/2 Subsystem
- ✦ Posix Subsystem
- ✦ Security Log
- ✦ Halt on Audit Failure
- ✦ Display Logon Message
- ✦ Last Username Display
- ✦ Shutdown Button
- ✦ Password Length
- ✦ Guest Account
- ✦ Networking
- ✦ Drive Letters & Printers
- ✦ Removable Media Drives
- ✦ Registry Security
- ✦ File System Security
- ✦ Other Security Items

An administrator can use the C2Config utility to harden an operating system without taking it to the C2 level of compliance. As a really good starting point, run each of the options listed previously except for Halt on Audit Failure, Networking, and Removable Media Drives.

Miscellaneous Windows Security Adjustments

In its relatively short history, Windows NT has been attacked numerous times. The following is a list of recommended adjustments suggested by Microsoft. These modifications are Microsoft's responses to known attacks:

✦ Caching of Logon Credentials

✦ Disabling Known Accounts

✦ Hiding the Username

✦ Printer Drivers

✦ Renaming Known Accounts

✦ Securing Shares

✦ The Pagefile

Each of these modifications is described in the following sections.

Caching of logon credentials

When a Windows NT system takes part in a domain model, the system relies on the domain controllers to authenticate it. A problem occurs, however, when the domain controllers are not available. To solve this problem, Windows NT will cache the user's logon information so that the user can be logged on if the network is unavailable. Hackers have found ways to recover this cached information.

To disable Windows NT from caching user credentials locally, add a new key called CachedLogonsCount of type REG_DWORD with a value of 0 to HKLM\Microsoft\Windows NT\CurrentVersion\Winlogon subkey in the Registry.

Disabling known accounts

Believe it or not, hackers actually install and play with the operating systems that they hack, so they usually have a good understanding what an OS does and does not do. One feature of Windows NT (and most Network Operating Systems [NOSs], for that matter) is the creation of a Guest account upon installation. While this Guest account does not have many rights, it also lacks a password.

To ensure that the Guest account is not used to access your network, you should assign it a password that would be difficult to crack, and make sure that the account is disabled.

Hiding the username

To make Windows NT easier to use, Microsoft decided to cache the last user to log onto the system. After the user has logged out of the system, their username is displayed in the logon box. To force Windows NT to clear out that username from the logon box, create a key called DontDisplayLastUserName of type REG_SZ with a value of 1 to the HKLM\Software\Microsoft\CurrentVersion\Winlogon subkey.

Print drivers

Users cannot live without printers. Removing printers from the network, therefore, is not feasible in most organizations. This can cause a problem with Windows NT, because print drivers run with system-level security, giving them full access to the network. Additionally, by default, any Windows NT user can install print drivers on the system. This means that a hacker can create a Trojan horse that appears to be a print driver but actually runs as the system and creates back doors or modifies system information to bring the server down.

To restrict printer driver installation to only Print Operators and Administrators add a key called AddPrintDrivers of type REG_DWORD with a value of 1 to the HKLM\System\CurrentControlSet\Control\Print\Providers\LanMan Print Service subkey.

Renaming known accounts

Hackers are well aware that Windows NT names its administrator account "Administrator." If you do not modify the name of the administrator account, you give the hacker an advantage. In order to log onto the network, you need a username and a password. By not changing the username, you give the hacker half the solution.

To rename the administrator account, follow these steps: create a new account called Administrator, give it no rights, an extremely long and complex password, and then disable it. This will keep the average hacker busy for some time.

Securing shares

By default, shared items under Windows NT (such as serial ports, parallel ports, or USB ports) are accessible to all users. You can restrict accessibility to the Administrators group only. Be ready to reverse this setting should an application complain or cease to function properly, as many applications will attempt to communicate with these shared objects.

To configure shared objects so that only the Administrators group can gain access to them, add a key named ProtectionMode of type REG_DWORD with a value of 1 to the HKLM\System\CurrentControlSet\Control\Session Manager subkey.

The pagefile

Windows NT uses the pagefile as extra memory. By default, when the system is shut down cleanly, the pagefile contents are left untouched. Should someone gain access to that pagefile, they may be able to extract restricted information. Windows NT has a feature that will erase the contents of the pagefile upon shutdown.

To configure Windows NT to clear out the pagefile upon shutdown, add a key named ClearPageFileAtShutdown of type REG_DWORD with a value of 1 to the HKLM\System\CurrentControlSet\Control\Session Manager\Memory Management subkey.

Dealing with Unnecessary UNIX Services

In much the same way that Windows NT uses Services, UNIX uses daemons. Because UNIX systems have been around longer and tend to have a more open architecture than that of Windows NT, many security holes have already been fixed. The wide range of UNIX systems makes it difficult to list each and every daemon that might be running on a UNIX system. Additionally, one version of UNIX may have a security hole with a specific daemon, whereas another does not. To ensure that your UNIX system is secure, apply any required security patches and secure the following services:

✦ Simple Mail Transfer Protocol (SMTP)

✦ Telnet

✦ Trivial File Transfer Protocol (TFTP)

Simple Mail Transfer Protocol

The Sendmail daemon is commonly used for sending e-mail on UNIX systems. Sendmail is the name of the application that brings SMTP to UNIX. A large number of Sendmail versions exist today, with version 8.11 being the most recent (as of this writing).

Although version 8.11 is fairly secure, many earlier versions were not. For example, earlier versions had debugging tools built into the daemon, many of which were later removed. Make sure you are running the most up-to-date version on your UNIX box.

Sendmail can be downloaded from `www.sendmail.com`.

Telnet

Every implementation of UNIX includes the Telnet tool. Most UNIX versions also automatically install and configure the Telnet Daemon, allowing remote users to "telnet" into the system. Telnet opens a session with the server and allows a user to execute commands directly on the server.

If Telnet is a requirement of your organization, make sure you have a strong password policy in place. Should a hacker gain access to your network using Telnet and then gain Root access, your system will be compromised.

Trivial File Transfer Protocol

The Trivial File Transfer Protocol (TFTP) is similar to the File Transfer Protocol, except that it requires no authentication. The main uses for TFTP are to boot diskless computers or to allow routers to pick up their configuration files without having to log into a system. TFTP is not used very often any more — since hackers can access files without having to authenticate on the server — and should be disabled.

Windows System Logging

Like most Network Operating Systems, Windows NT has a logging facility to log pertinent information about its operation. The Security Log logs security-specific information. The following sections introduce Windows NT logging options and the application used to monitor the logs.

Audit policies

Auditing in a Windows NT system will track access on the system. Simply activating auditing, however, does nothing but prepare the system to be audited. You have to choose what is to be audited.

Enable audit policies through the User Manager for Domain utility. Once auditing is enabled, you can audit user events or file and object access. The user events include success, failure, or both on the following events:

✦ Logon and Logoff

✦ File and Object Access

✦ Use of User Rights

✦ User and Group Management

✦ Security Policy Changes

✦ Restart, Shutdown, and System

✦ Process Tracking

As you can imagine, turning on all auditing features will very quickly fill up your log files and make the job of monitoring these logs a tedious and difficult task. Imagine auditing every successful logon and file access. Even on a small network, hundreds or thousands of events will be logged to the system daily.

At a minimum, you should audit all event failures, since that usually indicates either someone trying to gain access to your system or a misconfigured network component. You should probably log the successful User and Group Management, Security Policy Changes, and Restart, Shutdown, and System events.

Directory and file access logging have some different events to log, such as

✦ Read

✦ Write

✦ Execute

✦ Delete

✦ Change Permissions

✦ Take Ownership

While the user events are universal (for example, all users get audited), the file events are created on each file and/or folder. A user or group must be selected and the events to audit assigned to that user.

Working with Event Viewer

Once auditing has been enabled on your system, you need to monitor the logged information. Luckily, Windows NT includes a fairly functional tool, the Event Viewer, for performing this task.

The Event Viewer is included as one of the default Administrative tools and can be used to monitor and archive the information collected for the Application, System, and Security logs.

Key Point Summary

This chapter introduces you to some methods for securing your Windows NT and UNIX systems. Although this discussion is in no way comprehensive, it is an excellent starting point. The following points were covered:

✦ Windows NT has service packs that contain a large number of OS and security fixes, patches, and enhancements. Hot fixes are temporary fixes that are applied for a specific problem between service pack releases. On the UNIX side, each vendor has their own naming convention for these fixes, but all major vendors maintain the fixes online.

✦ One of the main security exploits in Windows NT is an application that modifies the Registry. This chapter introduces some of the tools used for editing the Registry (such as RegEdit and RegEdt32), as well as applying security.

✦ Several ways exist to deal with unwanted or unnecessary Services in Windows NT. You can physically remove Services using the SC command, remove them using the Network control panel, disable them using the Services control panel, or control them using the C2Config utility.

✦ Windows NT adjustments exist for further securing your network, including print driver, pagefile, and shared object security.

✦ Common UNIX services that pose a security threat and that you should watch out for include SMTP, Telnet, and TFTP.

✦ Finally, we looked at auditing events in Windows NT and monitoring them in the Event Viewer application. Checking these logs on a regular basis is an excellent way to ensure that your system is not being attacked from both internal or external sources.

✦   ✦   ✦

STUDY GUIDE

This Study Guide contains five assessment questions and three lab exercises to test your knowledge of the topics covered in this chapter.

Assessment Questions

1. Which Registry subtree contains the user information?

   A. HKLM

   B. HKU

   C. HKCR

   D. HKCC

2. Which Registry subtree contains current Windows NT configuration information?

   A. HKLM

   B. HKU

   C. HKCU

   D. HKCR

3. Which Registry subtree contains file extension mapping?

   A. HKU

   B. HKCU

   C. HKCR

   D. HKCC

4. Which groups are allowed to install printer drivers by default?

   A. Administrators

   B. Print Operators

   C. Everyone

   D. All of the above

5. In UNIX, what are network applications called?

   A. Services

   B. Components

   C. Daemons

   D. Applets

Lab Exercises

Lab 10-1 Installing a Windows NT Service Pack

1. Download the newest service pack from Microsoft's Web site.

2. Double-click on the downloaded file.

3. Accept the license agreement.

4. Choose the Backup option and click the Install button.

Lab 10-2 Securing the Registry using the C2Config tool

1. Select Start ⇨ Programs ⇨ Resource Kit 4.0 ⇨ Confirmation ⇨ C2.

2. Double-click the Registry Security entry.

3. Click the OK button to secure the Registry.

4. Click the OK button to confirm the process. After a few minutes, the C2Config tool will complete its configuration of the Registry.

Lab 10-3 Auditing user access

1. Select Start ⇨ Programs ⇨ Administrative Tools (Common) ⇨ User Manager for Domains.

2. From the Policy menu, choose Audit Policy.

3. Check any event that is to be audited (for success, failure, or both) and click OK.

Answers to Chapter Questions

Chapter Pre-Test

1. **False.** No matter how many security patches are applied, no Service is ever truly secure.

2. **True.** Although not complete, the C2Config tool is a great place to start.

3. **True.** As stated earlier, no operating system is truly secure.

4. **True.** You can physically remove installed services from Windows NT using the SC command.

5. **True.** Auditing every event under Windows NT will fill up the log files and will make the job of monitoring these logs a nearly impossible task.

Assessment Questions

1. **B.** HKU. For more information, see the section titled, "Registry Overview and Structure."

2. **A.** HKLM. For more information, see the section titled, "Registry Overview and Structure."

3. **C.** HKCR. For more information, see the section titled, "Registry Overview and Structure."

4. **D.** All of the above. For more information, see the section titled, "Print Drivers."

5. **C.** Daemons. For more information, see the section titled, "Dealing with Unnecessary UNIX Services."

For More Information

For more information on the topics covered in this chapter, visit the following sites:

✦ Windows NT/2000 Tips, Tricks, Registry Hacks, and more. . . . — http://www.jsiinc.com/reghack.htm. A site dedicated to Windows NT and 2000 Registry entries.

✦ *Managing the Windows NT Registry*, Robichaux, Paul, O'Reilly Press, April 1998, ISBN: 1-56592-378-2.

Securing File Systems and Resources

CHAPTER PRE-TEST

1. Windows NT does not have the ability to secure items to the file level, only to the folder level. True or False?

2. Moving files from one folder to another on the same partition does not affect its permissions. True or False?

3. When both NTFS and Share permissions are used on a folder, the least restrictive becomes the Effective permission. True or False?

4. Share permissions are more flexible than NTFS permissions. True or False?

5. Converting from FAT to NTFS is a one-way process. True or False?

Windows NT employs several methods for securing files. This chapter will introduce you to the difference between NTFS and Share permissions and explain how Windows NT handles permissions when they are combined.

Understanding File System Security Issues

One of the limitations of the Microsoft operating systems designed for the home user (such as Windows 95, Windows 98, and Windows Me) is that little or no security is available. You can test this limitation yourself by pressing the Escape key at the login prompt. The login will be aborted and the operating system desktop will appear. While you may not have access to the network, you have complete access to any and all files on the system.

The reason for this is simple. Windows 95, 98, and Me use either the File Allocation Table (FAT) or FAT32 file systems for writing and storing information on the hard drive. Neither of these file systems allows file- and folder-level permissions to be set. Therefore, anyone that gains access to the system automatically gains access to all the files and folders on that system. In fact, FAT is the most widely used file system in the world. Nearly every one of today's operating system can read and write to it.

Microsoft was well aware of this file system limitation when they developed Windows NT. They knew that no organization would implement a Network Operating System (NOS) that did not allow for individual files and folders to be protected from unauthorized access. A new file system, the Windows NT File System (NTFS) was developed. NTFS has several powerful features, including the aforementioned file- and folder-level security, the ability to compress individual files and folders on the fly (meaning that the files are uncompressed as soon as they are accessed and re-compressed when they are no longer being used), and the ability to self-heal, thereby protecting the system from errors on the hard disk.

You can implement NTFS on a Windows NT system in several ways:

✦ By formatting a new partition using NTFS during the installation process of Windows NT

✦ By converting an existing FAT partition to NTFS using the Windows NT Convert command

Tip   The FAT to NTFS conversion is a one-way process. The only "built-in" way to convert back is to reformat the partition. There are, however, third-party tools to accomplish this in a less destructive way.

Securing NTFS

The process of actually assigning NTFS permissions to files and folders simply uses the familiar Windows Explorer interface. Assigning permissions properly, however, is another matter. Before you can fully understand the implications of multiple permissions for multiple users and groups, you must understand the individual permissions themselves.

Understanding NTFS permissions

NTFS permissions can be divided into two similar but distinct sections: file and folder permissions. Six permissions exist at the file level:

✦ Read

✦ Write

✦ Execute

✦ Delete

✦ Change Permissions

✦ Take Ownership

These permissions are explained in greater detail in Table 11-1.

Table 11-1 The NTFS File-Level Permissions	
NTFS Permission	**Description**
Read (R)	Allows you to view a file, its attributes, and its permissions.
Write (W)	Allows you to view the owner and permissions assigned to a file, and modify its attributes or data.
Execute (X)	Allows you to run a file (assuming that it is an executable file) and view the file's attributes and permissions.
Delete (D)	Allows you to delete the file.
Change Permissions (P)	Allows you to modify the file's permissions.
Take Ownership (O)	Allows you to take ownership of the file and make it your own.

These same six permissions can be applied to folders on an NTFS partition, although they differ slightly from their file permission counterparts. Table 11-2 explains these differences.

Table 11-2
The NTFS Folder-Level Permissions

NTFS Permission	Description
Read (R)	Allows you to view the folder, its attributes, and its permissions.
Write (W)	Allows you to view the owner and permissions assigned to a folder, modify its attributes, and add files to the folder.
Execute (X)	Allows you to modify subfolders within this folder and view the folder's attributes and permissions.
Delete (D)	Allows you to delete the folder.
Change Permissions (P)	Allows you to modify the folder's permissions.
Take Ownership (O)	Allows you to take ownership of the folder and make it your own.

These six permissions can be used in any combinations that you desire. When this is done, Windows will display the permission as "Special Access" (see Figure 11-1).

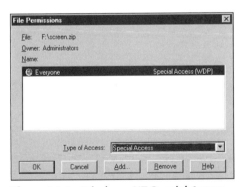

Figure 11-1: Windows NT Special Access

To simplify administration, Microsoft created combinations of these six permissions that make more sense. These permissions are known as *standard permissions* — five when dealing with files and seven when dealing with folders. Table 11-3 lists the file-level standard permissions.

Table 11-3
The NTFS Standard File Permissions

Standard Permission	NTFS Permission Combination
No Access	No Permission
Read	RX
Add and Read	RWX
Change	RWXD
Full Control	RWXDPO

Table 11-4 lists the seven folder-level standard permissions.

Table 11-4
The NTFS Standard Folder Permissions

Standard Permission	NTFS Permission Combination
No Access	No Permission
List	RX
Read	RX
Add	WX
Add and Read	RWX
Change	RWXD
Full Control	RWXDPO

You may have noticed that the default NTFS permission given to most files and folders on a Windows NT system is Full Control to the **Everyone** group. The reason for this is simple. When Microsoft entered the NOS market, they had a lot of catching up to do. Novell had a huge section of the NOS market (up to 85% of the market by some estimations) at the time, and many organizations and administrators were happy with the performance, stability, and features of Novell NetWare. They needed to make Windows NT as easy to use as possible. By configuring little security out of the box, the average user could install and configure a Windows NT system. This was radically different than their nearest competitors, UNIX and Novell NetWare, which required specialized (and usually expensive) consultants to get the systems configured.

The Full Control to the Everyone group can be an extremely dangerous setting, as it allows anyone accessing your system to modify almost everything. Many novice administrators quickly change the Full Control setting to No Access, not realizing that doing so can cause even more problems. The No Access permission in Windows NT is all-powerful. No permission setting can override it. Also, remember that the administrator belongs to the Everyone group. Therefore, if you assign Everyone No Access, the administrator will be denied access as well. You can take ownership of the object and give yourself back the permissions, but this requires an unnecessarily complex process.

To get around this problem, Microsoft defined the following two types of permissions:

✦ **Explicit permissions.** Whatever permissions are assigned are applied. For example, if a user, Joe, is assigned Read access, then the user, Joe, is granted Read access.

✦ **Implicit permissions.** If a user is not explicitly assigned a permission, then they will be implicitly denied. If the same user, Joe, is not given any rights to a folder, then Joe will be implicitly denied access to that folder. Therefore, instead of modifying the Everyone permission to No Access, removing the permission altogether will implicitly deny the Everyone group while allowing any explicit assignments.

Combining NTFS permissions

It is important to know what takes place when a user is granted multiple permissions based on their memberships. For example, assume that the user, Joe, belongs to the Everyone group and to the Sales group. Permissions are set on the Users folder as outlined in Table 11-5.

Table 11-5 Combining NTFS Permissions	
Group or User	*Assigned NTFS Permission*
Joe	Change
Everyone	Read
Sales	Full Control

When combining NTFS permissions from multiple group memberships, remember the following: the Effective NTFS permission is the least restrictive permission. Therefore, in the above example, Joe will be granted Full Control to the Users folder.

This rule holds true until a No Access permission is assigned. No Access always overrides other permissions. If Joe is also a member of the Payroll group, which has been granted the No Access permission, then Joe's effective permission becomes No Access, even though he has Full Control from the Sales group membership. Therefore, the actual rule of thumb is that the Effective NTFS permission is the least restrictive permission unless a No Access permission is assigned, at which point No Access becomes the Effective permission.

Permission-handling for move and copy operations

You can't avoid the fact that computers are constantly changing. As an administrator, you will find that having to move files and folders from one location to another is common. Once your file system is secured using NTFS, you will want to make sure that you understand what happens to those permissions when you change their location.

In situations like this, four different scenarios can occur:

✦ Copy a file or folder to another folder on the same partition.

✦ Move a file or folder to another folder on the same partition.

✦ Copy a file or folder to another folder on a different partition.

✦ Move a file or folder to another folder on a different partition.

Each of these scenarios is covered in the following sections.

Copy a file or folder to another folder on the same partition

Whenever the operating system performs a copy (in other words, writes a copy in the new location), the permissions are inherited from the destination folder. For example, if you copy the Users folder from the C:\File folder (which has the Everyone Full Control permission) to the C:\Data folder (which has the Everyone Read permission), then the Users folder will inherit the Everyone Read permission.

Move a file or folder to another folder on the same partition

When the operating system performs a move, it simply updates the pointer in the file system index. The file or folder is not actually moved, meaning that the file or folder itself does not change its position on the hard drive, only where it appears in the directory listing. You will notice that when you move a large folder from one location on your partition to another, the move occurs almost instantly.

If you were to move the Users folder from the C:\File folder (which has the Everyone Full Control permission) to the C:\Data folder (which has the Everyone Read permission), then the Users folder will retain its Everyone Full Control permission.

Copy a file or folder to another folder on a different partition

As with copying a file or folder within the same partition, copying to a different partition is a copy process, and the file or folder will therefore inherit the permission from the remote folder.

Move a file or folder to another folder on a different partition

If the previously stated rules apply, and you are performing a move process rather than a copy process, the file or folder should maintain its permissions. However, since you are actually writing a new copy of the file or folder in the destination partition and then deleting the original from the originating partition, you are actually performing a copy. Therefore, in this situation, the permissions are inherited from the destination partition.

Windows Share Security

NTFS permissions allow you to control access to files and folders when someone is interacting directly with the system (for example, sitting in front of the computer and typing on the keyboard). To allow access to files and folders on the system from a remote location, Window NT Shares are used. Shares simply broadcast the fact that a specific folder(s) is available on the network. The remote user's system then connects to the share and accesses the information contained within it.

Share permissions

Share permissions are similar to NTFS permissions, except that they are much simpler. In fact, there are only four possible permissions available for shares:

   ✦ No Access

   ✦ Read

   ✦ Change

   ✦ Full Control

Table 11-6 lists these permissions and the access they provide.

Table 11-6
Share Permissions

Permission	Access Provided
No Access	While a user will be able to connect to the share, they will not be able to access its content.
Read	User is allowed to view folders and files within the share, view their attributes, navigate the folder structure, and execute programs.
Change	User is allowed to add files and folders, modify file and folder attributes, modify files, delete files and folders, and all Read permissions.
Full Control	User is allowed to modify the file permissions, take ownership of files and folders that exist on an NTFS volume, and all Change permissions.

Share permissions can only be specified at the top level of the share. The permission that is granted (or denied) there gets inherited by all the subfolders and files within the folder hierarchy. This can cause a security flaw to appear in your structure.

```
C:\ (share: Cdrive)
C:\Users (share: Users)
C:\Data (share: Data)
C:\Data\Payroll (share: Payroll)
C:\Data\HR (share: HR)
```

In this situation, if a user attempts to connect to the Data share and is granted the Full Control permission, the user will be granted that same permission for the Data\Payroll and Data\HR shares, even though those shares may have more restrictive permissions assigned to them.

As with NTFS permissions, when a user belongs to multiple groups that are assigned permissions to a resource, the least restrictive permission will become the Effective permission unless a No Access permission is assigned, at which point the Effective permission will be No Access.

Combining NTFS and Share permissions

To solve the problem described in the previous section, you can combine NTFS and Share permissions. Once these two types of permissions are combined, the most restrictive of the two becomes the Effective permission. For example, a user, Joe, is granted Full Control through NTFS permissions and Read through Share permissions. His Effective permission will then become Read because it is more restrictive than Full Control.

This may seem complex, but in fact, it is not. One recommendation is to only use NTFS permissions and ignore the Share permissions. Since NTFS permissions are more flexible, with more options than Share permissions, simply secure the files and folders using NTFS and share the folder as Everyone Full Control. The most restrictive permission becomes the Effective permission, so the NTFS permission will always become the Effective permission.

Key Point Summary

This chapter introduces you to both NTFS and Share permissions:

✦ NTFS permissions are more flexible than Share permissions. There are six different NTFS permissions: Read, Write, Execute, Delete, Change Permission, and Take Ownership.

✦ When different NTFS permissions are assigned to groups to which a user is a member, the least restrictive permission becomes the Effective permission.

✦ A file system can be converted from FAT to NTFS once. To reverse the process, the partition must be re-created, or a third-party utility must be used.

✦ There are four Share permissions: No Access, Read, Change, and Full Control.

✦ When different Share permissions are assigned to groups to which a user is a member, the least restrictive permission becomes the Effective permission.

✦ When NTFS and Share permissions are combined, the most restrictive of the two becomes the Effective permission.

✦ When files are copied from one folder to another on the same partition, one folder to another on a different partition, or moved to another partition, the permissions are inherited from the destination partition.

✦ When files are moved from one folder to another on the same partition, the permissions are retained.

✦   ✦   ✦

STUDY GUIDE

This Study Guide presents five assessment questions and three lab exercises to test your knowledge of the exam objectives.

Assessment Questions

1. You would like to grant Joe permissions to add files to a folder, as well as change that folder's permissions. Which NTFS rights would you grant? (Choose all that apply)

   A. Read

   B. Write

   C. Change

   D. Take Ownership

2. When both NTFS and Share permissions are applied, what is the effective permission?

   A. Always NTFS

   B. Always Share

   C. Most restrictive

   D. Least restrictive

3. Joe is a member of both the Sales and Marketing groups. He attempts to access a file in the C:\Users directory. He is granted the Read permission, the Sales group is granted the Full Control permission, and the Marketing group is granted the No Access permission. What would be Joe's effective permission?

   A. Read

   B. Full Control

   C. Read/Write

   D. No Access

4. Mary belongs to both the Users and Management groups. She has been granted Full Control to the C:\documents folder. The Users group has been granted Read, and the Management group has been granted Change Permissions. What is Mary's Effective permission?

    A. Read

    B. Change

    C. Full Control

    D. No Access

5. When dealing with multiple share permissions, what becomes the Effective permission?

    A. First one accessed

    B. Least restrictive

    C. Most restrictive

    D. Share permissions does not allow for multiple share permissions.

Lab Exercises

Lab 11-1 Converting a FAT partition to NTFS

1. Select Start ➪ Run.

2. Type `Command` and click OK.

3. Type `Convert` *Drive*`:\ /fs:ntfs` and press Enter (where *Drive* is the FAT partition to be converted).

4. If you are presented with the following message: "Convert cannot gain exclusive access to *Drive:* drive, so it cannot convert it now. Would you like to schedule it to be converted the next time the system restarts (Y/N)?" then press Y. Otherwise, press Y to convert the partition to NTFS.

Lab 11-2 Assigning NTFS permissions on a folder

1. Open Windows Explorer.

2. Create a new folder called NTFSsample.

3. Right-click the newly created folder and choose the Properties from the drop-down list.

4. Choose the Security tab.

5. Click the Permissions button.

6. Add any desired user or group by clicking on the Add button, selecting the user or group, assigning them permissions, and clicking the OK button.

7. Remove any listed user or group by highlighting the desired group and clicking the Remove button, and then clicking the OK button.

Lab 11-3 Creating a Share and assigning it permissions

1. Open Windows Explorer.

2. Create a new folder called Sharesample.

3. Right-click the newly created folder and choose the Sharing option from the drop-down list.

4. Choose the Share As radio button.

5. Enter a name for the share in the Share Name field.

6. Click the Permissions button.

7. Add any desired user or group by clicking the Add button, selecting the user or group, assigning them permissions, and then clicking the OK button.

8. Remove any listed user or group by highlighting the desired group and clicking the Remove button, and then clicking the OK button.

Answers to Chapter Questions

Chapter Pre-Test

1. **False.** Windows NT does have the ability to secure objects down to the file level using NTFS permissions.

2. **True.** Moving files from one folder to another on the same partition does not affect its permissions.

3. **False.** When both Share and NTFS permissions are used, the Effective permission is the most restrictive.

4. **False.** NTFS permissions are more flexible and have more options than Share permissions.

5. **True.** Converting from FAT to NTFS is a one-way process.

Assessment Questions

1. **B, C.** For Joe to be given permission to both add files to a folder and change content, he requires both the Write and Change permissions.

2. **C.** When both Share and NTFS permissions are applied, the most restrictive permission becomes the effective permission.

3. **D.** As Joe is a member of the Marketing group and the Marketing group has the No Access permission assigned to it, Joe will have No Access to the objects.

4. **C.** As permissions are cumulative (except for No Access), Mary will be granted the Full Control permission to the folder.

5. **B.** When dealing with multiple share permissions, the least restrictive permission becomes the effective permission.

For More Information

For more information on the topics covered in this chapter, please visit the following sites:

✦ Microsoft TechNet site. www.microsoft.com/technet. Microsoft's online search engine for Windows NT topics.

✦ Windows NT Server 4.0 Server Resource Kit. *Microsoft Press*. November 1996. ISBN 1572313447

Securing User Accounts

+ Understand the relationship between account security and passwords

+ Explain the different methods to secure accounts under Windows NT

+ Explain the different methods to secure accounts under UNIX

+ Implement password policies under Windows NT

+ Audit changes in accounts

+ Audit unsuccessful logon attempts under Windows NT

+ Rename default accounts under Windows NT

+ Describe UNIX password security

+ Describe UNIX password file format

+ Identify how password aging works and the UNIX commands to accomplish password aging

+ Describe different UNIX security threats

+ Restrict account access and monitor accounts under UNIX

CHAPTER PRE-TEST

1. Identify three types of content that a strong password must contain.

2. Explain where UNIX passwords are stored.

3. Explain where Windows NT passwords are stored.

4. Name two utilities used to enforce strong passwords under Windows NT.

5. Describe how to protect the password file under UNIX.

✦ Answers to these questions can be found at the end of the chapter. ✦

User IDs and passwords are employed to authenticate users who log onto a network on a daily basis. For example, when you use an automatic teller machine, you present your bank card (user ID) and enter your PIN (password). Based on the information provided, the teller knows who you are and what transactions you are authorized to perform. The importance of such a system is obvious. No one would want someone else to access their bank account, let alone make withdrawals or transfers.

The same requirements apply to most network devices and operating systems. For instance, all varieties of UNIX and Windows NT-based operating systems include a simple authentication mechanism to verify each user's identity. As with banks, many companies do not want just anyone browsing the documents and resources on corporate networks, so user IDs and passwords are implemented. Unfortunately, many people must be forced to use a password, and they usually construct one that is easily guessed by others.

Password Security

 Understand the relationship between account security and passwords

Easily guessed passwords or blank passwords (passwords with no characters in them) lead to more system compromise than almost any other security issue. Some of the high-profile credit card database thefts over the last couple of years were the result of blank system administrator passwords on customer databases. The media often reports on hackers who deface a Web site or steal customer information. In reality, these perpetrators probably had low to average computer skills and simply found a blank password or easily guessed password on the network.

Passwords such as "welcome," "password," or "username" are easily guessed. Other common words that appear in the dictionary may not be easily guessed, but can be cracked with a dictionary attack. For example, the password "willow" may not be the first guess of an attacker unless the user account under attack is also named "willow," but a password-cracking program, such as L0phtCrack for Windows NT or Crack for UNIX, could crack the password in seconds.

The best way to prevent password security breaches is to implement a *strong password*—one that contains upper- and lowercase letters, numbers, and even other characters, such as %, !, or *. A strong password is unlikely to be manually guessed by an attacker, taking hours, sometimes days, to break. Keep in mind, however, that with an infinite amount of time—even with limited resources—any password can be cracked. The purpose of strong passwords is to slow an attacker down, or force him to give up, or prevent the password from being cracked before it is changed.

When devising a strong password, obey the following general rules:

✦ Passwords should not be common words or names.

✦ Passwords should not use personal information (such as a birth date).

✦ Passwords should not repeat letters or numbers.

✦ Passwords should not begin or end with a number.

✦ Passwords should be at least eight characters long.

✦ Passwords should expire every 30 days.

Many companies set a time limit of 120 days before passwords expire. Their management doesn't understand the security risk involved, thinking it is inconvenient to change passwords as often as every 45 days. Obviously, these companies need to find a balance between their security policies and their business requirements. Security professionals must educate employees about why shorter password expiration times are better, and be reasonable when deciding on a time period.

An attacker must know a person's user ID before he can attempt to crack the password. If a malicious password cracker is already an authorized user on the network, this is a very easy task because he has some internal access to network resources. An authorized user might want to crack the passwords of his own organization for any number of reasons, including the following:

✦ To read a manager's or co-worker's e-mails

✦ To access human resources records

✦ To access accounting records

✦ To sell marketing plans to competitors

An external attacker with no access to the corporate network can use a number of methods to gather valid user IDs. For one, he can simply gather possible usernames from e-mail addresses. Typically, but not in all cases, an e-mail address contains a person's username, especially if an organization uses employee IDs to assign usernames and e-mail addresses. (For example, you might have 15758@insecuredomain.com as an e-mail address, and a username of 15758 to log into the network.) An obvious recommendation is not to use this system in new implementations. Many medium- and large-sized organizations have assigned passwords this way and are now unable to effectively change to a better, more secure system. Windows NT and Windows 2000 provide multiple ways to collect user lists depending on the system's configuration, and the same goes for most versions of UNIX.

Windows NT Account Security

 Explain the different methods to secure accounts under Windows NT

The Windows NT architecture, explained in Chapter 9, is important to a discussion about authentication and user account security. In User Mode, you will find a number of memory-independent subsystems. The subsystems important to user authentication and account security are Winlogon, Local Security Authority (LSA), and Security Accounts Manager (SAM).

Windows NT authentication

 Audit changes in accounts

Audit unsuccessful logon attempts under Windows NT

Winlogon initiates all logon requests. It sends these requests to the Windows32 subsystem to generate the logon screen where users enter their usernames and passwords. It then sends those usernames and passwords to the security subsystem.

The LSA plays a key role in user authentication, processing the information received from the Windows32 subsystem by sending it to the SAM. The SAM is essentially a database containing the encrypted form of usernames and passwords. The LSA also controls security logging and determines which events will and will not be captured.

Authentication is probably the most critical process in terms of protecting any network operating system. Windows NT makes authentication mandatory by forcing the user to provide what is known as the *secure attention sequence* by pressing Ctrl+Alt+Delete. This process communicates directly with the LSA to help prevent the possibility of a Trojan program being inserted between the Logon screen and the SAM. The LSA will then call on an authentication process. Windows NT has the ability to use multiple authentication packages, but by default uses MSV1_0.

MSV1_0 is a challenge-response mechanism that involves two different parts: the authentication server that contains a copy of the authentication database to be used, and the client itself.

In a nutshell,

1. The client sends a request for authentication to a domain controller.
2. The domain controller sends a random challenge string, known as a *nonce,* back to the client.
3. The client encrypts the nonce with the appropriate password representation, and then sends the encrypted nonce back.

When logging in remotely, the client of the MSV1_0 package encrypts the password that the user has entered. By default, the server sends a random 8-byte nonce as the challenge string to the client. The client will then use a version of the Data Encryption Standard (DES) algorithm to encrypt the nonce with the password hash the following three times; with the first 7 bytes of the password representation, or hash. This can either be the NT hash, or in the case of Windows 9x workstations, the LAN Manager (LM) hash. The second encryption, independent of the results of the first encryption, uses the next 7 bytes of the password hash. Finally, the third encryption, which again is independent of the first and second encryptions, uses the last 2 bytes of the hash with an added 5 bytes of null characters used as filler.

Each step produces 8 bytes of ciphertext, a total of 24 bytes of ciphertext that the client sends to the server. During this process, the server encrypts a copy of the nonce it has sent to the client in exactly the same manner. If the two encrypted pieces do not match, the user will be unable to log in. This process is important to understand when dealing with password cracking and other user account–related attacks.

The SAM database is located in the Windows NT Registry. By default, even administrators do not have direct access to this part of the Registry. Password representations are created by two different protocols, depending on whether or not LM or NT hashes are used.

1. LM passwords are first converted to uppercase.
2. They are then padded with null characters to give them a length of 14 characters, if the password is less than 14 characters. For example, a password with a length of seven characters will have seven null characters added.
3. Each LM password is divided into two 7-byte halves from which two 8-byte odd parity DES keys are created.
4. The two 8-byte odd parity DES keys are hashed with a static value to produce a 16-byte result.

When Windows NT was first released, this static value was unknown to the general population, but has since been discovered to be based on the encryption of 0x4B7532140232425. NT passwords are first converted to Unicode characters, then hashed using the MD-4 encryption algorithm to produce a 16-byte result.

Unfortunately, although this process of encrypting and decrypting passwords originally appeared to be secure, multiple attacks against this process have been developed. One such attack was the creation of a program named L0phtCrack. L0phtCrack was created by a security research think tank known as L0pht Heavy Industries (L0pht has since been acquired by the consulting organization, @Stake and is located at www.10pht.com). Basically, with administrator privileges, L0phtCrack will take a copy of the SAM database and perform two types of attacks against it:

✦ The first attack involves the use of a dictionary file. L0phtCrack takes each word in the dictionary file, encrypts it using the same process that Windows NT does with passwords, and compares it to the retrieved password hash.

✦ The second attack is a brute-force attack where the program attempts to crack the password by using random characters.

Hackers and researchers have proven multiple times that no matter how strong your password, with current hardware and a little patience it will be cracked. Obviously, a password of "gP9#n8s" takes much longer to crack than a password like "welcome," but will eventually be cracked. As previously mentioned, to perform such an attack, administrator privileges are required on the computer containing the SAM database. However, a plethora of attacks can be used to temporarily escalate your privileges or steal the SAM database. In addition, L0phtCrack includes a powerful tool that allows the capturing of the encrypted password representations as they cross the network. Other tools, such as Dsniff (`www.monkey.org/~dugsong`), also allow for the capturing of password representations as they are sent across the network.

What is the point of strong passwords if they can all be cracked? The trick is to create passwords strong enough to deter the casual attacker. Obviously, if someone really wants into your network, they will get in. On the other hand, the random untargeted attacker will not spend the time required to crack a strong password.

One of the more difficult tasks for network administrators is to ensure that only authorized accounts are used and that they are only allowed to perform authorized functions. One of the most common ways to handle such a task is the creation of local and global groups.

Windows NT group security

A Windows NT group is a security entity to which users can be assigned a membership for the purpose of applying a broad set of group permissions to the user. By managing permissions for groups and assigning users to groups, rather than assigning permissions to individual users, security administrators can attempt to control large environments. A *global* group contains only users from within the domain, and a *local* group contains accounts that are local to a specific workstation or server. Local groups can also contain global groups. For example, if an administrator wanted to restrict access to a certain directory to only those users in the HR department, he could create a group named HR, place the appropriate users in that group, and then restrict the directory access control to only allow the HR global group access. On large networks, managing groups and security permissions is a large task and is usually difficult without the use of third-party utilities, or at least the *Windows NT Server 4 Resource Kit*.

Two of the primary challenges when managing groups are to ensure that unauthorized users are not being added to groups without the administrator's knowledge, and that unauthorized accounts are not being created. Using the built-in `net` commands is a simple, free way to manage this challenge. `net user` and `net group` will let you obtain a list of users and groups. By piping the output to a text file, it is easy to compare and identify differences. This process can also be easily automated by using either PERL or the `diff` command from the *Windows NT Server 4 Resource Kit.*

Windows NT default accounts

 Rename default accounts under Windows NT

You should rename the common default accounts — the Guest and Administrator user accounts — in Windows NT. While some in the security community feel doing so is unnecessary, it can be an essential security step.

First, you must understand how accounts are represented. When a user account is created, it is stored in the Registry as a numerical value known as a Security Identifier (SID). The SID is assigned to individual accounts and hosts and is unique within every domain, workstation, and server. An individual account SID is created with two parts: first, the SID of the primary domain controller (PDC), and second, the relative ID (RID). The RID is assigned as follows: the built-in Administrator account has a RID of 500 and the Guest account has a RID of 501. New accounts start with a RID of 1000 and change incrementally in the order that they are created. Once a SID is created, it can never be used on that domain again. An interesting note about the RID value is that even by renaming the Administrator or Guest account, the RID stays fixed at 500 and 501, respectively, and accounts created by copying either of the built-in accounts also retain the fixed RID. The following is an example SID:

```
S-1-5-21-1029464093-0329982144-59485500-500
```

As you can see from the last three numbers, this is the built-in Administrator account's SID, or a copy of it.

Depending on the configuration of the Windows NT Server, a remote user can retrieve user information complete with copies of each SID. So, simply renaming the Administrator account is not a good defense on a poorly configured server.

The Guest account should be disabled and not used. For accountability and auditing reasons, each network user — whether they are a temporary or permanent employee — should have a unique user ID and password. General purpose shared accounts are not a good idea, because they do not allow administrators to properly audit and hold a user accountable for his or her actions. As an administrator, who do you go after when you find an entire volume deleted by the Guest or an equivalent account?

The Administrator account is a little trickier.

1. Rename the account to something that is not descriptive. Why? Because there are many automated attack tools available that will attempt to brute force the Administrator account by using services such as FTP.

2. Assign a very strong password to the renamed account.

3. Create a second account to be used for administration. Do not simply copy the Administrator account; manually create an account and manually assign it the required permissions. This prevents the account from having the RID of 500. You may also want to create some regular user accounts prior to this, as attackers may assume that the first account created (RID 1000) is a new administration account.

4. Create another account named Administrator, adjust its access to be nil, and turn on all possible auditing options. This will alert system administrators to password cracking attempts if the fake Administrator account is continually locked out. A determined attacker will not be fooled, but taking this step will add a considerable amount of work to his attack.

Windows NT account policies

 Implement password policies under Windows NT

All of these security measures are useless if proper account policies are not in place. As with most security measures, a written policy should be in place and enforced, when applicable, by the technology. For example, Windows NT enforces a password and user account policy through the User Manager applet.

Windows NT allows the administrator to control several aspects of the Windows NT accounts. The first setting administrators are able to control is the password age, or how long a user's password will be valid before the user must change it. As previously mentioned, a correct balance between usability and security must be found. Changing a password every week would certainly minimize the possibility of security breaches, but the amount of time and energy to do so would be unreasonable. Forcing users to change their passwords too frequently leads to passwords that are written on sticky notes and posted on monitors. There have been incidents where an enterprising attacker snuck into an organization and searched cubicles for passwords and even usernames from the sticky notes posted on monitors. Most organizations require a password change somewhere between 30 and 90 days.

Minimum password age is another important value to set. Some users can't be bothered to remember their password — they will change their password and then change it back, defeating the purpose of expiring the password. Setting the minimum password age to one or two days is generally more than enough time to discourage users from resetting their passwords to an old one, while still allowing for passwords to be changed in other circumstances.

The third option is minimum password length. Before you decide on a limit to enforce, go back to the explanation on how passwords under Windows NT are stored in the SAM and how they are encrypted. A password of 14 characters is strongest and hardest to crack but is inconvenient to most users. The next best option, and a little more convenient to users, is a password of seven characters. Because of the password hashing technique used by Windows NT, a password of seven characters is much harder to crack than a password of nine characters.

Password history is another important option to set. This setting controls the number of previous passwords the system will remember and not allow the user to use. The purpose of this setting is to keep people from using the same few passwords over and over again. Be aware, however, that users will discover they can bypass this setting by simply adding a character, usually a number, to the end of the password. Still, this setting is beneficial because it prevents an attacker from using a previously cracked, and expired, password to access resources. A setting of 3 is usually sufficient.

The account lockout option prevents password-guessing attacks by allowing administrators to set the number of times a password can be attempted before the account is locked. There are two schools of thought when it comes to this option. Most agree that five attempts is a sufficient setting, but what action should be taken after an account is locked out? Some administrators feel that locking out the account indefinitely, requiring a manual reset, is best; others feel that locking the account out for a set amount of time — usually an hour — is enough to deter an attacker. The drawback to an indefinite lockout period is that an attacker can effectively cause a denial of service by purposely locking out every account on the server. The drawback to a set amount of time is, as with the other settings, finding a balance between security and usability. The lockout time must be long enough to deter an attacker but short enough to not inconvenience the user.

Unfortunately, the default options included with Windows NT do not enforce strong passwords. While it is easy to have a written policy asking users to devise strong passwords, if the technology does not enforce the policy, users will not adhere to it. Two utilities can help enforce strong passwords. One comes with the *Windows NT Server 4 Resource Kit* and the other is included with Service Pack 2; both are free.

✦ **Passprop** is the utility included with the Windows NT Resource Kit. By using Passprop, administrators gain the ability to enforce an account lockout policy on the Administrator account. On the downside, the utility is programmed to not enforce the Administrator account lockout if every other account on the server is already locked out. This is a safety feature to prevent an attacker from locking out every account — in particular, every account with administrative privileges.

✦ **Passfilt** is a DLL included with Service Pack 3 and a password filter that can help enforce specific password policies. The advantage to Passfilt is that it can be modified to suit your organization's needs.

Tip — Implementing both Passprop and Passfilt is quite easy and will be reviewed in the lab exercises at the end of the chapter.

UNIX Account Security

Explain the different methods to secure accounts under UNIX

Password cracking and account attacks under UNIX operating systems resemble those that are successful against Windows NT systems, but the format in which passwords are stored and the ways to protect accounts are much different.

Storing passwords and accounts on a UNIX system

Describe Unix password security

Identify how password aging works and the UNIX commands to accomplish password aging

Restrict account access and monitor accounts under UNIX

UNIX operating systems store passwords in a standard text file that is named passwd and stored in /etc. The default settings on this file make it readable by anyone. This "readable by anyone" setting is also called *world readable* under UNIX operating systems.

The structure of a password file is as follows:

```
testuser:GrRNrX6VS3QS7:501:100:Test User:/home/testuser:bin/bash
```

Each section is known as a field and the fields can be best explained as follows:

✦ **testuser** — The username of the user.

✦ **GrRNrX6VS3QS7** — The encrypted password along with any aging information.

✦ **501** — The user number, not to be confused with the UID or SID under Windows NT.

✦ **100** — The user group number.

✦ **Test User** — The user's full name as entered when the login ID was created.

✦ **/home/testuser** — The location of the user's home directory.

✦ **bin/bash** — The program that will be run upon login. This is usually a shell.

The password field is one-way encrypted using a highly modified DES algorithm. This means that decrypting the password would be difficult, if not impossible. The password field is 13 characters in length, with the first two characters being a "salt" (a value given to the username to give it a unique hash value) and the rest being the hash itself. The salt was added in order to prevent an attacker from encrypting a list of words, then comparing them to the field in the password file. The added salt creates 4096 possible matches to the hash stored in the file. This process does not make the password immune to cracking, but it does make the process a lot more time-consuming.

When a user attempts to log on, the password they supply is encrypted and compared to the field in the password file. If they match, the user is logged on; if not, the user is denied access and asked to re-enter the password.

As with Windows NT passwords, UNIX- and Linux-based systems are vulnerable to password cracking. A UNIX password cracker will take a list of words, or dictionary file, encrypt each word, and compare it to the hash in the password file. More advanced password crackers will also reverse the dictionary words, add characters, and change case.

UNIX has a built-in process, which makes use of *shadow passwords,* to protect the password file. This technique still allows a user to have the required read access, but the contents of the encrypted password field are not displayed. This technique can be used to foil some password-cracking techniques. When shadow passwords are enabled, the contents of the passwd file are as follows:

```
testuser:x:0:1:100:Test User:/home/testuser:bin/bash
```

This feature is implemented by creating a file called /ect/shadow, which, unlike the passwd file, is only accessible by those with root privileges. As shown in the previous code, the passwd file is still visible to all users, but the field that normally contains the salted password hash is replaced by a default value that is not the result of any encryption process. Obviously, if an attacker gains root privileges on the system, he or she will be able to access the shadow passwords.

UNIX operating systems contain many of the same features as Windows NT when setting password policy and protecting passwords. As with Windows NT, UNIX operating systems can implement a password aging policy. The purpose of such a policy is to help prevent passwords that have been compromised or cracked from being used. Unfortunately, the general user population cannot be trusted to make frequent password changes on their own and must be forced by the software to do so.

Between Solaris and LINUX distributions, the commands to accomplish these password policies are quite different. On Solaris (UNIX) distributions, the command is as follows:

```
% passwd -n <min_days> -x <max_days> -w <warning days> USERNAME
```

The first switch, -n, is the minimum number of days between password changes. This setting is the same as the Windows NT password age setting and enforces the minimum amount of time a user must stick with a new password.

The second switch, -x, sets the maximum number of days that the password will be valid. This is similar to the password expiration setting in Windows NT.

The third switch, -w, sets the amount of time, in days, that a user will begin getting warnings that their password will expire. For example, if this value is set to 5, and the -x value is set to 30, then on day 25 the user will begin getting warnings to change his password.

If you want to enforce a password policy that forces users to change their password every 45 days, use the new password for 2 days, and be warned 5 days before it expires, you would use the following command:

```
% passwd -n 2 -x 45 -w 5 USERNAME
```

USERNAME is the name of the user to which you want to apply the password aging policy. Other options not previously covered include -s, which allows you to query the password aging information of a specific user, and -f username, which forces a specific user to change his or her password.

The proper syntax when using the -s feature is as follows:

```
% passwd -s steve
```

You should expect the output to look similar to the following:

```
steve PS 04/01/01 2 45 5
```

In this output,

- ✦ steve is the user name.
- ✦ PS means Password Status.
- ✦ 04/01/01 is the last date the password was changed.
- ✦ 2 is the minimum password age.
- ✦ 45 is the maximum password age.
- ✦ 5 is the warning threshold.

If the administrator then issued the following command

```
% passwd -f steve
```

the user, in this case, steve, would be forced to change his password regardless of the current settings.

Another command that is very useful on Solaris installations is the `logins` command:

```
% logins -p
```

This command shows an administrator a list of accounts that do not have a password set.

In Linux distributions, the command and syntax are a bit different. Instead of using the `passwd` command, Linux uses the `chage` command, like this:

```
% chage -m 2 -M 45 -W 5 steve
```

This command will enforce a password aging policy on the account `steve`. The switches are as follows:

✦ `-m` is the minimum number of days between password changes.

✦ `-M` is the maximum number of days between password changes.

✦ `-W` is the warning message threshold.

Other options include the following:

✦ `-E` will set an expiration date on the account and can be used in MM/DD/YY format, or MONTH, DAY, YEAR format, as well.

✦ `-I` automatically disables an account if it is inactive for a specified number of days.

✦ `-L` will list the current password settings. The `-L` switch can also be used by unprivileged users to determine when their accounts will expire.

Various installations of UNIX will have built-in accounts that are known as system accounts. One account that is common across all installations is "root." It has the highest privileges on a UNIX system. Any other account with a UID of zero can also be considered the equivalent of root.

There are a number of ways to discover what accounts are valid on a UNIX host. A poorly protected password file is probably the easiest. Other methods depend on the configuration of the system. (These other methods are discussed in the following sections.)

The `finger` command, if allowed by the system, can be used to identify users that are currently logged in. When you type `finger @hostname`, a list of currently logged in users will be returned. You can also use the `finger` command to gain information on accounts that are already known.

The `Rusers` command returns remote user information if the service is running on the system. The Ruser method is a bit time-consuming, but has been used in the past with success. If the UNIX system is running mail services, an attacker can Telnet to the SMTP port 25 and issue some commonly known SMTP commands to verify users on the system.

UNIX has the ability to log unsuccessful password attempts. On Solaris systems, administrators must create a file, /var/adm/loginlog, allowing the system to log each login. Administrators should watch this file for frequent unsuccessful logins. Administrators of larger environments automate this process to avoid missing potential security issues.

Linux systems use a Syslog daemon and record login failures in /var/log/messages. Invalid attempts are marked with the indicator, `PAM_pwdb`, that indicates that the message originated with the Portable Authentication Module password checker. By using the `grep` command, a system administrator can easily list all invalid login attempts. For example,

```
$ grep login /var/log/messages
```

gives output similar to the following:

```
March 18 06:12:45 steve PAM_pwdb [13718]: failed login from
workstation.securesolutions.org [192.168.0.27], steve
March 19 09:01:23 steve PAM_pwdb [13718]: failed login from
labbox1.securesolutions.org [10.0.1.50], steve
```

Other UNIX security concerns

 Describe different UNIX security threats

Those of you familiar with Microsoft DOS, or even Windows NT, are probably familiar with path statements. A path statement tells the computer where to search for commands if they are not present in the current directory. Under UNIX, the search path variable is used to look up popular commands in a similar fashion. A common trick performed by attackers is to modify the search path to launch Trojan applications in place of the desired application. For example, to obtain the SU password, one could adjust the search path to launch a Trojan SU, steal the password, and pass the data to the proper SU command to prevent suspicion.

Some administrators will attempt to rename the root account to prevent attacks, but will find that unless they are prepared to adjust the programming code on a multitude of applications and services, many programs will fail because they depend on the actual account name of `root`.

Another option is to restrict the ability to log in as root remotely. This means that you will force administrators who require the use of the root account to actually log on at the console. This will also force remote users who require root privileges to log in with their regular accounts and use the SU command.

In Solaris systems, administrators must edit the default console access file located in /etc/default/login and change the line that begins with `CONSOLE` to look like this:

```
CONSOLE=/dev/console
```

A second change that is recommended is editing the /etc/default/su file to contain the following line:

```
SULOG=/var/adm/sulog
```

The advantage of making this change is that all logins using the root command and all usage of the SU command will be logged to /var/adm/sulog.

Linux systems administrators can control root logins by using the file, /etc/securetty. This file lists all devices that allow root to log into. By adding the following line, administrators can force root logins to console only:

```
cat /etc/securetty console
```

Tip   Administrators should be sure to make the securetty file readable and writeable to root only.

Another important option that administrators might want to consider is restricting remote user access by restricting the shell, such as rksh, which is a restricted version of the Korn Shell. rksh allows almost all of the features of a regular shell except the redirection of I/O, changing of directories, changing of environment variable, and checking of path names. Using a restricted shell prevents users from accidentally running malicious programs that might compromise or weaken security.

As with Windows NT systems, UNIX system administrators should constantly monitor user accounts and pay close attention to any patterns that suggest suspicious activity. Suspicious activity can include, but is not limited to, multiple failed login attempts and logins at odd hours. Most UNIX operating systems have a daemon process known as syslogd. Syslogd will listen to multiple log processes and consolidate them into one log, either in a local file or on a remote system. The advantage of using syslogd is that it keeps important information in a central repository and can be easily reviewed by administrators. The configuration file for syslogd is located at /etc/syslog.conf.

Other UNIX-based system files

 Describe UNIX password file format

There is a chance that you may run into a different UNIX operating system than the ones discussed in detail here. The following is a short list of log file locations on other UNIX operating systems:

✦ **/etc/wtmp** — Contains a record of login dates and file change dates. Used on Sun, Solaris, HP, and other Berkeley systems.

✦ **/var/adm/acct** — Once enabled, is used to audit processes.

✦ **/var/adm/pact** — Also used to audit processes once enabled.

✦ **/usr/etc/accton** — Used by FreeBSD systems to log system processes.

✦ **/usr/lib/acct** — Also used by FreeBSD to log system processes.

✦ **/usr/adm/sulog** — Used by various systems to track su usage.

✦ **/etc/remote** — Keeps track of UUCP usage.

✦ **/var/spool/uucp/.Admin** — Also used to track UUCP usage.

FTP, HTTP, and other services will also have separate logs that should be monitored on a daily basis.

Key Point Summary

This chapter stresses the importance of user accounts to the entire security posture of an organization. It discusses how there must be a trade-off between proper business reason and security implementation, as well as the following:

✦ How Windows NT passwords and usernames are stored, including how the Windows NT hash is created.

✦ The popular password-cracking tool L0phtCrack was introduced and its usage explained.

✦ Multiple ways to protect a Windows NT system, including built-in policy options and additional tools from the Window NT Resource Kit were described.

✦ The process used by UNIX to store and hash usernames and password.

✦ Ways to control password and login policies were outlined along with logging and log locations.

✦   ✦   ✦

STUDY GUIDE

This Study Guide presents assessment questions and lab exercises to test your knowledge of the chapter objectives.

Assessment Questions

1. Where are the UNIX usernames stored?

   A. /etc/SAM

   B. /etc/passwd

   C. /etc/usernames

   D. /etc/secret

2. Where are the usernames stored under Windows NT?

   A. SAM

   B. passwd

   C. usernames

   D. secret

3. How can you secure the /etc/passwd file under UNIX?

   A. Implement a shadow file.

   B. Implement a secure file.

   C. Encrypt the passwd file.

   D. This cannot be done under UNIX.

Lab Exercises

Lab 12-1 Enabling auditing events under Windows NT

This exercise reviews how to enable specific auditing events under Windows NT.

1. Launch *User Manager For Domains,* which can be found on the Start menu under Start ➪ Programs ➪ Administrative Tools (Common) ➪ User Manager for Domains.

2. Click on Policies, then Audit.

3. Now you can select which events you wish to audit and whether or not you wish to audit successful or failed attempts.

Lab 12-2 Specifying password policies under Windows NT

This exercise reviews how to specify the password policies under Windows NT.

1. Launch *User Manager For Domains,* which can be found on the Start menu under Start ➪ Programs ➪ Administrative Tools (Common) ➪ User Manager for Domains.

2. Click on Policies, then Account.

3. You can now configure all the different password policies under Windows NT.

Answers to Chapter Questions

Chapter Pre-Test

1. Three types of content that must exist in a password for it to be recognized as a strong password are uppercase characters, numbers, and special characters.

2. Under UNIX, passwords are stored in the /etc/passwd file, which carries the "default word readable" permission.

3. Under Windows NT, passwords are stored in the SAM database.

4. Two utilities that may be used to enforce strong passwords under Windows NT are Passprop and Passfilt.DLL.

5. To protect the password file under UNIX, you should enable password shadowing.

Assessment Questions

1. B. UNIX usernames are stored in the /etc/passwd file.

2. A. Under Windows NT, usernames are stored in the SAM database.

3. A. To secure the /etc/passwd file under UNIX, you should implement a shadow file.

Intrusion Detection and Response

P A R T

IV

✦ ✦ ✦ ✦

In This Part

Chapter 13
Defeating Network
and Server Attacks
and Penetration

Chapter 14
Intrusion Detection
and Prevention

Chapter 15
Intrusion Detection
Systems

Chapter 16
Handling Security
Incidents

✦ ✦ ✦ ✦

This part of the book explains how to detect an intrusion and what to do after you have identified an intrusion.

Defeating Network and Server Attacks and Penetration examines threats to operating system security, through identifying penetrations and related attacks. This process is simplified with an understanding of attack signatures and common targets for attacks to facilitate setting up auditing on system bugs, vulnerabilities, trapdoors, DoS attacks, illicit servers, Trojan horses, viruses, and worms. The chapter takes a look inside the mind of a nefarious user by coordinating multiple points of attack, such as establishing a strategy for penetration, hijacking, and IP spoofing and related attacks.

Intrusion Detection and Prevention explores intrusion detection in more detail. This examination includes discussions on automating IDS, using login scripts, automating audit analysis, and system scanning/checksum analysis. The chapter takes a look at how to distract intruders with dummy elements, tripwires, and jails. The chapter also discusses how to handle a detected intruder.

Intrusion Detection Systems begins with a general discussion of intrusion detection systems, including information on the different types of IDSs and rules for intrusion detection. The chapter explores how to select an IDS for an organization, and how to use it for security auditing.

Handling Security Incidents examines security in terms of incident management. This discussion begins with an examination of how to prepare in advance for an attack and how to establish incident-handling procedures. The chapter concludes with a discussion on how to analyze collected information and learn from experience.

Defeating Network and Server Attacks and Penetration

CHAPTER PRE-TEST

1. Select three of the most common targets of attack from the list below.
   A. Routers
   B. Web servers
   C. User workstations
   D. E-mail servers

2. What is the first thing a hacker would probably do to engage in IP spoofing?

3. What is a trapdoor, and how could it pose a risk?

4. What is a good way to find Trojan horse programs running on your system?

5. Which of the selections below are popular DoS-style system attacks? Choose all that apply.
   A. Smurf
   B. Teardrop
   C. Fraggle
   D. SYN Flood
   E. Ping of Death

✦ Answers to these questions can be found at the end of the chapter. ✦

Knowing the points of attack for your systems and servers before hackers know them is half the battle. Finding the vulnerabilities in your network and establishing fixes or a plan of defense is one of the most important considerations when auditing a network's security. Currently, DoS attacks, viruses, and intrusion through backdoors in software are relatively easy for hackers to exploit and use. This can make properly locking down systems to keep up with all the various types of attacks and intrusion methods a time-consuming job. However, knowing the system and establishing a good security model from the start will go a long way to ensuring solid system security.

Identifying Penetrations and Related Attempts

With the vast array of tools available today, hackers don't need a lot of time to establish the weak link in your network's security. Once they do, they are likely to target the weakest vulnerability first — or the one that can be exploited with the hackers' tools. Generally, the best points of attack from a hacker's point-of-view are weak software or operating systems that usually have the most penetration tools designed to make the hacker's job easier. Thankfully, average hackers use only a small group of attacks to try and exploit your vulnerabilities before moving on to the next point of penetration. Depending on the hacker's skill, he or she may design a custom attack tool if a pre-made tool won't do the job. As a security auditor or administrator, you should make sure that you know the key points of attack of a given network and that you implement ways to protect it accordingly.

Understanding attack signatures

Attack signatures are just like human fingerprints. Different attacks cause different results to occur while the attack is going on. Using a network scanner or one of the many security/intrusion scanners on today's market is one way to watch for attacks. However, you can identify the signatures in other ways, without the aid of additional software. Some common attacks that hackers may use include the following:

✦ **Dictionary attacks** — Dictionary attacks are typically used against network resources in an effort to obtain access by guessing passwords for accounts that may provide a door into the system. Although network intrusion software will help audit such an attack, you can monitor this kind of activity without going through the added expense of a software package.

✦ **Man-in-the-middle-attacks** — By placing a network-sniffing package between two systems, a hacker hopes to obtain usernames and passwords to network resources without having to directly attack systems. The best way to protect against such attacks is to implement strong encryption technologies to secure sensitive account information.

✦ **Hijacking attacks** — Hackers can use hijacking to interrupt an already established connection between two systems and remove one of the systems from the connection to establish a foothold on the network. Although this is by no means the best way to defend against such attacks, utilizing strong encryption is a good way to protect connections.

✦ **Viruses** — These all too common pests have been used more and more often to house potentially damaging programs that can disrupt service on your network or, even worse, plant backdoor programs on your systems to gain access to the network from the inside. A "number one" priority in any audit should be recommendation of an anti-virus package that can protect the various types of operating systems and software packages that the site has. Anti-virus software is an oft-forgotten component to a sound security policy that should be mandatory on any system. Educating users is also an essential part of protecting against anti-virus attacks, although with the multitude of recent high-profile attacks, users are being educated the hard way.

✦ **Illicit servers** — Hand-in-hand with viruses, illicit servers are backdoor programs or services that allow access to your network, or create a vulnerability that can be exploited when needed at a later date.

✦ **Denial of Service (DoS)** — Essentially, a DoS attack is an attack that limits system resources in such a way that proper system functions are interrupted. Viruses, such as Love Letter and Melissa, are a type of DoS attack against mail servers that utilize packet attacks to drain bandwidth from Web sites, effectively taking them offline.

Common Targets for Attack

 Identifying common targets

Attacks are usually directed against certain types of systems or network hardware to either gain access to the network, or modify or obtain data from information servers. Typical points of attack include network routers, network services, such as DNS and Windows Internet Name Server (WINS), and user-oriented services, such as Web and FTP servers.

Routers

Routers are perfect targets for attack because they are always exposed to the rest of the network or the Internet. Routers often use Simple Network Management Protocol (SNMP) to manage their feature sets. However, this can be used against them, especially if they utilize SNMP version 1, because hackers can employ widely available network management software to gain access and manipulate the router with little effort. The one major security faux pas is to leave Telnet open or unprotected on any network resource. The security issue becomes even worse with routers, because with Telnet, a hacker can gain access to the unit and glean information to help profile the attack against the router. After a hacker has control of a router, he or she has the ability to entirely disable the unit or reconfigure the unit to pass the hurdle that the router can represent, or even change settings that would limit the router's performance (a form of DoS attack). Because routers are hardware, they are often not considered to be at risk from physical attacks, but besides the obvious vandalism of the hardware, most routers feature an access port of some type on the unit that allows for local administration of the router. Gaining access to one of these ports could allow someone to tamper with the router configuration.

Filtering Telnet ports on your firewall is an excellent way to protect your routers from outside tampering from the Internet. Telnet uses default ports 161 and 162. By limiting access to these ports in your firewall software, you can help prevent attacks against the router. As a rule, disabling or limiting Telnet access on any router or system is good security because you probably don't need to maintain usage of Telnet beyond initial configuration.

With the attacks against large Web sites (such as www.ebay.com and www.CNN.com) during late 2000 and early 2001, the alarming reality is that router security and configuration is more important than ever. Being able to reconfigure an affected router quickly will mean the difference between a quick repair and costly downtime. Unfortunately, many sites use offsite Internet Service Providers (ISPs) to house their Internet or Web server services, which can limit access to the routers during a Distributed DoS attack. During the course of an audit, you will want to determine how long it would take to access offsite routers if the client has such a setup. You will learn how to defend your routers against DoS attacks later in this book.

 In-depth coverage of DoS attacks is discussed in Chapter 5.

Common tools to facilitate DoS attacks against routers are:

✦ Tribal Flood Network (TFN and TFN2K)

✦ Stacheldraht (a powerful variant of TFN)

✦ Trin00 (the first DoS attack tool to be widely used and the most widely known)

Databases

Databases are ripe for attack because they typically contain the most valuable company information that a hacker may be searching for. Companies usually store the most valuable information in databases for ease of accessibility and functionality. Unfortunately, this is a well-known fact that provides hackers with an instant target of interest.

The following information can all be found in company databases:

✦ Employee salaries

✦ Addresses

✦ Marketing and client information

✦ Company product development information

✦ Various company financial records

This information can be used to formulate further attacks, blackmail material, or industrial espionage.

Software, like network attacks, has identifying fingerprints, and database packages are no exception. Because many databases operate on a central server with clients connecting to retrieve or enter information, they must have an open form of communication on the server. If a hacker knows which ports are typically used by different applications, he or she can identify the fingerprint of a particular piece of software to narrow the scope of the attack. When performing an audit on a site, determine whether software servers (a database server, for example) are protected by a firewall with the appropriate ports blocked from outside access to the application.

Due to the nature of database software, you should also investigate any particular security vulnerabilities that a package may have and use the vendor information to patch any holes above and beyond simply protecting access to the software from the Internet. Remember that database applications may still be open to exploitation if the hacker obtained access to the network in another fashion and was able to take advantage of a software flaw. Database security is something that is rarely performed; it should receive some scrutiny in a system audit.

Web and FTP servers

Web and FTP servers are typically the most attacked targets for two reasons:

✦ They are usually exposed to the Internet without protection from a firewall, which helps cut down the amount of time needed to break in.

✦ They are usually not locked down properly, which makes them easier to get into when so many security issues are related to them.

In general, users access Web and FTP services from a public source like the Internet. Because many servers are not locked down properly — and because most client systems have horrible security — hackers are given many opportunities to glean the data required to break in. Consider the amount of data that is transferred around unencrypted, and you can see why these servers are such easy prey for hackers.

Many Web servers were launched before security became a major concern. The resulting lack of security provides an abundance of possibilities because security is something that must be applied consistently and many people don't take it seriously until after a problem occurs.

Web graffiti, a popular activity for Web server hackers, usually involves breaking into a server and changing information on the Web site. Many graffiti attacks are motivated simply by self-promotion, and may only be a notice that the system has been broken. A new Web graffiti trend involves modifying Web sites for personal or political mandates. Many activists have used this form of hacking to get their point across. Regardless of its intent, Web site owners can lose a lot of revenue and money spent correcting the problem.

E-mail servers

Like Web and FTP servers, the major failing of e-mail is that most servers reside exposed to the Internet. A few products geared toward encrypting data sent by e-mail have been developed. However, the installation base for these products is still relatively small. With encryption technologies becoming much more affordable and easier to use, more sites are incorporating e-mail protection packages, such as Pretty Good Privacy (PGP), to ensure that e-mail reaches its intended recipient unmolested.

Another problem with e-mail servers is that the username and password are usually sent to the server in clear text, meaning that anyone with a packet sniffer on your network can capture the passwords and use them to their advantage. This can be particularly dangerous because users often use the same password for many resources, and hackers can use this information to potentially exploit other systems on the network.

Because most e-mail services were designed many years ago (before security was an issue), they have many weaknesses that a hacker can exploit. Weaknesses such as exploitable code and poor account security can contribute to the vulnerabilities of a typical e-mail server.

E-mail servers allow relaying of messages from one server to another. This can be a real problem with the vast array of e-mail borne viruses and backdoor programs that can be proliferated around the world in very short order by using a hijacked e-mail server. Using a hijacked e-mail server, hackers can effectively hide the source of spam e-mail or viruses. If the affected server is a corporate e-mail server with many users that have full address books, these attacks will spread faster than anyone can stop them. Thankfully, relaying isn't always needed and can even be disabled. In most cases, however, relaying isn't disabled, so it is something that you want to look for during an audit.

Name servers

Almost all of the common targets of attack are exposed to the Internet. DNS servers are no exception, and although many people may not consider DNS servers to be much of a target, valuable information can be obtained from a DNS server, and even more DoS-style attacks can be mounted. DNS communicates with UDP, which is a typically weak protocol. Given most administrators' lack of knowledge in how to properly configure firewalls to lock down UDP communications, DNS servers quite often stay exposed and vulnerable, even though they don't have to be.

Some typical attacks against DNS servers include:

✦ **Unauthorized zone transfers** are basically a type of DoS attack. Time is spent whenever a DNS zone change request is transferred to various DNS servers. A hacker can conceivably mess around and change the zone settings, effectively causing more zone transfers than are needed — this in turn is considered a DoS attack.

✦ **DNS poisoning** is a method by which a hacker can enter false data about the DNS address of a server. The purpose of this type of attack is to either prevent users from reaching the site in question or to substitute one site for another. DNS poisoning can work hand-in-hand with Web graffiti. Connecting a Web surfer to a Web server put up for nefarious activities, which has been redirected from a legitimate Web site by poisoning the DNS, can conceivably redirect revenue-generating traffic from the intended server to another. DNS poisoning can be technically challenging, and DNS entries can be fixed with relative ease — once the attack has been noticed. The widespread effects of such an attack were once thought to be minimal, because these types of attacks are rare. However, given recent Microsoft DNS server problems, DNS poisoning has become an issue that must be addressed so that it doesn't get out of hand. Most security analysts are surprised that this type of attack hasn't happened more often.

✦ **DoS attacks** can encompass many different forms. Notwithstanding the attacks mentioned previously, packet or ping flood attacks can be effective in slowing down or limiting DNS activity as well.

Additional name services can be exploited, including WINS and SMB servers. Attacks against these targets may include the following:

✦ DoS attacks against WINS servers, varying from straight ping flood attacks to WINS server spoofing attacks that confuse client systems into changing their names, which can result in loss of service to that system.

✦ Server Message Blocks (SMB) services are typically vulnerable to man-in-the-middle-attacks, or allowing authentication data to be captured by using a network sniffer. SMB is used whenever servers make file, print, or mail services available to clients over a network. Whenever a client connects to one of these resources, the server must check that the user has authentication to access it. It is at these moments during the authentication that a hacker is most likely to step in and capture or intercept useful user and server information.

✦ NFS and NIS are Windows NT/UNIX services that are also susceptible to network sniffer use because they pass authentication information from UNIX servers to Windows NT Servers to allow access to files and directory services.

If you find any of these services on a network that you are auditing, check for available patches to ensure that they have the best possible protection.

Exam Tip   For the exam, know the common targets of attack.

Auditing for System Bugs and Vulnerabilities

As a security auditor or administrator, staying informed is very important. Thankfully, due to the amount of hacking and security problems that exist, the amount of information on vulnerabilities and weaknesses is growing every day. You should stay informed about security issues and problems that may affect your site. Many Web sites and print documents are updated on a regular basis and should be consulted to find out new information on the systems that you have.

For instance, it seems like the number of vulnerabilities to Microsoft IIS servers increases daily—problems that range from executing command lines from the address bar to having IIS run illicit code to perform a variety of nefarious activities. If you aren't informed about these issues, you give hackers an upper hand—after all, they are keeping their eyes open, always looking for a way to exploit the slow-moving security administrator or auditor.

Updates to the affected software are usually the best and most common solution to security problems. However, test the software updates on an unessential installation to ensure that they don't do anything you don't want them to do.

Although maintaining security may seem like a daunting task, the best news is that you aren't alone. Others like yourself have security-related jobs and interests; interacting with these individuals can help you solve a complex security issue, or introduce you to the newest version of a particular product that may also resolve your problem. Many security issue-related sites host forums and mailing lists that can help put you in touch with others like yourself. Two popular sites are www.windowsitsecurity.com and www.securityfocus.com. It is likely that someone has "been there before." Keeping in touch with like-minded individuals can mean the difference between getting your security hole fixed quickly, and having it exploited.

When performing any patch to a system, research the patch fully before implementing it to see what changes it will make. There is nothing worse than applying a patch to fix a small security hole, and then having an even larger one open after updating your software. Thankfully, most large patches include information on what was changed and what was fixed. Letting other people perform the patches first is probably a good idea—you can learn from their experience. When you do implement a patch or fix, fully test the implementation to ensure that you won't have any surprises a day or two after the server is out and exposed to potentially hostile traffic.

Auditing Trap Doors and Documented Exploits

Trapdoors and root kits are often tricky to catch during system audits because they are not visible to casual scrutiny. Trapdoors, in particular, are hard to nail down because they are typically bugs in software that are generated by normal use. Once known, hackers can attempt to take advantage of unexpected results that the software puts out while it is working normally. For instance, one older UNIX-based sendmail package allowed scripts to be run with root user authentication if you ran debug on the software. This is a rather large vulnerability because, once exploited, a hacker can own the system from one end to the other and plant numerous backdoors and user accounts that would take forever to root out. This allows the hacker all the time that he or she needs to infiltrate the server and other systems on the network.

Root kits are essentially software that is utilized in place of actual system programs, such as a Trojan horse. Root kits disguise themselves as a typical software package, but launch a backdoor program or reconfigure a system setting to allow access that wouldn't normally exist. Root kits are most often designed for UNIX/Linux, but they can exist for Windows systems as well. Root kits for Windows are called "backdoor programs," and are classified as something like NetBus or BackOrifice, which are two very handy hacking utilities that allow fairly complete access to an infected system. Software packages like these can be detected and removed with current anti-virus software. Unfortunately, most people don't keep anti-virus signatures up to date, let alone actually have the anti-virus software running all the time.

When auditing a system that may have root kit software installed, keep in mind that even if a hacker has made inroads into disguising the backdoor utility from anti-virus software, root kits usually have open ports so the hacker can reconnect to the system. If you identify the open ports and trace them back to the software by using these ports, you can determine if a back-door utility is active on the system, and then try to figure out what the package is and where it is installed. If the hacker covered his or her tracks, this process may be time-consuming. In most cases, however, root kits can be caught fairly quickly.

A *backdoor* is best described as a glitch in code, or a purposefully written exploit that allows access to a system by exploiting that code. Many backdoor exploits with Web servers have been documented in the past — in Windows operating systems, mail servers, routers, and even games.

Backdoors can be present in any type of software package, professionally written or not. Backdoors are often present in custom software packages as a way to let the programmer gain access to perform software maintenance or troubleshooting that can't be performed otherwise without re-compiling the entire program, such as a setting or component modification. More often than not, these purposeful backdoors are either poorly covered up or not covered at all. Reportedly, many routers have backdoors that allow access to the settings inside by simply entering a specific username and password combination.

Even games can be subject to backdoors. The popular games DOOM and Quake both have versions of the software that allow unauthorized entry. Although it's highly unlikely that administrators would allow such games to be installed on critical servers, they may sometimes slip through the cracks if hidden well enough.

When auditing a system, try not to take for granted the security of any software package. Games and professional and custom-made applications can all be vulnerable. The best plan of defense is to document how the software installs and to discuss the package with others that may be using it. Reading security-related Web sites for past vulnerabilities on a questionable software package doesn't hurt either.

Tip If a backdoor program is in use and allows access from the outside world, there must be a port listening. Use of a network sniffer program, or appropriate port-scanning package, will provide information about open ports.

Auditing DoS Attacks

Objective Identify and analyze specific brute force, social engineering, and DoS attacks

DoS attacks have risen in popularity in the past year due to the vast array of vulnerable servers out there and the often-limited defense that some systems have to these attacks. Although most typical DoS attacks are directed at Windows-related systems, there are now DoS-style attacks for almost any operating system or network-attached hardware, such as a network router. Windows systems are targeted because of Microsoft's high profile in the computer industry. Microsoft is known for having many exploitable bugs in its software.

When auditing Windows NT systems, consider placing the servers behind a firewall to help protect the servers from malicious inbound traffic. Spending time applying the latest service packs and software patches is also critical to providing the best protection for vulnerable NT systems, because new ways to exploit or crash Windows NT servers are developed all the time. Ultimately, because most security administrators rarely have the time that they need when dealing with large networks, adding an intrusion and vulnerability scanning software package can make your life easier when it comes time to audit or protect generally weak Windows NT servers.

UNIX/Linux systems have long been vulnerable to DoS attacks. Due to UNIX's relative complexity, it was assumed that most users would have some skills and would take the time to secure the system properly, although this doesn't happen as often as one would hope. An important service to look for on UNIX systems is the Finger service, which can be a weak link in UNIX due to its vulnerability to buffer overflow attacks.

Exam Tip Knowing the "how and why" of DoS attacks and their possible consequences will help you tackle the exam.

Buffer overflow

Those of you around long enough to remember using DOS and Windows 3.*x* will remember buffer overflows. Those little errors that brought systems to their knees have been making a comeback and can present one of the more important security concerns that you may come across while auditing. Here's a brief explanation of how a buffer overflow happens: Software requires memory address space to be allocated while it is running. Usually, operating systems manage these memory spaces, but sometimes they can fail in their operation — either by poor OS design or poor application programming.

C and C++ are quite vulnerable to buffer overflows, and there is a very large collection of software written in these languages. Software programs that are written in these languages make direct memory calls without asking the operating system if the memory that they require is available. As such, when the program makes a grab for the memory that it wants, it gets the memory regardless of its availability. An application that isn't written properly will take the memory that it wants — memory that can be in use by another application — thus causing a buffer overflow and either making one or more of the applications or operating systems crash.

Although crashing software is bad enough, a residual result of the crashed software is that when one of these applications crashes, it can be exploited. Sometimes, when the operating system or application goes down from a buffer overflow attack, it can leave behind the remnants of a system shell that may have user or administrative privileges to the operating system. Hackers with access to leftover system shells can sometimes, by using the shell's operating-system rights, execute code right on the system.

Buffer overflow attacks are growing in popularity due to the poor software design that many programmers implement these days to get the product out by deadline. As the saying goes, it will probably get worse before it gets better, so arm yourself with all the information that you can get on buffer overflow attacks because they pose a big security risk. A great paper on buffer overflows can be found at `www-4.ibm.com/software/developer/library/overflows/index.html`.

WinNuke attacks

WinNuke attacks were very popular at one time, but have fallen off somewhat in their usage. WinNuke works by exploiting a well-known bug in the Windows 9*x*/Windows NT networking code to continually send bad clumps of data to port 139 on the target system. Although some versions of the software require software compiling to run, newer and easier-to-use versions of the software run under Windows and only require that you enter the address and click a single button. Microsoft was quick to issue fixes to its major operating systems. When auditing systems, look to see if Windows 9x has the most up-to-date dial-up networking update installed, and that Windows NT 4 has at least Service Pack 3 or later installed (although in most cases, this isn't an issue). If you are unsure whether or not the systems are protected, patches and information to fix this vulnerability are available on Microsoft's Web site.

Tip   Microsoft released an updated IP package called Dial Up Networking Update Version 1.3, or DUN 1.3. This updates Windows 95 systems with a new IP stack and protect against most DoS-style attacks. Windows 98 doesn't require this update.

Preventing DoS attacks

Objective   Implementing methods to thwart penetration

DoS attacks are difficult to stop, but as a security administrator or auditor, you can prevent yourself from becoming a potential DoS victim. You can defend against DoS attacks in the following ways:

✦ Implement tested patches for the various operating systems on the network.

✦ If you have employees or vendors creating specialized software applications, make sure that they are creating the most secure code possible.

✦ Use only known, secure operating systems and hardware. Although this is easier said than done, researching the security features of a new server or operating system before implementing it can go a long way to preventing future problems.

✦ Establish time-outs on connections that don't send appropriate requests to limit the amount of erroneous data that can possibly affect the system.

✦ Implement a strong firewall and keep it updated with the latest patches and fixes.

Auditing Illicit Servers

Illicit servers are the type of programs referred to in this chapter's sections on backdoors and root kits. Illicit servers typically open up a port on the host system and provide access to the system without requiring authentication. Some popular illicit servers are:

✦ NetBus

✦ BackOrifice and BackOrifice 2000 (An updated version for use under NT)

✦ Girlfriend

Many more types of illicit servers are available that can provide access to FTP, Telnet, and HTTP services, as well as different programs that can create hidden shares, or that can be useful to disguise or hide other backdoors, illicit servers, and Trojan horses.

Many of the aforementioned illicit servers can serve multiple duties — acting as a backdoor program or Trojan horse, for example, or allowing creation of services, such as FTP or HTTP on the host system. Once again, auditing such services goes back to monitoring open ports that don't belong on the system. Knowing the regular system ports, and which ports are used by the installed software, will help speed up auditing for these types of software. In this kind of "hunt-and-chase" auditing, a packet sniffer or vulnerability scanner can go a long way to finding the rogue application. An up-to-date anti-virus scanner can also help stop some of the more popular illicit servers, such as NetBus or BackOrifice.

Tip   If NetBus is installed on a Windows 98, NT, or 2000 system and was installed with the default PATCH.EXE program, you can check the task manager to see if the application "patch" is running as a process. This is a quick and easy way to check for illicit servers. Keep in mind that hackers can find ways to hide or change the names of the executable, so this is not entirely reliable.

An example of NetBus can be seen in Figure 13-1.

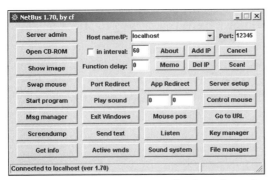

Figure 13-1: NetBus server application allows for easy exploitation of the victim's system.

Auditing Trojan Horses, Viruses, and Worms

The three most common types of attacks are Trojan horses, viruses, and worms. The following sections examine how to deal with these malicious programs and protect your system from them.

Trojan horses

Trojan horses can take many forms, and in many cases, they may be one of the larger annoyances for anyone performing a security audit. Trojan horses can be regular software that is activated by use of another legitimate program, or can even be packed into a legitimate program that activates the Trojan horse when the system or user runs it. A variety of utilities or programs may act as Trojan horses, including anything from root kits and backdoor programs to keystroke-capture software that can be installed into a system or program. Lately, popular Trojan horses have been keystroke capturers or password grabbers that can intercept password hashes and usernames and e-mail them back to the hacker. Trojan horses can be particularly dangerous if not caught right away, because the hacker can spread them around, making it difficult to find all of them.

Auditing Trojan horses is much the same as auditing any backdoor program: Watch for suspicious open ports, such as a listening or sending port, on the system in question. After these types of ports are installed, some Trojan horses may only send information out, instead of allowing the hacker to regain access by using the tool. Pay particular attention to port activity on the system, because it can divulge valuable information. Another useful tip is to limit the amount of software that is installed and keep a list of what ports the software uses so that later on, when you are re-auditing the system, you don't treat the port as a security problem if it should actually be open.

Viruses

Auditing viruses is a relatively easy science. As mentioned before, keeping a solid anti-virus package installed on your servers and workstations will help root out almost any virus. Installing an anti-virus package or snap-in for e-mail servers is very important when performing security administration or a long-term audit. Many corporate anti-virus packages include snap-ins or agents for e-mail servers like Exchange. If working properly, these anti-virus packages do a great job.

If the network doesn't have an appropriate up-to-date anti-virus package installed, make sure that you throw up a big red flag, because viruses can deliver Trojan horses or perform DoS attacks against corporate e-mail servers and will only get more popular as time goes on.

Worms

Worms, such as the Melissa Virus or the Love Bug, can wreak havoc and highlight the inherent weaknesses in today's networks. When performing an audit, you should know how to configure firewalls to protect against both general and specific attacks in order to properly protect against worm attacks. As a security administrator or auditor, you would be well advised to take a course on some of the more popular firewall packages, or at a minimum, spend some time configuring and testing the various packages on the market. Knowing what ports are particularly vulnerable to attack can become very important when trying to explain what needs to be locked down when performing an audit.

Worms typically rely on specific software to perform their functions. Recently, two popular programs, Microsoft Outlook and Outlook Express, have been particularly vulnerable to worm attacks. Both have been hit with a rash of attacks, including the Melting worm, which was first discovered in the spring of 2000. Melting is a particularly nasty and persistent worm; once it has infected the system, it can cause permanent system instability until a complete wipe and re-install is performed. It is naïve to think that only Microsoft software will be affected by worms and similar attacks, as it is only a matter of time before other vendors' applications and e-mail software are targeted by hackers.

In the Real World A good virus scanning software package for e-mail servers is a must. Ensuring that the package has a "plug-in" for the e-mail server is also helpful to curb the spread of worms and viruses.

Coordinating Multiple Points of Attack

Serious hackers will work from more than one system to fully attack a network. Although they may use one system to profile your network, yet another system may be employed to attack. When time is of the essence, and if the network has even a modicum of security, hackers must work fast to find a way in. Hackers may use more than one operating system as well, because utilities for 9*x*, NT, and Linux may not be available for the other operating systems, or they may simply work better under a particular OS. Combining attacks makes sense from a hacker's point of view, because although they use one system to perform a DoS attack on the victim and slow down response on the server, they use another system to perform a man-in-the-middle attack to capture password hashes, and then yet another system to brute force attack the password with a password hacker, such as L0phtcrack.

Quite often when a hacker is attacking a system, the first two initial attacks will be a system profile. After the hacker has a handle on the target, the hacker will likely perform a DoS attack. A hacker will use a DoS attack to stop the server from attempting to connect back to the attacker, essentially performing IP spoofing in the process.

Strategies for penetration

Objective Understanding penetration strategies and methods

Now that you have read about the types of commonly attacked systems and network hardware and heard about the various types of attacks, think about how hackers combine these attacks to penetrate a target network. When you understand how hackers combine the different attack methods into a final, successful attack, you will be able to develop a complete audit strategy. Keep in mind that almost every successful attack uses a combination of the strategies discussed here.

Physical

 Potential physical, operating system, and TCP/IP stack attacks

If potential hackers have physical, unsupervised access to servers, you may as well hang up your hat, because it can't get much easier for them. Hackers can use the many utilities available to gain administrative access or execute programs that can help bypass login security. A typical physical attack involves manually rebooting a Windows NT Server, and inserting a bootable floppy disc with a utility, such as NTFS for DOS, that allows the user to boot into DOS and gain access to NTFS partitions. NTFS partitions are typically unreadable by anything other than a Windows NT system without special software like NTFSforDOS. Once inside the file system, a hacker can glean any amount of information about the server, including access to the user account and password lists. The lists can be copied onto a floppy and put to task with a brute-force password cracking utility, such as L0phtcrack.

Copying the password lists onto a floppy works great for hackers, because they have all the time that they need to crack the passwords on a separate system instead of trying to break in at the local console, with the possibility of being caught. In this case, a hacker's only concern would be if someone noticed the system was rebooted, became suspicious, and forced password changes before the hacker could get the necessary passwords. With the speed at which most brute-force hackers work, it probably wouldn't take long to gain at least one administrative account and password — unless the site practices strong password policies.

Physical attacks are not limited to subterfuge. Even walking up to a Windows 9x system with a locked or unlocked screensaver and rebooting to gain access to the computer is a type of physical attack that, depending on the security level of the user, can prove to be quite useful for a hacker.

Most people think that a hacker's purpose is to gain access to networks and cause harm. This is frequently true, but sometimes a hacker attempts a different type of DoS attack: The physical DoS attack. If the system in question doesn't have any physical security, a hacker can bypass all the time-consuming password cracking and software loading and simply take the side off of the server and either remove or damage critical system components. It will take time for less experienced system administrators to figure out what happened, and may even cost tens of thousands of dollars to fix the system, given the cost of replacement parts for servers. If the server is using an SCSI RAID card that gets removed, the server may be effectively dead (unless the administrators have complete and secure backups).

 Every job site should have a secure, locked room for their servers and networking equipment that includes appropriate air conditioning and ventilation systems.

Operating system

Operating system infiltration auditing will consume much of your time as a security administrator or analyst. Hacking utilities and vulnerabilities are widespread for almost any operating system on the planet. Operating system penetration can take many forms, and describing them all is beyond the scope of this book. However, your responsibility as a security professional is to know your operating system as well as or better than hackers; otherwise, you may find yourself explaining to the company president why a teenager broke into the Web server and posted Web graffiti. This type of activity can touch any organization.

Take, for instance, the White House Web site at www.whitehouse.gov. This Web site was infiltrated a couple of years ago by a fairly inexperienced hacker, who was able to identify vulnerabilities in the Web servers' operating system, Solaris 7. In general, Solaris 7 is a secure operating system, but in this case, the administrator forgot to change some default settings that allowed the hacker to gain access. The administrator had set a tripwire to catch hackers or software that made unauthorized changes, but a tripwire is only good if someone pays attention to it, or if it is set to automatically restore the changed setting. In this case, the hacker was detected, but only after he modified some pages on the White House's Web site.

Bad password policies

By now, the advantage of creating a strong password policy has probably been pounded into your head, but system administrators sometimes get lazy and forget to mind the policies set forth for their users. In the case of the White House intrusion, the system administrator had been using FTP services to update and maintain the server instead of performing the updating and maintenance locally on the server itself. (FTP services are not secure because they use clear text to transfer authentication information between the server and user, although if set up properly, they can be quite useful as a service or administrative tool.) The administrator likely forgot that if someone set up a packet sniffer, they could capture authentication information transferring from the server and client. Users and administrators often use the same password for many resources and, in this case, once the hacker obtained the password for the FTP server, he had access to practically the entire server.

The bottom line: You can implement strong password policies in many ways, but they are only effective if everyone follows them, administrators included.

Tip   Make your passwords at least seven or eight characters long, preferably mixing special characters, such as ', *, and $, with letters and numbers. Don't use repetitive characters. Also, avoid using real words or names that can be found in a dictionary, regardless of the language.

NetBIOS Authentication Tool (NAT)

NetBIOS Authentication Tool (NAT, not to be confused with Network Address Translation) warrants some mention because it enables hackers, as well as system auditors, to test the current state of password security on the audited network. NAT is a simple utility that runs under UNIX/Linux and Windows 9x/NT/2000 operating systems. The UNIX/Linux version runs from the command line. The Windows version has a nice clean graphical user interface for those who have grown attached to their mice. NAT is popular because it can quickly perform a brute-force dictionary attack on the target system(s) and because it requires little system overhead to run.

Even if the administrator has implemented some typical security settings, such as password aging and bad password lockout, a hacker can still cause grief. All a hacker has to do on a system that locks out accounts after bad password attempts is to continually attack accounts until they are locked out, generating many problems for administrators and users, who then have to reset the lockout to continue operation. Imagine having to unlock several hundred or several thousand accounts and you will understand how annoying and time-consuming an attack like this would be. Administrators often forego enforcing account lockout policies due to the effect of this type of attack.

Tip   If account lockouts are a security measure that your company or client intends to pursue, consider restricting them to servers that don't process network or domain authentications in order to limit negative effects.

Bad system policies

One of the main problems for any security auditor is poor system security policy. A system administrator can perform all the tricks in the book to block potential infiltrations, but security will still be jeopardized if the users don't practice good system security measures. A bad security policy — or no security policy at all — will lead to bad passwords and a general lack of effort to perform even the minimum amount of local security on workstations. Enforcing security can be a time-consuming proposition for network administrators and users alike; however, an appropriate security policy — including account lockout or minimum password-length requirements — can go a long way towards easing the burden for everyone. These caveats may seem like common sense, but more often than not, security policies are created or enforced only after an incident has occurred.

Auditing file system weaknesses

Every proponent of a certain operating system likes to think that this operating system has advantages that the others lack. However, almost every file system available today has a vulnerable point. Microsoft's FAT and NTFS file systems both have security weak points. FAT-type file systems have no inherent security features at all.

NTFS file systems can be secure, but Microsoft's Windows NT has been the target of many utilities that allow access to files located on NTFS volumes, thereby bypassing most security features. NTFS is weak at the very least, because when you create a new folder, by default it allows full access to anyone connected to the system. So, unless people take time to set the permissions properly, NTFS is almost as open as a FAT-type file system.

UNIX systems with Network File System (NFS) enabled are vulnerable as well, and a common recommendation is that if you don't require the functionality that NFS and its related utilities provide, you should disable it. Setting up proper client and user access control lists is a far more secure method to provide access to network resources. If you do require that NFS be enabled, don't allow the servers' local IP address to mount the file system. As always, applying the latest available patches and service packs can help strengthen file system security.

IP spoofing and hijacking

Spoofing is a popular form of attack that allows hackers to bypass system authentication measures. IP spoofing is often used in conjunction with other attacks as part of a larger infiltration. IP spoofing is also a great way for a hacker to try to cover his tracks — or at least try to trick any intrusion detection software into thinking the attack is coming from somewhere else or is an entirely different type of attack. The Internet was never designed with the current use in mind. As such, the network has a very open and often insecure method of addressing.

By nature, UNIX systems have an established trust between other UNIX systems, and as such can be exploited much more easily by IP spoofing. Servers that use TCP/IP assume that all incoming IP addresses are the actual address of the sender. By taking advantage of TCP/IP's trusting nature, a hacker can write or use a program that generates forged IP packets labeled with an IP that is either unlike anything that the hacker is connecting with, or is one of a trusted system. By doing so, a hacker can either confuse the server or pretend to be a legitimate client connecting to the server.

Most UNIX-type systems have rhost and rlogin entries that generate trusted connections between servers and systems over external networks like the Internet. This method of maintaining connections is used often, because it can help cut down on the amount of time that administrators use to maintain trusted connections to outside servers. Although this type of setup is typically secure from most forms of attacks (because it uses UNIX authentication methods with a fixed IP), it incorrectly assumes that the IP address can't be spoofed and that the system that it is talking to is, in fact, the trusted system in its rhost authorized list. As you now know, a hacker with knowledge of authorized systems can easily defeat this type of scheme. Infiltrating one system often means finding a connection to another. Using this method, a hacker can spread quickly between several trusted servers.

IP spoofing was used in widespread Distributed DoS attacks against Web sites such as www.yahoo.com and www.CNN.com. When the attacks commenced, the packets that were sent had spoofed source addresses. When the routers or servers received a packet, they tried to respond to the source address with no luck. Not only does attempting to respond tie up the network resource with response packets, it can also have an effect on whatever source IP address the hacker spoofed in the first place, thereby hitting two birds with one stone. More information on DoS attacks involving IP spoofing can be found at `www.landfield.com/rfcs/rfc2267.html`.

Hope is on the horizon — the latest incarnation of TCP/IP is in development and will bring about standards changes to help combat IP spoofing. Methods of protecting against IP spoofing attacks currently exist, but they are rarely foolproof. For now, you should use a firewall package and block out any obviously spoofed addresses. Most firewalls have anti-spoofing enabled by default, but it doesn't hurt to check that rogue addresses are being filtered out.

Blind and non-blind spoofing

Blind and non-blind spoofing differ only in their execution. Non-blind spoofing requires that the hacker fiddle with a connection that exists on the same subnet or physical network connection as the target system. Blind spoofing occurs when the hacker fiddles or manipulates packets destined to a foreign network or separate physical network connection. Although both types of attack are common, blind spoofing is more difficult to pull off.

When hackers attempt an IP spoofing attack, they need a few programs or utilities to aid in their attack. The first is a packet sniffer software package, and the second is a TCP connection manipulation program. The TCP manipulation package must be able to generate a TCP connection, spoof IP packets, and kill TCP connections. Although there are utilities that will perform each of these tasks separately, "Swiss Army-like" utilities exist that will provide all the required functions in one useful package.

IP spoofing usually involves three separate hosts. As previously discussed, if the servers use authentication that requires a trusted IP address, a trust relationship must be set between the two servers. If the servers don't have any real security measures, then spoofing the servers into accepting the forged packets is a much easier job for the hacker.

Hackers must have access to raw network sockets (as compared to cooked network sockets) in order to properly spoof IP addresses. Cooked network sockets, which are provided by the operating system for applications that request them, already include the appropriate IP information. Raw ports allow the hacker to include his own header and IP information in the packets being sent. Both UNIX and Windows NT support raw packets, and both usually require root or administrative access to open raw network sockets. This is typically not a problem once a system has been cracked.

Take, for example, this IP spoofing scenario: You have three hosts (1, 2, and 3) communicating with one another. Host 1 is a UNIX server and will be the hacker's target. Host 1 thinks it has established a TCP SYN connection to open a connection to a legitimate client system named Host 2. However, Host 2 has been taken out by a DoS attack initiated by the hacker, using Host 3. Host 3 then uses forged IP packets to assume that the identity of Host 2, with Host 1 none the wiser. This type of attack is quite common, given the number of improperly set-up UNIX systems connected to the Internet.

If you perform a network audit and find this particular vulnerability at the site, it's unlikely that you will be able to convince the network administrator to stop using trusted connections by IP address, due to its convenience level. However, do recommend a firewall package to help block potential DoS and IP spoofing attacks from taking down or hijacking one of the systems.

Exam Tip   The exam will probably have at least a couple of questions about IP spoofing.

IP-Based Attacks

Objective   Understand potential physical, operating system, and TCP/IP stack attacks

As an auditor or security administrator watching over your flock, you should know what different IP-based attacks look like in progress. Like any other type of attack, IP attacks usually leave a fingerprint that provides information about the type of attack that the system was hit with or is currently being attacked with. Knowing how popular attacks, such as SYN floods, Teardrop, Smurf, and Fraggle, act will help you quickly determine an appropriate course of action. IP-based attacks typically encompass one form of DoS or another, and each has its own twist on limiting or disabling access to certain TCP/IP services and ports.

SYN flood

SYN flood is a common form of attack usually used to attack Web servers. SYN floods can be classified as a popular Distributed DoS attack. SYN floods work by taking a normal TCP/IP handshake connection attempt, and using it to take advantage of the target system by exploiting how the target system accepts and handles incoming packets. To execute a SYN flood attack, a hacker will create a half-open TCP connection. When the hacker sends the packet to the server, the server attempts to open a port and accept the connection. The hacker then stops the connection to the server with the port still partly open and establishes yet another connection. This carries on repeatedly until the server has partially opened hundreds upon thousands of ports.

Not only can SYN floods cause a connection problem for legitimate systems wanting to connect to the resource, but every time a system opens a port, it uses system resources, such as CPU cycles and memory. If enough ports are left half-open, the system can experience resource starvation, as well as a slowdown or denial of connections for legitimate client systems.

Most servers can maintain hundreds of connections on a single port, but many are only designed to sustain a certain amount of half-open connection requests. This is more of a design limitation than a flaw. If enough half-open requests are left, and enough resource starvation is present, the server can crash or go down entirely. You can protect against SYN flood attacks in the following ways:

✦ Keep the TCP connection timeouts to a shorter interval to help the server clear out failed connections.

✦ Increase the size of the connection queue.

Both ways will help the server handle a SYN flood attack, but neither is an optimal solution to the problem. Employing any available vendor-provided patches is a good way to protect against these attacks. Most up-to-date operating systems incorporate some type of SYN flood detection and prevention methods.

SYN flood attacks are among the most common types of attacks that you will experience as an auditor, due to their relative ease and ability to produce effective results against unprotected systems. SYN flood attacks can be a precursor to or part of a larger spoofing attack.

Smurf and Fraggle

Smurf attacks use Internet Control Message Protocol (ICMP) packets. ICMP is the type of protocol that is used when a system pings another system, requesting a response. To start a Smurf attack, a hacker will create an invalid packet that has the return address of the victim's system. The hacker then sends the packet to another system — usually an innocent bystander — and that recipient responds to the ICMP ping request with a response, which goes to the target's system instead of the hacker's. To give the attack real stopping power, a hacker will send as many ICMP ping requests to as many systems as he or she can, overwhelming the target computer and either slowing it down or crashing the system entirely.

Smurf attacks are one of the more powerful attacks in existence, due to the snowball effect of the attack. All a hacker has to do is send a broadcast ping to a network of hosts and all of those systems will respond back. Imagine sending such an attack to several thousand clients attached to a larger ISP — the results could be devastating to the network or server under attack.

Fraggle attacks are very similar to Smurf attacks, except they use User Datagram Protocol (UDP) ports instead of ICMP traffic. Typically, a Fraggle attack is targeted at port 7, but almost any Fraggle attack package will allow full customization of the attack, including which port it will target. The Fraggle attack will work whether or not ECHO is enabled on the bystander systems. If ECHO is not enabled, the system will report back to the victim that ICMP is unreachable, and the attack will still consume the same amount of network resources.

A good rule when protecting against Smurf and Fraggle attacks is to use a firewall package and disable all ICMP traffic. Alternatively, you could disable the ability to ping servers; however, keep in mind that this could cause difficulties when trying to diagnose a possible network problem down the road. To limit the involvement of your systems as possible innocents in an attack, directed broadcast functionality should be disabled on the outermost router on your network connection to the Internet. If you are not using a hardware router, it's a good idea to implement a router and ensure that the appropriate security settings are applied. Some different types of UNIX and Linux implementations can also be set to quietly discard ICMP packets with some minor configuration changes.

If a hacker employs broadcast addresses in Smurf or Fraggle attacks, they can turn the attack from a minor annoyance into a full-blown assault. Broadcast addresses are those addresses that end in .255 or .0 on a network and are often used in troubleshooting networks, because you can send one packet to a broadcast address and see what systems are live on the entire network. This works well with the hacker's plans, because with a couple of hundred systems available on any given subnet, mass attacks are easy.

When you audit a network, you should recommend disabling directed broadcast pings on the network's routers to help curb possible participation in Smurf and Fraggle attacks. If you want to learn more about these types of attacks or directed broadcasts, visit `http://netscan.org`.

Teardrop/Teardrop2

Teardrop attacks (a type of DoS attack) take advantage of bad code involved with software that doesn't handle reassembly of fragmented or overlapping UDP packets properly. Teardrop attacks typically effect systems that utilize the IDENT protocol that is primarily used by systems to match TCP connections to a particular user. IDENT is used quite often in user authentication to system services, such as sendmail under Linux.

Linux, Windows NT, and Windows 9x are vulnerable to both Teardrop and Teardrop2 attacks, but many patches are available now to help protect systems. Typically, the end result of a Teardrop attack is the now infamous Blue Screen of Death, which reports something to the effect of a STOP error at address space 0x0000000A on Windows systems.

During a Teardrop attack against a Windows system, an undersized UPD packet will be sent to the host, which won't be able to re-create the information properly. Usually, this will cause a Blue Screen Of Death (BSOD), effectively crashing the system.

Teardrop and Teardrop2 only differ in Teardrop2's use of larger packets of data and UDP packet length spoofing. Teardrop was patched by most major vendors right away, but, unfortunately, not well enough, which is why Teardrop2 can still cause problems with newer "fixed" systems. At a minimum, a Teardrop attack against a patched target can still cause processor and bandwidth resource depletion. If you are looking for more information on these attacks, they are often referenced by different names — "Boink" for Teardrop and "Bonk" for Teardrop2.

Ping of Death

Ping of Death attacks are easy to deploy and can be an effective DoS attack against a host. Ping of Death works by sending a spoofed packet that is larger than 65,536 bytes. Usually, sending a packet of this size over IP is impossible, but the packets can be broken up into parts, allowing the packet to be sent and reassembled on the victim's side. Not only can this cause a system slowdown, it is usually effective in causing a buffer overflow on the victim's computer, possibly crashing it.

A variation of this attack, called Ping of Death2, works exactly the same as Ping of Death except instead of sending one oversized packet, it sends a flurry of oversized packets that quickly and effectively lock the target system up.

To protect against Ping of death attacks, limit inbound ICMP packets from untrusted networks such as the Internet and perform all available service packs and patches available for either Linux or Windows-based operating systems.

Another fun and software free version of the Ping of death is to continually ping a system with large packets of around 60,000 bytes. This usually won't cause the target system to crash, but it will perform a minor DoS attack, usually eating up processor cycles on the victim's system.

Land attack

Land attacks are formulated when a hacker inserts the same source port, destination port, and IP address of the victim's system into a spoofed packet and then sends the packet to the victim's computer. The targeted system will busily try to respond to itself, resulting in either a slowdown or complete system crash. Most operating systems have been patched and protected against these attacks, but as with all the other attacks discussed in this section, make sure that all appropriate service packs and patches have been applied.

Exam Tip   For the exam, know the various types of DoS attacks. You will probably be asked questions about each type — from SYN flood to Smurf.

Key Point Summary

This chapter discusses the how and why of auditing networks, as well as some common ways to make auditing network penetrations and attacks easier. Keep the following points in mind when you review this chapter:

✦ Hacker attacks leave "fingerprints" behind that are unique identifiers that administrators can use to help identify an attack. Knowing what different attack fingerprints look like will make your life as an auditor much easier.

✦ Knowing common targets of attack will help shorten the chase in most cases. Although focusing in on the various popular targets is a good way to start understanding common targets of attack, total network security should be the ultimate goal.

✦ Routers are a common target for hackers. Usually, they are entirely outside the target network, which means hackers encounter them first. It is important to ensure that routers are configured properly to block inappropriate access, and also to ensure that hardware is physically secure.

✦ Databases, which are likely to contain valuable company information, are popular targets for hackers. Databases are typically insecure and rarely have any practical security settings enabled.

✦ Because Web and FTP servers are open targets on the Internet, auditing them is a lengthy process. Web servers are among the most attacked servers around, so they have a slew of vulnerabilities. It is time-consuming to tighten down these services, but their security should be a top priority for companies. With the number of high-profile Web graffiti attacks on the rise, these Web graffiti attacks will constitute a majority of activity for the near future.

✦ Security options for e-mail servers are on the rise; using services such as PGP will help secure e-mail traffic. Allowing e-mail servers to relay messages from untrusted sources is a major concern, because it contributes to the distribution of e-mail–borne virus DoS attacks. Fixing this vulnerability to e-mail virus DoS attacks should be one of the first recommendations in any e-mail server audit.

✦ Name Server attacks are on the rise. Given the problems that Microsoft has had recently with DNS poisoning, attention should be paid to DNS activity on the network. This problem will get worse before it gets better, due to the inherent security problems that the current DNS system brings.

✦ Keeping informed is the best action any auditor can take when auditing for system bugs and vulnerabilities. You can stay ahead of the curve by reading the various security Web sites on the Internet and subscribing to security-related mailing lists.

✦ Trap doors and system bugs, which are usually hidden fairly well or are a result of regular software design and activity, tend to be difficult to audit. Of the two, trap doors are easier to audit because they often leave an open port for a hacker to use. Any type of software can be subject to trap doors, even game software. If the company obtains special software written for the company, make sure that the programmers keep the code tight and free of backdoors.

✦ DoS attacks are still very popular because they are an effective way to attack or possibly infiltrate a target network. DoS attacks are typically geared towards Windows-based operating systems, although other popular operating systems are not immune to their devastating effects.

✦ Buffer overflow attacks represent a dangerous type of DoS attack because they can leave the system in an unstable state, with the possibility that the hacker could arbitrarily execute code on the target system and thus gain full access. Buffer overflow attacks are usually the result of poor software writing.

✦ WinNuke used to be a popular DoS attack but has waned because most current operating systems are immune or at least resilient to its effects. WinNuke still sees some active duty occasionally, because many new users are getting on the Internet with totally un-patched, unsecured systems.

✦ Protecting against DoS attacks isn't an exact science, but you can take a few important steps. First, have a good firewall system implemented to protect the network. Second, ensure that the software that the company uses is patched with the latest security fixes. Third, establish time-outs on port activity to ward off possible attacks.

✦ Illicit servers can be useful tools for hackers who want to infiltrate the target system. Most illicit servers leave a fingerprint, such as an open port. Also, most current anti-virus packages will detect many popular illicit server programs, such as Back Orifice and NetBus.

✦ Trojan horses, viruses, and worms all tend to fall into a general category for detection. A good anti-virus program will detect most of them. Anti-virus packages should be a standard recommendation in any security audit. To protect against worms, ensure that users are informed about the various types of e-mail borne worms, such as Melissa and Love Bug.

✦ Most successful hackers will implement a multiple-point attack against a network to get the best results. Using one system to spoof the network, another to profile the system, and yet another to attack is common activity these days.

✦ Physical system penetration is something that most people don't think of as a potential threat, but if systems are out in the open, it's possible for hackers to do some damage, either on the server level or by physically doing damage to the hardware itself. Physical attacks can be dangerous and costly.

✦ It's important to secure Linux and Windows-based operating systems, because they are among the primary targets for hackers, next to Web servers. If a hacker knows a particular vulnerability in an operating systems' code, he or she will likely use it.

✦ Bad security policies will sink any organization. Most sites don't implement appropriate plans until after an incident has occurred. Creating strong passwords from the start will go a long way to providing a more complete security implementation.

✦ Knowing inherent weaknesses in different file systems is important because most operating systems have at least one security failing and ensuring that the administrators know what they are will be a key issue in a security audit.

✦ With the rise and relative performance of IP spoofing attacks, setting appropriate limits on inbound traffic is key to prevent yourself from being the victim of an attack. IP spoofing is used in almost every full-scale attack, including all of the major distributed DoS attacks in the last two years.

✦ SYN flood attacks constitute the majority of TCP/IP-based attacks. Most of these attacks are a variation of other previously designed attacks. They all typically provide erroneous data to a port in either a varying size or simply punish the port with more data than it can handle. These types of attacks are effective in either diverting attention from the main thrust or simply taking out the target in question. The latest operating system patches can protect you from the most popular attacks, such as Smurf, Fraggle, Ping of Death, Teardrop, and the like. However, these attacks can be rather effective against even patched systems when performing resource-depleting attacks or as middlemen in a larger distributed DoS attack. Using a properly setup firewall can help curb these type of attacks.

✦   ✦   ✦

STUDY GUIDE

This Study Guide presents ten assessment questions and four labs to test your knowledge of the exam objectives.

Assessment Questions

1. Why are routers common targets of attacks?

   A. They are a physical access point on the network.

   B. They are easily broken.

   C. They are usually the first item that a hacker comes to.

   D. They capture all inbound traffic and are susceptible to viruses.

2. Why are system bugs and trap doors hard to audit?

   A. They often are results of regular system operation.

   B. Programmers are malicious and tend to hide flaws.

   C. They are both invisible to detection by anti-virus software.

   D. They are only found in games.

3. Why are buffer overflow attacks so dangerous?

   A. They crash the system permanently.

   B. They upload system files while you reboot from the crash.

   C. They erase all the data in the boot sector.

   D. They launch malicious code in the leftover shell of a program.

4. What is the best way to catch Trojan horses, backdoor programs, and viruses?

   A. Watch the system logs for unauthorized logins.

   B. Lock down physical security around the server.

   C. Install a firewall package on the network.

   D. Use an up-to-date anti-virus package.

5. Ultimately, what is the most important thing to do as a security auditor?

   A. Install a firewall package on the network.

   B. Practice good security policy procedures.

   C. Keep on top of security problems and fixes on a regular basis.

   D. Practice DoS attacks on test servers to see how they affect systems.

6. Why do hackers often target databases?

   A. Databases have weak security.

   B. Databases usually contain a wealth of information.

   C. Databases are usually outside of a network's firewall.

   D. Databases are poorly written and vulnerable to buffer overflow attacks.

7. UNIX operating systems are typically very secure and thus require little security administration and attention. True or False?

8. E-mail viruses can be a form of DoS attack. True or False?

9. Hackers usually attack with a couple of different systems to help cover their tracks. True or False?

10. Illicit servers will usually close ports on the victim's system to stop access to system services. True or False?

Lab Exercises

Lab 13-1 Using NAT (NetBIOS Authentication Tool) to test password integrity

In this lab, you will use the command-line version of NAT to test brute force password attacks.

1. Copy all appropriate NAT files to a folder on your hard drive.

2. Run a command prompt and change to the NAT folder.

3. Pick a system to attack, preferably a system on your test network or a friend's system (make sure that your friend knows you are going to attack first).

4. Run the following command line to execute the attack:

   ```
   Nat 192.168.1.1 -o out.txt -u userlist.txt - p passlist.txt
   ```

   This command line assumes that certain file names for the password list and username list. Substitute when necessary. Press Enter.

5. You will see some text flash by. Depending on how many usernames and passwords you have in your files, this may take anywhere from seconds to hours. After the command has completed, use Notepad or DOS Edit to view the `out.txt` file.

6. Observe the output provided by NAT. If there is a successful password verification, it will notify you in the file. Otherwise, it will just say that it tried to connect.

7. If the target system has password failure lockouts set, you can attempt to run NAT a few more times until the server locks out the accounts, effectively providing a DoS attack. Otherwise, you may get lucky and crack a weak password. Usually, the administrator account can't be locked out for this very reason, so an administrator can at least log in and start unlocking accounts as needed.

Lab 13-2 Using WinNuke to attempt a DoS attack

1. Obtain a WinNuke GUI and unzip/install it to a folder on your system. You can also obtain WinNuke as a script for Linux/UNIX or Windows.

2. Go to the WinNuke folder and execute `WinNuke.exe`. A GUI pops up that asks you to insert an IP address and enter a message to display on the screen when the nuke is successful. Type an IP address for a Windows 9*x* system that can be attacked safely. (Either a friend's or a test system on your network.)

3. Click the NUKE button. After a few seconds, either WinNuke will report back a successful nuke or it will say, "Nuke failed" or "Couldn't connect," if the system is either patched or was an unrecognized operating system.

4. If the nuke was successful, the client machine should show, at a minimum, the attack message that you entered in a pop-up box. The system should either have a General Protection error on the screen or be entirely unstable and crash after a little bit of usage.

Keep in mind that these types of attacks are quite rare now, but NUKE is a good example of the ease in which a hacker can execute a DoS attack with widely available tools.

Lab 13-3 Using NetBus to backdoor a system

To complete this lab, you must first Obtain NetBus and unzip it to a folder on your test system.

1. Run Server.exe and you will see many different buttons in front of you. Each button has a useful task, but first you will want to ensure that the address bar

says "localhost" or 127.0.0.1 and then click the Connect button. After the connection is made, you can experiment with the various buttons.

2. NetBus can be very powerful if installed on a victim's system. Not all the functions work for every operating system, but try the different options and see what they can do. Easy ones to test are the Go To URL button, where you can remotely launch a Web site of your choosing, Open/Close CDROM, and Start Program.

3. If you are not going to use NetBus any longer, it's a good idea to remove it from your system. Click the "Server Admin" button and then select Remove Server to uninstall NetBus. It is advisable to delete the folder that you installed NetBus to as well, due to the risk that someone could install it again to your system and create a new vulnerability. If you are going to complete Lab 13-4, leave the NetBus folder where it is for now.

4. This type of hacking can be fun when performed against friends or other users on your home network. Messing around with their systems can be a way to learn about the hacking process. Back Orifice performs many of the same functions as NetBus, but NetBus has the best and easiest to use interface (hands-down!). It's a good idea to check out both packages to see which of the two you like better.

Lab 13-4 Checking for suspicious ports from backdoor programs under Windows

You can use many utilities to do port scans that can be used on your servers to figure out what ports are open on your system. However, a free utility is included with Windows that does the job just fine.

1. Run a command prompt. Under Windows NT, click Start ➪ Run, then type **cmd** and press Enter. (Under Windows 9*x*, you should follow the same steps, except instead of typing cmd, type **command**.)

2. At the command prompt, type the following command to scan for open TCP ports: **Netstat –a –p tcp**.

3. This action will output the list of open TCP ports on the system. Conversely, by replacing TCP with UPD, you will get a list of those ports. Not including the –p switch with a type of port will provide all open ports. Some ports will be labeled with their function, and some just with a port number.

4. If you left NetBus installed from the previous lab, you should see port 12345 and 12346 open on the system. By default, these ports are the typical NetBus ports, but keep in mind that most Trojan horses will allow for customization of what ports it uses to accept connections.

5. Knowing the programs on your system and the ports that they use can help you figure out what each port does. Sometimes you can connect to the port in question with a Telnet program and receive a banner that may give more information about what the port is used for. Trial-and-error is the name of the game here, although using a professional system scanning utility or anti-virus package are the quickest ways to catch backdoors, such as NetBus.

Answers to Chapter Questions

Chapter Pre-Test

1. Routers, Web servers, and e-mail servers are three common targets of attack, because they usually reside on the outside of a network.

2. A trap door is a system bug where regular system operation can result in an unexpected condition or vulnerability.

3. A very good way to find Trojan horses residing on systems is to use an updated anti-virus software package. Another is to watch for suspicious port activity.

4. Hackers engage in IP spoofing to either distract from the actual attack or to cover their tracks.

5. Three popular DoS-style attacks are: Smurf, Teardrop, and SYN Flood. A couple of other popular types are Fraggle and Ping of Death.

Assessment Questions

1. **C.** They are usually the first item that a hacker comes to. Typically, items exposed to the Internet will be first hit because it's easier for a hacker to get to.

2. **A.** They often are results of regular system operation. Often a trap door can lead to an unexpected vulnerability due to the software performing normally.

3. **D.** Launch malicious code in the leftover shell of a program. Often, when a buffer overflow occurs, a hacker may launch code in the leftover shell of the program attacked. Sometimes, this shell will have administrative or system access.

4. **D.** Use an up-to-date anti-virus package. A good anti-virus software package can catch most common Trojan horses, or stop new ones from being installed.

5. **C.** Keep on top of security problems and fixes on a regular basis. Knowing as much as you can about problems and how to fix them is important because hackers can obtain the same information you can. When performing an audit, thinking like a hacker and knowing where the problems lie will make the difference between a good audit and a poor one.

6. **B.** You can usually find a wealth of information in them. Companies keep most of their valuable information — such as client lists, financial information, and personnel data — in databases.

7. **B.** False. UNIX operating systems are typically just as weak as any other popular operating system. The same amount of attention must be paid to UNIX, Linux, Novell, or Microsoft operating systems.

8. **A.** True. Viruses like Melissa and Love Letter can propagate using contact lists on user's workstations. They can flood e-mail servers with messages, possibly taking them entirely offline or slowing the flow of messages to a trickle.

9. **A.** True. Using one system to perform IP spoofing and yet another to perform a DoS attack can help cover where the actual infiltration is coming from.

10. **B.** False. Illicit servers usually open ports to allow remote connections to the victim's system.

For More Information

For more information on the topics in this chapter, take a look at these links:

✦ www-106.ibm.com/developerworks/library/overflows/index.html — This site helps you learn the basics of buffer overflows.

✦ www.windowsitsecurity.com — This site provides up-to-date security articles and bulletins.

✦ www.microsoft.com/security — This site is the best source for Microsoft security issues.

Intrusion Detection and Prevention

EXAM OBJECTIVES

- ✦ Understand the principles of intrusion detection
- ✦ Implement proactive detection
- ✦ Know how to distract intruders and contain their activity
- ✦ Setting traps
- ✦ Using a tripwire
- ✦ Jail usage and considerations

CHAPTER PRE-TEST

1. What are three common ways to distract intruders once they have gained access to a system?

2. What is a jail used for in system security?

3. When dealing with crackers, is it best to take a wait-and-see approach or a proactive approach?

4. Can login scripts be used to implement security features?

5. Is using dummy password files a good idea in a Windows NT network?

✦ Answers to these questions can be found at the end of the chapter. ✦

Detecting and containing intruder activities on networks is as important as securing them. This chapter looks at ways to detect cracking attempts and activity on networks, and ways to contain or trap intruders in the act. Understanding these detection and containment methods should be one of your primary goals as a security administrator or auditor.

Understanding Intrusion Detection

 Understand the principles of intrusion detection

The need for intrusion detection should be readily apparent to anyone who has witnessed the rash of Web site break-ins and vandalism of Web sites in the past two years. Even sites that are incredibly secure, such as Yahoo.com or Amazon.com, have been victimized by vigilant crackers who managed to find their loopholes. For example, back in late 1997, crackers penetrated Yahoo!'s search engine site and left Web graffiti demanding the release of convicted Kevin Mitnick—possibly the most famous cracker of them all. When the security administrator at Yahoo! was asked about the event, he stated that no site is completely secure.

The main problem for most security administrators is time. Simply put, administrators don't have enough time to keep up with every security vulnerability. As it is, most security administrators do double duty as network administrators or help desk personnel with nary a moment to perform the most basic patching on vulnerable servers.

Even if you have dedicated security staff and the latest and greatest hardware and software, it is likely that you will have a vulnerability or two. Additionally, if you're dealing with a high-profile site like Amazon.com or Microsoft.com, the number of attempted security breaches goes up. As you have learned, security threats arise from many different sources—for example, from outside professional attackers, company employees poking around where they shouldn't, or joy riders playing around with the latest cracking utility or script release. As pessimistic as it sounds, you should be prepared for the worst.

Automating IDS

 Implement proactive detection

Most computer cracking and intrusion happens at night. This is because most system administrators and security analysts are home at that time, not monitoring the systems the way they are during the day.

Being proactive in your detection techniques gives you a leg up on the crackers. A good rule is to at least enable system event auditing. Even if you aren't going to use an aftermarket software package, you should track what is going on with the system while you aren't there watching over it. Event logging and auditing will help make the tracking of new and existing security problems easier and should be the cornerstone of active intrusion detection on your systems.

Striking a balance between security monitoring and inconvenience is always a battle, especially if your network has odd usage hours. In most cases, you should be able to schedule your scans for late evening or early morning so you don't affect user operations. If you don't plan on using an aftermarket security-scanning package, consider using a program such as NT Scheduler. An intruder could use NT Scheduler to execute malicious batch files, but it can also be used to execute batch files of your own. These scripts can be designed to log current connections and resources in use, which can make tracking unusual activity much easier.

You can program your batch files to do many things — you are only as limited as your ability to perform batch programming. You can find many programs on the Internet that will help you write quick and effective batch programs. One very popular scripting package is Kixtart, which is available for download at www.kixtart. org. Another very useful script writing software package is Perl, which is available for download at www.perl.com.

> **Tip**
>
> Be flexible with your schedule when automating intrusion detection. Not scanning when you should, or disrupting users while they are trying to perform their jobs can cost your company time and money.

Batch scripting can be a very useful tool in your security implementation. A well-written batch file or two can save many hours when compared to manually tracking activity during off hours. Batch files can even be programmed to respond to data collected during a scan. Implementing setups like this can take a lot of time, but are worth it in the long run.

Having batch files output their results to a text file provides a wealth of information on the specific areas you set up to have scanned. If you have tried to read through Windows NT's cryptic event logs, you will understand very quickly the time saved by performing custom and direct automated batch file scans. When planning scheduled batch file scans of your network, consider this: Running the Windows NT Task Scheduler from a secure administrative system that is safe inside your network, rather than directly on the servers themselves, may be more secure.

> **Caution**
>
> Using the Windows Scheduler involves security risks. In Windows NT, the Scheduler runs with full system rights by default. Crackers can use Task Scheduler to execute any type of batch file they want. Limit NT Scheduler's permissions to Read-Only if you plan on implementing this setting. If not, disable NT Scheduler entirely for the best security.

Using login scripts

Normally, login scripts are used to customize user settings or apply updates and security policies on the network. As covered in the last section, batch files are very powerful and can be used to perform a variety of actions, such as scheduling system audit scans or gathering software and operating system event log data. They can also be used to enhance a network's security features. Login scripts only run when a user has properly logged into the network. Because crackers want to have an authorized login account on the network to compromise Root or administrative access, login scripts give security administrators an opportunity to build in a few security features to catch them. You can have several system auditing tools execute to check the validity of the user trying to log in.

A typical option is to create a login script that runs when an administrator logs in. The batch file can log the connecting IP address and host name and store them for scrutiny at a later date. After you have gathered information on logins, you can reference IP address and host names for systems that don't match the typical administrator login activity and look for suspicious connections. The best thing about this type of logging is that an intruder is likely to be unaware of anyone tracking his or her connection, which will add an element of surprise when you want to trap or punish the intruder later.

Login scripts shouldn't be limited to auditing administrative or system accounts. Using similar techniques on regular user accounts is also a good idea. Attackers won't be able to gain administrative access right off the bat because of strong passwords — or because of their concern that those accounts are monitored more closely than a standard user account. They may go after regular user accounts first and then try to obtain administrative access from there. Crackers can often use tricks and utilities to alter permissions on standard user accounts, or to glean more information about what type of security exists on the system before attempting a full-fledged attack. Therefore, using this type of scanning on administrative, user, and system accounts is a great way to provide global auditing. Additionally, performing global auditing during a login script allows for execution of any type of security scanning that you want to design when an account is activated.

System accounts are usually not used to log on to the network like a regular user, and you will probably notice if a system account is being used in this way. You could have the login script activate some kind of SNMP notification by network message or e-mail if someone tries to log in using this type of account. Even if you aren't close to the system or it's after business hours, have the login script send an alert to your e-mail account at home. This way, you can be notified immediately if one of these critical accounts has been compromised. At any rate, it's a good idea to identify normal activity on these accounts so that you aren't setting up false alerts on regular login activity.

Login scripts are only limited by your ability to write in simple scripting languages. Microsoft has provided the robust and useful Kixtart batch programming utility, which is available for download at http://www.kixtart.org. You can also check message boards or ask experienced batch file coders for tips on your batch file needs and problems.

Login scripts and batch files for security auditing are free and enabled on almost every operating system that is currently available. This means that it should be easy to persuade management to implement scripting solutions.

Automating audit analysis

Establishing detailed logging can provide the largest wealth of information for any security administrator trying to get a handle on network security. The data logged by the system in security logs can provide extra protection against intrusions. Remember, as a security administrator, you must know your vulnerabilities before intruders do, and logging security activity can provide the upper hand when monitoring network access. It is often a daunting task to select what gets logged and audited. Many system events and activities can be logged and many are important. Enabling logging of login failures and/or successes is a good start. If the server has shares that are secured, setting file access logging to watch those shares is probably a good idea.

Monitoring behavior and logging activity on your network hardware will also provide helpful information if you are monitoring inbound or outbound traffic on your network. Proactive auditing can take a lot of time out of any administrator's day, but, by automating event log scanning with automated scripts, you can help recover some of that time.

Scripts can be used to scan files and report on a particular occurrence, such as a login from an unknown IP address or a user logging in from a system that they shouldn't be connecting to. As mentioned in the last section, scripts can be designed to do anything that you program them to do. Designing a script to alleviate the chore of administering security on a network will go a long way toward making sure that other areas of weak security are cared for properly. For example, by lessening the amount of time spent gathering log files using a script, you can spend more time researching additional patches or security fixes for other areas of your servers and network.

In the Real World

When selecting which items to log and which items to generate audits on, the best practice is to gather more information than you think you need. When you "over log," you increase the likelihood that you will be alerted to suspicious events that you may not have considered logging in the first place. Don't limit your auditing to only logins and file access.

System scanning and checksum analysis

Most crackers will attempt to use some type of Trojan horse program to secure access on systems and servers. This can be done out in the open or it can be hidden. The "out-in-the-open" method drops the Trojan horse on the system as it was made, making the intrusion visible and increasing the likelihood of being caught by an antivirus scanner if the system is so equipped. The "hidden" method involves incorporating the Trojan horse into an already existing executable or system file. Hidden in common system executables, they will either be run by the user at some point or are system files that will execute upon the next reboot.

Usually, intruders will hide the backdoor in an application such as calc.exe or explorer.exe, hoping that an unsuspecting user will execute either of these files and activate the software that allows the intruders in. You can audit for Trojan horses on your servers and systems with a *checksum analysis*.

Analyzing the checksum data, (date, time, file version number, file size, and so on) enables you to monitor files that may have been affected. If any of these programs have changed in size — or have the wrong time stamp on them — the files are likely infected with a virus or Trojan horse of some type. To perform a checksum analysis, you must have some idea of what properties the file originally had. It may be advisable to record the checksum information when you first build the system or install software that you want to watch. Also, remember to update the checksum information after any upgrades, patches, or software installations to ensure that the information hasn't changed.

Caution   Some executables change in size spontaneously as applications use them. However, this isn't the norm, and most executables stay the same size.

Most anti-virus and system security scanners employ file checksums for monitoring systems. Using these types of anti-virus scanning software can save you a tremendous amount of time and effort. However, if you operate your security implementation on a tight budget, a checksum analysis can be incorporated into scripts by selecting a few key files to monitor manually. Also, having an antivirus software package scanning the servers and systems should be mandatory regardless of the implementation.

If you run across a file that appears to have been changed and is either infected by a virus or Trojan horse, replace the affected file right away with a known good version. At this point, you should also try to figure out where the cracker infiltrated the network so you can lock down the vulnerability.

Although checksum analysis can be a very time-consuming process, it can yield good results when dealing with rogue viruses or Trojan horses. If you perform regular system logging as discussed in the previous section, you can quickly and easily track down when and where a cracker has made changes. Instead of turning every single rock over, you can audit the logs and narrow down the file and user rights activity to that particular file.

Distracting Intruders

 Know how to distract crackers and contain their activity

Although the focus of this chapter has thus far been directed toward stopping an intruder or cleaning up after an attack, there are ways to help security administrators slow down, stop, or distract crackers when they attempt to break into a network. You want to distract intruders for several reasons: First, to redirect them from the actual data that you are trying to protect, and second, to keep them connected to your network and systems long enough to find the intruder's location or catch the cracker in the act.

This type of "bait and switch" activity is similar to what you would see in a spy movie, where the FBI or CIA attempt to keep the perpetrator on the line as long as possible to pinpoint the origin of the call. The longer the intruder is connected to your network, the better chance you have to gain information. This information will help the authorities when they begin their investigation of the attack or intrusion and will also help you formulate your defense.

You have many options for distracting intruders on your network. A common method is to set a rule on your firewall that takes potential crackers to a second empty system that is clear of any access to the main network. In effect, this allows the cracker to play in the network equivalent of a kiddie pool. If the crackers realize that they can't benefit from further exploitation of your "dummy" system, they will most likely go in search of a better target.

Medium to large networks often incorporate some type of distraction technology, which can vary from specialized software to full-blown systems with a variety of distractions or misinformation to keep the cracker poking around long enough to tighten their own noose.

Distractions can vary from decoy files and databases to dummy user accounts and systems. Systems and software used in this manner are often called *honey pots* because they pose as a sweet opportunity to crackers if set up properly.

 Setting up honey pots or distractions carries risks that may not be evident on the surface. If intruders realize that they are involved in a honey pot, they may end up leaving; however, if they took offense, they may level an even stronger attack, bypassing the honey pot completely. It may be best to just end the cracker's connection entirely — hopefully, the cracker will get the hint to back off.

Attracting interest to dummy elements

 Setting traps

An early target for most crackers is testing the default system settings and accounts. For a cracker, finding a server on a network with the default administrator's password and security settings is the stuff that dreams are made of. Tricky security administrators can use this type of approach to take a cracker's intrusion and turn it against them, as discussed in the following sections.

Dummy accounts

A default setting typically attacked first is the venerable Administrator account. As you have probably learned, the first step in account management is to rename the Administrator account to limit possible attacks. Then modify the Administrator account and either give it very limited rights or disable the account entirely. The account will still show up and respond to login requests, but it will never authenticate properly — or, if the account is active but with limited rights, users won't be able to cause any damage while logged in. The next step is to enable account access logging and auditing on the Administrator account, so if anyone tries to log in to the Administrator account, the event log can send off alerts to administrators, informing them that people are poking around in an account that never gets used.

This approach can also be applied to network shares. Create network shares with eye-catching names, such as "employee pay databases" or "customer lists." Then, set auditing on these folders to notify you when someone tries to access them; leave a file inside that says, "You have illegally accessed a restricted area. This event has been logged. We reserve the right to prosecute any intruders on this network." This type of scare will probably send most, if not all, crackers off your servers very quickly.

Dummy accounts can be very effective in stopping most casual crackers from gaining access to networks, and the best part of this solution is that it is free and should only take about five minutes to set up

Tip   Changing the name of the Administrator account can cause problems if the account is used by certain system services or software to gain access to server resources. Most major applications will typically create their own system account and don't need to use the Administrator account, but it is a good idea to perform a cursory check first.

Dummy files

If you want to take the distraction theme one step further, consider implementing dummy files on potentially high-risk systems. You can make many different types of files; for example, create a dummy spreadsheet with fake information in it and label it with an obvious name. You can do the same for client databases, inventory pricing lists, prototype product development, and more. If the cracker in question is a spy or someone from a competing company looking for information, these dummy files could keep them busy for a while.

Creating the dummy files and placing them on servers at this point isn't going far enough. Place the files in obvious locations, but don't make it look like a trap. If you want to make the cracker's life even more difficult, try either encrypting the file or locking it with a password if it's a Microsoft Office document. After you have placed the files where you want them, set the appropriate security around the files to monitor for activity.

Dummy password files

After a hacker has taken root in your systems, he or she may attempt to obtain a copy of your password lists. Setting up dummy password files, such as dummy administrative accounts and dummy files, simply makes good sense. When you set up dummy password files, make sure that you use accounts that are realistic but not in use anywhere else on the system.

Tip

Setting up dummy password files isn't possible under Windows NT, due to the design of the password structure. All accounts and passwords are housed in one SAM with no way of pointing it to an alternate file. Fortunately, most varieties of UNIX allow you to set up dummy password files.

Attackers will use various brute-force password cracking software packages to try to gain passwords for accounts located in the password files. Programs such as L0phtcrack for Windows NT and CRACK for UNIX systems try every combination of a password, in the form of a password hash. These password hashes are tried over and over again on various accounts until a successful password match is found. Programs such as L0phtcrack can take anywhere from mere seconds to weeks to complete, depending on the speed of the computer and the complexity of the password. If strong passwords are maintained, this process can take a long time. In the UNIX world, if a dummy password file with strong passwords is used, the process can be extremely long and fruitless for the attacker. In most cases, attackers will give up if no usable accounts or passwords are cracked in a reasonable amount of time.

In the Real World

The best practice for securing Windows NT passwords is ensuring that strong password policies are observed across the network, especially on administrative accounts of any type. Under UNIX, it is advisable to enable shadowing of passwords and to use a dummy password file list. Although most passwords can eventually be broken, chances are that if breaking the password takes too long, the hacker will either move on, or the password will have expired or been changed anyway.

Tripwires

Objective ▶ Using a tripwire

Setting a tripwire to watch over critical system assets is happening more and more these days as honey pots and dummy files become more popular. When an intruder "trips" the protection in a certain area, he or she will trigger whatever security setting you have enabled. Suppose, for instance, that an intruder penetrates your network defenses and tries to adjust a setting to gain administrative access. If you set a tripwire to monitor a particular point, such as administrative password files, you can set up a number of different tricks and alerts to shore up system security.

You can set up tripwires to perform a wide variety of tasks, such as:

◆ Logging the intruder's connection information

◆ Tracking changes to system configuration

◆ Disconnecting the intruder

◆ Alerting the administrator that the wire has been tripped

◆ Bringing down the hacked system entirely

Take care when setting up tripwires that can trap or potentially cause damage to the server. Setting up a tripwire that disconnects the system or brings it down entirely could cause problems with other systems and servers. If the tripwires are set up in an area where they can be easily tripped over by an administrator or user, problems may arise if a tripwire disconnects the server right away. If you set up a tripwire that will retaliate against an intruder, you must take care to assess the possible ramifications of taking the attack to an intruder.

> **Tip**　When setting up tripwires, it's a good idea to test them on a *non-production server* (one that won't affect network data).

An intruder's ultimate goal when manipulating system files is to accomplish the change without being detected — even after the change is in effect. Programs such as Tripwire for Windows NT or UNIX allow for quick and easy tripwire settings. However, locating important system files in read-only directories, media, or hard drives to limit any possible manipulation of important system files is advisable. Keep in mind that many system files are constantly updated by the operating system and may not be able to relocate to a read-only area.

You can set up tripwires for free in several ways; for example, batch files can perform system audits based on security logs, or Windows NT can be set up to audit login failure and success. A utility included in most versions of Windows operating systems is Performance Monitor. Performance Monitor can be used to analyze system resource activity, and can also be set to send an alert to an administrative account if certain activities occur. For example, have Performance Monitor send an alert to your account if someone tries to unsuccessfully access a certain file or user account several times. This type of alert can be set up for almost any type of system activity that can be monitored. You can also set Performance Monitor to alert you when CPU or network usage hits a specified level, possibly indicating a DoS attack against that system.

> **Tip**　Performance Monitor may not be installed by default when you install Windows. To install it, go to Start ⇨ Settings ⇨ Control Panel ⇨ Add/Remove Programs ⇨ Windows Setup, and select Performance Monitor from the appropriate category. To quickly check to see if it is installed, Click Start and then Run. In the command box, type **perfmon.exe** and press Enter. If it loads, it is installed on your system.

Choosing and monitoring important system files, user accounts, and activity can help cut down on the amount of time that you spend watching every minute detail on every server on your network. The time it takes to set tripwires is minimal compared to the amount of time they will eventually save you.

Creating a jail

 Jail usage and considerations

Network administrators often create an active jail on a network to provide extra time in case of attack to gain information on the intruders. This information can be used in order to either catch them or launch a counterattack. Jails typically contain dummy files or information, such as fake human resources databases or spreadsheets with false username and password information, which pique the crackers' interest long enough for the administrator to gather information on the intruders. Jails, however, can be a double-edged sword.

Jails, like honey pots, are usually set up on a network and contain false information, but unlike honey pots, they are generally located on or somewhere near the main network that you are trying to protect. Also unlike a honey pot, a jail is designed to keep and hold an intruder in place long enough to get the necessary information, rather than just act as a diversion. If an intruder recognizes a jail—or gets bored with the information that he or she is looking at—then the intruder may disconnect immediately, thus preventing the administrator from potentially gaining data on the attacker. Moreover, the intruder may break out of the jail and into your main network, where there is more opportunity to really do some damage.

Setting up a jail should be allowed in any security implementation, but it often conflicts with standing security policies. Before you implement jails on the network, make sure that everyone involved understands their purpose; also, be sure that your actions are permissible.

 All security implementations should be brought up with the head of the IT department and the board of directors or company principals. Making a financial and benefits case that is clear and easy to understand will help greatly when trying to sell them on the importance of implementing a jail.

Jails can be particularly useful to a large network. Before intruders can break into your network, they will probably have to work their way through several other networks or sites. Tracking a cracker's origin (in other words, gaining the trace route back to the intruder's network and obtaining packet data from that source) may take you a considerable amount of time. Like a phone tap, these procedures can take a while to establish and gain the necessary information. If you use a jail setup, you will likely slow the cracker down long enough to obtain the necessary data.

Experienced crackers will usually only touch on a network for a very short period of time, maybe five or so minutes per session. They may also be active on several different systems or networks at once. This can cloak their activities and make the intrusion activity appear more infrequent and less of a threat. Rarely will you see an intruder perform an information sweep and then commence an attack right away; usually, they will prod other areas on the network so they have a better idea of what they are getting into. Intruders will disguise their attacks, making it more difficult for administrators to locate and stop them.

Tip Many security administrators get a bit squeamish when they think about practicing cracking methods. However, practicing these methods will help you see overall network security from a cracker's point of view, thus making it easier for you to implement effective security.

Ultimately, a proactive approach to security will help you realize the best protection for your network. Good security administrators are paranoid about "what could go wrong." The best way to lessen this paranoia is to research and *know with certainty* what could go wrong. Setting up as many traps and jails as possible will also conceal sensitive information from crackers, perhaps keeping them off your network entirely. The jails and traps discussed in this chapter are only the tip of the iceberg. More good methods are being developed and even more software packages are being designed to help administrators perform proactive security on networks.

Handling Intruders

When handling an intruder, it's not enough to simply drop the connection. Some intruders may think the disconnection is a network anomaly and try again. Distracting and detaining intruders are essential components in a strong security implementation, but they probably won't stop intruders entirely. The best way to stop and keep intruders away for the long term is to punish them.

Caution Punishing intruders will most likely get rid of them permanently. However, be prepared for the cracker that considers punishment an insult and continues — with renewed energy — to crack your system.

Principals of deterrence

Successfully detecting and slowing down the advance of an intruder is limited by:

✦ Your ability to think like an intruder

✦ Your knowledge of cracker tools

✦ Your knowledge of the network's security vulnerabilities, its failings, and its strong points

You can deter cracker activity on your network in many ways. WinNuke is especially helpful, for example. Use it in a script that will attack the intruder when they attempt to connect or when they set off a tripwire in your network. However, WinNuke will rarely work on most up-to-date operating systems. Another good idea is to perform a reverse DoS attack by using the Chargen service on your system.

Chargen, which is rarely used anymore, is an old connection troubleshooting tool that sends a constant stream of characters until the opposite end disconnects or falls off the network. You could effectively set Chargen to a port (such as the FTP port 21 or Web server port 80, if they aren't already in use). When an intruder attempts to connect to the port, your system sends a Chargen stream of characters to their system that will usually crash the application that they are using to scan or attack with. Because the Chargen client service is not designed to handle the sheer amount of characters that it will send, the application or operating system will typically freeze up. If the cracker's system isn't configured very well or is taxed as it is, a reverse Chargen attack could entirely emancipate the resources of the cracker's computer or crash it entirely.

When you set up Chargen attacks, don't set them on a port that is in use for another service. A good idea is to enable this type of reverse attack on a honey pot or decoy system that houses dummy files and services. You are only limited by your creativity — this is the time when your knowledge of crackers' attack tools comes in handy, helping you to create an effective counterattack.

Detection tools

The number of intrusion and network vulnerability tools and software packages has exploded in recent years. These types of tools can vary from simple network packet sniffers to full-blown intrusion detection software that monitors your network and servers in real time. Although you have learned about the appropriate use of these tools to date, figuring out new ways to use them will provide you with an opportunity to develop a solid detection and deterrence strategy.

Depending on how they are configured, these tools can help you determine whether an intruder has made an attempt to breach your security — or has actually done so. Some software packages can even monitor sequences of events that match the blueprint of an intruder's attack and notify you of an impending attack before it even happens. Exploring these types of packages to enhance your network's security is time well spent.

Caution   Many people think that by simply installing a single security scanner or intrusion detection software package, they are completely safe from attack. Although doing so will help shore up security, a solid plan — including the aforementioned techniques and diligence in fixing known and new security holes — will bring about stronger security. As with anti-virus software, keeping your security canning and intrusion software up to date is important, as new security vulnerabilities are found every day.

These types of aftermarket intrusion detection and vulnerability scanning software packages can produce a wide variety of responses to attacks and intrusion. Some software packages may simply notify the administrator of the event, while others may take action on their own and root out information about the cracker trying to intrude on your system. And some may alert you to vulnerabilities that you weren't aware of, helping you tighten security on your network and firewalls.

The "Inverse Golden Rule"

As you have undoubtedly heard time and time again, knowledge is power. Thus, knowing your vulnerabilities is very important to your continued network security. You should attempt cracking methods on your own network and servers on a regular basis. This is called the *inverse golden rule*: "Do unto yourself as others do unto you."

In practice, the inverse golden rule requires a lot of time, research, and effort to ensure that you are fixed up with the latest patches for vulnerabilities and holes in your security. After you have made any type of major change to your network or security, test to see if, by accident, a change that you made has left you vulnerable to attack.

The best plan of action to promote security is to read industry material, visit security-related Web sites, and try out cracker utilities and tools. When you start, you may want to set up a test system that mimics the server or servers that you have on your network and then use a variety of tools and scripts to try to crack your setup.

Microsoft and third-party security-related companies often release security bulletins on a specific vulnerability, and you may see code or tools designed to exploit that vulnerability. Stay informed about such matters, and test the tools on your setup — you will gain a better understanding of what your network looks like from an intruder's point of view.

If you can't obtain a system that is identical to your server due to budget restraints, get your hands on a workstation that can be set up similarly to the other server. You don't necessarily need identical hardware, but the workstation should have the same operating system settings, services such as IIS, and database settings.

In the Real World

What crackers hope for the most is a network that ignores or pays little attention to its network security. Network security is a full-time endeavor; you can't simply install patches and hot fixes when you build the system and expect it to stay secure forever. Keeping yourself in the know and trying out different types of security, such as setting up a jail or performing vigilante attacks against intruders, will give you a leg up on crackers.

Key Point Summary

This chapter discussed various methods of distracting and punishing crackers. You can protect and take action against intruders in many ways, and you are only limited by your knowledge and ability to think ahead. Proactive security will always produce the best results. Keep the following points in mind:

✦ Intrusion detection is an important element in any network security implementation. Even fairly secure networks on large organizations such as Yahoo! and eBay are vulnerable to intrusions.

✦ Time is a constant battle for any security administrator. You must balance the time that you spend researching new vulnerabilities with time spent maintaining and updating your current security while keeping on top of old ones. Utilizing available software and techniques will help you reclaim lost time.

✦ Regardless of the number of personnel in your company or the quality of your hardware, you are likely to have a vulnerability or two.

✦ A security administrator can't simply focus on protecting against attacks from the Internet. Attacks can be initiated from many places — from inside your company on your own network, or even from a contractor working on equipment in your server area. Considering the big security picture is as important as installing the latest fix.

✦ The vast majority of cracking happens at night, for obvious reasons. At most sites, security and network administrators are usually at home during the night hours — unless they run a 24-hour vigil on the server hardware.

✦ It doesn't take much effort to be proactive in your network security implementation. Tasks as simple as enabling login and resource auditing can keep one eye on your network and one eye on your security. Enabling logging and auditing will help identify existing and potential problems before they occur.

✦ Finding a way to scan your network when it won't interfere with regular network usage can be tricky. Plan to monitor when your typical network activities drop off. In most cases, late night monitoring may work best, because this is the time when most problems occur anyway.

✦ Take advantage of the free utilities that come with operating systems, such as NT Scheduler. NT Scheduler can help run automated scripts that can take the burden of scanning your networks and help recover lost time weeding through the many meaningless logs that your auditing will generate. Be careful to know the potential vulnerabilities that your helper tool may create; for example, NT scheduler can be used by crackers to execute malicious code on your system if they gain access.

✦ When writing your own scripts and batch files to perform security functions on your network, you are only limited by your creativity or your ability to write scripts. If writing scripts isn't your forte, you can find many good resources on the Internet to help you. A good rule of thumb when running any script to scan your network is to always execute the scripts from a secure administrative machine that resides inside your network.

✦ Login scripts are not only used to provide appropriate network resources to authenticated users; they can also be used to perform various security and administrative tasks. Login scripts can be used to call in smaller security-oriented scripts when a particular user or member of a group logs in. Don't hesitate to use this handy resource.

✦ Login scripts can be set up to log connection information and even active alerts if failed logins occur. The great thing about login scripts is that they can be customized like any other script to do almost anything you want. Another benefit of login scripts (and scripts in general) is that they are free. Therefore, they are an easy sell to any management committee when trying to get approval to implement.

✦ Enabling logging on your network will give you current and past data on network activity and allow you to make the right decisions when planning your next security implementation. Selecting what to log and audit is a daunting task, but monitoring login and file activity should be first on the list.

✦ Checksum analysis can be tedious if you try to perform it manually. Using anti-virus software can help ferret out most common Trojan horses these days, however some are very cleverly contained within system software that may not normally be scanned. Note the appropriate size of various system utilities and executables in order to figure out if your network has been penetrated.

✦ If you find that you are, in fact, host to one or more Trojan horses, simply replace the affected file (if any) with a legitimate version from backups, source media, or a similar system. Keep in mind while watching checksums that some executables change all the time while the system is using them. Monitoring these files for a while is advisable before replacing them.

✦ Distracting crackers bound for your network is as much an art as a science. There are many ways to detour crackers who are breaking in. A popular way is to set up a rule on a firewall to redirect crackers to empty or useless systems, putting them off on some harmless system.

✦ Distractions can include vulnerable-looking systems to decoy files and other sources of information, such as database files. However, be cautious when setting up distractions, because some crackers may take offense if they find out they have been duped, redoubling their efforts to break in.

✦ Setting up dummy accounts is an age-old trick in the security world. While not always entirely effective, it can slow down or stop many crackers from getting anywhere when trying to break in. You can also enable auditing on the dummy account so that if someone tries to use it, you have a pretty good idea it's an intruder.

✦ Dummy files can be set up on a variety of systems, even important ones inside your network. Consider setting up dummy employee wage spreadsheets or customer information databases and placing them in obvious locations that are far removed from the real information. Thus, if crackers manage to break in, they may go for the dummy files and ignore the legitimate ones.

✦ Consider setting up dummy password files on your servers. While this type of decoy won't work the way that Windows NT handles accounts, you can use it under UNIX-type operating systems and it should be considered for almost any system. For the best implementation, combine this technique with shadowing of the password lists and strong account passwords.

✦ Tripwires can be useful tools in your security toolkit. Some tripwires can simply notify you when an issue arises; others can replace altered files or settings. Furthermore, you can have tripwires perform system functions, such as dropping connections and taking the system offline entirely. When setting up tripwires, always keep in mind the potential ramifications if someone inside the network sets off the tripwire by accident.

✦ You can set up tripwires in many different ways; even system auditing is a type of tripwire. Not all tripwires cost money to install, but many good tripwire software packages are available that can help automate the process and take some of the burden off your shoulders.

✦ Setting up jails is useful for a couple of reasons. First, you can trap the cracker long enough to obtain the necessary information to either retaliate or inform the authorities. Second, you can possibly punish the cracker for intruding on your network. Be aware, however, that jails must be used with care. As with distractions and honey pots, crackers may take offense when they see a jail, breaking out and causing even more havoc.

✦ Before putting any plans in place to punish crackers that have intruded on your network, think of the potential ramifications — legal and otherwise. Vigilante strikes by security administrators is still a new issue that hasn't entirely been fleshed out by the courts. Always take in the big picture before launching a retaliatory attack.

✦ Utilizing automated security scanning and detection software has gained momentum in the last couple of years, due to the time restraints involved in monitoring security on large networks. Today, many good software packages are on the market and even more are on the way. It is advisable to explore these resources and see if they can help your implementation.

✦ Practicing cracking on your own system is a good way to understand a cracker's perspective and also to better understand your network security. Security administrators shouldn't feel like they are above performing actual cracking on their own network or test system.

✦   ✦   ✦

STUDY GUIDE

This Study Guide presents ten assessment questions and four lab exercises to test your knowledge of the exam topic area.

Assessment Questions

1. Why is proactive detection of problems on your network important?

   A. Break-ins usually occur when you are not around to monitor your network.

   B. Crackers are always trying to break in.

   C. If you aren't proactive, your security will fail from neglect.

   D. Someone who is proactive will take your job.

2. In addition to helping apply resources to users logging in, login scripts can also _____.

   A. Monitor people's login habits

   B. Display nice login screens for the user's enjoyment

   C. Allow access to secure resources

   D. Run other security scripts when a user connects

3. When performing checksum analysis, you usually know that a file is infected with a Trojan horse when _____.

   A. It has the extension .TRJ on the end of the file after .EXE.

   B. The size of the file is too large or too small, or the time stamp is wrong.

   C. The file is deleted.

   D. The file has an .SRC file extension.

4. When setting up a dummy account, what system account is the most important to rename?

   A. Administrator

   B. Guest

   C. Your account

   D. Exa-admin

5. The security surrounding dummy files isn't important. True or False?

6. It is smart to implement dummy password files under UNIX. True or False?

7. Tripwires can cause damage or downtime to your network servers or systems. True or False?

8. Typically, jails are used to achieve what result?

　　A. Create a protected area for administrative files

　　B. Punish users for forgetting their password

　　C. Keep crackers online long enough to obtain connection information

　　D. Rehabilitation of crackers once they have been caught

9. When punishing an intruder, there is little worry about recourse. True or False?

10. Constantly updating your servers, software, and skill sets are among the most important things you can do for your network's security. True or False?

Lab Exercises

Lab 14-1 Creating a dummy decoy account

1. You can create a dummy account in many ways. The quickest and most effective way overall is to create another account and disable the existing administrator. Under NT4, start by opening User Manager and single-clicking the administrator account.

2. Click the User menu and then select Rename from the drop-down menu.

3. In the window that pops up, enter your new name for the administrator account. It should be something that isn't too obvious, preferably something that sounds like a regular user name.

4. Now create another user account. Click the User menu and select New Account from the drop-down menu.

5. In the next screen, fill in the user information just as the default administrator account is set up. In this case, however, change the group membership for the account to "Guest." You can disable the account if you want (this depends on whether you want to try to catch people logging in on the account).

6. You will now have a renamed administrator account and a dummy administrator account. You can set up auditing and monitor for successful or failed logins, as shown in Figure 14-1.

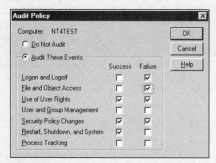

Figure 14-1: Renamed administrator accounts can be a great way to trick hackers or delay hacking attempts.

Creating a disabled or low rights account called Administrator and renaming the original Administrator account is a great idea and can help trick hackers or delay possible account cracking attempts.

Lab 14-2 Setting up auditing under Windows NT

Setting up auditing to monitor failed and successful events in Windows NT is quick and easy, and should be set up for — at a minimum — successful account login/logout auditing.

1. Open User Manager. Select Policies from the menu and Audit from the drop-down menu.

2. If auditing isn't enabled already, select the "Audit These Events" radio button. The check boxes are now ready to be selected.

3. At a minimum, place a check in the failure checkmark box for Logon and Logoff. This will place an alert in the logs for any failures to log in, possibly notifying you of attempts to brute force crack passwords on your system.

4. You have many different options to select here. Some smart choices include: Security Policy Changes, Restart, Shutdown and System, and User and Group Management. Selecting these options could help monitor possible security changes or suspicious events that you didn't know about before. See Figure 14-2.

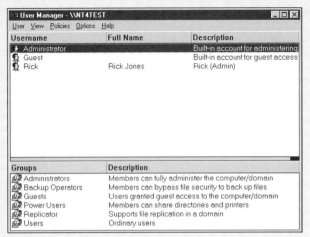

Figure 14-2: Enabling basic auditing under Windows NT is quick and easy.

Lab 14-3 Enabling Scheduler to automate batch file processing of your logs

1. Open up the Services dialog box and locate the Schedule service. By default, it should have the Startup option set to Manual. The Schedule service may be called Task Scheduler, depending on your version of NT.

2. Double-click Schedule and look at the new window that opens. Set the startup type to Automatic so that Windows loads the schedule service automatically whenever Windows starts. Close the Open window and return to the services window.

3. In the services window, make sure that Schedule is selected and then click the Start button on the right side of the window. After a moment, the service starts. Close the services window.

4. Click the Start button on the taskbar and select Run. In the command window, type **cmd**, and then hit Enter. A command prompt window opens. You must enter the command to enable the scheduled execution of a batch file or program.

5. In the command prompt, type the following: at **computer_name time to run schedule /interactive "c:\testbatch.bat"** (for example, **nttest 13:51 /interactive c:\testbatch.bat**). You have now set up an automatic job to execute at 1:51 in the afternoon that will run the file testbatch.bat.

Many jobs can be spooled up if you want to run the same job at different times, or if you have different scripts to run at different times. See Figure 14-3.

Figure 14-3: Setting up scheduled execution of scripts is quick and easy and can be done at any time.

Lab 14-4 How to set up a basic alert when a dummy administrator account is used

1. Create a new text file with an alert message. In the text file, enter the following code:

```
@echo off
net send istc "Your alert message"
```

   Something like "Unauthorized access!" will be fine. Save this text file in a convenient place and call it alert.bat. Copy it to the winnt\system32\repl\import\scripts folder (the netlogon share on your Windows NT system).

2. Open User Manager and locate the dummy administrator account that you created. Double-click it. Now click the Profiles button on the bottom and type **alert.bat** in the "Login Script Name" line. Click OK and exit User Manager.

3. To test your new alert, log out of your session and log in as your dummy administrator account. The system that is logged in as the actual administrator should receive an alert message that says "Unauthorized access!"

These types of basic alerts can be used on all types of dummy accounts that you can set up.

Answers to Chapter Questions

Chapter Pre-Test

1. Three common ways to distract intruders include the use of dummy accounts, dummy files, and dummy password files.

2. A jail is used to distract an intruder long enough to allow system administrators to obtain information about the cracker's source.

3. When dealing with crackers, it is always best to take a proactive approach.

4. Yes, login scripts can be used to enable a wide variety of security-oriented scripts at login, such as source IP logging.

5. Using dummy password lists is not feasible due to the account/password architecture of Windows NT.

Assessment Questions

1. **A.** A, B, & D are all possible answers, but in this case, A is the correct answer. Proactive detection of problems is important, because crackers will typically work when you don't, always researching new vulnerabilities and trying new things out. Being proactive will help you keep up with crackers — it may even help you gain the upper hand.

2. **D.** Running other security scripts when the user logs in. As you have learned, you can run many different types of security scripts when a user logs in. Some of these scripts can alert administrators to login anomalies, and some will log connection information so an administrator can go back after the fact and do some investigation after a possible break-in.

3. **B.** The file size is too small or large, or the time stamp is wrong. Typically, an intruder will embed a Trojan in another file, thus changing the actual file size; sometimes, intruders aren't observant enough and will forget to change the time stamp on the file, which is a good tip-off as well.

4. **A.** Administrator is the first and probably most important account that you should rename or create a decoy for. Other administrative accounts are important to rename or decoy, but at the very least, the common accounts such as Administrator and Guest or service administrative accounts for programs like Backup Exec should be considered.

5. **False.** It is important to set security on the dummy files just like you would on any other file so you don't draw attention to them. If it's easy to obtain access to important files, but hard to get to everything else, chances are that crackers will realize something is up.

6. **True.** Setting up dummy password files is a great idea under UNIX. Other methods are available under UNIX to secure the password list even more, such as enabling shadowing of the password file and obviously strong passwords.

7. **True.** Tripwires need to be set up with some caution and tested before implemented. If a tripwire only sends out alerts or logs information, this isn't too much to worry about, but when a tripwire can reboot a server or disconnect it from the network, it's important to see what possible problems could arise.

8. **C.** Jails can be used for many things, but most often they are used to obtain more information on the cracker and the source of the attack.

9. **False.** You do face a risk of possible recourse by intruders. An intruder may get annoyed and come back with a more concerted attack. Legal issues may also be involved with turning around and attacking an intruder's network.

10. **True.** Being proactive with security doesn't stop with server settings or new software. Training yourself with the newest skills and keeping up-to-date with new vulnerabilities will give you a leg up on crackers.

For More Information

For more information on the topics in this chapter, take a look at these links:

✦ For a good start on scripting — http://www.perl.com/pub.

✦ For a wide variety of security tips and guides on a wide variety of security topics — http://www.secadministrator.com/.

✦ An excellent site with lots of security information, utilities, and scripts available for download — http://www.technotronic.com/.

✦ A great security site providing information on security from the cracker's point of view — http://project.honeynet.org/.

✦ A site specializing in security news and information from many different sources for many different operating systems and networks — http://www.securitynews.org/index2.html.dx.

Intrusion Detection Systems

EXAM OBJECTIVES

- ✦ Define intrusion detection
- ✦ Differentiate between intrusion detection and automated scanning
- ✦ Understand the various categories of intrusion detection systems
- ✦ Understand IDS errors

CHAPTER PRE-TEST

1. What is an intrusion detection system?

2. What is the difference between network and host intrusion detection?

3. What are false positives?

4. What are false negatives?

5. Where should you place an IDS to see as much traffic as possible?

✦ Answers to these questions can be found at the end of the chapter. ✦

Previous chapters have discussed firewalls, OS hardening, and other ways to secure your systems, but inevitably, intruders will get by these protective measures and onto your network. How do you know where they have been and what they have been doing? Intrusion detection systems (IDSs) are the answer.

What Is Intrusion Detection?

 Define intrusion detection

Differentiate between intrusion detection and automated scanning

IDSs are software applications that monitor networks and computer systems for signs of intrusion or misuse. They are quickly becoming a core component of any security infrastructure as the standard solution for monitoring and recognizing attacks.

 Tip   *Intrusion* refers to an unauthorized user attacking your resources. *Misuse* refers to an authorized user doing something they should not be doing, as outlined in your security policy.

IDSs work in the background, continuously monitoring network traffic and system log files for suspicious activity. When an IDS encounters suspicious activity, alerts are sent to the appropriate individuals, often by e-mail, page, or SNMP trap.

An IDS differs from a vulnerability scanner, which looks for existing vulnerabilities by comparing configuration to an attack-signatures database. A vulnerability scanner focuses on specific configuration weaknesses, not on actual network activity. Even if a vulnerability scanner was running on a targeted host, the scanner would not recognize an attack.

Remember that intruders can originate from both inside and outside your network. An IDS' strength is that it can help detect malicious activity from your own internal users. As discussed in earlier chapters, over 80 percent of intrusions and attacks arise from inside an organization, because users may know your network architecture and the security mechanisms that are in place.

Categories of Intrusion Analysis

Intrusions can be categorized into three main classes: signature, statistical, and integrity. These categories provide different techniques to analyze network traffic and identify attacks.

Signature intrusions

Signature intrusion analysis looks for specific attacks against known weak points of a system. Some attacks have unique signatures that can be easily identified. Signature analysis systems look for these unique characteristics to identify the attack.

The majority of commercial IDS products are based on examining network traffic and looking for well-known patterns of attack. This means that for every recognized attack technique, the product developers code a signature, into the system. This signature can be as simple as a pattern match, such as `/cgi-bin/phf?`, which might indicate somebody attempting to access the vulnerable CGI script on a Web server. Or it can be as complex as a security state transition (changing access levels) written as a formal mathematical expression.

To utilize these signatures, the IDS performs signature analysis on the information it obtains. Signature analysis is pattern matching of system settings and user activities against a database of known attacks. Commercial IDS products include databases that contain hundreds (or thousands) of attack signatures.

Statistical intrusion

Statistical intrusion analysis observes deviations from normal system usage patterns. These deviations are detected by defining a profile of the system being monitored and detecting significant deviations from this profile. System administrators define this profile based on the system's functionality and past performance.

The idea behind this approach is to measure a baseline of stats, such as CPU utilization, disk activity, user logins, file activity, and so on. The system alerts you when there is a deviation from this baseline. The benefit of this approach is that it can detect anomalies without having to understand the underlying cause. For example, take a situation where you monitor traffic from individual workstations. One day, each system starts sending information to an external site at 3 a.m — an event that should be noted and investigated. The transferred information could be keylog files, password lists, sensitive documents, and so on.

Anomalous intrusions are detected by the Intrusion Detection System by observing significant deviations from normal behavior. The classic model for anomaly detection, developed by Dorothy Denning, contains metrics derived from system operation. A metric is defined as a random variable x representing a quantitative measure accumulated over a period of time. Metrics are computed from available system parameters, such as average CPU load, number of network connections per minute, and number of processes per user.

An anomaly may be a symptom of a possible intrusion. Given a set of metrics that can define normal system usage, you can assume that exploitation of a system's vulnerabilities involves abnormal use of the system; therefore, security violations could be detected from abnormal patterns of system usage.

Anomalous intrusions are difficult to detect. No fixed patterns exist that can be easily identified. Ideally, you would like a system that combines human-like pattern matching capabilities with the vigilance of a computer program. The IDS would always monitor systems for potential intrusions, but would be able to ignore false intrusions if they resulted from legitimate user actions.

To create the baseline, many intrusion detection systems rely on the analysis of operating system audit trails. This convenient data source forms a footprint of system usage over time that is readily available on most systems. From this baseline and from continuous observation, the IDS will compute metrics about the system's overall state, and decide whether an intrusion is occurring.

An IDS may also perform its own system monitoring and keep aggregate statistics that give a system usage profile. These statistics can be derived from a variety of sources, such as CPU usage, disk I/O, memory usage, activities by users, and number of attempted logins. These statistics must be continually updated to reflect the current system state. They are correlated with an internal model that will allow the IDS to determine if a series of actions constitute a potential intrusion. This model may describe a set of intrusion scenarios or use the profile of a clean system as a baseline.

Integrity analysis

Integrity analysis focuses on whether a file or object has been altered. This analysis often utilizes strong cryptographic hash algorithms to determine if anything has been modified.

Implementing these analysis methods in an IDS can take many forms, such as the Tripwire application.

Characteristics of a Good Intrusion Detection System

Before delving into the various types of intrusion detection systems, you should be aware of the basic characteristics any IDS must have to be effective.

✦ The IDS must run continually without supervision.

✦ The IDS must be fault-tolerant. If a system crash occurs, an IDS should not lose its data or have its knowledge base rebuilt at restart.

✦ The IDS must not use excessive system resources. An IDS that slows a computer to a crawl will simply not be used.

✦ The IDS must observe deviations from normal behavior.

✦ The IDS must cope with changing system behavior over time. As new applications are added, the system profile will change and the IDS must be able to adapt.

✦ The IDS must be accurate.

Errors

 Understand IDS errors

This last point brings up an important issue: errors that are likely to occur with an IDS. Errors can be categorized in one of three ways.

✦ **False positive** — A false positive occurs when the IDS classifies an action as anomalous (a possible intrusion) when the action is actually legitimate.

✦ **False negative** — A false negative occurs when an intrusive action takes place but the IDS allows the action to pass as non-intrusive behavior.

✦ **Subversion** — A subversion error occurs when an intruder modifies the operation of an IDS to force false negatives to occur.

False positives

False positive errors are a real issue with IDSs and lead users to ignore their output. You should try to minimize, if not eliminate, as many of these errors as possible. If too many false positives are generated, you will begin to ignore the output of the system, which may lead to an actual intrusion being detected but not investigated.

False negatives

False negative errors are more serious than false positive errors because they give a misleading sense of security. If intrusion actions proceed, the IDS becomes a liability, as the security of the system is less than it was before the IDS system was installed. You rely on the IDS to alert you to intrusions. If you receive no alert, you do not expect that an intrusion has occurred.

Subversion

Subversion errors are more complex, but closely related to false negatives. An intruder could use knowledge about the internal settings of an IDS to alter its operation, allowing anomalous behavior to proceed. The alteration may be discovered by an administrator examining the logs from the IDS, but overall, the system will appear to be functioning properly.

Fooling a system over time represents another form of subversion. As the detection system observes behavior, it may be possible to carry out operations that, taken individually, pose no threat, but taken as an aggregate, form a threat to system integrity. As mentioned previously, the detection system continually updates its notion of normal system usage. As time goes by, a change in system usage patterns is expected and the detection system must adapt. If an intruder performs actions over time just slightly outside of normal system usage, the actions could be accepted as legitimate when they really form part of an intrusion attempt. The detection system accepts each of the individual actions as slightly suspicious, but not as a threat to the system. However, it can't see that the *combination* of these actions poses a serious threat.

Packet fragmentation is a good example of subversion. Packet fragmentation allows a user to break packets into smaller components. An IDS cannot assemble the packets for evaluation, so an attacker can fragment the TCP/IP packets of an attack and easily elude the IDS.

Intrusion Detection Categories

 Understand the various categories of intrusion detection systems

Several categories of intrusion detection exist, including application, host, network, and integrated. Each category has advantages and disadvantages, which are discussed in the following sections.

Application intrusion detection

Application intrusion detection collects information at the application level. Examples include logs generated by database management software, Web servers, and firewalls. Sensors placed in the application collect and analyze information. Most IDSs provide centralized management, so the information can be sent to a centralized repository for review and analysis.

 Tip Sensors are the component of an IDS that collects data from a remote data source. They are also referred to as agents.

While not currently popular, application intrusion detection's use and importance in the security infrastructure will probably increase in the next several years. The advantage of such a system is that it offers a high degree of control. Application intrusion detection provides a high level of granularity. You can easily monitor any number of application attributes or functionality. On the other hand, having too many applications to support is a disadvantage. Thousands of applications exist on the market, and developing sensors for each one is impossible. Vendors will focus on developing products for the most-used applications, even though they might not be the best solution for your environment.

Host intrusion detection

Host intrusion detection collects information about the activity of a specific system. Sensors are installed on each monitored system. These sensors collect and analyze information from the host. Some may report to a central management server for consolidation and analysis. The information obtained from the host can include operating system audit trails, system logs, and any other information included in audit and logging mechanisms.

A good example of host intrusion detection is the Linux Intrusion Detection System (LIDS). LIDS is a free software package for Linux to protect against root account intrusions. In order for LIDS to properly secure the server operating system, it must restrict the use of modules, raw memory/disk access, protect boot files, and prevent access to I/O Ports. LIDS logs every denied access attempt, locks routing tables/firewall rules, and restricts mounting. LIDS can also hide system processes. Users logged into the system will not be able to execute a simple command such as `ps aux` to reveal running daemons. LIDS has been proven an effective tool in both intrusion detection and prevention.

The advantages of host intrusion detection are as follows:

✦ **Verifies success or failure of an attack.** Because host-based IDSs use logs containing events that have actually occurred, they can measure whether an attack was successful or not with greater accuracy and fewer false positives than network-based systems.

✦ **Monitors specific system activities.** Host-based IDSs monitor user and file access activity, including file accesses, changes to file permissions, attempts to install new executables, and attempts to access privileged services. For example, a host-based IDS can monitor all user logon and logoff activity, as well as what each user does while connected to the network. Host-based technology can also monitor activities that are normally executed only by an administrator. For example, operating systems can log any event where user accounts are added, deleted, or modified. The host-based IDS can detect and alert you to an improper change as soon as the change is executed. Host-based IDSs can also audit policy changes that affect what systems track in their logs. Finally, host-based systems can monitor changes to key system files and executables. Attempts to overwrite vital system files, or to install Trojan horses or backdoors, can be detected.

✦ **Detects attacks that network-based systems miss.** Host-based systems can detect attacks that cannot be seen by network-based systems. For example, attacks from the keyboard of a critical server do not cross the network and cannot be seen by a network-based intrusion detection system.

✦ **Well-suited for encrypted and switched environments.** Because host-based systems reside on various hosts throughout an enterprise, they can overcome some of the deployment challenges faced by network-based intrusion detection in switched and encrypted environments. Host-based intrusion detection provides greater visibility in a switched environment by residing on as many critical hosts as needed. Certain types of encryption also present challenges to network-based intrusion detection. Depending on where the encryption resides within the protocol stack, it may leave a network-based system blind to certain attacks. Host-based IDSs do not have this limitation. By the time the data reaches the operating system, and therefore the host-based system, the data stream has already been de-encrypted and can be analyzed.

✦ **Requires no additional hardware.** Host-based intrusion detection resides on your existing network infrastructure, including file servers, Web servers, and other shared resources. This efficiency can make host-based systems very cost-effective because they do not require another box on the network that must be addressed, maintained, and managed.

✦ **Lower cost of entry.** Deploying a single network intrusion detection system can cost more than $10,000. Host-based intrusion detection systems, on the other hand, are often priced in the hundreds of dollars for a single agent and can be deployed with limited initial capital outlay. Start by protecting your most critical servers and you will greatly increase the effectiveness of your security infrastructure for little cost.

The disadvantages to host intrusion detection include the following:

✦ **Network activity is not visible to host-based sensors.** Because agents run on hosts and analyze system files, they do not see network traffic and may miss some early warning signs that help prevent intrusion.

✦ **Running audit mechanisms can use additional resources.** If your system generates a high amount of log file or audit activities, you may see a substantial performance degradation.

✦ **When audit trails are used as data sources, they can take up significant storage.** If you have a lot of activity on your system, audit trails can be huge. The hardware necessary to accommodate these files may significantly increase the overall cost of the system.

✦ **Host-based sensors must be platform-specific.** Because they work hand-in-hand with the system, agents are platform-specific. You cannot install the same agent on Windows and Solaris. Some vendors only support Windows and Linux, whereas others only support Windows and Solaris. A few support only Windows systems. Finding a product for your environment that supports multiple operating systems can be a difficult task. If you are running BSD, AIX, or HP-UX, you may be hard-pressed to find a solution.

✦ **Complex management and deployment.** Because host sensors must be physically installed on each monitored system, deployment is more complex than that of a network IDS. This process can be time-consuming if you plan on monitoring a large number of systems.

Network intrusion detection

Network intrusion detection collects information directly from the network. Sensors gather information by packet sniffing and analyze it for suspicious activity. Network sensors can be installed on a server or they can be stand-alone, dedicated devices. Cisco Secure is an example of a network intrusion detection product. Snort is a free network IDS that runs on Linux and a variety of other platforms.

The advantages of network intrusion detection include the following:

✦ **Lowers cost of ownership**. A network-based IDS can be strategically deployed in your network to view network traffic for multiple systems. As a result, network-based systems do not require software to be loaded and managed on a large number of hosts. Because fewer detection points are required, the total cost of ownership can be lower for an enterprise environment.

✦ **Detects attacks that host-based systems miss**. A network-based IDS examines all packet headers for signs of malicious and suspicious activity. Host-based IDSs do not see packet headers, so they cannot detect these types of attacks. For example, many IP-based denial-of-service (DoS) attacks can only be identified by looking at the packet headers as they travel across a network. This type of attack can be quickly identified by a network-based system looking at the packet stream in real-time. A network-based IDS can also investigate the content of the payload, looking for commands or syntax used in specific attacks. An attacker probing for the new BackOrifice exploit on systems not yet infected with the BackOrifice software can be detected by examining the packet payload. Host-based systems do not see the payload and are not able to recognize embedded payload attacks.

✦ **Difficult for an attacker to remove evidence.** Network-based IDSs use live network traffic for real-time attack detection. Captured data includes not only the method of attack, but also information that may help lead to identification and prosecution. Unless attackers can compromise the IDS, they cannot remove the evidence. Because many hackers understand audit logs, they know how to manipulate these files to cover their tracks, frustrating host-based systems that need this information to detect an intrusion.

✦ **Fast detection and response.** Network-based IDSs detect malicious and suspicious attacks as they occur, providing faster notification and response. For example, a hacker initiating a network-based Denial of Service (DoS) can be stopped by having a TCP reset sent to terminate the attack before it crashes or damages the targeted host. Host-based systems usually do not recognize an attack or take action until after a suspicious log entry has been written. By this time, critical systems may already be compromised, or the system running the host-based IDS may have crashed.

✦ **Detects unsuccessful attacks and malicious intent.** Network-based IDSs add valuable data for determining malicious intent. A network-based IDS placed outside a firewall can detect attacks intended for resources behind the firewall, even though the firewall may be rejecting these attempts. This information can be critical in evaluating and refining security policies.

✦ **Creates operating system independence.** Network-based IDSs are not dependent on host operating systems as detection sources. If you run a multiplatform environment, you should not have any trouble finding a network IDS to use.

The disadvantages to network intrusion detection include the following:

✦ **Unable to determine outcome.** Although some network intrusion detection systems can infer from network traffic what is happening on hosts, they cannot tell the outcome of commands executed on the host. This is an issue in detection, distinguishing between user error and malfeasance. A command execution, such as cmd.asp on a Windows system, might look harmless, but if executed after a successful privilege escalation attack, it can be very dangerous.

✦ **Unable to read encrypted traffic.** Network agents cannot scan protocols or content if network traffic is encrypted. If the sensor cannot read the packed payload, it has no idea what is included.

✦ **Unable to save all packets on a switched network.** Network intrusion detection does not work well on switched networks. Switched networks establish a network segment for each host; therefore, network agents are reduced to monitoring a single host. Network switches that support a monitoring or scanning port can mitigate this issue.

✦ **Unable to handle high-speed networks.** Current network intrusion detection approaches cannot handle high-speed networks. When overloaded, they do not process all packets. A few attacks may be allowed to pass undetected, providing you with a false sense of security. Technology is rapidly advancing in this area, though. Modern IDSs can handle much faster networks. A few vendors, such as Network ICE, even support Gigabit traffic.

Integrated intrusion detection

Some intrusion detection products combine categories, most commonly host and network intrusion detection sensors. Like hybrid firewalls, *integrated intrusion detection* solutions provide the advantages of each category and attempt to mitigate the disadvantages. From my previous discussion on network and host intrusion detection systems, you can easily see that they complement each other and that the level of detection with an integrated solution is much higher than with either as a stand-alone.

In some cases, such as with ISS's RealSecure and Network ICE's ICE Pac suite, the product is integrated and includes both network and host agents. Otherwise, you must purchase two separate products, one host-based and the other network-based, to implement an integrated solution. Vendor interoperability, as usual, is desired. If the two products cannot work together, you are no better off than if you had one solution or the other. Because they are unable to talk to each other and combine information, you lose the benefits of analyzing host and network traffic together to gain a better understanding of what is occurring on your network.

The primary advantage of integrated intrusion detection is trend analysis, which enables you to see patterns of attacks over time and across the network space.

The disadvantage of integrated intrusion detection is that you will have to deal with interoperability issues. There are no industry standards with regards to interoperability of intrusion detection components, so it is difficult, if not impossible, to integrate components from different vendors. Additionally, exploits and vulnerabilities have different names at each vendor. CVE (Common Vulnerabilities and Exposures; at `cve.mitre.org`) is changing this by developing a dictionary of exploits.

Table 15-1 compares the abilities of IDS categories.

Table 15-1 IDS Functionality				
IDS Ability	**IDS Category**			
	Application	**Host**	**Network**	**Integrated**
Unauthorized access to file and system resources	X	X		
Discover violation of security policy	X	X	X	X
Discover Trojan horses and malicious software		X		X
Network service attacks			X	X
DoS attacks			X	X
Failure or misconfiguration of firewalls	X		X	
Attacks on encrypted or switched networks	X	X		X

What Is Intrusion Detection Capable of Doing?

Intrusion detection systems can increase the security of your network and become a valuable component of your security infrastructure, but, unlike many vendors' claims, they cannot protect you from everything. You should understand the limitations of an IDS so you know which areas of your infrastructure need additional security measures.

Intrusion detection *can*:

✦ **Add security integrity to your existing security infrastructure.** IDSs do provide an additional layer of protection that works well in conjunction with firewalls, operating system hardening, and various other security mechanisms.

✦ **Help you better understand what is happening on your systems.** Operating system audit trails and other system logs contain tons of information about your systems. Making sense of that information is another issue. A host IDS can help you organize and comprehend this information so it is valuable to you and helps you improve and strengthen your security infrastructure.

✦ **Trace activity from point-of-origin to point-of-attack.** An IDS allows you to follow an attacker's trail. Without an IDS, you may know that an attacker has penetrated the mail server, but you may not be aware that the file server has also been compromised. An IDS can provide a detailed account of what occurred on a system or a network.

✦ **Be managed by individuals without security expertise.** Many IDS products provide user-friendly GUI management interfaces as well as built-in best practice configurations and guidelines to help even the most novice administrators add a strong level of security to their infrastructure.

Intrusion detection *cannot*:

✦ **Compensate for poor authentication mechanisms.** Although an IDS can tell you if an unauthorized user performed a specific action on a server, it cannot help you against an administrator that uses an easily guessable password. The IDS only looks for suspicious activity; an Administrator account adding users is not considered a suspicious or uncommon action (unless the IDS is specifically told to look for this type of activity).

✦ **Conduct an attack investigation without your help.** The IDS can provide you with valuable data regarding an attack, but you still need to follow your incident response plan.

✦ **Intuitively determine your security policy.** An IDS can monitor traffic and activities to help enforce your security policy, but it must know what your policy is. Use your security policy as a guideline when configuring an IDS for your organization.

✦ **Overcome network protocol weaknesses.** An IDS is only as strong as the protocol it is monitoring. For example, TCP/IP does not authenticate source and destination IP addresses. A spoofed packet will most likely pass through the IDS. Your firewall is the best place to stop these attacks.

✦ **Improve "garbage" data.** If an attacker is able to modify your system logs, any analysis and reporting performed by the IDS will be useless.

Network Architecture with Intrusion Detection

Where does intrusion detection fit into your network architecture? The answer largely depends on the purpose of the IDS in your organization. Figure 15-1 shows a common configuration.

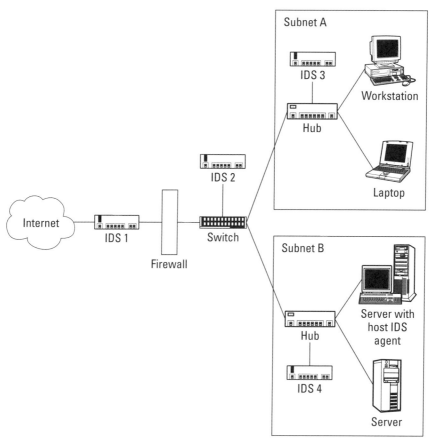

Figure 15-1: The placement of your IDS greatly depends on the role it plays in your security infrastructure.

If you are interested in seeing what attacks are targeted at your company, you can place a network IDS in front of your firewall (IDS 1 in Figure 15-1). Be prepared to deal with a long list of alarms, though. You might want to consider just monitoring return traffic (from your network to the Internet) to find out about potential successful attacks or the hacking practices of your employees.

Some people like to place a network sensor on their firewall. Doing so will most likely interfere and degrade your firewall performance. If you want to monitor all activity on your network, you should place network sensors on each subnet (IDS 3 and 4 in Figure 15-1). Make sure that if you have a switched network, your switch provides a monitoring port, or you may be out of luck (IDS 2 in Figure 15-1). Installing host IDS agents is easy. Simply select the systems you want protected and you will be ready to analyze data and watch for alerts.

Managed Services

Most likely, you do not have the in-house resources or knowledge to take full advantage of your IDS. Log files can provide valuable information about probes and attacks launched against your system if you understand how to read and analyze them. Many companies now provide services to monitor and evaluate your IDS logs and alerts around the clock.

IDS data evaluation is a great component of your security infrastructure to outsource. For a small monthly fee, you can receive expert knowledge and assistance in a highly specialized area of security.

Problems with Intrusion Detection

Intrusion detection systems are useful, but they do have their problems. As discussed previously, these systems can be circumvented by attackers. Additional problems include lack of real-time response and dated signature databases.

IDSs usually alert you to a suspicious event after the event has occurred. This is especially true with host IDSs, which base their alerts on log file analysis. After the fact may be too late. Host IDS response time has improved. In the first IDSs, the host reported alerts at set intervals. Now, most systems make interrupt calls to the operating system when a log event is recorded to speed up the alert process and make it as real-time as possible.

Network intrusion detection systems provide more real-time information than host intrusion detection systems, but they still have problems. Many network systems still cannot detect an attack in its early stages.

IDSs simply monitor traffic and activities and alert you to suspicious activity. They cannot prevent attacks from occurring unless you respond quickly to an alert.

Finally, signature-based IDSs are often out-of-date. Some vendors only update their signature databases once a quarter. What do you do about the new Web server exploit released last week? You can't wait another two months for your IDS vendor to provide protection. You must be proactive and vigilant in your monitoring of new exploits and vulnerabilities.

Key Point Summary

This chapter discusses intrusion detection and how you may use it in your environment.

✦ IDSs monitor networks and computer systems for signs of intrusion or misuse. They work in the background, continuously monitoring network traffic and system log files for suspicious activity. When they find something, alerts are sent to the appropriate individuals, often by e-mail, page, or SNMP trap.

✦ An IDS is different from a vulnerability scanner. A vulnerability scanner looks for existing vulnerabilities by comparing configuration to an attack-signatures database. It focuses on specific configuration weaknesses, not actual network activity. Even if a vulnerability scanner were running on a targeted host, the scanner would not recognize an attack.

✦ Intrusions can be categorized into three main classes: signature, statistical, and integrity.

✦ Signature intrusions look for specific attacks against known weak points of a system. They can be detected by watching for certain actions being performed on certain objects.

✦ To utilize these signatures, the IDS performs signature analysis on the information it obtains. Signature analysis is pattern matching of system settings and user activities against a database of known attacks. Commercial IDS products include databases that contain hundreds (or thousands) of attack signatures.

✦ Statistical intrusion analysis is based on observations of deviations from normal system usage patterns. These deviations are detected by defining a profile of the system being monitored and detecting significant deviations from this profile.

✦ Anomalous intrusions are detected by observing significant deviations from normal behavior. The classic model for anomaly detection, developed by Denning, contains metrics that are derived from system operation. A metric is defined as a random variable x representing a quantitative measure accumulated over a period. These metrics are computed from available system parameters, such as average CPU load, number of network connections per minute, and number of processes per user.

✦ An anomaly may be a symptom of a possible intrusion. Given a set of metrics which can define normal system usage, you can assume that exploitation of a system's vulnerabilities involves abnormal use of the system; therefore, security violations could be detected from abnormal patterns of system usage.

✦ Anomalous intrusions are hard to detect. There are no fixed patterns that can be easily identified.

✦ To create the baseline, many intrusion detection systems rely on the analysis of operating system audit trails. This data forms a footprint of system usage over time. It is a convenient source of data and is readily available on most systems. From this baseline and continuous observation, the IDS will compute metrics about the system's overall state and decide whether an intrusion is occurring.

✦ An IDS may also perform its own system monitoring. It may keep aggregate statistics that give a system usage profile. These statistics can be derived from a variety of sources, such as CPU usage, disk I/O, memory usage, activities by users, and number of attempted logins. These statistics must be continually updated to reflect the current system state. They are correlated with an internal model that will allow the IDS to determine if a series of actions constitute a potential intrusion. This model may describe a set of intrusion scenarios or use the profile of a clean system as a baseline.

✦ Integrity analysis focuses on whether a file or object has been altered. This often utilizes strong cryptographic hash algorithms to determine if anything has been modified.

✦ A good IDS must run continually without supervision, be fault-tolerant, not use excessive system resources, observe deviations from normal behavior, cope with changing system behavior over time, and be accurate.

✦ A false positive occurs when the IDS classifies an action as anomalous (a possible intrusion) when it is actually a legitimate action.

✦ A false negative occurs when an intrusive action has taken place but the IDS allows it to pass as non-intrusive behavior.

✦ A subversion error occurs when an intruder modifies the operation of the IDS to force false negatives to occur.

✦ Application intrusion detection collects information at the application level. Examples include logs generated by database management software, Web servers, and firewalls. Sensors placed in the application collect and analyze information. Most IDSs provide centralized management, so the information could be sent to a centralized repository for review and analysis.

✦ Host intrusion detection collects information about the activity of a specific system. Sensors are installed on each monitored system. These sensors collect and analyze information from the host. Some may report to a central management server for consolidation and analysis. The information obtained from the host can include operating system audit trails, system logs, and any other information included in audit and logging mechanisms.

✦ Network intrusion detection collects information directly from the network. Sensors gather information by packet sniffing and analyze it for suspicious activity. Network sensors can be installed on a server or they can be standalone, dedicated devices. Cisco Secure is an example of a network intrusion detection product. Snort is a free network IDS that runs on Linux and a variety of other platforms.

✦ Some intrusion detection products combine categories, most commonly host and network intrusion detection sensors. Like hybrid firewalls, integrated intrusion detection solutions provide the advantages of each category and attempt to mitigate the disadvantages. From my previous discussion on network and host intrusion detection systems, you can easily see that they complement each other and the level of detection with an integrated solution is much higher than with either as a stand-alone.

✦ IDS can add security integrity to your existing security infrastructure, help you better understand what is happening on your systems, trace activity from point-of-origin to point-of-attack, and be managed by individuals without security expertise.

✦ IDS cannot compensate for poor authentication mechanisms, conduct an attack investigation without your help, intuitively determine your security policy, overcome network protocol weaknesses, or improve "garbage" data.

✦ If you are interested in seeing what attacks are targeted at your company, you can place a network IDS in front of your firewall.

✦ If you want to monitor all activity on your network, you should place network sensors on each subnet.

✦ The most difficult aspect of an IDS is analyzing and understanding the alerts and log files you receive at all hours of the day. Most likely, you do not have the resources or the knowledge in-house to take full advantage of your IDS. Log files can provide valuable information about probes and attacks launched against your system if you understand how to read and analyze them. Many companies now provide services to monitor and evaluate your IDS logs and alerts 24 hours a day, 7 days a week.

✦ With an IDS, you are usually alerted to a suspicious event after it has occurred. This is especially true with host IDSs. Because the majority of their alerts are based on log file analysis, you do not know something has occurred until after the fact. By then, it may be too late. Host IDS response time has improved. In the first IDSs, the host reported alerts at set intervals. Now, most systems make interrupt calls to the operating system when a log event is recorded to speed up the alert process and make it as real-time as possible.

✦ Network intrusion detection systems provide more real-time information than host intrusion detection systems, but they still have problems. A lot of systems cannot detect an attack in its early stages. By the time it recognizes the attack, it may be too late. The attack may have already occurred.

✦ IDSs simply monitor traffic and activities and alert you to suspicious activity. They cannot prevent attacks from occurring unless you respond quickly to an alert.

✦ Signature-based IDSs are often out-of-date. Some vendors only update their signature databases once a quarter. What do you do about the new Web server exploit released last week? You can't wait another two months for your IDS vendor to provide protection. You still need to be proactive and vigilant in your monitoring of new exploits and vulnerabilities.

✦   ✦   ✦

STUDY GUIDE

This Study Guide presents five assessment questions to test your knowledge of the exam objectives.

Assessment Questions

1. Which IDS category can see all network traffic?

    A. Host IDS

    B. Application IDS

    C. Network IDS

    D. Integrated IDS

2. What is an advantage of a host IDS?

    A. It works well in encrypted or switched environments.

    B. It cannot see network traffic.

    C. It is platform-specific.

    D. It uses additional system resources.

3. Why would you not want to consider managed services?

    A. Money is not an issue for deployment.

    B. You do not have any security expertise.

    C. You need around-the-clock, 24x7 monitoring.

    D. You already have an in-house expert.

4. What is the worst type of error?

    A. False negative

    B. False positive

    C. Subversion

    D. None of the above

5. Which of the following is *not* a characteristic of a good IDS?

   A. IDS must run continuously without supervision.

   B. IDS must be accurate.

   C. IDS must be static.

   D. IDS must be fault-tolerant.

Answers to Chapter Questions

Chapter Pre-Test

1. IDSs monitor networks and computer systems for signs of intrusion or misuse.

2. A vulnerability scanner looks for existing vulnerabilities by comparing configuration to an attack-signatures database. It focuses on specific configuration weaknesses, not actual network activity.

3. A false positive occurs when the IDS classifies an action as anomalous (a possible intrusion) when the action is actually legitimate.

4. A false negative occurs when an intrusive action has taken place but the IDS allows the action to pass as non-intrusive behavior.

5. You should place your IDS sensor outside your firewall to see all the external attacks launched against your network.

Assessment Questions

1. **C**. A network IDS can see all network traffic.

2. **A**. A host IDS works well in encrypted or switched environments.

3. **D**. If you already have an in-house IDS expert, you may not need to use a managed service.

4. **A**. A false negative is the worst type of error. Here, you have an attack you do not know about and to which you cannot respond.

5. **C**. An IDS must not be static. It must be able to continuously evolve and adapt to a changing environment.

Handling Security Incidents

EXAM OBJECTIVES

- ✦ Understand the importance of a formalized incident response policy
- ✦ Learn how to develop your own incident response plan
- ✦ Understand how to appropriately respond to a security incident
- ✦ Identify groups and organizations that can help you in the event of a security incident
- ✦ Identify critical resources for the Incident Response Policy
- ✦ Understand how you can learn valuable lessons from each incident

CHAPTER PRE-TEST

1. What is an incident response policy?
2. Who should be one of the first people contacted in the event of a security incident?
3. What is the most important thing not to do during a security incident?
4. What is an incident response plan?
5. What is the most important thing to do during a security incident?

What happens when you discover someone was able to compromise your network? Chapter 5 discussed the types of security vulnerabilities that exist, but what happens when you recognize one of those attacks on your own network? Maybe you just see some strange network traffic and decide to investigate, or maybe you receive an anonymous e-mail from the attacker stating they have complete control of your network. Regardless of the situation, you need to have a detailed plan in place, both policies and procedures, to help your organization deal with the security breach.

Understanding Incident Management

 Understand the importance of a formalized incident response policy

The concept of incident response stems from the great worm of 1988. The Morris worm crippled the Internet, then made up of a meager 60,000 systems. After recovering from this incident, the general consensus was that the Internet needed a single trusted body to help deal with security situations. This consensus led to the formation of the Computer Emergency Response Team Coordination Center (CERT/CC; www.cert.org) in November of 1988 at Carnegie Mellon University.

CERT was originally under the control of the U.S. Department of Defense, Defense Advanced Research Projects Agency (DARPA) and charged with collaborating with the Internet community on security issues, providing technical assistance to organizations that have been attacked, and announcing security risks and vulnerabilities to the public.

This model worked well at first, but as the Internet began to grow exponentially in size, having one central response agency became infeasible. Around 1998, the Internet had an estimated 36 million hosts. Organizations similar to CERT sprang up all over the world, and companies began creating their own Computer Security Incident Response Teams (CSIRTs).

Today, CSIRTs are a necessary component for any security infrastructure. They provide a central location to report or obtain information regarding security incidents. This centralized approach simplifies containment and evidence gathering and coordinating efforts with third parties, such as law enforcement. Incident response teams are often composed of members of the security and IT staff. This works great because these individuals are often the most knowledgeable about a company's systems and infrastructure.

In addition to providing their main service, incident response, CSIRTs can use their security expertise to provide additional services to their organization, such as the following:

✦ Disseminate information on potential security threats

✦ Report security vulnerabilities to the appropriate group for elimination or at least mitigation

✦ Promote security awareness

✦ Track security incidents

✦ Monitor intrusion detection systems

✦ Support system and network auditing through processes such as penetration testing

✦ Analyze new technologies for security vulnerabilities and risks

✦ Provide security consulting

✦ Develop security tools

Building an Incident Response Plan of Attack

 Objective   Learn how to develop your own incident response plan

Building an incident response plan should not be taken lightly, nor should it be postponed; in fact, advance preparation is essential. Most companies put it off until their systems are compromised and the damage has already been done. Implementing a plan and CSIRT then to guard against the next attack still requires recovery from the initial incident first.

Preparation is key for an effective and efficient incident response plan. The main thing you want to avoid is making critical decisions during the middle of a crisis. People tend to make poor decisions in crisis mode unless everything has been specifically predefined in a policy and procedures document. This document is the crutch for everyone to lean on in times of crisis.

The incident response plan document should be as detailed as possible. Plan everything from naming the individuals (or job positions) that will be involved in the plan to specifying steps for removing a compromised system from the network.

 In the Real World   Like a professional sports team going into a big game, preparation is often the biggest key to success. Sports teams spend hours poring over available information about the opponent, then countless more hours going over possible plays and situations. Incident response planning is not much different — planning ahead will gain the best results overall.

Define policies

Before detailing procedures in an incident response plan, you first need to define incident response policies. This is the most important step in creating an incident response plan because everything is based on these policies. The procedures to follow, the parties to contact, and the tools to use in investigating the attack are all defined based on the policy.

Just like information security policies, an incident response policy should be written in very general terms. The incident response plan details the exact steps that should be taken in each scenario.

Select a CSIRT leader

The first thing to define in the policy is who should act as the CSIRT leader. This person is the focal point for the entire incident's decision-making process. Should it be the IS Manager, the CTO, the CEO, or the CSO? This decision varies from company to company, but it is important and should be carefully analyzed. This person is also responsible for deciding when the incident response plan should be activated.

Select CSIRT members

Next, define who is involved in the CSIRT. Generally, you want to limit the list to job titles, because people move around frequently. Feel free to use names, but if you do, make sure you keep the policy up-to-date and modify it whenever something changes. The team usually consists of three to five individuals with positions in security, IT, legal, or management.

The size of the team often depends on the size of the company (the bigger the company, the bigger the team). You might want to consider including some team alternates that can be called on in case of a huge incident. For example, if the majority of the systems on a network are compromised, you might need more than three to five people to help deal with the breach. Again, the skills and size of the team depend on your organization. Nothing is set in stone regarding CSIRTs, so make the decision that is best for your company.

Who should be contacted?

Defining everyone who must be contacted in the event of a security incident is often an arduous process. Depending on who makes up the CSIRT, this list could include upper management, legal, PR, federal authorities, local authorities, and CERT/CC. This list varies from company to company, but is very important. Decide who needs to be "in the know" when a security incident occurs and document this in the policy. Specific contact information should be included in the detailed procedures document.

Define appropriate action

What will you do when an incident occurs? Will you immediately remove the compromised system from the network? Do you feel it is necessary to watch the intruder for a period of time to obtain more information? Will you contact the authorities? Who has the right to contact authorities and which agency will be contacted? Who will speak to the media? All these questions need to be addressed in the incident response policy. Each company has different views on how to handle security incidents, so meet with the team members and upper management to develop the best policies for your company.

Specific procedures

After defining the policies, the next step is to create detailed procedures that will be followed by each team member in the event of a security incident. I discuss this in detail in the following section.

Establishing the Incident Response Plan

The policy is created so you know what you should and should not do at a general theoretical level. This section details the creation of incident response procedures that will be followed during a security incident.

Assess your circumstance

Identify critical resources for the incident response policy

What exactly is going on? What tipped you off to a possible attack? Was it an intrusion detection alert? Sometimes, intrusion detection software can create false positive intrusion alerts. Therefore, you need to have a more definite idea of the real situation before calling out the dogs and firing up the incident response plan. Define a few steps to be taken to better assess the situation. Make sure questions like the following are answered:

✦ Is it just one server that is compromised?

✦ Have multiple servers been affected?

✦ Is it a false alarm?

You might want to include a list of logs or specific servers to look at to see if you can gain any valuable information regarding the current state of the network or system compromise.

Start contacting people

Most likely, the first individuals you need to contact are upper management. If they are not directly involved in the plan, then they should be the first to know when something is going on with the company's electronic assets. Contact the CSIRT and get them on the scene if required. The remainder of the contact list depends on your company policy. Some feel now is the best time to contact the authorities, although others prefer to wait until they have a chance to gather more evidence.

Contain the damage

In most cases, containing the damage means immediately removing the compromised system(s) from the network for further investigation. Some people refuse to do this; they are often the ones that repeatedly find themselves under attack or find the intruder has been able to compromise another system while the first system was still connected to the network.

Often, when the compromised systems are not taken offline, the original attacker or other hackers can further intrude, using the affected system, if they find the system in a weakened state. It is also a good idea to take the system off the network for the simple reason of having the time required to properly repair the damage done, and to limit potential loss of incident information.

Once the system is removed from the network, take it to a safe place for analysis. If it needs to be connected to a network, connect it to a subnet that has no Internet access and, ideally, no real corporate network access. (The intruder might be an insider.) Some companies take a complete image of the drive for analysis, whereas others ship the hard drive off for a forensics analysis.

The decision to image or ship the entire hard drive often hinges on the amount of resources available to the company. If they have a backup server or a spare system lying around that can replace the affected server, they are more likely to perform a thorough analysis because they have the time and not a strong demand to return the server to service. Companies that are critically low on electronic resources will scream if they have to remove a server from the system. These are the groups that image the affected server and put it back in service, using the image for analysis.

Caution Some individuals feel it is necessary to keep the compromised system attached to the network and monitor the attacker. Some even feel the need to attack the hacker in return. In addition to not being very effective, and potentially inviting further attack, this approach can run the risk of getting you involved in costly legal battles.

Analyze the compromise and system integrity

After you have contained the compromised systems, you need to figure out what happened by answering the following kinds of questions:

✦ What accounts were affected?

✦ What files were affected?

✦ Is there evidence that this was an inside job?

✦ Is there evidence that more servers are compromised?

In general, you want to trace the activities on your system. If you are using a file integrity tool such as TripWire, you can easily tell which files have been modified.

One of the most important aspects of this series of procedures is defining what tools should be used. You want to be thorough and act fast. Prepare a detailed list of tools to use and the locations where they can be found (so you are not searching all over the place for software and applications during the middle of a crisis). You may even consider having one system, whether it is a desktop or laptop that has as many of these tools installed as possible. When an incident occurs, fire up the laptop and off you go.

Protect the evidence

Protecting the evidence of the attack is very important, but often overlooked. Most people are so focused on getting the server cleaned up and back into service that they do not think about the possible prosecution of the attacker. For the prosecution to proceed, you need evidence.

Defining the steps to be taken to protect evidence varies from company to company because it largely depends on the environment. Will you use a burned image of the system's hard drive as your evidence? The best option is to leave the system out of service and have it available as evidence, but this is generally not the option most used. Will you just record what changes were made on the system and keep only the system log files? This is what most companies do, but it may leave out important aspects of the attack, such as the recorded source address of the attacker, host name, last known network connection for that system, activities on the system(s), and related information that could further aid in prosecution.

One of the most important aspects of this series of procedures is defining who is responsible for what. The last thing you want is each person thinking someone else is responsible for the preservation of the evidence when the attack occurs. When no one takes the responsibility for the evidence, nothing gets done, and valuable evidence is either lost or destroyed.

In the Real World   If a hacker has broken in and gained control, he or she will usually alter or remove any logs showing activity related to the break-in. Depending on when you first notice the intruder, you may still be able to retain this valuable information before it is lost.

Media inquiries

In today's world, computer attacks are big news, so, depending on the size and stature of your company, prepare for a media onslaught. Select one person to act as the spokesperson for the company. This is usually a public relations (PR) expert. This person may need to get assistance from a more technical person to help explain what happened. The main point is to have only one person speaking to the media to control the information being released to the public, including stories, who is speaking, what is being said, and the accuracy of the pertinent details

What you tell the media depends on your company. Some companies, though not very many, feel full disclosure is important. A few others fall in the other extreme, never mentioning a word to the public unless the story is leaked to the press.

Be as honest as you can. If the attacker obtains credit card numbers or other sensitive information, notify these individuals involved immediately. Compromises of this magnitude can greatly hinder consumer confidence in your company.

Detail these steps in the incident response plan, including who will act as the company spokesperson, what the spokesperson can and cannot say, the order in which people will be notified (for example, customers first and then the media), and how the information will be disseminated (for example, press conference, press release, and AP Newswire).

Communicate

 Identify groups and organizations that can help you in the event of a security incident

A system compromise should not be hidden away, in the hope that no one will find out. You need to communicate with various groups to help gain control of the situation and prepare for possible future legal action. The first group to communicate with should be your Internet service provider (ISP). They may be able to stop the attack and help track the culprit for prosecution. Your incident response plan should contain the detailed contact information for your ISP.

The next group to contact should be the authorities. Your company needs to decide who will be involved first — federal or local authorities. This decision might depend on the nature of the compromise. If you can tell the attacker came from overseas, you might contact the federal authorities first. Some experts feel it is best to always contact the local authorities first and let them bring in the Feds. Whatever you decide, include the details of all contact information in your plan.

The last place that should be contacted is CERT. They have a wealth of knowledge regarding attacks and may have experience with an attack similar to yours. If so, they can save you time by pointing you in the right direction for evidence gathering. Their contact information, cert@cert.org or 412-268-7090, should be included in your plan.

Recover from compromise

The next step involves system recovery. How will you restore the machine to a trusted state? Restore from backup? Rebuild? Whatever you decide, completely document each step. You want to make sure you do not forget any security patches, updates, or configurations on the system. If you do, you might leave yourself wide open for another attack. Ideally, you should have a disaster recovery plan in place that you can use in this situation.

 In the Real World   It is likely these days that companies and organizations will have at least a somewhat basic backup in place. Make sure that the essential data that is required for recovery is kept in a safe place, but is still accessible if the issue arises.

Prepare a report

Write a report about the entire experience. The best way to learn is from experience. You do not want to repeat your mistakes, so taking a step back to look at the big picture is good.

Make the report a specific step in the plan to help ensure that it is not forgotten. If the plan ends with system recovery (which is where most people stop), you lose a great chance to learn a few valuable lessons from the experience. The plan should outline what must be included in the report. This helps ensure consistency from incident to incident. At a minimum, include a copy of the activity log file that was kept during the response period (covered in more detail in the next section). Include a few thoughts on what went well and what didn't and a discussion of the incident itself. What allowed the attack to succeed? How can you prevent future attacks? Distribute this report to all parties involved in the incident and any others that should be aware of the situation.

Evaluate lessons learned

 Objective   Understand how you can learn valuable lessons from each incident

Once the report has been distributed and reviewed, meet with all parties involved and discuss the incident. Ask questions, such as the following, to evaluate the handling of the attack:

- ✦ What went right and what went wrong?
- ✦ What things should be changed?
- ✦ Do you need to add team members?
- ✦ Do you need to remove team members?
- ✦ Do you need to add new tools?
- ✦ Should you change your entire approach?

Update policies and procedures

Based on the incident and the after-the-fact analysis, update the policies and procedures to reflect any changes that were made or any new approaches and findings developed.

The plan should discuss how the policy and procedure update process works. How should the policy and procedures be updated? Who has to approve changes? Who do you contact to communicate the changes?

The development of the incident response plan is an ongoing process. The plan will need to be refined and adjusted as the environment and the attacks change.

Table 16-1 lists the major components of an incident response plan.

Table 16-1
Incident Response Plan Components

Task	Process
Assess your circumstance.	What steps should be taken to identify the situation? Is this really the result of a successful attack or is it a false alarm? Define these procedures very carefully. You do not want to be activating your CSIRT every day, but neither do you want to be so lax that you miss an attack.
Start contacting people.	The first person who should be contacted, besides the CSIRT leader, is the CEO. Keep him or her informed at all times. Also, detail all other parties that should be informed of the security breach. Should the authorities be contacted now or later?
Contain the damage.	Remove the affected servers from the network!
Analyze the compromise and system integrity.	Thoroughly detail the steps to analyze a compromised system. What files do you look at; what logs do you look at? What tools do you use? This is the step in which you gather the majority of the information regarding the attack, so make it count.
Protect the evidence.	This is very important if you are planning to prosecute the attacker. Ideally, you want to keep the system off the network and available for analysis, but if you cannot do that, make copies of important log files, system files, and so on.

Continued

Table 16-1 *(continued)*

Task	Process
Have a set plan on how to respond to and deal with media inquiries.	The media loves security incidents so be prepared to handle them. Name one person to act as spokesperson and detail what information will and will not be released to the public and at what times.
Communicate.	Inform your ISP, the authorities, and CERT about the incident. All of these parties can help you resolve the problem. You can always use more help.
Recover from the compromise.	Detail the steps to restore the system to its trusted state and put it back into service.
Prepare a report.	Document your thoughts and analysis on the event after the fact. Learn something from the experience. Detail what should be included in the report in your incident response plan, so each report follows the same format. Include this as a step in the plan to make sure it gets completed.
Evaluate lessons learned.	Meet with all parties involved in the incident. Discuss the report and the lessons learned from the incident. What should be changed? Again, include this as a step in the plan to make sure it gets completed.
Update policies and procedures.	Based on the contents of the report and the outcome of the meeting, update the incident response policies and procedures as necessary. The plan should detail the steps to be followed to achieve this. Who must approve changes? Who should be contacted to communicate the changes?

When an Incident Occurs

 Understand how to appropriately respond to a security incident

When an incident occurs, there are some things you should remember.

Don't panic

First and foremost, do not panic when a security incident occurs. If you have adequately planned and rehearsed your incident response procedures, you are already ahead of the game.

If you do enter a state of panic, you will not make logical, rational decisions regarding the incident. Rash decisions could cause more problems than the compromise itself.

Document everything

Write everything down. Have each team member keep a detailed log of all actions they take during and after the incident. Do not lose these logs because they can be valuable during a review of the incident and prosecution of the attacker.

For example, one log entry could read: "On December 21, 2000, at 12:21 a.m., I analyzed the compromised system's system log and noticed an entry for su to root by an individual who does not know the root password. I suspect the attacker gained control of this user's account or this user exploited the system to gain root access."

Tip   Keeping accurate logs and information can ultimately help an administrator repair the damage after an attack. If set up properly, logs can point toward modified permissions, changed system settings, and more.

Assess the situation

When you first feel you have been compromised, take a step back and look at the big picture. Before invoking the incident response plan, have a fairly strong feeling that you are indeed under attack.

Often, perceived security incidents can actually be regular administrative activity by another administrator on the network, or even the result of normal system operation. Knowing your systems and network and how they regularly behave will go a long way toward avoiding potential false alarms.

Remember, when something occurs that is a potential security issue, it can cause even the most experienced people to act rash or draw conclusions without looking at the whole situation.

Stop or limit the intrusion

Once an attack has been detected, an important step is to stop or limit any further activities by the hacker. Often, this dictates limiting or directing the scope of activity a hacker may get involved in. This can be approached in several different ways; however, keep in mind that attempting to contain or hold a hacker may backfire, and if this path is chosen, make sure you have a good idea what to do when you have the intruder "boxed in."

Invoke the incident response plan

If an attack is occurring, invoke the plan and follow the detailed procedures that you outlined during your incident response plan preparation.

Tip   Follow the response plan as closely as possible. If you do this and the plan is solid, you will likely have a much easier time stopping further intrusion and recovering from the incident.

Key Point Summary

This chapter discussed the importance of an incident response policy as well as what should be included in an incident response plan and how to handle security incidents.

✦ Incident response procedures stem from the Morris worm of 1988. This worm showed the world that security should be taken a bit more seriously. It also brought to light a few pressing issues related to common components used on UNIX type operating systems.

✦ CERT/CC was formed as a result of the Morris worm to provide a central organization to handle security incidents.

✦ Today, many companies develop their own Computer Security Incident Response Teams. These teams may only consist of one person, but many larger organizations will have many people working in several security teams to effectively handle incidents, which for some may be regular occurrences.

✦ In addition to incident response, CSIRTs can perform a variety of functions for a company, such as the following:

  • Disseminate information on potential security threats

  • Report security vulnerabilities to the appropriate group for elimination or at least mitigation

  • Promote security awareness

  • Track security incidents

  • Monitor intrusion detection systems

  • Support system and network auditing through processes such as penetration testing

  • Analyze new technologies for security vulnerabilities and risks

  • Provide security consulting

  • Develop security tools

✦ Advance preparation is essential to an effective, efficient incident response plan. It is hard to properly put into effect a plan that pays attention to every detail at the last minute or during the heat of the incident. Plan ahead and let cooler heads prevail.

✦ Creating an incident response policy is the first step. A properly outlined and detailed incident response policy is a necessity when trying to properly outline the requirements on how to deal with these types of situations.

✦ The incident response policy includes information on the CSIRT leader and members, who should be contacted, and what defines appropriate action.

✦ The incident response policy is the basis for developing the incident response plan, a detailed listing of procedures.

✦ An incident response plan should contain the following major steps:

1. Assess your circumstance.

2. Start contacting people.

3. Contain the damage.

4. Analyze the compromise and system integrity.

5. the evidence.

6. Have a set plan on how to respond to and deal with media inquiries.

7. Communicate.

8. Recover from compromise.

9. Prepare a report.

10. Evaluate lessons learned.

11. Update policies and procedures.

✦ When an incident occurs, don't panic! By panicking, you could miss things that could be important down the road, including valuable log information. Even worse, you could act upon an incident that was nothing more than a false alert caused by a legitimate action elsewhere on your network.

✦ Document everything and keep thorough logs. Such logs can assist you in rebuilding after the incident. Also, they can provide valuable information to the authorities should there be a need or desire to track down the intruder.

✦   ✦   ✦

STUDY GUIDE

This Study Guide presents ten assessment questions and one lab exercise to test your knowledge of the chapter objectives.

Assessment Questions

1. When you realize one of your systems has been compromised, you:

    A. Invoke the incident response plan

    B. Call the newspaper

    C. Hide under your desk

    D. All of the above

2. What should you never do during a security incident?

    A. Panic

    B. Document everything

    C. Call the CEO

    D. Invoke the incident response plan

3. What is the first step in creating an incident response plan of action?

    A. Create an incident response policy

    B. Create an incident response plan

    C. Call the CEO

    D. Define acceptable and unacceptable activities

4. After protecting the evidence of the attack, what is the next step in the incident response plan?

    A. Preparing the report

    B. Assessing the situation

    C. Communication

    D. System recovery

5. If you do only one thing during an incident, what should it be?

   A. Call CERT

   B. Call the CEO

   C. Document everything

   D. Call the authorities

6. The best time to develop your incident response plan of action is when the incident occurs. True or False?

7. It is important to remove a compromised system from the network to contain further damage or intrusion. True or False?

8. Preserving the evidence for investigators isn't that important because they likely won't be able to actually prosecute the intruder with the information obtained from your systems. True or False?

9. If critical data has been compromised, it is best to let anyone who may be affected by this data know about the situation so appropriate action can be taken. True or False?

10. After an incident has occurred, it is best to repair the damage and go on with regular operation, leaving the incident undocumented. True or False?

Lab Exercise

Lab 16-1 Subscribing to the CERT Alert Service

Using and participating in e-mail services, such as the CERT alert service or other vulnerability services like NT Bugtraq, can keep you informed of new security issues. It can also help you continually update your incident response plan with the appropriate information for your network and configuration. This lab shows you the quick way to subscribe to the CERT e-mail service.

1. Open your mail application.

2. Create a new e-mail and enter `majordomo@cert.org` in the To: address bar. You should leave the subject line blank. In the body of the e-mail, type the following:

   ```
   subscribe cert-advisory
   ```

   Click Send.

3. You should receive a response e-mail back, notifying you that you have successfully subscribed. In this e-mail, there will likely also be further guidelines and tips on how to best utilize the e-mail service. Make sure to keep these for future reference.

Answers to Chapter Questions

Chapter Pre-Test

1. An incident response policy is a high-level list of things that should be done and people who should be contacted during a security incident. Specific names and procedures are not included in the policy.

2. The CEO should be the first person contacted. Because he or she is the main representative of the company, he or she must always know what is going on, what the status of the situation is, and how it is being resolved.

3. The most important thing not to do during a security incident is to panic. This only makes the situation worse. Follow your exquisitely planned incident response procedures, and you will do fine.

4. An incident response plan is the detailed list of procedures that should be performed during a security incident. This varies from an incident response policy in its detail. A policy is not detailed; it discusses the company's approach and philosophy. The plan is the implementation of that philosophy and provides the steps to achieve that.

5. The most important thing to do during a security incident is to document everything. The more information you have documented, the easier your life is when speaking with the authorities or going over the incident in an after-the-fact analysis meeting. This extra information will also help fix whatever problems facilitated the intrusion in the first place.

Assessment Questions

1. **A.** When you realize one of your systems has been compromised, you should invoke the incident response plan.

2. **A.** You should not panic during a security incident. This only makes your job harder and less effective.

3. **A.** The first step in creating an incident response plan of action is to create an incident response policy. The incident response plan is developed after the policy is complete.

4. **D.** After protecting the evidence of the attack, the next step in the incident response plan is to perform a system recovery. After protecting the evidence, you can put the system back into a trusted configuration and put it back into service.

5. **C.** If you do only one thing during an incident, document everything. This way, if you do talk to the authorities or CERT after the incident, you have specific details to discuss with them.

6. **B.** False. The best time to develop your incident response plan of action is well before any incident occurs. This enables you to be better prepared and properly act upon the situation in a timely fashion.

7. **A.** True. When a system has been compromised, it is important to remove the compromised system from the network to contain further damage or intrusion.

8. **B.** False. Preserving the evidence for investigators is important because they will not be able to prosecute the intruder without the information obtained from your systems or network.

9. **A.** True. If critical data has been compromised, it is best to let anyone who may be affected by this data know about the situation so appropriate action can be taken.

10. **B.** False. It is important to take a step back after the situation has been handled and document the entire event. This way you can get a better overall grasp of what happened, as well as a better idea of how to avoid another potential situation from happening again. Learn from your mistakes!

For More Information

For more information on handling security incidents, take a look at the following resources:

✦ *Handbook for Computer Security Incident Response Teams* by Moira J. West-Brown, Don Stikvoort, and Klaus-Peter Kossakowski. Available at `www.sei.cmu.edu/publications/documents/98.reports/98hb001/98hb 001abstract.html`

✦ CERT/CC at `www.cert.org`

✦ Forum of Incident Response and Security Teams (FIRST) at `www.first.org`

✦ `www.sans.org/topten.htm`. This SANS Web site outlines the top ten vulnerabilities seen on networks, and how to best go about eliminating them from your network.

Security Auditing, Analysis, and Intrusion Detection

This part of the book shows you how to gather information regarding intrusion and what to do with that information.

Principles of Security Auditing explores the role of a security auditor, and how to assess security risks via the use of a formal security policy, categorizing and prioritizing resources, and customization of security for an organization. This chapter also discusses risk management techniques; including mapping, scanning, and footprinting intrusions, and how to establish control after a system has been violated.

System Security Scanning and Discovery explores security scanning in detail. This includes examinations of fingerprinting utilities, network- and server-discovery tools, fingerprinting IP stacks, share scans, Telnet inquiries, SNMP vulnerabilities, TCP/IP service vulnerabilities, simple TCP/IP services, and security scanning suites. The chapter also takes a look at how to assess information and system security.

Creating and Managing Security Control Procedures begins with a general discussion of how intruders can establish security control. This discussion includes information on the different phases and methods of control. The chapter concludes with an examination of how to use auditing to prevent unwanted control.

(continued)

Continued

Auditing System and Security Logs explores log analysis, how to build a baseline, and how to use key logs for analysis. The chapter takes a look at how to detect suspicious activities and secure log storage. Finally, the chapter examines the impacts of logging on your system.

Acting on Audit Results shows you how to understand the results of the auditing process. This discussion includes information on using an auditing assessment report, and ensuring and confirming security compliance. The chapter discusses auditing and security standards, using proactive intrusion detection, effective host-auditing strategies, and how to improve overall security by strengthening system and network services.

Principles of
Security Auditing

◆ ◆ ◆ ◆

EXAM OBJECTIVES

+ Understand an auditor's duties

+ Understand the importance of a risk assessment

+ Define risk

+ Understand the roles of an auditor

CHAPTER PRE-TEST

1. What does an auditor do?

2. What is a risk assessment?

3. What is risk?

4. What two approaches can an auditor take?

5. What is transferring risk?

Auditors play a very important role in an organization. Although this role may vary between companies — and even within the same company — the basics remain the same. Auditors evaluate risk, design audit strategies, and present recommendations to mitigate identified risk.

What Is an Auditor?

At the most basic level, an auditor is an individual (or group of individuals) who assesses the effectiveness of a network's security by conducting a risk assessment. Effective security means that networks are reasonably secure and that employees can still perform their job duties. The most effective auditors work from two approaches:

✦ They think like attackers and look for weaknesses in the infrastructure.

✦ They think like employees and evaluate how security measures will affect their work.

What Is Risk?

 Understand risk

Risk, defined by `http://www.dictionary.com` as "the possibility of harm or loss," is used to express uncertainty about events and outcomes that could have an undesirable effect on your organization and its goals. Risks range from the sudden death of the CEO, to an earthquake that destroys your office building, to an attacker deleting your entire customer database. Some risks are voluntary and some are involuntary, but they must all be identified, minimized, and managed to the greatest extent possible.

The central element of risk is uncertainty, generally defined as the possibility of experiencing loss as a result of a threatening event. Risk is the probability of an undesirable outcome in the face of an uncertain situation. For example, will your servers be attacked when you connect them to the Internet? They may be successfully hacked or they may never even be targeted. The outcome is uncertain, but the threat is very real. Identifying and understanding risk enables you to manage the threats that result in negative outcomes.

Risk management

Although inherent in all aspects of business, risk is especially prevalent in e-business. After you connect your systems to the Internet, you are connected to the world. Everyone else on the Internet can be perceived as a potential threat. The Internet age forces companies to be much more proactive and cutting edge when implementing new products and applications; it also compels businesses to take on more risk to conduct business in the wired and wireless world. Companies must anticipate how network systems and information can be manipulated, corrupted, misappropriated, and used against them or for someone else's benefit; they must then determine how to combat those risks. The risks involved with the Internet may appear daunting, but they can be removed, mitigated, or transferred.

The entire purpose of security in an organization, especially an e-business organization, is to manage risk, whether real or perceived. Risk management provides the tools to decide between action and inaction by comparing the cost of taking action against the risk of potential losses due to inaction. Security does not exist in a vacuum; it is only beneficial if it complies with the goals and direction of your business. Without security, your company can lose revenue, but with too much security, you can increase your operating costs. The goal of security risk management is to achieve a balance between these two areas. Your security infrastructure is the physical embodiment of your risk management plan.

Risk management helps answer questions such as the following:

✦ Will passing up the new database upgrade increase your chances of being hacked?

✦ Do you really need to implement that secure e-mail system?

✦ Will you reduce the likelihood of a successful attack on your Web server if you purchase the latest intrusion detection technology?

Additionally, risk management helps you prioritize issues. Prioritization helps you identify the most critical issues so that you can allocate resources to these areas first. Prioritization is especially helpful if you have a limited amount of resources and cannot address all areas immediately.

Embracing risk

To survive in today's global Internet economy, you need to embrace risk, and more importantly, embrace it intelligently. Take on only those risks that you can handle and that will provide the most benefit to your organization. The voluntary risk your company assumes is often termed *opportunity risk*, which is risk that provides new opportunities for your organization in the marketplace. In today's environment, e-businesses are assuming larger opportunity risks than their old economy predecessors. The risks are much greater, but the payoffs can be equally great. Some organizations still prefer to avoid as much risk as possible.

Opportunity risk exposes you to dangers, such as malicious employees and crackers, that you do not voluntarily assume; rather, these dangers exist as a necessary part of doing business. To adequately deal with these risks, quantify the impact they have on your business and prioritize the implementation of safeguards and controls to remove, mitigate, or transfer these risks.

Removing a risk means implementing a solution or control that removes the threat. For example, if you fear that network sniffers on your internal network will capture sensitive user ids and passwords, you can encrypt all network communications to remove the risk.

Mitigating a risk means implementing a safeguard or control that lessens the severity of the risk. Connecting your systems to the Internet is a huge risk, but installing a firewall and intrusion detection system lessens the chance that unauthorized individuals will enter your network and systems.

Transferring a risk means moving the consequences of risk from your organization to a third party. Insurance policies are the best example of transferring risk. If you purchase a "hacker" insurance policy to protect yourself from break-ins, you are transferring this risk from your organization to the insurance company.

The rapid rate of technological change, coupled with the growing number of threats on the Internet, dictates that risk management, like security, cannot be a static, one-time event. Risk management must be a continuous and adaptable process.

What Does an Auditor Do?

 Understand an auditor's duties

Auditors help mitigate risk and ensure that security measures are properly implemented and followed. To accomplish these goals, auditors work with system administrators to determine *compliance*. In other words, are the users following the posted security policies? If not, why not?

The second activity an auditor performs is a risk analysis. A risk analysis includes, at a minimum, the following steps:

1. Understand the business of the organization.
2. Read the written security policy (if available).
3. Evaluate existing management and control architecture.
4. Conduct a security audit.
5. Identify and prioritize at-risk systems, including databases, Web servers, routers, and user account databases.
6. Write and deliver a detailed findings report.

What Is a Risk Assessment?

 Understand the importance of a risk assessment

The best way to analyze your organization's security risk is to perform periodic information security assessments. A security assessment helps you identify, understand, and quantify the risks to your company assets. Understanding these risks is the first step in building a security infrastructure.

Numerous risk assessment methodologies exist, but the most common is the *ad hoc* method, in which someone believes a risk exists, convinces management the risk exists, and recommends a means to address it. This process often immediately follows a security incident or news story about a new threat. Although this method works for some organizations, it is not a systematic approach, and critical threats can often be overlooked.

The risk assessment process is the crucial step in building a security infrastructure that links security issues to business needs. The risk assessment shows the impact of specific, defined events to the confidentiality, integrity, and availability of critical business processes. Every security control has a cost, so there should be a business purpose for every control that is implemented. A risk assessment provides you with the business purpose, as well as the priority for implementation.

At the very least, a risk assessment should answer seven categorical questions.

✦ **Threat events:** What can go wrong?

✦ **Single loss exposure value:** If the event occurred, how bad could it be?

✦ **Frequency:** How often might the event happen?

✦ **Uncertainty:** How sure are the answers to the first three questions?

✦ **Safeguards and controls:** What can be done to remove, mitigate, or transfer risk?

✦ **Cost control:** How much will it cost to control the risk versus the potential damage if the risk were to actually take place?

✦ **Cost/Benefit or Return on investment (ROI) analysis:** How efficient is the risk management?

In real life, risk assessments are much more complex, but you get the general idea. The risk assessment process for this book consists of the following six steps:

1. Inventory, definition, and requirements

2. Vulnerability and threat assessment

3. Evaluation of controls

4. Analysis, decision, and documentation

5. Communication

6. Monitoring

The risk assessment process should include both technical and non-technical individuals to ensure that all areas are adequately covered. Technical folks do not always understand the business aspects of the organization, and vice versa.

Phase 1: Inventory, definition, and requirements

The first phase of the risk assessment process helps you understand the function of each asset in your organization so you can accurately measure the potential impact a risk will have.

Assets include anything subject to protection, such as information, databases, personnel, facilities, software, computers, and networks. Start the risk assessment process by identifying your organization's critical business. Questions you should answer include:

✦ How do you generate revenue?

✦ What is your main means of corporate communication?

✦ Where is your key data stored and how do you modify that data?

✦ Where is your source code stored and how do you modify it?

After you identify your critical business processes, identify the assets that comprise those processes. Besides the physical assets, such as servers, routers, mail servers, and Web servers, you should also consider the following:

✦ Network services and protocols (HTTP, SMTP, SSL, and so on)

✦ Remote access locations (employees at home or traveling, branch offices)

✦ What information is traveling over the Intranet? Internet?

✦ Who should be able to access what, and when should they be able to access it?

Make sure the asset list you create is exhaustive, but manageable. Omitting key assets will lead to a flawed decision-making process, although including everything under the sun makes the entire process unwieldy and difficult to complete.

Next, place a value on the assets — or somehow quantify their importance to your organization. This key step in the risk-assessment process plays a big role in determining priority. Involve business-process owners in this step because they can provide you with more accurate data regarding the value of the processes and their corresponding assets.

Phase 2: Vulnerability and threat assessment

Carefully and thoroughly analyze your systems to determine vulnerabilities that could be exploited and the probability that these vulnerabilities will be successfully exploited. Make sure you include not only electronic risks, such as network attacks, but also physical risks, such as someone popping in a floppy to steal data or modify the system.

Look at the applications running on the systems, such as Web servers and e-mail servers. The majority of successful attacks today come through misconfigured or unpatched Web servers. This analysis step helps you cover the majority of the points of attack for your network and systems.

Many tools exist to help automate this analysis process. Some are commercial, whereas others are free. Although you could manually analyze all your systems for vulnerabilities, automation tools speed up the process, producing a report of known vulnerabilities on your system that you can use as a starting point for your analysis.

Phase 3: Evaluation of controls

Look at your threats, the probability of that threat, and ways you can remove, mitigate, or transfer the risk of the threat. No decisions are made in this phase, just brainstorming on potential safeguards and controls and their associated costs. Controls can be technical, such as implementing a security product, or policy-based, such as requiring employees to request and justify Internet access. You can rarely reduce the risk of the threat to zero; residual risk almost always exists. The risk assessment process does, however, allow you to *control* your amount of residual risk.

View potential controls as a risk/value proposition. You do not want the control to cost more than the threat. Remember that the cost of the control is more than just the cost of acquisition and implementation; it also includes operations, maintenance, usability, scalability, and performance.

Analyzing your vulnerabilities with an eye toward potential safeguards and controls gives you a holistic view of your business and associated risk, allowing you to maximize your security investment and get more bang for your buck. Many e-businesses focus on point solutions, fixing holes and threats only as they arise. This is not the most efficient, secure, or cost-effective approach.

Phase 4: Analysis, decision, and documentation

Evaluate the cost of controls versus the value of the assets you are protecting and the amount of residual risk. Implementing a control that is more expensive than the revenue generated by the business processes being protected is poor business.

Analyze the list of options that you developed in Phase 3 and make a decision on which control should be implemented. Use the information gathered during the risk assessment process as the basis for your decision.

During this phase, involve a wide range of people, including:

✦ Management

✦ Business process owners

✦ Technical personnel

✦ Non-technical personnel

Being involved gives everyone a sense of ownership. Additionally, the business process owners best understand the processes and which controls will work best in your environment.

The final step of this phase is to formalize the process by documenting the work that was performed, as well as the results of the assessment. The better your documentation, the easier the process becomes next time.

Phase 5: Communication

Communicate the results of the risk assessment to management, process owners, and users. Your final report is your means of gaining management buy-in and user awareness to successfully implement the controls (security infrastructure).

Communicating results also ensures that the risks are understood throughout your organization and may even bring new vulnerabilities to light that had gone previously unnoticed.

Phase 6: Monitoring

Ongoing monitoring of controls is critical. As your organization changes, your threats also change. Continuously update your risk assessment to maintain relevancy. When something in the organization changes, such as launching an e-business initiative, start the entire risk assessment process from the beginning.

You might also consider performing mini risk assessments on a project-by-project basis to ensure the impact on the security infrastructure is understood, documented, and accounted for.

Your risk assessment is now complete. Hopefully, you have a thorough understanding of the potential threats faced by your organization and a list of controls to remove, mitigate, or transfer the risk of those threats.

Auditor Roles and Perspectives

 Objective   Understand the roles of an auditor

Auditors evaluate security from two perspectives: from that of an attacker and from that of a manager. These roles are explored in the sections that follow.

Auditor as security manager

As a security manager, you know how the network is configured and how everything works. You have detailed, inside information that can help you find weaknesses. This insider monitoring is also called *administrative auditing*.

Auditing from the administrative perspective allows you to test the network for insider attacks, which are estimated to constitute over 80 percent of the attacks against your network. These audits focus on servers and workstations and are usually performed inside the firewall.

A security manager can also analyze security from outside the firewall to see what is able to pass.

Auditor as consultant

Approaching an audit as a consultant (independent third party), you can analyze the security of the network without the insider's knowledge. You can see the network from the eyes of an external attacker.

As a consultant, you can also analyze the network from both inside and outside the firewall to scout the vulnerabilities and weaknesses internal and external attackers are likely to use.

You can also approach this analysis as an insider. In this case, you would meet with the security manager or security administrator before beginning the audit to help you understand the architecture, policies, and technology used by the organization.

Most often, consultants combine the two approaches to provide the best information and most thorough audit to their clients.

Insurance

As mentioned earlier in the chapter, insurance is a good way to transfer risk. In the past, all a business needed was error and omission, business interruption, and property damage insurance. However, in the Age of the Internet and e-commerce, the rules and risks have changed. Insurance policies have not.

Why do you need insurance? If you use a patented idea on your Web site, such as the one-click functionality that is currently being disputed, you could pay three times the profit you made from the site to the patent holder. If a court finds you guilty of improperly using someone's trademark online, you could face a fine of up to $100,000 per infringement. What happens when someone uses your network as a launch point for an attack?

A few regular insurance policies cover losses incurred by these instances. What businesses are more concerned about, though, are losses due to the acts of hackers. In some cases, hacker losses are covered under loss-of-business or act-of-vandalism clauses, but there are few policies written to specifically cover hacker attacks. For those that do, premiums often start at $100,000 and can run as high as $3 million. Analysts expect the hacker insurance market to grow to billions of dollars in annual premiums in the next few years because of the growth and increased reliance on e-commerce.

Several companies offer technology insurance, including Managed Security Service Providers (MSSPs). Counterpane, the leading security monitoring company, has teamed up with Lloyd's of London to offer hacker insurance. As quoted from their press release, they offer, a "direct financial reimbursement in the event a hacker breaks through its defenses and uses customer data." A $20,000 annual premium provides coverage for $1 million in hacker losses, and a $75,000 premium provides coverage for $10 million in losses. The price for any additional coverage, up to $100 million, must be negotiated with Lloyd's of London.

If you are looking for a policy to cover your servers, you have several options and the list grows longer each day. INSURETrust.com is one option. This company launched a new policy in September 2000, EXPRESSTrust, aimed specifically at companies launching an e-business initiative.

Prospective insurance clients typically must perform a risk assessment to determine coverage rates, and known security gaps must be fixed before a policy can be issued. Around-the-clock monitoring is also a common condition for coverage.

Key Point Summary

This chapter discusses auditors and their role in the organization as the risk mitigator.

✦ At the most basic level, an auditor is an individual or group of individuals that assess risk. Auditors determine the effective security of a network by conducting a risk assessment.

✦ The most effective auditors work from two approaches:

• They think like attackers and look for weaknesses in the infrastructure.

• They think like employees and evaluate how security measures will affect their work.

✦ *Risk,* defined by Dictionary.com as "the possibility of harm or loss," is used to express uncertainty about events and outcomes that could have an undesirable effect on your organization and its goals.

✦ The central element of risk is *uncertainty,* generally defined as the probability of experiencing loss as a result of a threat event.

✦ To survive in today's global Internet economy, you need to not only embrace risk, but to embrace it intelligently. Take on only the risks that can provide the most benefit to your organization and that you can best handle.

✦ The entire purpose of security in an organization, especially an e-business organization, is to manage risk, whether real or perceived.

✦ Some risks are voluntary and some are involuntary, but they must all be identified, minimized, and managed to the greatest extent possible.

✦ Companies must anticipate how their systems and information can be manipulated, corrupted, misappropriated, and used against them for someone else's benefit; they must then determine how to combat those risks.

✦ Risk management provides the decision tools to help decide between inaction and action, comparing the losses incurred with inaction to the cost of action taken to reduce risks.

✦ To adequately deal with risks, you need to quantify the impact they have on your business and prioritize the implementation of safeguards and controls to remove, mitigate, or transfer these risks.

✦ Mitigating a risk is implementing a safeguard or control that lessens the severity of the risk.

✦ Transferring a risk is moving the consequences from your organization to a third party. Insurance policies are the best example of transferring risk.

✦ Security does not exist in a vacuum; it must fall in line with the goals and direction of the business to be beneficial. Without security, your company can lose revenue, but with too much security, you can increase your operating costs.

✦ The voluntary risk your company assumes is often termed *opportunity risk* because assuming this risk provides new opportunities for your organization in the marketplace.

✦ Risk management cannot be a static, one-time event. It is an ongoing, continuous process that needs to be adaptable and able react to changes quickly.

✦ Auditors help mitigate risk and ensure security measures are properly implemented and followed. To accomplish this, they work with system administrators to determine compliance.

✦ The best way to analyze your organization's security risk is to perform periodic information security assessments.

✦ A security assessment helps you identify, understand, and quantify the risks to your company assets. Understanding these risks is the first step in building a security infrastructure.

✦ Numerous risk assessment methodologies exist, but the most common by far is the ad hoc method. In the ad hoc method someone believes a risk exists, convinces management the risk exists, and recommends a means to address the risk. Although this method works for some organizations, it is not a very systematic approach and leaves room for missing some very important threats.

✦ The risk assessment process is the crucial step in building a security infrastructure that links security issues to business needs.

✦ The risk assessment shows the impact to the confidentiality, integrity, and availability of critical business processes.

✦ Every security control has a cost and there must be a business purpose for the control to be implemented. A risk assessment provides you with the business purpose as well as the priority for implementation.

✦ The risk assessment process for this book will contain the following six steps:

1. Inventory, definition, and requirements

2. Vulnerability and threat assessment

3. Evaluation of controls

4. Analysis, decision, and documentation

5. Communication

6. Monitoring

✦ The risk assessment process should include both technical and nontechnical individuals. This helps ensure all areas are adequately covered.

✦ The first phase of the risk assessment process helps you understand the function of each asset in your organization. This is necessary to accurately measure the potential impact a risk will have.

✦ Assets include anything subject to protection such as information, databases, personnel, facilities, software, computers, and networks.

✦ Start the risk assessment process by identifying your organizations' critical business.

✦ After you have identified your critical business processes, identify the assets that comprise those processes.

✦ Omitting key assets will lead to a flawed decision-making process, whereas including everything under the sun makes the entire process unwieldy and not likely to be completed.

✦ In phase 2, carefully and thoroughly analyze your systems for vulnerabilities that could be exploited and the probability the vulnerability will be successfully exploited. Make sure you include not only electronic risks such as network attacks, but also physical risks such as someone popping in a floppy and stealing data or modifying the system.

✦ In phase three, look at your threats, the probability of that threat, and ways you can remove, mitigate, or transfer the risk of the threat.

✦ No decisions are made in this phase; just brainstorming on potential safeguards and controls and their associated cost.

✦ Controls can be technical, such as implementing a security product, or policy-based, such as requiring employees to request and justify Internet access.

✦ You can rarely reduce the risk of the threat to zero; residual risk will almost always exist. What the risk assessment process allows you to do is control the amount of residual risk you have.

✦ Potential controls need to be viewed as a risk/value proposition. Remember the cost of the control is more than just the cost of acquisition and implementation; it also includes operations, maintenance, usability, scalability, and performance costs.

✦ Phase four is where you will evaluate the cost of a control versus the value of assets you are protecting and amount of residual risk. It is rather poor business to implement a control that is more expensive than the revenue generated by the business processes it is meant to protect.

✦ Phase 5, the most important step, communicates the results to the appropriate parties.

✦ The results need to be communicated to management, process owners, and users. Your final report is your means of gaining management buy-in and user awareness to help successfully implement the controls (security infrastructure).

✦ Communicating the results of the assessment process makes sure the risks are understood throughout your organization as well as possibly bringing new vulnerabilities to light that had gone previously unnoticed.

✦ Ongoing monitoring of controls is critical. As your organization changes, your threats will also change. Your risk assessment needs to be continuously updated to maintain relevancy. When something in the organization changes, such as launching an e-business initiative, you need to start the entire risk assessment process from the beginning.

✦ Auditors evaluate security from two perspectives, that of an attacker and that of a manager.

✦ As a security manager, you know how the network is configured and how everything works. You have detailed, inside information that can help you find weaknesses. This is also called administrative auditing.

✦ Approaching an audit as a consultant (independent third party), you can analyze the security of the network without the insider's knowledge. You can see the network from the eyes of an external attacker.

✦ You can also approach this analysis as an insider. In this case, you would meet with the security manager or security administrator before beginning the audit and understand the architecture, policies, and technology in use by the organization.

✦ Insurance is a good way to transfer risk. In the past, all a business needed was errors and omissions, business interruption, and property damage insurance.

✦ Prospective insurance clients typically must perform a risk assessment to determine coverage rates and known security gaps must be fixed before a policy can be issued. Around-the-clock monitoring is also a common condition for coverage.

✦ ✦ ✦

STUDY GUIDE

The following Study Guide provides five assessment questions to test your knowledge of the exam topic area.

Assessment Questions

1. What does it mean to remove a risk?

    A. Removing a risk is the process of implementing a solution or control that removes the threat.

    B. Removing a risk is implementing a safeguard or control that lessens the severity of the risk.

    C. Removing a risk is moving the consequences from your organization to a third party.

    D. None of the above.

2. What does it mean to mitigate a risk?

    A. Mitigating a risk is the process of implementing a solution or control that removes the threat.

    B. Mitigating a risk is implementing a safeguard or control that lessens the severity of the risk.

    C. Mitigating a risk is moving the consequences from your organization to a third party.

    D. None of the above.

3. What is transferring a risk?

    A. Transferring a risk is the process of implementing a solution or control that removes the threat.

    B. Transferring a risk is implementing a safeguard or control that lessens the severity of the risk.

    C. Transferring a risk is moving the consequences from your organization to a third party.

    D. None of the above.

4. What is the main purpose of an auditor?

    A. To fire employees for non-compliance

    B. To develop applications

    C. To take notes

    D. To assess risk

5. Compliance reviews ensure that _____.

    A. Employees are following the security policy

    B. Employees are eating lunch every day

    C. Employees are being security-conscious

    D. Employees are not taking home confidential information

Answers to Chapter Questions

Chapter Pre-Test

1. Auditors help mitigate risk and ensure security measures are properly implemented and followed.

2. A security risk assessment helps you identify, understand, and quantify the risks to your company assets.

3. Risk, defined by www.dictionary.com as "the possibility of harm or loss," is used to express uncertainty about events and outcomes that could have an undesirable effect on your organization and its goals.

4. Auditors evaluate security from two perspectives, that of an attacker and that of a manager.

5. Transferring a risk is moving the consequences from your organization to a third party.

Assessment Questions

1. **A**. Removing a risk is the process of implementing a solution or control that removes the threat.

2. **B**. Mitigating a risk is implementing a safeguard or control that lessens the severity of the risk.

3. C. Transferring a risk is moving the consequences from your organization to a third party.

4. D. The main purpose of an auditor is to assess risk.

5. A. Compliance reviews ensure employees are following the company's stated security policy.

System Security Scanning and Discovery

+ Understand footprinting and network discovery tools

+ Scan for shares

+ Deploy an enterprise scanner

+ Describe host scanning versus network scanning

+ Describe TCP/IP service vulnerabilities

+ Explain how to discover system hosts and the services they run

+ Implement network and vulnerability scanners

+ Describe stack fingerprinting

CHAPTER PRE-TEST

1. How can ping be used to discover hosts on a network?

2. How can Telnet be used to discover applications running on a system?

3. What is stack fingerprinting?

4. From a security standpoint, what makes TFTP a particularly risky utility to have installed?

5. Why can social engineering be such an effective hacking method?

The first step in auditing (or hacking) a network is to find out what systems and applications are in place. This is achieved through *scanning*, the process of gathering as much information as possible about the network and systems being audited. Numerous utilities and approaches exist for scanning a network. Many of these are discussed in this chapter.

Some tools focus on a specific area, such as NetBIOS scanning or ping sweeping, whereas others are more general and perform a variety of functions. Although some tools are freely available on the Internet, others are enterprise class commercial applications. As always, if you don't find the tool you need, you can create your own using Perl, Java, C, C++, or your favorite language.

Footprinting Utilities

 Understand footprinting and network discovery tools

Scanning begins with finding the active IP addresses on a network. This process is commonly referred to as footprinting. Through footprinting, you can find DNS servers, physical location of servers, mail servers, and "live" IP addresses.

Whois

Whois is a service that gives you information on domain names and DNS servers by querying whois servers on the Internet. The default server in most systems is `whois.crsnic.net`, but this can be easily changed to any available whois server in most utilities. UNIX and Linux systems include a whois client, as shown in Figure 18-1. Numerous clients are available for the Windows platform, including WS_Ping Pro Pack.

From the initial whois query, you can determine the domain you need to focus on. If you already know what domains are owned by the target network, you can perform a whois query on the full domain name to receive a listing of DNS servers, as shown in Figure 18-2.

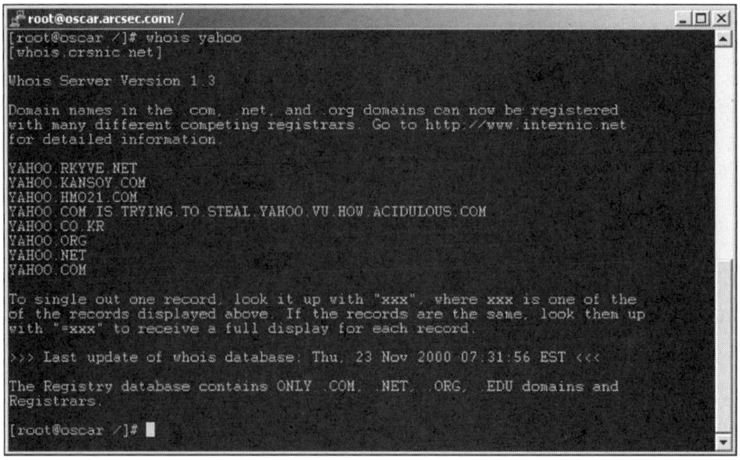

Figure 18-1: Performing a whois query on a name will list all domains containing that name. In this example, we performed a query on `www.yahoo.com`.

Figure 18-2: Performing a whois query on a complete domain name lists DNS servers as well as the registrar for the domain (Network Solutions, Inc., in this example).

Now that you know who the registrar is for the target domain, you can query that server to gain more detailed information on physical location, DNS IP addresses, and contact information. For Linux systems, you specify a whois server by appending the address after an "@" symbol: `whois yahoo.net@whois.networksolutions.com`, as shown in Figure 18-3.

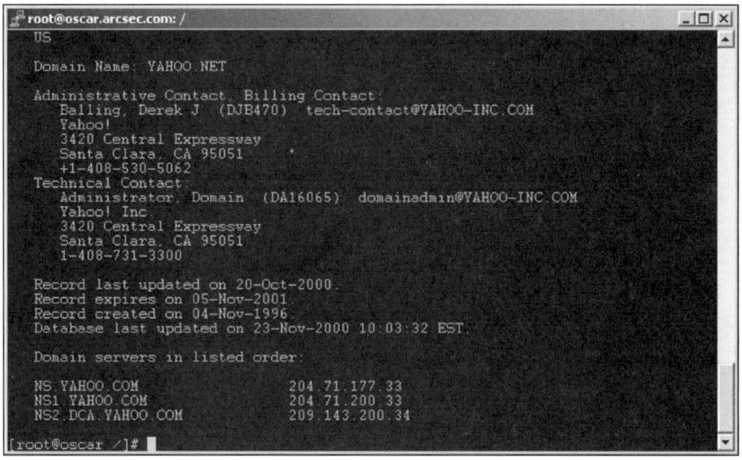

Figure 18-3: This is the result of performing a query on the Network Solutions whois server for `www.yahoo.net`. Here, you can see the IP address of the primary and secondary domain name servers.

Nslookup

Nslookup was meant to be a DNS troubleshooting tool, but it is very useful in obtaining detailed information about a network's configuration. By looking at the DNS table, you can find very valuable information regarding IP addresses, servers, applications, and so on.

Nslookup performs a zone transfer. A zone transfer allows a secondary server to update its information from the primary server, to provide redundancy in case the primary server goes down. When performing an nslookup query, you are requesting that the primary domain server send you all the information it has for the requested domain. In most cases, the name server is misconfigured and will send you, an untrusted party, all the information it has in its zone file. You can obtain very useful information with this, such as internal IP address ranges and subnets, system functions (`mail.target.com`), and comments describing what applications are running on each system (Exchange, IIS, and so on).

As with most tools, Linux contains an nslookup client. Windows also includes an nslookup client, but many better tools for Windows exist on the Internet.

Tip
Among some of the better nslookup clients available as shareware or freeware are NetScanTools from Northwest Performance Software, Inc. (for Windows) and AGNetTools from WildPackets, Inc. (for Macintosh operating systems).

To perform a zone transfer, follow these steps:

1. Find the name of the primary name server by performing a whois query on the target network. You should receive a listing of name servers, such as ns1.target.com.

2. Open the nslookup client. Change the default server to the target network's server by issuing the following command:

   ```
   server ns1.target.com
   ```

   This command connects you to the target's primary name server.

3. Once connected, ask the primary name server to send you the zone file contents for the target network by issuing the following command:

   ```
   ls target.com
   ```

If the server is properly configured to deny zone transfers, this command will not yield any particularly useful information.

UNIX host command

Linux systems contain the *host command*, which looks for information about hosts on the Internet. Basically, it converts IP addresses to host names and vice versa. Entering a system name will give you the IP address and entering a system IP address will give you the system name.

Using the -t or -a option will perform a zone transfer for the target domain. The host command is an easy way to learn about the target's mail (MX) servers. Issuing the following command gives you all the information available on the target's mail server:

```
Host -t mx target.com
```

Traceroute

Traceroute is a tool that shows the path an IP packet takes from one host to another. Linux and Windows contain a command line traceroute program, and many more traceroute programs are available for download, such as VisualRoute (www.visualroute.com), as shown in Figure 18-4.

Traceroute helps you learn a network's physical layout, displaying routers, ISPs, and firewalls in use by the target network. By understanding the physical layout, you can create a better, more targeted network audit.

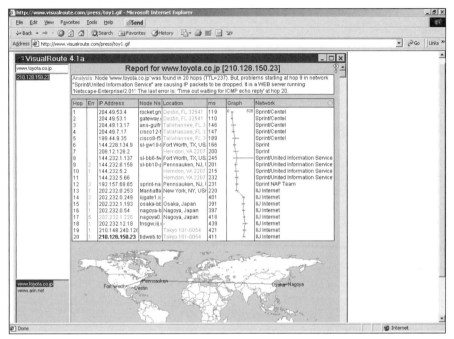

Figure 18-4: VisualRoute provides a graphical interface to traceroute, showing each hop geographically as well as performing whois lookups and gathering banner information for Web servers.

Ping sweeps

Whois, nslookup, and traceroute gather information on the target's systems and structure, showing the domain servers, mail servers, IP address ranges, and any other information contained in the zone transfer file. Now you need to find out which systems are accessible from the Internet.

Ping scanning helps you create a more detailed diagram of the target's network. Pinging a system is the process of sending an ICMP ECHO request and waiting for an ICMP ECHO_REPLY. You can further isolate the systems by finding IP addresses with live systems attached by scanning a range of IP addresses known to belong to the target's network. The example scan in Figure 18-5 shows 11 hosts in the 10.10.10.1-254 range.

Linux and Windows each include a basic ping program, but neither scales very well when used for larger scans. `Fping` for Linux (`http://packetstorm.securify.com/Exploit_Code_Archive/fping.tar.gz`) is the best tool to use when you are looking for a solid ping utility for Linux operating systems. For Windows operating systems, you can use a great graphical tool called Pinger that was written by Rhino9, shown in Figure 18-5 (`www.nmrc.org/files/snt`).

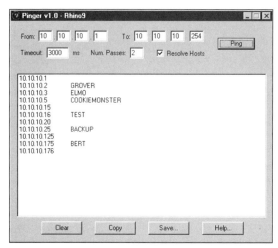

Figure 18-5: Pinger by Rhino9 is a fast, efficient ping sweeper.

Port scanning

With a ping scan, you find which systems are up and running. With a *port scan*, you take the level of detail one step further to find what TCP and UDP ports are open on a system. This helps target an audit to the specific services in place on the target network. In Figure 18-6, you can see that the system at 10.10.10.2 has five ports open.

Many port scanning tools exist for Linux and Windows. NMAP is the best all around port scanner for Linux (with a recent port to Windows). For Windows fans, SuperScan is a fast, free port scanner (`www.foundstone.com`).

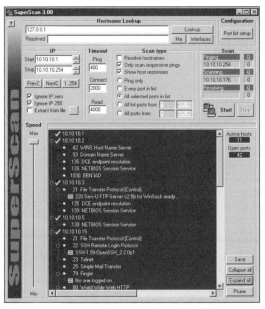

Figure 18-6: SuperScan is a free, flexible port scanner for Windows.

Network and Server Discovery Tools

 Explain how to discover system hosts and the services they run

With a port scan, you can find which systems are running Web servers, mail servers, FTP servers, and Windows machines with file sharing enabled (port 139). Several applications exist that perform all the functions I have discussed so far. Although keeping an arsenal of individual tools gives you best-of-breed performance, it is sometimes easier to have a centralized location for your scanning needs.

Ping Pro and NetScan

WS_Ping Pro, shown in Figure 18-7 and available at www.ipswitch.com, can perform ping sweeps, limited port scanning, nslookup, whois queries, and packet analysis. One of Ping Pro's downfalls is its limitation of being able to only scan the subnet it exists on, severely limiting the effectiveness of the software.

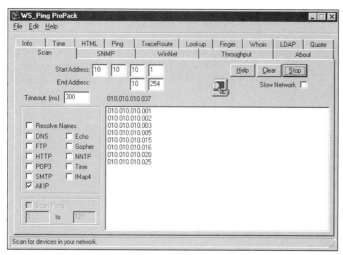

Figure 18-7: WS_Ping Pro provides a one-stop shop for footprinting and scanning tools.

NetScanTools, shown in Figure 18-8 and available at www.netscantools.com, is a shareware application that is much more powerful than WS_Ping Pro. NetScanTools provides nslookup, ping, traceroute, whois, finger, database, and NetBIOS utilities.

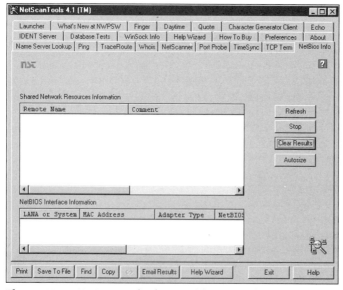

Figure 18-8: NetScanTools also provides many footprinting and scanning utilities in one application.

NetScanTools Pro 2000—a very thorough, expensive, scanning application—is also available, but is probably better suited for people who will use this package on a frequent basis, due to its cost.

Nbtstat

Nbtstat is a command line utility included with Windows that can help find out a remote systems name table, cache of names, and any local NetBIOS names the machine has. Although somewhat archaic, nbtstat can be very useful as a network scanning utility.

Netstat

Netstat is a very helpful command line utility built into Windows that can provide information on what open ports and connections a system has. Netstat can also tell you the routing tables of the target system if desired, thus giving some possible leads to a hacker to other important networks or systems the target system is connected to.

Not only is netstat great for checking out other systems, it can be used on your own systems to see if there are Trojans or other rogue software packages running on your system that shouldn't be there.

Netcat

Netcat was originally a UNIX/Linux tool that would allow for effective TCP/IP exploration. Recently, Netcat has been ported to a Windows version. Netcat allows for quick and efficient scanning of a system, including providing a port redirection feature that can allow redirection of a legitimate port to a port with netcat listening, thereby allowing a hacker to gain access again later. By using this access point, a hacker can then make an informed decision on the worthiness or difficulty of the target system, and come and go freely.

Stack Fingerprinting

 Describe stack fingerprinting

Usually, an auditor or hacker uses *banner grabbing* to discover what operating system a host is running. I discuss the specifics of banner grabbing a little later in the "Telnet Inquiries" section, but what is important to mention here is that system administrators have wised up to this technique and disabled banners. How do you find what is running on a system now? The answer is *stack fingerprinting*. Stack fingerprinting is the art of looking at a host's TCP/IP stack to discover what operating system it is running. Each operating system makes subtle changes to the TCP/IP stack, making it possible to distinguish one operating system from another. It is very difficult, if not virtually impossible, for a system administrator to control these changes, so stack fingerprinting is a reliable method for gathering information.

How exactly does stack fingerprinting work? In general, you send strange TCP/IP packets and see how the system responds.

Tip   The best paper on the subject was written by Fyodor and first published in *Phrack Magazine*. It can be found at `www.insecure.org/nmap/nmap-fingerprinting-article.html`.

Several applications exist for stack fingerprinting. One of the older OS-checking programs is checkOS. CheckOS contains basic fingerprinting functionality, but is not used very often in light of more recently released applications. One of the newer fingerprint applications, queso, made many advances in stack fingerprinting, including moving the fingerprint information out of the code and into a separate configuration file.

NMAP

The most well-known and oft-used fingerprint application is NMAP by Fyodor. NMAP (shown in Figure 18-9) is a powerful, free port scanner, as well as a stack fingerprinting application. It has a significant database of OS fingerprints. Besides recognizing server operating systems, NMAP can identify routers, firewalls, dial-up devices, and wireless LAN gateways. Additionally, NMAP is designed to defeat perimeter security mechanisms, such as firewalls or router ACLs, by fragmenting its scans. By utilizing its stealth option, you can effectively bypass the checks on many of today's common firewall products, a feature that has been used to great effect.

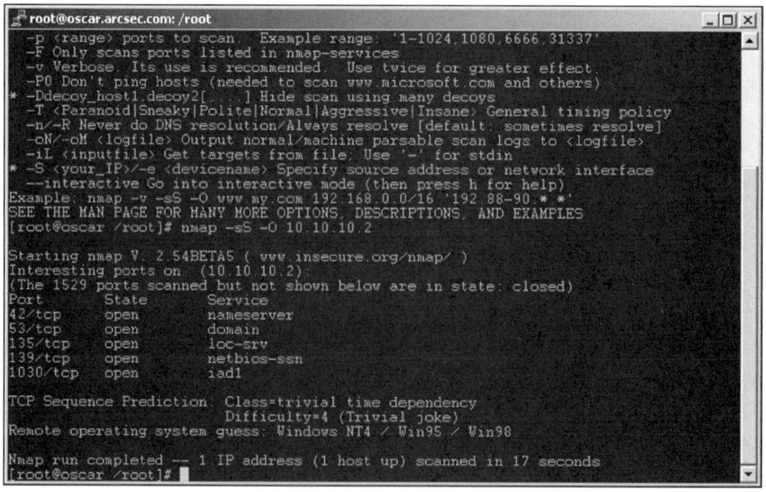

Figure 18-9: NMAP is the best stack fingerprinting application available.

NMAP runs best on Linux systems, but was recently ported to Windows by the eEye Digital Security team. The Windows version is available at www.eeye.com/html/Databases/Software/index.html. NMAP is easy to use and provides great instructions. Issuing the nmap -h command lists all the options and commands available.

Share Scans

 Scan for shares

Scanning for Windows shares is easily accomplished with the tools available. Many users open shares with no password protection or other security measure, making their directories easy targets.

Share scans function by looking at TCP and UDP ports 135-139. These are the ports Microsoft uses for communication. Both WS_Ping Pro and NetScanTools (refer to Figure 18-8) provide share scanning functionality. These tools only find network shares. Other tools actually attempt to break into shares, guessing passwords if the share is password protected. RedButton, shown in Figure 18-10, is one such share scanning tool. RedButton enumerates Windows shares, gains access to resources available to Everyone, determines the current name of the built-in Administrator account, and lists all shares (even hidden ones).

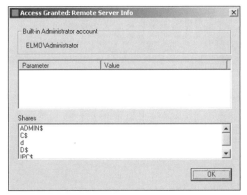

Figure 18-10: RedButton enumerates Windows shares.

Telnet Inquiries

Telnet is a very useful auditing tool for OS/application detection. Telnet was developed to run on port 25 and to allow a user to work on a remote computer as if she or he were sitting in front of the console. You can use Telnet to connect to any port on a system, though. In a command line Telnet client, the following command will connect you to port 80 on the target server:

```
telnet www.target.com 80
```

Figure 18-11 shows what you see when connected to port 80 on a system running IIS. Once you have connected to port 80, press Enter a few times and you will see a similar output to Figure 18-11. This technique is known as *banner grabbing*, and can be quite useful for hackers when they are poking around, trying to gather information about what specific applications are running on a server. By observing the output of such banner grabbing techniques, a hacker can get a pretty good idea of what type of system and services the target is running. Some scanning tools incorporate banner grabbing in the scan. YAPS is one scanner that does this. Banner grabbing is a great way to identify server versions, as long as the administrator has not disabled this feature on the application. This is not often the case, but as administrators grow more security conscious, less banner information will be available. As previously mentioned, stack fingerprinting comes in handy in cases where banner information is unavailable.

Figure 18-11: Using Telnet to connect to a port gives you valuable information about what application is running on the system.

You can also use Telnet to connect to a server and use the SYST command to discern what operating system that server is running.

SNMP Vulnerabilities

The *Simple Network Management Protocol (SNMP)* is the protocol that governs network management and monitoring of network devices and their functions. SNMP is used to gather information on TCP/IP as well as other services running on servers, workstations, and routers.

Three versions of SNMP exist today, SNMPv1 through v3, with SNMPv1 being the most common, but also the least secure. SNMP uses *trivial authentication*, which is a string of text sent over the network in clear text. This communication mechanism makes packet sniffers the perfect tool to compromise SNMP community strings. Additionally, many SNMP-enabled devices come preconfigured with a community name, often "public," thus allowing a hacker to break in with little to no effort.

You can use SNMP to reconfigure devices using the `setRequest` command, including stopping and starting services. If you are using SNMPv1 and someone gains access to the community name, he or she can change device configurations.

SNMPv3 contains many additional security features, including encryption and stronger authentication.

SNMP does you no good without an application that can make use of the information it provides. The most common SNMP software are as follows:

✦ **HP OpenView** — Available from Hewlett-Packard

✦ **SNMPUTIL** — Available in the Windows NT Resource Kit

✦ **WS_Ping Pro** — Available from Ipswitch and shown in Figure 18-12

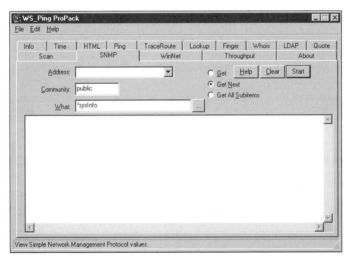

Figure 18-12: WS_Ping Pro can be used to gather SNMP information.

TCP/IP Services

 Describe TCP/IP service vulnerabilities

Each of the TCP/IP services, such as FTP, SMTP, HTTP, POP3, LDAP, contains their own security mechanism, some offering more security than the others. For example, SMTP and POP3 still send clear-text passwords, making network sniffers valuable tools for password grabbing. Other services are vulnerable to buffer overflow attacks.

LDAP

Lightweight Directory Access Protocol (LDAP) servers often contain valuable user data. Protecting the server should be a top priority for administrators, but such protection often gets overlooked, especially the process of keeping current with updates and patches. LDAP servers are also notorious for buffer overflow vulnerabilities.

TFTP

Any system running *Trivial FTP (TFTP)* should cause concern because TFTP does not require any authentication. TFTP is also vulnerable to denial-of-service attacks.

Finger

Finger servers allow you to find information about users, including user names, e-mail addresses, and the user's current login status. This information can be valuable to an attacker for use in social engineering or other discovery techniques.

Security Scanning Suites

 Implement network and vulnerability scanners

The problem with most of the tools previously discussed in this chapter is that they do not scale well for use in an enterprise environment. Trying to scan hundreds or thousands of hosts is difficult with many of the tools we have previously discussed, due to limitations of options or the speed of the network scans. Although many of these tools could be used for enterprise scanning, most take too long to perform the scan to be of any value.

Host versus network

 Describe host scanning versus network scanning

Two types of scanning applications exist: host and network. Host-based applications scan individual workstations for vulnerabilities and misconfigurations. Network-scanning applications scan servers (such as e-mail servers and Web servers), routers, firewalls, and operating systems. The combination of these two scanning types provides a strong basis for audit and analysis. Many companies provide both types in a suite of applications.

Needs of the enterprise

 Deploy an enterprise scanner

Enterprise networks are large, complex systems that often require different tools in order to perform a thorough, accurate analysis. Most enterprise networks contain numerous subnets, or groups of small networks. To scan multiple subnets, you normally must install a tool on each subnet, but some enterprise class scanners have the ability to scan multiple subnets from one central location.

All security tools support the TCP/IP protocol, but some enterprises may use other protocols, such as IPX/SPX, NetBEUI, and AppleTalk. An enterprise scanner should support multiple protocols.

Another consideration is the operating system platform. Some scanners run only on specific operating systems; consider this when looking for a solution. Traditionally, the most powerful scanners run on UNIX; however, there have been many recent developments in the Windows arena.

Scan levels

Most enterprise scanners allow the user to set scan levels to low, medium, or high. A low-level scan is the quickest, but least thorough option. Usually, a low-level scan looks for vulnerabilities and misconfigurations, such as poor password configuration, patch installations, well-known security weaknesses, and well-known ports. Medium- and high-level scans take more time, but search more thoroughly for more items, such as scanning all ports, analyzing the complete configuration of the system, and searching for all known security weaknesses.

Scan profiles

Most commercial enterprise scanners come with default scan profiles. For example, the ISS Internet Scanner from Internet Security Systems, shown in Figure 18-13, comes preconfigured with scans for Windows NT Servers (with and without IIS) and UNIX servers, to name a few.

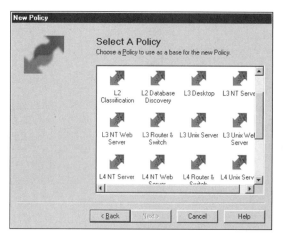

Figure 18-13: ISS Internet Scanner includes many preconfigured policies.

Enterprise scanners also give the administrator the ability to create unique scan profiles depending on the needs of the enterprise. You can see ISS Internet Scanner's policy configuration wizard in Figure 18-14.

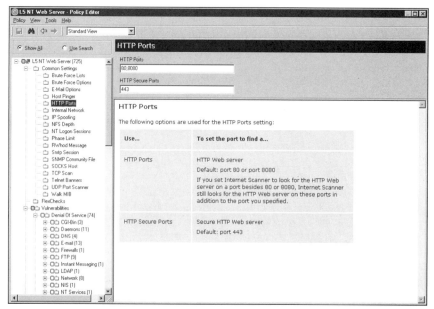

Figure 18-14: ISS Internet Scanner, like many other enterprise scanners, gives you the ability to configure your own scan policy.

Reporting

One area that usually sets enterprise scanners apart from the freeware/shareware applications is reporting. Enterprise scanners often provide very detailed reports in a variety of formats, including HTML, ASCII, RTF, DOC, EXL, and PDF, for administrators to analyze. See an example of ISS Internet Scanner's report in Figure 18-15.

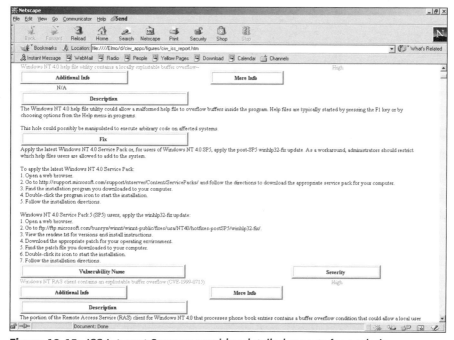

Figure 18-15: ISS Internet Scanner provides detailed reports for analysis.

Reports often categorize vulnerabilities by risk level to give the administrator an idea of how critical a threat is to the network. High-risk threats should be corrected immediately, whereas medium- and low-risk threats should be analyzed regarding business purpose and overall cost. That's not to say that low-level risks should be ignored. Just make sure the cost of fixing the security hole is not more than the value of the information and resources being protected.

Internet Security Systems

ISS developed the SAFESuite line of scanning products; these include Internet Scanner and System Scanner. Internet Scanner is a network scanner, and System Scanner is a host scanner. Internet Scanner was one of the first scanning applications available and is still one of the most popular applications today. This scanner is available for both Linux and Windows systems. Download an evaluation version at www.iss.net.

As shown earlier in the chapter (refer to Figures 18-13 and 18-14), Internet Scanner contains default policies and the ability to design your own custom policies. ISS scanners look for security configurations and known vulnerabilities. Comprehensive reports (refer to Figure 18-15) provide administrators with all of the information they need to fix vulnerabilities and threats. Currently, Internet Scanner looks for 728 vulnerabilities, including the following:

✦ 47 backdoors (GetAdmin, SubSeven, and so on)

✦ 50 daemons (rlogin, fingerd, and so on)

✦ 38 CGI-bin (ColdFusion, PHP, cgiexec, and so on)

✦ 51 NT patches (PPTP3, SSL, NT RAS overflow, and so on)

✦ 50 e-mail checks (popimap, buffer overflows, and so on)

Kane Security Analyst

Intrusion.com's Kane Security Analyst, shown in Figure 18-16, analyzes systems in six critical security areas: password strength, access control, user account restrictions, system monitoring, data integrity, and data confidentiality. This scanner does not look for specific vulnerabilities, but does provide a basis for auditing a system against a series of best practices. Kane Security Analyst comes preconfigured with security standards; however, these can be modified as appropriate for the enterprise. Go to `www.intrusion.com` for more information.

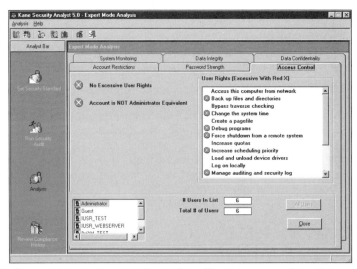

Figure 18-16: Kane Security Analyst allows you to analyze six security areas against defined best practices.

WebTrends Security Analyzer

WebTrends Security Analyzer, available at `www.webtrends.com`, scans Linux and Windows servers, firewalls, and routers for numerous threats, configuration issues, and vulnerabilities. Figure 18-17 shows the WebTrends interface, the starting point for scans, whether the scans are predefined or customized for the enterprise.

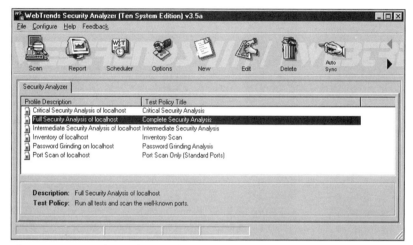

Figure 18-17: WebTrends Security Analyzer scans networks for vulnerabilities and configuration.

WebTrends HTML reports are known as the best on the market due to their clean presentation and useful information. Shown in Figure 18-18, they provide an easy-to-read description of each vulnerability, broken out by risk level. The report also provides recommended steps to eliminate security issues and help protect the system from further vulnerabilities.

Symantec NetRecon

Symantec recently bought Axent and their NetRecon product. NetRecon is a system vulnerability scanner that performs the regular gamut of vulnerability scanning; however, it generates reports a little differently.

When detailing a particular vulnerability, the software will help show the root of the issue that could show where other vulnerabilities may occur due to the issues that it has found initially. Thus, NetRecon can provide information on potential vulnerabilities that exist due to other known vulnerabilities and also a path to properly understanding the current issues the system faces.

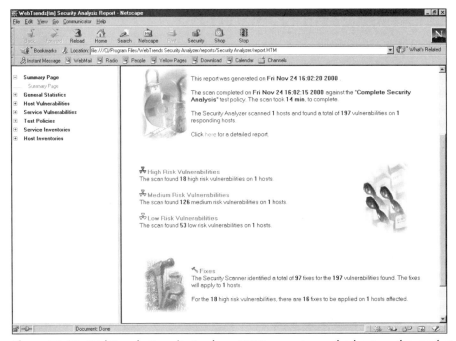

Figure 18-18: WebTrends Security Analyzer HTML reports are the best on the market.

PGP Security's CyberCop Scanner

CyberCop can perform hundreds of security tests on your systems and network, even providing perimeter vulnerability scanning on your network's firewall. Like most other vulnerability scanners, CyberCop can generate reports for auditors and security administrators alike. Included in these audits is information on the problems encountered and the possible fixes for the vulnerabilities.

CyberCop Scanner is currently available for Windows NT, Windows 2000, and Linux operating systems and is regarded as one of the better "enterprise" security scanners on the market.

BindView's bv-control for Internet Security

BindView recently changed the name of its HackerShield product to bv-control for Internet Security. This long name aside, HackerShield is undoubtedly one of the best products on the market for enterprise security scanning and reporting. bv-control is quick and performs security scans that can really help the average security administrator prepare for a security audit when the time arises. The reports generated by bv-control for Internet Security are clean, detailed, and well suited for presentations.

BindView facilitates new updates for its bv-control products with the Razor security team, which researches the latest vulnerabilities and hacking methods to provide one of the most complete scanning products available.

Additional scanning products

Numerous enterprise network vulnerability scanning products exist on the market, including the following:

✦ eEye's Retina scanner software (www.eeye.com)

✦ HP Presidium WebEnforcer (www.hp.com)

Social Engineering

Social engineering means using human resources to find information about a network or resource. By using the footprinting and scanning techniques discussed in this chapter, you get a good idea of what the network looks like. Because humans are the weakest link in a security infrastructure, with a little research you have a high probability of getting some valuable information out of someone at the target company.

E-mail

Sending e-mail messages with innocent-looking attachments, such as an animated greeting, are a great way into an unsuspecting user's system. A malicious user could attach a Trojan, such as BackOrifice, to the program, giving him/her free reign on the system once the attachment is opened. Less intrusive scenarios include asking users for userids and passwords, credit card numbers, or Social Security numbers.

Telephone

With all of the technological advances in the past decade, it is still easiest to pick up the phone and ask for information. Why go to all the work performing scans and analyzing data when you could make one phone call to find out the target has an IIS server at address 192.168.0.1?

If a hacker has done a little homework with a network discovery tool and learned the head network administrator's name from a DNS lookup, it wouldn't be hard for the hacker to use this name in a conversation with someone to obtain additional confidential information.

For instance, a hacker could call up and pretend to be a software reseller: "I was talking to Joe and he asked me to call you and ask what you think of the firewall product you are running." With the appropriate questions, the hacker could figure out what type of firewall software is running, and maybe even if there have been problems locking it down or with it crashing after a particular type of attack. The possibilities are endless.

Fighting social engineering

Education is the key to fighting social engineering. All employees should be aware of what administrators will and will not ask a user for over the phone or e-mail. For example, if someone receives a phone call asking for a password, the user should be aware that company policy does not allow discussion of passwords over the phone.

Procuring tool approval

A fine line exists between legal and illegal network scanning. Mainly, scanning with the intent of malicious activity or without the approval of the targeted company is not ethical, and may be illegal. Many of the tools discussed in this chapter are also used by attackers with malicious intent. The only difference between auditing and cracking is the intent of the user. When using these tools, make sure the target company is aware and approves of the audit approach you are taking. It is always best to get something in writing.

Many of the enterprise scanning applications, besides eating bandwidth, include some security mechanisms to track the origin of network scans. This helps administrators in tracking down the source of unauthorized scans.

Key Point Summary

This chapter discusses the first steps of the audit process, identifying the systems and services running on a network.

✦ Footprinting is the first phase in auditing where you find the range of IP addresses associated with the target network and which of those addresses are active.

✦ Footprinting tools include whois and nslookups, traceroute, ping sweeps, and port scanning.

✦ Network discovery tools, such as WS_Ping Pro and NetScanTools, perform a variety of functions and provide a one-stop shop for footprinting and analysis tools. These applications include basic footprinting utilities as well as SNMP and Windows share utilities.

✦ Stack fingerprinting is the process of analyzing the behavior of TCP/IP to determine the operating system running on a target system. NMAP is the best stack fingerprinting tool available today.

✦ Share scans search a network for shared directories on Windows systems. Many users share directories without password protection, making information gathering a rather simple process. Tools such as RedButton can be used to perform share scans.

✦ Telnet can be used for banner grabbing to help determine what application is running on a system on a specific port. Some administrators are beginning to remove application banner displays, though.

✦ Simple Network Management Protocol (SNMP) is used to monitor and control network devices. SNMPv1 contains numerous security vulnerabilities, including transmitting the SNMP community name in cleartext. SNMPv3 contains more security features, such as encryption and stronger authentication, but it is not widely deployed.

✦ TCP/IP services such as SMTP, POP, LDAP, FTP, and finger are full of security issues, such as sending passwords in cleartext and buffer overflows.

✦ Security scanning suites help the enterprise alleviate the complications and administrative overhead of auditing large, complex networks.

✦ Enterprise scanning applications come in two varieties, host and network. Host scanning focuses on individual systems. Network scanning focuses on network devices, such as firewalls, routers, Web servers, and mail servers.

✦ Enterprises have differing needs. Commercial scanning products generally meet these needs, such as the ability to scan multiple subnets, support a variety of operating systems and network protocols, and provide detailed reporting.

✦ Enterprise scanning suites come with scanning profiles preinstalled, but give administrators the opportunity to create custom profiles to better fit their enterprise needs.

✦ Internet Security Systems developed the Internet Scanner and System Scanner products, part of their SAFESuite security package. These applications scan hosts and networks for known vulnerabilities and recommend system configurations based on industry best practices.

✦ Kane Security Analyst analyzes systems in six critical security areas: password strength, access control, user account restrictions, system monitoring, data integrity, and data confidentiality. The results are compared to predefined security standards. You have the option of defining your own standards.

✦ WebTrends Security Analyzer is similar to ISS in that it analyzes networks and hosts for known vulnerabilities and misconfigurations. WebTrends differentiates itself mainly in its reporting capabilities.

✦ Social engineering is a very effective discovery tool that is fought only with end-user education.

✦   ✦   ✦

STUDY GUIDE

This Study Guide provides ten assessment questions and three lab exercises to test your knowledge of the chapter objectives.

Assessment Questions

1. Which of the following is not a part of the footprinting and discovery process?

    A. Whois query

    B. Analyzing firewall logs

    C. Ping sweep

    D. Share scan

2. Windows systems communicate over which port?

    A. 139

    B. 21

    C. 113

    D. 80

3. Which of the following is not considered social engineering?

    A. Calling the CEO's secretary and asking when the CEO will be in the office

    B. Sending an e-mail to all users saying they need to change their system password to "test"

    C. Performing a port scan on the system at 10.10.10.2

    D. Calling an employee pretending to be a network administrator

4. Most freeware/shareware tools are better than enterprise scanning software because enterprise applications:

    A. Use a lot of network bandwidth

    B. Support multiple network protocols

    C. Support multiple operating systems

    D. Provide better reporting capabilities

5. Using Telnet to connect to a specific port on a system may provide what information?

   A. The date the system was placed in service

   B. A list of all the applications running on the system

   C. The root/administrator password

   D. The application running on the system on that port

6. Ping sweeps can help hackers find out what systems are accessible from the Internet. True or False?

7. Telnet banner grabbing techniques rarely produce enough useful information about the design of the system for hackers to draw an accurate conclusion. True or False?

8. Protecting LDAP servers should be a major concern and priority for system administrators. True or False?

9. Education is the best defense against hackers trying to utilize social engineering methods. True or False?

10. The security needs of small networks are typically greater than the needs of larger corporations, since smaller network setups are harder to monitor. True or False?

Lab Exercises

Lab 18-1 Using NMAP on a Linux system for stack fingerprinting

1. Download and install the NMAP RPM from www.insecure.org.

2. Perform the stack analysis on a specific system by typing the following command:

   `nmap -O 10.10.10.15`

   Note: Replace IP address with that of a system on your network.

3. The results should look similar to those shown in Figure 18-19. Besides performing stack fingerprinting, NMAP performs port scans. You can also specify a range of IP addresses.

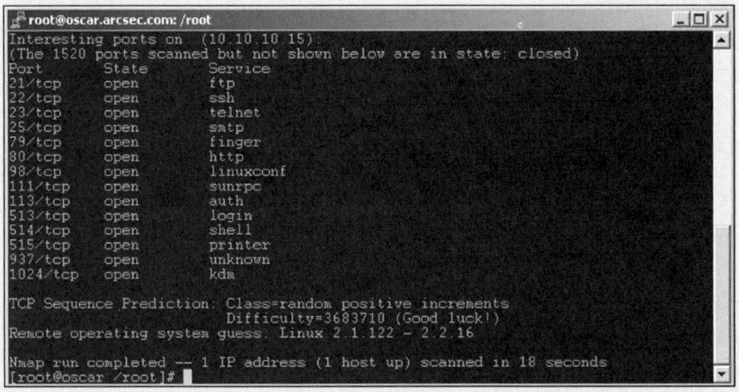

Figure 18-19: NMAP helps you identify the operating system running on a remote system through stack fingerprinting.

Lab 18-2 Using WebTrends Security Analyzer to scan the systems on a network

1. Download the evaluation version of Security Analyzer at www.webtrends.com.

2. Run the installation program.

3. Start WebTrends Security Analyzer. You should see the screen shown in Figure 18-20.

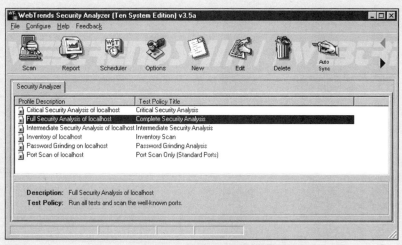

Figure 18-20: WebTrends Security Analyzer main menu

4. Click New to define a new scan profile.

5. Give the new profile a name and select a predefined Test Policy from the main drop-down menu, shown in Figure 18-21, or configure your own Test Policy. Click Next.

Figure 18-21: WebTrends Security Analyzer gives you the opportunity to select a predefined Test Policy or configure your own.

6. Click Add and select devices to be scanned by IP address or host name, as shown in Figure 18-22.

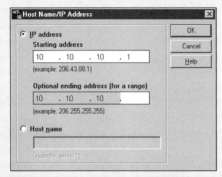

Figure 18-22: WebTrends Security Analyzer lets you define devices by host name or IP address.

The resulting list will look something like Figure 18-23. Click Finish.

Figure 18-23: Listing of hosts to be scanned by WebTrends Security Analyzer

7. Make sure your newly defined policy is selected. Click Scan to start the analysis. When the scan is complete, WebTrends Security Analyzer will open a Web browser with the finished report for your review.

Lab 18-3 Using traceroute under Windows to learn more about a network's setup and possible targets

1. First, open a command prompt window, either by clicking the icon, or by clicking Start ➪ Run and then typing `cmd.exe` (NT/2000) or `command.com` (Windows 9x).

2. Next, type the following command:

   `tracert destination address`

   Press Enter. (Replace `destination address` with any address you desire; it can be either an IP or Web address.)

3. The trace route should track through the various network connections between you and your destination address.

   This can be useful to see where routers and servers exist between you and your target, and also for delving deeper into networks now that you have names and addresses.

Answers to Chapter Questions

Chapter Pre-Test

1. Pinging a range of IP addresses known to belong to the target network can provide you with a list of addresses with active systems connected to them.

2. Using Telnet to connect to a specific port on a system can provide valuable information about the application running on that port.

3. Stack fingerprinting is the process of analyzing the behavior of TCP/IP on various devices to determine what operating system is running on the system.

4. TFTP is a particularly risky service to install because it does not require any authentication to utilize. It is also particularly vulnerable to denial-of-service attacks.

5. Social engineering can be an effective hacking method because it relies on the knowledge of humans, not the settings in a piece of software. In other words, hackers can leverage the general ignorance of the average user into useful results.

Assessment Questions

1. **B.** Analyzing firewall logs is not part of the footprinting/discovery process. This is part of the monitoring process to help determine if a security breach has occurred.

2. **A.** Port 139 is one of the ports Windows uses to communicate.

3. **C.** Running a port scan is not considered social engineering.

4. **A.** Enterprise scanning software is very noisy and consumes a good deal of bandwidth. Freeware/shareware applications are usually very lean, efficient applications.

5. **D.** Using Telnet to connect to a port on a system may show the application running on the port on that system.

6. **A.** True. Ping sweeps can help hackers find out what systems are accessible from the Internet.

7. **B.** False. Telnet banner grabbing techniques can produce useful information about the design of the system; however, there are now typically faster ways to obtain the information.

8. **A.** True. Protecting LDAP servers should be a major concern and priority for system administrators, mainly due to the critical user information contained within.

9. **A.** True. Education is the best defense against hackers trying to use social engineering methods.

10. **B.** False. The security needs of small networks are usually less than the needs of larger corporations, because larger networks are harder to monitor in respect to more stations, servers, outside network services and potential hacks from the inside.

For More Information

✦ Go to www.insecure.org to obtain the great TCP/IP fingerprinting utility, NMAP, and to partake in the NMAP-oriented user discussion forums.

✦ Go to www.technotronic.com/ for a wide selection of utilities, software packages, and information on the topics in this chapter.

✦ www.windowsitsecurity.com contains a wide array of articles, reviews, and other information on security software and security-related issues.

✦ Go to www.@stake.com/research/tools/index.html for a good selection of system scanning and testing software utilities.

Creating and Managing Security Control Procedures

EXAM OBJECTIVES

+ Define control phases

+ Learn methods of control

+ Audit unwanted control procedures and methods

CHAPTER PRE-TEST

1. When an intruder gains entry into a system, he will try to gain full control of the system. What two things will he do to maintain control?

2. Which file do intruders that want to crack NT passwords using L0phtCrack covet the most?

3. What are two ways to detect if NetBus has compromised your system?

4. What is the main difference between BackOrifice and BackOrifice 2000?

5. What is a keylogger used for and how can it quickly compromise a system?

✦ Answers to these questions can be found at the end of the chapter. ✦

Previous chapters explored a wide range of topics, including security auditing, network fingerprinting, and methods for breaking into networks. As a security administrator or auditor, you must keep yourself informed of the various ways that the network can be compromised. As an auditor, you have a duty to inform the client of security issues. To be a *good* auditor or security administrator, you must have a firm grasp of the various concepts, utilities, software, and methods to successfully gain access and control over a target network. Often, the best way to improve your understanding of security — and the various weaknesses that plague most networks today — is to attempt to compromise security yourself. This chapter uncovers the various ways an intruder can gain control and takes a look at how NetBus operates so you can better understand illicit network attack methods.

Phases of Control

 Define control phases

When an intruder has broken through the security measures placed on your system, he or she will try to gain as much control as possible to obtain sensitive information, make any wanted changes, and conceal the break-in.

The typical goals of an intruder at this initial stage of control are as follows:

- ✦ To gain root access (UNIX/Linux).
- ✦ To gain administrator privileges (NT).
- ✦ To gather information on the operating system and related software.
- ✦ To open or reopen new security holes and vulnerabilities.
- ✦ To cover their tracks and any evidence of the break-in.
- ✦ To propagate to other computers on the network or elsewhere.

The cracker is similar to a master thief casing the joint by obtaining information on the site and leaving behind points of access for a later intrusion. If an intruder can be successful at even a couple of these goals, he or she stands a good chance of not being detected, or at least of not being stopped if you become alerted to the intrusion. If the intruder is skillful, he or she will constantly move around the system, planting little backdoors or vulnerabilities to provide access at a time when your defenses are lowered. If an intruder gains access to other servers and systems on your network, the problem can become even worse — getting rid of an intruder with good control of one system is hard enough, let alone getting rid of one who has control over a couple of servers or workstations. The intruder might re-infiltrate the original system later. To put it simply, this kind of "cat-and-mouse game" could go on for quite a while.

Gaining root or administrative access

When penetrating a UNIX/Linux system, the ultimate goal of any would-be intruder is to obtain *root access*. Root access is the account that allows for full and unrestricted access to the system; it represents a big open door for anyone with the rights that the root account provides.

In Windows NT, the term for root access is *administrative access*. With root or administrative access, an intruder can manipulate security settings, services, and programs, and also plant backdoors for future access. When root or administrative access is compromised, the system is a sitting duck.

 In the Real World   Root and administrative access are one in the same; however, when discussing these concepts with individuals who are Windows-centric, keep the terminology distinction in mind — they may not have any idea what root access is!

Intruders can gain root access on UNIX/Linux systems in many ways. Many implementations of UNIX/Linux are vulnerable to trap doors in system software or buffer overflow attacks that allow for scripts or programs to be run with heightened access levels. The use of illicit servers, such as BackOrifice or NetBus, can allow for increased system access in Windows 9*x*. In Windows NT, there are similar types of illicit servers and methods to gain administrative access to the system with little effort.

 Cross-Reference   Many of these illicit servers and methods, such as NetBus or BackOrifice, are explained in Chapter 13. It is likely that many more will exist by the time you read this.

Illicit servers in software can allow an intruder to use a valid user account as a method of upgrading permissions to system resources or user accounts. Users often think that because their root or administrative accounts have strong passwords, there is little risk of heightened user access. However, if an intruder can obtain a legitimate user account, it is often much easier to use various buffer overflow or vulnerabilities to escalate the security of the regular user account than it is to get direct access to root or administrator. The following sections discuss the other intruder benefits of user accounts.

Creating additional accounts

Once an intruder gains root or administrative control of a system, he or she is reluctant to lose this control. Thus, the best way to maintain control is to create many different accounts. The intruder will try to spread the creation out a bit and obscure the account names in an effort to make everything look normal on the surface.

Other than leading administrators on a wild goose chase, additional accounts give intruders another backdoor into the system in case they are detected. Often, in larger or poorly run networks, there is so much infiltration that the IT departments or security administrators have no idea which accounts are legitimate and which are planted by intruders to the network.

Tip   The first task of any security administrator should be setting up account access and creating logging. This implementation is quick and easy in Windows NT, and as long as the event logs are monitored, and User Manager watched with some regularity, the task of catching fake accounts will involve much less guesswork.

One remaining fake account is all an intruder needs to regain access and spread himself out again. Detection on a return visit is unlikely until the user lists become fragmented again and someone attempts to weed out the unnecessary accounts, assuming the organization hasn't implemented a tripwire or decided to start watching the audit logs by this point in time.

One way both intruders and administrators can make several accounts at the same time is to use a batch file. Many people think that using the User Manager for Domains is the only way to create users in Windows NT; however, you can perform almost any administrative task through a command prompt window. By using a batch file, an intruder can enter several predefined accounts, including what group or groups they belong to and what administrative rights they have, and execute them on a system over which the intruder has gained control. A typical add user command looks like this:

```
net user fakeuser fakepassword /add
net localgroup administrators fakeuser /add
```

When you execute these lines, you will create a user called `fakeuser`, with the password `fakepassword` and added the account to the Administrators group. Now, all an intruder has to do is take these two lines and enter them over and over again in a simple batch file with different username/password combinations. He or she will then have quick and easy propagation of ready-to-use accounts on your system.

This batch file can be called whatever you want, as long as it ends with a `.bat` file extension (for example, `user.bat`). You should also be aware that the accounts created by the batch file can be created without a password at all. Simply not including the password after the username creates the account with no password. However, depending on how they audit their network, administrators may use a software package that identifies accounts without passwords, and an account with no password may be a dead giveaway if stringent password policies are in place.

If administrators enforce accounts with full details included in the user account, by inserting data of some type in the description information box, fake accounts may be routed out if administrators peruse User Manager for Domains and see half a dozen accounts with administrative access and no descriptions. All of this depends on how observant an administrator is when auditing the network. If you don't pay attention to small details, intruders will be able to sneak behind your back and take full control of your systems.

Tip   For the aforementioned technique to work, the user that is logged in must have administrative rights, or at least have the rights to write to the Registry (which holds the key that contains passwords). If this type of access is not available, you can still use the Scheduler service in Windows NT. Simply place the file in `\winnt\profiles\administrator\start    menu\programs\startup`. Once the administrator logs in, the batch file will be executed and the accounts added. However, the steps in the batch file will work only if the administrator account is actually in use. If the account has been renamed, try to figure out which account is active and place the file there.

Obtaining sensitive information

Some intruders break into systems for the challenge. Other intruders are looking for information once they have obtained root access to your systems. Once inside, these intruders will scan your system for useful information contained in documents, files, or databases. Common targets are typically human resources database files, accounts payable/receivable files, and systems that belong to people in power or management that may hold valuable company secrets. If an intruder has reached this point of control and access, he or she usually has only one goal in mind — exploiting the information found on the system.

Once the intruder has obtained control, their gathering of information will tend to be more methodical than the earlier fingerprinting technique, in which a "shotgun approach" was employed to find weaknesses. Once the intruder has control and is effectively inside the system or network he or she can target areas where sensitive information may be held. In many cases, users dump the files in the most obvious places, or in the default location for file storage, depending on the software. The only upside is that if intruders are looking for information, they will typically leave the network once they have the desired data. Intruders with malicious intentions may trash or damage the system in some way before leaving, but this is not typical of information seekers.

 In the Real World   Although some information gathering may appear to be a discovery activity, the information gathering will be more deliberate and directed than a typical discovery activity that is after a more broad range of information. Thus, the information gathering steps are usually included as part of the penetration process. The information an intruder can gather during the information gathering stage will give insight into what the system is and what kind of other information the intruder will find. Plus, the intruder may glean how the system operates and what type of additional security they may encounter.

Hackers can obtain information in a variety of ways, including by using a Web browser. Every operating system shipped in the last five years has been accompanied by some type of Web browser, and most networks have Internet Web browsing enabled. Many IT departments don't consider HTTP traffic dangerous to the average user and usually allow full access to HTTP services.

The truth is a Web browser can open up real security issues. One such issue is the cross-frame browsing bug, a problem found in both Netscape and Microsoft Web browsers. Web browsers are also vulnerable to particularly nasty buffer overflow attacks that allow an intruder to launch a DoS attack against systems with Web browsers open. If the intruder is successful in crippling the system with a buffer overflow, he or she can then execute scripts that allow penetration and control of the victim's system.

The cross-frame browsing bug can enable a malicious Web site operator (or anyone who may administer or work for the Web site) to create a rogue Web site to scavenge information from the victim's system. This exploit exists on both the 4.*x* and 5.*x* versions of Netscape and Microsoft Internet Explorer Web browsers. The one catch is that intruders must know where the files are located. By using known locations and save points, an intruder can often get useful information.

In the Real World   The cross-frame's limitation of having to know where the files are located may seem like a big hurdle to overcome, but keep in mind that most users leave files in the location suggested. For example, most intruders would know that the default path for critical UNIX/Linux files is in the `/etc` directory, for sensitive Windows NT files is in `\winnt\`, and for IIS files is in `\inetpub\wwwroot`.

Many users of Microsoft Office will use the My Documents folder to store their documents and many other sensitive files, which is always stored in the same place in Windows 9*x* (`\windows\desktop\my documents`). In Windows 98, the directory is usually found in the root (`\my documents`), whereas Windows 2000 usually stores this directory in the user's profile, so gaining access to this folder can be difficult unless you know the user account.

The My Documents folder may contain any variety of documents, spreadsheets, and databases ripe for the picking, it may even hold resumes, financial records, and incriminating photographs. Even if the intruder hasn't spent much time casing the system, or the user, the intruder will know where system files and applications are based on the operating system installed.

As they do with the Windows NT scheduler service, intruders may find the `\Windows\Start Menu\Programs\Startup` folder handy to execute illicit servers or batch files that will either root out more information or provide a quick and easy backdoor into the system. If the user has been complaining of weird activity or something not running properly when their computer starts up in the morning, take a look through their startup folders to make sure they don't contain anything that shouldn't be there.

Tip   To provide backward compatibility, Windows 9*x* and NT still use the two system files, `system.ini` and `win.ini`. Either of these files can be used to execute programs or batch files, as with the Startup folder. If you aren't having any luck identifying where an illicit server or batch file is executing from, take a look in these files.

Although using such a Web browser manipulation does not give an intruder real control of the system, it does facilitate further steps in the infiltration and eventual control of the target system. The data that can be had from a cross-frame browsing bug attack can be much more detailed than what is found during network fingerprinting or initial system penetration.

If the system is on a network, reading files obtained from the appropriate directories can provide a wealth of information about the network or servers. The only recourse for a security administrator or IT department at that point is to drastically reconfigure the server architecture or network design, and that can be done only if they know what information was nabbed in the first place.

Caution   In the current enterprise environment, most mission-critical servers are UNIX-based and not necessarily vulnerable to the aforementioned file-grabbing techniques. However, remember that most workstations on those enterprise networks are Windows-based, and, once infiltrated, can be used to further weaken other network systems at an intruder's leisure.

Auditing file system changes

Many utilities on the market — such as a good anti-virus scanner — can help audit or monitor the file system on your servers quickly and easily. However, nothing beats monitoring the directories yourself, especially if you are trying to get your head around the security ins and outs of your systems.

UNIX file systems

A large selection of root kits can be found on the Internet. Type `root kit` into any search engine and a wide array of these useful hacking tools will pop up. Root kits are very difficult to find and remove once they have been installed properly. In its most basic form, a root kit is several Trojan horse programs that are disguised as one valid useful utility.

Root kits will typically replace the original `ls`, `su`, and `ps` utilities with altered versions that can perform a wide variety of nefarious tasks, such as discovering system settings, digging out passwords, or altering security settings.

The best rule when auditing root kits in UNIX/Linux is to check that the files typically tampered with (`ls`, `su`, `ps`) all work the way they should. Usually, when a root kit replaces one of the files, the program will act strangely, perhaps by appearing to execute twice or by having unusual characters appear on the screen, or the file checksum (the size of the file or the date) will be different than the original file. Not everyone is going to take notice, but it is worthwhile knowing what to look for in these types of files. Trying to remember or list out what files are what sizes and the dates they held may seem tedious, but retaining that knowledge will make it easier to track down odd behavioral patterns in your critical system files.

The most useful files to monitor under UNIX/Linux are the following:

✦ **/:** The root directory. (Often, files are dumped here out of laziness.)

✦ **/sbin:** Administrative commands are found here.

✦ **/bin:** User commands are found here (usually a shortcut to /usr/bin).

✦ **/usr:** The majority of the operating system is kept here.

✦ **/user/bin:** The majority of the system-related commands are kept here.

✦ **/usr/local:** This is where software packages that have been installed locally are stored.

✦ **/usr/include:** This is where the include files (used for software development) are held.

✦ **/usr/src:** This is the location for the operating system installation source code.

✦ **/usr/local/src:** This is the location for the source code for locally installed programs.

✦ **/usr/sbin:** Administrative commands are found here.

✦ **/var:** This is a general data directory that usually holds log files and spooler files.

✦ **/var/log:** This is the directory where Log files are typically found.

✦ **/export:** This directory will help detail file systems that will be shared.

✦ **/home:** This is where the system's user home directories are found.

✦ **/opt:** This directory contains any optional software that may have been included with the OS.

✦ **/tmp:** Typically this directory will often be used for OS or installed software temporary files.

✦ **/proc:** This directory is utilized as a folder for the OS to access kernel variables.

Auditing NT systems

Root kits in Windows NT are typically Trojan horse illicit servers, such as BackOrifice 2000, SubSeven, or NetBus. Such utilities can be quite dangerous if an intruder gains access to your system with these programs. Additionally, because of the proliferation of viruses these days, many of these programs can be packaged with legitimate operating system components and easily take root in your file system.

The most critical areas of the Windows NT file system are as follows:

✦ **\winnt:** Where system files are stored (contains Regedit and Registry logs).

✦ **\winnt\system32:** Contains the vast majority of the NT OS and Event Logs.

✦ **\winnt\profiles:** Holds user info and settings for all users (even Admin).

✦ **winnt\system32\config:** Holds valuable SAM and SAM.log files.

✦ **winnt\inetpub:** The default installation point for IIS 4.0 settings and files.

✦ **Program Files:** Standard installation directory for almost any program.

L0phtCrack

L0phtCrack is the most recognized security auditing utility available today. Not only has L0phtCrack earned its reputation as an effective tool for auditing passwords on your systems and servers, it has proven to be just as useful to intruders.

L0phtCrack is a very efficient program that can perform dictionary and brute force attacks against NT's SAM file. L0phtCrack has become faster and faster with each new version. It's almost a guarantee that if you wait long enough, L0phtCrack will break every password in the SAM, no matter how good.

L0phtCrack can use a dictionary-style attack that will try various passwords from a predefined word list. You can use the included list or you can customize one with your own words. Once L0phtCrack has achieved what it can from a dictionary attack, it can switch gears and employ a brute-force attack to try to crack the tougher passwords. Although brute-force attacks can take much longer, the combination of the two attacks (dictionary and brute-force) allows L0phtCrack to obtain passwords much faster than similar products on the market. L0phtCrack can be used in a couple of different ways. The first way is to enter the IP address of the system you want to crack. Because L0phtCrack is trying to gain access to sensitive information, the system running L0phtCrack has to be logged in on the target systems first.

Tip   When attempting brute-force password attacks, always remember to choose the appropriate character set. The default set only checks regular characters and numbers, whereas other character sets include special characters such as @, !, #, %, and *. Keep in mind that selecting the sets with special characters causes the brute-force attacks to take longer, but they will generate better results.

The second way L0phtCrack can be used is by running it against a copy of the SAM file from the target system. There are two ways to obtain the password hashes locally on the system:

✦ Obtain a copy of the SAM file by copying it from `\Winnt\Repair`. You can also copy it from a repair disk if one is handy.

✦ Perform a Registry dump. By performing a Registry dump, you can obtain essentially the same information as what is in the SAM file, but obtaining the passwords is much quicker than exporting the SAM file and tends to get the most current password hashes.

L0phtCrack can also be used to glean passwords from a computer on the same segment as the target system. L0phtCrack essentially becomes a network password sniffer. In this mode, L0phtCrack watches traffic on the network segment for passwords as they zip by. Once you have captured a few password hashes, they can be employed by L0phtCrack in the same way that you would have attacked the SAM or Registry dump. To use this handy tool, you have to use Windows NT (not Windows 9*x*), and you must be "between" the two systems that are passing the passwords back and forth.

In the Real World
L0phtCrack can take up to 30 days to crack well-designed passwords. Password complexity dictates the amount of time needed to break a password. However, with faster and faster systems on the market, the amount of time needed drops exponentially with every processor upgrade.

UNIX Password File Issues

In UNIX/Linux operating systems, the password file is found in the `/etc/passwd` directory, which holds all of the openly readable account information on the system. All unencrypted password data is held in this directory. Although this may seem like a major vulnerability, the unencrypted password data is required to be there for certain system and software processes. These processes need to be able to take UID numbers from the password lists and convert them to user names, and vice versa. These files will also tell the system which directory is the users' home directory.

The architecture of the `/etc/passwd` file is a text file with fields that are separated by colons. Every line in the file contains the same information on every user and follows this syntax:

```
Username:x:UID:GID:Full Name:Home Directory:Shell
```

The following record is an example of an actual account:

```
sporter:x:100:100:Shawn Porter:/home/sporter:/bin/bash
```

The breakdown of the first line is as follows:

✦ **Username:** sporter

✦ **UID:** 100

✦ **GID:** 100

✦ **Full Name:** Shawn Porter

✦ **Home Directory:** /home/sporter

✦ **Shell:** /bin/bash

Tip

Sometimes, the full name field can be called the GECOS field (although not very often anymore). GECOS is an outdated OS that is no longer in widespread use.

When you apply rights to the password file, it must be kept publicly readable; however, you must make sure that the file isn't writeable by anyone except the root administrative account. Also, the /etc directory should be kept as writeable only for the root administrative account, not for general users on the system.

Shadow password files

Older implementations of UNIX, such as SunOS, had a slightly different design in their /etc/passwd file structure. The passwd file included encrypted versions of the users' login passwords, as well as unencrypted versions of the accounts. Originally, the encrypted password was kept in the spot marked with the x in the above account line, between the username and the UID markers. As the passwords were encrypted, it was impossible to figure out the user's password simply by reading the passwd file.

As with Windows NT, this password hash could be used in a dictionary attack, in which the software takes known words from a dictionary and encrypts them. The cracker would try the new passwords and compare them to the hash from the passwd file; if one matched, that password was broken. Because users traditionally practice poor password selection, a simple dictionary-style attack will usually yield good results.

Realizing the inherent weakness in this type of password security, UNIX-based operating systems adopted the *shadow passwords* method. The encrypted passwords were moved from the /etc/passwd file to a new file called /etc/shadow (sometimes, different variants of UNIX/Linux use a different term). This file is now protected, so it can be read only by the root account and, because the file is not readable by any other user on the system, the passwords are tucked away from the general public and cannot fall victim to a potentially compromising dictionary attack.

As you can see from the following list, the name of the shadow password file will be different on an OS-by-OS basis:

✦ **Linux, Solaris:** /etc/shadow

✦ **AIX:** /etc/security/passwd

✦ **HP UNIX (Version 9):** /.secure/etc/passwd

✦ **HP UNIX (Version 10):** This version of HP UNIX uses another different approach, protected password database files.

Not only does it contain encrypted password information, the shadow password file can house any password aging or expiry settings that may be applied to the users passwords on the systems. Password aging or expiries can force users to change their passwords after a set period of time or after a special set of conditions happens.

By executing the `passwd` command under UNIX/Linux, the root account can insert encrypted passwords into the `/etc/shadow` file (or similar variant). The root administrative account can run `passwd` with a username argument to set the password for any user on the system, regardless of whether or not the administrator is logged in with that user account. If you execute `passwd` without a username argument, the system will prompt you to input one. Here is an example of the way this simple utility can be used:

✦ `/etc/ passwd sporter`

✦ Password: (The password will be hidden)

✦ Re-type: (The confirmation password will be hidden as well)

Once this utility has been executed and the passwords entered matched, the user will have a new password.

Tip   As it is being typed in, the password will usually show up blank, not as asterisks (*). Therefore, make sure you type the password correctly the first time.

Crack and John the Ripper

Two of the most popular brute-force password attack programs available for UNIX-based operating systems are John the Ripper and Crack. Either program can extract passwords from UNIX password files. Either program is easy to find. Search for "John the Ripper" on any search engine and many links will show up for a variety of hacking or UNIX security Web sites.

In the Real World   Be careful what sites you download from. Although some sites may appear to be a good resource for security utilities, they could be rogue hacker sites waiting for you to download a utility with a Trojan horse planted inside. As always, practice common sense and use an up-to-date anti-virus scanner.

As previously discussed, the password files for UNIX are always kept in the same place (`/etc/passwd` or `/etc/shadow`) and reside in the same place on all UNIX systems. Some Linux systems will differ. These files must have read access for every user for UNIX to operate properly.

Similar to L0phtCrack's popularity for cracking passwords under NT, John the Ripper and Crack are the most popular brute-force applications for rooting passwords out of the `passwd` and `shadow` password lists under UNIX or Linux. Also like L0phtCrack, they try all combinations of passwords, encrypt them, and match them up against the password hashes in the `passwd` or `shadow` file until a match is made and the password is broken.

Although there are many ways to audit passwords on UNIX systems, a software package such as John the Ripper or Crack is useful to determine how strong the passwords are on your site. Although many of the new commercial or free system security scanners will attempt to simulate brute-force password attacks, they rarely work as well as a dedicated scanner like John the Ripper or Crack.

In the Real World

You will find that professional security auditors do not rely on basic cracking utilities, but instead turn to well-used, time-proven solutions, such as L0phtCrack, John the Ripper, and Crack, to provide the best password auditing results.

Windows NT Registry password cracks

Several Windows NT Registry vulnerabilities are known to date. The first is the auto login at boot Registry key. Auto login allows a server operator to set a login account and password to automatically log in when the system is booted up. Often, these accounts are an administrative account or an account with elevated privileges. Although a simple utility like auto login can provide quicker and easier access for the legitimate system administrator, it also provides a dangerous hole that can be exploited. The problem with auto login is that it stores the login and password in an unencrypted Registry key (HKLM\SOFTWARE\Microsoft\Windows NT\CurrentVersion\Winlogin\DefaultDomainName, DefaultUserName, as well as DefaultPassword). If someone were to gain access to the information in the Registry, they could obtain administrative access to your system. To get around this problem, simply delete the DefaultPassword information stored here. You can also delete the AutoLogin key or set the value associated to it to 0.

Caution

The handy, but dangerous, auto login utility is available as part of the *Windows NT Server 4 Resource Kit*. By installing all the applications in the *Resource Kit*, you could facilitate a possible security problem. Make sure that the file autolog.exe is not present on your system. Remove the key if it is present or executed to help prevent this issue from becoming a problem.

The second Registry-related issue is that the scheduler key in the Registry has incorrect permissions. The scheduler key allows read and write privileges to users in the server admin group. When NT Scheduler runs, it does so with system user control. If a rogue server administrator or hacker with control of that type of account wants, they can enter a batch file that would allow them to escalate privileges from server administrator to full administrator. The best way to fix this problem is to run the Registry editor and change the privileges for server administrators for this key (HKEY Local Machine\System\CurrentControlSet\Services\Schedule) from read/write to read only.

Several other keys are known to have poor rights assigned to them in the NT Registry, including the RAS (Remote Access Server) administration key, the MTS (Microsoft Transaction Server), and SNMP (Simple Network Management Protocol).

These keys can present a problem because they are used for management of important resources; two of these resources are for remote access to the server. With escalated privileges, an intruder could facilitate a full-scale assault on your servers. Microsoft has released a patch for these issues; however, it is likely that these patches have not yet been downloaded or installed on many systems.

Establish spurious services

Once an intruder has gained control of a system, he or she may first try to establish redirection of ports or software applications. The act of port or software redirection is sometimes called creating spurious services, or illegitimate services, because it creates a false port that looks and acts like the legitimate one.

For instance, an intruder could take down the legitimate FTP server on the system and establish a port redirect for an entirely different system's FTP server, presumably one they have control of or own. As users attempt to use the service, the intruder can start to obtain connection information and files from people that may be uploading to the system, assuming it's the original, legitimate server.

Many similar possibilities exist with port and application redirecting. Take, for instance, the SMTP port. If redirected, this port could provide substantial sensitive information. Web-based commerce sites, such as eBay, sometimes use an SMTP system to relay information from their front-end commerce servers back to the shipping department's customer lists. An intruder could intercept this information, which might include customers' credit card numbers. Even if the data were encrypted, the intruder could still break into the information, given today's strong encryption cracking techniques.

Create backdoors or alternate control methods

As previously discussed, intruders will often open up numerous front doors to regain access to a system later on, often by creating more login accounts. Intruders can also try to establish backdoors into a system. These backdoors are often installed as a contingency plan in the event the intruder's front doors are discovered and removed. Like system administrators, intruders will always want a contingency plan in case regular access is lost.

As a security administrator or auditor, you must always be watching for any possible alternative methods of control that an intruder may have planted for their contingency plans.

 Tip The methods for monitoring backdoor programs include topics discussed in previous chapters, including anti-virus scanners, batch file/script auditing, professional security scanning software, and regular review of system auditing log files.

Automating account creation

A recommended step with security auditing is to monitor user accounts and watch for accounts with modified permissions, any new accounts, and altered system policies. Keep in mind, however, that taking these steps will not remove the risk that older or original system accounts can and will get compromised by intruders.

Even if unauthorized new accounts are quickly taken care of by the administrator, skillful intruders can still work around this minor inconvenience by automating the new account creation process. As discussed earlier in this chapter, intruders can use batch files to automate the creation of accounts on a system. By using the system's scheduling service, an intruder can have the accounts automatically re-created on a set schedule. Because most system administrators aren't always watching the server, an intruder could easily evade the administrator until the next scan of users. It could take some time before the administrator found out why the accounts were being constantly re-created or modified.

 In the Real World If you set up your operating system to audit successful or failed creation of users or modification of rights, you stand a better chance of quickly spotting the rogue accounts. It may also lead you to the account where the user creation is occurring.

Hackers can also use backdoor programs, such as NetBus or BackOrifice 2000, to bypass the authentication process entirely. These programs operate with system permissions without any regard for who is logged or what permissions they have. These types of programs are covered in more depth later in this chapter.

Covering the tracks of penetration

At this point, you have likely implemented auditing on your systems or servers. If you enable the appropriate auditing, you should have solid logs of an intruder's activities on your systems. These types of logs are quite handy because an intruder must usually make repeated attempts to enter a system. Any hacker that doesn't want to be seen, or needs to cover their activity, will hunt down these logs and attempt to destroy the evidence related to their nefarious activities. If an intruder can successfully manage to remove the evidence from the audit logs, it will be very difficult for security administrators or auditors to figure out what an intruder did or where they came from.

Important log files to monitor include the following:

✦ Web servers

✦ Firewalls

✦ SMTP (e-mail) servers

✦ FTP servers

✦ Database servers (Oracle, SQL)

✦ Operating systems

Typically, these systems will have two or three types of log files, such as:

✦ **Event logs:** Can contain user access/creation and object access information

✦ **Application logs:** Can contain application usage and error information

✦ **Security logs:** Can contain access failures and other security-related information

Tip

The logs just listed don't include any logs that may be kept by the ISP (Internet service provider) or on any network routers. Intruders may find that eradicating all information related to their activities on your systems is difficult. If they succeed in removing these key logs, it will be much harder to track down the intruder. Without these logs it will also be much harder to determine what the intruders may have manipulated during their intrusion of your network.

Attack other systems

The goal of an intruder when breaking into your network may not always be to glean information from your systems. Sometimes, an intruder may want to access systems or other networks to which you have trusted access. A good example is the NASA network. NASA is a constant target of attack, not just for the information it possesses, but for the trusted connection NASA has to other government networks, such as the Department of Defense. Sometimes attacking other systems may simply be a way of spoofing where the actual hacking is coming from by using other compromised systems to attack the real target. If an intruder gets routed into enough networks, he can cause a lot of trouble for any security auditor trying to locate the intruder's origin.

Because diversionary attacks and attacks from compromised systems happen with fair amount of regularity, the government requires that any company or organization connected directly to a government network implement security standards that the government has laid out. A series of books called the *Rainbow Series*, which was first implemented in the 1970s, helps the government determine the guidelines that organizations and companies must follow in order to securely connect to their networks.

Tip

The *Rainbow Series* books take their name from their different colored covers. These books specify security and other types of guidelines for the U.S. government to follow when implementing standards.

The most commonly referred to book in the *Rainbow Series* is the Orange book, entitled the *Department of Defense Trusted Computer Systems Evaluation Criteria*. The C2 Standard, which you may have heard about before, is one of the standards implemented in the Orange book to indicate a certain level of trust and security ability in networks and operating systems that connect to government networks. The C2 Standard is the integrity level that forms the basis of the C2 Manager Service that is an option in the Microsoft NT Service Pack and *Windows NT Server 4 Resource Kit*.

The file included in the Service Pack or the *Windows NT Server 4 Resource Kit* is called `c2config.exe`, and if the various options inside are implemented, an administrator can make the appropriate security changes to Windows NT to bring it up to C2 compliance. Due to its age, the original series of books is currently being updated. The book entitled *Federal Criteria for Information Technology Security* takes the standards set out in the *Rainbow Series* one step further.

In the Real World   In spite of all its security features, Windows NT scores very low on the government's standards list. Out of the box, NT requires the C2 configuration to be performed to even bring it up to a slightly better level. One of the only ways to get an A class configuration is to disconnect the system from the network entirely.

Port misdirection

Like IP spoofing, port misdirection is a technique that intruders will use to cover their activities while they work on your network. Intruders will often employ multiple Telnet, FTP, or Web sessions to create a series of connections that each take time to trace to their source.

If used properly, port redirection can be just as effective as IP spoofing because it can take longer to figure out exactly where the port has been misdirected. Once the legitimate port is located, a trace would have to be performed back to the host, assuming that the potential legitimate host is not actually another system that was misdirected by the intruder, and so on and so on.

Methods of Control

Objective   Learn methods of control

Due to system and software updates and the large-scale changes involved in many of these updates, new security issues will undoubtedly be generated. These new security issues are ripe for exploitation by intruders of all types, and both the hacking and security communities are constantly working to discover new vulnerabilities. Once these issues are found, the security community usually informs the software manufacturer to allow them to issue a patch before knowledge of the exploit is made public.

The hacking community will sometimes keep the exploit low key, allowing a smaller group of people to use the exploit until the problem is discovered. After that, many casual intruders will try to use the exploit with the assumption that administrators haven't patched their systems yet. This section discusses the various methods of control and how intruders use them.

Exploit weak configurations and defaults

Default configurations for most operating systems, software, and hardware may as well have a big sign on them saying, "Hack Me!" The standard implementation for most software is usually geared for ease of product support and/or ease of use. Often these settings will not be altered due to inexperience or lack of knowledge. For intruders, systems with default configurations will typically be the holy grail of system hacking because exploiting systems and networks is that much easier when everything is set to the default configuration.

Even though altering the system from its defaults is a fairly easy process, many administrators don't bother to — or simply don't know how. Unfortunately, this is the case in many of today's time-strapped IT departments. With very little time to dedicate to everyday tasks, tackling proper security, no matter how minimal, can be daunting.

 Even performing quick and easy tasks, such as hiding the administrator account, enabling auditing of logins and object management, applying the latest service pack and security updates, and disabling unneeded services, can improve security dramatically. Furthermore, performing these changes on most NT systems can take less than half an hour.

Attack weak services, daemons, or executables

Security can be a double-edged sword and so can the way different operating systems handle system services. Windows NT uses services and UNIX/Linux makes use of daemons, and unfortunately, these services and daemons can be used against the operating systems they are supposed to be helping operate.

As discussed earlier in this chapter, the Windows NT Scheduler service can be used by intruders to run programs and scripts with full system access. Hackers can use these services to gain access to other areas of the system and to run other useful services that will help the intruders cause even more damage. Disabling services that are not required, or at least applying the appropriate security to them, will help lessen the chance of an intruder using system services to maintain or establish control.

Add illicit services, daemons, or executables

Once intruders have gained control, they often set up camp and plan to stay in control of their new conquest. Hackers may do this by creating and inserting daemons and programs that can impede security.

There are different types of such programs. Some can log passwords and then e-mail them quietly out to a waiting hacker. Some packages, such as root kits, bypass the established security and provide full access to the system. For

Windows-based operating systems, two similar utilities — NetBus and BackOrifice — can provide the aforementioned services and more. Although NetBus and BackOrifice are not new to the hacking scene, they still provide a good look into the how's and why's of system control.

All about NetBus

If you have been involved in any way with computers over the past five years, chances are good that you have heard of or seen NetBus. If not, take it upon your-self to explore this interesting piece of control software. NetBus touts itself as a remote network management utility and was first introduced in March of 1996. NetBus is intended to control Windows 9x and NT operating systems and has become popular with a variety of intruders.

The first version of NetBus was 1.5, released in 1996. Versions 1.6 and 1.7 have since been released. NetBus can go around regular system security, and its main function is to let a remote user control many aspects of the system operation from another workstation. NetBus can enable another user to perform a wide variety of actions with the same rights as the user that is currently logged into the system. In Windows 9x, this means almost complete control of the operating system. Figure 19-1 shows NetBus and its simple user interface.

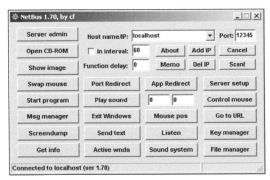

Figure 19-1: NetBus has a simple interface with many buttons for quick and easy use.

The newest version of NetBus, 2.10 Pro, isn't as widespread as the older versions of NetBus. This is due to more diligent protection against Trojan horses by anti-virus scanning software today, as compared to the late 1990s when older versions of NetBus were more prevalent. Version 2.10 Pro has more features than previous ver-sions, including a more detailed logging system, but requires more configuration to operate than the older versions. It also takes up more space, but it keeps much more detailed logs.

In an effort to make their remote management utility a bit more legitimate, and used by administrators for its original purpose, UltraAccess Networks, Inc., the authors of NetBus, decided to turn NetBus into a shareware product. Recently, certain anti-virus firms like Symantec removed NetBus 2.10 Pro from their anti-virus definition. You will likely come across the older versions of NetBus rather than version 2.10 Pro.

All versions of NetBus enable you to set a password to protect the remote server from unwanted entry. If your system is subverted with NetBus, or you have intentionally installed it for remote management, you or an intruder can perform the following actions:

✦ Launch applications

✦ Force a shutdown and/or restart of the system

✦ Log out the logged-in user

✦ Control the default Web browser, including launching any URL

✦ Send keystrokes to an open application

✦ Capture keystrokes (Not all can be captures when under NT.)

✦ Redirect ports and applications

✦ Provide information on the current session, such as username, system name, and the number of clients connected to the system at that point in time

✦ Upload, download, and delete files

✦ Remotely control the server, as well as upload updates

✦ Alter password protection for NetBus

✦ Show, kill, and focus active windows that are open on the system

By default, NetBus communicates by port 12345 via TCP. A popular choice for the listening port is 12631, although the server can be configured to listen on any port you choose. If an intruder has installed the software on its default port, it will be fairly easy to find and catch. However, if the intruder has changed any of the default settings, locating the intruder's server can be quite difficult.

Tip   NetBus does not encrypt data sent back and forth from the server to the client, so if you are using the program for remote management, keep this security risk in mind. The one upside to NetBus not encrypting transferred data is that if you are using a port scanner with packet capture turned on, you may be lucky enough to locate the server.

The following list provides detailed information about the default names and sizes for the various components of NetBus to help identify the version and, more importantly, what NetBus looks like.

For Version 1.5 and 1.6:

- ✦ **NetBus.exe (the client):** 567,296K
- ✦ **Patch.exe (the server):** 472.576K
- ✦ **Keyhook.dll (server .dll):** 54,784K

For Version 1.7:

- ✦ **NetBus.exe (the client):** 599,552K
- ✦ **Patch.exe (the server):** 494,592K
- ✦ **Keyhook.dll (server .dll):** 54,784K

Version 2.10 Pro uses more files, which can make this version of NetBus easier to locate and remove. The following files are the counterparts to those in older versions:

- ✦ **NetBus.exe (the client):** 1,241,600K
- ✦ **NBSvr.exe (the server):** 624,640K
- ✦ **NBHelp.dll (app. .dll):** 71,680K

The larger-size version of 2.10 Pro is a dead giveaway for the version that's installed, and the extra files (not listed) make version 2.10 much less stealthy and less popular with intruders. Also worth mentioning is the fact that any of these program files can be renamed to something completely different, and there are several utilities to repackage NetBus into different forms.

Tip   As previously mentioned, any up-to-date anti-virus package should locate and remove any instance of NetBus it finds; however, remember the recently lifted scanning for NetBus 2.10 Pro by a few of the larger anti-virus firms.

NetBus will use Registry entries to ensure that the server loads into memory each time the system starts, enabling intruders to connect when the system is online.

- ✦ Any version 1.x installation of NetBus will have the following Registry entry (the executable listed at the end can vary but will likely be patch.exe in most cases):
  `HKEY_LOCAL_MACHINE\SOFTWARE\Microsoft\Windows\CurrentVersion\Run\patch.exe`

- ✦ If the intruder or administrator has implemented a password on the NetBus server, it will be located here:
  `HKEY_CURRENT_USER\Patch\Settings\ServerPwd`

- ✦ Under certain versions of NetBus, mainly in version 1.7, but occasionally in some version 2.10 Pro installations, as well, the following Registry entry will exist to aid in the software's operation:
  `HKEY_LOCAL_MACHINE\SOFTWARE\Microsoft\Windows\CurrentVersion\RunServices`

Detection and removal of NetBus

In addition to anti-virus scanning, there are a few ways to locate and detect NetBus. One good way is to use a packet sniffer software package, such as Sniffer Pro, TCP-DUMP, or NetXRay to search for the default ports of 12345 and 12346 for good measure. Regardless of whether or not your network is using network intrusion detection software, it isn't a bad idea to do a sweep of the system from time to time to ensure that the system is clean.

If you happen to be scanning through directories or Windows Explorer while in Windows, you can keep a watch for NetBus servers by knowing what the icons look like.

✦ Version 1.6 of NetBus looks like a flaming Olympic torch.

✦ Version 1.7 looks like a satellite dish with a white background.

✦ Version 2.10 Pro looks like a satellite dish facing the other way; the background of the icon is black.

Knowing what appearances and tendencies to look for when trying to locate NetBus can yield some lucky finds, and informing users on the network what the icons look like can limit the amount of mistaken clicks on the file attachment, reducing the risk of infecting their system.

NetBus icons, file names, and active ports can be disguised in many ways. Two such disguise programs are SaranWrap and SilkRope, both of which can be used to make the software appear to be any number of different types of programs or software packages. This can work to an intruder's advantage, because intruders can easily trick users into installing the server, as the user will think the program is a legitimate software package.

 In the Real World SilkRope and SaranWrap are easily available on the Internet at a wide variety of sites. These types of programs can sometimes foil anti-virus packages, depending on how the software scans for viruses. If the anti-virus packages don't perform file-content scans looking for specific data patterns in files, then it could be possible to get NetBus by the scanner.

Removing NetBus from your system isn't always as easy as locating the server application and deleting it. Quite often, if the server application is running, Windows will not allow you to simply delete the file. It will become necessary at this point to enter the Windows Task Manager and end the running process (usually called `patch.exe`). After this, you can usually remove any instances of the file from the system.

If the server isn't password-protected, you can attempt to connect with the same version of client software and click the Remove Server button to remove the software from the server. Either way, you should reboot the system and perform additional scans to ensure that the server was, in fact, removed from the system.

Other methods of removing the server usually require more effort. Usually, the best way is to end the process and delete any files and Registry entries associated with the installation.

 Caution   Many so-called NetBus cleaning or removal utilities are available for download. Make sure, however, that these utilities are coming from a trusted source, because all they may do is infect your system with NetBus instead of actually removing it.

NetBus components

A few key NetBus components include the following:

✦ **The listener utility** can be used as a keystroke logger when there is an active connection from the server to the client. It could also be used to capture login names and passwords.

✦ **The file manager utility** can enable you to insert and grab files from the remote server system and is as easy to use as a standard Windows Explorer window. To use the file manager, first hit the Scan button to scan the hard drive for its directory and file structure, then use the download, upload, and delete buttons to make use of this utility.

✦ **The start program button** simulates clicking the Start button and clicking on Run. From here, an intruder could easily execute any batch file or application on the system.

✦ **The server setup button** does exactly what it sounds like. From here, you can alter the following software settings:

• The port the server runs on

• What password you want on the server (if any)

• Whether you want activity logging

• Whether you want the server to send an SMTP notification when the server has connected with a client

Many of these options should be considered mandatory if the server is actually being used for remote administration.

✦ **The port redirect button** allows port redirection for any output destined for one port to be directed to another port entirely.

✦ **The app redirect button** allows the intruder to redirect output from a software application to a specified port. Similar to the port redirect button, the app redirect button allows an intruder to use Telnet to connect to the port and then redirect the output to a TCP port. Once established, the intruder could access the command prompt on the system as if he or she were sitting at the computer by redirecting command.com to a TCP port.

The only requirement to execute any of these illicit servers or activities is that the user must be logged into the system. There is no need for any action by a user on the server software's system for the client software to perform these actions.

All about BackOrifice and BackOrifice 2000

BackOrifice is similar to NetBus in that it allows an intruder to gain control over an infected system. BackOrifice works only with Windows 9x systems, whereas the BackOrifice 2000 release functions on Windows NT systems (which, until this release, had been largely unaffected by anything other than NetBus). A pair of these illicit servers were brought to the Internet by a group called the Cult of the Dead Cow. Although NetBus and BackOrifice do not represent any direct threat to UNIX/Linux operating systems, they do show the dangers that Windows systems face. Like any other intrusion, if Windows clients are attached to a UNIX/Linux network, there is a chance that the intruder will use information gleaned in a BackOrifice or NetBus attack to gain access to the UNIX/Linux network. Anyone who connects to BackOrifice can gain information about the system and any open network connections that may exist. Like NetBus, BackOrifice can be used to gain unauthorized access to a wide variety of systems and networks and is readily available on the Internet.

Like NetBus, BackOrifice uses the same client/server application design, and the client can be operated from UNIX, Linux, Windows 9x, and Windows NT operating systems to connect to infected servers.

Also like NetBus, BackOrifice allows intruders to use a wide variety of functions, including:

✦ Obtain system information, including user, CPU type, Windows version, memory statistics, drive specs, and connected network information

✦ Gain user and password information, including the screen saver password and other passwords that may be saved for Web sites and other programs

✦ Full file and application control on the system, including application launching, Registry access, and network connection management

✦ Port and application redirection

✦ File uploading and downloading using HTTP through a Web browser

Caution   Keep in mind that users will use the same passwords for many resources, so even finding only one or two passwords when looking may allow an intruder to gain access to many more resources on the network or system.

By default, BackOrifice listens on UDP port 31337, but as with NetBus, the listening port can be altered so that BackOrifice listens on any port that isn't reserved by another application. BackOrifice 2000 can allow the transferred data to be encrypted and can also use any port on the system.

Usually, the BackOrifice client uses port 1049 to connect, but if the client is connected to the BackOrifice HTTP server, the client communicates through port 1056. An intruder could connect through the command line interface and change the port by using the -p command, which can make tracking down BackOrifice much harder.

Although many people prefer the cleaner interface of NetBus, BackOrifice offers the same basic components (with the exception of the additional network control options).

Keystroke logging

Keystroke logging is a useful utility for any hacker, because it can log any and all keystrokes input into the keyboard and save them to a simple text file that can be read easily. Keystroke loggers are installed in a similar fashion to illicit servers and can be installed by attachments to e-mails or other trickery. Finding keystroke loggers can be difficult, as they may not necessarily be found by scanning for viruses.

Auditing to Prevent Unwanted Control

 Audit unwanted control procedures and methods

A well-rounded security auditor will use a wide variety of scanning utilities, vulnerability scanners, and audit logs. You should know what suspicious traffic and activities look like. Traffic can originate from all over, including illegal NMAP and SATAN usage, illicit servers such as NetBus, or utilities that aren't widely known to the industry.

The main difference between auditor and hacker at this stage is that the auditor will rarely enter the control phase, whereas the intruder will try to do so more often than not. When auditing, remember to create detailed reports of your findings and the actions that should have been taken to circumvent the problems. Don't leave any real trace of your presence or illicit server utilities on the network, as doing so may cross the fine line between hacking and auditing.

There are many ways to report possible issues when control may be compromised. The most professional solutions allow you to prove your theories and provide detailed information to the client. The best approaches include the following:

✦ Providing presentations and reports from professional security scanning programs, such as NetRecon, Retina, IIS Scanner, or similar software packages.

✦ Generating network traffic that produces an example entry in the audit logs, then presenting this information as a possible r result of an attack or intrusion.

✦ Showing captured packets that contain details on IP addresses, port numbers, and other information.

✦ Taking as many screenshots as you can of areas that you have penetrated in your audit (if the audit requires test penetration).

Don't practice these control techniques on another person's system or on any network that you may be auditing. If you want to learn more about various control techniques, practice on your own network or systems.

Key Point Summary

This chapter discussed the various control phases that an intruder will go through to establish and maintain control of your systems and networks. Learning these methods will help you look for and limit the various methods that intruders use.

✦ Understanding how intruders gain control of your systems and networks is imperative if you want to provide a complete depiction of network security for your clients while performing an audit.

✦ Once intruders have taken root in your system, they will likely attempt to solidify control of the system to further infiltrate it.

✦ The initial steps an intruder will take when establishing control over your systems include gaining administrative/root access and gathering more information on the system and software that is installed.

✦ Hackers will also try to open new security breaches and backdoors to your system. Once they are done, they will try to cover their tracks.

✦ Gaining root access (UNIX/Linux) or administrator access (NT) is the Holy Grail of hacking. This type of break-in is often referred to as "front door entry," because you are gaining access to the system through "normal" means. Once root/administrative access has been obtained, there is no limit to how much control the intruder may have over your systems.

✦ There are many ways intruders can gain root access to a system, from root kits to buffer overflow attacks. In Windows 9*x,* the options are more limited. However, utilities such as NetBus and BackOrifice control can be even more convenient and quicker than trying to utilize root kits or complicated buffer overflow attacks.

✦ Once intruders have managed to gain administrative access, they will often attempt to generate more accounts that will allow them entry at a later time.

✦ Most people think that Web browsers can't cause any security issues. However, a host of vulnerabilities and potential control issues can arise from unpatched and insecure Web browsers.

✦ Auditing file system changes can often tip you off to an intruder's presence on your systems.

✦ Windows NT password vulnerabilities don't stop at the password SAM. A few password vulnerabilities exist in other areas of the operating system, such as the Registry (the place where the actual SAM file generates its passwords). Always make sure to cover the entire system when looking at password security.

✦ Hackers will generate backdoors into systems to help maintain control. Usually, if intruders have administrative access, they will first try to use the front door accounts, relying on backdoors as a secondary approach if the front doors are closed.

✦ To cover their tracks, intruders will have to clear up logs on a variety of different sources. The OS, FTP, Web, mail servers, and database programs, for example, can generate a log. If they are turned on, an intruder will go around and either alter the data inside or delete the files entirely to limit the possibilities of easily finding out what the intruders did.

✦ When intruders have gained control, they will usually try to attack other systems connected to the victim. They may even attack other systems that aren't directly in the same network as the victim's system.

✦ When connecting to a governmental site, the C2 configuration guides developed by the government must be followed to facilitate a secure connection.

✦ A hacker will attempt to exploit default and weak operating systems, hoping that the user will not have spent any time changing the defaults. Other than knowing what the default settings and passwords may be, the default configuration on most operating systems can be very weak.

✦ NetBus is a very handy tool that allows intruders to easily control a system remotely. NetBus has a wide variety of included options and utilities. Typically, older versions (up to 1.7) are quickly picked up by most current anti-virus scanners, although the new version 2.10 Pro is attempting to make a go as a legitimate network maintenance tool, and as such, may not be found out by your anti-virus software packages.

✦ NetBus can be disguised as any other program, using different freeware software utilities called SilkRope and SaranWrap. Either of these programs can be used to package up NetBus and disguise it in another software program, making it much harder to remove. Often, your only chance to catch a repackaged NetBus file can be to search for mysterious files with certain file size characteristics.

✦ BackOrifice and BackOrifice 2000 are software packages that are similar to NetBus in operation and abilities. BackOrifice does have some differences, like encrypted data and a few other skills that NetBus doesn't posses. BackOrifice also is picked up fairly easily by most anti-virus software.

✦ Keystroke loggers can be very dangerous Trojans if one gets planted on your system. These loggers can capture anything from text being entered into a file to login accounts and passwords.

✦ It is recommended that you practice control techniques, but only on your own system or test network. It would be unprofessional to perform these activities on clients' systems.

✦ Providing detailed professional reports (created manually or by a commercially available security scanning software), captured packet data, and lots of screenshots of your findings will help provide the best overall security audit for the site and its owners.

✦   ✦   ✦

STUDY GUIDE

This Study Guide presents ten assessment questions and four lab exercises to test your knowledge of the exam objectives.

Assessment Questions

1. When intruders try to gain control of a system, why is it important for them to open new security holes?

   A. They will use these holes to gain access at a later date.

   B. They will open these holes so their buddies can join in.

   C. They will open these holes to cause system resource leakage.

   D. It can help bypass anti-virus software scanners.

2. What is usually the first and primary goal of intruders when they intrude on your system?

   A. Finding pictures that could be used for extortion

   B. Locating connections to other networks

   C. Gaining root or administrative access

   D. Deleting critical system files

3. When auditing a UNIX/Linux file system, where is the bulk of the operating system usually kept?

   A. / (root directory)

   B. /usr

   C. /home

   D. /proc

4. When auditing a Windows NT file system, where does regedit.exe usually reside?

   A. \winnt\system32

   B. \winnt\system32\config

   C. \winnt\profiles

   D. \winnt

5. Which of the following is not a way L0phtCrack can obtain the password hashes?

    A. Reading passwords from the SAM file taken from a repair disk (rdisk)

    B. Scanning the Registry of the local or remote system (with permissions)

    C. Connecting to each workstation and requesting passwords from the user

    D. Acting as man-in-the-middle and catching passwords as they go between clients and servers

6. Windows NT systems use password-shadowing methods. True or False?

7. The Red book is the volume of the *Rainbow Series* that deals with system security standards in the U.S. Government. True or False?

8. NetBus is a single executable solution that requires only one file on the remote system. True or False?

9. Most versions of NetBus and BackOrifice can be detected with anti-virus scanners. True or False?

10. Keyloggers can capture most data that is entered through a keyboard, including passwords. True or False?

Lab Exercises

Lab 19-1 Using L0phtCrack to obtain passwords

1. Obtain the latest version of L0phtCrack and install it on a Windows NT PC. (Other Windows operating systems can be used.)

2. Create a test account with User Manager called "test" and give it the password "windows."

3. Open L0phtCrack, click the Tools menu, and select Dump Passwords from Registry. Type the name of the NT system you are on and click OK.

4. The accounts on your system should show up on the left side of the window, with the passwords in the middle and the hashes on the right. Click on the Tools menu and select Run Crack.

5. L0phtCrack should go to work and crack at least the test password within a few seconds. Other passwords may take longer, depending on how complex or strong they are.

6. Try passwords of varying strengths on your test accounts and experiment to see how long it takes for L0phtCrack to break them.

Lab 19-2 Using NetBus to execute applications on a system

1. Install NetBus client and server on your test system and execute `patch.exe`.

2. Run `server.exe` and you will see many different buttons in front of you. Each button has a nefarious task, but first you will want to ensure that in the address bar you see "localhost" or "127.0.0.1" and then click the Connect button. Once connected, you can try the various buttons to see what they do.

3. NetBus can be very powerful if installed on a victim's system. Not all the functions work for every operating system, but try the different options and see what they can do. Easy options to test are the "Go To URL" button, where you can remotely launch a Web site of your choosing, "Open/Close CD-ROM," and "Start Program."

4. Click the Start Program button and explore launching various applications, such as `calc.exe`, `notepad.exe`, `usrmgr.exe`, and so on. You can also try clicking the Active Wnds button and performing a refresh to see the active programs on the system.

5. Once you have tested the various buttons, if you are not going to use NetBus any longer, it is a good idea to remove it from your system. Click the Server Admin button and then select Remove Server to uninstall NetBus. For the purposes of this review, it is a good idea to leave NetBus installed until after Lab 19-4. However, you should remove the installation and delete the folder you installed NetBus to as well, due to the risk that someone may install it again to your system and create a new vulnerability.

This type of hacking can be fun when performed against friends or other users on your home network. Messing around with their systems can be a useful way to learn about the hacking process. However, you shouldn't perform this type of hacking on any client's systems without their prior authorization.

Lab 19-3 Using NetBus to capture keystrokes

1. Open NetBus and connect to the local system (127.0.0.1). Once inside, click the Listen button.

2. Perform a variety of activities on the system, such as creating new accounts with passwords, opening up a notepad file and entering some text, and so on. In other words, explore those activities that require text entry.

3. You will notice the text log fill up with data entered by your activities. You can then use this information to gain access to resources or possibly to capture sensitive information.

4. You can also disable the remote systems keyboard entirely. A reboot of your system will be required to re-enable the keyboard if you attempt these steps on your own system. When you are done, you can reinstate control over the keyboard the same way you disabled it.

Lab 19-4 Using NetBus to gain control of a system

1. Open NetBus and connect to the local system (127.0.0.1). Once inside, click the App Redirect button.

2. Enter the following line: `c:\winnt\system32\cmd.exe`.

3. In the I/O port dialog box, enter 4455 as the port to redirect to.

4. Click the Start button and open Telnet.

5. Connect to the local system on port 4455.

6. You should see the command prompt in your Telnet window. Sometimes, the command prompt won't show up right away, and you may have to repeat steps 4 and 5 a few times. From here you should be able to execute any command like you would normally from the command prompt.

7. Practice directing different applications to different ports and see how they operate.

Answers to Chapter Questions

Chapter Pre-Test

1. Intruders will maintain control by:
   - Gaining Root/Administrative access
   - Opening new security holes

2. The file that NT L0phtCrackers covet the most is the SAM file, which is derived from the SAM Registry key.

3. One way to check is to look for open ports 12345 and 12346. Another way is to use the old standby, an anti-virus scanner.

4. The main difference between BackOrifice and BackOrifice2000 is that BackOrifice works only on Windows 9x systems, while BackOrifice2000 works on both Windows 9x and Windows NT systems.

5. Keyloggers are used to log keystrokes, which might include logging passwords and other sensitive data that could be used to break into other secure areas on the system and network.

Assessment Questions

1. **A.** A hacker will use the new holes to gain access at a later date. Hackers will open new holes once they have intruded into your system to facilitate entry later on.

2. **C.** Gaining root or administrative access. Hackers will usually make a beeline for the administrative accounts. Although many nasty deeds can be done without administrative access, there are many obvious benefits to having it.

3. **B.** /usr. This is where UNIX stores most of its system files. Although some may be moved around, /usr is typically the default location.

4. **D.** \winnt. Regedit.exe is stored in this directory.

5. **C.** Connecting to each workstation and requesting passwords from the user (social engineering). L0phtCrack cannot perform this function, although the other methods of getting password hashes are quite useful.

6. **False.** Unfortunately, the SAM design does not facilitate password shadowing This is an option available only in UNIX/Linux-type operating systems.

7. **False.** The color of the book that covers system security standards in the U.S. government's *Rainbow Series* is called the Orange book.

8. **False.** Most versions of NetBus require three files to do the job: one server executable, one client executable, and a .dll file. Version 2.10 Pro actually requires several files and usually a couple of subdirectories.

9. **True.** While there are methods of disguising NetBus and BackOrifice from anti-virus software packages, most people will be affected by the standard installation.

10. **True.** Keyloggers are very dangerous utilities and can capture much sensitive information. Thankfully, keyloggers aren't widespread, although they are built into NetBus and BackOrifice.

For More Information

For more information on the topics in this chapter, check out these links:

✦ Matt's UNIX Security Site. Many of the utilities we discussed in this chapter can be found here, plus many more. `http://www.deter.com/unix/index.html`

✦ NMRC.com contains many files, bulletins, and information. This particular page contains many well-written FAQs on various operating system hacking methods. `http://www.nmrc.org/faqs/index.html`

✦ Packet Storm contains many great links, files, and information for any security auditor. `http://packetstorm.securify.com/`

✦ A great site to get information on and download John the Ripper password cracker for UNIX/Linux systems. `http://www.openwall.com/john/`

Auditing System and Security Logs

+ Understand the different types of logs and what they can contain

+ Understand the difference between default logging and auditing systems

+ Establish a baseline for log analysis

+ Know how to perform a log analysis, as well as identify critical security events

+ Be able to use log filtering to view specific event types

+ Be able to set up auditing on a machine, and configure it to audit specific types of events

CHAPTER PRE-TEST

1. What is a baseline? How do you create one?

2. What system is used for Linux logging? How do you control what is logged and where?

3. Where do you enable Windows NT auditing?

4. Where are the default logs kept for Linux?

5. What are the default Windows NT logs?

6. What are the two keys to building an auditing baseline?

7. What are the key information points from firewall and router logs?

8. What are the three Windows event logs and what do they contain?

9. How can you tell the difference between a clean and dirty shutdown in the Event Viewer?

10. What is the default location of system logs on UNIX? Windows NT?

✦ Answers to these questions can be found at the end of the chapter. ✦

*L*og analysis involves reviewing system logs to determine the occurrence of some event. Log analysis is performed for troubleshooting, performance monitoring, resource utilization and expansion planning, and security. This chapter focuses on logging and log analysis for security purposes.

Understanding Log Analysis

 Know how to perform a log analysis, as well as identify critical security events

Before you can start, you need to do two things. First, you need to determine what you are going to log, because you can't log everything. Second, you need to establish a *baseline* for the things you do log. A baseline is simply a measurement of network behavior during normal usage.

What to log

The first question most people ask is "What should I be auditing/logging?" The following is a minimal starting point of events to log:

- ✦ All successful and unsuccessful login and logout events
- ✦ All modifications to system-specific files (configuration files, system binaries, and libraries)
- ✦ All administrative actions (user adds, host changes, password changes, and so on)
- ✦ All system-type events (reboots, eeprom changes, and so on)
- ✦ Firewall, router, and other network traffic–related software and hardware activity logs

This set gives you a very good, though not complete, picture of your system at any given point in time. Logging these events will prove invaluable in auditing a system from a security standpoint.

Building a baseline

 Establish a baseline for log analysis

Before you can determine what is inappropriate activity, you must determine what is appropriate activity. This is accomplished by two main methods:

✦ **Understanding your company policy** — By understanding your company policy, you will know what is and is not acceptable behavior and what constitutes a potential security incident or event within your organization. For example, if you know that your company policy requires all route access to be done via the console, and you notice that there are successful Telnet logins to the router from an internal host, this would be a notable security event that may not be discernable from just looking at the logs.

✦ **Examining what current activity exists on your network and systems** — By examining logs and having an understanding of normal usage patterns for users and networks, you get a better handle on what should and should not be happening. For example, if there is normally a low amount of Internet traffic at 2:00 a.m. and then one day you see traffic at 50 percent capacity, a security issue is likely related to the increase. Start with an overview and then get more specific.

It is important to understand that most of this analysis will, and should, be done using automated tools to sort, filter, and combine information into digestible chunks that can be properly assessed by the person viewing them. You should perform this baseline collection over a representative period of time, say monitoring 24 hours a day for two weeks. This should give you a representative sample of the normal usage patterns. Do not choose a time where normal activity may be interrupted (for example, during an extended holiday period).

Again, two of the key baselines you need to understand are the following:

✦ Overall traffic patterns
✦ Periods of high and light traffic use

Key Logs for Analysis

 Objective Understand the different types of logs and what they can contain

A number of logs and sources for those logs should be evaluated and monitored when doing an analysis. Some of the more important ones are described in this section.

Firewall and router logs

You should be reviewing the logs generated by your routers, firewalls, and Internet perimeter systems. This information is invaluable from the standpoint of determining the potential cause of an attack and for detecting an impending attack. Things that are important to observe and note from these logs are the following:

✦ Source and destination of the traffic, in terms of interfaces (especially on routers) and IP addresses.

✦ Protocols that are passing through the systems. Look for things that may be of limited business use or are known attacker favorites, such as MP3, Instant Messenger, IRC, FTP, heavy ICMP between two systems, and other "interesting" TCP or UDP traffic.

✦ Usage patterns on interfaces that might indicate scans or blocked attacks from external sources.

✦ Access to specific Trojan horse ports, such as 6711–6713 (SubSeven) and 8787 and 31337 (BackOrifice 2000).

Don't forget to ensure that the logs that you want to analyze are actually being created. For example, by default, Cisco routers do not log, so you will have to enable logging as well as configure an external system (for instance, Syslog server) to send logs to for later analysis.

Operating system logs

 Understand the difference between default logging and auditing systems

Operating system logs are an invaluable resource when performing analysis. Consequently, I will cover how to enable them and what they can contain. For the exam, Linux and Windows NT are the reference systems.

By default, Windows NT supports three categories of logs through its Event Log service:

✦ **Application** — Applications record their information on this log (C:\Winnt\ System32\config\AppEvent.evt). If an application does not call the audit system, then no logs are created. Logging to this log is enabled by default and can be stopped only by stopping the Event Log service.

✦ **System** — This log (C:\Winnt\System32\config\SysEvent.evt) records system- and system service–related events, such as startup, shutdown, Netlogon, and Print. Logging to the system log is enabled by default and can be stopped only by halting the Event Log service.

✦ **Security** — This log (C:\systemroot\System32\config\SecEvent.evt) records security-related events, such as login, file access, addition of users, and process tracking. Logging to the security log is not enabled by default and must explicitly be turned on.

 Tip   You enable security auditing in Windows 2000 through the Active Directory Users and Computers administrative tool.

From within Active Directory Users and Computers, you can audit the following events:

✦ **Logon and Logoff** — Success and failure

✦ **File and Object Access** — Success and failure (See discussion of usage following this bulleted list.)

✦ **Use of User Rights** — Failure

✦ **User and Group Management** — Success and failure

✦ **Security Policy Changes** — Success and failure

✦ **Restart, Shutdown, and System** — Success and failure

✦ **Process Tracking** — None

Auditing files and directories allows you to track their usage. For a particular file or directory, you can specify which groups or users and which actions to audit. You can audit both successful and failed actions. To audit files and directories, you must set the audit policy to audit File and Object Access. You can then use the Windows Explorer to set auditing on objects (right-click the object and then select Properties ⇨ Auditing). You can granularly select the user and groups that you want to audit on a directory (and subtrees) and/or files. Once you select the user/group, then you can select the event to audit. The following is a list of auditable events:

✦ **Read** — Display filenames, attributes, permissions, and owner

✦ **Write** — Creation of subdirectories and files, changes to attributes, and display of permissions and owner

✦ **Execute** — Display of attributes, permissions, and owner and changes to subdirectories

✦ **Delete** — Deletion of the directory

✦ **Change Permissions** — Changes to directory permissions

✦ **Take Ownership** — Changes to directory ownership

You must determine which directories and files should be audited on your system, but a good option is to audit "write" attempts to files in the \%systemroot%\system32\ folder. To do this, follow these steps:

1. Select the Properties option on the folder.

2. Select Security Auditing, and then click the Add button.

3. Add the Everyone group from the list and select the following checkboxes: Write; Success and Failure; Replace on existing files; and Do not replace on existing subdirectories.

Caution Performing too much auditing on files and directories (or Registry entries described next) can cause a denial of service by consuming a large portion (if not all) of your system's resources.

Auditing the Registry

Part of the "File and Object Auditing" option allows you to audit the Registry as well. It is configured with `Regedt32.exe`. From the main menu of this tool, select Security. The method for setting up auditing is the same as for files and directories, but the auditable events are different. The events that can be audited in the Registry are as follows:

✦ **Query Value** — Read the value of a key.

✦ **Set Value** — Set or modify the value of a key.

✦ **Create Subkey** — Create a subkey.

✦ **Enumerate Subkeys** — Display the keys immediately below a key.

✦ **Notify** — Set the notify property.

✦ **Create Link** — Link the values of two keys.

✦ **Delete** — Delete a key.

✦ **Write DAC** — Change the ACL (Access Control List) to a key.

✦ **Write Owner** — Take ownership of a key.

✦ **Read Control** — Determine the owner of a key.As with file and directory auditing, you will need to determine which Registry keys to audit.

Viewing the audit events

The main Windows NT–based tool for viewing auditing data is the Event Viewer. It allows you not only to view individual log entries, but also to set log parameters (such as size and rotation options, which are described later).

Exam Tip There are six event types that you need to know for the exam. They are listed in Table 20-1 with their descriptions. It is important to note that event IDs can be added between service packs and operating system releases. These events are correct as of Service Pack 4 (SP4). To determine your system's service pack level, use the `winver` command-line utility.

Table 20-1
Windows NT Event Types and Their Descriptions and Logs

NT Event ID	Description	Log
517	Security log cleared.	Security
529	Logon failure.	Security
560	Object access failure.	Security
6005	System restart.	System
6006	Clean shutdown.	System
6007	Failed shutdown request, due to inadequate permissions.	System
6008	Dirty shutdown. Happens when system is not shut down properly.	System
6009	OS information: Version, build number, service packs, and other information.	System

Tip   A number of third-party tools can be used to view Windows NT events. One such tool is the Event Log module for Win32 Perl. Another good idea is to have Windows automate the gathering of log files using a custom script and NT scheduler to automate the gathering of the log files to help save some of your time. There are also several smaller utilities that can help in this process, available on the Internet or in the *Windows NT Server 4 Resource Kit* from Microsoft Press.

Linux Logs

By default, Linux (and most UNIX variants) support the following logs:

✦ `wtmp/utmp` — This file holds user login information. There may be more users currently using this system than it will initially look like, because not all programs use `utmp` logging.

✦ `btmp` — This file, if it exists, contains all the unsuccessful login attempts.

✦ `syslog` — This service actually creates any number of files, in addition to sending logs to other destinations. `Syslog` is the main logging tool for UNIX systems.

Exam Tip   All the logs are located in the `/var/log` directory by default.

Syslog basics

Syslog is the most common source of log information on a UNIX system. It has the single purpose of providing a method for programs to log to a central service. Syslog uses two factors in determining where and if to log messages: facility and priority.

Facility factor

The *facility* describes the category or subsystem that produced the message. For example, all kernel level messages will be logged with the "kern" facility (LOG_KERN). The available facilities are as follows:

+ **Auth** — Security/authorization messages (depreciated)

+ **Authpriv** — Security/authorization messages

+ **Cron** — Cron and at jobs

+ **Daemon** — Other system daemons (sshd, inetd, pppd, and so on)

+ **Kern** — Kernel messages

+ **Lpr** — Line printer subsystem

+ **Mail** — Mail subsystem (for example, sendmail)

+ **Mark** — For internal use only

+ **News** — Usenet news messages

+ **Security** — Security/authorization messages (depreciated)

+ **Syslog** — Internal syslog messages

+ **User** — Generic user-level messages

+ **Uucp** — UUCP subsystem

+ **local0–local7** — Locally defined levels

Priority factor

The *priority* defines the severity of the log message. The following priorities are listed in order of importance, with Emerg being the highest.

1. **Emerg** — System is unusable

2. **Alert** — Action must be taken posthaste

3. **Crit** — Critical conditions

4. **Err** — Error conditions

5. **Warning** — Warning conditions

6. **Notice** — Normal but significant conditions

7. **Info** — Informational messages

8. **Debug** — Debugging messages

Syslog configuration

The `Syslog` service is configured with the `Syslog.conf` file (usually located in `/etc`), which allows you to specify where messages go, depending on the facility and priority. Every entry is considered a rule, which consists of two fields, a selector field and a logfile field. One or more spaces or tabs separate the selector and logfile.

```
facility.loglevel      logfile
```

Tip

Using tabs is a safer bet; some older `Syslog` services do not understand spaces.

The selector

The selector field specifies a pattern of facilities and priorities for which you want to take a desired action. A selector has the following format:

```
<Facility>.<Priority>
```

When forming the selector, you must understand the following rules:

✦ All messages of the specified priority and higher are processed according to the given action.

✦ An asterisk ("*") stands for all facilities or all priorities, depending on where it is used (before or after the period).

✦ The keyword *none* indicates no priority of the given facility, so do not log anything for that facility.

✦ You can group multiple facilities with the same priority pattern in one selector using the comma (,) operator.

✦ You can group multiple selectors for a single action using the semicolon (;) separator. Selectors are evaluated in order, so a latter selector can overwrite the preceding ones.

✦ You can use the equal sign (=) to specify only a single priority and not any of the above.

The logfile

The logfile field of a rule describes where the message should be sent. Most of the time, the logfile is an actual text file, but it does not have to be. The following are descriptions of the logfile that is specified in the action location:

✦ **Regular file** — This logs messages to the file specified. There must be a full pathname, beginning with a slash (/). You can prefix an entry with the minus sign (–) to omit syncing the file after every logging. Take note, however, that you might lose information if the system crashes right after a write.

✦ **Named pipes** — The messages will be written to the named pipe specified. (This is good for filtering with an external program.)

```
/path/to/named_pipe
```

✦ **Terminal and console** — You can send messages to a connected terminal, such as `/dev/console`.

✦ **Remote machine** — You can forward messages to a remote `Syslog` server by prepending the hostname with the at sign (@). You can use this to have all systems log to a central server.

✦ **List of users** — This will send a "wall" message to a specified user(s). You can specify a list of users by separating them with commas (,). If they're logged in they will receive the message, and if not, they won't.

✦ **Everyone logged on** — Like the list of users just described, this logfile will send a "wall" message, but the message will go to all users currently logged on. To specify this feature, use an asterisk (*).

Caution

The @loghost target for logging messages is a simple way to have your logs go to more than one machine. However, since `Syslog` uses UDP as a transport, it can be unreliable, and messages are not guaranteed to arrive at all of the target machines. Also, remember that these messages pass over the network in clear text.

Comments and blank lines

When processing the file, the `Syslog` server will ignore blank lines and any line that starts with a hash mark (#). Hash marks are considered comments. Furthermore, most current versions of `Syslog` can also understand the extended syntax, where a single rule can be divided into several lines if the leading line is terminated with a backslash (\).

The following is an example of a real `syslog.conf` file on a production Linux system. Each rule is preceded by a description:

```
# This is a comment

# Log all kernel messages in /var/adm/kernel. Then send
# anything that is at critical priority or above to
# the system "mainserver". As well as send anything that is
# at critical priority or above to the console. Finally log
# anything that is at info priority or above (except err
# priority) to /var/adm/kernel-info
kern.*                     /var/adm/kernel
kern.crit                  @mainserver
kern.crit                  /dev/console
kern.info;kern.!err        /var/adm/kernel-info
```

```
# Log all messages (except mail and private authentication
# messages) at info priority or higher in to the file
# /var/log/messages This is kind of the log dumping grounds

*.info;mail.none;authpriv.none        /var/log/messages

# Log all private authentication messages (authpriv) to a
# different file, so we can restrict access.
authpriv.*           /var/log/secure

# Log all the mail messages to maillog.
mail.*           /var/log/maillog

# Log all critical mail messages to root and user phil_cox.
mail.=crit          root,phil_cox

# Everybody gets emergency messages
*.emerg            *

# Save mail and news errors of level err and higher in a
# special file.
uucp,news.crit           /var/log/spooler

# Store all messages, except kernel,  with a
# critical priority in the critical file
*.=crit;kern.none           /var/adm/critical
```

See the `syslog.conf` main page for more options available to make your logging even more specific.

Exam Tip   Know the purpose of the `cron`, `messages`, `secure`, and `maillog` files in `Syslog`.

Syslog messages format

`Syslog` formats the messages it receives as follows:

```
Month Day Time source-hostname processname[pid]: log_record
```

So, an example snippet could look like this:

```
Dec 20 09:16:22 RH62 login[2460]: FAILED LOGIN SESSION FROM
10.0.0.9 FOR , User not known to the underlying authentication
module
Dec 20 09:16:22 RH62 PAM_pwdb[2460]: 1 more authentication
failure; (uid=0) -> vcox for login service
Dec 20 09:16:22 RH62 inetd[480]: pid 2459: exit status 1
Dec 20 09:16:26 RH62 PAM_pwdb[2435]: (login) session closed for
user pcox
```

```
Dec 20 09:16:26 RH62 inetd[480]: pid 2434: exit status 1
Dec 20 09:16:34 RH62 PAM_pwdb[2462]: password for (vcox/502)
changed by (root/0)
Dec 20 09:16:41 RH62 PAM_pwdb[2463]: new password not
acceptable
Dec 20 09:16:49 RH62 PAM_pwdb[2464]: password for (admin/503)
changed by (root/0)
Dec 20 09:17:04 RH62 PAM_pwdb[2467]: (login) session opened for
user pcox by (uid=0)
Dec 20 09:17:12 RH62 PAM_pwdb[2492]: (login) session opened for
user vcox by (uid=0)
Dec 20 09:17:21 RH62 PAM_pwdb[2517]: (login) session opened for
user admin by (uid=0)
```

Log commands

UNIX systems have many tools to help view log data. These include the following:

✦ last — Searches back through the file /var/log/wtmp (or the file designated by the -f option) and displays a list of all users logged in (and out) since that file was created, as well as the user's terminal, location, date, and time. There will be a user named reboot in the log each time the system is rebooted.

✦ lastb — Is the same as previous tool, except that by default it shows a log of the file /var/log/btmp, which contains all unsuccessful login attempts.

✦ w — Shows currently logged-in users and their processes. w uses the /var/log/utmp for login information and /proc for process information. The header shows the current time, system uptime, and the number of currently logged on users.

✦ who — Like w, shows who is logged on, but unlike w, it does not show process information. By default, who uses information from utmp/wtmp.

✦ lastlog — Displays the login name, port, and last login time of users who have logged in. It uses the information from /var/log/lastlog. If the user has never logged in the message **Never logged in** will be displayed instead of the port and time.

✦ grep and tail — Can be used to select particular expressions to match, as well as look at the number of entries in a file.

Other logs worth inspecting

Two other logs can be used in your analysis.

✦ **Service logs** — These contain logs from services such as Web servers, database servers, and remote access servers. Authentication servers usually have their own log files with a special format. You should keep this in mind when considering where to look for information.

✦ **Intrusion detection logs**—Your IDS system should have valuable information regarding potential exploits attempted against your system. They should be reviewed as part of an overall strategy as well.

Filtering Logs

 Be able to use log filtering to view specific event types

It is important to know what events you are and are not looking for. Sometimes you know what events are normal, so you are looking for things that are abnormal. For instance, a user failing to log in once in the morning would be considered normal, whereas the same user failing to log in ten times in quick succession would be considered abnormal. At other times, you will be looking for a specific event. This section discusses methods to accomplish event log filtering in both Windows NT and Linux.

Linux

This section will discuss the tools mentioned earlier in this chapter. These tools are intended only for Linux use and can assist in establishing event log filtering.

last

Usage for last is as follows:

```
last [-R] [-num] [ -n num ] [-adiox] [ -f file ] [name...]
[tty...]
```

The last command has many options available to it. The most useful are the following:

✦ last -n <num>—This is a count telling last how many lines to show.

✦ last -x—Displays the system shutdown entries and run level changes.

✦ last -x reboot—Displays the system reboots.

✦ last -x shutdown—Displays the system shutdowns.

✦ last -x <user>—Displays login information for the specific user.

✦ last -a—Displays the hostname in the last column.

✦ last -d—Displays remote logins.

The following is an example of using the `last` command to see all reboots:

```
[RH62]# last -x reboot
reboot   system boot  2.2.14-5.0   Wed Dec 20 08:40   (00:09)
reboot   system boot  2.2.14-5.0   Tue Dec 19 02:33   (00:05)
reboot   system boot  2.2.14-5.0   Wed Nov 15 01:59   (06:02)
reboot   system boot  2.2.14-5.0   Tue Nov 14 01:12   (16:40)
reboot   system boot  2.2.14-5.0   Mon Nov 13 07:11   (00:14)

wtmp begins Mon Nov 13 07:01:19 2000
```

lastb

This command has the same options as `last`, but only focuses on failures.
Remember that the `/var/log/btmp` must exist for the file to contain information.
Its usage is as follows:

```
last [-R][-num][ -n num ][-adiox][ -f file ][name. . .][tty. . .]
```

The following is an example of using the `lastb` command to see all failed root login attempts:

```
[RH62]# lastb -a root
root     pts/1    Wed Dec 20 08:56 - 08:56   (00:00) 10.0.0.2
root     pts/1    Wed Dec 20 08:56 - 08:56   (00:00) 10.0.0.2
root     pts/1    Wed Dec 20 08:56 - 08:56   (00:00) 10.0.0.2
root     pts/1    Wed Dec 20 08:56 - 08:56   (00:00) 10.0.0.2
root     pts/1    Wed Dec 20 08:56 - 08:56   (00:00) 10.0.0.2
root     pts/1    Wed Dec 20 08:55 - 08:55   (00:00) 10.0.0.2
root     pts/1    Wed Dec 20 08:55 - 08:55   (00:00) 10.0.0.2
root     pts/1    Wed Dec 20 08:55 - 08:55   (00:00) 10.0.0.2
root     pts/1    Wed Dec 20 08:55 - 08:55   (00:00) 10.0.0.2

btmp begins Wed Dec 20 08:53:12 2000
```

w

Usage for `w` is as follows:

```
w - [husfV] [user]
```

The `w` command has many options available to it; the most useful are the following:

✦ `w -h` — Keeps header from printing.

✦ `w -u` — Displays only system information.

✦ `w -s` — Keeps login time, JCPU, or PCPU times from displaying.

✦ `w -f` — Keeps the from (remote hostname) field from displaying.

✦ `w user` — Displays information about the specified user only.

The following is an example of using the w command to see all logged-in users:

```
[RH62]# w
9:17am  up 37 min, 5 users, load average: 0.07, 0.02, 0.00
USER   TTY    FROM        LOGIN@  IDLE  JCPU   PCPU   WHAT
root   tty1   -           9:14am  3.00s 0.40s  0.06s  man nmap
pcc    pts/0  10.0.0.2    8:58am  0.00s 0.99s  ?      -
pcox   pts/1  10.0.0.7    9:13am  3.00s 0.38s  0.04s  gcc smurf.c
vcox   pts/2  10.0.0.12   9:16am  3.00s 0.32s  0.03s  emacs
admin  pts/3  10.0.0.3    9:17am  3.00s 0.31s  0.14s  -bash
```

who

Usage for who is as follows:

```
who [option] . . . [File|arg1 arg2]
```

The who command has many options available to it. The most useful are as follows:

✦ who -H—Prints a line of column headings.

✦ who -I—Adds user idle time as HOURS:MINUTES.

✦ who -m—Shows only hostname and user associated with the console.

✦ who -q—Summarily displays all login names and number of logged-in users.

The following is an example of using the who command to see all logged-in users and their idle time:

```
[RH62]# who -HI
USER      LINE     LOGIN-TIME     IDLE  FROM
root      tty1     Dec 20 09:14   00:06
pcc       pts/0    Dec 20 08:48   .
pcox      pts/1    Dec 20 09:13   00:09
vcox      pts/2    Dec 20 09:16   00:07
admin     pts/3    Dec 20 09:17   00:06
```

lastlog

Usage for lastlog is as follows:

```
lastlog [-u uid] [-t days]
```

The lastlog command has two options available to it:

✦ lastlog -u <login-name>—Prints a lastlog record for the specified user.

✦ lastlog -t <#days>—Prints a lastlog record for logins more recent than the number specified with the #days augment. The -t flag overrides the use of -u.

The following is an example of using the `lastlog` command to see all logins in the last three days:

```
[RH62]# lastlog -t 3
Username   Port   From        Latest
root       tty1               Wed Dec 20 09:14:04 -0800 2000
pcc        0      10.0.0.2    Wed Dec 20 08:58:25 -0800 2000
pcox       1      10.0.0.7    Wed Dec 20 09:13:04 -0800 2000
vcox       2      10.0.0.12   Wed Dec 20 09:16:12 -0800 2000
admin      3      10.0.0.3    Wed Dec 20 09:17:21 -0800 2000
```

grep and tail

You should become very familiar with the `grep` and `tail` commands, as you will use them extensively while doing analysis.

The usage for `grep` is very complex, and for the purposes of this book, only a couple of commands are listed here. Usage for `grep` is as follows:

```
grep  [-v] <regular expression>  [file...]
```

The `grep` command has two options that you will use frequently:

✦ `grep -v` — Displays everything that does not match the expression.

✦ **Regular expressions** — You will use regular expressions to match data in a file.

The following example uses `grep` to find all occurrences of an `su` in the `messages` file:

```
[RH62]# grep "(su) session" messages
Dec 20 08:52:59 RH62 PAM_pwdb[2288]: (su) session opened for
user root by pcc(uid=500)
Dec 20 09:14:22 RH62 PAM_pwdb[2393]: (su) session opened for
user gopher by root(uid=0)
Dec 20 09:14:52 RH62 PAM_pwdb[2414]: (su) session opened for
user root by root(uid=13)
Dec 20 09:15:06 RH62 PAM_pwdb[2414]: (su) session closed for
user root
Dec 20 09:15:08 RH62 PAM_pwdb[2393]: (su) session closed for
user gopher
Dec 20 10:43:32 RH62 PAM_pwdb[2288]: (su) session closed for
user root
Dec 21 09:22:59 RH62 PAM_pwdb[668]: (su) session opened for
user root by pcc(uid=500)
```

An alternative method would be to run the following command. It produces the same output:

```
[RH62]# cat /var/log/messages | grep \(su\)
```

Tip   You should check both the `messages` and `secure` file for information on services that you run.

Usage for the `tail` command is as follows:

```
tail [OPTION]... [FILE]...
```

The `tail` command has many options available to it. The most useful are as follows:

✦ `tail -f`—Outputs appended data as the file grows.

✦ `tail -n <#lines>`—Outputs the number of lines, instead of the default last 10.

The following example uses the `-f` option of `tail` to continually monitor the log entries in the `/var/log/messages` file:

```
[RH62]# tail -f messages
Dec 20 09:16:26 RH62 PAM_pwdb[2435]: (login) session closed for
user pcox
Dec 20 09:16:26 RH62 inetd[480]: pid 2434: exit status 1
Dec 20 09:16:34 RH62 PAM_pwdb[2462]: password for (vcox/502)
changed by (root/0)
Dec 20 09:16:41 RH62 PAM_pwdb[2463]: new password not
acceptable
Dec 20 09:16:49 RH62 PAM_pwdb[2464]: password for (admin/503)
changed by (root/0)
Dec 20 09:16:59 RH62 PAM_pwdb[2467]: authentication failure;
(uid=0) -> pcox for login service
Dec 20 09:17:00 RH62 login[2467]: FAILED LOGIN 1 FROM 10.0.0.9
FOR pcox, Authentication failure
Dec 20 09:17:04 RH62 PAM_pwdb[2467]: (login) session opened for
user pcox by (uid=0)
Dec 20 09:17:12 RH62 PAM_pwdb[2492]: (login) session opened for
user vcox by (uid=0)
Dec 20 09:17:21 RH62 PAM_pwdb[2517]: (login) session opened for
user admin by (uid=0)
```

Exam Tip   For the exam, understand how to use `grep` and `tail`.

Windows NT

Filtering with Windows NT is much simpler, as there is only one method involved: the Event Viewer filter. To filter events, run the Event Viewer. Then, on the main menu, select View ➪ Filter Events. From this screen you can select the following:

✦ **View From and View Through**—Search for entries with a specific time period, down to the second.

✦ **Event type** — Search for entries with a specific type. Types include Information, Warning, Error, Success Audit, and Failure Audit (the first three are used in the Application and System logs, the latter two for the Security log).

✦ **Source** — Search for entries related to a specific Windows NT subsystem that created the log entry.

✦ **Category** — Search for entries within a specific category. Categories are Account Management, Detailed Tracking, Logon/Logoff, Object Access, Policy Change, Privilege Use, or System Event.

✦ **User** — Search for entries with a specific user or group.

✦ **Computer** — Search for entries with a specific computer account. (This is the NetBIOS name for the computer.)

✦ **Event ID** — Search for a specific event ID.

 Tip

Remember that if you set your filters incorrectly, you may miss valuable log entries. So proper planning and event filter configuration are essential to get the most out of your systems logging activities.

Detecting Suspicious Activities

When an incident occurs, if you don't have good logs (that is, auditing), you'd better have good luck. The chances of figuring out what happened without good auditing are few and far between.

You will be looking for suspicious or abnormal activity. This could, and probably does, mean a number of things to different people. If you are protecting nuclear secrets, then outgoing e-mail may be a "suspicious" activity, whereas in most commercial corporations, it would not be.

Read your log files periodically to check for warning activity. This includes hacking attempts (many failed logins for a user may be a sign of hacking) or nonsecurity-related problems (for example, running out of swap space). The logs' sole purpose is to help the administrator. Ignoring logs renders them useless.

Items to be sensitive to while reviewing the logs include the following:

✦ The appearance of new accounts

✦ Unusual account activities, such as access to unauthorized resources, logins at strange hours, or logins from unauthorized systems

✦ Unscheduled system restarts

✦ Performance degradation with no apparent cause

✦ Missing files or rapidly increasing disk space

✦ Multiple login failures

In the Real World

Probably the most important factor in detecting suspicious activity is the understanding of what "normally" happens on your systems, and to know that you must regularly review the logs. The best method for review is to use a log-reducing program such as `watcher` or `swatch` on Linux. For Windows NT you will need a third-party tool such as Centrax Log Analyzer.

Securing Log Storage

Because attackers will target a log for modification to hide their tracks, you need to protect your logs in some manner. Table 20-2 lists the most practical ways of protecting your log files.

Table 20-2		
Protecting Log Files		
Action	*Linux*	*Windows NT*
Send logs to a central server.	Use `Syslog` and the "@" logfile.	Windows NT does not have this capability. You need to use third-party tools.
Write logs to alternative storage (CD-ROM, backup tapes).	Use appropriate file system drivers. Performance may be an issue, depending on the log activity.	Save Event Log data to alternative media.
Save logs to hard copy.	Log to a printer device.	Select events and print them out.

Tip

Hard copy is an unrealistic alternative and should be considered only if a very specific need arises. Searching for an event on a CD or log server is infinitely easier than looking through a hard copy.

Linux log file permissions

In conjunction with the above listed items, you should make sure your logs are not readable by everyone. Logs should be owned and writeable by root and readable by a logging group. No permissions should exist for the world account. The people who need to review the logs can be made members of the logging group so that they can read the files.

Windows NT log file permissions

The Windows NT Event Log service exclusively locks the files while the system is running; therefore, the default security on the files is adequate.

Managing Audit Logs

A number of administrative functions, such as log maintenance and service validation, must be performed for logging to be successful.

Windows NT logs

You will need to configure the Event Log settings for all three logs (Application, System, and Security). You set these in the Event Viewer. From the main menu select Log and Log Settings. For each of the logs, you can set the following:

✦ **Maximum Log Size** — Sets the maximum size for the log.

✦ **Event Log Wrapping** — Set as follows:

- **Overwrite Events as Needed** — Causes the oldest events to be written over when the log reaches its maximum size. This method is safe, but may be used by an attacker to overwrite critical entries by flooding the logs. Use this option only if you do not have any log maintenance programs in place.

- **Overwrite Events Older than** — Causes events that are older than the specified number of days to be overwritten if the log fills. If the log reaches its file size limit before the time period has been reached, then subsequent events will not be logged until the specified time has passed, thereby protecting old event entries, but possibly losing valuable newer ones. This is an acceptable setting if you have a large enough file to handle the events for a given period. It will not overwrite past critical events as the previous setting will, but it can be exploited to fill the logs and then be unable to log the remainder of an attacker's actions, so use this option with care.

- **Do Not Overwrite Events (Clear Logs Manually)** — You must clear the logs manually. All events are kept until the administrator clears them. This option has the same problem as "Overwrite Events Older than" in that once the logs are full, no more events are written until the log is cleared. Use this method if you regularly review your logs.

The Event Log service

You will need to ensure that the Event Log service is running. You can do this by performing the following steps.

1. Open Control Panel, then double-click the Services icon. Once the Services window has opened, locate the Event Log service.

2. Double-click the service. From here, you can see the status of the service and the option to reconfigure it.

3. For example, you can change the start-up type to Automatic, Manual, or Disabled. You can also start and stop the service, or even observe the service's dependencies on other services, if any.

Linux logs

Linux logs will utilize the disk on which they reside. Unlike Windows NT, Linux logs do not have individual log settings. Linux logs will consume disk space until the space runs out. However, a daily cron job can be run to rotate the logs (/etc/cron.daily/Logrotate). Logrotate can also be invoked with the -f option to force Logrotate to run immediately.

Logrotate uses a configuration file (default is /etc/Logrotate.conf) and can be configured to rotate specific logs at different intervals or following different trigger events. The following is a slightly edited sample Logrotate configuration file from the man page:

```
# This is a comment line
# These are global options, used on all files specified.

# any errors that occur during logfile processing
# are  mailed  to sysadmin@my.org and logs are compressed
# after they are rotated

errors sysadmin@my.org
compress

# Defined how to handle the log file /var/log/messages.
# The log will go through five weekly rotations before
# being removed. After the log file has been rotated
# (but before the old version of the log has been
# compressed), the command
# /sbin/killall -HUP syslogd will be executed

/var/log/messages {
rotate 5
weekly
postrotate
/sbin/killall -HUP syslogd
endscript
}
```

```
# Rotate the log whenever it grows over 100k in size
# Mail old logs files to www@my.org after going through
# 5 rotations, rather then being removed.
# Any errors that occur while processing the log file are
# also mailed to  www@my.org (overriding global setting)

"/var/log/httpd/access.log" {
rotate 5
mail www@my.org
errors www@my.org
size=100k
postrotate
/sbin/killall -HUP httpd
endscript
}

# Each file in the directory is rotated on a monthly basis,
# and errors are mailed to newsadmin@my.org
# If a file is missing, keep processing
# The log files are not compressed

/var/log/news/* {
monthly
rotate 2
missingok
errors newsadmin@my.org
postrotate
kill -HUP `cat /var/run/inn.pid`
endscript
nocompress
}
```

Make sure that the `syslog` service is running on your Linux box. The easiest way to do that is by viewing the output of the `ps -x` command and looking for `syslog`. If `syslog` is not running, you can start (restart) it by invoking the `/etc/rc.d/rc2.d/S30syslog` script:

Usage for `syslog` is as follows:

```
/etc/rc.d/rc2.d/S30syslog {start|stop|status|restart}
```

Impact of Logging

Logging, like any process, consumes resources. The resources consumed can be relatively small and unnoticeable, or they can literally bring the system to its knees. Take performance into consideration when configuring your system logs.

Remember the corollary: the more logging, the bigger the impact. Some issues to keep in mind include the following:

✦ **Performance** — Consider your CPU, your disk bandwidth, and your network bandwidth if logging to a remote system.

✦ **Hardware resources** — How much disk space is available?

✦ **Staff resources** — How much staff does it take to use your tools (if you have them) or to perform the analysis if you don't?

In the Real World

One final thought — not for the course, but for practicality. If it has not already hit you, auditing and logging are not simple, quick tasks. Logs take a lot of time, a concerted effort, and an ongoing diligence to keep current. If you start the job, then make sure you have the time and resources to finish it. Take the time, learn your systems, and set up auditing that is adequate and appropriate for your systems.

Key Point Summary

This chapter discussed logging on Windows NT and Linux; covered the importance of establishing a baseline and how to create one; and examined log services on Windows NT and Linux, how to filter logs, how to identify suspicious activity and what tools can help. This chapter also considered the importance of proper logging settings.

✦ A baseline provides a basis for understanding what is and is not acceptable behavior and what constitutes a potential security incident or event for your company.

✦ Two main factors in an event activity baseline are overall traffic patterns and periods of high and light traffic use.

✦ Many sources exist for logs, such as firewall and router logs, operating system logs, application and service logs, and intrusion detection logs.

✦ Knowing how different programs behave can lead toward what would be considered normal traffic on your network. For instance, instant messengers generate a substantial amount of ICMP packets.

✦ The primary logging service in Windows NT is the Event Log service, which logs to the Application, System, and Security logs. Events are viewed with the Event Viewer.

✦ Under Windows NT, if you have file and object access auditing enabled, you can further audit your system by auditing activity in the Registry. By applying auditing to Registry keys, you can monitor if there has been unauthorized installation of software or other changes to system settings.

✦ The primary logging service in Linux is `Syslog`, which is supplemented with `utmp` and `lastlog`. Events are viewed with various commands (`w`, `last`, `lastlog`, `lastb`, `who`, and so on) and used in conjunction with `grep` and `tail`.

✦ Archive log files to a secure medium such as CD-ROM or backup tapes.

✦ Look into service logs from various services such as Web, database, and RAS servers. Other logs to monitor are those generated from any intrusion detection software that you may have installed on the network.

✦ Filtering logs can be a real time saver. Whether you do it manually, or have a script or a third-party program do it for you, filtering security logs for content will go a long way toward minimizing time spent scrolling through endless events.

✦ Obviously, monitoring the logs for unusual activity will help you not only figure out which activities are normal, but help you identify abnormal activity much more often. You may even be clued into a larger attack by seeing some activities that indicate a hacker probing your network.

✦ Improper logging configurations will adversely impact performance. Also there will usually be an impact on performance on your organization's networks. This can be the case even more so with larger enterprise scanning packages that perform a larger degree of scans and audits when the network isn't up to the task.

✦   ✦   ✦

STUDY GUIDE

This Study Guide will present five assessment questions and six lab exercises to test your understanding of the exam objectives.

Assessment Questions

1. Windows NT event logging separates its logs into three main categories. Which of the following groups is correct?

   A. System, Security, and Application

   B. Software, Application, and Network

   C. User, Application, and Network

   D. Machine, Software, and Login

2. What is the correct event number for a clean shutdown event?

   A. Event ID: 529

   B. Event ID: 6006

   C. Event ID: 6008

   D. Event ID: 6009

3. An example of suspicious activity would be the primary domain controller rebooting in the early morning hours. True or false?

4. It is a good idea to regularly take a copy of your system event logs from their normal location and put them in an alternate location for safekeeping. True or false?

5. Which side effect of system event auditing will most likely occur?

   A. Nothing, system event auditing will not affect normal system operation.

   B. Depending on the amount of system event logging, a substantial amount of system resources could be utilized, possibly slowing the system.

   C. Available network bandwidth could be consumed, resulting in network utilization exceeding recommended limits.

   D. With event logging enabled, the system will run better with the additional information provided in the logs.

Lab Exercises

The following labs will help solidify some of the things covered in this chapter. The first four labs deal with Windows NT and build on each other. The last two are Linux-based.

Lab 20-1 Enable Windows NT auditing

 Objective   Be able to set up auditing on a machine, and configure it to audit specific types of events

In this lesson, you will enable and configure auditing on Windows NT. (If you get stuck, see the "Operating system logs" section earlier in this chapter.)

1. Open the User Manager tool.
2. From the main menu, select Policies ➪ Audit.
3. Click Audit These Events.
4. Select success and failure for Logon and Logoff and File and Object Access.
5. Then click OK.

Lab 20-2 Enable directory auditing in Windows NT

In this lesson, you will set up auditing on the C:\WINNT\Repair directory. This directory is highly desirable from an attacker's standpoint because it often contains a copy of the NT password database.

1. Use the Windows Explorer to open the Properties (right-click) on C:\WINNT\Repair.
2. Click the Security tab and then the Audit button.
3. Click Add and then select the Everyone group.
4. Configure the Events to Audit to capture all successful and unsuccessful actions.
5. Select the options to Replace Auditing on Subdirectories and Replace Auditing on Existing Files.
6. Click OK.

You have now generated an event for which Windows will create an Event Log entry whenever someone attempts access to the directory or files in the directory.

Lab 20-3 Detect failed file access attempts

In this lab, you will study a successful access of the `Repair` directory. Make sure that there are files in the `C:\WINNT\Repair` directory by running the Rdisk utility.

1. Log in as Administrator.
2. With Windows Explorer, set the permissions on the `C:\WINNT\Repair\sam` file to Everyone: No Access.
3. Log out.
4. Log in as a normal user.
5. With the Windows Explorer, try to copy the `C:\WINNT\Repair\sam` file to another directory.
6. Log out.
7. Log in as Administrator.
8. Open the Event Viewer.
9. Select Log ⇨ Security and view the Security log.
10. Search for failed object access (event ID 560).

You should now see the failed access to the SAM file.

Lab 20-4 Identify failed login attempts

In this lab, you will study unsuccessful Windows NT login attempts.

1. Fail log in as Administrator five to ten times.
2. Log in as Administrator.
3. Open the Event Viewer.
4. Go to Log ⇨ Security and view the Security log.
5. Search for failed logon attempts (event ID 529).

You should now see the failed login attempts.

Lab 20-5 Identify su root attempts

In this lab, you will study `su root` attempts.

1. Log in as a normal user.
2. Perform multiple `su root` commands (if you have the root password, then make one successful).

3. Change into the /var/log directory by typing cd /var/log and pressing Enter.

4. Run the following:

```
grep "(su) session" messages
```

You should now see the failed, then successful, su root attempts. Note that this represents a typical attack scenario, in which an attacker obtains a normal user account (say via sniffing) and then once logged in, attempts to guess the root password.

Lab 20-6 Identify failed root login attempts

In this lab, you will study failed su root attempts.

1. Fail root login five to ten times.

2. Log in as a normal user.

3. Change into the /var/log directory by typing cd /var/log and pressing Enter.

4. Run the following command:

```
grep "FAILED LOGIN " messages
```

You should now see the failed logins. An alternative would be to run the lastb root command.

Answers to Chapter Questions

Chapter Pre-Test

1. A set of data that defines normal and acceptable usage for a system. You create one by monitoring system usage over a representative period of time.

2. Syslog is the main Linux logging service, supplemented with lastlog and utmp. Syslog is configured with the Syslog.conf file located in /etc.

3. User Manager tool.

4. /Var/log.

5. Application, System, and Security.

6. Understanding your company policy and examining what current activity exists on your network and systems (overall traffic patterns and periods of high and light traffic use).

7. Key information points are source and destination of the traffic, protocols that are passing through the systems, usage patterns on interfaces that might indicate scans or blocked attacks from external sources, and external access to specific Trojan horse ports.

8. The Application log contains application-related events. The System log contains system- and system service–related events. The Security log contains security-related events.

9. The dirty shutdown has event ID 6008, and the clean shutdown has event ID 6006.

10. UNIX: `/var/log/`   Windows NT: `C:\WINNT\SYSTEM32\Config`

Assessment Questions

1. **A.** Windows NT event logging separates its logs into three main categories: System, Security, and Application.

2. **B.** Event ID 6006 is the correct ID for a clean shutdown event and can be found in the system event log. 529 is for unsuccessful login, 6007 is for an improper shutdown request, and 6008 is for a dirty shutdown event.

3. **True.** An example of suspicious activity would be the primary domain controller rebooting in the early morning hours.

4. **True.** It is a very good idea to regularly take a copy of your system event logs from their normal location and put them in an alternate location for safekeeping.

5. **C.** A possible side effect of system event logging could be the possibility of available network bandwidth being consumed, resulting in network utilization exceeding recommended limits. This may be especially true for enterprise class auditing utilities, such as Axent's Enterprise Security Manager.

For More Information

For more information on the topics covered in this chapter, please visit the following sites:

✦ Windows NT Event Log FAQ: `www.heysoft.de/nt/eventlog/faq.html`

✦ *The System Logging Daemons,* `syslogd` *and* `klog`:
`www2.linuxjournal.com/lj-issues/issue75/4036.html`

✦ "Linux's Tell-Tale Heart, Part 1" (*Linux Journal*): `http://www2.linuxjournal.com/articles/sysadmin/035.html`

✦ "Linux's Tell-Tale Heart, Part 2" (*Linux Journal*): `http://www2.linuxjournal.com/articles/sysadmin/036.html`

✦ Murray, James D. and Debby Russell. *Windows NT Event Logging,* O'Reilly Nutshell, September 1998. ISBN: 1-565-92514-9.

✦ Northcutt, Stephen. *Network Intrusion Detection, An Analyst's Handbook*, New Riders, August 1999. ISBN: 0-735-70868-1

Acting on Audit Results

EXAM OBJECTIVES

- ✦ Develop solutions drawn from specific network issues
- ✦ Suggest a plan to improve security policy compliance
- ✦ Generate security assessment reports
- ✦ Learn security assurance standards
- ✦ Install aftermarket security software, such as personal firewalls
- ✦ Set up auditing policies
- ✦ Strengthen system and network services

CHAPTER PRE-TEST

1. What is a very important first step in securing a router?

2. What is the difference between proactive detection and passive intrusion detection?

3. What piece of software can detect a network card that is running in promiscuous mode?

4. When auditing systems, why is cleaning up after poorly executed installations an important step?

5. What two things are personal firewall software packages particularly useful for?

6. SSH services can provide two fundamental services. Name one of these services and why it is useful.

7. What utility can you use that is included in every standard Windows operating system to track down illicit servers?

8. By implementing IPv6, what are the possible ramifications for the network?

9. IPSec is growing in popularity and is starting to spread in the corporate world. Name one product that is a basic implementation of IPSec that has been around for a decade.

10. SSH requires one other system service to function properly. Identify this service.

✦ Answers to these questions can be found at the end of the chapter. ✦

Understanding the Results of the Auditing Process

 Develop solutions drawn from specific network issues

Suggest a plan to improve security policy compliance

Previous chapters in this book discussed the many tools and techniques that allow for effective audits of client networks. The next step is to generate a well-documented, detailed, written recommendation that can be understood by your client.

The three main areas that should be covered in your recommendations are:

✦ Various ways to implement or extend auditing on the network to make it more efficient. These ways of implementing or extending auditing are mainly to root out the difference between recommended security policies and the actual implementation and follow-through of security.

✦ The location and removal of viruses, worms, Trojan backdoor programs, and various system vulnerabilities.

✦ Recommendations for improvements and changes required to enhance or improve security, such as:

- Changing router settings to remove possible security issues

- Setting up or reconfiguring firewall settings and rules

- Patching and implementing service packs for the operating system and software

- Removing outdated software, services, and network stacks that may compromise security

- Increasing the quality of network auditing and monitoring

- Setting up automation of security and auditing for the internal and external network zones

- Setting up intrusion detection software

- Improving physical security in and around essential servers and network devices

- Implementing or improving anti-virus protection on clients and servers

- Implementing user grade encryption for client systems

- Removing all extraneous user accounts, system services, and software

- Installing all current and required Microsoft hot fixes (NT/2000)

Four general topic areas can help segment your auditing and report generating methods. You are not limited to these particular suggestions, but they can help sort the report out into useful categories.

The four topic areas are as follows:

✦ Firewalls

✦ Intrusion detection

✦ Host and personal security

✦ Policy enforcement

Specific recommendations under each of these four areas include:

✦ **Firewalls**

• Make sure that proper packet filtering is implemented.

• Check current firewall rule configuration.

• Scan the DMZ (if implemented) for problem members.

✦ **Intrusion detection**

• Update intrusion-detection software security settings.

• Scan and discover systems that may not have been covered before and that may need to be monitored for intrusion detection.

✦ **Host and personal security**

• Implement client-level encryption methods.

• Install personal firewall software packages on remote client systems that connect to your network to limit the risk of intrusion from remote users' systems.

• Monitor unused or suspicious user accounts and remove them as necessary.

• Implement system patches and service packs to provide broad implementation of security fixes.

• Upgrade the TCP/IP stack to the newer "patched" version to minimize vulnerabilities associated with older implementations.

✦ **Policy enforcement**

• Implement system monitoring and security management software.

• Recommend complete regularly scheduled audits of the systems, networks, and physical premises.

The Auditing Assessment Report

 Generate security assessment reports

The auditing report you present to clients should follow a consistent layout that doesn't jump in a disorganized way from one topic to the next, and should exhibit a clear sense of readability. Expect to spend some time fine-tuning your audit report, because a presentable, thorough product can help get you back in for follow-up audits or more work at other locations. A good report will cover both the problems that were found and your recommendations for change.

The key components of a successful audit report include:

✦ A general outline of the network security (if any) that is currently in place. You should state whether you thought the security was at a low, medium, or high level. You should also mention what hardware and software was tested during the audit, including servers, operating systems, special applications, and network hardware.

✦ Optionally, an estimate of how long it would take hackers of varying skill levels to break into the different areas of the systems or network.

✦ A brief blurb on the critical areas of the network — those that you think require immediate attention.

✦ A fully detailed report on the methods and tools you used, as well as the actions you took during the audit. Make sure you mention anything that piqued your interest. Describe anything that was found during the discovery, penetration, and control audits that you feel should be brought up.

✦ Suggest changes for settings on the network, including routing equipment, system or firewall ports, user accounts, and software settings. Don't forget to suggest ways to improve physical security at the client's site.

✦ An outline of the cause and effect of not implementing the changes that you have recommended.

✦ A brief outline of terminology used in the body of the report.

 When discussing physical security, remember that many business and IT departments have inherited poor locales for their sensitive server and network equipment. With this in mind, make suggestions that are realistic, but do outline what the best physical security would be, and let the client choose how important physical security is to them. Quite often, secretaries can be the only line of defense between your network and a hacker.

For example, at a site I worked at, a security auditor was able to walk by the receptionist into a sensitive area with a laptop under his arm. He proceeded to walk right up to the server area and could have gained easy access to an active network port. The auditor was never challenged and the receptionist was never introduced beforehand. The receptionist assumed that because the auditor had a laptop, he was supposed to be there. Think how dangerous that could be!

There are non-IT people who will read your report and assess the points you make. Because much of the information in the report may be over their heads, make sure you present it clearly and concisely, in a way that most people can understand. Consider creating a separate section at the end of the report that contains more detailed, technical suggestions for the benefit of the IT personnel.

When you have completed the security audit and generated your report, consider the security of the report itself. It is likely to contain much confidential information. If you are delivering the document by mail, consider using a secure courier company and placing the document in a sealed container that lets the recipient know whether the document has been tampered with. If you are sending the document by e-mail, consider using encryption.

Ensuring Compliance

During the reporting process, you will need to mention problem areas and suggest ways they can be remedied. In general, there will be a set quantity of common areas that will require beefed-up security. The following sections cover the various levels of compliance that you may want to make known to your client.

The following list summarizes the initial steps that your clients should take to continue the security standards that you have implemented.

✦ Outline an effective security policy that will be enforced.

✦ Design internal support systems that will delegate the responsibilities for the various areas of security to the appropriate people. Establish someone as the security manager.

✦ Detail the various network components and organize them in appropriate classes and groups for more effective management.

✦ Create appropriate security guidelines that will be followed by employees, which should include password strength, workstation security, installed software, and safe security practices in general.

✦ Outline server security, including methods to secure services, operating systems, network equipment, and related software.

✦ Establish or improve upon access control management techniques.

✦ Set up and maintain security methods for continual auditing and security risk management.

✦ Make sure the network will allow the company to work in the capacity they require, while still maintaining the level of security they need.

✦ Apply the security policies and periodically test whether the network, systems, and employees are complying with them. Adjust the policies as necessary.

◆ Perform the aforementioned steps again as needed. Performing these types of audits every six months is recommended. Make sure the client is aware that implemented security does not stay secure forever.

Tip   This list shouldn't stay static. Always redefine the recommendations to encompass any special circumstances the site may have and any new security-related issues that may have popped up.

These security methods should be considered mandatory for network and system security. In fact, many international bodies require that every step be followed for compliance with their security standards policymakers.

Several different international standards exist that security auditors and administrators can follow, including the ISO 7498-2 standard and the British Standard 7799. These two standards, and others, will be covered in more detail a little later in this chapter. In general, it is a good idea to follow at least one of them.

Auditing and Security Standards

Objective   Learn security assurance standards

There are no less than three international security standards that auditors can use to help develop a logical and efficient approach to generating a report for their client. The standards discussed in this section are among the most respected standards in the field. Keep an eye on them, as they may be updated and revised on a semi-frequent basis.

Knowing how the various standards work and what they encompass can help you write a presentable, informative report that allows your client to draw an educated conclusion.

Some security auditors may play down the need for standards, claiming that they are too vague and may not necessarily apply to any or all networks. A large part of the problem with some security auditors not wanting to utilize standards is that keeping a guideline such as an international security standard in mind while trying to keep the myriad of other problems in check can be a losing battle for auditors. Implementing theory in everyday practical network environments can be difficult.

Often, the end result of auditors not utilizing the various international standards that are available is that the security standards become more difficult to apply, and at the same time, more important to implement. Many businesses, both large and small, now want to see that a certain level of security standard has been implemented in your company before they do business with you, notwithstanding any special standards that may be in place when you do business with a government organization.

Most governing bodies require that some level of security is implemented. For instance, the U.S. government has published the *Rainbow Series*, outlining security standards, and the British government has adopted the BS 7799 standard practices.

The ISO 7498-2 standard

The International Standards Organization, or ISO, is responsible for providing standards for a wide variety of industries, such as manufacturing or engineering. ISO has established the 7498 series of standards to help standardize network deployment and implementation. The second document or subcategory to the 7498 standard is 7498-2, which describes ways to implement security on systems or networks and outlines ways to develop a sound plan for implementing security auditing techniques.

The 7498-2 standard is titled *Information Processing Systems, Open System Interconnecting, and Basic Reference Model Part 2: Security Architecture.* This standard was one of the first that applied a standard step-by-step approach to network security.

BS 7799 – (British Standard 7799)

The BS 7799 standard further outlines how to secure network systems properly. The standard is titled *A Code of Practice for Information Security Management,* and the 1999 version consists of two separate parts. BS 7799-1 looks at the steps needed to secure a network properly, while BS 7799-2 goes into more depth, outlining the individual steps required to apply the Information Security Management System (ISMS).

Even though the BS 7799 standard originated in Britain, it is accepted and implemented in a wide array of non-British companies, organizations, and governing bodies because it discusses the following three critical areas of security:

✦ Designing a plan

✦ Implementing the plan

✦ Documenting the results of the plan

This outline greatly helps security and network management workers tackle the often-daunting task of applying this standard to your network security.

Tip The British Standard 7799 and the ISO 9000 series of documents (probably the one ISO standard known by most people) are closely mated and are designed as such to let companies work together with secure networks, similar or identical security standards, and various other business practices.

ISMS helps implement policies and standards that will increase security related to any information used by a company or organization to the highest possible level. Security considerations must encompass all forms in your company or organization. Every facet of your business or activities must come under scrutiny, including the various departments that interact with your information technology infrastructure, such as telephony, information filing, network data transportation, and the like.

Implementing and outlining ISMS can be a very difficult and time-consuming process because you must not only look at network security, but also at any other branches of the company that interact with that department. Once you have outlined other areas that need to be secured, you must document and categorize any part of the business that can be used to generate information, including even standard office supplies. Define a scope so you can focus only on specific areas that will be direct and urgent to your network's security.

The process of defining ISMS for your network will encompass several different steps:

✦ Define and design a specific security policy for your needs.

✦ Decide on the actual scope of your ISMS implementation.

✦ Assess risk related to your scope, and document as necessary.

✦ Develop a plan to manage and resolve risks about which you have prior knowledge.

These steps have been covered in earlier chapters (see Chapter 20). When it comes time to implement a security standard such as BS 7799 or ISO 7498-2, you will need to be able to associate the skills involved with these steps with the standards. Following or implementing these types of standards successfully will greatly help you develop your credibility and skill as a security auditor.

 In the Real World

Companies and organizations are usually as interested in industry standards as they are in certifications. If you can tuck a reputable certification or two under your belt, that's great; but as a security auditor, your ability to implement pertinent standards will provide an extra edge over other applicants for security auditing work.

Both ISO 7498-2 and BS 7799 outline a multitude of steps involved with properly implementing the standards. Both standards are similar in nature, and both effectively discuss the steps that should be taken to obtain proper standards compliance:

1. Outline and publish a written security policy and implement it.

2. Develop and output a list of people who are responsible for the various areas of security management.

3. Train personnel in the hows and whys of proper computer and network security measures (an informed employee will make your work much easier).

4. Lay out guidelines that can be used by users and administrators to report security-related events.

5. Research and implement a solid anti-virus software package for all applicable systems, and ensure that the software is effective and kept up-to-date.

6. When applying the various security policies and protection methods, make sure they do not interfere with core business goals.

7. Establish measures to control the installation of unlicensed software and ensure that existing unlicensed software is taken care of in an appropriate manner.

8. Ensure that data relating to company procedures, sensitive documents, and other technology-related data is physically secured offsite, if possible.

9. Generate a system that protects new information produced by the company, including regular data backups that are taken to offsite, environmentally-controlled, secured storage.

10. Develop a means to monitor compliance with the implemented security policies and track actual compliance to written security policies.

The BS 7799 standard will go on to outline many more steps and goals that should be reached to obtain that standard.

Common Criteria

The Common Criteria (CC) is a set of common points of comparison for evaluating and selecting security solutions for a particular network. ISO has put its name behind the Common Criteria, which gives it the same clout as the ISO 9000 series. Following the CC allows for a verifiable process to be followed and performed to ensure repeatable security implementation.

The Orange Book standards were brought about by the U.S. government some time ago and have become outdated by today's standards. The Common Criteria is intended to supersede or replace the Orange Book and to unify ITSEC and TCSEC. The CC is commonly known as ISO standard 15408 (IS15408), but it is also referred to as the Common Criteria 2.1 document. This document covers various objectives and ways to implement proper security. It is broken into the following three parts:

✦ **Part One:** Discusses how to generate proper security objectives and requirements. Also covers the general terminology used in the document.

✦ **Part Two:** Covers the details of the requirements lists that can help a company or organization communicate in a more secure fashion. It also shows how to sort the requirements into appropriate classes (such as authentication, encryption, and so on), families, which are more specific requirements (such as user and process authentication), and components (such as Kerberos and other items like Secure ID cards).

✦ **Part Three:** Discusses the procedures for the creation of "assurance components," which help a company address its current security requirements. Also outlines seven different Evaluation Assurance Level (EAL) requirements, which get progressively more detailed and extensive by level.

The three parts to the CC are very detailed and complex, but time spent reading the CC will benefit you as an auditor because you should know and understand the basics contained therein. IT professionals and security auditors use the information in the CC to perform the following tasks:

1. Outline the security needs and requirements of the company.

2. Specify a common vocabulary that everyone in IT and security can understand and use to convey the requirements of the organization's security needs.

3. Show the need to implement common procedures that will help evaluate a network, site, or security product.

4. Help verify the features and abilities that various security software and hardware manufacturers supply with their products.

The following list outlines the terminology and concepts that security auditors should know.

✦ **Protection Profile (PP):** An organized list of network services and components that are required by the network or systems. This profile can include security objectives.

✦ **Security Objectives:** A general statement that describes a rough outline of how to fix a particular vulnerability. Keep in mind that the statement should be general, as there will usually be a more detailed outline on how to fix the vulnerability later in the report.

✦ **Security Target (ST):** The ST lists the abilities that have been specified by a software manufacturer to measure the usefulness of their particular security tool(s). This list is different from a security objective or security requirement; a requirement is the actual specifications that have been placed upon a product, and the objective is the overall security goal that has been outlined by the security auditor.

✦ **Target of Evaluation (TOE):** The actual system(s), network, hardware, or piece of software that will be the object of your security audits. Using the security objectives, combined with the security target, should help you figure out if the TOE meets the set objectives and if it actually performs its intended functions.

✦ **Packages:** Any reusable component (software or otherwise) that will allow a security auditor to implement the requirements of a security objective. An example of a package is the seven Evaluation Assurance Levels. It is quite common and acceptable to combine any number of the seven evaluation levels to ensure that security targets or requirements are met or exceeded.

✦ **Evaluation Assurance Level (EAL):** The seven packages that have been outlined to help security auditors and IT personnel look at and evaluate security on existing networks and systems, as well as networks and systems on the drawing board. The following section looks at the various EAL levels.

Evaluation Assurance Levels

The Evaluation Assurance Levels provide a universally acceptable way to outline and profile the security behavioral patterns of a system or network. The EAL works on a rising scale — the higher the number, the more stringent the requirements are to meet that level.

EAL level 1 may only require that any claims of the TOE are verified by the manufacturers. EAL level 7 requires that the security auditor actually verify and completely document every step taken when implementing the various TOE. Whenever the EAL level increases in number (for example, 1 to 2) two requirements in the EAL always get more detailed and stringent in their application:

✦ **Verification of design and abilities.** At EAL level 1, the only requirement is that the product documentation be read and understood. At EAL level 7, the software or hardware needs to be fully inspected, documented, and confirmed to work as it should.

✦ **The ability to withstand inbound attacks against the system.** EAL level 1 only requires that the software or hardware claim that it will offer the ability to protect against attacks. EAL level 7 requires that the software or hardware undergo a rigorous battery of attacks and tests to see if system integrity, data, and general provision of services can be kept intact.

The following list provides a general outline of the seven different EAL categories and shows the increasing scrutiny each level provides.

✦ **EAL level 1:** At this level, the product is only tested for functionality. This level requires basic investigation into the product's intended abilities, usually with a test installation of the TOE.

✦ **EAL level 2:** At this level, the product is required to be structurally tested. This usually means that someone with the appropriate qualifications, such as an application developer or expert, tests the key abilities of the TOE.

✦ **EAL level 3:** At this level, the product should be tested and verified in a planned and efficient manner. EAL level 3 usually requires that the person that performs the tests fall under certain, stricter guidelines than are in EAL level 2. For instance, you could have an engineer who is certified with the product perform the tests. Now, all main components of the system must be tested and verified independently of each other, although it is not required that every component be tested.

✦ **EAL level 4:** Level 4 takes a large step forward, requiring that the TOE be methodically tested and reviewed in a well-designed format. This is the highest level of assurance that can be obtained while still using existing applications and systems that were previously deployed to implement the EAL assurance levels. EAL level 4 also requires that any existing and new systems weather a low-level set of attacks without failure.

✦ **EAL level 5:** This level takes the core outline from Level 4 and adds to it. To gain this level, the software or system must be designed and tested under semi-formal conditions. Software and systems must also handle a slightly more difficult series of attacks.

✦ **EAL level 6:** Software or systems must be semi-formally designed and tested, and the results must be verified. Level 6 is the same as level 5, except that a third party must verify the TOE design and abilities.

✦ **EAL level 7:** The system has to be completely reviewed, fully tested, and able to weather the most sophisticated attacks. At this level, the product must be formally verified and tested to ensure that the process used to develop the product is properly and completely structured. A third party should not only verify, but document, all related procedures, including any correspondence used during the testing and verifying stages.

Router Security Upgrades

Security routers on the client's network should be among the top items included in your security audit. A few simple steps improve security on routers. The following four points should be kept in mind with basic router security:

✦ Ensure that proper physical security is followed. All the security settings in the world won't do any good if someone can easily plug in to the router.

✦ When dealing with software-based routers, such as Windows NT, multi-homed routing setups, and hardware router operating system software like Cisco's IOS, make sure to download the latest patches and system upgrades that are designed to improve security.

✦ Make sure that the router isn't vulnerable to DoS or DDoS attacks. A router that is susceptible to these types of attacks can be taken out with relative ease by just about anyone. One way to improve its defense against DoS attacks is to disable broadcasting on the router.

The information in the following section outlines detailed steps to ensure that your routers are not vulnerable to the types of crippling DoS and DDoS attacks mentioned earlier.

Ingress and Egress filtering

Set up your router to only route outgoing packets if they have a valid internal IP address. By rule, your routers should disregard and drop any outgoing packet that isn't originating from a valid internal IP address. When you perform this setting change, you will effectively prevent your network from becoming a participant in any spoofing attacks.

Set up your routers to drop any packets that originate from the list below:

✦ Historical Low End Broadcast: 0.0.0.0/8

✦ Limited Broadcast: 255.255.255.255/32

✦ RFC 1918 Private Network: 10.0.0.0/8

✦ RFC 1918 Private Network: 172.16.0.0/12

✦ RFC 1918 Private Network: 192.168.0.0/16

✦ The Loop back (test) address: 127.0.0.0/8

✦ Link Local Networks: 169.254.0.0/16

✦ Class D Addresses: 224.0.0.0/4

✦ Class E Reserved Address: 240.0.0.0/5

✦ Unallocated Address: 248.0.0.0/5

There may be other addresses that need to be blocked by your router. However, the addresses listed above should provide good protection against DoS and/or spoofing attacks.

Disable broadcast filtering

DoS attacks and Distributed DoS attacks often gain more clout if a hacker can use many routers that have been set up to provide directed IP broadcasts; this includes most DoS attacks, including the Smurf attack covered in previous chapters. You can quickly discern if the router in question will respond to these types of addresses by sending a ping to either the network address (for example, 192.168.4.0) or the network broadcast address (for example, 192.168.4.225).

Tip   With the rise in popularity of DoS and DDoS attacks, many sites will have already made the appropriate adjustments to these router settings. However, always make sure that they have been adjusted accordingly. Also, keep informed about the latest vulnerabilities that may affect your router's security (software or otherwise).

Using Proactive Intrusion Detection

As discussed in previous sections, proactive detection enables a security auditor to implement specific strategies that allow the target network to turn a hacker's activities against him, instead of just stopping the attack.

Like any good intrusion detection policy, proactive intrusion detection should include auditing of system, objects, and access. It should further assist in detecting problem areas and help determine solutions to the problems you have encountered by deduction.

Scan detection, honey pots, and jails

Many intrusion detection or honey pot software packages on the market allow you to generate dummy accounts, files, system services, and sometimes even fake networks that will appear to be running valid targets, ripe for infiltration. If set up properly, these dummy accounts will be irresistible to a hacker.

False networks or honey pot systems will usually cause a hacker to run around in circles, limiting the progress he can make into the valuable areas of the network or systems. Once the hackers have gained access to a honey pot or a false network, a tripwire or alarm will usually notify the system administrator or security management team to the intrusion. At this point, logging information on the hacker's activities and connection information should be considered mandatory.

Honey pot systems or jails that assist administrators in counterintelligence and attacks against hackers will usually involve setting up a server as an open server with very weak security levels, although some software allows configuration of these options. These types of software packages and systems can also allow for these additional settings:

✦ Promiscuous mode scans.

✦ Fake database files.

✦ Dummy or bogus shadow password files.

✦ Dummy files in general (for example, spreadsheets containing employee data).

✦ Dummy administrator accounts, which should be a mandatory setting on any system.

✦ A firewall entry that will automatically take the hacker into a decoy network.

✦ Tripwires that alert administrators to the presence of hackers, or any number of automated actions.

✦ Reverse tracking of the hacker's location and network information. If possible, trace back to the exact originating network port or telephone line. (This usually requires assistance from your ISP or phone company.)

✦ Packet traces in order to locate the real legitimate origin of the packet, not the spoofed one (if the hacker used a spoofed IP).

Caution   Performing some of the aforementioned methods of proactive security intrusion detection may not be in your best interest. Some counterattacks may end up harming innocent parties, or hackers may take offence, causing them to redouble their efforts or damage the system in other ways. Don't suggest overly dramatic or vigilante forms of proactive security to your clients.

Detecting a network interface card in promiscuous mode

There are ways to ensure that you do not have a network interface card (NIC) operating in promiscuous mode on your systems or network. An NIC operating in promiscuous mode is an NIC that has been set up to "sniff" the network packets going by to try and catch information that is traveling from workstations to servers. To set an NIC in promiscuous mode, you must install a sniffing software program, such as Sniffer Pro, and set the software to collect data as it passes to and from the NIC. If the network is using hubs to connect all the systems together on the network, an NIC in promiscuous mode can catch a considerable amount of data as it passes through, and can allow a hacker to obtain login accounts, passwords, and other sensitive data.

On a regular un-switched network, every packet of data is sent to every system on the network until the appropriate system that requested the packet is found. If a hacker is watching, he can see most, if not all, data passed on the network. This can be prevented to a large degree by implementing switches on your network to replace any network hubs. Network switches route packets to the appropriate port and destination system, increasing network performance, and limiting potential sniffing activity.

Many common network sniffer applications, such as AntiSniff or Sniffer Pro, use three different methods to locate an NIC that is running in promiscuous mode.

   ✦ Detecting specific changes in the NIC's electrical field can indicate to the detection package that an NIC is running in promiscuous mode.

   ✦ As with fingerprinting a system, detection methods can include sending out various packet types, such as ARP requests, ICMP packets, DNS queries, TCP SYN floods, and more. If packets are coming back that have taken a long time to reply from a particular host, and the packets don't appear to have been read or modified by the recipient, then the software can usually determine if the target's system is operating its NIC in promiscuous mode.

   ✦ The software can also wrap a fake ICMP request within an invalid Ethernet header. Usually, most systems will reject just a fake header. However, if the NIC is running in promiscuous mode, it will likely return the fake request.

Because these types of sniffer programs use a small range of triggers to deduce whether an NIC is running in promiscuous mode, it is possible that the software will generate false positive results. Care should be taken when attempting to correct the "assumed" problem NIC.

When setting up automated, scheduled security audits, perform promiscuous mode detection sweeps. There are a few utilities that can be used for setting up the automated scans. L0pht Heavy Industries (@stake) even has its own scheduler program. However, you can also use Windows NT's built-in Scheduler service (if not disabled already) or the UNIX/Linux cron program. Any of these types of programs can be used to automate the promiscuous scans of your network.

Tip   LOpht Heavy Industries (@Stake) offers a UNIX version of AntiSniff, but it will compile and run only on FreeBSD Linux and Solaris UNIX–type operating systems.

Effective Host Auditing Strategies

Because every business and network is different, you must keep your audits as
close to your plan as possible, but also take these differences into consideration.
By keeping your clients' specific business needs in mind, you can develop a specialized audit that will determine the information you really need. Besides the specialized areas you may need to look at during an audit, you can always make the
following recommendations:

✦ **Implement native auditing.** Although there are many solid aftermarket auditing and logging utilities, recommending those built into the operating systems
is a good place to start and provide, at minimum, basic (often cryptic) logging. Event Viewer for Windows NT, for example, would be a form of native
auditing.

✦ **Install a security auditing monitoring software package.** Several very good
security-auditing packages exist on the market. Each go about their job in
slightly different ways, but setting up any of them to monitor security thresh-
olds on networks or systems is a great idea. Because network administrators
and security auditors can't be everywhere at once, these types of software
can notify administrators when something isn't right.

✦ **Clean up after poor installation practices.** Automated software installers may
not clean up after themselves very well, so inspect any temporary folders and
remove any leftover temporary files that you find. These files may also contain sensitive information, including administrative accounts, system services
accounts, and passwords.

✦ **Cleaning and re-instatement of compromised systems.** Sometimes you may
be called in after a hacker has been through some of the systems or network.
Check for and remove viruses, backdoor programs, and illicit servers such as
NetBus or BackOrifice that may be compromising the system. Once found,
document and remove them.

✦ **Replacing or updating services.** Some services can be replaced with more
secure services (for example, Telnet for SSH). Finding out if there is a security
update available for a specific service is a good start.

✦ **Installing add-ons and updates.** Fix known problems that can be patched or
repaired with fixes and service packs. While patching the operating system is
great, don't forget to check the installed applications as well.

In the
Real World   Make sure that both you and the client understand what will happen in the course
of your audit. For example, on some occasions, your clients may assume that you
will be fixing any problems that exist, whereas you may simply be performing an
assessment and giving recommendations. Performing a general outline of what
you will or will not do before you start is in the best interests of both parties.

Most anti-virus software packages do an effective job of locating and removing backdoor Trojan horses, viruses, and the like. Sometimes, though, anti-virus scanners can let something slip if they haven't been updated in time to catch the latest infection roaming the Internet. Other ways to discover and remove these types of rogue or stealth infections include:

✦ Using common, free TCP/IP network troubleshooting tools, such as netstat or even ping.

✦ Watching Windows Task Manager for unusual system resource usage, or unusual programs running as tasks.

✦ Using Telnet to inspect and test the status of conspicuous network ports.

✦ Continuing to use anti-virus software. (Ensure that it is kept up-to-date.)

Improving Overall Security

There is more to security than locking down corporate servers and routers. Looking at other areas of security, such as workstation or home user system security, can be just as important to your overall network security implementation.

Personal firewall software

 Install aftermarket security software, such as personal firewalls

Although the abilities of personal firewall software packages are usually pared down from their larger corporate-level brethren, much of today's personal firewall software is becoming more and more capable with every revision of this affordable software. Personal firewall software often has three important functions for home or small office users who are exposed to the Internet:

✦ Port blocking or filtering

✦ Connection trace to intruder or attacker

✦ Attack logging

Not only can personal firewall packages perform these duties, they can also be used to block certain IP address. This can be useful if you notice someone has been performing several attacks or probes, which can hint towards a larger, more concerted attack.

The market has been flooded with a wide array of personal firewall packages in recent months. Some of the more popular choices include:

✦ Network Ice's Black Ice (sometimes called Black Ice Defender)

✦ McAffee's Personal Firewall (formerly called ConSeal)

✦ Zone Lab's Zone Alarm

✦ Norton Internet Security 2001

An example of a popular personal firewall software package is Black Ice Defender, shown in Figure 21-1.

 Caution These software packages, once installed, can disable or limit access to services on some NT systems. If settings are not properly set during installation or are tampered with afterward, legitimate Internet access may be limited or disabled entirely.

Figure 21-1: Black Ice Defender is a fairly able personal firewall package that can effectively monitor and protect small networks.

Most of the self-touted personal firewall software packages are intended for single system or small office implementations. However, many of these newer packages, such as Black Ice, can be successfully used in larger environments.

Software companies that have a personal firewall package will usually offer a corporate-level package that should be used for larger networks or networks with sensitive data. These types of packages can often perform more duties than simple port filtering or IP blocking and should be considered mandatory on any medium to large network. A popular choice in corporate firewall software is Firewall-1 by Checkpoint Software.

IP security

Companies often look internally for possible hacking problems, and rightfully so. Users are far more computer savvy than they were five years ago. Thankfully, advances in network security can be implemented to stop hacking by internal as well as external sources.

One such advance is IPSec. PGP is a prime example of a basic IPSec implementation that has been around for over a decade. Windows 2000 also offers IPSec as part of its new network and system security features, which should merit some attention.

Several encryption packages are now available for personal or home use. Programs such as BestCrypt can help organizations and users ensure that the data in their directories or hard drives remains private and untouched. Most of these types of applications (like BestCrypt and PGP) are add-ons to existing system software or operating system components and are a large step forward in providing network and personal security and data encryption techniques.

End-to-end encryption

Companies may not want individual users to use personal encryption or security packages because the company or organization will not be able to control use or obtain access to important information if the user leaves that business. In addition, if data needs to be restored from backup after a long period of time, the software once used by an individual employee may not be in use anymore.

When recommending such products to clients, explain the benefits and manageability concerns of the product to ensure that they understand the possible risks and benefits. Most types of file or data encryption software will now allow for centralized management and/or an administrative "key" to unlock the encryption on a file if need be. Windows 2000 offers such a setup with their new Encrypting File System (EFS).

Auditing policies

 Set up auditing policies

Auditing is an essential part of any security implementation, which doesn't just stop at the operating system level. Auditing should (and can) be implemented for software, hardware, and other system and network components.

Although auditing could be applied on a Windows primary domain controller to audit the entire domain, local operating system security can be audited for failed logins, access control, system shutdowns, and other such activities. Auditing can even be applied to file and directory access on local systems and network shares.

Install security patches and fixes

Be aware of the major bugs that exist on systems and software today and know how to address them. Most operating system vendors offer hot fixes, patches, and service packs on a fairly frequent basis (some more often that others). Consider implementing IPv6 as previously discussed, or at least ensure that the latest functional TCP/IP stack is in use.

Tip   The Windows 95 TCP/IP stack has many security holes and vulnerabilities to DoS attacks and similar attacks that can be fixed with an update that patches not only the IP stack, but other related system networking components, and should be mandatory if the user is using VPN access to the host network.

Windows NT implementations prior to NT4 Service Pack 5 used a very predictable TCP sequencing scheme. Hackers could exploit this flaw by predicting the sequence and then hijacking the connection. Every number after the first randomly assigned sequence number increments by one, making the number easy to predict.

Although the new and improved sequencing brought in by SP5 is better, it still isn't as solid as that offered in current UNIX/Linux implementations. However, the current sequencing is a step forward, and updating past Service Pack 4 (currently SP6a) is a good idea.

Consider IPv6

IPv6 isn't ready for widespread distribution yet, because much of the Internet is still using older IP implementations. By switching to IPv6, you may take your system out of the loop entirely. However, the good news is that more and more is being done to bring this improved IP setup to mainstream use. IPv6 enables encryption and authentication and is supported by most major operating systems, including NT, Linux 6.1, and Solaris UNIX. Currently, using IPv6 may cause Internet-related services on the network to not work at all, or work with limited functionality. However, if the network is somewhat isolated from the Internet, it may be worthwhile to consider securing the network from some outside and internal hacking attempts.

IPv6 can provide:

✦ **Improved authentication:** A new authentication header improves protection from spoofing and hijacking of network connections.

✦ **Data encryption:** Using the new Encrypted Security Payload (ESP) header, IPv6 can help lessen exposure to network sniffing or exploratory network monitoring practices.

IPv6 is more detailed than what can be covered here, though there are many Request For Comments (RFC), Web sites, and white papers regarding this topic on the Internet.

Strengthening System and Network Services

 Strengthen system and network services

Undoubtedly, you will spend some time updating, removing, and replacing services on the systems and network. Keep the following items in mind when updating services:

✦ Don't just install a replacement service without looking into it a bit. When you install an untested service, you may encounter more problems than you think there are.

✦ Try to figure out how much time you will need to properly apply the changes or replacement services.

✦ Try to test the services or updates on a non-production server, rather than risk causing a problem on your live systems.

✦ Don't pay so much attention to one service that you don't find out if this service will affect anything else on the system — other services, software, or otherwise.

✦ Assess whether the changes will require additional user training.

Secure Shell

Secure Shell (SSH) can help secure useful services, such as Telnet or rlogin. By default, these services can cause security issues, but are useful for remote management of systems. The main problem with these services is that they send all the data in clear text, which will let anyone sniffing the connection to intercept the data being sent. Quite often, administrators will relegate themselves to disabling or removing these utilities from their systems for the sake of security; however they don't have to if they implement SSH to replace these types of services with secure types. SSH is more secure, due to its use of Public Key Encryption techniques.

Versions of SSH now exist for Macintosh Telnet implementations as well. The newer version, SSH2, is not directly compatible with SSH1 out of the box, so if you are operating with a mixed SSH setup, there are some additional settings that must be taken care of first.

Two valuable services are provided by implementing SSH.

✦ **Data privacy:** Data sent is encrypted. When data is sent, the server will initially send the server's public key to the client. Once the client has the key, it will encrypt the data against the server's key. The now encrypted data is sent back, and the server decrypts it using its private key that matches the public key sent initially.

✦ **Authentication services**: During this process, SSH will use keys that are different from the ones used during the data privacy stage. When users are trying to authenticate, they can send each other their keys to gain access to the necessary resources. The real benefit of this system is that no password or account information is transmitted across the wire at all — only keys.

Naturally, the authentication keys that are exchanged during the data transfer are not just sent out unprotected across the network; they are encrypted first in the data channel to ensure integrity of the keys.

SSH uses port 22 by default and is set up to allow usage of public-key encryption methods. The encryption method that SSH uses is similar in design to the RSA algorithm, but is not proprietary in design like RSA. SSH can now use RSA as well, because it has been made publicly available.

SSH was originally designed for secure UNIX/Linux communications, but there are now several Windows clients that support and can connect to a UNIX/Linux system that is using SSH.

Encryption and authentication using SSH

Once the initial encryption process is performed, further transactions between the systems are automatically encrypted for the session. SSH will first try to use the available public keys during authentication. If these keys are not found, SSH will switch over and use standard user names and passwords that are found in the standard UNIX/Linux password files. By default, SSH keys are usually kept in the $HOME/.ssh directory under each user's home drive (for example, /home/james/ .ssh2). This directory, for security reasons, will always be hidden so people can't easily find the keys if casually browsing directories.

Make sure that anyone using SSH has a proper key in their home directory. If SSH can't find the key, it will use normal account/password authentication, creating a risk that the password hashes will be captured along the way.

There are several components to SSH2; the following list shows some of the UNIX/Linux and NT components.

✦ **/usr/local/bin/ssh2:** Contains the actual SSH2 client program.

✦ **SSH Secure Shell Client:** Usually found under Program Files. There are many different types of Windows SSH clients available today.

✦ **/usr/local/bin/ssh-keygen2:** The key generator to create a pair of keys for every user.

✦ **/usr/local/bin/scp2:** The client that will allow execution of remote commands using SSH.

✦ **/usr/local/sbin/sshd2:** The main SSH2 daemon.

✦ **/usr/local/bin/ssh-agent2:** If you have a trust relationship with the server, this agent will allow logins without using passwords by saving the public keys in memory.

✦ **/usr/local/bin/sftp-server2:** A secure FTP server used by SSHD2. Some Windows clients can use this secure server.

✦ **/usr/local/bin/sftp2:** The main secure FTP client program.

One requirement of SSH is that there is an operating DNS structure set up to facilitate SSH. The DNS server is used to perform reverse DNS lookups, and if the DNS structure isn't working properly, the SSH implementation may fail to authenticate clients properly, or you may experience unpredictable behavior. This requirement shouldn't be out of line for most UNIX/Linux setups, because they usually require a proper DNS setup to authenticate connections.

Tip   If you have a mixed SSH and SSH2 environment, you can follow the instructions in the SSH2.quickstart file, which should be included with the product's documentation to facilitate a smooth and compatible SSH2 setup with existing SSH1 clients.

Upgrading to Windows 2000

Upgrading to Windows 2000 can bring about a wide range of security options; only a few extra security-related utilities that can be used in an upgrade to Windows 2000 have been previously mentioned. Although vulnerabilities may exist that have not been uncovered with Windows 2000, you do benefit from the fact that Windows 2000 is a relatively un-hacked operating system. That is not to say that Windows 2000 hasn't had its share of security issues. Numerous hot fixes and two service packs have already been released.

A wide range of features and possible pitfalls exist with an upgrade, and you would do well to read up on these issues before jumping headlong into an upgrade of any type. However, if you do decide to upgrade, you can take advantage of Active Directory with Group Policies. Group Policies are set up like the easier to manage Novell network operating system. You can also take advantage of Public Key Encryption, Encrypted File System, Kerberos authentication, and built-in IPSec.

If you do implement Windows 2000, you will be given a host of new and useful security features to play with, such as IPSec and Encrypted File System. As a security auditor, you should install and test the new features and see if they can benefit your client or fit in with their needs. Clients may not be willing to upgrade right away, but they can put it on the table after they have improved their overall network security.

Tip Windows 2000 security isn't much different than it was in Windows NT 4. Auditing, hiding administrator accounts, strong passwords, secure file systems such as NTFS, access control lists, operating system patching, and anti-virus protection are all still required elements for a successful, secure Windows 2000 upgrade.

Some people discount Windows 2000 security. They would prefer to have a properly hardened NT 4 server running, instead of a locked-down Windows 2000 system, because much of the holes in NT 4 are known and have a solution. This idea certainly has some merit, but it is up to you to draw an appropriate, educated stance on the subject.

Taking the time to research Windows 2000 security issues and other new security implementations, software, or hardware, will be worth your while and will ultimately help you become a more efficient security auditor.

Key Point Summary

This chapter discusses the various ways to assess the results of your audit. Once you have completed your audit, it is time to make your recommendations to the client. Knowing what options are available and how to present this data in a proper manner will go a long way towards shoring up your credibility as a security auditor.

✦ The three main areas that must be covered during your security audit are:

- Ways to implement appropriate security auditing on the host network.

- Location and removal of viruses and Trojan horse software.

- Recommendations geared towards the client's networks needs.

✦ Always include categories concerning firewalls, intrusion detection, host and personal security measures, and policy enforcement in your audit reports.

✦ Include a section in your audit report on the importance of good physical security measures.

✦ When writing auditing reports, keep the target audience in mind. The report should be written in such a way that non-technophiles could understand it.

✦ Government organizations and international standards organizations, such as the ISO, have generated sets of security standards in an effort to standardize security around the globe. Take some time to learn about the various government standards and those provided by other organizations.

✦ Learn the various security standards that are available. Understanding the Common Criteria can prove to be beneficial to understanding what the overall flow of a security implementation should be.

✦ Routers are vulnerable to many different attacks and should be paid attention to whenever possible. The first step is to ensure that the basic operating and system software is kept up-to-date. Then, make various configuration changes to help limit the chance of DoS and spoofing attacks using the router or attacking the router.

✦ Two items to look at when protecting your routers from attacks are Ingress and Egress filtering so that the router will only route packets that are actually from the host network. You should also disable broadcast filtering to limit the possibility of DoS and DDoS attacks.

✦ Proactive detection can be a very beneficial activity if used properly. Proactive detection enables a security administrator to locate the source of attacks or intrusions on the network or systems. Also, proactive detection can help ferret out security issues before they are even known.

✦ Honey pots and jails are a form of proactive detection that can help gather valuable information on a hacker and their activities. One caveat: if honey pots aren't operating properly, they can cause more trouble than good — for example, a honey pot can allow for reverse lookup of the hacker's address, but this could potentially be the address of an innocent bystander that was infiltrated.

✦ Caution should be used whenever proactive detection is in place, because it may sometimes cause hackers to detect traps that are set in place. Hackers may take offense at these traps, redoubling their efforts to break in or causing some other sort of damage.

✦ There are a few decent methods to detecting an NIC in promiscuous mode. These methods are typically performed in an effort to locate systems that may be set up to sniff your network. Network monitoring packages, such as Sniffer Pro, can often route out promiscuous network cards by using a set base of rules to compare their findings with. Although sometimes this information may be false, the information can help locate rogue sniffers.

✦ When developing host auditing strategies, try to stick to your usual plan of action, always keeping your client's specific business needs and desires in mind. Some security standards or settings can be applied to one site but not to another.

✦ When outlining the planned auditing strategy for the client's network, make sure that you and the client are both aware of the expectations and coverage the audit will encompass. Communicating your expectations upfront will limit possible incidents once the audit is complete.

✦ Personal firewall software is usually only intended for home use or small offices, but many new personal firewall products can do almost as much as some of the larger enterprise products.

✦ Besides port and IP filtering, personal firewalls can provide useful information about the attacker that can be used to either limit his activities or provide necessary information about these activities to the authorities.

✦ Personal firewalls should only be used for small networks and home users, whereas larger enterprise-class software should be used on medium- to large-sized networks, because they have a wider array of configuration options and built-in utilities, such as secure VPN access.

✦ IPSec can help network security by encrypting data sent to and from clients and servers. Although there are many different IPSec implementations available, including PGP and BestCrypt, newer operating systems like Windows 2000 are starting to include their own IPSec implementations.

✦ File encryption is becoming more common these days, although network management may have concerns over the ability to manage encrypted files in case of backup or loss of the original key used to lock it. Most file encryption methods will include some type of key management that allows for centralized control over key access. Learning the different options available will help you explain this topic to your clients more effectively.

✦ IPv6 is gathering a larger and larger audience. Keep in mind that by implementing IPv6 now, you may cause the loss of most Internet services, if not all of them, on your network. However, IPv6 will likely become even more popular, due to the various problems that are being found with older implementations of the IP stack.

✦ Old methods are good methods; take the time to recommend implementation of auditing, operating system, and software patches and updates. All of these areas must be taken care of before large-scale implementation of security can commence.

✦ SSH offers a more secure method of allowing use of Telnet and other regularly vulnerable but useful administrative utilities. Keep in mind that SSH is intended for UNIX/Linux use, but there are many Windows and some Macintosh clients available for use with UNIX/Linux servers.

✦ Upgrading to Windows 2000 can be a worthwhile effort if planned and applied accordingly. Windows 2000 offers many new security-geared features, such as IPSec, EFS, and Kerberos authentication. Securing Windows 2000 systems isn't much different than for NT 4 and other operating systems. However, attention must be paid to new vulnerabilities and their possible ramifications because Windows 2000 is a relatively new OS.

✦   ✦   ✦

STUDY GUIDE

This Study Guide presents eight assessment questions and one lab exercise to test your knowledge of the exam objectives.

Assessment Questions

1. Why is learning the various popular security standards an important step in trying to best assess the security needs of your clients?

    A. Allows for more complete reporting.

    B. Shows the client what you can do.

    C. Clients may require one or more of the standards in place.

    D. The government may audit your report for accuracy.

2. What is the main goal of the Common Criteria?

    A. Providing further validation of your security auditing skill set.

    B. To help choose and evaluate security solutions.

    C. To show how to implement government security standards.

    D. The CC is required by the ISO for ISO 9000 certification.

3. Of the following items, which is NOT usually a function of proactive intrusion detection packages or setups?

    A. Fake databases as a decoy

    B. Dummy administrative accounts and passwords

    C. Physical line tracing of intruders

    D. Reverse DoS attacks against intruders

4. What is the main problem with older implementations of NT TCP sequencing?

    A. After the initial random sequence, all following numbers in the sequence were the initial number plus one.

    B. The first number was randomized in a predictable pattern.

    C. It wasn't compatible with Windows 9x sequencing.

    D. It would send the data in clear text when prompted to.

5. Personal firewall software packages can be used on enterprise servers. True or False?

6. Telnet can be used to help clean up or detect backdoor or Trojan software. True or False?

7. Audit reports should be full of lingo and technical information to impress the client. True or False?

8. EAL categories get tougher and more stringent the lower the number (for example, EAL level 4 is more involved that EAL level 5). True or False?

Lab Exercise

Lab 21-1 Installing an SSH server to replace Telnet under UNIX/Linux

1. Obtain the SSH installation files (for quick and easy access, you can download them from www.ssh.com).

2. Once you have received the files, unzip and untar them. (For example, gunzip ssh-2.0.x.tar.gz and then tar –xvf ssh-2.0.x.tar)

3. When the files are unpacked, gunzip should create a directory named after the tar file (ssh-2.0.x). Change into this directory and compile SSH using the ./configure command. Issue the make command to finish the building process.

4. The make process may take a few minutes, but once it's done, you will want to install SSH. Issue the make install command and SSH will generate the public and private keys for the server itself.

5. Once the keys have been generated, start the server by executing /usr/local/sbin/sshd2. The SSH server should now be active and waiting for use.

6. You may want to add the above command line to the rc.local file using a text editor so that Linux will launch the SSH server every time the system is booted up.

Answers to Chapter Questions

Chapter Pre-Test

1. A very important first step in securing a router is ensuring that physical access to the router is restricted or secured in one way or another. If the router can be accessed, it's easy for someone to connect in with a laptop and make changes or even worse, physically vandalize the unit.

2. The main difference between passive and proactive intrusion detection is that with proactive detection, you use the hacker's strategies against him, instead of just stopping an attack in progress or simply monitoring the activity.

3. A few pieces of software can locate NICs that are in promiscuous mode; among the popular choices are AntiSniff or Sniffer Pro.

4. Often, when there have been poor installation practices, temp files and the like may contain user account information, including passwords to sensitive system services and administrative accounts.

5. Personal firewall software is useful for blocking port activity (both inbound and outbound), and performing connection traces back to the intruder, thus helping source more information on the nature of the attack.

6. One key function that SSH provides is data privacy. By encrypting the data channel, the SSH server can perform authentication in a secure channel, minimizing possible sniffing of network logins and passwords. Another useful function of SSH is authentication using public keys so account information isn't sent over the wire.

7. Among the utilities you can use to help clean up infections, Trojan horse programs, and backdoor software packages, is TCP/IP software, such as netstat — included in every Windows installation since Windows 95. Another useful utility is Telnet, which can be used to connect to ports located with netstat.

8. When implementing IPv6, there is always the possibility that you could lose the use of one or more Internet services, with the chance that you may take the network "offline" entirely.

9. The one piece of software that is a basic implementation of IPSec technology is PGP. PGP has been around for more than ten years, making it one of the veterans of Internet security utilities.

10. SSH requires DNS to operate properly (because it uses DNS to authenticate systems properly). Most versions of UNIX/Linux use DNS anyway, so just make sure that the DNS services are installed properly and functioning correctly.

Assessment Questions

1. **C.** Clients may require one or more of the standards in place. Learning about the various security standards that are available is useful, because clients may already have implemented some or all of the standards and you may be required to pick up the security standards implementation where someone else left off. Clients may also quiz you on the standards if they have been considering that path when they hired you.

2. **B.** Helps choose and evaluate security solutions. By using the Common Criteria outlines, you can properly assess what security solutions you will use and which will benefit your client the most.

3. **D.** Reverse DoS attacks against the intruder. Although a vigilante security administrator may use the information gleaned from proactive intrusion detection to perform a DoS attack, it isn't usually a feature that is implemented in any type of proactive intrusion detection software package.

4. **A.** After the initial random sequence, all numbers after the initial number generated were plus one. This method of sequencing often allowed patient hackers the ability to hijack connections once they figured out the initial random number in the sequence, because all later numbers were always in a predictable format, not randomized like the initial number.

5. **A.** True. This is a bit of a trick question. Personal firewall software packages can be used on enterprise class servers. However, it is recommended that you don't do so. Although they can provide the basics of firewall security, they usually lack the robustness and features of a proper enterprise class firewall package.

6. **A.** True. Telnet can be used to connect to ports that you are unsure of. NetBus and the like always have ports open to listen for connections. If you have done a scan and find odd ports, you can try using Telnet to connect to the port and see what answers.

7. **B.** False. People with little to no technical knowledge usually end up reading audit reports. Although there should be technical information included for the IT department and managers, the main report should read like a business presentation, with just the right amount of lingo and technical information to give a proper presentation, but not so much to make people go to sleep.

8. **B.** False. Evaluation Assurance Levels always become more stringent the higher the number. (For example, EAL level 7 is the highest, whereas EAL level 1 is the lowest).

For More Information

For more information on the topics in this chapter, look at the following links.

✦ To gather more information on ISO standards, check out `www.iso.ch`.

✦ For one of the best places to learn about the Common Criteria, check out `http://csrc.nist.gov/cc/index.html`.

✦ More information on protecting against DoS attacks can be found at the informative SANS site `www.sans.org/dosstep/index.html`.

✦ Extensive information on Ipv6, including any and all RFC (Request for Comments) documents, can be had at `www.ipv6.org`.

What's on the CD-ROM

This appendix details the contents of the CD-ROM that accompanies this book.

Foundstone

The following Foundstone products are on the CD:

- ◆ SuperScan 3.0
- ◆ Vision
- ◆ The Forensic ToolkitTM
- ◆ NTLast
- ◆ DDoSPing
- ◆ FScan
- ◆ UDPFlood
- ◆ Blast
- ◆ NTOMax

Descriptions for these products follow.

SuperScan 3.0

SuperScan 3.0 is a TCP port scanner, pinger, and hostname resolver.

For additional product information, visit http://www.foundstone.com/rdlabs/proddesc/superscan.html.

Vision

Vision checks all open TC and UDP ports, and documents activity on them.

For additional product information, visit `http://www.foundstone.com/products/proddesc/vision.html`.

The Forensic Toolkit

The Forensic Toolkit is a file properties analyzer that examines files for unauthorized activity, lists files by their last access time, searches for access times during specified time frames, and scans for hidden files, data streams, dump files, and security attributes.

For additional product information, visit `http://www.foundstone.com/rdlabs/proddesc/forensic-toolkit.html`.

NTLast

NT Last is a security log analyzer that identifies and tracks system access and documents the details. It also provides advanced auditing and tracking features.

For additional product information, visit `http://www.foundstone.com/rdlabs/proddesc/ntlast.html`.

DDoSPing

DDoSPing is a network administration utility that is able to remotely detect many common DDoS programs.

For additional product information, visit `http://www.foundstone.com/rdlabs/proddesc/ddosping.html`.

FScan

The Windows-based FScan utility is a command-line port scanner that scans over 200 TCP and UDP ports per second.

For additional product information, visit `http://www.foundstone.com/rdlabs/proddesc/fscan.html`.

UDPFlood

UDPFlood sends a controlled rate of UDP packets to a specified IP address.

For additional product information, visit http://www.foundstone.com/rdlabs/ proddesc/udpflood.html.

Blast

Blast is a tool that performs stress tests on the TCP service to identify potential weaknesses.

For additional product information, visit http://www.foundstone.com/rdlabs/ proddesc/blast.html.

NTOMax

NTOMax is a server stress-testing tool that takes a text file as input and runs your network server through tests based on that input to find buffer overflows.

For additional product information, visit http://www.foundstone.com/rdlabs/ proddesc/ntomax.html.

eEye Digital Security's Retina

Retina is a network security scanner that inspects your network for intrusions, including DoS attacks, Trojan horses, and viruses. Retina also secures vulnerable system services, such as protocols, Registries, and network and database services.

For additional product information, visit http://www.eeye.com/html/Products/ Retina/index.html.

Visualware Inc.'s VisualRoute

VisualRoute incorporates a number of utilities to analyze and secure Internet connections.

For additional product information, visit http://www.visualware.com/ visualroute/index.html.

Internet Security Systems, Inc.'s ISS Internet Scanner

Internet Scanner 6.1 performs an analysis of network services and devices to determine their status and vulnerabilities. In addition to its scanning and analysis capabilities, Internet Scanner 6.1 is able to suggest corrective action when breaches are discovered.

For additional product information, visit http://documents.iss.net/manuals/IS_UG_6.1.pdf.

Fyodor's NMAP

NMAP is a comprehensive port-scanning utility that checks for just about every type of security hole. Additionally, it has a dedicated newsgroup that discusses the product and security issues; subscribe at nmap-hackers-subscribe@insecure.org.

For additional product information, visit http://www.insecure.org/nmap/index.html.

Fping for Linux

Fping, similar to an FTP application, is an ICMP-based utility that determines whether a host is responsive.

For additional product information, visit http://www.fping.com/.

Adobe Systems, Inc.'s Acrobat Reader 5.0

Acrobat Reader 5 allows you to view files in Adobe PDF format.

For additional product information, visit http://www.adobe.com/products/acrobat/readstep.html.

✦   ✦   ✦

Objective Map

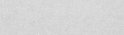

The following table lists the exam objectives for the CIW Security Professional certification exam. It is an exhaustive cross-reference that links each exam objective to the corresponding chapter and section in this book where the subject matter is covered.

Exam Objective	Chapter	Section
Discuss data integrity	1	Integrity
Define data confidentiality	1	Confidentiality
Explain the need for security	1	What are You Protecting Against?
List hacker motivations	1	Sources of Attacks
Describe how increased security mechanisms can result in increased latency	1	Understanding Security Issues and Risks
Define authentication; explain access control; discuss data integrity; define data confidentiality; explain non-repudiation	1	Security Services
Identify security-related organizations, warning services, and certifications	1	Security Organizations
Understand the major Authentication authentication methods	2	User
Identify the three main encryption methods	2	Encryption
Understand the need for access control	2	Access Control
Understand the function Listsof an access control list	2	Access Control
Understand the purpose of auditing	2	Auditing

Continued

Exam Objective	Chapter	Section (continued)
Understand the business impact of security solutions	2	Business Issues for Security
Understand the importance of trusts	3	Understanding Encryption and Trusts
Understand symmetric, asymmetric, and hash encryption	3	Encryption Techniques and Technologies
Understand different encryption algorithms	3	Symmetric-key encryption
Understand how digital signatures work	3	Digital Signatures
Understand the use of digital certificates and signatures	3	Digital Certificates
Deploy PGP in Windows NT and Linux	3	PGP
Understand how SSL and S-HTTP work	3	Web Server Encryption
Deploy PGP in Windows NT and Linux	3	Lab 3-1
Deploy PGP in Windows NT and Linux	3	Lab 3-6
Understand the TCP/IP protocol stack	4	TCP/IP Security Issues
Explore the OSI Model	4	TCP/IP DARPA Model and the OSI Model
Examine specific protocols and their exploits	4	Security issues with TCP/IP— DARPA in depth
Understand TCP/IP handshaking	4	TCP Handshake
Review common TCP and UDP ports and their use	4	TCP/IP Servers and Daemons
Understand IP address classes	4	TCP/IP Addressing
Deconstruct TCP/IP packets	4	The TCP/IP Packet Structure
Categorize Denial-of-Service attacks	4	Denial-of-Service Attacks

Exam Objective	Chapter	Section
Understand the different types of security attacks	5	Understanding Attacks and Security Incidents
Identify attack incidents	5	Understanding Attacks and Security Incidents
List the main types of viruses	5	Viruses
Understand why buffer overflow attacks are so dangerous	5	Buffer Overflows
List the contents of a root kit	5	Root Kits
Understand how humans are the weakest link	5	Social Engineering
Understand the importance of controlling information leakage	5	Unauthorized Access to Sensitive Information
Define and describe a firewall	6	What is a Firewall?
Understand the purpose of a firewall and the role it plays in a company's security policy	6	What Does a Firewall Do?
Define common firewall terms, such as NAT and DMZ	6	Firewall Terminology
Understand packet filters	6	Packet Filters
Understand stateful inspection	6	Stateful Inspection
Understand circuit-level gateways	6	Circuit-Level Gateways
Understand application-level gateways	6	Application-Level Gateways
Describe some advanced firewall functions and features	6	Advanced Firewall Features
Understand bastion hosts	7	Types of Bastion Hosts
Understand screened subnets	7	Common Firewall Designs
Understand screening routers	7	Screening Routers
Understand screened host	7	Screened Host Firewall (Single-Homed Bastion)

Continued

Exam Objective	Chapter	Section (continued)
Identify security issues and solutions specific to Windows NT	8	Windows NT Security Risks — Insecure Defaults
Identify security issues and solutions specific to Windows 2000	8	Windows 2000 Security Risks
Understand system scanning and footprinting	8	System Scanning and Footprinting
Identify security issues and solutions specific to UNIX	8	UNIX Security Risks
Examine security using the Network File System	8	Network File System
Understand the need for security in UNIX and Windows NT environments	9	Why is Security so Important?
Examine industry evaluation criteria used for security	9	Why is Security so Important?
Set guidelines for determining three general security levels	9	Levels of System Security
Implement security system mechanisms	9	Security Mechanisms
Explore the three different areas of security management	9	Managing System Security
Understand Windows NT default security	9	Windows NT "Out of the Box" Security
Use tools to evaluate Windows NT security	9	Tools to Evaluate Windows NT Security
Identify general threats to UNIX systems	9	UNIX and Linux Security
Implement operating system bug fixes and patches	10	OS Patches, Fixes, Uprevs, and Updates
Understand the Windows NT Registry and its security	10	Securing the Windows Registry
Describe the process of controlling Windows NT Services and Daemons	10	Dealing with Unnecessary Windows Services

Exam Objective	Chapter	Section
Describe the process of controlling UNIX Services and Daemons	10	Dealing with Unnecessary UNIX Services
Understand how to use audit logs in Windows NT to monitor your systems	10	Windows System Logging
Assign NTFS permissions	11	Securing NTFS
Understand the effects on permission of copying and moving files and folders	11	Permission-Handling for Move and Copy Operations
Control permissions for shares	11	Windows Share Security
Combine NTFS and Share permissions	11	Combining NTFS and Share Permissions
Create shares	11	Lab 11-3
Understand the relationship between account security and passwords	12	Password Security
Explain the different methods to secure accounts under Windows NT	12	Windows NT Account Security
Audit changes in accounts	12	Windows NT Authentication
Audit unsuccessful logon attempts under Windows NT	12	Windows NT Authentication
Rename default accounts under Windows NT	12	Windows NT Default Accounts
Implement password policies under Windows NT	12	Windows NT Account Policies
Explain the different methods to secure accounts under UNIX	12	UNIX Account Security
Describe UNIX password security	12	Storing Passwords and Accounts on a UNIX System
Identify how password aging works and the UNIX commands to accomplish password aging	12	Storing Passwords and Accounts on a UNIX System
Restrict account access and monitor accounts under UNIX	12	Storing Passwords and Accounts on a UNIX System

Continued

Exam Objective	Chapter	Section (continued)
Describe different UNIX security threats	12	Other UNIX Security Concerns
Describe UNIX password file format	12	Other UNIX-Based System Files
Identify common targets	13	Common Targets for Attack
Identify and analyze specific brute force, social engineering, and DoS attacks	13	Audit DoS Attacks
Implement methods to thwart penetration	13	Preventing DoS attacks
Understand penetration strategies and methods	13	Strategies for Penetration
Identify potential physical, operating system, and TCP/IP stack attacks	13	Physical
Understand the principles of intrusion detection	14	Understanding Intrusion Detection
Implement proactive detection	14	Automating IDS
Know how to distract crackers and contain their activity	14	Distracting Intruders
Set traps	14	Attracting Interest to Dummy Elements
Use a tripwire	14	Tripwires
Jail usage and considerations	14	Creating a Jail
Define intrusion detection	15	What is Intrusion Detection?
Differentiate between intrusion detection and automated scanning	15	What is Intrusion Detection?
Understand IDS errors	15	Errors
Understand the various categories of intrusion detection systems	15	Intrusion Detection Categories
Understand the importance of a formalized incident response policy	16	Understanding Incident Management
Learn how to develop your own incident response plan	16	Building an Incident Response Plan of Attack

Exam Objective	Chapter	Section
Identify critical resources for the Incident Response Policy	16	Assess your Circumstance
Identify groups and organizations that can help you in the event of a security incident	16	Communicate
Understand how you can learn valuable lessons from each incident	16	Evaluate Lessons Learned
Understand how to appropriately respond to a security incident	16	When an Incident Occurs
Understand risk	17	What is Risk?
Understand an auditor's duties	17	What Does an Auditor Do?
Understand the importance of a risk assessment	17	What is a Risk Assessment?
Understand the roles of an auditor	17	Auditor Roles and Perspectives
Understand footprinting and network discovery tools	18	Footprinting Utilities
Explain how to discover system hosts and the services they run	18	Network and Server Discovery Tools
Describe stack fingerprinting	18	Stack Fingerprinting
Scan for shares	18	Share Scans
Describe TCP/IP service vulnerabilities	18	TCP/IP Services
Implement network and vulnerability scanners	18	Security Scanning Suites
Describe host scanning versus network scanning	18	Host versus network
Deploy an enterprise scanner	18	Needs of the Enterprise
Define control phases	19	Phases of Control
Learn methods of control	19	Methods of Control
Audit unwanted control procedures and methods	19	Auditing to Prevent Unwanted Control

Continued

Exam Objective	Chapter	Section (continued)
Know how to perform a log analysis and identify critical security events	20	Understanding Log Analysis
Establish a baseline for log analysis	20	Building a Baseline
Understand the different types of logs and what they can contain	20	Key Logs for Analysis
Understand the difference betweendefault logging and auditing systems	20	Operating System Logs
Be able to use log filtering to view specific event types	20	Filtering Logs
Be able to set up auditing on a machine, and configure it to audit specific types of events	20	Enable Windows NT Auditing
Develop solutions drawn from specific network issues	21	Understanding the Results of the Auditing Process
Suggest a plan to improve security policy compliance	21	Understanding the Results of the Auditing Process
Generate security assessment reports	21	The Auditing Assessment Report
Learn security assurance standards	21	Auditing and Security Standards
Install aftermarket security software, such as personal firewalls	21	Personal Firewall Software
Set up auditing policies	21	Auditing Policies
Strengthen system and network services	21	Strengthening System and Network Services

✦   ✦   ✦

APPENDIX

Sample Exam

The sample exam included in this appendix will help prepare you for the exam. These questions are designed to reflect the style and content of the actual exam. Answers and explanations can be found at the end of the exam.

Sample Exam

1. What is a masquerading attack?

   A. An attack that records network information, modifies it, and sends it back to the network

   B. An attack that prevents legitimate users from accessing a server or service

   C. An attack in which the malicious program or host attempts to disguise their true identity

   D. An attack that is executed by another user, thereby creating a backdoor to the system

2. With which system security level is Windows NT compliant?

   A. A1

   B. B1

   C. C1

   D. C2

   E. D

3. In UNIX, what are the network applications called?

   A. Services

   B. Components

   C. Daemons

   D. Applets

4. Windows NT has the ability to secure items at the:

    A. Directory level

    B. File level

    C. File and directory level

    D. None of the above

5. Where are NT passwords stored?

    A. SAM database

    B. Registry

    C. Password file

    D. Password folder

6. Why are routers common targets of attack?

    A. They are funny looking.

    B. They are easily broken.

    C. They are usually the first item a hacker encounters.

    D. They capture all inbound traffic and are susceptible to viruses.

7. Why is proactive detection of problems on your network important?

    A. Break-ins usually occur when you are not around to monitor your network.

    B. Hackers are always trying to break in.

    C. If you aren't proactive, your security will fail from neglect.

    D. Someone who is proactive will take your job.

8. What IDS category can see all network traffic?

    A. Host IDS

    B. Application IDS

    C. Network IDS

    D. Integrated IDS

9. What should you never do during a security incident?

    A. Panic

    B. Document everything

    C. Call the CEO

    D. Invoke the Incident Response Plan

10. What is mitigating a risk?

    A. The process of implementing a solution or control that removes the threat

    B. Implementing a safeguard or control that lessens the severity of the risk

    C. Moving the consequences from your organization to a third party

    D. None of the above

11. Which of the following is not a part of the footprinting and discovery process?

    A. Whois queries

    B. Analyzing firewall logs

    C. Ping sweeps

    D. Share scans

12. What is usually the first and primary goal of intruders when they intrude on your system?

    A. To find pictures that could be used for extortion

    B. To locate connections to other networks

    C. To gain root or administrative access

    D. To delete critical system files

13. Where do you enable NT auditing?

    A. User Manager Tool

    B. System Monitor

    C. User Administrator

    D. Services

14. Why is learning the various popular security standards an important step in trying to best assess the security needs of your clients?

    A. It allows for more complete reporting.

    B. It shows the client what you can do.

    C. Clients may require one or more of the standards in place.

    D. The government may audit your report for accuracy.

15. A good security plan should be:

    A. Long and complicated

    B. Flexible, scalable, easy-to-use, and informative

    C. Scalable and easy-to-use

    D. Informative and flexible

16. Which of the following is an example of passive auditing?

    A. Disabling a login when attackers start port scanning the network

    B. Blocking access to a pornographic site when employees are discovered accessing it during the workday

    C. Shutting down the Telnet server discovered in a routine network port scan

    D. Examining log of invalid login attempts

17. You want to share large encrypted files with a small number of people. What encryption method should you choose?

    A. Symmetric

    B. Asymmetric

    C. Hash

    D. Digital

18. Which of the following protocols does NOT use plain text for communication?

    A. SMTP

    B. SSL

    C. Telnet

    D. HTTP

19. Your system resources suddenly skyrocket to 100 percent. You have most likely been the target of what type of attack?

    A. Trojan horse

    B. Denial of Service

    C. Spoof

    D. Man-in-the-middle

20. What firewall type provides no direct communication between the Internet and your internal network?

    A. Stateful inspection

    B. Packet filter

    C. Application-level gateway

    D. NAT

21. What firewall design is the most secure?

    A. Screened host, single-homed

    B. Screened host, dual-homed

    C. Screening router

    D. Screened subnet

22. What utility can be used to determine the operating system of a remote server?

    A. Ping

    B. Tracert

    C. Telnet

    D. Ifconfig

23. Which of the following is not a Windows NT object?

    A. File

    B. Process

    C. Floppy drive

    D. Printer

    E. Memory

24. Which groups are allowed to install printer drivers by default?

    A. Administrators

    B. Print operators

    C. Everyone

    D. All of the above

25. Which of the following is not an option for NTFS file level permissions?

    A. Read

    B. Execute

    C. Change permission

    D. Revoke ownership

26. What utility can be used to enforce strong passwords on Windows NT?

    A. L0phtcrack

    B. John the Ripper

    C. GetAdmin

    D. Passprop

27. Why are system bugs and trap doors hard to audit?

    A. They are often the result of regular system operation.

    B. Programmers are malicious and tend to hide flaws.

    C. They are both invisible to detection by anti-virus software.

    D. These types of problems are only found in games.

28. When setting up a dummy account, what system account should be the most important to rename?

    A. Administrator

    B. Guest

    C. Your account

    D. Exadmin

29. What is the worst type of error?

    A. False negative

    B. False positive

    C. Subversion

    D. None of the above

30. If you only do one thing during a security incident, what should it be?

    A. Call CERT

    B. Call the CEO

    C. Document everything

    D. Call the authorities

31. What is the purpose of an auditor?

    A. Fire employees for non-compliance

    B. Develop applications

    C. Take notes

    D. Assess risk

32. Windows systems communicate over which port?

    A. 139

    B. 21

    C. 113

    D. 80

33. There are different ways to obtain passwords. Which of the following is not a way that L0phtCrack can obtain the password hashes?

    A. Reading passwords from the SAM file taken from a repair disk (rdisk)

    B. Scanning the Registry of the local or remote system (with permissions)

    C. Connecting to each workstation and requesting passwords from the user (social engineering)

    D. Acting as man-in-the-middle and catching passwords as they go between clients and servers

34. Where are the default logs for Linux stored?

    A. /etc/services/log

    B. /Var/log

    C. /etc/http

    D. /usr/log

35. What is the main goal of the Common Criteria?

    A. Creates another standard set

    B. Helps choose and evaluate security solutions

    C. Shows how to implement government security standards

    D. Is required by the ISO for ISO 9000 certification

36. What security service provides a means of proving that a transaction occurred?

    A. Access control

    B. Authentication

    C. Non-repudiation

    D. Data confidentiality

37. You want to provide a strong, but accurate, level of authentication. Which is the best method to use?

    A. Fingerprints

    B. SecurID

    C. Reverse DNS

    D. Password

38. Which of the following algorithms is used for creating hash values?

    A. RSA

    B. DSA

    C. SHA

    D. DES

39. What port does SMTP use?

    A. 21

    B. 23

    C. 25

    D. 80

40. You receive a cartoon as an e-mail attachment that also installs a backdoor on your system when executed. What type of attack is this?

    A. Trojan horse

    B. Denial of Service

    C. Spoof

    D. Man-in-the-middle

41. Circuit-level gateways provide what key functionality?

    A. IP address translation

    B. Authentication

    C. Remote access

    D. VPN

42. What should you not remove from your bastion host?

    A. Unnecessary daemons and services

    B. NIC

    C. Administration programs

    D. Guest account

43. What are the two security threat categories?

    A. Accidental

    B. Controlled

    C. Intentional

    D. None of the above

44. What type of Access Control List (ACL) stores user and group permissions?

    A. Discretionary

    B. User

    C. System

    D. Secure

45. Which Registry subtree contains the user information?

    A. HKLM

    B. HKU

    C. HKCR

    D. HKCC

46. When you copy a file on an NTFS partition from one folder to another, what are the final permissions on the copied file?

    A. They are the same as they were in the original folder.

    B. Permissions are inherited from the destination folder.

    C. Permissions are inherited from another file in the destination folder.

    D. None of the above.

47. UNIX passwords, if not being shadowed, are stored in what file?

    A. /etc/user

    B. /etc/passwd

    C. /etc/account

    D. /etc/group

48. Buffer overflow attacks are dangerous because a hacker can do what?

    A. Crash the system permanently

    B. Upload system files while you reboot from the crash

    C. Erase all the data in the boot sector

    D. Launch malicious code in the leftover shell of a program

49. Typically, jails are used to achieve what result?

    A. Create a protected area for administrative files

    B. Punish users for forgetting their password

    C. Keep hackers online long enough to obtain connection information

    D. Rehabilitate hackers once they have been caught

50. Which of the following is not a characteristic of a good IDS?

    A. IDS must run continuously without supervision

    B. IDS must be accurate

    C. IDS must be static

    D. IDS must be fault-tolerant

51. After protecting the evidence of the attack, what is the next step in the Incident Response Plan?

    A. Preparing the report

    B. Assessing the situation

    C. Communication

    D. System recovery

52. What do compliance reviews ensure?

    A. Employees are following the security policy

    B. Employees are eating lunch every day

    C. Employees are being security-conscious

    D. Employees are not taking home confidential information

53. Which of the following is not considered social engineering?

    A. Calling the CEO's secretary and asking when the CEO will be in the office

    B. Sending an e-mail to all users saying they need to change their system password to "test"

    C. Performing a port scan on the system at 10.10.10.2

    D. Calling an employee and pretending to be a network administrator

54. What security mechanism disguises data characteristics to protect against traffic analysis?

    A. Authentication exchange

    B. Data integrity checks

    C. Digital signatures

    D. Traffic padding

55. What is the first step in creating a security policy?

    A. Classify your systems

    B. Determine security priorities

    C. Assign risk factors

    D. Define acceptable and unacceptable activities

56. Which of the following does asymmetric encryption use?

    A. The same key for encryption and decryption

    B. A different key for encryption and a different key for decryption

    C. A total of three keys

    D. A total of four keys

57. What port does the Telnet protocol use?

    A. 21

    B. 23

    C. 25

    D. 80

58. Which of the following is not considered a type of attack?

    A. Frontdoor or backdoor

    B. Active or passive

    C. Open or closed

    D. Internal or external

59. If you require specialized client software to communicate with servers on the Internet, what type of firewall do you have?

    A. Application-level gateway

    B. Packet filter

    C. Stateful inspection

    D. Screening router

60. What is a dual-homed host?

    A. A system with at least two network interfaces

    B. An application server

    C. A system with two monitors

    D. A system with no network interfaces

Answers

  1. C. In a masquerading attack, the malicious host or program attempts to access a secure system by pretending to be a trusted system.

  2. D. Windows NT can be configured to be C2-compliant.

  3. C. In UNIX, network applications are called daemons.

  4. C. Windows NT can secure at both the file and directory level when using the NTFS file system.

  5. A. Windows NT passwords are stored in the SAM database.

  6. C. Routers are usually the first item a hacker encounters. Typically, items exposed to the Internet will be hit first because they're easier for a hacker access.

  7. A. Proactive detection of problems is important because hackers will typically work when you are not. They are night owls and are always researching new vulnerabilities. Being proactive will help you keep up with the hackers — it might even gain you the upper hand.

  8. C. A network IDS can see all network traffic.

9. **A.** You should not panic during a security incident. This will only make you a less effective worker.

10. **B.** Mitigating a risk is implementing a safeguard or control that lessens the severity of the risk.

11. **B.** Analyzing firewall logs is not part of the footprinting/discovery process. It is part of the monitoring process that helps determine if a security breach has occurred.

12. **C.** The correct choice is gaining root or administrative access. Hackers will usually make a beeline for the administrative accounts. Although many nasty deeds can be done without administrative access, there are many obvious benefits to having it.

13. **A.** User Manager is used to enable auditing in Windows NT.

14. **C.** Clients may require one or more of the standards in place. Learning about the various security standards that are available can be useful, since clients may already have implemented some or all of the standards and you may be required to pick up where someone else left off.

15. **B.** A good security plan should be flexible, scalable, easy-to-use, and informative.

16. **D.** Passive auditing involves examining log files or other documents after the fact, looking for anomalies.

17. **A.** Symmetric encryption is much faster than asymmetric encryption. Since you have a small group of people, it is easy to manage the required keys.

18. **B.** SSL is the only protocol listed that uses encryption when sending data (such as usernames and passwords) over the network. The others use plain text.

19. **B.** A Denial-of-Service (DoS) attack can cause your system resources to increase to 100 percent.

20. **C.** An application-level gateway provides no direct access between the Internet and your internal network.

21. **D.** The screened subnet design is the most secure.

22. **C.** The Telnet utility can be used to access any open port on a remote system.

23. **C.** A floppy drive is not a Windows NT object.

24. **D.** All of the above.

25. **D.** You can take ownership, but you cannot revoke ownership.

26. **D.** Passprop can be used to help enforce strong passwords on Windows NT.

27. **A.** System bugs and trap doors often are results of regular system operation. Often, a trap door can lead to an unexpected vulnerability, due to the fact that the software does what it is supposed to.

28. A. Administrator is the first and probably most important account you should rename or create a decoy for. Other administrative accounts are important to rename or decoy, but at the very least, the common accounts such as Administrator and Guest should be modified, as well as service administrative accounts for programs like Backup Exec.

29. A. A false negative is the worst type of error. In this case, you have an attack you do not know about and cannot respond to.

30. C. Document everything. If you only do one thing during an incident, document everything. That way, if you talk to the authorities or CERT after the incident, you can give them specific details.

31. D. The main purpose of an auditor is to assess risk.

32. A. Port 139 is one of the ports Windows uses to communicate.

33. C. Connecting to each workstation and requesting passwords from the user (social engineering) is the correct answer. L0phtCrack cannot perform this function, although the other methods of getting password hashes are quite useful and usually work fine.

34. B. Default log files are stored on Linux in /Var/log.

35. B. The main goal is to help you choose and evaluate security solutions. By utilizing the Common Criteria outlines, you can properly assess what security solutions you will use and which will benefit your client the most.

36. C. Non-repudiation is the security service that proves a transaction occurred.

37. B. SecurID, or two-factor authentication, is the best answer. Biometrics provides strong authentication, but the technology is not very accurate. Passwords are more accurate than biometrics if the password is chosen well, but two-factor authentication provides a stronger level of authentication than a simple password. Reverse DNS is very weak and should never be considered as a means of authentication on a system containing information of any value.

38. C. SHA is a hashing algorithm.

39. C. The SMTP protocol uses port 25 for its communication.

40. A. A Trojan horse is an attack that appears to be benign, but actually performs a malicious act on your system.

41. A. Circuit-level gateways provide IP translations, also known as NAT.

42. B. You should not remove the NIC from a bastion host. This is what connects the system to the network.

43. A and C. The two threat categories are accidental and intentional.

44. A. User and group permissions are stored in the Discretionary ACL.

45. B. The correct answer is HKU.

46. B. Permissions are inherited from the destination folder.

47. B. UNIX passwords are stored in /etc/passwd.

48. D. Launch malicious code in the leftover shell of a program. Often when a buffer overflow occurs, a hacker may launch code in the leftover shell of the attacked program. Sometimes, this shell will have administrative or system access.

49. C. Jails can be used for many things, but most often they are used to obtain more information on the hacker and the source of the attack.

50. C. An IDS must not be static. It must be able to continuously evolve and adapt to a changing environment.

51. D. System Recovery is the correct answer. After protecting the evidence, you can put the system back into a trusted configuration and back into service.

52. A. Compliance reviews ensure that employees are following the companies' stated security policy.

53. C. Running a port scan is not considered social engineering.

54. D. Traffic padding is the security mechanism that disguises data characteristics to provide protection against traffic analysis.

55. A. Classifying your systems is the first step in developing a corporate security policy.

56. B. Asymmetric encryption uses a different key for encryption and decryption.

57. B. The Telnet protocol uses port 23 for its communication.

58. C. Open or closed is not an option for an attack.

59. A. Application-level gateways require special client software to connect to services on the Internet.

60. A. A dual-homed host is a system with at least two network interfaces.

✦   ✦   ✦

Exam Tips

Exam Prerequisites

The CIW Foundation Exam (1D0-410) is the prerequisite for the CIW Security Professional Exam. To achieve CIW Security Professional certification, you must pass both exams. Passing the Security Professional Exam alone will not result in certification.

Registration and Test Locations

Similar to all CIW exams, the Security Professional Exam is available worldwide through VUE and Prometric testing centers. You must register with either VUE or Prometric, schedule an exam appointment, and pay the candidate fee (price of the exam). Information on VUE and Prometric locations can be found at their respective Web sites:

- ◆ http://www.prometric.com/
- ◆ http://www.vue.com/

VUE

To register with VUE, obtain a CIW VUE login. After completing this process, register for the exam by clicking "Register for an exam."

Prometric

Obtain a Prometric Web User login from their Web site. When you have a login, select "Information Technology Certifications" from the drop-down menu.

Canceling an Exam Appointment

After you have registered for the exam, you will receive a confirmation, along with instructions on how to cancel the exam appointment. General cancellation information is provided in the following sections. Please defer to the instructions in your exam appointment confirmation materials in case of any discrepancies.

VUE

After you have registered for the exam, you can cancel it on the VUE Web site with 24 hours notice. If your appointment is less than 24-hours away, contact the testing center or a VUE agent directly. To locate the VUE agent closest to you, check out the VUE Telephone Directory, located on their Web site.

Prometric

Exams can be cancelled one business day prior to your scheduled exam appointment, before 7:00 p.m. CST.

Exam Cost

As of this writing, the fee for a CIW exam in the United States and Canada is $125. The exam fee outside the United States and Canada is approximately US $125, depending upon local currency exchange rates. Contact your testing center to determine the exact rate in your local currency.

Exam Length and Protocol

You have 75 minutes to complete the exam, which consists of 60 questions.

You are not allowed to bring any materials into the testing center. A pencil and scratch paper are available on request.

Getting Your Results

After you complete the exam, the results will be displayed on your testing station computer screen. A printed copy of your exam score is also available from the testing center staff. Make sure you save this copy for your records.

Passing the Exam

If you have already passed the Foundations Exam (1D0-410), you will be awarded Certified Internet Webmaster Professional (CIWP) status. You will receive your certificate four to eight weeks after passing the exam.

Failing the Exam

If you fail the exam, take notes on the exam topics you found especially difficult. Study these topics closely until you feel prepared to take the exam again.

You may retake the exam as many times as you like. However, you will have to pay the candidate fee ($125) each time you take it, so be sure you are prepared before you schedule another appointment.

What to Do If You Have a Problem or a Question on the Test

Thorough information on all CIW exams can be found at the CIW Web site.

If you cannot find the answer to your question there, contact the CIW Exam and Certification Department by sending an e-mail to exam@CIWcertified.com.

Other Exams

Once you pass the Server Administrator (1D0-450) and Internetworking Professional (1D0-460) exams, you will obtain Master CIW Administrator status.

✦   ✦   ✦

APPENDIX

Well-Known Ports

There are 65,536 different ports that can be used by applications to communicate over the network. These ports are divided into three groups:

- ✦ Well-known ports (0 through 1023)
- ✦ Registered ports (1024 through 49151)
- ✦ Dyname or Private ports (49152 through 65535)

All the well-known ports are listed in Table E-1. These ports are assigned by The Internet Assigned Number Authority (IANA), located at www.iana.org.

Table E-1 Well-Known Ports		
Keyword	**Decimal**	**Description**
Reserved	0/tcp	Reserved
Reserved	0/udp	Reserved
tcpmux	1/tcp	TCP Port Service Multiplexer
tcpmux	1/udp	TCP Port Service Multiplexer
compressnet	2/tcp	Management Utility
compressnet	2/udp	Management Utility
compressnet	3/tcp	Compression Process
compressnet	3/udp	Compression Process
Unassigned	4/tcp	Unassigned
Unassigned	4/udp	Unassigned
rje	5/tcp	Remote Job Entry
rje	5/udp	Remote Job Entry
Unassigned	6/tcp	Unassigned
Unassigned	6/udp	Unassigned

Continued

Table E-1 *(continued)*

Keyword	Decimal	Description
echo	7/tcp	Echo
echo	7/udp	Echo
Unassigned	8/tcp	Unassigned
Unassigned	8/udp	Unassigned
discard	9/tcp	Discard
discard	9/udp	Discard
Unassigned	10/tcp	Unassigned
Unassigned	10/udp	Unassigned
systat	11/tcp	Active Users
systat	11/udp	Active Users
Unassigned	12/tcp	Unassigned
Unassigned	12/udp	Unassigned
daytime	13/tcp	Daytime (RFC 867)
daytime	13/udp	Daytime (RFC 867)
Unassigned	14/tcp	Unassigned
Unassigned	14/udp	Unassigned
Unassigned	15/tcp	Unassigned
Unassigned	15/udp	Unassigned
Unassigned	16/tcp	Unassigned
Unassigned	16/udp	Unassigned
qotd	17/tcp	Quote of the Day
qotd	17/udp	Quote of the Day
msp	18/tcp	Message Send Protocol
msp	18/udp	Message Send Protocol
chargen	19/tcp	Character Generator
chargen	19/udp	Character Generator
ftp-data	20/tcp	File Transfer [Default Data]
ftp-data	20/udp	File Transfer [Default Data]
ftp	21/tcp	File Transfer [Control]
ftp	21/udp	File Transfer [Control]

Keyword	Decimal	Description
ssh	22/tcp	SSH Remote Login Protocol
ssh	22/udp	SSH Remote Login Protocol
telnet	23/tcp	Telnet
telnet	23/udp	Telnet
	24/tcp	Any private mail system
	24/udp	Any private mail system
smtp	25/tcp	Simple Mail Transfer Protocol
smtp	25/udp	Simple Mail Transfer Protocol
Unassigned	26/tcp	Unassigned
Unassigned	26/udp	Unassigned
nsw-fe	27/tcp	NSW User System FE
nsw-fe	27/udp	NSW User System FE
Unassigned	28/tcp	Unassigned
Unassigned	28/udp	Unassigned
msg-icp	29/tcp	MSG ICP
msg-icp	29/udp	MSG ICP
Unassigned	30/tcp	Unassigned
Unassigned	30/udp	Unassigned
msg-auth	31/tcp	MSG Authentication
msg-auth	31/udp	MSG Authentication
Unassigned	32/tcp	Unassigned
Unassigned	32/udp	Unassigned
dsp	33/tcp	Display Support Protocol
dsp	33/udp	Display Support Protocol
Unassigned	34/tcp	Unassigned
Unassigned	34/udp	Unassigned
	35/tcp	Any private printer server
	35/udp	Any private printer server
Unassigned	36/tcp	Unassigned
Unassigned	36/udp	Unassigned

Continued

Table E-1 *(continued)*

Keyword	Decimal	Description
time	37/tcp	Time
time	37/udp	Time
rap	38/tcp	Route Access Protocol
rap	38/udp	Route Access Protocol
rlp	39/tcp	Resource Location Protocol
rlp	39/udp	Resource Location Protocol
Unassigned	40/tcp	Unassigned
Unassigned	40/udp	Unassigned
graphics	41/tcp	Graphics
graphics	41/udp	Graphics
name	42/tcp	Host Name Server
name	42/udp	Host Name Server
nameserver	42/tcp	Host Name Server
nameserver	42/udp	Host Name Server
nicname	43/tcp	Who Is
nicname	43/udp	Who Is
mpm-flags	44/tcp	MPM FLAGS Protocol
mpm-flags	44/udp	MPM FLAGS Protocol
mpm	45/tcp	Message Processing Module [recv]
mpm	45/udp	Message Processing Module [recv]
mpm-snd	46/tcp	MPM [default send]
mpm-snd	46/udp	MPM [default send]
ni-ftp	47/tcp	NI FTP
ni-ftp	47/udp	NI FTP
auditd	48/tcp	Digital Audit Daemon
auditd	48/udp	Digital Audit Daemon
tacacs	49/tcp	Login Host Protocol (TACACS)
tacacs	49/udp	Login Host Protocol (TACACS)
re-mail-ck	50/tcp	Remote Mail Checking Protocol
re-mail-ck	50/udp	Remote Mail Checking Protocol

Keyword	Decimal	Description
la-maint	51/tcp	IMP Logical Address Maintenance
la-maint	51/udp	IMP Logical Address Maintenance
xns-time	52/tcp	XNS Time Protocol
xns-time	52/udp	XNS Time Protocol
domain	53/tcp	Domain Name Server
domain	53/udp	Domain Name Server
xns-ch	54/tcp	XNS Clearinghouse
xns-ch	54/udp	XNS Clearinghouse
isi-gl	55/tcp	ISI Graphics Language
isi-gl	55/udp	ISI Graphics Language
xns-auth	56/tcp	XNS Authentication
xns-auth	56/udp	XNS Authentication
	57/tcp	any private terminal access
	57/udp	any private terminal access
xns-mail	58/tcp	XNS Mail
xns-mail	58/udp	XNS Mail
	59/tcp	any private file service
	59/udp	any private file service
Unassigned	60/tcp	Unassigned
Unassigned	60/udp	Unassigned
ni-mail	61/tcp	NI MAIL
ni-mail	61/udp	NI MAIL
acas	62/tcp	ACA Services
acas	62/udp	ACA Services
whois++	63/tcp	whois++
whois++	63/udp	whois++
covia	64/tcp	Communications Integrator (CI)
covia	64/udp	Communications Integrator (CI)
tacacs-ds	65/tcp	TACACS-Database Service
tacacs-ds	65/udp	TACACS-Database Service

Continued

Table E-1 *(continued)*

Keyword	Decimal	Description
sql*net	66/tcp	Oracle SQL*NET
sql*net	66/udp	Oracle SQL*NET
bootps	67/tcp	Bootstrap Protocol Server
bootps	67/udp	Bootstrap Protocol Server
bootpc	68/tcp	Bootstrap Protocol Client
bootpc	68/udp	Bootstrap Protocol Client
tftp	69/tcp	Trivial File Transfer
tftp	69/udp	Trivial File Transfer
gopher	70/tcp	Gopher
gopher	70/udp	Gopher
netrjs-1	71/tcp	Remote Job Service
netrjs-1	71/udp	Remote Job Service
netrjs-2	72/tcp	Remote Job Service
netrjs-2	72/udp	Remote Job Service
netrjs-3	73/tcp	Remote Job Service
netrjs-3	73/udp	Remote Job Service
netrjs-4	74/tcp	Remote Job Service
netrjs-4	74/udp	Remote Job Service
	75/tcp	Any private dial out service
	75/udp	Any private dial out service
deos	76/tcp	Distributed External Object Store
deos	76/udp	Distributed External Object Store
	77/tcp	any private RJE service
	77/udp	any private RJE service
vettcp	78/tcp	vettcp
vettcp	78/udp	vettcp
finger	79/tcp	Finger
finger	79/udp	Finger
http	80/tcp	World Wide Web HTTP
http	80/udp	World Wide Web HTTP

Keyword	Decimal	Description
www	80/tcp	World Wide Web HTTP
www	80/udp	World Wide Web HTTP
www-http	80/tcp	World Wide Web HTTP
www-http	80/udp	World Wide Web HTTP
hosts2-ns	81/tcp	HOSTS2 Name Server
hosts2-ns	81/udp	HOSTS2 Name Server
xfer	82/tcp	XFER Utility
xfer	82/udp	XFER Utility
mit-ml-dev	83/tcp	MIT ML Device
mit-ml-dev	83/udp	MIT ML Device
ctf	84/tcp	Common Trace Facility
ctf	84/udp	Common Trace Facility
mit-ml-dev	85/tcp	MIT ML Device
mit-ml-dev	85/udp	MIT ML Device
mfcobol	86/tcp	Micro Focus Cobol
mfcobol	86/udp	Micro Focus Cobol
	87/tcp	any private terminal link
	87/udp	any private terminal link
kerberos	88/tcp	Kerberos
kerberos	88/udp	Kerberos
su-mit-tg	89/tcp	SU/MIT Telnet Gateway
su-mit-tg	89/udp	SU/MIT Telnet Gateway
dnsix	90/tcp	DNSIX Securit Attribute Token Map
dnsix	90/udp	DNSIX Securit Attribute Token Map
mit-dov	91/tcp	MIT Dover Spooler
mit-dov	91/udp	MIT Dover Spooler
npp	92/tcp	Network Printing Protocol
npp	92/udp	Network Printing Protocol
dcp	93/tcp	Device Control Protocol
dcp	93/udp	Device Control Protocol

Continued

Table E-1 *(continued)*

Keyword	Decimal	Description
objcall	94/tcp	Tivoli Object Dispatcher
objcall	94/udp	Tivoli Object Dispatcher
supdup	95/tcp	SUPDUP
supdup	95/udp	SUPDUP
dixie	96/tcp	DIXIE Protocol Specification
dixie	96/udp	DIXIE Protocol Specification
swift-rvf	97/tcp	Swift Remote Virtural File Protocol
swift-rvf	97/udp	Swift Remote Virtural File Protocol
tacnews	98/tcp	TAC News
tacnews	98/udp	TAC News
metagram	99/tcp	Metagram Relay
metagram	99/udp	Metagram Relay
newacct	100/tcp	[unauthorized use]
hostname	101/tcp	NIC Host Name Server
hostname	101/udp	NIC Host Name Server
iso-tsap	102/tcp	ISO-TSAP Class 0
iso-tsap	102/udp	ISO-TSAP Class 0
gppitnp	103/tcp	Genesis Point-to-Point Trans Net
gppitnp	103/udp	Genesis Point-to-Point Trans Net
acr-nema	104/tcp	ACR-NEMA Digital Imag. & Comm. 300
acr-nema	104/udp	ACR-NEMA Digital Imag. & Comm. 300
cso	105/tcp	CCSO name server protocol
cso	105/udp	CCSO name server protocol
csnet-ns	105/tcp	Mailbox Name Nameserver
csnet-ns	105/udp	Mailbox Name Nameserver
3com-tsmux	106/tcp	3COM-TSMUX
3com-tsmux	106/udp	3COM-TSMUX
rtelnet	107/tcp	Remote Telnet Service
rtelnet	107/udp	Remote Telnet Service
snagas	108/tcp	SNA Gateway Access Server

Keyword	Decimal	Description
snagas	108/udp	SNA Gateway Access Server
pop2	109/tcp	Post Office Protocol - Version 2
pop2	109/udp	Post Office Protocol - Version 2
pop3	110/tcp	Post Office Protocol - Version 3
pop3	110/udp	Post Office Protocol - Version 3
sunrpc	111/tcp	SUN Remote Procedure Call
sunrpc	111/udp	SUN Remote Procedure Call
mcidas	112/tcp	McIDAS Data Transmission Protocol
mcidas	112/udp	McIDAS Data Transmission Protocol
ident	113/tcp	Ident service
auth	113/tcp	Authentication Service
auth	113/udp	Authentication Service
audionews	114/tcp	Audio News Multicast
audionews	114/udp	Audio News Multicast
sftp	115/tcp	Simple File Transfer Protocol
sftp	115/udp	Simple File Transfer Protocol
ansanotify	116/tcp	ANSA REX Notify
ansanotify	116/udp	ANSA REX Notify
uucp-path	117/tcp	UUCP Path Service
uucp-path	117/udp	UUCP Path Service
sqlserv	118/tcp	SQL Services
sqlserv	118/udp	SQL Services
nntp	119/tcp	Network News Transfer Protocol
nntp	119/udp	Network News Transfer Protocol
cfdptkt	120/tcp	CFDPTKT
cfdptkt	120/udp	CFDPTKT
erpc	121/tcp	Encore Expedited Remote Pro.Call
erpc	121/udp	Encore Expedited Remote Pro.Call
smakynet	122/tcp	SMAKYNET
smakynet	122/udp	SMAKYNET

Continued

Table E-1 *(continued)*

Keyword	Decimal	Description
ntp	123/tcp	Network Time Protocol
ntp	123/udp	Network Time Protocol
ansatrader	124/tcp	ANSA REX Trader
ansatrader	124/udp	ANSA REX Trader
locus-map	125/tcp	Locus PC-Interface Net Map Ser
locus-map	125/udp	Locus PC-Interface Net Map Ser
nxedit	126/tcp	NXEdit
nxedit	126/udp	NXEdit
locus-con	127/tcp	Locus PC-Interface Conn Server
locus-con	127/udp	Locus PC-Interface Conn Server
gss-xlicen	128/tcp	GSS X License Verification
gss-xlicen	128/udp	GSS X License Verification
pwdgen	129/tcp	Password Generator Protocol
pwdgen	129/udp	Password Generator Protocol
cisco-fna	130/tcp	cisco FNATIVE
cisco-fna	130/udp	cisco FNATIVE
cisco-tna	131/tcp	cisco TNATIVE
cisco-tna	131/udp	cisco TNATIVE
cisco-sys	132/tcp	cisco SYSMAINT
cisco-sys	132/udp	cisco SYSMAINT
statsrv	133/tcp	Statistics Service
statsrv	133/udp	Statistics Service
ingres-net	134/tcp	INGRES-NET Service
ingres-net	134/udp	INGRES-NET Service
epmap	135/tcp	DCE endpoint resolution
epmap	135/udp	DCE endpoint resolution
profile	136/tcp	PROFILE Naming System
profile	136/udp	PROFILE Naming System
netbios-ns	137/tcp	NETBIOS Name Service
netbios-ns	137/udp	NETBIOS Name Service

Keyword	Decimal	Description
netbios-dgm	138/tcp	NETBIOS Datagram Service
netbios-dgm	138/udp	NETBIOS Datagram Service
netbios-ssn	139/tcp	NETBIOS Session Service
netbios-ssn	139/udp	NETBIOS Session Service
emfis-data	140/tcp	EMFIS Data Service
emfis-data	140/udp	EMFIS Data Service
emfis-cntl	141/tcp	EMFIS Control Service
emfis-cntl	141/udp	EMFIS Control Service
bl-idm	142/tcp	Britton-Lee IDM
bl-idm	142/udp	Britton-Lee IDM
imap	143/tcp	Internet Message Access Protocol
imap	143/udp	Internet Message Access Protocol
uma	144/tcp	Universal Management Architecture
uma	144/udp	Universal Management Architecture
uaac	145/tcp	UAAC Protocol
uaac	145/udp	UAAC Protocol
iso-tp0	146/tcp	ISO-IP0
iso-tp0	146/udp	ISO-IP0
iso-ip	147/tcp	ISO-IP
iso-ip	147/udp	ISO-IP
jargon	148/tcp	Jargon
jargon	148/udp	Jargon
aed-512	149/tcp	AED 512 Emulation Service
aed-512	149/udp	AED 512 Emulation Service
sql-net	150/tcp	SQL-NET
sql-net	150/udp	SQL-NET
hems	151/tcp	HEMS
hems	151/udp	HEMS
bftp	152/tcp	Background File Transfer Program
bftp	152/udp	Background File Transfer Program

Continued

Table E-1 *(continued)*		
Keyword	*Decimal*	*Description*
sgmp	153/tcp	SGMP
sgmp	153/udp	SGMP
netsc-prod	154/tcp	NETSC
netsc-prod	154/udp	NETSC
netsc-dev	155/tcp	NETSC
netsc-dev	155/udp	NETSC
sqlsrv	156/tcp	SQL Service
sqlsrv	156/udp	SQL Service
knet-cmp	157/tcp	KNET/VM Command/Message Protocol
knet-cmp	157/udp	KNET/VM Command/Message Protocol
pcmail-srv	158/tcp	PCMail Server
pcmail-srv	158/udp	PCMail Server
nss-routing	159/tcp	NSS-Routing
nss-routing	159/udp	NSS-Routing
sgmp-traps	160/tcp	SGMP-TRAPS
sgmp-traps	160/udp	SGMP-TRAPS
snmp	161/tcp	SNMP
snmp	161/udp	SNMP
snmptrap	162/tcp	SNMPTRAP
snmptrap	162/udp	SNMPTRAP
cmip-man	163/tcp	CMIP/TCP Manager
cmip-man	163/udp	CMIP/TCP Manager
cmip-agent	164/tcp	CMIP/TCP Agent
smip-agent	164/udp	CMIP/TCP Agent
xns-courier	165/tcp	Xerox
xns-courier	165/udp	Xerox
s-net	166/tcp	Sirius Systems
s-net	166/udp	Sirius Systems
namp	167/tcp	NAMP
namp	167/udp	NAMP

Keyword	Decimal	Description
rsvd	168/tcp	RSVD
rsvd	168/udp	RSVD
send	169/tcp	SEND
send	169/udp	SEND
print-srv	170/tcp	Network PostScript
print-srv	170/udp	Network PostScript
multiplex	171/tcp	Network Innovations Multiplex
multiplex	171/udp	Network Innovations Multiplex
cl/1	172/tcp	Network Innovations CL/1
cl/1	172/udp	Network Innovations CL/1
xyplex-mux	173/tcp	Xyplex
xyplex-mux	173/udp	Xyplex
mailq	174/tcp	MAILQ
mailq	174/udp	MAILQ
vmnet	175/tcp	VMNET
vmnet	175/udp	VMNET
genrad-mux	176/tcp	GENRAD-MUX
genrad-mux	176/udp	GENRAD-MUX
xdmcp	177/tcp	X Display Manager Control Protocol
xdmcp	177/udp	X Display Manager Control Protocol
nextstep	178/tcp	NextStep Window Server
nextstep	178/udp	NextStep Window Server
bgp	179/tcp	Border Gateway Protocol
bgp	179/udp	Border Gateway Protocol
ris	180/tcp	Intergraph
ris	180/udp	Intergraph
unify	181/tcp	Unify
unify	181/udp	Unify
audit	182/tcp	Unisys Audit SITP
audit	182/udp	Unisys Audit SITP

Continued

Table E-1 (continued)

Keyword	Decimal	Description
ocbinder	183/tcp	OCBinder
ocbinder	183/udp	OCBinder
ocserver	184/tcp	OCServer
ocserver	184/udp	OCServer
remote-kis	185/tcp	Remote-KIS
remote-kis	185/udp	Remote-KIS
kis	186/tcp	KIS Protocol
kis	186/udp	KIS Protocol
aci	187/tcp	Application Communication Interface
aci	187/udp	Application Communication Interface
mumps	188/tcp	Plus Five's MUMPS
mumps	188/udp	Plus Five's MUMPS
qft	189/tcp	Queued File Transport
qft	189/udp	Queued File Transport
gacp	190/tcp	Gateway Access Control Protocol
gacp	190/udp	Gateway Access Control Protocol
prospero	191/tcp	Prospero Directory Service
prospero	191/udp	Prospero Directory Service
osu-nms	192/tcp	OSU Network Monitoring System
osu-nms	192/udp	OSU Network Monitoring System
srmp	193/tcp	Spider Remote Monitoring Protocol
srmp	193/udp	Spider Remote Monitoring Protocol
irc	194/tcp	Internet Relay Chat Protocol
irc	194/udp	Internet Relay Chat Protocol
dn6-nlm-aud	195/tcp	DNSIX Network Level Module Audit
dn6-nlm-aud	195/udp	DNSIX Network Level Module Audit
dn6-smm-red	196/tcp	DNSIX Session Mgt Module Audit Redir
dn6-smm-red	196/udp	DNSIX Session Mgt Module Audit Redir
dls	197/tcp	Directory Location Service
dls	197/udp	Directory Location Service

Keyword	Decimal	Description
dls-mon	198/tcp	Directory Location Service Monitor
dls-mon	198/udp	Directory Location Service Monitor
smux	199/tcp	SMUX
smux	199/udp	SMUX
src	200/tcp	IBM System Resource Controller
src	200/udp	IBM System Resource Controller
at-rtmp	201/tcp	AppleTalk Routing Maintenance
at-rtmp	201/udp	AppleTalk Routing Maintenance
at-nbp	202/tcp	AppleTalk Name Binding
at-nbp	202/udp	AppleTalk Name Binding
at-3	203/tcp	AppleTalk Unused
at-3	203/udp	AppleTalk Unused
at-echo	204/tcp	AppleTalk Echo
at-echo	204/udp	AppleTalk Echo
at-5	205/tcp	AppleTalk Unused
at-5	205/udp	AppleTalk Unused
at-zis	206/tcp	AppleTalk Zone Information
at-zis	206/udp	AppleTalk Zone Information
at-7	207/tcp	AppleTalk Unused
at-7	207/udp	AppleTalk Unused
at-8	208/tcp	AppleTalk Unused
at-8	208/udp	AppleTalk Unused
qmtp	209/tcp	The Quick Mail Transfer Protocol
qmtp	209/udp	The Quick Mail Transfer Protocol
z39.50	210/tcp	ANSI Z39.50
z39.50	210/udp	ANSI Z39.50
914c/g	211/tcp	Texas Instruments 914C/G Terminal
914c/g	211/udp	Texas Instruments 914C/G Terminal
anet	212/tcp	ATEXSSTR
anet	212/udp	ATEXSSTR

Continued

Table E-1 *(continued)*

Keyword	Decimal	Description
ipx	213/tcp	IPX
ipx	213/udp	IPX
vmpwscs	214/tcp	VM PWSCS
vmpwscs	214/udp	VM PWSCS
softpc	215/tcp	Insignia Solutions
softpc	215/udp	Insignia Solutions
CAIlic	216/tcp	Computer Associates Int'l License Server
CAIlic	216/udp	Computer Associates Int'l License Server
dbase	217/tcp	dBASE Unix
dbase	217/udp	dBASE Unix
mpp	218/tcp	Netix Message Posting Protocol
mpp	218/udp	Netix Message Posting Protocol
uarps	219/tcp	Unisys ARPs
uarps	219/udp	Unisys ARPs
imap3	220/tcp	Interactive Mail Access Protocol v3
imap3	220/udp	Interactive Mail Access Protocol v3
fln-spx	221/tcp	Berkeley rlogind with SPX auth
fln-spx	221/udp	Berkeley rlogind with SPX auth
rsh-spx	222/tcp	Berkeley rshd with SPX auth
rsh-spx	222/udp	Berkeley rshd with SPX auth
cdc	223/tcp	Certificate Distribution Center
cdc	223/udp	Certificate Distribution Center
masqdialer	224/tcp	masqdialer
masqdialer	224/udp	masqdialer
Reserved	225-241	Reserved
direct	242/tcp	Direct
direct	242/udp	Direct
sur-meas	243/tcp	Survey Measurement
sur-meas	243/udp	Survey Measurement
dayna	244/tcp	Dayna

Keyword	Decimal	Description
dayna	244/udp	Dayna
link	245/tcp	LINK
link	245/udp	LINK
dsp3270	246/tcp	Display Systems Protocol
dsp3270	246/udp	Display Systems Protocol
subntbcst_tftp	247/tcp	SUBNTBCST_TFTP
subntbcst_tftp	247/udp	SUBNTBCST_TFTP
bhfhs	248/tcp	bhfhs
bhfhs	248/udp	bhfhs
Reserved	249-255	Reserved
rap	256/tcp	RAP
rap	256/udp	RAP
set	257/tcp	Secure Electronic Transaction
set	257/udp	Secure Electronic Transaction
yak-chat	258/tcp	Yak Winsock Personal Chat
yak-chat	258/udp	Yak Winsock Personal Chat
esro-gen	259/tcp	Efficient Short Remote Operations
esro-gen	259/udp	Efficient Short Remote Operations
openport	260/tcp	Openport
openport	260/udp	Openport
nsiiops	261/tcp	IIOP Name Service over TLS/SSL
nsiiops	261/udp	IIOP Name Service over TLS/SSL
arcisdms	262/tcp	Arcisdms
arcisdms	262/udp	Arcisdms
hdap	263/tcp	HDAP
hdap	263/udp	HDAP
bgmp	264/tcp	BGMP
bgmp	264/udp	BGMP
Unassigned	265-279	Unassigned
http-mgmt	280/tcp	http-mgmt

Continued

Table E-1 *(continued)*

Keyword	Decimal	Description
http-mgmt	280/udp	http-mgmt
personal-link	281/tcp	Personal Link
personal-link	281/udp	Personal Link
cableport-ax	282/tcp	Cable Port A/X
cableport-ax	282/udp	Cable Port A/X
rescap	283/tcp	rescap
rescap	283/udp	rescap
corerjd	284/tcp	corerjd
corerjd	284/udp	corerjd
Unassigned	285-307	Unassigned
novastorbakcup	308/tcp	Novastor Backup
novastorbakcup	308/udp	Novastor Backup
entrusttime	309/tcp	EntrustTime
entrusttime	309/udp	EntrustTime
bhmds	310/tcp	bhmds
bhmds	310/udp	bhmds
asip-webadmin	311/tcp	AppleShare IP WebAdmin
asip-webadmin	311/udp	AppleShare IP WebAdmin
vslmp	312/tcp	VSLMP
vslmp	312/udp	VSLMP
magenta-logic	313/tcp	Magenta Logic
magenta-logic	313/udp	Magenta Logic
opalis-robot	314/tcp	Opalis Robot
opalis-robot	314/udp	Opalis Robot
dpsi	315/tcp	DPSI
dpsi	315/udp	DPSI
decauth	316/tcp	decAuth
decauth	316/udp	decAuth
zannet	317/tcp	Zannet
zannet	317/udp	Zannet

Keyword	Decimal	Description
pkix-timestamp	318/tcp	PKIX TimeStamp
pkix-timestamp	318/udp	PKIX TimeStamp
ptp-event	319/tcp	PTP Event
ptp-event	319/udp	PTP Event
ptp-general	320/tcp	PTP General
ptp-general	320/udp	PTP General
pip	321/tcp	PIP
pip	321/udp	PIP
rtsps	322/tcp	RTSPS
rtsps	322/udp	RTSPS
Unassigned	323-343	Unassigned
pdap	344/tcp	Prospero Data Access Protocol
pdap	344/udp	Prospero Data Access Protocol
pawserv	345/tcp	Perf Analysis Workbench
pawserv	345/udp	Perf Analysis Workbench
zserv	346/tcp	Zebra server
zserv	346/udp	Zebra server
fatserv	347/tcp	Fatmen Server
fatserv	347/udp	Fatmen Server
csi-sgwp	348/tcp	Cabletron Management Protocol
csi-sgwp	348/udp	Cabletron Management Protocol
mftp	349/tcp	mftp
mftp	349/udp	mftp
matip-type-a	350/tcp	MATIP Type A
matip-type-a	350/udp	MATIP Type A
matip-type-b	351/tcp	MATIP Type B
matip-type-b	351/udp	MATIP Type B
bhoetty	351/tcp	bhoetty
bhoetty	351/udp	bhoetty
dtag-ste-sb	352/tcp	DTAG

Continued

Table E-1 *(continued)*		
Keyword	*Decimal*	*Description*
dtag-ste-sb	352/udp	DTAG
bhoedap4	352/tcp	bhoedap4
bhoedap4	352/udp	bhoedap4
ndsauth	353/tcp	NDSAUTH
ndsauth	353/udp	NDSAUTH
bh611	354/tcp	bh611
bh611	354/udp	bh611
datex-asn	355/tcp	DATEX-ASN
datex-asn	355/udp	DATEX-ASN
cloanto-net-1	356/tcp	Cloanto Net 1
cloanto-net-1	356/udp	Cloanto Net 1
bhevent	357/tcp	bhevent
bhevent	357/udp	bhevent
shrinkwrap	358/tcp	Shrinkwrap
shrinkwrap	358/udp	Shrinkwrap
tenebris_nts	359/tcp	Tenebris Network Trace Service
tenebris_nts	359/udp	Tenebris Network Trace Service
scoi2odialog	360/tcp	scoi2odialog
scoi2odialog	360/udp	scoi2odialog
semantix	361/tcp	Semantix
semantix	361/udp	Semantix
srssend	362/tcp	SRS Send
srssend	362/udp	SRS Send
rsvp_tunnel	363/tcp	RSVP Tunnel
rsvp_tunnel	363/udp	RSVP Tunnel
aurora-cmgr	364/tcp	Aurora CMGR
aurora-cmgr	364/udp	Aurora CMGR
dtk	365/tcp	DTK
dtk	365/udp	DTK
odmr	366/tcp	ODMR

Keyword	Decimal	Description
odmr	366/udp	ODMR
mortgageware	367/tcp	MortgageWare
mortgageware	367/udp	MortgageWare
qbikgdp	368/tcp	QbikGDP
qbikgdp	368/udp	QbikGDP
rpc2portmap	369/tcp	rpc2portmap
rpc2portmap	369/udp	rpc2portmap
codaauth2	370/tcp	codaauth2
codaauth2	370/udp	codaauth2
clearcase	371/tcp	Clearcase
clearcase	371/udp	Clearcase
ulistproc	372/tcp	ListProcessor
ulistproc	372/udp	ListProcessor
legent-1	373/tcp	Legent Corporation
legent-1	373/udp	Legent Corporation
legent-2	374/tcp	Legent Corporation
legent-2	374/udp	Legent Corporation
hassle	375/tcp	Hassle
hassle	375/udp	Hassle
nip	376/tcp	Amiga Envoy Network Inquiry Protocol
nip	376/udp	Amiga Envoy Network Inquiry Protocol
tnETOS	377/tcp	NEC Corporation
tnETOS	377/udp	NEC Corporation
dsETOS	378/tcp	NEC Corporation
dsETOS	378/udp	NEC Corporation
is99c	379/tcp	TIA/EIA/IS-99 modem client
is99c	379/udp	TIA/EIA/IS-99 modem client
is99s	380/tcp	TIA/EIA/IS-99 modem server
is99s	380/udp	TIA/EIA/IS-99 modem server
hp-collector	381/tcp	hp performance data collector

Continued

Table E-1 *(continued)*

Keyword	Decimal	Description
hp-collector	381/udp	hp performance data collector
hp-managed-node	382/tcp	hp performance data managed node
hp-managed-node	382/udp	hp performance data managed node
hp-alarm-mgr	383/tcp	hp performance data alarm manager
hp-alarm-mgr	383/udp	hp performance data alarm manager
arns	384/tcp	A Remote Network Server System
arns	384/udp	A Remote Network Server System
ibm-app	385/tcp	IBM Application
ibm-app	385/udp	IBM Application
asa	386/tcp	ASA Message Router Object Def.
asa	386/udp	ASA Message Router Object Def.
aurp	387/tcp	Appletalk Update-Based Routing Pro.
aurp	387/udp	Appletalk Update-Based Routing Pro.
unidata-ldm	388/tcp	Unidata LDM Version 4
unidata-ldm	388/udp	Unidata LDM Version 4
ldap	389/tcp	Lightweight Directory Access Protocol
ldap	389/udp	Lightweight Directory Access Protocol
uis	390/tcp	UIS
uis	390/udp	UIS
synotics-relay	391/tcp	SynOptics SNMP Relay Port
synotics-relay	391/udp	SynOptics SNMP Relay Port
synotics-broker	392/tcp	SynOptics Port Broker Port
synotics-broker	392/udp	SynOptics Port Broker Port
dis	393/tcp	Data Interpretation System
dis	393/udp	Data Interpretation System
embl-ndt	394/tcp	EMBL Nucleic Data Transfer
embl-ndt	394/udp	EMBL Nucleic Data Transfer
netcp	395/tcp	NETscout Control Protocol
netcp	395/udp	NETscout Control Protocol
netware-ip	396/tcp	Novell Netware over IP

Keyword	Decimal	Description
netware-ip	396/udp	Novell Netware over IP
mptn	397/tcp	Multi Protocol Trans. Net.
mptn	397/udp	Multi Protocol Trans. Net.
kryptolan	398/tcp	Kryptolan
kryptolan	398/udp	Kryptolan
iso-tsap-c2	399/tcp	ISO Transport Class 2 Non-Control over TCP
iso-tsap-c2	399/udp	ISO Transport Class 2 Non-Control over TCP
work-sol	400/tcp	Workstation Solutions
work-sol	400/udp	Workstation Solutions
ups	401/tcp	Uninterruptible Power Supply
ups	401/udp	Uninterruptible Power Supply
genie	402/tcp	Genie Protocol
genie	402/udp	Genie Protocol
decap	403/tcp	decap
decap	403/udp	decap
nced	404/tcp	nced
nced	404/udp	nced
ncld	405/tcp	ncld
ncld	405/udp	ncld
imsp	406/tcp	Interactive Mail Support Protocol
imsp	406/udp	Interactive Mail Support Protocol
timbuktu	407/tcp	Timbuktu
timbuktu	407/udp	Timbuktu
prm-sm	408/tcp	Prospero Resource Manager Sys. Man.
prm-sm	408/udp	Prospero Resource Manager Sys. Man.
prm-nm	409/tcp	Prospero Resource Manager Node Man.
prm-nm	409/udp	Prospero Resource Manager Node Man.
decladebug	410/tcp	DECLadebug Remote Debug Protocol
decladebug	410/udp	DECLadebug Remote Debug Protocol
rmt	411/tcp	Remote MT Protocol

Continued

Table E-1 *(continued)*

Keyword	Decimal	Description
rmt	411/udp	Remote MT Protocol
synoptics-trap	412/tcp	Trap Convention Port
synoptics-trap	412/udp	Trap Convention Port
smsp	413/tcp	SMSP
smsp	413/udp	SMSP
infoseek	414/tcp	InfoSeek
infoseek	414/udp	InfoSeek
bnet	415/tcp	BNet
bnet	415/udp	BNet
silverplatter	416/tcp	Silverplatter
silverplatter	416/udp	Silverplatter
onmux	417/tcp	Onmux
onmux	417/udp	Onmux
hyper-g	418/tcp	Hyper-G
hyper-g	418/udp	Hyper-G
ariel1	419/tcp	Ariel
ariel1	419/udp	Ariel
smpte	420/tcp	SMPTE
smpte	420/udp	SMPTE
ariel2	421/tcp	Ariel
ariel2	421/udp	Ariel
ariel3	422/tcp	Ariel
ariel3	422/udp	Ariel
opc-job-start	423/tcp	IBM Operations Planning and Control Start
opc-job-start	423/udp	IBM Operations Planning and Control Start
opc-job-track	424/tcp	IBM Operations Planning and Control Track
opc-job-track	424/udp	IBM Operations Planning and Control Track
icad-el	425/tcp	ICAD
icad-el	425/udp	ICAD
smartsdp	426/tcp	smartsdp

Keyword	Decimal	Description
smartsdp	426/udp	smartsdp
svrloc	427/tcp	Server Location
svrloc	427/udp	Server Location
ocs_cmu	428/tcp	OCS_CMU
ocs_cmu	428/udp	OCS_CMU
ocs_amu	429/tcp	OCS_AMU
ocs_amu	429/udp	OCS_AMU
utmpsd	430/tcp	UTMPSD
utmpsd	430/udp	UTMPSD
utmpcd	431/tcp	UTMPCD
utmpcd	431/udp	UTMPCD
iasd	432/tcp	IASD
iasd	432/udp	IASD
nnsp	433/tcp	NNSP
nnsp	433/udp	NNSP
mobileip-agent	434/tcp	MobileIP-Agent
mobileip-agent	434/udp	MobileIP-Agent
mobilip-mn	435/tcp	MobilIP-MN
mobilip-mn	435/udp	MobilIP-MN
dna-cml	436/tcp	DNA-CML
dna-cml	436/udp	DNA-CML
comscm	437/tcp	comscm
comscm	437/udp	comscm
dsfgw	438/tcp	dsfgw
dsfgw	438/udp	dsfgw
dasp	439/tcp	dasp
dasp	439/udp	dasp
sgcp	440/tcp	sgcp
sgcp	440/udp	sgcp
decvms-sysmgt	441/tcp	decvms-sysmgt

Continued

Table E-1 *(continued)*

Keyword	Decimal	Description
decvms-sysmgt	441/udp	decvms-sysmgt
cvc_hostd	442/tcp	cvc_hostd
cvc_hostd	442/udp	cvc_hostd
https	443/tcp	http protocol over TLS/SSL
https	443/udp	http protocol over TLS/SSL
snpp	444/tcp	Simple Network Paging Protocol
snpp	444/udp	Simple Network Paging Protocol
microsoft-ds	445/tcp	Microsoft-DS
microsoft-ds	445/udp	Microsoft-DS
ddm-rdb	446/tcp	DDM-RDB
ddm-rdb	446/udp	DDM-RDB
ddm-dfm	447/tcp	DDM-RFM
ddm-dfm	447/udp	DDM-RFM
ddm-ssl	448/tcp	DDM-SSL
ddm-ssl	448/udp	DDM-SSL
as-servermap	449/tcp	AS Server Mapper
as-servermap	449/udp	AS Server Mapper
tserver	450/tcp	TServer
tserver	450/udp	TServer
sfs-smp-net	451/tcp	Cray Network Semaphore server
sfs-smp-net	451/udp	Cray Network Semaphore server
sfs-config	452/tcp	Cray SFS config server
sfs-config	452/udp	Cray SFS config server
creativeserver	453/tcp	CreativeServer
creativeserver	453/udp	CreativeServer
contentserver	454/tcp	ContentServer
contentserver	454/udp	ContentServer
creativepartnr	455/tcp	CreativePartnr
creativepartnr	455/udp	CreativePartnr
macon-tcp	456/tcp	macon-tcp

Keyword	Decimal	Description
macon-udp	456/udp	macon-udp
scohelp	457/tcp	scohelp
scohelp	457/udp	scohelp
appleqtc	458/tcp	apple quick time
appleqtc	458/udp	apple quick time
ampr-rcmd	459/tcp	ampr-rcmd
ampr-rcmd	459/udp	ampr-rcmd
skronk	460/tcp	skronk
skronk	460/udp	skronk
datasurfsrv	461/tcp	DataRampSrv
datasurfsrv	461/udp	DataRampSrv
datasurfsrvsec	462/tcp	DataRampSrvSec
datasurfsrvsec	462/udp	DataRampSrvSec
alpes	463/tcp	alpes
alpes	463/udp	alpes
kpasswd	464/tcp	kpasswd
kpasswd	464/udp	kpasswd
digital-vrc	466/tcp	digital-vrc
digital-vrc	466/udp	digital-vrc
mylex-mapd	467/tcp	mylex-mapd
mylex-mapd	467/udp	mylex-mapd
photuris	468/tcp	proturis
photuris	468/udp	proturis
rcp	469/tcp	Radio Control Protocol
rcp	469/udp	Radio Control Protocol
scx-proxy	470/tcp	scx-proxy
scx-proxy	470/udp	scx-proxy
mondex	471/tcp	Mondex
mondex	471/udp	Mondex
ljk-login	472/tcp	ljk-login

Continued

Table E-1 *(continued)*		
Keyword	*Decimal*	*Description*
ljk-login	472/udp	ljk-login
hybrid-pop	473/tcp	hybrid-pop
hybrid-pop	473/udp	hybrid-pop
tn-tl-w1	474/tcp	tn-tl-w1
tn-tl-w2	474/udp	tn-tl-w2
tcpnethaspsrv	475/tcp	tcpnethaspsrv
tcpnethaspsrv	475/udp	tcpnethaspsrv
tn-tl-fd1	476/tcp	tn-tl-fd1
tn-tl-fd1	476/udp	tn-tl-fd1
ss7ns	477/tcp	ss7ns
ss7ns	477/udp	ss7ns
spsc	478/tcp	spsc
spsc	478/udp	spsc
iafserver	479/tcp	iafserver
iafserver	479/udp	iafserver
iafdbase	480/tcp	iafdbase
iafdbase	480/udp	iafdbase
ph	481/tcp	Ph service
ph	481/udp	Ph service
bgs-nsi	482/tcp	bgs-nsi
bgs-nsi	482/udp	bgs-nsi
ulpnet	483/tcp	ulpnet
ulpnet	483/udp	ulpnet
integra-sme	484/tcp	Integra Software Management Environment
integra-sme	484/udp	Integra Software Management Environment
powerburst	485/tcp	Air Soft Power Burst
powerburst	485/udp	Air Soft Power Burst
avian	486/tcp	avian
avian	486/udp	avian
saft	487/tcp	saft Simple Asynchronous File Transfer

Keyword	Decimal	Description
saft	487/udp	saft Simple Asynchronous File Transfer
gss-http	488/tcp	gss-http
gss-http	488/udp	gss-http
nest-protocol	489/tcp	nest-protocol
nest-protocol	489/udp	nest-protocol
micom-pfs	490/tcp	micom-pfs
micom-pfs	490/udp	micom-pfs
go-login	491/tcp	go-login
go-login	491/udp	go-login
ticf-1	492/tcp	Transport Independent Convergence for FNA
ticf-1	492/udp	Transport Independent Convergence for FNA
ticf-2	493/tcp	Transport Independent Convergence for FNA
ticf-2	493/udp	Transport Independent Convergence for FNA
pov-ray	494/tcp	POV-Ray
pov-ray	494/udp	POV-Ray
intecourier	495/tcp	intecourier
intecourier	495/udp	intecourier
pim-rp-disc	496/tcp	PIM-RP-DISC
pim-rp-disc	496/udp	PIM-RP-DISC
dantz	497/tcp	dantz
dantz	497/udp	dantz
siam	498/tcp	siam
siam	498/udp	siam
iso-ill	499/tcp	ISO ILL Protocol
iso-ill	499/udp	ISO ILL Protocol
isakmp	500/tcp	isakmp
isakmp	500/udp	isakmp
stmf	501/tcp	STMF
stmf	501/udp	STMF
asa-appl-proto	502/tcp	asa-appl-proto

Continued

Table E-1 *(continued)*

Keyword	Decimal	Description
asa-appl-proto	502/udp	asa-appl-proto
intrinsa	503/tcp	Intrinsa
intrinsa	503/udp	Intrinsa
citadel	504/tcp	citadel
citadel	504/udp	citadel
mailbox-lm	505/tcp	mailbox-lm
mailbox-lm	505/udp	mailbox-lm
ohimsrv	506/tcp	ohimsrv
ohimsrv	506/udp	ohimsrv
crs	507/tcp	crs
crs	507/udp	crs
xvttp	508/tcp	xvttp
xvttp	508/udp	xvttp
snare	509/tcp	snare
snare	509/udp	snare
fcp	510/tcp	FirstClass Protocol
fcp	510/udp	FirstClass Protocol
passgo	511/tcp	PassGo
passgo	511/udp	PassGo
exec	512/tcp	remote process execution; authentication performed using passwords and UNIX loppgin names
comsat	512/udp	
biff	512/udp	used by mail system to notify users of new mail received; currently receives messages only from processes on the same machine
login	513/tcp	remote login a la Telnet; automatic authentication performed based on privileged port numbers and distributed databases which identify "authentication domains"
who	513/udp	maintains databases showing who's logged in to machines on a local net and the load average of the machine

Keyword	Decimal	Description
shell	514/tcp	cmd like exec, but automatic authentication is performed as for login server
syslog	514/udp	
printer	515/tcp	spooler
printer	515/udp	spooler
videotex	516/tcp	videotex
videotex	516/udp	videotex
talk	517/tcp	like tenex link, but across machine. Unfortunately, doesn't use link protocol (this is actually just a rendezvous port from which a tcp connection is established)
talk	517/udp	like tenex link, but across machine. Unfortunately, doesn't use link protocol (this is actually just a rendezvous port from which a tcp connection is established)
ntalk	518/tcp	
ntalk	518/udp	
utime	519/tcp	unixtime
utime	519/udp	unixtime
efs	520/tcp	extended file name server
router	520/udp	local routing process (on site); uses variant of Xerox NS Routing Information Protocol (RIP)
ripng	521/tcp	ripng
ripng	521/udp	ripng
ulp	522/tcp	ULP
ulp	522/udp	ULP
ibm-db2	523/tcp	IBM-DB2
ibm-db2	523/udp	IBM-DB2
ncp	524/tcp	NCP
ncp	524/udp	NCP
timed	525/tcp	timeserver
timed	525/udp	timeserver
tempo	526/tcp	newdate

Continued

Table E-1 *(continued)*

Keyword	Decimal	Description
tempo	526/udp	newdate
stx	527/tcp	Stock IXChange
stx	527/udp	Stock IXChange
custix	528/tcp	Customer IXChange
custix	528/udp	Customer IXChange
irc-serv	529/tcp	IRC-SERV
irc-serv	529/udp	IRC-SERV
courier	530/tcp	rpc
courier	530/udp	rpc
conference	531/tcp	chat
conference	531/udp	chat
netnews	532/tcp	readnews
netnews	532/udp	readnews
netwall	533/tcp	for emergency broadcasts
netwall	533/udp	for emergency broadcasts
mm-admin	534/tcp	MegaMedia Admin
mm-admin	534/udp	MegaMedia Admin
iiop	535/tcp	iiop
iiop	535/udp	iiop
opalis-rdv	536/tcp	opalis-rdv
opalis-rdv	536/udp	opalis-rdv
nmsp	537/tcp	Networked Media Streaming Protocol
nmsp	537/udp	Networked Media Streaming Protocol
gdomap	538/tcp	gdomap
gdomap	538/udp	gdomap
apertus-ldp	539/tcp	Apertus Technologies Load Determination
apertus-ldp	539/udp	Apertus Technologies Load Determination
uucp	540/tcp	uucpd
uucp	540/udp	uucpd
uucp-rlogin	541/tcp	uucp-rlogin

Keyword	Decimal	Description
uucp-rlogin	541/udp	uucp-rlogin
commerce	542/tcp	commerce
commerce	542/udp	commerce
klogin	543/tcp	KLogin
klogin	543/udp	KLogin
kshell	544/tcp	krcmd
kshell	544/udp	krcmd
appleqtcsrvr	545/tcp	appleqtcsrvr
appleqtcsrvr	545/udp	appleqtcsrvr
dhcpv6-client	546/tcp	DHCPv6 Client
dhcpv6-client	546/udp	DHCPv6 Client
dhcpv6-server	547/tcp	DHCPv6 Server
dhcpv6-server	547/udp	DHCPv6 Server
afpovertcp	548/tcp	AFP over TCP
afpovertcp	548/udp	AFP over TCP
idfp	549/tcp	IDFP
idfp	549/udp	IDFP
new-rwho	550/tcp	new-who
new-rwho	550/udp	new-who
cybercash	551/tcp	cybercash
cybercash	551/udp	cybercash
deviceshare	552/tcp	deviceshare
deviceshare	552/udp	deviceshare
pirp	553/tcp	pirp
pirp	553/udp	pirp
rtsp	554/tcp	Real Time Stream Control Protocol
rtsp	554/udp	Real Time Stream Control Protocol
dsf	555/tcp	
dsf	555/udp	
remotefs	556/tcp	rfs server

Continued

Table E-1 *(continued)*		
Keyword	*Decimal*	*Description*
remotefs	556/udp	rfs server
openvms-sysipc	557/tcp	openvms-sysipc
openvms-sysipc	557/udp	openvms-sysipc
sdnskmp	558/tcp	SDNSKMP
sdnskmp	558/udp	SDNSKMP
teedtap	559/tcp	TEEDTAP
teedtap	559/udp	TEEDTAP
rmonitor	560/tcp	rmonitord
rmonitor	560/udp	rmonitord
monitor	561/tcp	
monitor	561/udp	
chshell	562/tcp	chcmd
chshell	562/udp	chcmd
nntps	563/tcp	nntp protocol over TLS/SSL (was snntp)
nntps	563/udp	nntp protocol over TLS/SSL (was snntp)
9pfs	564/tcp	plan 9 file service
9pfs	564/udp	plan 9 file service
whoami	565/tcp	whoami
whoami	565/udp	whoami
streettalk	566/tcp	streettalk
streettalk	566/udp	streettalk
banyan-rpc	567/tcp	banyan-rpc
banyan-rpc	567/udp	banyan-rpc
ms-shuttle	568/tcp	microsoft shuttle
ms-shuttle	568/udp	microsoft shuttle
ms-rome	569/tcp	microsoft rome
ms-rome	569/udp	microsoft rome
meter	570/tcp	demon
meter	570/udp	demon
meter	571/tcp	udemon

Keyword	Decimal	Description
meter	571/udp	udemon
sonar	572/tcp	sonar
sonar	572/udp	sonar
banyan-vip	573/tcp	banyan-vip
banyan-vip	573/udp	banyan-vip
ftp-agent	574/tcp	FTP Software Agent System
ftp-agent	574/udp	FTP Software Agent System
vemmi	575/tcp	VEMMI
vemmi	575/udp	VEMMI
ipcd	576/tcp	ipcd
ipcd	576/udp	ipcd
vnas	577/tcp	vnas
vnas	577/udp	vnas
ipdd	578/tcp	ipdd
ipdd	578/udp	ipdd
decbsrv	579/tcp	decbsrv
decbsrv	579/udp	decbsrv
sntp-heartbeat	580/tcp	SNTP HEARTBEAT
sntp-heartbeat	580/udp	SNTP HEARTBEAT
bdp	581/tcp	Bundle Discovery Protocol
bdp	581/udp	Bundle Discovery Protocol
scc-security	582/tcp	SCC Security
scc-security	582/udp	SCC Security
philips-vc	583/tcp	Philips Video-Conferencing
philips-vc	583/udp	Philips Video-Conferencing
keyserver	584/tcp	Key Server
keyserver	584/udp	Key Server
imap4-ssl	585/tcp	IMAP4+SSL (use 993 instead)
imap4-ssl	585/udp	IMAP4+SSL (use 993 instead)
password-chg	586/tcp	Password Change

Continued

Table E-1 (continued)

Keyword	Decimal	Description
password-chg	586/udp	Password Change
submission	587/tcp	Submission
submission	587/udp	Submission
cal	588/tcp	CAL
cal	588/udp	CAL
eyelink	589/tcp	EyeLink
eyelink	589/udp	EyeLink
tns-cml	590/tcp	TNS CML
tns-cml	590/udp	TNS CML
http-alt	591/tcp	FileMaker, Inc. - HTTP Alternate (see Port 80)
http-alt	591/udp	FileMaker, Inc. - HTTP Alternate (see Port 80)
eudora-set	592/tcp	Eudora Set
eudora-set	592/udp	Eudora Set
http-rpc-epmap	593/tcp	HTTP RPC Ep Map
http-rpc-epmap	593/udp	HTTP RPC Ep Map
tpip	594/tcp	TPIP
tpip	594/udp	TPIP
cab-protocol	595/tcp	CAB Protocol
cab-protocol	595/udp	CAB Protocol
smsd	596/tcp	SMSD
smsd	596/udp	SMSD
ptcnameservice	597/tcp	PTC Name Service
ptcnameservice	597/udp	PTC Name Service
sco-websrvrmg3	598/tcp	SCO Web Server Manager 3
sco-websrvrmg3	598/udp	SCO Web Server Manager 3
acp	599/tcp	Aeolon Core Protocol
acp	599/udp	Aeolon Core Protocol
ipcserver	600/tcp	Sun IPC server
ipcserver	600/udp	Sun IPC server
urm	606/tcp	Cray Unified Resource Manager

Keyword	Decimal	Description
urm	606/udp	Cray Unified Resource Manager
nqs	607/tcp	nqs
nqs	607/udp	nqs
sift-uft	608/tcp	Sender-Initiated/Unsolicited File Transfer
sift-uft	608/udp	Sender-Initiated/Unsolicited File Transfer
npmp-trap	609/tcp	npmp-trap
npmp-trap	609/udp	npmp-trap
npmp-local	610/tcp	npmp-local
npmp-local	610/udp	npmp-local
npmp-gui	611/tcp	npmp-gui
npmp-gui	611/udp	npmp-gui
hmmp-ind	612/tcp	HMMP Indication
hmmp-ind	612/udp HMMP	Indication
hmmp-op	613/tcp	HMMP Operation
hmmp-op	613/udpHMMP	Operation
sshell	614/tcp	SSLshell
sshell	614/udp	SSLshell
sco-inetmgr	615/tcp	Internet Configuration Manager
sco-inetmgr	615/udp	Internet Configuration Manager
sco-sysmgr	616/tcp	SCO System Administration Server
sco-sysmgr	616/udp	SCO System Administration Server
sco-dtmgr	617/tcp	SCO Desktop Administration Server
sco-dtmgr	617/udp	SCO Desktop Administration Server
dei-icda	618/tcp	DEI-ICDA
dei-icda	618/udp	DEI-ICDA
digital-evm	619/tcp	Digital EVM
digital-evm	619/udp	Digital EVM
sco-websrvrmgr	620/tcp	SCO WebServer Manager

Continued

Table E-1 *(continued)*

Keyword	Decimal	Description
sco-websrvrmgr	620/udp	SCO WebServer Manager
escp-ip	621/tcp	ESCP
escp-ip	621/udp	ESCP
collaborator	622/tcp	Collaborator
collaborator	622/udp	Collaborator
aux_bus_shunt	623/tcp	Aux Bus Shunt
aux_bus_shunt	623/udp	Aux Bus Shunt
cryptoadmin	624/tcp	Crypto Admin
cryptoadmin	624/udp	Crypto Admin
dec_dlm	625/tcp	DEC DLM
dec_dlm	625/udp	DEC DLM
asia	626/tcp	ASIA
asia	626/udp	ASIA
passgo-tivoli	627/tcp	PassGo Tivoli
passgo-tivoli	627/udp	PassGo Tivoli
qmqp	628/tcp	QMQP
qmqp	628/udp	QMQP
3com-amp3	629/tcp	3Com AMP3
3com-amp3	629/udp	3Com AMP3
rda	630/tcp	RDA
rda	630/udp	RDA
ipp	631/tcp	IPP (Internet Printing Protocol)
ipp	631/udp	IPP (Internet Printing Protocol)
bmpp	632/tcp	bmpp
bmpp	632/udp	bmpp
servstat	633/tcp	Service Status update (Sterling Software)
servstat	633/udp	Service Status update (Sterling Software)
ginad	634/tcp	ginad
ginad	634/udp	ginad
rlzdbase	635/tcp	RLZ DBase

Keyword	Decimal	Description
rlzdbase	635/udp	RLZ DBase
ldaps	636/tcp	ldap protocol over TLS/SSL
ldaps	636/udp	ldap protocol over TLS/SSL
lanserver	637/tcp	lanserver
lanserver	637/udp	lanserver
mcns-sec	638/tcp	mcns-sec
mcns-sec	638/udp	mcns-sec
msdp	639/tcp	MSDP
msdp	639/udp	MSDP
entrust-sps	640/tcp	entrust-sps
entrust-sps	640/udp	entrust-sps
repcmd	641/tcp	repcmd
repcmd	641/udp	repcmd
esro-emsdp	642/tcp	ESRO-EMSDP V1.3
esro-emsdp	642/udp	ESRO-EMSDP V1.3
sanity	643/tcp	SANity
sanity	643/udp	SANity
dwr	644/tcp	dwr
dwr	644/udp	dwr
pssc	645/tcp	PSSC
pssc	645/udp	PSSC
ldp	646/tcp	LDP
ldp	646/udp	LDP
dhcp-failover	647/tcp	DHCP Failover
dhcp-failover	647/udp	DHCP Failover
rrp	648/tcp	Registry Registrar Protocol (RRP)
rrp	648/udp	Registry Registrar Protocol (RRP)
aminet	649/tcp	Aminet
aminet	649/udp	Aminet
obex	650/tcp	OBEX

Continued

Table E-1 *(continued)*

Keyword	Decimal	Description
obex	650/udp	OBEX
ieee-mms	651/tcp	IEEE MMS
ieee-mms	651/udp	IEEE MMS
udlr-dtcp	652/tcp	UDLR_DTCP
udlr-dtcp	652/udp	UDLR_DTCP
repscmd	653/tcp	RepCmd
repscmd	653/udp	RepCmd
aodv	654/tcp	AODV
aodv	654/udp	AODV
tinc	655/tcp	TINC
tinc	655/udp	TINC
spmp	656/tcp	SPMP
spmp	656/udp	SPMP
rmc	657/tcp	RMC
rmc	657/udp	RMC
tenfold	658/tcp	TenFold
tenfold	658/udp	TenFold
url-rendezvous	659/tcp	URL Rendezvous
url-rendezvous	659/udp	URL Rendezvous
mac-srvr-admin	660/tcp	MacOS Server Admin
mac-srvr-admin	660/udp	MacOS Server Admin
hap	661/tcp	HAP
hap	661/udp	HAP
pftp	662/tcp	PFTP
pftp	662/udp	PFTP
purenoise	663/tcp	PureNoise
purenoise	663/udp	PureNoise
secure-aux-bus	664/tcp	Secure Aux Bus
secure-aux-bus	664/udp	Secure Aux Bus
Unassigned	665	Unassigned

Keyword	Decimal	Description
mdqs	666/tcp	
mdqs	666/udp	
doom	666/tcp	doom Id Software
doom	666/udp	doom Id Software
disclose	667/tcp	campaign contribution disclosures – SDR Technologies
disclose	667/udp	campaign contribution disclosures – SDRTechnologies
mecomm	668/tcp	MeComm
mecomm	668/udp	MeComm
meregister	669/tcp	MeRegister
meregister	669/udp	MeRegister
vacdsm-sws	670/tcp	VACDSM-SWS
vacdsm-sws	670/udp	VACDSM-SWS
vacdsm-app	671/tcp	VACDSM-APP
vacdsm-app	671/udp	VACDSM-APP
vpps-qua	672/tcp	VPPS-QUA
vpps-qua	672/udp	VPPS-QUA
cimplex	673/tcp	CIMPLEX
cimplex	673/udp	CIMPLEX
acap	674/tcp	ACAP
acap	674/udp	ACAP
dctp	675/tcp	DCTP
dctp	675/udp	DCTP
vpps-via	676/tcp	VPPS Via
vpps-via	676/udp	VPPS Via
vpp	677/tcp	Virtual Presence Protocol
vpp	677/udp	Virtual Presence Protocol
ggf-ncp	678/tcp	GNU Gereration Foundation NCP
ggf-ncp	678/udp	GNU Generation Foundation NCP

Continued

Table E-1 *(continued)*

Keyword	Decimal	Description
mrm	679/tcp	MRM
mrm	679/udp	MRM
entrust-aaas	680/tcp	entrust-aaas
entrust-aaas	680/udp	entrust-aaas
entrust-aams	681/tcp	entrust-aams
entrust-aams	681/udp	entrust-aams
xfr	682/tcp	XFR
xfr	682/udp	XFR
corba-iiop	683/tcp	CORBA IIOP
corba-iiop	683/udp	CORBA IIOP
corba-iiop-ssl	684/tcp	CORBA IIOP SSL
corba-iiop-ssl	684/udp	CORBA IIOP SSL
mdc-portmapper	685/tcp	MDC Port Mapper
mdc-portmapper	685/udp	MDC Port Mapper
hcp-wismar	686/tcp	Hardware Control Protocol Wismar
hcp-wismar	686/udp	Hardware Control Protocol Wismar
asipregistry	687/tcp	asipregistry
asipregistry	687/udp	asipregistry
realm-rusd	688/tcp	REALM-RUSD
realm-rusd	688/udp	REALM-RUSD
Unassigned	689-703	Unassigned
elcsd	704/tcp	errlog copy/server daemon
elcsd	704/udp	errlog copy/server daemon
agentx	705/tcp	AgentX
agentx	705/udp	AgentX
Unassigned	706	Unassigned
borland-dsj	707/tcp	Borland DSJ
borland-dsj	707/udp	Borland DSJ
Unassigned	708	Unassigned
entrust-kmsh	709/tcp	Entrust Key Management Service Handler

Keyword	Decimal	Description
entrust-kmsh	709/udp	Entrust Key Management Service Handler
entrust-ash	710/tcp	Entrust Administration Service Handler
entrust-ash	710/udp	Entrust Administration Service Handler
cisco-tdp	711/tcp	Cisco TDP
cisco-tdp	711/udp	Cisco TDP
Unassigned	712-728	Unassigned
netviewdm1	729/tcp	IBM NetView DM/6000 Server/Client
netviewdm1	729/udp	IBM NetView DM/6000 Server/Client
netviewdm2	730/tcp	IBM NetView DM/6000 send/tcp
netviewdm2	730/udp	IBM NetView DM/6000 send/tcp
netviewdm3	731/tcp	IBM NetView DM/6000 receive/tcp
netviewdm3	731/udp	IBM NetView DM/6000 receive/tcp
netgw	741/tcp	netGW
netgw	741/udp	netGW
netrcs	742/tcp	Network based Rev. Cont. Sys.
netrcs	742/udp	Network based Rev. Cont. Sys.
flexlm	744/tcp	Flexible License Manager
flexlm	744/udp	Flexible License Manager
fujitsu-dev	747/tcp	Fujitsu Device Control
fujitsu-dev	747/udp	Fujitsu Device Control
ris-cm	748/tcp	Russell Info Sci Calendar Manager
ris-cm	748/udp	Russell Info Sci Calendar Manager
kerberos-adm	749/tcp	kerberos administration
kerberos-adm	749/udp	kerberos administration
rfile	750/tcp	
loadav	750/udp	
kerberos-iv	750/udp	kerberos version iv
pump	751/tcp	
pump	751/udp	
qrh	752/tcp	

Continued

Table E-1 *(continued)*		
Keyword	**Decimal**	**Description**
qrh	752/udp	
rrh	753/tcp	
rrh	753/udp	
tell	754/tcp	send
tell	754/udp	send
nlogin	758/tcp	
nlogin	758/udp	
con	759/tcp	
con	759/udp	
ns	760/tcp	
ns	760/udp	
rxe	761/tcp	
rxe	761/udp	
quotad	762/tcp	
quotad	762/udp	
cycleserv	763/tcp	
cycleserv	763/udp	
omserv	764/tcp	
omserv	764/udp	
webster	765/tcp	
webster	765/udp	
phonebook	767/tcp	phone
phonebook	767/udp	phone
vid	769/tcp	
vid	769/udp	
cadlock	770/tcp	
cadlock	770/udp	
rtip	771/tcp	
rtip	771/udp	
cycleserv2	772/tcp	

Keyword	Decimal	Description
cycleserv2	772/udp	
submit	773/tcp	
notify	773/udp	
rpasswd	774/tcp	
acmaint_dbd	774/udp	
entomb	775/tcp	
acmaint_transd	775/udp	
wpages	776/tcp	
wpages	776/udp	
multiling-http	777/tcp	Multiling HTTP
multiling-http	777/udp	Multiling HTTP
Unassigned	778-779	Unassigned
wpgs	780/tcp	
wpgs	780/udp	
concert	786/tcp	Concert
concert	786/udp	Concert
qsc	787/tcp	QSC
qsc	787/udp	QSC
Unassigned	788-799	Unassigned
mdbs_daemon	800/tcp	
mdbs_daemon	800/udp	
device	801/tcp	
device	801/udp	
Unassigned	802-809	Unassigned
fcp-udp	810/tcp	FCP
fcp-udp	810/udp	FCP Datagram
Unassigned	811-827	Unassigned
itm-mcell-s	828/tcp	itm-mcell-s
itm-mcell-s	828/udp	itm-mcell-s
pkix-3-ca-ra	829/tcp	PKIX-3 CA/RA

Continued

Table E-1 (continued)

Keyword	Decimal	Description
pkix-3-ca-ra	829/udp	PKIX-3 CA/RA
Unassigned	830-872	Unassigned
rsync	873/tcp	rsync
rsync	873/udp	rsync
Unassigned	875-885	Unassigned
iclcnet-locate	886/tcp	ICL coNETion locate server
iclcnet-locate	886/udp	ICL coNETion locate server
iclcnet_svinfo	887/tcp	ICL coNETion server info
iclcnet_svinfo	887/udp	ICL coNETion server info
accessbuilder	888/tcp	AccessBuilder
accessbuilder	888/udp	AccessBuilder
Unassigned	889-899	Unassigned
omginitialrefs	900/tcp	OMG Initial Refs
omginitialrefs	900/udp	OMG Initial Refs
Unassigned	901-910	Unassigned
xact-backup	911/tcp	xact-backup
xact-backup	911/udp	xact-backup
Unassigned	912-988	Unassigned
ftps-data	989/tcp	ftp protocol, data, over TLS/SSL
ftps-data	989/udp	ftp protocol, data, over TLS/SSL
ftps	990/tcp	ftp protocol, control, over TLS/SSL
ftps	990/udp	ftp protocol, control, over TLS/SSL
nas	991/tcp	Netnews Administration System
nas	991/udp	Netnews Administration System
telnets	992/tcp	telnet protocol over TLS/SSL
telnets	992/udp	telnet protocol over TLS/SSL
imaps	993/tcp	imap4 protocol over TLS/SSL
imaps	993/udp	imap4 protocol over TLS/SSL
ircs	994/tcp	irc protocol over TLS/SSL
ircs	994/udp	irc protocol over TLS/SSL

Keyword	Decimal	Description
pop3s	995/tcp	pop3 protocol over TLS/SSL
pop3s	995/udp	pop3 protocol over TLS/SSL
vsinet	996/tcp	vsinet
vsinet	996/udp	vsinet
maitrd	997/tcp	
maitrd	997/udp	
busboy	998/tcp	
puparp	998/udp	
garcon	999/tcp	
applix	999/udp	Applix ac
puprouter	999/tcp	
puprouter	999/udp	
cadlock	1000/tcp	
ock	1000/udp	
Unassigned	1001-1009	Unassigned
surf	1010/tcp	surf
surf	1010/udp	surf
Reserved	1011-1022	Reserved
Reserved	1023/tcp	Reserved
Reserved	1023/udp	Reserved

✦   ✦   ✦

Web Resources for Security Professionals

This appendix provides Web resources for various security topics.

General Security Resources

✦ http://www.gocsi.com — This Web site is the home of the Computer Security Institute, which trains security professionals, holds conferences, and so on. Look for their "Firewall Product Matrix" for a good comparison of firewall products.

✦ http://www.securtekcorporation.com/ InfoResources.htm — This Web site, home of the Information Security Resources list and maintained by SecurTek Corporation, is a great place to start your own computer security surfing adventures.

✦ http://www.alw.nih.gov/Security/security-groups.html — The Feds maintain an excellent list of Security Groups and Organizations at the Center for Information Technology at NIH.

✦ http://www.trusecure.com — This Web site is the home of the TruSecure Corporation, which offers all kinds of information and certification services for hardware and security technology, as well as computer security-related information. TruSecure also publishes a magazine, called *Information Security* (http://www.infosecuritymag.com), which is worth checking out.

✦ http://www.bxa.doc.gov/Encryption/regs.htm — This Web site is the home of the Department of Commerce, which makes its Commercial Encryption Export Controls Regulations available to the public.

◆ `http://www.securityfocus.com`—This Web site is a premier resource for security news and information online.

◆ `http://www.attrition.org`—This is a computer security Web site dedicated to the collection, dissemination, and distribution of information about the industry for anyone interested in the subject. They maintain one of the largest catalogs of security advisories, cryptography, text files, and Denial of Service attack information. They are also known for the largest mirror of Web site defacements and their crusade to expose industry frauds and inform the public about incorrect information in computer security articles.

◆ `http://www.cauce.org`—This Web site is the home of CAUCE, the Coalition Against Unsolicited Commercial Email, which handles all kinds of e-mail and SPAM-related matters, including the occasional security item.

◆ `http://www.securityportal.com/closet/`—This Web page is the home of Kurt Seifried's monthly column on Security Techniques and Survivability—a must-read resource in this area. Overall, `www.securityportal.com` is a great general security resource as well.

◆ `http://www.cs.auckland.ac.nz/~pgut001/`—This Web site is the undertaking of Peter Gutmann, a member of the Computer Science faculty at the University of Aukland. He maintains a giant compendium of security pointers on this home page.

◆ `http://www.nipc.gov/warnings/advisories/1999/99-024.htm`—This Web site is the home of The National Infrastructure Protection Center (NIPC).

◆ `http://www.nmrc.org`—This is the homepage of Nomad Mobile Research Centre (NMRC), which contains multiple Windows-specific tools for testing security, as well as resources for UNIX and Novell NetWare security.

◆ `http://project.honeynet.org`—The Honeynet project is a group of thirty security professionals dedicated to learning the tools, tactics, and motives of the blackhat community and sharing the lessons they have learned.

◆ `http://www.all.net/dtk/`—The Deception Toolkit is a toolkit designed to give defenders a couple of orders of magnitude advantage over attackers.

◆ `http://www.recourse.com/products/mantrap/trap.html`—ManTrap extends the honeypot concept by creating an entire network of deception hosts that lure the attacker away from production systems and into the confines of the ManTrap cage.

◆ `http://www.pgp.com/products/cybercop-sting/default.asp`—CyberCop Sting is a revolutionary decoy system that simulates a virtual network on a single machine. This innovative "honeypot" technology redirects hackers away from your critical systems.

◆ `http://www.simovits.com/nyheter9902.html`—Simovits Consulting maintains a comprehensive list of ports used by Trojan horses, which is worth consulting when scanning your own network and strange or unexpected port usage patterns emerge.

Denial-of-Service attacks

✦ `http://www.cert.org/advisories/CA-2000-01.html` — This is the Computer Emergency Response Team Coordination Center (CERT/CC) Web page that deals with DoS attacks.

✦ `http://www.denialinfo.com/` — The Denial of Service Attack Resources site documents known DoS attack strategies and tools, along with related repairs and workarounds.

Windows security

✦ `http://www.microsoft.com/security` — Microsoft's security Web site contains information on new vulnerabilities and how to patch them.

✦ `http://www.windowsitsecurity.com` — This site, focused on Microsoft security, contains information on new vulnerabilities and security tips and tricks. The site also provides the full disclosure mailing list on Microsoft security issues, Win2KSecAdvice.

✦ `http://www.wiretrip.net/rfp` — This is the homepage of Rain.Forrest. Puppy (RFP). The penetration expert, known only as Rain.Forest.Puppy, published one of the best explanations of the heavily reported "Netscape engineers are weenies!" exploit against Microsoft FrontPage extensions. If you use FP extensions, be sure to check this out. RFP has discovered multiple security vulnerabilities, including the now famous MSADC/RDS vulnerability.

✦ `http://www.microsoft.com/downloads/` — This area of the MS Web site hosts Microsoft's Download Center, which is the company's primary repository for Service Packs, Hotfixes, and other important security and software updates. For Windows 2000, you access this area automatically when you invoke the Windows Update utility from the Start menu.

✦ `http://www.microsoft.com/technet/` — Access TechNet subscription information online to obtain one of the premier sources of Windows NT information of all kinds. You can also find lots of good security-related manual chapters, white papers, tech notes, and training materials on the TechNet CDs.

✦ `http://support.microsoft.com/directory/` — Search the Microsoft Knowledge Base (KB) for all kinds of security-related Windows NT and 2000 information online.

✦ `news:msnews.microsoft.com` — This is the home of Microsoft's News Server, which includes a number of security-related newsgroups, including: microsoft.public.iis-4.beta.security, Microsoft.public.inetexplorer.ie4.security, microsoft.public.java.security, and a whole collection of newsgroups under the microsoft.public.windowsnt.* umbrella. They also operate a security mailing list at `secure@microsoft.com`.

✦ The following is the home of Microsoft's Step-by-Step Guide to Configuring Enterprise Security Policies for Windows 2000: `http://www.microsoft.com/windows2000/techinfo/planning/security/entsecsteps.asp`.

✦ `http://www.microsoft.com/technet/security/iischk.asp`—This Web page hosts Microsoft's IIS Security Checklist.

✦ `http://www.microsoft.com/technet/security/tools.asp`—This site hosts a fabulous collection of pointers to Microsoft security checklists, tools, and updates.

✦ `http://oliver.efri.hr/~crv/security/bugs/NT/nt.html`—The Windows NT Systems Bug List includes numerous pointers to security-related matters, but a lack of descriptions for the bug fixes means that inspection of each element is required to determine what's security-related, and what's not. The site also provides a giant collection of security-related mailing lists that's worth checking out as well (`http://oliver.efri.hr/~crv/security/mlist/mlist.html`).

✦ `http://www.ntbugtraq.com`—Russ Cooper's NT Bugtraq is widely regarded as one of the best sources for information about NT bugs and security holes available online today.

✦ `http://www.c2.net/products/sh3/index.php3`—C2 Software, acquired by Red Hat, Inc. in September of 2000, is the maker of a secure version of Apache called Stronghold and now offers a beta version of this software for Windows, available as a free download.

✦ `http://www.entmag.com`—*Windows NT & Windows 2000 News* is another NT-focused trade magazine that covers most security news and information.

✦ `http://www.it.kth.se/~rom/ntsec.html`—Robert Malmgren, of the Royal Institute of Technology, maintains a Windows NT Security FAQ that is worth a regular visit, owing to its frequency of updates.

✦ `http://www.pedestalsoftware.com/ntsec/index.htm`—Pedestal Software offers some of the most useful command-line file and directory manipulation tools we've ever seen for managing ACLs and shares and manipulating the Registry. If you're into using batch files to get things done, these tools are a must-have! (Thanks to Peter Sturm of Siemens, München, for pointing these tools out to us.)

✦ `http://www.sysinternals.com`—Sysinternals (shareware) and Winternals (commercial versions, located at `http://www.winternals.com`) provide a way for Mark Russinovich and Bryce Cogswell to market their wares. Since their tools include NTFSDOS, ERD Commander, Remote recover, NT Locksmith, and much, much more, these are two sites you should check out for yourself.

✦ `http://www.securitysoftwaretech.com`—This Web site provides a download of the L0phtCrack password cracking tool.

✦ `http://www.quakenbush.com`— The Quakenbush Password Appraiser will review your account and password data and comment on its strengths and weaknesses.

✦ `http://www.webspan.net/~tas/pwdump2/` — This Web site hosts the pwdump2 SAM database extraction and cracking tool.

✦ `http://www.paperbits.com`— Paperbits is a great online resource for Windows NT and Windows 2000 information.

✦ `http://www.jsiinc.com/reghack.htm`— This Web site hosts Windows NT/2000 Tips, Tricks, Registry Hacks, and more.

✦ `http://www.smallwonders.com`— This Web site hosts Small Wonders Software of Orlando, developers of Security Explorer.

✦ `http://grc.com`— Online port vulnerability scanner from Gibson Research Corporation, called ShieldsUP!, provides an external scan of any site from which the Web page is invoked; a very handy tool.

✦ `http://www.netinnovation.com/nt/WebServerSecurity.html` — Windows NT Web Server Security Issues reproduced by permission from Sanjaya Hettihewa's book *Windows NT 4 Web Development* (SAMS Publishing).

✦ `http://www.ir.com`— Integrated Research's PROGNOSIS NT is a multi-platform network management tool based on Windows NT and Windows 2000.

✦ `http://www.emf.net/~ddonahue/NThacks/ntexploits.htm`— This site hosts Bill Stout's Known NT Exploits.

✦ `http://www.ntfaq.com`— This site is home to John Savill's famous Windows NT/2000 FAQ, which covers just about any base you can even *think* of!

✦ `http://searchwin2000.techtarget.com`— TechTarget's outstanding Search Windows 2000 Web site includes a very useful section on Security.

UNIX security/Linux security

✦ `http://www.slashdot.org`— This Web site, dedicated to the Linux community, provides Linux-specific information, including security information.

✦ `http://www.sourceforge.net` — This Web site, dedicated to the open source community, is home to multiple security projects.

✦ `http://www.slackware.com`— This Web site is the home of Slackware Linux.

✦ `http://www.redhat.com`— This Web site is the home of Red Hat Linux.

✦ `http://www.trinux.org`— This Web site is the home of the Trinux Linux Security Toolkit.

✦ `http://www.freebsd.org`— This Web site is the home of the Free BSD project.

Security Mailing Lists

- ✦ http://www.windowsitsecurity.com—This Web site is the home of Win2KSecAdvice and HowTo Security Admin.

- ✦ http://www.securityfocus.com—This Web site is the home of Bugtraq and multiple other mailing lists.

- ✦ http://archives.neohapsis.com—This Web site is an archive site for most of the popular mailing lists.

Security Tool Web Sites

- ✦ http://www.insecure.org—This Web site is the home of the Nmap scanner and a vulnerability listing for most operating systems.

- ✦ http://packetstorm.securify.com—This Web site provides security tools and a script archive for most operating systems.

Commercial Security Products

- ✦ http://www.bindview.com—This Web site is the home of BindView Corporation.

- ✦ http://www.symantec.com—This Web site is the home of Symantec and AXENT.

- ✦ http://ntsecurity.nu/toolbox/winzapper/—WinZapper is a hacking tool that permits records to be deleted from the Event Manager's security log, a hacking tool you should investigate (and look for, if you scan systems).

- ✦ http://www.intrusion.com—The Security Analyst from Intrusion.com scans many aspects of a network's security apparatus and assesses vulnerabilities.

- ✦ http://www.aelita.net—Aelita Software offers a number of interesting products, including the Domain Migration Wizard (this tool also handles migrating information from one Windows NT domain to another, and promises to help when moving data from Windows NT 4.0 domains to Win2K domains). Check out their ERDisk product, which offers networked creation and access to ERDs for any and all NT systems on that network.

- ✦ http://www.engarde.com—En Garde Systems T-Sight is a manual intrusion detection system, while IP-Watcher is an "active sniffer" that can not only observe network traffic, but also can hijack ongoing IP-based sessions.

✦ `ftp://ciac.llnl.gov/pub/ciac/sectools/unix/satan/`—The infamous Security Administrator Tool for Analyzing Networks (SATAN) runs only on UNIX but is an excellent public domain scanning and analysis tool.

✦ `http://www.bluelance.com`—Blue Lance builds an audit and security product called LT Auditor+ that handles and analyzes Windows NT and 2000 Audit data to issue alerts and take protective actions.

✦ `http://www.pgp.com/products/cybercop-scanner/default.asp`—Network Associates acquired and renamed HayStack Lab's WebStalker utility to CyberCop; it remains an excellent security monitoring and response tool.

✦ `http://www.iss.net/securing_e-business/security_products/security_management/decisions/index.php`—Internet Security Systems SAFEsuite Decisions is regarded by many as the best general-purpose, NT-based Internet security scanning tool. The company that makes this tool also makes a product named Internet Scanner that is an "attack simulator"—it automatically scans all networked machines and examines each for weaknesses, holes, and misconfigurations. They also offer some useful white papers on intrusion detection and assessment.

✦ `http://www.iss.net/securing_e-business/security_products/intrusion_detection/index.php`—Internet Security Systems also offers a product family called RealSecure that includes a real-time attack recognition and response capability, along with more conventional security monitoring and auditing facilities.

✦ `http://www.cybersafe.com`—Cybersafe Corporation makes a product called the Centrax Computer Security Suite that can monitor and respond to intrusion attempts, and that provides an analysis of your site's security weaknesses.

✦ `http://www.somarsoft.com`—Frank Ramos runs an operation called Somarsoft that offers a number of tools, the most useful of which is DumpACL. As its name suggests, DumpACL dumps a comprehensive listing of all file and folder ACLs on a per-volume basis. Be sure to check out Ramos' DumpEvt (Event Log Report) and DumpReg (Registry contents report) utilities as well. Now available at no charge (used to be shareware). Also includes pointers to lots of other good security and Windows NT resources. Now a part of `www.systemtools.com`.

✦ `http://www.distinct.com/rpc/docs/PortMapperandRPCInformation.htm`—Distinct Corporation offers a 32-bit Windows RPC port scanner called RPCINF32.EXE that can map out any RPC ports in use, from address 0 through address 65,535.

✦ `http://netsecurity.about.com/compute/netsecurity/cs/ntsecurityissues/index.htm`—Visit NetSecurity.com's NT Security Issues page for all kinds of useful references, including one on "Hacker Tools" that includes a wide variety of password crackers, scanners, and packet sniffers. Be sure to check out their other security pages as well.

✦ `http://www.nfr.com`—Marcus Ranum is one of the reigning gurus in the areas of network and Internet security. Check out his famous Network Flight Recorder, and related tools, to see what this guy can do!

✦ `http://www.hummingbird.at/hcl.at/dokus/thinclients/relnotes/Relnote_jump.htm`—Hummingbird makes a network/connectivity management product called JuMP that can impose an idle timeout on user connections, among many other capabilities. We're not sure this capability justifies the product by itself, but it's one of the few such products that advertises this capability.

✦ `http://www.stbernard.com`—St. Bernard Software makes a package called SPQuery that can report on and manage Service Packs and Hotfixes on a Windows NT or 2000 machine.

✦ `http://www.abbottsys.com/cowin.html`—Abbott Systems, Inc., makes a cross-platform product called CanOpener that can read or extract data from infected files without launching or activating an attached or embedded virus. Be sure to check the site for their Macintosh version (`http://www.abbottsys.com/co.html`) if it's of interest to you.

✦ `http://www.officerecovery.com`—Use OfficeRecovery.com to recover data from damaged MS Office documents.

✦ `http://www.insecure.org/nmap/`—Both nmap and its companion tool, nlog (`http://www.securiteam.com/tools/NLog__log_analyzer_for_NMap.html`), are Perl libraries. Thus, you should be able to download and compile these tools to run on a Windows NT or 2000 box, but as the first Web page indicates, nobody has bothered to do this yet. Unless you're the pioneering type, stick to one of the other native Windows tools for the job.

✦ `http://www.slacker.org`—The Legion scanner is a native Win32 tool, so it shares none of the portability problems associated with nmap and nlog.

✦ `http://www.antigame.com`—Search for unapproved software and games with AntiGame.

✦ `http://www.protect-me.com/dl/`—DeviceLock allows network administrators to specify which users can access which devices (ports, floppies, MOs, and so on) on the local computer. Once DeviceLock is installed, administrators can assign permissions to LPT ports, CD-ROMs, COM Ports, or any other device, just as they would to any share on the hard disk.

✦ `http://www.zonelabs.com`—Zone Labs' ZoneAlarm is a network security software package aimed at users or networks that use technologies that are always on, like DSL or Cable Modem, and comes in several varieties designed for single machines, small, or medium- to large-sized networks.

✦ `http://www.tenmax.com/teleport/pro/home.htm`—Tenmax.com offers a great Webspider called Teleport Pro that can scan comments and code for possible security exposures, in addition to checking links and so forth.

✦ `http://www.nessus.org`—Nessus is a powerful, free security scanner that's worth downloading and trying out on your systems.

✦ `http://www.eeye.com/html/` — eEye's nmapNT, Retina, Iris, and Blink.

✦ `http://www.pcguardian.com` — PC Guardian's Encryption Plus for Hard Disks (EPHD).

✦ `http://www.sans.org/infosecFAQ/win2000/ipsec_w2k.htm` — *IP Security in Windows 2000: Step-by-Step* by Timothy J. Rogers.

✦ `http://www.microsoft.com/ISAServer/` — Microsoft's ISA Server.

✦ `http://img.cmpnet.com/nc/1201/graphics/f1-detect-results.pdf` — Vulnerability Scanners: Detection Results.

Hacking tools

✦ `http://www.antionline.com` — AntiCode and AntiOnline are sources of hacking news, code, and information.

✦ `http://www.cerberus-infosec.co.uk/cis.shtml` — Cerberus Internet Scanner (CIS) is a general-purpose security scanner that covers 300 separate scanning tasks, can run in a background batch file, and creates easy-to-read HTML-based reports.

✦ `http://www.digicrime.com/dc.html` — Digicrime.com advertises itself as "... the industry leader in the digital underworld." Makes us curious about what they're up to. You should be curious, too!

✦ `http://www.holodeck.f9.co.uk/elitewrap/` — eLiTeWrap is a tool that is designed to create customized Trojan horse programs. Need we say more?

✦ `http://www.indiesoft.com` — Genius is a shareware collection of online and offline security scanning and analysis utilities that includes a nifty graphical traceroute tool.

✦ `http://www.amecisco.com/iksnt.htm` — Invisible KeyLogger Stealth is a keystroke recorder that can even capture the so-called Secure Attention Sequence (Ctrul+Alt+Del); also includes instructions to "...provide the maximum stealth."

✦ `http://www.10pht.com/~weld/netcat/` — Netcat is a popular, all-purpose port and service scanning tool that's great for "footprinting" a Windows system.

✦ `http://www.ibt.ku.dk/jesper/NetViewX/default.htm` — NetviewX is a handy tool that lists servers in a domain or a workgroup.

✦ `http://users.aol.com/jpeschel/crack.htm` — Joe Peschel has put together the most comprehensive list of software cracking tools we've seen anywhere, including lots of password and other kinds of crackers.

✦ `http://www.accessdata.com` — AccessData offers a powerful password recovery tool that can recover passwords from PKZip, WinZip, Word, Excel, WordPerfect, Lotus1-2-3, Paradox, Q&A, Quattro-Pro, Ami Pro, Approach, QuickBooks, Act!, Access, Word Pro, dBase, Symphony, Outlook, Express, MSMoney, Quicken, Scheduler+, Ascend, Netware, and Windows NT server/workstation. No ability to crack Windows 2000 passwords yet!

- `http://www.s0ftpj.org/tools/pippa_v1.txt` — Pippa provides a mechanism to redirect data to different, nonstandard TCP or UDP port numbers. This is a common technique used to penetrate firewalls once internal systems have been compromised.

- `http://www.snadboy.com` — Revelation can very often exchange the asterisks that show up for cached or saved passwords with their clear-text equivalents, when run on a Windows machine.

- `http://samspade.org/ssw/` — Sam Spade is a general-purpose freeware Internet scanning and monitoring tool that includes all kinds of IP functionality, plus e-mail and other high-level scanning and analysis capabilities.

- `http://www.solarwinds.net/` — SolarWinds 2000 is a mid-priced ($125 to $595, plus yearly maintenance), general-purpose network monitoring and management tool. A nice all-in-one package, at an attractive price.

- `http://www.visualware.com/visualroute/index.html` — VisualRoute is a handy, cheap ($37.50 for a single-user license), shareware utility that combines the functionality of ping, whois, and traceroute, and performs connectivity analyses for automatic graphic display.

Security devices

- `http://www.activcard.com/activ/index.html` — ActivCard's token devices for computers and communications.

- `http://enterprisesecurity.symantec.com/products/products.cfm?ProductID=51` — Symantec's Defender is a well-known dialback system that adds extra security for remote access services of all kinds.

- `http://cardshow.com/EN/Login.html` — CardShow is a tradeshow with a substantial Web presence that specializes in Smart Card technologies.

- `http://www.datakey.com` — Datakey, Inc., offers all kinds of secure hardware products, including Smart Cards that integrate PKI support, digital signature and electronic lock technologies, and more.

- `http://www.ibutton.com` — The Java-based iButton is being used for a variety of security-based hardware applications.

- `http://www.securecomputing.com` — Secure Computing's SafeWord provides advanced, software-based authentication services suitable for Web and other Internet use.

- `http://www.rsasecurity.com/products/securid/` — Security Dynamics, Inc., is now part of RSA Security. Their SecurID Cards are just one of this growing company's many security enhancement tools, products, and technologies.

- `http://www.teleport.com/~samc/scard.html` — "The Electronic Wallet: Smart Cards arrive in the United States" is a general overview piece from Teleport.com, a leading purveyor of Smart Card technologies in the Europe and the U.S.

✦ http://www.vasco.com/Main/Frameset.asp?lang=en&reference=01-01&sess=1005515281& — Vasco's Digipass products use Smart Card technology to support secure user login and authentication.

Security Organizations, Conferences, and Certifications

✦ http://nsi.org/compsec.html — The National Security Institute provides a plethora of TCP/IP-related security issues and references to other sites.

✦ http://www.cert.org — Computer Emergency Response Team (CERT) provides advisories, security tips, intrusion countermeasures, and more.

✦ http://www.trusecure.com — The International Computer Security Association, or ICSA, once known as NCSA (National Computer Security Association), is also one of the leading security organizations worldwide, in addition to being a great information resource (hence the double listing).

✦ http://www.sans.org/newlook/home.htm — The SANS Institute offers all kinds of security and best-practices information to the public, including a series of shows and seminars devoted to Windows NT Security matters.

✦ http://www.issa-intl.org — Information Systems Security Association is an international organization that delivers educational information, materials, and publications related to computer security.

✦ http://tisc.corecom.com — The Internet Security Conference (TISC) is a yearly security conference that covers all kinds of interesting topics, and usually has great speakers like Stephen Kent, Marcus Ranum, Phil Cox, and others (heck, we teach for them, too). They also publish lots of great articles and white papers throughout the year. Information about all of these topics appears on their Web site.

✦ http://www.isc2.org — The International Information Systems Security Certification Consortium (in other words, "ICS-squared") offers one of the best-known security certifications, the Certified Information Systems Security Professional (CISSP) credential, to a global audience.

✦ http://www.ciwcertified.com/exams/1d0470.asp — ProsoftTraining's Certified Internet WebMaster (CIW) program includes the 1D0-470 Security Professional exam as part of its Master CIW Administrator track.

✦   ✦   ✦

Index

Continued

Hungry Minds, Inc.
End-User License Agreement

READ THIS. You should carefully read these terms and conditions before opening the software packet(s) included with this book ("Book"). This is a license agreement ("Agreement") between you and Hungry Minds, Inc. ("HMI"). By opening the accompanying software packet(s), you acknowledge that you have read and accept the following terms and conditions. If you do not agree and do not want to be bound by such terms and conditions, promptly return the Book and the unopened software packet(s) to the place you obtained them for a full refund.

1. **License Grant.** HMI grants to you (either an individual or entity) a nonexclusive license to use one copy of the enclosed software program(s) (collectively, the "Software") solely for your own personal or business purposes on a single computer (whether a standard computer or a workstation component of a multi-user network). The Software is in use on a computer when it is loaded into temporary memory (RAM) or installed into permanent memory (hard disk, CD-ROM, or other storage device). HMI reserves all rights not expressly granted herein.

2. **Ownership.** HMI is the owner of all right, title, and interest, including copyright, in and to the compilation of the Software recorded on the disk(s) or CD-ROM ("Software Media"). Copyright to the individual programs recorded on the Software Media is owned by the author or other authorized copyright owner of each program. Ownership of the Software and all proprietary rights relating thereto remain with HMI and its licensers.

3. **Restrictions On Use and Transfer.**

   (a) You may only (i) make one copy of the Software for backup or archival purposes, or (ii) transfer the Software to a single hard disk, provided that you keep the original for backup or archival purposes. You may not (i) rent or lease the Software, (ii) copy or reproduce the Software through a LAN or other network system or through any computer subscriber system or bulletin-board system, or (iii) modify, adapt, or create derivative works based on the Software.

   (b) You may not reverse engineer, decompile, or disassemble the Software. You may transfer the Software and user documentation on a permanent basis, provided that the transferee agrees to accept the terms and conditions of this Agreement and you retain no copies. If the Software is an update or has been updated, any transfer must include the most recent update and all prior versions.

4. Restrictions on Use of Individual Programs. You must follow the individual requirements and restrictions detailed for each individual program in Appendix A of this Book. These limitations are also contained in the individual license agreements recorded on the Software Media. These limitations may include a requirement that after using the program for a specified period of time, the user must pay a registration fee or discontinue use. By opening the Software packet(s), you will be agreeing to abide by the licenses and restrictions for these individual programs that are detailed in Appendix A and on the Software Media. None of the material on this Software Media or listed in this Book may ever be redistributed, in original or modified form, for commercial purposes.

5. Limited Warranty.

(a) HMI warrants that the Software and Software Media are free from defects in materials and workmanship under normal use for a period of sixty (60) days from the date of purchase of this Book. If HMI receives notification within the warranty period of defects in materials or workmanship, HMI will replace the defective Software Media.

(b) **HMI AND THE AUTHOR OF THE BOOK DISCLAIM ALL OTHER WARRANTIES, EXPRESS OR IMPLIED, INCLUDING WITHOUT LIMITATION IMPLIED WARRANTIES OF MERCHANTABILITY AND FITNESS FOR A PARTICULAR PURPOSE, WITH RESPECT TO THE SOFTWARE, THE PROGRAMS, THE SOURCE CODE CONTAINED THEREIN, AND/OR THE TECHNIQUES DESCRIBED IN THIS BOOK. HMI DOES NOT WARRANT THAT THE FUNCTIONS CONTAINED IN THE SOFTWARE WILL MEET YOUR REQUIREMENTS OR THAT THE OPERATION OF THE SOFTWARE WILL BE ERROR FREE.**

(c) This limited warranty gives you specific legal rights, and you may have other rights that vary from jurisdiction to jurisdiction.

6. Remedies.

(a) HMI's entire liability and your exclusive remedy for defects in materials and workmanship shall be limited to replacement of the Software Media, which may be returned to HMI with a copy of your receipt at the following address: Software Media Fulfillment Department, Attn.: *CIW Security Professional Certification Bible*, Hungry Minds, Inc., 10475 Crosspoint Blvd., Indianapolis, IN 46256, or call 1-800-762-2974. Please allow four to six weeks for delivery. This Limited Warranty is void if failure of the Software Media has resulted from accident, abuse, or misapplication. Any replacement Software Media will be warranted for the remainder of the original warranty period or thirty (30) days, whichever is longer.

(b) In no event shall HMI or the author be liable for any damages whatso-ever (including without limitation damages for loss of business profits, business interruption, loss of business information, or any other pecu-niary loss) arising from the use of or inability to use the Book or the Software, even if HMI has been advised of the possibility of such damages.

(c) Because some jurisdictions do not allow the exclusion or limitation of liability for consequential or incidental damages, the above limitation or exclusion may not apply to you.

7. **U.S. Government Restricted Rights.** Use, duplication, or disclosure of the Software for or on behalf of the United States of America, its agencies and/or instrumentalities (the "U.S. Government") is subject to restrictions as stated in paragraph (c)(1)(ii) of the Rights in Technical Data and Computer Software clause of DFARS 252.227-7013, or subparagraphs (c) (1) and (2) of the Commercial Computer Software - Restricted Rights clause at FAR 52.227-19, and in similar clauses in the NASA FAR supplement, as applicable.

8. **General.** This Agreement constitutes the entire understanding of the parties and revokes and supersedes all prior agreements, oral or written, between them and may not be modified or amended except in a writing signed by both parties hereto that specifically refers to this Agreement. This Agreement shall take precedence over any other documents that may be in conflict herewith. If any one or more provisions contained in this Agreement are held by any court or tribunal to be invalid, illegal, or otherwise unenforceable, each and every other provision shall remain in full force and effect.

CD-ROM Installation Instructions

These instructions provide a quick start for installing the CD-ROM included with this book. The CD contains a variety of security software discussed throughout the book.

Before installing the CD, make sure your computer meets the minimum system requirements listed in Appendix A. Although Windows versions of the software are included on the CD, many of these products are also available for Linux and the Mac OS.

+ **Microsoft Windows.** To install the items from the CD on your hard drive, follow these steps:

    1. Insert the CD into your computer's CD-ROM drive.

    2. View the contents of the CD-ROM using Windows Explorer or by clicking the My Computer icon on your desktop.

    3. Locate the software you wish to install.

    4. Either double-click the program's installation program to install it, or follow the directions contained in the readme file in the CD directory for the program.

+ **Linux.** To open the items from the CD, follow these steps:

    1. Log in as root.

    2. Insert the CD into your computer's CD-ROM drive.

    3. Mount the CD-ROM.

    4. Launch a graphical file manager to view the items on the CD.

+ **Mac OS.** To open the items from the CD, follow these steps:

    1. Insert the CD into your computer's CD-ROM drive.

    2. Double-click the CD icon on your desktop.

    3. Locate the item you wish to view.

    4. Double-click the file you want to open, or use the Open command from the appropriate program.